MILESTONES
IN MASS
COMMUNICATION
RESEARCH

SECOND EDITION

MILESTONES
IN MASS
COMMUNICATION
RESEARCH

M E D I A   E F F E C T S

Shearon A. Lowery   and
Associate Professor
Department of Sociology
Florida International University

Melvin L. De Fleur
John Ben Snow Professor
S.I. Newhouse School of Communications
Syracuse University

Longman
New York & London

Milestones in Mass Communication Research: Media Effects
Second edition

Longman Inc., 95 Church Street, White Plains, N.Y. 10601

Associated companies:
Longman Group Ltd., London
Longman Chesire Pty., Melbourne
Longman Paul Pty., Auckland
Copp Clark Pitman, Toronto
Pitman Publishing Inc., New York

Executive editor: Gordon T. R. Anderson
Production editor: Elsa van Bergen
Text and cover design: Steven August Krastin
Production supervisor: Judith Stern
Compositor: Best-Set Typesetter Limited
Printer and binder: Maple-Vail Book Manufacturing Group

Library of Congress Cataloging-in-Publication Data
Lowery, Shearon.
    Milestones in mass communication research.
    Includes bibliographical references and index.
    1. Mass media.   2. Mass society.   I. De Fleur,
Melvin L. (Melvin Lawrence), 1923–   .   II. Title.
HM258.L68   1987   302.2'34   86-33759
ISBN 0-8013-0039-8
ISBN 0-8013-0038-X (pbk.)

89 90 9 8 7 6 5 4 3

Contents

Foreword

Mass communication research is today increasingly looking toward its past in order to understand its present and future. The second edition of Shearon Lowery and Melvin L. De Fleur's book, *Milestones in Mass Communication Research: Media Effects,* is an important indicator of this trend to looking backward to where we have come. Other recent scholarly works on the history of mass communication science are chapters in Daniel J. Czitrom's *Media and the American Mind* (University of North Carolina Press, 1982), Willard D. Rowland's *Politics of TV Violence* (Sage, 1982), and my own *Communication Technology* (Free Press, 1986). These historical analyses focus on certain scholars who founded mass communication research—Harold Lasswell, Kurt Lewin, Carl Hovland, Paul F. Lazarsfeld, and Wilbur Schramm—rather than on their theories or on the landmark research studies that they accomplished. Stressed are the key scholars and the historical context in which they operated, rather than the substantive content of what these pioneering researchers actually found.

Milestones takes quite a different approach to this history of mass communication research. A distinctive aspect of the present book is that it organizes the history of our field by "milestones." What is a milestone? The term derives from the stone markers placed along ancient roads like the Romans' Appian Way to inform travelers of how far they had come, and thus how far they had yet to go toward their eventual goal. The thirteen milestones featured here provide the reader with a scholarly roadmap of the path taken by mass communication research. For the new student of mass communication, the present book answers such questions as Where did we come from? and How did we get here? and suggests responses to Where are we? and Where are we going? I have used the first edition of *Milestones* in my courses at Stanford University and at the University of Southern California, and I found my students very interested in these classics. The field of mass communication is presently mature enough to have a substantial intellectual history. *Milestones* presents this past in an interesting and effective manner, so that the reader grasps the multidisciplinary foundations from which mass communication research has emerged.

Focus on Media Effects
As the subtitle of this book states, the main focus in the thirteen milestone studies is upon mass media *effects*. Mass communication research has been dom-

inated by an effects-orientation over the 50– or 60–year period covered by this book. This dominant concern with media effects is guided by a one-way model of mass communication, originally proposed by Claude Shannon's *A Mathematical Theory of Communication* (University of Illinois Press, 1949). This one-way model came on the intellectual scene only about halfway through the sequence of the thirteen milestones detailed here, but it fit well with the existing concerns of mass communication scholars. The mass media in a nation like the United States reach such huge audiences with such rapidity that any observer of these media naturally turns to questioning whether they have strong effects. Most advertisers and mass media professionals (and many laypeople) believe in strong media effects. Many scholars of mass communication (1) come from background experience as media professionals, and/or (2) are influenced by government or other policy concerns with media effects (much of the funding for mass communication research comes from research sponsors who are primarily interested in media effects issues).

Given this dominant orientation toward determining media effects, the Shannon model was interpreted by mass communication scholars into an effects framework (even though that interpretation of his model was not intended by Shannon). Source variables, channel variables, message variables, and receiver variables were investigated as they explained media effects. Such aspects of Shannon's model as feedback were largely ignored or de-emphasized by mass communication scholars because the study of feedback did not fit with an effects-orientation. Further, applications of the Shannon model by mass communication scholars tended to remove much of the human subjectivity of the communication process that was originally intended by Shannon. He felt that the encoding of an idea into a message and the decoding of the message into an idea by a receiver involved a great deal of subjectivity, so that the receiver usually decodes an idea out of the communication process different from the idea originally encoded by the source. Only in the 1980s have certain mass communication scholars begun to more fully appreciate that human communication involves giving meaning to information. Mass communication is thus a process of constructivism as the participants in the process seek to create their own reality out of the information that they exchange with others.

Advances in the Epistemology of Mass Communication Research

The 60-year era spanned by the thirteen milestones was punctuated by important methodological advances that allowed mass communication scholars to study the effect question with greater precision. Survey design, multivariate statistical methods, and new measurement techniques were incorporated in scholarly studies of media effects. Paul F. Lazarsfeld, one of the four main founders of mass communication science (and the chief investigator in two of the thirteen milestone studies reported here), pioneered several of these methodological improvements. For example, Lazarsfeld and his colleagues in the People's Choice study utilized a panel design with 600 research interviews each month for six months prior to the 1940 presidential election. The panel design allowed scholars to trace changes in voting intentions due to mass media influences. The sharpening of the media effects question that ensued from this improved research design led Lazarsfeld and his colleagues to the then-surprising conclusion that the mass media had relatively weak effects in a political campaign (we should remember that the Erie County, Ohio study was conducted in the pre-television days, and the project's results might be different today).

Multidisciplinary Roots and the Institutionalization of Communication Research

In the main, the thirteen milestone studies of media effects are empirical, quantitative social science investigations, carried out in the mainline academic tradition of North American functionalist theory. These thirteen soundings in the academic river of mass communication research illustrate the nature and directions of multidisciplinary social science research in the United States, as it grew in size and scientific sophistication across the five or six most recent decades. Halfway through this period, about the time that the Shannon model appeared, the first Ph.D. degrees in mass communication were awarded, first at the University of Illinois, then at Stanford, and soon thereafter at many other large universities. Prior to this time, scholars who studied mass communication were social psychologists, sociologists, political scientists, and others, attracted to investigate the media effects question. After conducting research on this issue, the scholar often left mass communication research to move back into the center of his or her disciplinary concerns. As Wilbur Schramm noted, communication research was a place where many tarried, but few remained. Schramm himself played a key role in changing this in-and-out venturing in mass communication research, when he launched the first doctoral programs at Illinois and at Stanford.

Once mass communication research became institutionalized in university departments, schools, and research institutes, the field began to display greater consistency, and moved toward becoming a discipline. Communication scientists today have their own scholarly journals, scientific associations, textbooks, and the other trappings of a discipline. Many contributors to mass communication research today, however, earned their doctorates in another discipline (the author of this foreword is an example), and communication science remains open to intellectual contributions by many scholars who were trained in other fields. No other social science discipline today is so open to external intellectual influences as is communication.

The university institutionalization of mass communication research impacts the thirteen milestones. The first eight milestone studies were conducted by scholars attracted by the media effects question from various social sciences, but who had not earned Ph.D. degrees in this new discipline (most could not have done so if they wished to, because such degree programs did not then

exist). The last five of the thirteen milestone studies were mainly carried out
by Ph.Ds in mass communication (Ed Parker, Jack Lyle, Max McCombs, and
Steve Chaffee, for example). How the later milestone studies were thus different
from the preceding studies is a matter of conjecture.

Certainly these thirteen studies helped toward the institutionalization of
the communication discipline. These milestones are read today by every doctoral
student in the field, and thus provide a core focus for the academic study of
mass communication. The multidisciplinary roots of communication science,
illustrated particularly by the early milestones, lends a pluralistic quality (the
intellectual belief that all viewpoints deserve to be heard and considered) to
contemporary mass communication research.

The Role of New Communication Technologies

Obviously, American society was changing in very major ways during the 50
to 60 years covered by the thirteen milestones: For example, the components
of the U.S. labor force altered so that we became an information society (with
a majority of the work force becoming information workers in about 1955; the
proportion has increased since). Urbanization, transportation changes, com-
puterization, and other major social changes have occurred. Many of these alterations in society influence the degree to which media effects occur in various
situations. For instance, we have previously mentioned that the lack of strong
media effects in the Erie County study of the 1940 presidential election might
have been related to the absence of television political spots, which have more
recently been found to have certain effects on voters.

One of the most important changes across the 50 or 60 years has been the
new communication technologies that have in turn taken center stage in the
directions of mass communication research: first film, followed by radio, comic
books, television, and, today, computer-related interactive communication
technologies. Each of these media (except the most current) have in turn dominated the research attention of mass communication scholars, as is illustrated
by the thirteen milestones. Research on the effects of each communication technology usually focuses, particularly at first, on *children* perhaps because (1) this
youthful audience is especially affected, and (2) public policy concerns often
center on children, who are viewed as more defenseless than adults. The present
milestone studies illustrate this focus of mass communication research on the
effects of a medium on children: six of the thirteen studies concern children.
And, not surprisingly, scholarly work on the new interactive technologies in
the 1980s deals heavily with the effects of computers on children.

Thus we see that communication scholars over recent decades have displayed
(in the topics they select to study) a certain degree of *technological determinism,*
the belief that technology is a cause of social change in society. Most U.S. mass
communication scientists are probably "soft" technological determinists, believing that communication technology is *one* cause, along with others, of social
change in American society.

The focus on children in certain of the milestone studies also suggest that mass communication scholars often regard media effects with a critical stance, looking for possibly harmful impacts (like those of television violence on children's aggressive behavior). Certainly, critics of mass communication research cannot accuse these scholars of assuming that media effects are usually positive for the audience individuals of study.

Thirteen Milestones of Mass Communication Research

It happens that the period covered by thirteen milestones of mass communication research coincides with my lifetime. Perhaps this coincidence makes it appropriate for me to comment on the milestone studies in a rather personal way, drawing on my memories for the context of these milestones.

The Payne Fund studies of the effects of film on children represent the first real communication research, although it lacked the methodological sophistication that was to follow in later decades. About 75 percent of U.S. films in the early 1930s dealt with themes of love, sex, and crime. No wonder that parents (like mine) and public officials were concerned. At that time, I was a child growing up in rural Iowa, the buckle on the Bible belt. Tickets to Saturday matinees cost 5 cents, and my little friends and I attended often. Some violent movies gave me bad dreams, as I remember (the effect of movies disturbing the sleep of children was one index utilized by the Payne Fund studies). I can recall my mother taking her children to a movie, and then forcing us all to leave the theatre when the theme of the violent film became obvious. Little did I know at that time that such parental protest was sparking the Payne Fund studies, setting off the field of communication research that was to command my adult career.

In October 1938, my family and I were among the 6 million Americans who listened to Orson Welles' "Mercury Theatre of the Air," but I was not among the many in the audience who panicked (I heard Orson announce at the top of the program that it was all a Halloween spoof). A huge (by today's standards) vacuum-tube radio was the center of our family's evening entertainment, and we listened regularly to programs like "Fibber McGee and Molly," "The Bob Hope Show," Fred Allen, and "The Great Gildersleeve." And, on Sunday evenings, to Orson Welles' Mercury Theatre. Fortunately for today's students of mass communication, a quick-acting Princeton University psychologist, Hadley Cantril, mounted an investigation of the effects of "The Invasion from Mars" in the weeks immediately following this broadcast. Such strong effects on a mass audience were to occur only infrequently in the years to follow, and so it is to our field's intellectual benefit that Cantril capitalized on this happening. He was able to conduct this firehouse research because of his affiliation with Princeton's Office of Radio Research, the first University-based communication research institute. Cantril, of course, found strong media effects, as had the earlier Payne Fund research. The conventional belief in strong effects was shortly to be challenged, however, by the Erie County study conducted by Paul F. Lazarsfeld and his colleagues in the Columbia University Bureau of Applied Social Research, a direct descendant of Princeton's Office of Radio Research. As we have seen, his research team found very little *direct* media effect on voting behavior.

World War II was a time of intellectual flowering for mass communication research, and one of its important advances is represented by a series of experiments concerning the effects of military training films on U.S. soldiers' morale. A brilliant young psychologist from Yale University, Carl Hovland, directed these persuasion studies. The Army films had only limited effects, as might seem reasonable to anyone who has seen military training films. Note that Hovland's experimental findings of limited media effects matched Lazarsfeld's panel survey results. Mass communication research was entering an era of minimal effects.

In 1945, Hovland returned to Yale to direct a series of 50 or so experiments on media effects, substituting sophomores for sergeants and various media messages (such as front-page stories from *The New York Times* and *Pravda*) for military films. His Yale experiments on the persuasion effects of fear appeals, source credibility, and other conceptual variables marked the high water mark for communication experiments. These investigations were so thoroughly planned and executed, and so comprehensive in scope, that the experimental approach to mass media effects has languished since. There simply was not much left to study experimentally after Hovland published his work, which was cut short by his untimely death in 1959.

I remember replicating one of Hovland's experiments when I was studying for my Ph.D degree at Iowa State University in the mid-1950s. We showed a propaganda film about cooperatives (then a controversial issue among Iowans) with two different endings to treatment and control groups of Iowa State students. Our measure of media effects was a pre-post questionnaire indexing attitudes toward co-ops. Our results matched Hovland's, and unfortunately added little to this previous research. We never published the results. I have not carried out a laboratory experiment since, although the principles of research design that I learned then helped me in various field experiments and other studies later in my career. I was, however, more directly influenced by Lazarsfeld's Erie County study, and by his later milestone study of the two-step flow of communication in Decatur, Illinois (with Elihu Katz, now a colleague at USC's Annenberg School of Communications). The Decatur study investigated the role of interpersonal networks in the mass communication process, as media messages were passed along among the individual members of the media audience. Note the beginnings of research on the *indirect* effects of the media, inspired perhaps by the limited effects results of earlier mass communication research. In my doctoral dissertation research at Iowa State, an investigation of the diffusion of a new weed spray among farmers in an Iowa community, I sought to test certain of Katz and Lazarsfeld's formulations of the two-step flow and of opinion leadership.

Prior to studying for a Ph.D. in sociology, I had fulfilled military service in the U.S. Air Force unit that sponsored social science research. One such Air Force-funded study was Project Revere, carried out by a team of sociologists at the University of Washington from 1952 to 1954, one of whom was Melvin De Fleur. Certainly I did not know that the CIA may have been sponsoring Project Revere and using the Air Force as a front (I was just a young Air Force officer, serving as an aide to the official in charge of social science research). But I did absorb the diffusion research approach from the Revere studies, a scholarly specialty that I have pursued for the past 30 years or so. Certain of the mathematical formulae for the diffusion of air-dropped leaflets, worked out in Project Revere, are still useful in diffusion studies today. Like the Decatur study, Revere showed the importance of interpersonal networks in understanding the mass communication process.

Milestone study #8, on the Seduction of the Innocent, concerned the effects of crime comic books on children. Frederic Wertham launched this study with the firm assumption that comics were harmful to children, and that comic book publishers were villains. His results convinced the American public of his personal viewpoint. Although Wertham is hardly an exemplar of the objective communication scientist, his activities do suggest that media effects research can have policy impacts. A long-term consequence of the Seduction of the Innocent study may have been a public attitude of distrust toward the media (as Lowery and De Fleur point out).

During the decade of the 1950s, television diffused to most U.S. households, causing important changes in individuals' lifestyles, their time-use, and in patterns of exposure to other media such as radio, film, and magazines. The greatest effects were expected in the lives of U.S. children, as Wilbur Schramm, Jack Lyle, and Edwin Parker pointed out in their important study, Milestone #9. This Stanford University research team actually found that television had *some* effects on *some* children; these research results were generally in line with the limited effects model of the mass media then in vogue among mass communication scholars. The book by Schramm and others (published in 1962) set off a tremendous volume of researches on the effects of television, especially on children. Until 1970, 300 publications had appeared in English on this topic; 830 more reports were published between 1970 and 1975; and 1,670 additional publications appeared between 1976 and 1980. Many of these studies were conducted by psychologists or psychiatrists, but a large number were carried out by mass communication scholars.

This voluminous research is discussed here as Milestone #10, the Task Force Report on Violence and the Media (a content analysis showing that U.S. television programs contained a great deal of violence); Milestone #11, the Report to the U.S. Surgeon General on Television and Social Behavior (which synthesized a $1 million government-sponsored research program on the effects of TV violence); and Milestone #13, a summary of more recent research on television effects (including those of a prosocial nature, like teaching children to be polite and obedient). The 1962 study by Schramm and others (Milestone #9) formed the basic paradigm for the research on television effects that was to follow, investigations that have greatly broadened and sharpened the original study. This considerable body of television effects research represents the most important single contribution of mass communication research in the past several decades. If one indicator of a milestone's significance is the degree to which it sets off a stream of later research, the ninth study included here is our largest milestone.

What have these many studies told us about media effects? The television effects research shows little support for a catharsis effect, that TV violence purges the viewer of aggressive tendencies. Support *is* provided for a social learning model of television effects; viewers may identify with television roles, and thus learn certain of the behaviors depicted in television programs. At least for some individuals, such modeling leads to television effects on behavior.

While I have not conducted research on television effects myself (at least in the United States), it has been a major activity of certain of my colleagues and students at Michigan State, Michigan, and Stanford in the 1964–1985 period. Through this close association with TV research, I conclude that important lessons about mass communication effects were learned from the many television studies, as is indicated in the three milestone chapters describing attempts to synthesize this original research. On the other hand, I wonder if we really need a 2801*st* study of television effects.

Another important topic for mass communication research in the 1970s and 1980s is an indirect media effect, that of agenda-setting (Milestone #12). This field of research began with an investigation, by Max McCombs and Donald Shaw, of the 1968 U.S. presidential election. These scholars, then at the University of North Carolina, found that the mass media influenced the relative importance which the public attached to various political issues. In the 15 years since the McCombs-Shaw research was published, over 150 studies of the agenda-setting process have been completed. This research provides evidence that the media play an important role in influencing what the public *thinks about,* even though the media may not determine *what* we think. The scope of the original McCombs-Shaw research has been widened to explore (1) how the media agenda is set, and (2) how the public agenda (that is, what the public thinks are the most important issues and events) influences the policy agenda (what public officials and politicians think are the most important issues).

My recent synthesis of agenda-setting research (with a colleague, Jim Dearing) concludes that this indirect effect of the mass media was stimulated, in large part, by mass communication scholars' continuing search for media effects (and their general inability to find strong media effects of a direct nature, in the methodologically sophisticated research of the 1970s and 1980s). Perhaps mass communication researchers should investigate additional types of indirect media effects in the future.

The thirteen milestones in the second edition of this book represent a sampling of the outstanding breakthrough discoveries in mass communication research over the past five or six decades. Additional milestone chapters undoubtedly remain to be "written" by future investigators. We leave the fourteeth milestone study, however, for a possible third edition of this volume.

Everett M. Rogers
Annenberg School of Communications
University of Southern California

Preface

Consensus is by no means complete among communication scholars as to which research efforts make up our principal intellectual heritage. It was with some trepidation, therefore, that we selected the eleven studies that were reviewed in the first edition of the present book and characterized them as "milestones" in mass communication research. But in spite of fears that our colleagues would denounce us for selecting the wrong ones, the first edition was well received and our selection did not generate any noticeable controversy. On the contrary, the book appears to be serving a useful purpose by providing both a convenient summary of the major studies it reviews and interpretative framework that places each in the intellectual context of a developing field of research.

The criteria for identifying a particular work as a "milestone" are set forth in Chapter One. Briefly, our concern was with the effects of mass communication rather than with its process. Each project selected had to be of large scale and its findings published in book form. Such books had to have played a significant role in the development of the field. This could have been in terms of new concepts or theories, new methodology, or even the shaping of public beliefs about mass communication. Several did all of these.

Unfortunately, the criteria exclude many excellent studies of smaller scope, published in professional journals, that may have had their own significant impact. For such exclusions we can only say that such research reports become well known by other means and they are generally more readily available to scholars than most of the works reviewed in the present book.

Why was a second edition necessary? As in every field, the cutting edge continues to move forward. Therefore, it will come as no surprise that additional large-scale projects of significance to the field have come into prominence since the first edition was prepared. At least two major research efforts have become influential in providing direction to the field. These represent the major change that makes the second edition distinct from the first. In addition, the final chapter was replaced with a new version that attempts to bring together into a more cogent statement the major lessons that are provided by the thirteen research efforts now included.

One of the new "milestone" is the programmatic study of agenda-setting conducted by Donald L. Shaw, Maxwell E. McCombs, and their associates. It develops themes that are classic extensions of the great questions of the past concerning the role of the press in society. Its roots lie in the debates over the power of the press to shape political thinking that characterized the work of communication scholars before empirical research became the norm. The study of agenda-setting brings those questions forward into a contemporary world of research where the issues can be confronted through such strategies as survey techniques, probability samples, and cross-lagged correlations. The results indicate that the press—including both newspapers and broadcast news programs—is still a significant factor in the shaping of American public opinion.

The second addition to the book is the massive report, *Television and Behavior—Ten Years of Progress*, prepared and published in 1982 by the National Institute of Mental Health. That report claims that approximately 90 percent of the research ever done on the effects of television was conducted during the decade following the first Surgeon General's Report (which is summarized in our Chapter 12). In fact, the new report is so large that it is treated in two separate chapters in this new edition of our book. These two chapters try to bring together the major points that emerged from an examination of an enormous body of research on the influences of television on many aspects of behavior and social life.

Our final chapter provides both an overview of the major generalizations, focused theories, and broad paradigms to which these thirteen milestones contributed, and discussions of how they should be interpreted. It attempts to place the study of mass communication in a context of scientific investigation that is logically similar to that of other fields of knowledge.

It seems obvious that much of what was discovered over the half century represented by these research efforts is limited by the fact of *change*. The media have changed; their content has changed; their audiences have changed; and the society as a whole has changed.

Technological change is very obvious. The researchers who started it all by confronting the media at an earlier time would have been astounded if they could have looked into the future to see today's movies in color, stereo sound, FM radios, tiny portable receivers, color TV, multiple screen theaters, VCRs, digital disks, satellite transmissions, and all the rest. But change means more than advances in technology. What our media present to us has also changed. Media content that was seen decades ago as dangerous, immoral, or even shocking, may now seem routine and boring. People today have different standards of interpretation than those of earlier years. Audiences use new values and norms for judging human behavior generally. These, in turn, have emerged from broad social and cultural changes in the society as a whole—industrialization, urbanization, modernization, immigration, and so on.

An important question for researchers emerges from these considerations. How can we develop an accumulation of valid and reliable knowledge if what we study is constantly undergoing change? Do the findings and interpretations of earlier researchers have any significance for understanding the constantly changing society and constantly changing media? This issue is discussed in the final chapter and suggestions for integrating our accumulating research findings across time are offered.

Another interesting question concerns the implications of these milestone studies for the developing field of communication as an arena of specialized study. For one thing there is the nagging question of whether it is a discipline or merely an unfocused field. More than twenty years ago, De Fleur pointed out that the study of communication was beginning to assume the characteristics of a discipline in its own right. At that time, there were a number of transitions taking place that look even more important today than they might have during the 1960s. Prior to the 1960s, communication research was conducted for the most part by social scientists. They studied the media not to accumulate knowledge about the process and effects of mass communication but to gain insights into problems generated within their own disciplines—psychology, sociology, and political science. Many of the classic studies reviewed in the present book show that clearly.

But important changes have taken place. New academic systems for training people for the communication professions were developed. Schools and departments of communication brought together what had been a scattering of seemingly unrelated specialties. Graduate programs were founded. The number of students enrolled in communication majors and advanced degree programs increased sharply. These events provided a growing pool of positions for specialized teachers/researchers who increasingly made up communication faculties. Meanwhile, specialized journals, devoted solely to the publication of research on communication problems, were established. New kinds of textbooks began to appear to provide bodies of accumulated knowledge to study in increasingly standardized communication courses and specialties. Professional organizations grew. Some are regional; others are national or even international. All of these events moved the study of communication more closely toward the typical organization of a discipline.

As research slowly revealed insights and explanations of the process and effects of mass communication, the responsibility for designing and conducting research started to change hands. As the present book reveals, the founding studies were products of psychology and sociology, with minor input from political science. But a turning point came in 1961, when the first large-scale study of the effects of mass communication was published by investigators outside those fields. The work is summarized in our Chapter 10, which reviews *Television in the Lives of Our Children* by Wilbur Schramm, Jack Lyle, and Edwin Parker.

Today, at least some psychologists continue to pursue their traditional interests in violence and aggression in the context of media studies. They also probe media influences on various forms of prosocial behavior. But within psychology, the study of mass communication has marginal status at best. While some psychologists will probably continue to use media studies to test hypotheses about individual human behavior, their contributions to understanding our system of mass communication and its relationship to the society as a whole can be expected to be limited in the future. The situation of sociology is even more striking. Sociologists appear to have all but abandoned their interest in the study of mass communication. Whereas studies of the media were conducted by the most important scholars in the field just before and after World War II, few sociologists today continue that tradition. Political scientists have also discontinued media research after limited involvement in earlier years.

Communication scholars have now moved to center stage as the group responsible for conducting mass communication research. A corps of young men and women, well trained in schools and departments of communication are now the research specialists who will have to take up the challenge. It is they who inherit the intellectual tradition set forth in the present book. It is they who will produce the next milestones in mass communication research. It is they who will develop the theories that enable us to understand better the nature of our media, their role in society, and their influences on each of us. Those who participated in the development of their intellectual heritage can hardly wait to see what they will do.

Shearon A. Lowery   **Melvin L. De Fleur**

Acknowledgments

Figures 2.1 and 2 and Table 2.1 are from *Motion Pictures and the Social Attitudes of Children* by Ruth C. Peterson and L. L. Thurstone (New York: The Macmillan Company, 1933), and are reprinted by permission of W. W. Charters, Jr., Eugene, Oregon.

Segments in chapter 2 from *The Movies and Conduct* by Herbert Blumer (New York: The Macmillan Company, 1933) are reprinted by permission of W. W. Charters, Jr., Eugene, Oregon.

Excerpts from *Invasion from Mars,* a Mercury Theatre dramatization of H. G. Wells' *War of the Worlds,* are by Howard Koch. We have been unsuccessful in locating the copyright owner, and information as to same would be appreciated.

Tables 3.1 and 3.2 are from *The Invasion From Mars: A Study in the Psychology of Panic* by Hadley Cantril. Copyright 1940, copyright © renewed by Princeton University Press.

Figures 4.1, 4.2 and 4.3 are from *The People's Choice* by Paul F. Lazarsfeld, Bernard Berelson, and Hazel Gaudet © 1948 by Columbia University Press. Reprinted by permission.

Figures 5.1, 5.2, 5.3, and 5.4 and Tables 5.1 and 5.2 are from *Experiments on Mass Communication* by Carl I. Hovland, Arthur A. Lumsdaine, and Fred Sheffield. Copyright 1949 by Princeton University Press.

Tables 6.1, 6.2, 6.3, 6.4, and 6.5 are from *Communication and Persuasion* by Carl Hovland, Irving L. Janis, and Harold H. Kelley. Copyright 1953 by Yale University Press. Reprinted by permission.

Tables 7.1, 7.2, and 7.3 are from *Personal Influence* by Elihu Katz and Paul F. Lazarsfeld. Copyright 1955 by The Free Press, a Corporation. Reprinted with permission of Macmillan Publishing Co., Inc.

Figure 8.1 is from "Mass Communication and the Study of Rumor," by Melvin L. De Fleur, *Sociological Inquiry,* Vol. 32, No. 1, Winter 1962. Copyright 1962 by the University of Texas Press. Reprinted by permission.

Table 8.1 and Figures 8.2 and 8.3 are from "A Mass Communication Model of Stimulus Response Relationships: An Experiment in Leaflet Message Diffusion" by Melvin De Fleur in *Sociometry.* Vol. 19, No. 1, March 1956. Copyright 1956 by The American Sociological Association. Reprinted by permission.

Table 8.2 is from *The Flow of Information* by Melvin L. De Fleur and Otto N. Larson (New York: Harper and Brothers, 1958). Reprinted by permission of Melvin De Fleur.

Excerpts in chapter 9 from *Seduction of the Innocent* by Dr. Frederic Wertham. Copyright 1953, 1954 by Frederic Wertham. Reprinted by permission of Curtis Brown Associates, Ltd.

Figures 10.1, 10.2, 10.3, and 10.4 are from *Television in the Lives of Our Children* by Wilbur Schramm, Jack Lyle, and Edwin B. Parker. Reprinted with the permission of the publishers, Stanford University Press. © 1961 by the Board of Trustees of the Leland Stanford Junior University.

Tables 13.1, 13.2, 13.3 and Figures 13.1 and 13.2 are reprinted by permission from *The Emergence of American Political Issues* by Shaw and McCombs. Copyright © 1977 by West Publishing Company. All rights reserved.

1

Developing Frameworks for Studying Mass Communication

The American society is constantly changing. The mass media supported by that society are also changing. In some part, the process is reciprocal. That is, the society influences its media, but the media, once in place, sometimes modify the society. These facts make the search for stable generalizations about the personal, social, and cultural influence of mass communication a difficult one. For example, as will become clear from our examination of studies of the movies of the 1920s, such films apparently had a significant impact on the children of that particular period. But the films of the 1920s, and the responses made to them by young people during the time, offer few reliable guides to relationships between media and youth of more contemporary generations. Since the media first arrived, each succeeding decade has brought a different set of economic conditions, new technology, changing political demands, and a continuously developing culture. In this dynamic milieu, the media continued to change their form, content, and distribution. This, in turn, modified the influence that they had on the people who attended to them. The process continues, and it will go on into the foreseeable future.

What this means for the student of mass communication is that the question of what influence mass communication has on people is an extraordinarily complex one. There are few "eternal verities" that can adequately describe the effects of all mass media on all people during all historical periods. Even a conclusion about the influence of a particular medium that seems inescapably true for a specific category of people during a given period may prove to be invalid at a later time. This is not to say that no stable generalizations can be found through an examination of the major research studies of the past. As the present book indicates, we have learned a great deal about mass communication and how people are influenced by media in a given set of economic, political, and cultural conditions. There are also a few generalizations that appear to have wide applicability under a variety of times and circumstances.

But if there are only a limited number of timeless truths to be obtained from an examination of the research milestones of the past, why should they be reviewed in detail? Actually, there are a number of reasons. For example, such a review provides an intellectual history of mass communication as seen through the eyes of research scientists. That is a very different history from one understood from any other perspective. It shows the development of theories about cause and effect in the analysis of media influences on society as well as the progressive adaptation of an increasingly sophisticated research methodology to the study of mass communication. Such a review also reveals the evolution of a unique relationship between a community of communication scholars, a public interested in their findings, and a government increasingly willing to provide funds for research providing answers to socially significant questions.

Thus, a review of milestones of mass communication research is more than an effort to construct a list of propositions that spell out how the media influence people. It is a journey that starts at a unique point in the past. It was that point at which the media had developed to a degree where it seemed important to study their effects systematically because the public was concerned about their impact on their lives. It was also a point at which social science had developed the research tools needed for the task. It was during the late 1920s that the goal and the means came together. It was the beginning of an ever-expanding effort to assess the impact of mass communication through the use of scientific strategies.

What have been the major research studies that have shaped thinking about the nature and influence of mass communication in the United States since that beginning? A somewhat arbitrary answer to this question is given in the present book by our summaries of thirteen large-scale research projects, the findings of which have appeared in book form over the last half century. Why have we chosen these particular studies rather than a number of potential alternatives? The selection is somewhat arbitrary but by no means capricious. For example, the studies we have summarized have each made important contributions to the development of the field in at least one of three ways: (1) Some were investigations that led researchers to conceptualize the process of mass communication in a new and important way. (2) Others introduced innovative methodological procedures, techniques, or strategies that made a lasting contribution to the scientific study of mass communication. And (3) still others played a particularly important part in shaping the beliefs of the non-scientific public about the nature of media influences. Some of the studies we selected did only one of the foregoing. Others did two. At least a few did all three.

A second consideration in selecting what we have identified as milestones was that they all represent attempts to study the media within the framework of science. In some cases the research efforts we have selected were programs rather than single projects. Some were based on elaborate experiments; others used survey techniques. One was based on a purely clinical strategy. But above all, these thirteen appear to us as the ones that have made the most difference. They have been widely cited; they have stimulated extensive further research; some have created substantial controversies; but above all, they have attracted the attention of the community of communication scholars, and in many cases the general public, to provide important perspectives on the process and influences of mass communication.

In an ideal world, science would proceed very systematically to accomplish its twin goals of innovation and accumulation. In such a world, some studies would move forward the cutting edge of theory and method whereas others would replicate and confirm earlier findings. Such an ideal science would be self-policing, and the generalizations accumulated would be both reliable and valid.[1] Unfortunately, things seldom work out so neatly in the real world of scientific investigation. Studies in almost every field are undertaken for a bewildering variety of reasons, ranging from the trivial to the profound. Thus, the accumulation of knowledge is often frustratingly uncoordinated.

The study of mass communication has been particularly unsystematic. It is not a concisely defined field, and it has had only a relatively brief history. One problem has been that those who have studied the media in the past have come from several different disciplines. Only infrequently have they developed their research efforts in a "programmatic" manner. Typically they have almost never coordinated their efforts or built upon the results of previous research. Seldom have they been willing to abandon a theory because someone else's data failed to support it. Many investigations have been carried out simply because there was a substantial amount of money to do so, and the public wanted answers to some policy question. Many of those questions were not theoretically significant. In other words, media research did not move forward in a neat and orderly way following the ideal model of science. Our selection of milestone studies had to take this situation into account.

In spite of this unsystematic development, earlier studies did have at least *some* influence on later ones, and they represent the intellectual heritage of the present discipline. Over the years, there were identifiable changes in basic conceptualizations. There has also been an increase in the level of sophistication of methods and techniques used in media research. Generally, these advances paralleled developments in the social and behavioral sciences, mainly psychology and sociology. It is the purpose of the present chapter to present a brief overview of the progression of the general theoretical frameworks that have been used over the last half century for the study of mass communication. The chapter also presents a brief discussion of the changes in methodological strategies and procedures that have played a part in the conduct of media studies.

An essential beginning point for understanding the development of frameworks for the study of mass communication is to review the meaning of the term *mass society*. It is from this concept that came such derived terms as "mass" audience, "mass" media, and (of course) "mass" communication. Once the nature of this rather complex set of ideas has been clarified, the underlying thinking behind early theories of mass communication can be understood. This understanding sets the stage for changes in our central theories of the effects of mass communication that occurred both as a result of media research and findings from the parent social and behavioral sciences. Following the clarification of these theoretical issues in order to provide guidelines for the review of specific research efforts, the growth of the media of mass communication is briefly traced as it has occurred in American society.

CONCEPTUALIZING MASS SOCIETY

The term "mass," as used in "mass" society, is, as we have noted, the intellectual source from which we obtain the concepts of "mass" media and "mass" communication. Unless the mass concept is thoroughly understood, in both its historical and contemporary perspectives, theories about the nature and effects of mass communication cannot be fully grasped. It does not refer merely to large numbers. Many so-called mass societies happen to have large populations. However, the underlying features that distinguish this type of society from other forms (e.g., traditional society) have to do with the relationships between their members rather than the size of their populations. This idea of mass as a form of societal organization emerged from a century and a half of theoretical analyses by a number of pioneer social scientists. It remains important in the public's beliefs about the power and influence of the media.

The concept of mass society emerged from the study of fundamental social changes that took place in society over the last two centuries. These changes altered drastically the relationships that members of society have with others as they carry on their everyday lives. The changes were subtle, complex, and profound. It is not easy to capture their essential nature in a brief review. However, we can begin by summarizing the master trends that shaped the emerging mass society.

The Master Trends

Prior to the late eighteenth century, western society was what sociologists call "traditional" in its organization. It was changing only slowly. People remained rooted to the land, and agriculture was almost everyone's principal preoccupation. The production of goods from wood, metal, leather, and cloth was in the hands of individual artisans and craftsmen. There were a few cottage industries and entrepreneurs, but no factories and no vast systems for distribution and consumption of manufactured products. Water, wind, and muscle were the sources of power used to operate the few machines that existed.

In terms of social organization, people were tied to each other through family and kinship, loyalties to local rulers, or through deeply established beliefs, customs, and traditions that guided their behavior in almost all aspects of social life. Communication between people was, for the vast majority, a matter of word-of-mouth. Books were being printed, but only a few people were sufficiently affluent or literate to use them. Early forms of the newspaper had appeared in some cities, but they played little part in the daily affairs of the population at large.

By the end of the century, major changes that would drastically restructure this traditional type of society were beginning. The development and spread of mass communication would be part of those changes, but almost every aspect of social life was to undergo alteration. In retrospect, we can identify three master trends that were, and continue to be, at the heart of the change from traditional to modern society. These are *industrialization, urbanization,* and *modernization*. As the new society was developing, each of these trends had a profound influence on social relationships, material culture, social norms and the thoughtways of individuals.

Industrialization. Generally speaking, the Industrial Revolution began as the eighteenth century came to a close. It was not a sudden transition but a gradual acceleration of processes of change that had begun much earlier. The idea of producing goods for entrepreneurs to market was well-established in Europe long before the mid-1700s. Developments in science and engineering were about to yield new power sources and machinery. The next major step was to combine investment capital with the new machines that could spin, weave, grind, stamp, and cut with a stamina and precision that no craftsman could match. With these devices replacing human hands and muscles, goods could be produced far more rapidly, uniformly, and cheaply than ever before. Steam power derived from wood or coal soon replaced other sources of energy and transformed one industry after another.

Such applications spread through the western world all during the nineteenth century, and soon a great variety of manufactured goods was being produced. The social significance of this process is that it greatly changed relationships between people in terms of their work. Earlier, human beings made things for each other. The artisan or craftsman performed or controlled all phases of the production process, from assembling raw materials to selling the finished product to his customer. In the new industrial order, the process of production was divided into a host of ministeps, with machines doing most of the more demanding tasks. The human being became a kind of appendage to the machine, working at the machine's pace, feeding it raw products, or taking its finished goods away to be marketed by impersonal systems to unknown customers. In his classic analysis, Marx maintained that this system resulted in serious *alienation* of the industrial worker, not only from the work itself but from other people and even from himself.[2]

The industrial labor force required people with minimal skills who could be hired for minimal pay. They had to be free from traditional obligations to lands and landlords so that they could work when they were needed. In England, much earlier, many peasants had been evicted from their farms by the Enclosure Acts; they constituted just such a pool of free labor. It became clear quite early that using such workers was better than using slaves (who were available at the time). Even though the workers had to be paid, they could be dismissed in slack periods, which in the long run minimized the costs of production. In other countries there were somewhat similar poorly educated and unskilled populations that could make up an industrial labor force. In the United States, immigrants who had been driven out of other countries were welcomed as they entered at the "bottom of the ladder" in the mines, mills, and factories. Even many of those who went first to the farms later migrated to towns and cities to become part of the new labor force.

Two additional elements were especially significant in shaping the emerging social order. These were the *factory system* and the *corporation*. The factory system was a direct result of the economic advantages of "shop production." This meant housing the machinery, labor, and stages of the manufacturing process under one roof. Plants were located, logically enough, where materials, labor, and transportation could easily come together. The social significance of the early factory system was that new communities developed around the sites—communities with no history or traditions of their own. They drew their residents from diverse sources. Social relationships in such areas, even outside the plant, tended to be culturally rootless and personally anonymous.

As factories, marketing enterprises, transportation systems, and financial institutions grew larger, the importance of the corporation became increasingly clear. Corporations, as legal entities for sharing risks and protecting shareholders from personal liability, had existed prior to industrialization, but it was the spread of this form of sociolegal organization that made the industrial society possible. The majority of early factories were often financed by a single individual, or at most by a few partners or a family. But as industrial and commercial activities increased in scope, larger and larger amounts of capital were required. Through the sale of shares, it was possible to obtain funds from hundreds or even thousands of owners willing to risk their capital for a proportionate part of the profits.

The significance of the development of the corporate structure and the great expansion in the size of industrial-commercial groups is that they brought a new dependence on *bureaucracy* as a form of social organization. A small group can be informal and depend upon intuitive understanding of its rules and tasks in order to achieve its goals. A group of thousands, designed to achieve the goals of a factory, a retail chain, or even a newspaper, must be far more impersonal in its structure. Groups organized as bureaucracies are deliberately designed to achieve clear-cut goals in a rational and efficient manner. Aside from all of the bad jokes about bumbling bureaucrats and snarls of red tape, bureaucracy, in principle, is the most effective way in which large-scale social enterprises can be conducted. A bureaucratic group has written rules; the activities of each person's position are carefully set forth; patterns of power and authority are clearly defined; the system of rewards and punishments is specified in contractual agreements. There are no real alternatives to this form of social organization for enterprises of large scope. For this reason, we live in an age of bureaucracy. All large-scale activities in contemporary society—manufacturing, commercial, educational, military, religious, sports, medical and recreational—are carried out by groups that are bureaucratically organized. About the only exceptions are our families and friends.

Needless to say, the new types of human relationships resulting from the growth of bureaucracy were very different from the older forms based on friendship, kinship, or traditional loyalty. As the traditional society gave way to the industrial order, the bonds that united people were based less and less on such sentiments and more and more on the impersonal obligations of the legal contract.[3] People still had families and friends, but the increasingly mobile, differentiated, and bureaucratized society was one that tended to reduce close personal ties between people rather than strengthen them.

Urbanization. The social controls that traditional people exercise over each other decline sharply with the changes mentioned. People's customs and other rules for behavior give way to more formal means of control through civil or restitutive law and criminal justice systems with police, courts, and penal institutions. Deviant behavior becomes increasingly common as the older rules lose their force. The second master trend that has played a part in the emergence of mass society is urbanization. Defined very simply, urbanization is a process by which an increasing proportion of the population of a given area live in towns and cities. In the history of mankind, it is a relatively recent phenomenon. While human life in various forms goes back millions of years, people have been city dwellers for only a short part of that time. For example, the first known cities were established a mere 7000 years ago.[4] We think of Europe today as highly urbanized. However, 150 years ago it was still overwhelmingly rural. As late as the beginning of the nineteenth century, only 3 percent of the world's people lived in communities of 5000 or more.[5] Today, urbanization is one of the most significant trends of modern life. Even in the New World, cities reach 15 million or more (e.g., Mexico City). Dozens of cities in the United States have exceeded one million inhabitants. Today, less than 5 percent of the U.S. population is still in farming, and only about a quarter of the population lives in rural areas. These trends are very much in evidence in other parts of the globe. Some countries are considerably more urbanized than the United States.

This explosion in urban growth began and kept pace with the industrial revolution. But while the two master trends are closely linked, they are not simply different ways of looking at the same thing. In many areas, urbanization has proceeded without industrialization. Other areas have become industrialized without significant changes in the proportion of the population that is urban. The social significance of urbanization is that it changes the quality of life. Above all, it brings unlike people together. In the early days of industrialization, uprooted farm people were drawn to the new factory towns to seek work. They were joined there by others from different parts of the country and by people from the slums of established cities. These people did not relate to each other easily because of their social and psychological differences. Whereas the earlier rural and traditional social order was based on clear conceptions of the rules of social behavior, life in the new cities was characterized by a confusion of the rules, customs, and traditions, a condition called *anomie*.

The process of bringing unlike people together was accelerated greatly in the United States by heavy immigration from other lands. Not only were rural people going to the city to seek their fortunes, but millions of foreigners were arriving to enter at the bottom of the social ladder. The population of the United States grew very rapidly during the late nineteenth and early twentieth centuries as national policy sought to fill vacant land. A veritable tidal wave of immigration brought poorly educated and economically deprived people to the new world. Emma Lazarus' words inscribed at the base of the Statue of Liberty capture the essential characteristics of this inflow of humanity:

> Give me your tired, your poor,
> your huddled masses yearning to breathe free,
> the wretched refuse of your teeming shore—
> send these, the homeless, tempest-tossed to me:
> I lift my lamp beside the golden door.

And so they came. They poured in from northern, southern, and eastern Europe; from Asia and Africa; from Mexico and the dozens of lands to the south. They settled mainly in the cities, entered at the bottom of the labor force, and began their struggle upward. They spoke different languages, followed different customs, and subscribed to different values. They developed prejudices toward each other; called each other bad names; discriminated against each other; and sometimes fought each other in the streets. All the while, those who had arrived earlier deplored and rejected the later arrivals. The end product was what August Comte had called "a multitude of separate corporations."[6] They split up into enclaves where language and customs could be maintained and where dislike and distrust of "the others" could be kept alive. Emotion and sentiment became more significant than reason and rationality in decisions about behavior. As time went on, many of those who had entered at the bottom did move up the social ladder. The majority did not. The industrial labor force, its related commercial activities, and the opportunities provided by public education provided the basis for upward mobility for some and social differentiation for all. Urbanization, in other words, created great differences between people. These differences provided no basis for the older and traditional bonds, based on loyalty, trust, and fealty, to develop again and keep people together. The new social order was what Ferdinand Tönnies called the *Gesellschaft*.[7] Trust was replaced by *distrust*. In a society of distrust, the contract rather than the handshake becomes the principal basis for regulating obligations between people.

Modernization. As industrialization and urbanization continued, the life-styles of the inhabitants of modern societies underwent change. Hundreds and even thousands of *innovations* were adopted. Inventive people designed machines for every conceivable purpose. By the turn of the century, the industrial order was producing an incredible array of devices that the ordinary family could purchase and use. These ranged from basics, such as tools and clothing, to the exotic, such as ointments for bust development or electric devices guaranteed to restore hair on bald heads. Mechanical innovations— indoor plumbing, central heat, the automobile, refrigeration, electric lights, and so on—had an impact on every aspect of life. Not only were the objects of everday use undergoing change, but the very rhythm and meaning of life were different. Time scheduling assumed a new importance. Work, play, meals, education, and even worship started and stopped according to the clock.

Industrialization and urbanization had already created differences between people. Modernization was a force toward even greater distinctions. Material life-styles, based on consumption of the products of the new industries, were quite different at each level in the stratification system. Rich people had always lived differently from poor people, but the emerging industrial order brought a tremendous new diversity of goods. Those at the highest economic level could engage in conspicuous consumption and surround themselves with amenities never dreamed of by the affluent in more traditional societies.

Many of these new products served as status symbols and were adopted as quickly as possible by those who could afford them. Those lower in the system looked on with envy or used the new time-payment plans to acquire what they could. Between the economic elite at the top and the destitute poor at the bottom stretched numerous middle levels identified mainly by their patterns of consumption of the goods of modern society. In this way, modernization created another basis for social differentiation in addition to those stemming from regional, ethnic, and religious sources.

The process of modernization is closely linked with the growth of the mass media. Populations undergoing modernization not only increase their consumption of goods but their use of print, film, and broadcast media. Generally, they undergo a corresponding increase in literacy, which has an influence on their perceptions and participation in government.

Modern societies, then, are media-dependent societies. Their populations make use of the media for achieving a great many goals that are handled differently in the traditional society. The media provide information critical to economic, political, religious, and educational decisions in ways that are totally different from preindustrial societies. This flow of information further breaks people away from traditional ways of life and thrusts them into constantly changing ways of thinking about family obligations, sexual mores, basic values, and other central features of human existence.

Contemporary Society as Mass Society

Our review of the master trends underlying the transition from traditional to contemporary society has emphasized increases in social differentiation and psychological isolation in urban-industrial populations brought about by such factors as bureaucracy, contracts, migration, stratification, and the spread of innovation. It is said that all of these individual and social forces have worked to set people apart far more than to bring them together. The master trends, in one form or another, led social theorists of the last century to conceptualize the urban-industrial society as a *mass* society. The term "mass" in this context refers not to numbers but to a distinctive pattern of social organization, more precisely, a process of changing social organization that occurs when industrialization, urbanization, and modernization increasingly modify the social order. In other words, "mass" society emerges when the following changes take place:

1. Social differentiation in the society *increases* because of the growing division of labor, the bureaucratization of human groups, the mixing of unlike populations, and differential patterns of consumption.
2. The effectiveness of informal social controls *erodes* as the influence of traditional norms and values declines, leading to increases in the incidence of deviant behavior.
3. The use of formal social controls (the contract, restitutive law, and criminal justice systems) *rises* as the new impersonal society develops.
4. Conflicts *increase* because of social differences between people with opposing values and life-styles.
5. Open and easy communication as a basis of social solidarity between people becomes *more difficult* because of social differentiation, impersonality and distrust due to psychological alienation, the breakdown of meaningful social ties, and increasing anomie among the members.

Does this theoretical description provide an accurate picture of society today? Clearly it does not. There is much more to contemporary society than this portrayal of people psychologically and socially isolated from each other. Yet, the idea remains important. The concept of mass society is significant for the study of the media for two reasons. First, in spite of the fact that the theoretical picture it provides of contemporary society is overdrawn, we can recognize at least some of these trends around us. We *have* undergone industrialization, urbanization, and modernization. Life in contemporary society is very different because of these changes from what it was in the "good old days" of traditional society. The ideas embedded in the conceptualization of mass society do provide an understanding of at least some of the features of life in the urban-industrial social order. But more important, it was this conceptualization of mass society that dominated the thinking of those intellectuals who were first concerned about the effects of the new mass media.

As each new medium came into the society and was adopted for widespread use, there was an increasing level of concern about the influences of the mass communication process. As the newspapers and, later, films and broadcasting were increasingly criticized for their presumed undesirable influences, the idea that members of the mass society could easily be controlled by powerful media troubled the critics. It was assumed that the isolated and alienated individual was at the mercy of those who could control the media. The media were thought to have great power because of the absence of other competing social and psychological influences on people.

THE SPREAD OF THE MEDIA IN MASS SOCIETY

Our contemporary forms of mass communication emerged as a part of the development of mass society. The new media—newspapers for the ordinary citizen, movies as a form of family entertainment, radio and television as devices of daily use at home—were products of industrialization and modernization.[8] They would not have been possible without the gathering together of large audiences resulting from urbanization. There was no single date that marks the beginning of the age of mass communication, but it came with the development of the first mass newspaper. Print as a medium of communication had been around for centuries, but it was the mass newspaper that brought printed information to the ordinary citizen of the industrializing society. Magazines, film, and broadcast media followed later as social changes as well as scientific and technological advances made them possible.

Print

The techniques of writing have ancient roots. This skill was invented independently in several places in the world at various times. This important ability to communicate using written symbols spread slowly over the centuries as characters and alphabets became increasingly standardized and as lighter and more portable surfaces became available. The printing press and the process of manufacturing paper were important technological advances that eventually led to the use of print as a *mass* medium. However, it was not until the early part of the nineteenth century that ordinary people began to have direct experiences with the printed word.

Books, of course, are the oldest print medium. They were first produced by a press with moveable type in 1456. For centuries they remained a medium for the elite. Few ordinary people were literate, and still fewer could afford to buy a book even if they could read it. Increasingly, however, the use of books spread among the better educated segments of a society. Then, as education itself became more commonplace, the use of books increased until in the nineteenth century they became a mass medium. Today, they remain our most respected medium in terms of their use as college textbooks, works of literary merit, scholarship, or scientific importance. They are also a very popular medium in the form of cheap paperbacks produced for all taste levels.

The mass newspaper got its start in 1834 in New York when a printer put together a power press, a scheme for financing the paper through advertising, and a bureaucratic organization for gathering the news and distributing the paper. Earlier, there had been newspapers for the educated minority, but the new daily paper was aimed at those for whom literacy was a relatively new experience. By the time the first mass newspaper appeared, urbanization was well under way. Industrialization had produced a working class that was not tied to agriculture, and modernization had brought free public education to the children of the new industrial labor force. The new venture was profitable beyond the dreams of its publisher, and within months he had numerous imitators. Soon there was a mass newspaper in every major city, and the age of mass communication had begun.

The newspaper spread rapidly in the United States, not only in a geographic sense but in its increasing adoption by the public. Great newspaper empires were founded by pioneer journalists, such as William Gordon Bennett, Horace Greeley, and William Randolph Hearst. By the end of the century, the newspaper was not only a deeply established mass medium; it was "the only game in town." It had no real competitors until the growth of the movies and the development of broadcasting. The peak of newspaper usage in the United States was during the decade 1910–1920 (the period of World War I). Circulations were at an all-time high in terms of the number of daily newspapers produced and consumed per household. For example, in 1910 more than 1.3 daily newspapers were sold per household in the United States. Since that time, the newspaper has declined steadily but slowly. Today, the number of competing newspapers has been greatly reduced; the majority are owned by large newspaper chains, and circulation has dropped to about 0.8 per household.[9] However, the newspaper, with millions of daily readers, remains a major mass medium in contemporary society.

Magazines have a shorter history than either books or newspapers. Late in the last century, printing techniques and postal services had developed to a point where mass-circulation magazines were possible. Modernization had raised the literacy level, and the magazine provided a supplement to the briefer accounts of the newspaper. During the late nineteenth century and the first half of the twentieth, most magazines were aimed at a large and general readership. With circulations in the millions, they were a significant mass medium. In more recent times, the general and large-circulation magazines have all but disappeared. Today, there are some 10,000 different periodicals produced in the United States, but for the most part they are aimed at very specialized categories of readers. As social differentiation has increased, it is no longer financially profitable to produce a magazine that will appeal to everyone. Magazines now focus on interest groups; there is a magazine for every taste, hobby, and activity. These magazines range from *Skin Diver* and *Model Train* to *Penthouse* and *Gourmet*. Readership is high because issues are often passed on to others to be read again and again. Taken as a whole, magazines constitute a major mass medium, even though their readership is scattered across thousands of specialized topics and interests.

Film

As a mass medium, the film has had a relatively short history. While its technological roots lie in the distant past, it became a form of recreation for ordinary people in society less than a century ago. The lens, critical to both photography and projection, was understood and used as early as 600 B.C. However, the idea of projecting shadow images onto a screen through a transparency was not to become a reality until the 1600s. Then, as science moved slowly forward, the basic chemistry of photography was developed, and the light-sensitive photographic plate became available. It was not until 1839 that the first actual photographs were made, to astonish the world with their vivid detail. Progressing from still to motion pictures required an understanding of the physiology of the visual senses and the psychology of perceiving motion from a series of rapidly projected photographs. By the beginning of the 1900s, simple moving pictures of brief duration were being shown to paying audiences, and the stage was set for the movies to become a major mass medium.

The first family-oriented motion picture theaters were the simple and crude "nickelodeons." By 1910, there were some 10,000 such exhibition halls in various cities of the United States, and early motion picture production studios were supplying a variety of silent films for their use. But it was during the next decade that the movies blossomed into a major mass medium. More attractive theaters were built. Movies became longer and told stories. The star system was invented: sex gods and goddesses of the screen enthralled millions of fans. Although the movies were silent until about 1927, they were a major form of weekly entertainment for some 90 million as the 1920s came to a close.

The Golden Age came between 1930 and 1940. Movies had no competitors. The sale of tickets per household was at an all-time high of about 2.5 per week for every household in the United States. (Currently, it has dropped to a mere 0.27 per household per week.) The decline of the movies began when television started to reach the majority of households in the United States. At first, the black-and-white broadcasts made only minor inroads in the movie industry. Later, as color television brought free talking pictures into all corners of the nation, the popularity of the movies dropped greatly. Movies remain today mainly because they are a relatively inexpensive form of entertainment for children and young people of dating age. The film industry also makes money producing movies for the insatiable television industry. Yet, the future of the movies is less than clear. As TV increases its flexibility with new forms of cable and subscription broadcasts, the number of entertainment choices for most Americans will expand. Indeed, this expansion of choices will probably also occur in most other countries as satellites make broadcasts increasingly available. Therefore, the fate of the movies in their traditional form remains to be seen.

Broadcasting

The idea of instantaneous communication over long distances had fired the imagination of thinkers for centuries. It was not until 1844, however, that the dream was realized. In that year Samuel F.B. Morse sent a message along a copper wire between Washington, D.C. and Baltimore, Maryland to open the era of telecommunication. By the end of the century, radio waves had been discovered by Heinrich Hertz and adapted to a wireless telegraph by Guglielmo Marconi. When the waves were suitably interrupted to produce coded signals, they could telegraph information across vast distances without wires.

Transmission of the human voice was accomplished via the wireless telegraph by 1906, when a few additional devices (e.g., the vacuum tube) were added. The age of broadcasting had been made possible. However, at that time, radio was by no means a mass medium for household reception, but was used by military and commercial interests for a variety of purposes. A few amateurs were able to receive the signals at home, but the idea that radio could become a mass medium for ordinary people had not yet reached its time.

It was not until the early 1920s that home radio became a reality. It all happened in a remarkably brief time and in a totally unforeseen manner. A few manufacturers had experimented with building and marketing home receivers, and several thousand had been purchased by 1920. However, broadcasting was only sporadic; there were no regular "programs" to listen to. In November of that year the presidential election results were beamed through the evening sky to a handful of listeners from an experimental transmitter in Pittsburgh. It was little more than a novelty, but the event captured widespread attention. Soon the demand for sets increased greatly, and manufacturers began supplying them to an eager public. Transmitters were operated in several cities by manufacturers who wanted to stimulate sales. It was all great fun, and soon people built their own transmitters. They didn't cost very much. There were only a few legal restrictions and no effective control over frequency, use, power, and hours of operation.

Soon, the situation deteriorated; stations operated on the same frequencies, and the airwaves became a jumble of sound. New legislation was necessary to control the assignment of frequencies and the power of transmitters so that they did not interfere with each other. Such legislation was finally completed in the form of the Federal Communications Act of 1934. In revised form this remains the basic legal structure for broadcasting in the United States.

From only a few thousand in 1920, the number of home receivers rose sharply during the next decade. By 1925, four million sets were in use. By 1930, the number of sets had jumped to 13 million. The number of home receivers reached one per household in the United States in 1936, with a total of 30 million sets in the hands of the public. Radio had truly become a mass medium.

Today, Americans own an astonishing number of radio receivers. In the form of automobile, kitchen, bedside, and portable radios, the average is nearly eight sets per household. Thus, radio remains a mass medium in spite of its competition from television. It has a vast daytime and evening audience. There has been a substantial shift from AM broadcasting frequencies to static-free FM, which is now the dominant technology.

Radio's most significant period as a major medium was during the twenty years from 1930 to 1950. It had no direct competitor; its technology was sophisticated; live broadcasts could be received from all parts of the world. It provided rapid dissemination of the news, and it was central to the economic institution as an advertising medium; it was also one of the principal forms of home entertainment for millions of citizens. Even though it had to change when television came, radio continues to provide people with information and entertainment at times when attention to other media is inappropriate. With its timely news summaries, local focus, and broad range of music, it appears to have found a stable niche in an increasingly competitive media environment.

Television is a child of radio in many respects. However, the child has grown to dwarf its parent. The earliest television broadcasts outside the laboratory were experimental in nature and took place at various times in the late 1920s. During the 1930s, research continued, and the technology of the new medium was made more practical. Late in the decade, limited scheduled broadcasts to the public began from an experimental station in the Empire State Building. A few thousand people in the New York area had purchased sets and were anticipating the growth of the new phenomenon. However, the fledgling industry was grounded before it got into the air, so to speak. World War II intervened, and the electronics manufacturing capacities of the nation were devoted to producing the radio equipment and radar that were desperately needed for defense.

As the war closed, TV began to develop in earnest. In 1946, about 8000 sets were in the hands of the public. A mere five years later, more than 37 million home receivers were in use! The spread of transmitters matched this spectacular growth. They had been established in all major cities. But the federal government quickly stepped in, in order to avoid the chaos in broadcasting that had taken place during the early years of radio. Frequencies, levels of power, and times of operation needed to be controlled in a master plan for the entire country so that the signal of one station did not block out or interfere with that of another. The Federal Communications Commission placed a four-year freeze (1948–52) on new station licensing while engineers produced the master plan. This work was completed satisfactorily, and the rapid pattern of growth resumed during the remainder of the 1950s. By the end of the decade, there was slightly more than one television set per household in the United States, and a signal reached almost all parts of the country. Today, the figure has reached 1.5 sets per household, and virtually every corner of the country receives network television. Color sets have nearly replaced the older black and white receivers.

Today, television is a highly profitable industry. It inherited its advertising role from radio, along with the free entertainment function. With its penetration into the society, it is currently unmatched as an advertising vehicle for products of wide use. The gross revenues from advertising via the three major American networks are many millions of dollars annually. It can command audiences in the United States of 50 million for a single event (e.g., *Roots*). On a world-wide basis, with the aid of satellites, nearly a billion people can watch a live broadcast (e.g., the wedding of Prince Charles and Lady Diana of Great Britain in 1981).

On the other hand, the future may not be so rosy. Television may be about to face an era of turmoil. Cable systems, independent of the major networks, are rapidly being developed in American cities. For years Congress and the FCC protected the networks against their competition, but now all the barriers have been removed. A cable system can bring far more channels to the viewer than the usual four to six now typical in off-the-air reception. The range of material available across this large number of channels has the capability of dividing up the audience into many smaller ones, compared to the huge ones that now view programs produced by the three major networks. This splintering of the audience took place as magazines moved from huge general circulation periodicals to a large number of specialized audiences. What this will do to the networks financially is anyone's guess. Clearly, there is the possibility that advertisers will turn away from the networks when they can no longer command their huge audiences and try the more specialized forms of advertising strategies now used in magazines. In any case, the next several years represent an era of transition for the television industries.

Generally, then, in looking at all of the mass media in modern society, it is clear that they are a major feature of social life as we know it. They have a central role in the affairs of the urban-industrial society and bring modernizing influences to the most remote rural community. They have spread through the society, often with startling rapidity, and represent a part of the broader process of industrialization; their growth period covers more than a century.

However, their major development as a system of competing media has taken place within the last half century. Today they reach every eye and ear. Children and adults alike spend large proportions of their waking hours with the media in one form or another. They have made us dependent on their information in every sphere of life, from economics to religion. It is little wonder that many people are concerned about what they may be doing to us. Great debates have been carried on since the first newspapers appeared to be used by ordinary people. Are the effects of these media evil or good? Do they influence us in ways we do not want? Or do they serve us well by enlarging our consciousness and perspectives?

Such questions and many more have preoccupied the attention of critics, public leaders, scholars, researchers, and intelligent lay persons for many decades. Their curiosity and concerns have led to a number of research studies on various aspects of the media and their effects. However, it was not until the late 1920s that the first large-scale investigation was made. Somewhat predictably, it focused on the influences of motion pictures, a new medium that was growing with great rapidity and had a special appeal for children. The movies were a deep source of concern as millions of youngsters absorbed ideas from them every week. We need to look briefly at the growth in research capability that made it possible to do such a scientific study and at the theoretical perspectives on mass communication that were a product of the mass society theory outlined earlier.

THE DEVELOPMENT OF RESEARCH TECHNOLOGY

Prior to the 1920s, there was little in the way of systematic investigation of the effects of mass communication within what we would today call a scientific perspective. There was a great deal being written about the media. Most intellectuals of the nineteenth century denounced them at one time or another for their presumed destructive effects on the social order. Such critical claims continued in the twentieth century (and continue still). But these claims were just that—claims. Until well into the present century, it was not possible to approach the issue of media influences within a framework of objective, quantitative analysis where conclusions were based on value-free criteria. That is, it was not until scientific methods were available that research findings could replace speculation, accusation, and undocumented conclusions in the discussion of media effects. The development of those scientific methods did not come quickly or easily. They were part of the more general development of the social and behavioral sciences.

The Logical Foundations of Communication Research

Communication research is an extension of the methodology and theory-building strategies of the social and behavioral sciences. These in turn rest heavily upon the underlying logical strategies of the physical and biological sciences. Early in the nineteenth century, it became clear to many scholars concerned about human individual and social behavior that the research strategies of the physical sciences offered hope for the future in understanding people. Those research strategies were leading to great success in developing reliable and valid knowledge in such fields as physics, chemistry, and biology. For example, by the time that the first mass newspaper appeared, photography was about to become a reality. People were being vaccinated routinely against at least some serious diseases, and the telegraph had been in existence for five years. The social sciences, by comparison, were still in the age of Plato.

It was not that there was a lack of ideas about the individual or the social order. It was more like an embarrassment of riches. The wisdom of hundreds of philosophers was available. The problem was that they were all saying different things about human nature and society. There was no systematic and objective way to sort out valid conclusions from all the theories that could not be supported by facts. This was not so in the other sciences. Systematic observation, guided by reasoned theoretical perspectives and careful weighing of numerical evidence, had proved to be enormously successful in yielding reliable and valid generalizations. This procedure had brought Darwin to his historic conclusions about the origins of species; it was leading others to a host of discoveries in medicine, chemistry, astronomy, and physics. Was it not possible, and was it not wise, to try to adapt these strategies and procedures to study human beings in their individual and social activities?

Many scoffed at the idea or found it presumptuous. Some in well-established scientific fields dismissed such an effort as preposterous. Human behavior was too complex, they said, or too erratic and unpredictable. And how on earth could one quantify thoughts and emotions? Human activities did not follow immutable laws, they pointed out, as did the phenomena of the physical and biological world. Thus, the critics concluded, there were no regularities to be discovered by such a science even if the science might be possible. Others proclaimed that the whole idea was wicked. God had given human beings their destiny, and their behavior was the result of His divine plan. To presume that some sort of scientific approach could pry into such matters and see regular predictable patterns of action was little short of blasphemy!

Quantitative Procedures

In spite of the opposition of skeptics and critics, social and psychological pioneers did break away from the undisciplined philosophies of the past. They began to make measurements of limited forms of behavior. By the mid-nineteenth century, the psychologist Weber worked out a mathematically sophisticated system of "psychophysics" to describe patterns in people's perceptions of differences in the intensities of stimuli.[10] Toward the end of the century, the sociologist Durkheim assembled numerical data on deaths by suicide from various countries in Europe and developed an innovative theory concerning that ultimate act. It was not speculation; it was backed by impressive quantitative evidence.[11] Charles Booth used meticulous counting and classification to describe the way of life of London's poor in an early version of the survey.[12] Social psychologist Wilhelm Wundt in Leipzig developed the first laboratory for the precise measurement of human reaction times as early as 1879. He used a number of ingenious brass intruments and experiments.

As the new century began, these pioneering efforts led the way to the future. The social and behavioral sciences were about to become a reality. Still, it was clearly very difficult to use the experimental format or any other quantitative procedure for the study of anything but the most restricted forms of behavior. But new approaches were being developed by mathematicians and other scholars. These were the new techniques for examining the statistical parameters and distributions of numbers—their central tendencies, their scatter, and variability. Laws of probability had already been worked out, and these could be used to interpret the likelihood of any given pattern of differences between means. Pearson's new procedure, called the "product-moment coefficient of correlation," was another major breakthrough. Its index, r, summarized the tendency of two arrays of numbers to rise and fall jointly.

The beauty of these new statistical techniques was that they were universal in their application to scientific problems. It did not matter whether the numbers used represented observations from agriculture, biology, communication, psychology, sociology, or zoology. These statistical procedures, and the many more that have come since those early times, opened the scientific method to the social and behavioral sciences. Communication research followed these traditions and depends on them in the same manner.

By the beginning of the 1920s, the teaching of statistical techniques began in earnest in the social and behavioral sciences. Yet this generated considerable debate. More conservative scholars in the older traditions rejected the radical new procedures, claiming that they were sterile and atheoretical. How could one understand the delicacy and richness of human life, they asked, by looking at a table of numbers or a statistical index? In the end, however, the quantitative procedures found increasing acceptance. With them came the standardized questionnaire as a means of generating numerical data, the random sample that could fit the underlying assumptions of the new statistical procedures, and the probability considerations for deciding whether a given generalization was merely a reflection of chance.

As the movement toward quantification became more sophisticated, additional procedures were devised for probing into areas previously not accessible to scientific approaches. The attitude scales, pioneered by sociologist Emory Bogardus and psychologist L. L. Thurstone, made it possible to reduce people's psychological orientations to numerical scale values. This touched off a tidal wave of attitude studies. The techniques of partial and multiple correlation, the analysis of variance, and nonparametric statistics were added to the tools available for research.

Calculation of large data sets remained a laborious procedure, and ways were invented to make this easier. Before there were mechanical calculators and computers, there were Holerith cards with holes punched around their edges so that long wires could be inserted. Those with the holes punched out to the edge of the card would drop out of a pack. The others would remain. This is the same binary principle of the IBM card, and it worked well enough. Calculation from large data sets was also facilitated by grouping the data into class intervals and working with their midvalues. The quantitative procedures of content analysis were developed from this base. These procedures became very important in communication research. The frequency with which specific words, phrases, or themes appeared in a given communication could be counted; statistical relationships between these data and other factors could then be studied. It was a useful procedure for showing trends in the treatment of issues over time, or for comparing the treatment of a given type of content in various media.

It was not until these research tools began to be available that a scientific approach to the study of mass communication could get its start. But numbers alone are not enough: research cannot be done in a theoretical vacuum. The development of statistical procedures, measurement techniques, and research designs can only be effective in advancing a field if at the same time it develops hypotheses and theories that can be guides to what should be studied. For this reason, we need to understand how new frameworks emerged for understanding and explaining the influence of the media.

EMERGING THEORIES OF MEDIA EFFECTS

The ability to do research on the effects of mass communication was of enormous importance in developing theories to explain their role and significance in contemporary society. As investigators made use of increasingly sophisticated techniques and procedures, they began to come up with research findings that required them to modify earlier explanations of how, and to what extent, mass communication had effects on individuals and society. Research within the framework of science and in a large-scale sense began in the late 1920s. These early studies were based on a theory of the effects of mass communication derived directly from the assumptions of the nature of mass society noted earlier. This early theory assumed that the media had great power to influence every individual, more or less uniformly. As we will see, subsequent research increasingly called this idea into question. New theories that assumed more selective and less powerful effects had to be formulated. As research continued, these in turn were called into question as the study of short-term immediate influences of the media revealed a very mixed picture. Eventually, theories and research strategies were to be revised again and again to search for more indirect and long-term effects.

In the present section, we will review several significant theoretical formulations that emerged from research at various points in time over the last half century. Each advanced in some degree our understanding of how mass communication can influence individuals and society. For the most part, none of these theoretical explanations is totally "wrong." Some give more accurate and complete pictures of the effects of mass communication than others. But generally speaking, as research accumulates, increasingly valid and reliable generalizations about the effects of mass communication have emerged.

The Theory of Uniform Influences

It will be recalled that in the assumptions of the nature of mass society, urban-industrial populations were seen as diverse, differentiated, and free from binding social ties. Their members were said to act less on the basis of reason and rationality and more on impulse, sentiment, and emotion. Because of these assumptions, modern society was characterized as a "lonely crowd," a society composed of separate individuals not linked to each other but acting on the basis of their own individual psychological forces.[13] Even as early as 1895, Gustave Le Bon, the French social psychologist, characterized modern society as being in "the age of crowds."[14]

If it was indeed true that each individual was uninfluenced by social variables, each had an essentially similar human nature (based on the then current biological models), and each was like all others in terms of emotions and outlook, the mass media could be truly powerful sources of influence. Messages could be sent to every person to be received and understood more or less uniformly. Presumably, such messages would appeal to emotions and sentiments and sway the thinking or actions of each recipient in much the same way. Thus, the mass society concept yielded a theory of mass communication effects in which the media were seen as powerful, and their effects both uniform and direct among the members. Briefly, this theory can be summarized more formally in the following terms:

1. The media present messages to the members of the mass society who perceive them more or less uniformly.
2. Such messages are stimuli that influence the individual's emotions and sentiments strongly.
3. The stimuli lead individuals to respond in a somewhat uniform manner, creating changes in thought and action that are like those changes in other persons.
4. Because individuals are not held back by strong social controls from

others, such as shared customs and traditions, the effects of mass communication are powerful, uniform, and direct.

This set of ideas has often been called the *magic bullet theory* of media effects. It was the guiding perspective on the process and effects of mass communication prior to the beginnings of scientific research on the media. For example, the theory was current during World War I. Newspapers during the period were used to make people believe that the enemy was immoral and brutal. Atrocity stories played on the fears and other emotions of the masses. The stories described the hideous behavior of the enemy and convinced populations on each side that those whom they opposed were monsters.

After the war, a number of those who had engineered the deceptions were troubled by the part they had played in creating false beliefs. Their revelations, published in numerous books, created deep concern that the media could be used for all kinds of unacceptable purposes in the hands of the unscrupulous. Large-scale efforts were undertaken to educate the public regarding the insidious dangers of propaganda. From the close of World War I well into the present decade, college courses, textbooks, and learned treatises appeared under the general rubric of "propaganda analysis." It was a noble effort, a form of systematic if not scientific analysis clearly based on the beliefs of the magic bullet theory.

Today, little remains of the theory of uniform influences. It does appear in the beliefs of some members of the public who naively assume that the mass media exercise diabolical control over our minds. But, for the most part, the theory of uniform influences is important in that it provided a starting place for early research. As we will see, when reliable research findings began to accumulate, it had to give way to alternative theories of media effects that seemed to fit reality better.

Selective Influence Theories

A major problem of the magic bullet theory was that its underlying assumptions about people were inaccurate. It was soon discovered that people were active rather than passive receivers of information. Psychologists had begun to emphasize individual differences in people's needs, attitudes, values, and other personality variables. These, they said, led people to perceive the world in unique ways and to act on any stimulus in individually distinct ways. Human nature was not uniform but psychologically dissimilar from one person to another because of the selective influence of learning in society. The influence of the environment in shaping human nature began to be emphasized far more than the influence of our rather uniform biological endowment. This led to an emphasis on the selective manner in which people attended to the mass media and to the great variations in the way people could perceive and interpret the mass-mediated message. A new theoretical formulation began to replace the older theory of uniform effects. For the sake of convenience, it can be called the theory of selective influence based on individual differences. Its basic ideas can be summarized as follows:

1. The media present messages to the members of mass society, but those messages are received and interpreted selectively.
2. The basis of this selectivity lies in variations in habits of perception among members of the society.
3. Variations in habits of perception occur because each individual has a unique personal organization of beliefs, attitudes, values, needs, and modes of experiencing gratification that has been acquired through learning.
4. Because perception is selective, interpretation, retention, and response to media messages are also selective and variable.
5. Thus, the effects of the media are neither uniform, powerful, nor direct. Their influences are selective and limited by individual psychological differences.

As this view of the effects of the media became prominent, a search was undertaken for those psychological factors that operate as perceptual screens, letting some influences in but keeping others out. The idea had important policy implications: if only those magic keys to shaping people's behavior could be found, the media could incorporate them into its messages and could persuade people to buy, vote, donate, or at least think in desired ways. Thus, though the power of the media was less under this view, it was still there in a selective way.

As the selective nature of human perception was being realized by media researchers, another form of selective influence was found. This was what sociologists call *social categories*. People in different positions in the social structure act differently. This includes their mass communication behavior. The poor and the rich, the old and the young, males and females, the educated and the untutored, farmer, merchant, or Indian chief—all represent distinctive categories of people in the complex social system. However, the behavior *within* any category tends to be remarkably similar. Young, affluent females with reasonably high educational level read *Vogue*, *Glamour*, and similar magazines. Poor, black, male youths living in the inner city read comic books but not the editorial section of the newspaper. There is, in other words, a very powerful influence on selective mass communication exposure that comes about from such social differentiation. For the sake of convenience we can call this the *theory of selectivity based on social categories*. Its essential propositions can be summarized in the following terms:

1. The media present messages to the members of the mass society, but they are received and interpreted selectively.

2. An important basis of this selectivity lies in the location of the individual in the differentiated social structure.
3. That social structure is composed of numerous categories of people, defined by such factors as age, sex, income, education, and occupation.
4. Patterns of media attention and response are shaped by the factors that define these categories, making response to mass communication somewhat similar in each.
5. Thus, the effects of the media are neither uniform, powerful, nor direct, but are selective and limited by social category influences.

As research progressed, systematic efforts were undertaken to identify and measure the influence of these kinds of variables.

Another important discovery was that the audiences of the mass media were not simply isolated individuals, and not simply people who could be grouped into social categories. They remained tied to each other through friends, families, work associates, and membership in larger voluntary associations (e.g., lodges, clubs, political parties, and so on). In a rather dramatic way it was found that these social influences were a critical factor in the individual's exposure to the mass media. These influences produced selective effects that could not be attributed simply to psychological variables or to social categories. Some people were avid in their patterns of exposure to the media. Others attended very lightly, if at all. But through networks of social ties, it was found, some of those who attended heavily were influencing those who attended very little. Again, for the sake of convenience, we will call this set of ideas the *theory of selectivity based on social relationships*. The main ideas can be summarized as follows:

1. The media present messages to members of the mass society, but they are received and interpreted selectively.
2. An important basis of this selectivity lies in distinctive patterns of social influences on people from others with whom they have meaningful ties.
3. Such social influences are brought to bear when an individual's decisions regarding behavior toward mass communication are modified by family, friends, acquaintances, or others.
4. Patterns of media attention and response uniquely reflect the networks of meaningful social ties of each individual in the society.
5. Thus, the effects of the media are neither uniform, powerful, nor direct; they are greatly limited and shaped by the person's social interactions with others.

Obviously, this social relationships perspective on media effects represents a substantial movement away from the assumptions of the mass society. It is a product of a more complete understanding of the organizational nature of contemporary society, understandings that were not available at the beginning of the century when it appeared that the three master trends discussed earlier were leading to a rootless, anonymous, differentiated, and alienated social order.

Theories of Indirect Influence

One of the great disappointments of mass communication research as it accumulated was that it seemed to show that the media had only limited influences on their audiences, rather than the powerful influences feared by the critics. One reason why the research findings seemed to indicate this was that investigators had concentrated mainly on studies of specific effects that were supposed to be produced in a short-run sense by specific content in media messages. But as studies went on, this kind of influence was difficult to demonstrate. It was realized that the media could produce long-range and indirect influences, but these were difficult to study. The most popular research strategy was the experiment, modeled after the before–after studies used in the physical sciences. Tracing out indirect and long-term influences was not possible through the use of such an approach.

In later years, new theoretical formulations were developed that did direct research attention to long-range and indirect influences. One of those formulations came from psychology as an adaptation of social learning theory. Another came from sociology and anthropology as an adaptation of theories concerning the nature of symbolic interaction and the influence of language on behavior. The psychological theory is one of both short-term and long-term influences. However, its importance for our present purposes is that it showed how exposure to models of behavior in mass communication content could provide the individual with a learning source for the adoption of forms of action that could become a more or less permanent part of the person's mode of coping with recurring problems. This formulation has come to be called *modeling theory*. In simplified form, its principal assumptions are as follows:

1. The individual perceives a form of behavior described or portrayed by a character in media content.
2. The individual judges this behavior to be attractive and potentially useful for coping with some personal situation that has arisen or might arise.
3. The portrayed behavior is reproduced by the individual in a relevant personal situation.
4. The reproduced behavior proves useful or effective in coping with the situation, thereby rewarding the individual.
5. With further use, the modeled behavior becomes the person's habitual way of handling that type of situation, unless it is no longer effective and rewarding.

If the individual sees the behavior modeled in media content on numerous occasions, this will probably increase the probability of step 3 above. But the important idea is that the theory does not assume that people see some action in media content and then immediately and uniformly imitate that action. Modeling may come later, and the new behavior may slowly become a part of the person's repertoire, depending upon the frequency of relevant occasions for its use. Thus, in a population, at least some people can be influenced indirectly over a long period of time by behavior forms modeled in media content.

From anthropology came the conclusion that the language used by a given people had a profound influence on the manner in which they perceived, experienced, and acted upon the physical and social worlds around them. Language is a system of labels for aspects of reality, and the way in which we experience that reality depends upon the way we divide it up, establish cultural conventions for meaning, and use those conventions to interpret the world around us. Sociologists have very similar theories that emphasize the meanings attached to symbols by people through shared agreements that shape our interactions with others, the way we think about other people, society as a whole, and ourselves. These theories are very complex, and their full range of ideas cannot be expressed in a few sentences. However, the central idea is *meaning*. We respond toward any situation or object in terms of its meaning, as we interpret it. In large part, our personal meanings come to us through participation in our language community. We engage in the process of communication and learn the labels and associated meanings for everything with which we have to cope. The mass media are an important part of those processes of communication in modern society, and they can play a significant role in shaping and stabilizing the meanings we experience for the symbols of our language. We will use the phrase *meaning theory* (of media portrayals) to refer to these rather complex ideas. In summary form, the principal propositions of this meaning theory are as follows:

1. The individual perceives a situation described or portrayed in media content.
2. That situation is labelled by a standardized symbol or symbols from the shared language.
3. The media content effectively links the label and the portrayed meaning for the individual.
4. By such presentations, the media can establish new meanings, extend older ones to include new elements, substitute alternative meanings for older ones, or stabilize the language conventions concerning the shared meanings for symbols in the language community.
5. Since language (standardized labels and their shared meanings) is a critical factor shaping perception, interpretation, and decisions concerning action, the media can have powerful, indirect, and long-term effects.

Thus, a medium like television can by its portrayals show us how to interpret such labels as "women," "black people," "sexual attractiveness," and a host of other terms. It is difficult to assess the influence of the media in this respect within the format of an experiment, a one-shot survey, or even a content analysis of media messages. Nevertheless, it is probably in terms of such indirect and long-term influences that the media exercise their greatest influence.

In summary, the earliest theoretical views of the process and effects of mass communication incorporated assumptions from nineteenth-century psychology that postulated a strictly biological basis of individual human nature and others from sociology concerning a high level of impersonality in the emerging mass society. At first, communication researchers did not question these assumptions and based their magic bullet theory directly on them. However, as major research studies were undertaken, their findings seemed inconsistent with the magic bullet conceptualization of uniform influences. It became increasingly apparent that new theories were needed.

As the pace of mass communication research increased, selective influence explanations of how individuals attended to, perceived, remembered, and acted upon media messages soon came into vogue. While these still seem valid enough for certain purposes, they were eventually seen as narrow in focus and blind to long-range influences of the media. Insofar as they emphasized limited exposure to specific communications, rather than long-term influences of general categories of information, much of the research they stimulated produced disappointing results. Such research was mainly of an experimental nature, or based on one-time survey strategies. The usual situation was that few impressive effects of mass communication could be identified. Some distinguished researchers from sociology and psychology who had made important contributions in the early years simply gave up on mass communication research and moved into other areas of investigation.

Meanwhile, the society remained concerned about the mass media. The public was still deeply suspicious that they were producing unwanted effects. Because of that concern, support for mass communication studies remained, even though the research community had lost some of its enthusiasm. Eventually, of course, the federal government began to provide substantial sums for communication researchers investigating such topics as violence and pornography, along with other possible negative influences or even prosocial influences on children. With that stimulus, enthusiasm was rekindled, and communication researchers turned again to the task of unraveling the impact of mass communication on individuals and society. In addition, training for such research became increasingly focused, with new schools of communication turning out a growing number of specialists. As a result of these trends, mass communication research was no longer the exclusive domain of the parent social sciences.

During the half century represented by the investigations reviewed in the present book, there has generally been only a rather loose connection between the theories that we have summarized in the present chapter and the specific studies that are discussed in remaining chapters. The connection is there, but it is often difficult to see. In large part this is because the milestone studies were often undertaken for purposes other than pure theory-testing. Unfortunately, that is the nature of the practical world. There simply is no one standing in the wings ready to hand out money to communication researchers who want to test theories—even though it would be money well spent, and probably very practical in the long run. Most communication research has been supported because a need existed for practical information to try to address some nagging social problem, or because a concerned public put pressure on politicians to "do something" about the presumed bad influences of mass communication. Nevertheless, and to their credit, communication researchers have seldom ignored the central role of theory. Often they have had to tease theoretical implications out of the research results they have obtained for more pragmatic purposes.

In spite of the often tenuous relationship between theory and research in the scientific study of mass communication, important formulations have been developed, tested, and occasionally rejected. More often, they have simply been left in limbo because of a lack of truly definitive findings. In spite of the obstacles, progress has been made. We no longer give serious concern to magic bullet formulations. Furthermore, we have all but given up on the search for "magic keys" to persuasion—the hope that specific words or message organization can be used routinely to manipulate people's attitudes, beliefs, or behavior. At present, the newer "meaning" theories have emerged, based on the idea that the media in our society play a key role in providing us with "constructions of reality" that are derived from our participation in the collective communication process. Such influences on meanings are said to be long-range and indirect but potentially of great significance in shaping both ideas and actions. Further research will decide their fate.

Finally, although it is sometimes difficult to see the larger picture in the context of specific studies, the story of the changes we have noted in theoretical interpretations of how the media play a part in our lives is embedded in the projects and programs that we have chosen to call "milestones of mass communication research." In the chapters that follow, thirteen major investigations are described, with particular attention to why they were undertaken, what was studied, the research strategies used, the major findings, and their implications for our growing understanding of mass communication and its effects.

NOTES AND REFERENCES

1. Melvin L. De Fleur and Everette E. Dennis, *Understanding Mass Communication*, 3rd edition (Boston: Houghton Mifflin, 1987), chapter 14 (forthcoming).

2. Karl Marx, *Capital*, ed. by Friederich Engels (New York: International Publishers, 1967). This is a modern English translation of the original 19th-century work.

3. Ferdinand Tönnies, *Community and Society (Gemeinschaft und Gesellschaft)*, trans. by Charles P. Loomis (East Lansing: Michigan State University Press, 1957). This is an English translation of the original 19th-century work.

4. J. John Palen, *The Urban World* (New York: McGraw-Hill, 1975), p. 3.

5. Phillip Mauser and Leo Schnore, *The Study of Urbanization* (New York: John Wiley & Sons, 1965), p. 7.

6. Auguste Comte, *The Positive Philosophy*, trans. by Harriet Martineau (London: George Bell and Sons, 1915), p. 293. This is an English translation of the original 19th-century work.

7. Ferdinand Tönnies, op. cit.

8. Daniel Lerner, *The Passing of Traditional Society* (New York: The Free Press, 1958).

9. Melvin L. De Fleur and Sandra Ball-Rokeach, *Theories of Mass Communication*, 4th ed. (New York: Longman Inc., 1982). See Chapter 2, "Society and the Mass Press."

10. E. G. Boring, *A History of Experimental Psychology* (New York: Appleton-Century-Crofts, 1929), p. 279.

11. Emile Durkheim, *Suicide, A Study in Sociology* (Englewood Cliffs, N. J.: Prentice-Hall, 1968). First published in French in 1897.

12. The social survey in its modern sense is usually thought of as beginning with the work of Frederic Le Play, in his *Ouvriers Européens* (1855) or with Charles Booth's 17-volume *Life and Labour of the People of London* (produced between 1891 and 1897). For discussions of both works, see Pitirim Sorokin, *Contemporary Sociological Theories* (New York: Harper and Brothers, 1928).

13. David Riesman, *The Lonely Crowd* (New Haven, Conn.: Yale University Press, 1950).

14. Gustav Le Bon, *The Crowd: A Study of the Popular Mind* (London: Ernest Benn, Ltd., 1896).

2

The Payne Fund Studies:
The Effects of Movies on Children

During the 1920s, the motion picture industry suddenly thrust itself into the lives of virtually everyone in the United States. What was this new medium and what influence was it having on those who consumed its products? It was these questions that helped bring into existence one of the largest research projects ever undertaken in an effort to understand the relationship between a medium and a particular audience. Two additional trends taking place in the United States were to play important parts in establishing mass communication research as a field of scientific study. One was the increasing emphasis on the scientific method as a proper strategy for investigation in such fields as sociology, psychology, and education. The other was the extremely rapid rise in concern about the influence of the new motion picture industry. To understand why the first major scientific assessment of the effects of a mass medium was undertaken in the late 1920s, these two trends need to be understood.

One important factor of the times was the maturation of the social sciences. Following World War I, the social sciences began to undergo an important transformation. Increasing attention was being given to the use of quantitative research techniques. The trend was given a boost when procedures were devised for the measurement of aspects of individual human behavior that had previously been thought to be ephemeral. For example, Emory S. Bogardus began the movement to assess racial and ethnic attitudes with his "social distance scale" that was first published in 1924.[1] This was soon followed by the more sophisticated work of Thurstone and Chave with their "equal appearing intervals" scale for measuring almost any kind of attitude.[2]

The 1920s brought statistics to social science research. Important new techniques based on probability had been invented by mathematicians. These were advocated in journals, books, and courses by leading psychologists and sociologists of the period, who showed the applications of sampling, measures of central tendency, correlation, and probability to behavioral research problems.[3] Similar transformations had been taking place in educational research in addition to other social sciences.

It was a controversial time, and many traditional social scientists resisted the trend. Critics charged that the move toward quantification was merely an attempt to "ape" the physical sciences in a shameless grab for a share in the prestige of those sciences. They pronounced that the emphasis on numbers would "dehumanize" the study of human behavior; it would create mind-boggling accumulations of meaningless facts; and it would destroy efforts to build insightful theories. But in spite of these gloomy predictions, the trend continued. By the end of the decade, the scientific perspective, much as we know it today, had taken a strong foothold in both psychology and sociology.

During the same period, American movies took over the world film market. The new medium got its start as the century changed. At first, movies were little more than amusing novelties—pictures that appeared to move. By the end of the first decade, nickelodeons were attracting millions of unsophisticated viewers with slapstick films of short duration. By the time of World War I, the movies had become a widely accepted form of family entertainment. It was in the 1920s, however, that motion pictures matured into a major mass medium that was a part of the life of almost every citizen. Hollywood—previously a rather drab village on the suburban fringes of Los Angeles—became the glamour capital of the world. Its film studios ground out a veritable tidal wave of films (hundreds a year) to satisfy the insatiable demands of the public for the new form of entertainment. Its stars represented fantasy success stories that fascinated shop girls and factory workers across the nation. Obscure people were "discovered" by the studios and propelled into instant fame and fortune. Millions were eager to learn of the smallest details of the stars' lives. They became gods and goddesses, adored by publics eager to pay to see their features projected silently on the screen in black-and-white. It was the American Dream in a new form, and it rivalled even the most fanciful rags-to-riches stories of earlier times. By the end of the decade, sound tracks were added, making the movies even more attractive. Theaters had grown larger and more opulent as ticket sales soared.

Going to the movies was a frequent event for most families—they were great fun. Also, there were very few alternatives for inexpensive recreation. Homes had neither radios nor television sets. Some had pianos and windup victrolas; a few even had books. But for the majority of families with limited means, taking in a motion picture was an enjoyable and affordable evening out. For those of dating and courting age, movies were made to order: couples in dark theaters could do more than just watch the films. For children, the Saturday matinee was the high point of existence. Many a youngster behaved reasonably well for days in a row on the promise that he or she could go to the show with the other kids on Saturday afternoon.

All of these attractions had caused motion picture attendance to rise dramatically over a very short period of time. Data on movie attendance were not systematically gathered before 1922. During that year, some 40 million tickets were sold every week in the United States. By the end of the decade, the figure had more than doubled to 90 million! Among the movie-goers in 1929 were an estimated 40 million minors, and among those were approximately 17 million children under the age of fourteen.[4]

The content of the motion pictures produced in the 1920s was not much different than the content of movies today. There was less bare skin, sex, and blood, but the themes were very similar. Edgar Dale made an exhaustive study of the content of 1500 films of the period.[5] As we will note later in greater detail, their content could be grouped into ten major thematic categories. However, a mere three of these categories—love, crime, and sex—accounted for nearly three-fourths of the total!

Adults during the period did not quite know what to make of it all. In a single decade, the startling new medium had burgeoned into a national preoccupation. In a society that had barely emerged from the Victorian Age, the love, sex, and crime themes that dominated the films seemed to many to pose troublesome challenges to established moral standards. Above all, their great concern was what the movies were doing to the nation's children. A well-known educator of the time summarized the issues in the following terms:

> Motion pictures are not understood by the present generation of adults. They are new; they make an enormous appeal to children; and they present ideas and situations which parents may not like. Consequently when parents think of the welfare of their children who are exposed to these compelling situations, they wonder about the effects of the pictures upon the ideals and behavior of the children. Do the pictures really influence children in any direction? Are their conduct, ideals and attitudes affected by the movies? Are the scenes which are objectionable to adults understood by children, or at least by very young children? Do children eventually become sophisticated and grow superior to pictures? Are the emotions of children harmfully excited? In short, just what effect do motion pictures have upon children of different ages?[6]

Thus, the situation at the time was not unlike that faced by parents in the 1960s, when television had just emerged as a new national medium with a huge audience of children. The public was deeply concerned about effects, and it wanted answers.

By the mid 1920s, pressure began to mount on the motion picture industry. Numerous editorials, sermons, magazine articles, and other forms of public criticism raised questions and made charges that the movies were a negative influence on children. It became increasingly clear that research was needed. Social scientists were seeking opportunities to undertake assessments of the influence of movies on children. In 1928, William H. Short, Executive Director of the Motion Picture Research Council, invited a group of university psychologists, sociologists, and educators to design a series of studies assessing the influence of the movies on children; they responded enthusiastically. There was no government agency to which they could turn to obtain funds for such research, as there would be at a later time. However, a private philanthropic foundation (The Payne Fund) agreed to provide financial support. The end result was a series of thirteen specific studies, done by well-known researchers, on various aspects of the influence of the movies on children. The investigations, known as the Payne Fund Studies, were conducted over a three-year period from 1929 to 1932. They were published in the early 1930s in ten volumes. These classic works have recently been reprinted by the Arno Press and the New York Times (who generously provided a set of the reprints to the authors for purposes of the present book).

In retrospect, then, it was the coming together of two major social changes in the American society—the development of a more precise research capability in the social sciences and the deepening public concern over the mushrooming growth of the movies—that gave birth to the scientific study of mass communication. As we noted earlier, scholars had long been concerned with the influence of mass communication on individuals and society. However, this was largely in the context of "unmasking" the influence of propaganda, rather than in terms of uncovering cause-effect relationships within the framework of science. The Payne Fund Studies, therefore, represent the first major effort to bring such perspectives, strategies, and techniques to bear on the influence of a major medium on a specific category of people. In the section that follows, we present a brief summary of the individual studies.

OVERVIEW OF THE PAYNE FUND STUDIES

The question of influences of the motion pictures on children was posed in a variety of terms by the researchers who worked on the Payne Fund Studies. Over a dozen major investigations were undertaken simultaneously. Each was of relatively large scale; each had quite different goals. From the perspective of today, the majority of these studies are mainly of historical interest, in the sense that their findings would not be useful for understanding the influence of contemporary movies on modern youth. However, they all played a part in the development of mass communication research as a field of scientific investigation. Several of the studies remain important because they addressed problems that are still under active investigation today. It was these studies that provided a matrix of findings from which simple theoretical perspectives emerged, to be used in subsequent investigations for many years.

From the standpoint of their objectives, the Payne Fund Studies fall into two rather broad categories. In one category, the goals are to assess the content of the films and determine the size and composition of their audiences. The second category attempts to assess the effects on those audiences of their exposures to the themes and messages of motion pictures. There were several kinds of major effects under study. Stated briefly, these were: acquisition of information, change in attitudes, stimulation of emotions, harm to health, erosion of moral standards, and influence on conduct. In the paragraphs that follow, each of the specific investigations is described in very brief terms to give a more complete overview of the goals and scope of this pioneering research series.

The Audience and Content of the Films

No actual records of movie attendance by age-level were available during the period of the studies. To gain an understanding of the size and composition of the youthful audience, Edgar Dale, a well-known educator, used several different strategies and information sources to make estimates. Census data were, of course, available for every state and for the nation as a whole. The problem was to determine what proportion of the population at various age-levels attended the movies and how often. Dale made studies of actual movie attendance in over fifty Ohio communities in order to estimate the size and composition of their youthful audiences. He then used these data as a basis of projection for the nation as a whole. He found that even children of five to eight years were going to the movies with some frequency. Children of school age attended much more often; in fact, they went more frequently than adults. Boys attended more often than girls. The main finding was that on the average, children in 1929 and 1930 went to the movies once a week.[7] In a society that did not yet understand motion pictures and their potential influence on children, these figures caused considerable concern.

What did these children see? Again, a study by Dale provided clear answers.[8] He reviewed, classified, and analyzed 1500 films. Five hundred of these had been produced in 1920, another five hundred in 1925, and the remaining five hundred in 1930. He was able to classify their content into the following ten categories: crime, sex, love, mystery, war, children, history, travel, comedy, and social propaganda. Not only were the general themes of the stories studied, but their locales or settings; the nature of their heroes or heroines; the actors' clothing styles; their portrayals of how people met, loved, and married; how they engaged in crime; used vulgarity; consumed liquor and tobacco; and pursued goals identified as important in the films. In other words, it was a large-scale, systematic, and thorough content analysis of motion pictures produced and seen during a decade. The results were scarcely reassuring to critics of the movies. Over three-fourths of the films dealt with only three thematic categories—crime, sex, and love. More wholesome themes, such as travel, children's stories, and history, represented only an insignificant proportion of the total. The use of tobacco and liquor (in a period of prohibition) was openly protrayed.

Acquiring Information

To study the retention of factual information presented in motion pictures, P.W. Holaday and George D. Stoddard conducted a study of over 3000 children and adults.[9] It took them three years to complete their work. Seventeen full-length motion pictures were used as stimulus material. They tested audiences on details of the plots and on various kinds of information presented in the films. They found that even eight-year-old children acquired a substantial number of ideas from the movies (about 60 percent of the total learned by adults). In fact, retention of facts by all age groups was surprisingly high. Subjects were tested six weeks and three months after seeing the films. In some cases, retention was greater than the six-month period, suggesting a so-called sleeper effect that would be discovered again later (pp. 118; 145). The investigators concluded that movies provided a special learning format that led to unusually high retention of factual material, compared to the acquisition of facts in standard laboratory memory experiments.

Changing Attitudes

One of the more sophisticated investigations of the series was that of Ruth C. Peterson and L. L. Thurstone.[10] Their purpose was to assess the construction of attitude measures. Generally, the attitudes under study were the orientations of children toward selected ethnic groups, racial categories, and social issues. Regular commercial motion pictures were used as stimulus material. Children's attitudes were measured before exposure to the film or films and then remeasured with a parallel instrument after seeing the picture material. In many cases, attitude change was found. The details of this study and its implications for the research trends that it stimulated will be discussed more fully in a later section of the present chapter.

Stimulating Emotions

Studies of the capacity of films to arouse children's emotions were conducted by W.S. Dysinger and Christian A. Ruckmick.[11] They used both laboratory techniques and autobiographical case studies to assess the emotional impact of films. Several age categories of children were observed both in a lab setting and in actual theaters while viewing motion pictures. The 150 subjects used were selected to represent "average" intelligence levels. Some adults were also studied for comparison purposes. It was a dramatic form of research for the time. Electrodes and mechanical devices were attached to youthful viewers in order to record their galvanic skin responses and changes in their breathing patterns stimulated by the film content. These neurophysiological changes were used as indices of emotional arousal. Scenes of danger, conflict, or tragedy produced the greatest effects. Romantic and erotic scenes didn't seem to do much for very young children, but they blew the sixteen-year-olds off the graphs! Generally, males and females reacted similarly. By comparison, adults showed little emotional arousal to any of the scenes. The authors concluded that adults had learned to "discount" the films as fantasy, but children experienced substantial emotional arousal.

Harming Health

To study movies as a potential danger to health, psychologists Samuel Renshaw, Vernon L. Miller, and Dorothy P. Marquis devised ingenious experiments on children's sleep.[12] A total of 170 boys and girls in an Ohio state institution for juveniles participated in studies of sleep "motility." Special beds and other apparatus were used to measure how much they tossed and turned after seeing various categories of films. First, the researchers studied normal sleep patterns. Then they exposed their young subjects to motion pictures before bed time. A variety of controls and conditions were used to explore different kinds of influences on sleep. Briefly, certain kinds of films did result in disturbed sleep. Such consequences, the authors claimed, could be detrimental to normal health and growth.

Eroding Moral Standards

An elaborate study of the influence of motion pictures on standards of morality was conducted by Charles C. Peters.[13] His point of departure was the sociological theory of William Graham Sumner, whose analyses of folkways and mores were published at the beginning of the present century. Sumner's work on the nature and origins of such norms was so thorough that it has never been replicated and still stands as the definitive statement.[14] The goal of Peters' study was to determine whether specific kinds of actions or situations portrayed in the films paralleled or were in conflict with the standards of morality currently prevailing among several categories of subjects. He used written descriptions of movie scenes that included such actions as female aggressiveness in lovemaking (kissing and caressing in public), the portrayal of democratic practices and attitudes, and different forms of treatment of children by parents. Five categories of people responded to these descriptions in the preliminary standardization of the morality scale. These were college seniors, college faculty members and their wives, socially elite young women, factory working boys, and factory working girls. The result was a scale for "measuring the mores" of different kinds of people. The scale was then used to assess different patterns of approval and disapproval of samples of conduct taken from the films. Peters gathered such responses from seventeen different categories of subjects whose backgrounds ranged from poorly educated workers to upper-status professionals. The general conclusion from this complex study was that many of the depictions presented in the movies, especially in scenes of crime and sex (two of the most frequent themes) were contrary to the mores of the groups under study. Such findings were scarcely comforting to those who feared that the movies were providing unwanted influences on children.

Influencing Conduct

As might be suspected, the issue of motion picture influences on conduct received more attention than any other specific topic. Three separate studies were devoted to the impact of films on various forms of behavior. Each of these deserves separate comment. Two of these investigations will be discussed in some detail following the overviews.

Frank R. Shuttleworth and Mark A. May contrasted children who attended movies frequently ("fans") with a comparison group who seldom or never attended.[15] The study attempted to assess general conduct, deportment in school, and reputation among peers. In all, some 1400 children were studied. For the most part, it was a questionnaire study with a variety of paper and pencil questionnaires, rating scales, and other instruments used by both the children and their teachers. The investigators found that movie "fans" were usually rated lower in deportment by their teachers than those children who did not attend the movies frequently. The fans also had less positive reputations; they did worse in their academic work, and they were not as popular with their classmates as was the comparison group.

One of the most interesting of the conduct studies was an investigation by sociologist Herbert Blumer that probed the influences of motion pictures on general day-to-day behavior.[16] In this work, he depended primarily on the autobiographical method, in which subjects recalled earlier influences of the movies on their lives and on specific activities, such as play, modes of dress, hairstyles, and forms of communication. The autobiographical technique had been worked out to probe specific kinds of influences, including how the films had influenced the subjects' moods, emotions, interpretations of love and romance, ambitions, and temptations to behave in socially disapproved ways. Several hundred college students wrote such autobiographies, as did hundreds of high school youths, factory workers, and office personnel. Overall, the accounts seemed to indicate rather clearly that the content of the movies served as substantial influences on children. The subjects reported that they had imitated the movie characters openly in beautification, mannerism, and attempts at lovemaking.

The movies had also stimulated a great deal of daydreaming and fantasy. In particular, the films had aroused strong emotions in their youthful audiences, including terror, fright, sorrow, and pathos. Although this type of research was called "exploratory" by the investigator, and even though it was based on relatively unsophisticated methods, it remains one of the more significant studies of the series. Certainly, its findings reinforced the alarms raised by critics of the movies.

A widely discussed study of conduct was that of Herbert Blumer and another sociologist, Phillip Hauser.[17] Their central focus was on ways in which motion picture content stimulated children to commit acts of delinquency and crime. It was a wide-ranging study that included case histories, questionnaires, essays, and life histories of delinquency-prone youngsters. Reports on movie experiences were gathered from reformatory inmates, ex-convicts on parole, female delinquents in a training school, grade school boys and girls in high-delinquency neighborhoods, and several other categories of children and adolescents. Material was also obtained from the heads of penal institutions and other authorities. The methods and strategies used in this study have come under wide criticism from criminologists and specialists in deviant behavior. Nevertheless, at the time, the findings caused considerable concern. According to the authors, motion pictures played a direct role in shaping the delinquent and criminal careers of substantial segments of those studied. Once again, the worst fears of the public were confirmed. Movies appeared to be driving at least some children to a life of crime!

As can be seen from this brief overview, each of the investigations in the Payne Fund Studies was a work of substantial scope. Taken together, they constitute a research effort which would not be matched in size and diversity until forty years later, when the federal government funded studies of the influence of televised violence on children. The Payne Fund Studies, therefore, remain one of the largest scientific investigations of the influence of mass communication ever undertaken. In order to see in more detail the theoretical assumptions, the methodological strategies and techniques, and some of the major findings, the sections that follow present more detailed summaries of two of the Payne Fund investigations.

STUDIES OF SOCIAL ATTITUDES, GENERAL CONDUCT, AND DELINQUENT BEHAVIOR

While the highlights of the research by Peterson and Thurstone and by Herbert Blumer have been summarized above, these particular studies offer significant lessons regarding the development of both research methods and theory concerning the effects of mass communication. For this reason, the separate investigations are reviewed more fully in the sections that follow.

Motion Pictures and the Social Attitudes of Children

The purpose of the set of experiments by Peterson and Thurstone was to study the degree to which commercial motion pictures could change the attitudes of youthful subjects toward specific topics. Under investigation were attitudes toward people of different nationalities and races and attitudes toward socially significant topics such as crime, war, capital punishment, prohibition, and the treatment of criminals. The subjects were school children ranging from fourth-graders to college students.

The general strategy was straightforward. An initial measure was achieved by using a paired-comparisons scale developed around the particular attitude under study. The assessment was done in school classrooms in small communities near Chicago, with the cooperation of the authorities. The students participating were then given special tickets to the local movie theater.

Since the experiments were done in communities with only one theater, the subjects naturally attended the right movie, using their free tickets. The film seen by the subjects was one that had been specially selected by the experimenters and was being shown by prior arrangement with the local exhibitor.

To obtain suitable films, the investigators had examined more than 600 candidate pictures. Sixteen were selected because they presented particularly favorable or unfavorable views toward one of the attitude topics under investigation. For example, *All Quiet on the Western Front* was an antiwar film. *Birth of a Nation* was (in many respects) antiblack. Others were pro-Chinese, pro-Jewish, and so on.

Approximately two weeks after the first attitude assessment and the next day after seeing the film, the attitudes of the subjects were again measured. No direct connection was made between the attitude assessments and the movie experience. Controls were used to ensure that only subjects who had actually seen the film were included in the final determination of attitude change. (It can be noted in passing that no attempt was made to use control groups).

Within this general framework, two dozen experiments were completed. Some studied the effect of a *single* film on changing attitudes. Others studied the *cumulative* effect of two and even three pictures dealing with the same theme. Finally, a number of studies assessed the *persistence* of attitude changes over long periods of time. These periods ranged from two to nineteen months.

The Effect of Single Pictures. In a series of eleven separate experiments, the ability of a single exposure to a motion picture to modify attitudes was assessed. Under study were attitudes toward Germans, war, gambling, prohibition, the Chinese, capital punishment, treatment of criminals, and "the Negro" (the term would be "black" today). Each experiment followed the general strategy outlined earlier. The numbers of subjects ranged from 133 in a study of attitudes toward Germans to 522 in an investigation of attitudes toward the punishment of criminals. Because of the number of the experiments it is difficult to discuss the results in a simple way. However, in general, some of the experiments produced substantial attitude change. In others the subjects did not significantly change their orientations.

Two examples illustrate the nature of the results where significant change occurred. In Geneva, Illinois, 182 children in grades 9 through 12 saw a film entitled *Son of the Gods*. It was strongly pro-Chinese. The story concerned Sam Lee, a nice young Chinese-American who had been raised by an older Chinese man. The interpretation of Chinese life and culture was positive, and the characters presented were sympathetic. Figure 2.1 shows the results. The "before" mean was 6.72 and the "after" mean was 5.50. Statistically, a difference of 1.22 is 17.5 times its probable error. In short, there was a statistically significant attitude change in a favorable direction.

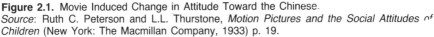

Figure 2.1. Movie Induced Change in Attitude Toward the Chinese.
Source: Ruth C. Peterson and L.L. Thurstone, *Motion Pictures and the Social Attitudes of Children* (New York: The Macmillan Company, 1933) p. 19.

Another experiment showed even more striking results. The film *Birth of a Nation* (updated from its original form with the addition of a sound track) was shown to 434 high school children in Crystal Lake, Illinois. The film portrays blacks in negative terms and is considered an antiblack statement. As it turned out, few of the subjects in the experiment had known or even seen a black. Figure 2.2 shows that at the outset the subjects were relatively favorable, with a mean score of 7.46. The mean after the film had shifted to 5.93, a more negative position. A difference of 1.48 is 25.5 times its probable error. Clearly, this particular movie had a substantial impact on the attitudes of its audience.

Cumulative Effects. A series of experiments were conducted in which subjects viewed two or more pictures dealing with the same issue between their before and after measures. In these studies, 750 children in grades 6–12 were in the various experiments. They were all residents of Mooseheart, a community for children of deceased members of a national organization. Two attitudes were

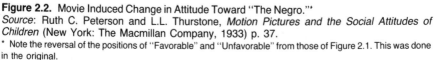

Figure 2.2. Movie Induced Change in Attitude Toward "The Negro."*
Source: Ruth C. Peterson and L.L. Thurstone, *Motion Pictures and the Social Attitudes of Children* (New York: The Macmillan Company, 1933) p. 37.
* Note the reversal of the positions of "Favorable" and "Unfavorable" from those of Figure 2.1. This was done in the original.

under study. In one set of experiments, the subjects saw two antiwar films—*All Quiet on the Western Front* and *Journey's End*. In another set of experiments, subjects saw three films dealing with the punishment of criminals. These were *The Big House, Numbered Men,* and *The Criminal Code.* Each was a relatively sympathetic treatment of the plight of men in prison.

Overall, the results of the cumulative studies were clear. The films shown singly had minor or no effects in terms of attitude change. However, two or three films on the same topic produced significant attitude modification among the subjects under study toward the view expressed in the films.

The Persistence of Attitude Changes. In eleven of the experiments selected from the studies of both single and multiple exposures, follow-ups were conducted at various intervals. In each case, parallel-form attitude scales measured the persistence of the changes achieved in the earlier experiment. The results of these studies can be seen in Table 2.1. The authors concluded that the effects of motion pictures on the social attitudes of children could persist for considerable periods of time. In one case, 60 percent of the original change was retained a year and a half later! In another case, the attitudes of the subjects had changed even more six months later than they had immediately following exposure to the film (a "sleeper" effect).

The general conclusions reached by Peterson and Thurstone were that the attitudes of children were definitely influenced by some films. These effects tended to be greater for younger children. Seeing two and three pictures treating the same topic in the same general way achieved greater results than was the case with a single film. Finally, attitude changes resulting from exposure to motion pictures can persist for long periods of time.[18]

These attitude change studies were of lasting importance for several reasons. The study of quantitative attitude scales was in its infancy; however, the measurement procedures used by the investigators were based on relatively

TABLE 2.1. THE PERSISTENCE OF ATTITUDE CHANGES

Place	Film	No. in Exp. Group	Interval	Percent of Effect Remaining
Watseka, Illinois	*The Criminal Code*	257	2½ months	87%
Watseka, Illinois	*The Criminal Code*	195	9 months	78%
Geneva, Illinois	*Son of the Gods*	117	5 months	62%
Geneva, Illinois	*Son of the Gods*	76	19 months	60%
Crystal Lake, Illinois	*The Birth of a Nation*	350	5 months	62%
Genoa, Illinois	*Four Sons*	87	6 months	123%
Paxton, Illinois	*All Quiet on the Western Front*	138	8 months	A change in the opposite direction.
Mooseheart, Illinois	*All Quiet on the Western Front and Journey's End*	572	2 months	52%
Mooseheart, Illinois	*All Quiet on the Western Front and Journey's End*	571	4 months	22%
Mooseheart, Illinois	*The Big House, Numbered Men, and The Criminal Code*	559	2 months	100%
Mooseheart, Illinois	*The Big House, Numbered Men, and The Criminal Code*	549	4 months	111%

Source: Ruth C. Peterson and L.L. Thurstone, *Motion Pictures and the Social Attitudes of Children* (New York: The Macmillan Company, 1933) p. 63.

sophisticated theories derived from the Law of Comparative Judgement. This formulation still remains the underlying rationale for attitude measurement. Thus, the movie studies were a highly visible application of the new technology to a socially significant issue. In addition, the experimental format used in the studies followed the model of science that was being enthusiastically adopted by psychology and sociology. For these reasons, and because the studies showed clear results, the Peterson and Thurstone research made a deep impact, both on the public and the scientific community.

Movies and Conduct

In a very different type of research, Herbert Blumer collected autobiographical accounts from more than 1800 young men and women, adolescents, and children. The general purpose of the study was to find out how motion pictures had influenced their childhood play, their attempts to imitate various elements of adult behavior, their daydreams, emotional experiences, and general life-styles. The goals of the research were sweeping. The methodology was *qualitative* rather than quantitative, and the findings can only be regarded as "exploratory" or "suggestive." Yet, in many ways, this is one of the most interesting of all of the Payne Fund Studies because it shows in rich detail the way in which the 1823 participants in the study thought that the movies had influenced their lives.

The researcher began his investigation with a preliminary study to help design a general format for the personal autobiographies. Students in university classes were "asked merely to write in as natural and truthful a manner, accounts of their prior experiences with movies, as best as these could be recalled."[19] These were extensive documents that required several weeks to prepare. From these accounts, Blumer constructed a set of guidelines for the preparation of autobiographies by the main body of his subjects. These guidelines focused the subject on his or her interest in the movies during childhood. They asked the subject to recall influences on emotions or moods, patterns of imitation of the actors, the subject's remembered interest in love and romantic films, ambitions and temptations which, in recollection, had been aroused by motion pictures.

These accounts were gathered from 634 university students, 481 college and junior college youths, 583 high school students, 67 office workers, and 58 factory workers. Considerable care was taken to preserve anonymity, ensure honesty, and encourage full disclosure. The statements were checked for internal consistency and what we would today call "face validity."

To these personal autobiographies, the investigator added information obtained in personal interviews with 135 of the subjects. In addition, information was derived from conversations among groups of students as they discussed the movies. Finally, data were obtained from structured question-naires administered to 1200 grade school children in the Chicago area.

This mass of material was not reduced to quantitative form. As the author explained it, the general plan of procedure followed in the report was to *let the facts speak for themselves.* This was accomplished by the liberal use of quotations from the autobiographies and general descriptions of the central themes that seemed to emerge from the materials.

Influences on Childhood Play. Nearly all the subjects studied reported that the movies had been a rich source from which they drew ideas for play. They liberally impersonated screen characters in their games of "Cowboys and Indians" and "Cops and Robbers." Depending upon what they had seen that week they became Robin Hood, Joan of Arc, Rudolph Valentino, a royal knight, a princess in a far-off land, or an African big game hunter. At other times, they played at being a daring fighter pilot, Mata Hari, Dracula, Mary Queen of Scots, or the Phantom of the Opera.

> *Male, 19, Jewish, white, college sophomore:* In my childhood it was common for one to imitate consciously heroes of the screen. For instance, I would climb the lone tree that was in the yard of the Catholic school near us and hang by one hand or hammer my chest shouting "Tarzan" and the like. Jumping over fences on a run as did the heroes of the screen was usual in my young life. Fighting with one another, and after conquering him, placing one foot on his chest and raising our arms to the sky as Tarzan did was also common.[20]

Not only had the subjects impersonated actors and their screen roles, but they modeled their games on the plots seen in the pictures. Thus, one day some of the kids would attack a fort with wooden swords and "pretend" shields that were really the tops of wash boilers or garbage cans. The defenders would resist with lances made of sticks and helmets devised from old cooking pots. Auto races could be recreated among makeshift cars devised from apple crates; cavalry charges seen on the screen could be relived on the backs of trusty steeds that were really mops and brooms. Or, daring aviators could duel in the skies over Germany.

> *A boy of 11 years:* The picture I saw was *The Dawn Patrol.* After I came home, we played it. I pretended I was Richard Barthelmess. I pretended I was bombing the German ammunition dumps. Then I went over the airports and bombed the planes and killed the men. Then three German planes came after me. Von Richter, the best German aviator, came up too, and I shot him down and shot his pal also. But the other aviator came from the back and shot me.[21]

Girls of the period pretended to be the pampered darlings of rich parents, with dozens of suitors and fantastic wardrobes. They acted out the part of

Juliet, or that of beautiful captives of handsome sheiks. Generally, costumes, weapons, and other artifacts seen in the films were improvised in addition to behavior patterns and social relationships. In short, the movies had a complex set of influences on children's play. The subjects, on the whole, recalled these influences with warmth and pleasure. Whether or not such effects were harmful in any way is not clear. In all likelihood, they were not.

Imitation by Adolescents. Motion picture influences on childhood play were largely in the realm of fantasy and make-believe. Among adolescent movie-goers, however, a somewhat different type of influence was widespread. Forms of conduct such as beautification, personal mannerisms, and social techniques were imitated from movie portrayals and incorporated into the day-to-day behavior patterns of youthful audiences. The styles of dress and hair arrangements used by female stars in the films were a particular source of fascination for female adolescents. In searching for means to bring beauty into their own lives, they experimented enthusiastically with what they had seen on the screen.

> *Female, 19, Jewish, white, college sophomore:* I remember that I got my first striking illumination through the movies of the difference clothes may make in appearance. It was *Daddy Long-Legs* where Mary Pickford paraded for five scenes, bare-legged, in dark brown cast-offs, pig-tailed, and freckled-faced, good, sweet, but hardly beautiful; and then in the final scene, after a visit from Daddy and a bath in milk, with the curls down, the gangly knees covered, the ankles silk-shod, in pink satin, a pearl-studded dress, a reborn gorgeous queen, she emerged as striking as the caterpillar-butterfly transition. At home that night I tentatively hinted about putting my daily glass of milk to better use, wound my straight black hair in tortuous curl papers, draped myself in red gauze, and compared effects. Since then I have carefully studied, attempted, and compared the effects of these past mistresses of the art of dressing and make-up. They are always first with the latest, my most reliable guide to styles, colors, accessories, combinations, lines, and general effects.[22]

Another important area of influence was in those mannerisms that become identified as attractive or sophisticated in every age. Thus, the movies taught a generation of males how to light a cigarette in a "manly" manner; how to tip one's hat to a lady in a gallant way; or how to offer her one's arm properly. They taught girls how to purse their lips coyly; how to lower their eyelids enticingly; how to sit gracefully; or how to shed a dainty tear for maximum effect.

The films served also to bring some semblance of social polish to upwardly mobile youths who might not have had other role models in their daily lives.

> *Male, 21, white, college senior:* As I got into high school and into my sixteenth and seventeenth year I began to use the movies as a school of

etiquette. I began to observe the table manners of the actors in the eating scenes. I watched for the proper way in which to conduct oneself at a night club, because I began to have ideas that way. The fact that the leading man's coat was single-breasted or double-breasted, the number of buttons on it, and the cut of its lapel all influenced me in the choice of my own suits.[23]

The adoption of behavior patterns from adult models is a normal part of the socialization process during childhood and adolescence. The movie stars, however, appeared to be particularly attractive sources from which to obtain modeling influences.

> *Female, 18, Negro, high-school senior:* Movies are the means by which a great many people obtain poise. This is especially true as far as girls are concerned. I am sure I haven't the poise of my movie idols, but I am trying to develop a more ladylike composure as I grow older. My father has caught me several times, as I stood before the mirror trying to tilt my head and hold my arms as the girls on the screen would do. He does not know that I am trying to create that sophisticated manner, which is essential for social success.[24]

Generally, then, the stars and their portrayals were imitated freely by millions of young Americans in the 1920s. In many cases, the forms of beautification, the mannerisms, or the techniques of social adaptation modeled from the movies were but brief experiments that were soon abandoned. In other cases, the people studied felt that these influences had been incorporated more permanently into their daily behavior patterns.

The preoccupation of the films of the period with themes of love and sex has already been noted. Lovemaking in the movies did not have much attraction for the younger children.

> *Male, 20, white, college sophomore:* Love stories and pictures never held much attraction for me at this time (age 12)...Whenever we boys would go to see a love picture and the hero kissed the heroine we would always make a lot of noise and smack our lips very loudly.[25]

Among adolescents, however, the love and romance themes of the movies found an enthusiastic audience. In an era when there were only a limited number of sources from which young people could learn ways of relating to the opposite sex, and especially about techniques of kissing or the meaning of love and romance, the films provided fascinating lessons.

> *Male, 21, white, college senior:* The technique of making love to a girl received considerable of my attention, and it was directly through the movies that I learned to kiss a girl on her ears, neck, and cheeks, as well as on the mouth.[26]

It was, of course, a more innocent time, and "making-love" meant merely kissing and hugging. Nevertheless, the motion pictures were a training vehicle that provided not only models for intimate interpersonal behavior, but media-constructed conceptions of passion, romance, courtship, flirting, and other forms of relationship between males and females.

Daydreaming and Fantasy. The movies were a rich source for adolescent daydreams and fantasies. Two thirds of the autobiographies studied discussed the films as a source of stimulation used during childhood to imagine playing fantastic adult roles: The boys rescued beautiful maidens, danced the tango in smart tuxedos, shot it out with desperados, and drove dog sleds across Alaska. The girls reveled in fabulous wardrobes, toyed with handsome admirers, bedecked themselves with jewels, and succumbed to tall, dark, Latin lovers.

The majority of the audience actually led rather dull lives. It was not unusual, therefore, that the vivid scenes of travel, adventure, glamour, wealth, luxury, success, romance, and heroism depicted in the films would be used in imagination as a basis for Walter Mitty-like constructions of deeply satisfying dreams. Contemporary students of the uses and gratifications provided by media content still pursue this line of inquiry.

Emotional Possession. One of the more pronounced influences of film content of the 1920s on their youthful audiences was termed "emotional possession." The concept refers to a situation where an individual's emotions are aroused so strongly that he or she loses some measure of self-control. Seeing dramatic motion picture portrayals led young audience members to suffer in empathy, cower in horror, or to feel overpowering affection. Such feelings were both strongly stimulated and made manifest in overt behavior (tears, screams, hiding, adulation, and so on) by some forms of communication content.

Powerful responses might be quite difficult to stimulate today among our more media-hardened youthful population. But during the 1920s, being frightened out of one's wits by a movie was a common phenomenon.

> *Female, 15, white, high-school sophomore: The Phantom of the Opera,* with Lon Chaney as the phantom, frightened me more than any other motion picture I have seen. He was made up as the most horrible creature with long teeth, glaring eyes, and a bald head. When he was unmasked by the heroine, I gasped and almost screamed. Although I tried to draw my eyes away from his terrible face, I couldn't; his ugliness was so fascinating. The entire picture was so weird and fantastic that the shivers ran up and down my back. For a long time after that, I dared not go near dark places, particularly the cellar. I did not let anyone else know I was frightened for fear they would call me silly.[27]

Another frequent response to films was to experience grief and sorrow over the plight of a movie character. Two thirds of those who prepared autobiographies recalled such moving emotions vividly. Typical was the following report.

> *Female, 20, white, college junior:* The first picture that I ever cried at was *Uncle Tom's Cabin*, with Marguerite Clarke playing the part of little Eva. I didn't want to cry and tried my best to fight against my emotions, but it was of no use, the tears rolled down just the same. I read the story of *Wings* and in spite of myself I cried over it. When I saw the movie I tried to tell myself that I wouldn't cry as I had already read the book and could have myself steeled against any display of sorrow. It all went well until one of the last scenes and I found myself crying. Most any picture with a touch of pathos to it has me using my handkerchief a great deal.[28]

For some viewers, crying at the movies seemed to have a therapeutic effect. Many reported that they resisted such displays of emotion, but after crying profusely over the agonies portrayed in the plot, they often felt better.

Other Emotional Influences. There were a number of other reported emotional reactions to film content that testified to the strong impact of films on children as they viewed them. Feelings of love and passion were clearly aroused for some. In many cases these emotions were attached to the shadowy figures on the screen as boys and girls fell madly in love with their favorite star. In other cases, the portrayed actions of lovers in the films stimulated strong interpersonal feelings among couples in the audience.

> In the gloom of the Fox Theater, I sat with my gang, and I gasped in pleasurable anticipation as the tense moment approached. The hero placed his hands about the heroine's divinely small waist and pulled her half-fiercely toward him. Her beautiful lips parted slightly; he looked into her heavenly eyes with infinite adoration and their kiss was perfect. My response was inevitable. My hand clutched Vera's; we thrilled in ecstasy.[29]

Although the autobiographies do not "contain graphic accounts of physical relationships," the movies clearly stimulated strong desires. Whether or not those pressures led to "the inevitable" is anybody's guess, but given the sexual norms of the time, they probably did not. The critics of the movies of the period were sorely concerned that the films were indeed inflaming the "baser passions." The author may have reinforced those concerns when he concluded that "emotional possession induced by passionate love pictures represents an attack on the mores of our contemporary life."[30]

Sheer thrills and generalized excitement were also a part of children's emotional response patterns to the movies. They shouted their relief when the hero escaped from danger; they groaned when things went badly. During the Saturday matinee, with audiences composed almost exclusively of children, whistles, screaming, laughter, cheers, shouts, and big sighs of relief were a normal part of the viewing experience. Nails were bitten, seats were clutched, eyes were covered, and caps were wrung into shreds.

Perhaps the most significant aspect of "emotional possession" in all its forms (according to Blumer) was that it often provided frameworks for perception and behavior choice long after the film had been seen. A familiar example is the reluctance of many children to enter dark rooms or to pass by graveyards at night, after seeing horror films and spook shows. Another familiar example was the young female who derived definitions of romance and court-ship mainly from the films. Carrying these conceptualizations into real-life relationships with suitors sometimes led to disappointments. It was this type of long-term and indirect influence that was of concern to the researcher—although it could clearly not be established in an experimental design.

Long-Term Influences. In the final sections of his report, Blumer tried to pull together in a general way the long-term and overall influences on children provided by their motion picture viewing. In so doing, he anticipated two theories of mass communication influence that have become more systemati-cally developed in recent years. One is the "meaning theory of media portrayals advanced by De Fleur and Plax.[31] The other is the modeling theory of Albert Bandura.[32]

Blumer did not have these formulations available at the time. However, in commenting on the role of media portrayals in providing socially constructed meanings for various aspects of reality, he anticipated the central thesis of meaning theory.

> One would expect that movies would be effective in shaping the images which people form of their world and in giving form to the schemes of conduct which they come to develop. Motion pictures depict types of life which are unfamiliar to many people and consequently shape their conceptions of such a life.[33]

In terms of modeling, the author noted that the films "show situations and various forms of conduct in very attractive ways." Because of that attractive quality, social relationships, patterns of behavior, or attitudes and values depicted in the movies provide clear lessons for children to copy—models for imitation and incorporation into one's own life-style.

Blumer found evidence in his autobiographies that motion pictures had indeed shaped modes of thinking and interpretation of many aspects of his subjects' worlds. These modes included stereotypes of ethnic and racial groups; of villains and heroes; of rich and poor; of wrongdoers and the righteous, and many other social categories. The movies provided conceptions of war, family life, work, sexual mores, romantic behavior, religious belief, the roles of men and women, parent-child relationships, college life, and hundreds of other social activities and arrangements. These depictions not only served as bases for belief and interpretation regarding activities removed from the lives of the subjects, but as guidelines for daily conduct as subjects actually participated in real-life versions of what had been modeled on the screen.

Overall, then, Blumer's work *The Movies and Conduct* emerges as perhaps the most significant of all of the Payne Fund Studies, in view of its early concern with two processes that have recently become the focus of both theory and research. Both meaning theory and modeling theory are now central to the analysis of the *long-term* influences of the media content on human behavior. We can also note that Blumer's work delved into other aspects of the effects of mass communication. For example, in the context of the motion pictures of the era, he made a very detailed analysis of the uses and gratifications provided by movie content for his youthful subjects. Movies were used in play, as a source of daydreams, as guides to etiquette, dress, mannerisms, and beautification.

The limitations of the research are many by the standards of experimentation and quantification that came to dominate media research in the decades that followed. Yet, those strategies—with their emphasis on stimulus-response conceptions, short-term effects, and point-by-point correspondence between components of a message and specific forms of response—are themselves being seriously questioned today. There is a real possibility that the detailed, subjective, and analytical procedures used by Blumer in his "exploratory study" revealed a greater richness and insight into the effects of the films than the "scientific" studies that were done at the same time.

CONCLUSIONS AND IMPLICATIONS

What can we learn from this fascinating series of studies done when the movies were young? First, we can gain a profound respect for the imagination and diligence of the researchers who designed, conducted, and reported on the individual investigations. These were truly massive research efforts, involving (in total) tens of thousands of subjects. The investigators made use of the best research procedures, strategies, and techniques available at the time. Those strategies ranged from laboratory-type efforts (e.g., those of Dysinger and Ruckmick) with elaborate controls and apparatus, to content analyses, surveys, field experiments, and the autobiographical approach of Blumer.

Interpreting the findings of this massive effort presents a very difficult picture. At the time they seemed relatively clear! The movies did seem to bring new ideas to children; to influence their attitudes; stimulate their emotions; present moral standards different from those of many adults; disturb sleep; and influence interpretations of the world and day-to-day conduct.

These conclusions may well have been quite correct at the time. America was not a media society except in a limited sense during the 1920s. The only mature medium was the newspaper. Radio was only a toy. The movies came with a rush—almost overnight—to delight, frighten, thrill, and fascinate an audience of millions of children who had never seen anything like them. The idea that this new medium, suddenly thrust upon a society just emerging from the Victorian Age, could have profound and visible effects upon such an audience does not seem far-fetched.

This does not mean that the findings of the Payne Fund Studies provide useful guides for understanding media influences on children today. Contemporary society bears only a faint resemblance, in terms of media presence, to the simpler times of the 1920s. Today's children and adolescents are surrounded by media content to a degree unimaginable fifty years ago.

The importance of the Payne Fund Studies lies elsewhere. Clearly, they were the great pioneering effort that established media research as a serious scientific field. They brought together in one extraordinary group of studies a major problem of public concern and the perspectives of young sciences. The fact that various disciplines participated in the research was a harbinger of things to come; the fact that a broad range of topics was studied with many different techniques was also an indicator of future directions.

When the findings of the Payne Fund Studies were published they confirmed the worst fears of the critics of the medium and the movie industry. W.W. Charters, who wrote a volume summarizing the main findings, concluded that "the commercial movies are an unsavory mess," and that "the producers ought to have heart" over their bad influences on children.[34]

Such conclusions played a part in reinforcing the *legacy of fear* that had been kept alive by strident denunciations of the evils of propaganda during the same decade and by the widely held beliefs about the horrors of newspaper influence current during the late nineteenth century. This legacy of fear was the key factor in bringing public pressure to bear on the movies to "clean up their act." By the early 1930s, the motion picture industry strengthened its Production Code and began enforcing it more rigidly through its Hays Office. After establishing such self-censorship, in which all the major producers cooperated, the movies of the mid and late 1930s altered greatly the degree to which they portrayed socially controversial scenes. The Payne Fund Studies were part of the effort by which this change was achieved.

In summary, the Payne Fund Studies undoubtedly presented a reasonably valid picture of the influences of the movies of the 1920s on the youth of that period. The films were an influence on attitudes; they provided models for behavior; they shaped interpretations of life. They probably had as many prosocial influences (or at least harmless influences) as those that disturbed adults of the time. The Payne Fund Studies were clearly the pioneer efforts that established the field of media research within the perspectives of science. They anticipated contemporary interest in meaning theory and the influence of models and focused the new field on such topics as attitude change, the sleeper effect, uses and gratifications, content analysis, modeling influences, and the social construction of reality. They placed an emphasis on quantitative, experimental, and survey methodologies, but they still made use of more qualitative approaches. Above all, the studies shifted the long-standing pattern of concern on the part of communication scholars with propaganda criticism that represented an earlier rhetorical form of analysis. In these senses, the Payne Fund Studies will remain one of the most significant milestones in the development of mass communication as a scientific field of study.

NOTES AND REFERENCES

1. For a full description of the history of this concept and its measurement, see Emory S. Bogardus, *Social Distance* (Yellow Springs, Ohio: Antioch Press, 1959).
2. L.L. Thurstone and E.J. Chave, *The Measurement of Attitude* (Chicago: The University of Chicago Press, 1929).
3. Basing their ideas on the work of such pioneers as G. Udny Yule and R.A. Fisher, sociologists and psychologists were transforming their fields by advocating quantitative approaches to the study of human behavior. See F. Stuart Chapin, *Field Work and Social Statistics* (New York: The Century Company, 1920); Robert R. Burgess, *Introduction to the Mathematics of Statistics* (Boston: Houghton Mifflin, 1927); Louis L. Thurstone, *The Fundamentals of Statistics* (New York: The Macmillan Company, 1925).
4. Edgar Dale, *Children's Attendance at Motion Pictures* (New York: The Macmillan Company, 1935), pp. 71–72.
5. Edgar Dale, *The Content of Motion Pictures* (New York: The Macmillan Company, 1935), p. 8.
6. W.W. Charters, *Motion Pictures and Youth: A Summary* (New York: The Macmillan Company, 1933), p. v.
7. Edgar Dale, *Children's Attendance at Motion Pictures* (New York: The Macmillan Company, 1935), pp. 30–73. See also Henry James Forman, *Our Movie Made Children* (New York: The Macmillan Company, 1935), pp. 12–27.
8. Edgar Dale, *The Content of Motion Pictures* (New York: The Macmillan Company, 1935). Note especially Table 2, p. 17.
9. P.W. Holaday and George D. Stoddard, *Getting Ideas From the Movies* (New York: The Macmillan Company, 1933), pp. 65–66.
10. Ruth C. Peterson and L.L. Thurstone, *Motion Pictures and the Social Attitudes of Children* (New York: The Macmillan Company, 1933).
11. W.S. Dysinger and Christian A. Ruckmick, *The Emotional Responses of Children to the Motion Picture Situation* (New York: The Macmillan Company, 1933), pp. 110–119.
12. Samuel Renshaw, Vernon L. Miller, and Dorothy P. Marquis, *Children's Sleep* (New York: The Macmillan Company, 1939), pp. 153–155 and 183–186.
13. Charles C. Peters, *Motion Pictures and Standards of Morality* (New York: The Macmillan Company, 1933).

14. William Graham Sumner, *Folkways* (London: Ginn and Company, 1906).

15. Frank K. Shuttleworth and Mark A. May, *The Social Conduct and Attitudes of Movie Fans* (New York: The Macmillan Company, 1933).

16. Herbert Blumer, *The Movies and Conduct* (New York: The Macmillan Company, 1933).

17. Herbert Blumer and Philip M.Hauser, *Movies, Delinquency, and Crime* (New York: The Macmillan Company, 1933).

18. Ruth C. Peterson and L.L. Thurstone, op. cit., pp. 64–66.

19. Herbert Blumer, op. cit., pp. 3–12.

20. Ibid., p. 22.

21. Ibid., p. 23.

22. Ibid., p. 31.

23. Ibid., pp. 38–39.

24. Ibid., p. 40.

25. Ibid., p. 45.

26. Ibid., p. 47.

27. Ibid., p. 88.

28. Ibid., p. 96.

29. Ibid., p. 105.

30. Ibid., p. 116.

31. Melvin L. De Fleur and Everette E. Dennis, *Understanding Mass Communication* (Boston: Houghton Mifflin, 1981), pp. 26–27.

32. Albert Bandura, *Social Learning Theory* (Englewood Cliffs, N.J.: Prentice-Hall, 1977), p. 25.

33. Ibid., p. 141.

34. W.W. Charters, *Motion Pictures and Youth: A Summary* (New York: The Macmillan Company, 1933), p. 54.

3

The Invasion from Mars:
Radio Panics America

On October 30, 1938, the United States was at war—invaded by monstrous creatures from Mars. At least that was the firm belief of a large segment of the six million people who were listening that night to CBS' "Mercury Theatre on the Air." What they heard was, of course, a radio drama—a chilling adaptation of H.G. Wells's science fiction masterpiece, *War of the Worlds*. Because the dramatization was presented in a clever newscast style, many listeners believed that the Martians were actually taking over. Others were driven to panic because the invasion seemed a direct threat to their lives. Many thought their world was ending; terrified people cried, hid, prayed, or fled into the countryside. The panic was, of course, an accident; there was no intent to frighten anyone. Nevertheless, what occurred that October night was one of the most remarkable media events of all time. If nothing else was proved that night, it was demonstrated to many people that radio could have a powerful impact on its audience. The broadcast also provided a unique opportunity for social scientists to study panic behavior triggered by a mass communication event. Before we begin a discussion of that research, it is important to take note of two features of the times that probably had a significant impact on the effect of the broadcast: (1) the popularity of radio and (2) the contemporary world situation (i.e., the historical setting).

Much to the dismay of newspapermen, radio had become the primary mode of mass communication and entertainment in the late 1930s, and the popularity of newspapers had begun to fade. It was estimated that of the 32 million families in the United States in 1938, 27 million had radios. Thus, a greater proportion of the population at that time had radios than had telephones, automobiles, plumbing, electricity, newspapers, or magazines.[1] The ownership of radios had been increasing dramatically; the number of radio sets owned by Americans had doubled almost every five years.[2]

Overall, radio had a deeply established role in the lives of Americans. It provided entertainment and brought the news of the world to the public almost as it happened. British Prime Minister Chamberlain explained the Munich concessions; President Roosevelt instilled confidence in the American population with his "fireside chats" in which he seemed to be speaking to each American personally. Radio made Edgar Bergen and Charlie McCarthy stars, popularized the music of the big bands and stars like Benny Goodman, and introduced millions of Americans to performers and performances of classical music. Thus, radio brought drama, soap operas, sports broadcasts, and music into the American home, but it also brought rapid and dramatic coverage of news events in a very tense and troubled time—the last was perhaps its most significant service.

The misery of the worst years of the Depression in the early 1930s was still vivid in people's minds in 1938. Many Americans had experienced the loss of their jobs or their farms or businesses. Many had seen their families hungry and even homeless; banks had foreclosed mortgages on a vast scale. For many, the solid rock upon which our social structure had been built turned out to be shifting sand. Although conditions had begun to improve by 1938, many people still wondered whether or not they would ever regain any sense of economic security. The complexity of modern finance and government, and the disagreements in the economic and political proposals of the various "experts" created an environment which the average American was unable to interpret.

The ominous and growing shadow of war added to these economic anxieties. On October 30, 1938, the Munich Crisis was still fresh in the memories of most Americans. The rise of Hitler and his transformation of Germany created anxiety for many. And if the threat of Fascism were not enough, there was also Communism. Both of these rising philosophies of government and politics were alien to the beliefs of most Americans. Indeed, at the time of the *War of the Worlds* broadcast, the American people had been hanging on the words of the radio broadcasts for weeks. They eagerly sought the most current international news. To facilitate the dissemination of this news, the broadcast industry had developed a new technique—"on the spot" reporting. Radio played a crucial role in keeping a nervous and news-hungry populace informed. Thus, it is no mere coincidence that the Halloween eve panic was created by a radio broadcast.

THE MERCURY THEATRE AND *THE WAR OF THE WORLDS*

"Mercury Theatre on the Air," sponsored by CBS, had been broadcasting since June of 1938. (The program lacked a commercial sponsor until the week following the *War of the Worlds* broadcast, when it obtained a lucrative contract with Campbell Soups). The program was aired on Sunday evenings between 8 and 9 P.M. Eastern Standard Time. The dramatic programs were built around the name and talents of Orson Welles, cofounder, with John Houseman, of Mercury Theatre. Welles and Houseman selected the shows; Howard Koch wrote the dramatic scripts.

Interestingly, the panic broadcast almost did not come off. On the Tuesday preceding the broadcast, Howard Koch had not yet finished the show. He was having problems adapting Wells' novel into a dramatic format. A particularly troublesome problem was the novel's setting (England); in addition, it was written in narrative style. Koch recalled:

> I realized that I could use practically nothing but the author's idea of a Martian invasion and his description of their appearance and their machines. In short, I was being asked to do an almost original hour-length play in six days.[3]

At the time, Koch felt that under no circumstances could the story be made "interesting or in any way credible to modern American ears."[4] Koch pleaded with Houseman to have his assignment changed to another play. This might have been done if an interesting alternative project had been available. Houseman recalled that the "only possible alternative for that week was a dreary one—*Lorna Doone*.[5] At the first rehearsal of the show, on Thursday, all involved agreed that the show was extremely dull. They thought that the only chance of success for the show would be to emphasize its newscast style—its simultaneous, eyewitness quality. Koch went back to work on the script, spicing up the newscast style with circumstantial allusions and authentic detail.

The revised script was rehearsed Saturday afternoon with sound effects but without its star. Welles did telephone later to find out how things were going. During that call, a CBS employee told him that it was "frankly not one of our better shows." Confidentially, according to this man, "it just didn't come off."[6] Twenty-seven hours later, many CBS executives would have been a good deal happier had that evaluation turned out to be accurate.

The Broadcast

The Mercury Theatre always began with its theme. As 8 P.M. approached, Welles finished drinking his pineapple juice in the studio and poised himself, amid the debris of the frenzied preparation, to throw the cue to begin the theme. He signaled, and Tchaikovsky's *Piano Concerto #1 in B Flat Minor* began; when the music faded, routine introductions were made. Then an announcer indicated that a dramatization of H.G. Wells' *War of the Worlds* would be performed. About one minute into the hour—intoning as only he could—Welles began his narration:

> We know now that in the early years of the twentieth century, this world was being watched closely by intelligences greater than man's and yet as mortal as his own. We know now that as human beings busied themselves about their various concerns they were scrutinized and studied, perhaps almost as narrowly as a man with a microscope might scrutinize the transient creatures that swarm and multiply in a drop of water. With infinite

complacence people went to and fro over the earth about their little affairs, serene in the assurance of their dominion over this small spinning fragment of solar driftwood which by chance or design man has inherited out of the dark mystery of Time and Space. Yet across an immense ethereal gulf minds that are to our minds as ours are to the beasts in the jungle, intellects vast, cool, and unsympathetic regarded this earth with envious eyes and slowly and surely drew their plans against us. In the thirty-ninth year of the twentieth century came the great disillusionment.

It was near the end of October. Business was better. The war scare was over. More men were back at work. Sales were picking up. On this particular evening, October 30, the Crossley service estimated that 32 million people were listening to their radios.[7]

Then, very smoothly, without perceptible transition, an anonymous announcer followed him on the air delivering a very routine bulletin:

> ...for the next twenty-four hours not much change in temperature. A slight atmospheric disturbance of undetermined origin is reported over Nova Scotia, causing a low pressure area to move down rather rapidly over the northeastern states, bringing a forecast of rain, accompanied by winds of light gale force. Maximum temperature 66; minimum 48. This weather report comes to you from the Government Weather Bureau.... We now take you to the Meridian Room in the Hotel Park Plaza in downtown New York, where you will be entertained by the music of Ramon Raquello and his orchestra.

The audience then heard a CBS house orchestra playing the tango, *La Cumparsita*.

It is evident that the first few minutes of the broadcast were strictly realistic in regard to time-frame and were perfectly credible, although somewhat boring. The adapted script of *War of the Worlds* started very slowly and continued to move at a snail's pace. There were some meteorological and astronomical bulletins, alternating with musical interludes and a rather dull scientific interview. These first few minutes were *intended* to bore or lull the listener into a false sense of security and furnish a solid base of real time from which to accelerate later into dramatic time. Some twelve minutes into the show, there was a news flash that "a huge, flaming object, believed to be a meteorite, fell on a farm in the neighborhood of Grover's Mill, New Jersey, twenty-two miles from Trenton."[8]

Musical interludes were then alternated with interviews with people on the scene. A few minutes later, the Martians reared their ugly heads and the scene was set. The dramatic action picked up speed after the audience had been significantly conditioned to additional scientific observations interspersed with a program of dance music. The program suddenly shifted from real time to the condensed and telescoped time required of dramatic presentations. The transition to dramatic time was outstanding, executed with such technical and dramatic skill that it was all but imperceptible.

Perhaps the skill of the transition helps to explain why much of the audience accepted a large number of events contained in a single broadcast as real, events that would have taken days, weeks, or longer to have occurred in fact. Within a span of 45 minutes, the Martians had blasted off their planet, set up their destructive machines, defeated our armies, disrupted our communications, demoralized the population, and occupied whole sections of the country! In addition, the United States had mobilized large bodies of troops; reporters had traveled great distances; government cabinet meetings were held; and savage battles were fought on land and in the air. Yet, it is estimated that approximately one million people believed all this to have taken place!

Because the actions of the Martians and the defenders of the country were compressed in time, it seemed unlikely that most people would mistake the broadcast for an actual occurrence—especially if they had heard the program introduction, which clearly stated that a dramatization of the Wells novel would follow. The entire "hoax" could easily have been recognized in these early minutes—except that few people were listening. Instead, they were being entertained by Charlie McCarthy and Edgar Bergen, then at the height of their popularity, on another network. The Crossley survey of listeners taken the week before the broadcast gave 34.7 percent of the listening audience to "The Edgar Bergen Show" and only 3.6 percent to the "Mercury Theatre." The critical factor here was the American listener's habit of *dial-twisting*. That particular evening Edgar Bergen had an unpopular guest who went on at approximately 8:12 P.M.; listeners began changing stations. By that time, the mysterious meteorite had already fallen on Grover's Mill, New Jersey; shortly thereafter, the Martians had shown their foul, leathery heads, and the New Jersey police authorities had rushed to the scene.

What made things more credible to the newly tuned listeners was the genuine-sounding appeal by the Secretary of the Interior around 8:31, at the height of the crisis:

> Citizens of the nation: I shall not try to conceal the gravity of the situation that confronts the country, nor the concern of your Government in protecting the lives and property of its people. However, I wish to impress upon you—private citizens and public officials, all of you—the urgent need of calm and resourceful action. Fortunately, this formidable enemy is still confined to a comparatively small area, and we may place our faith in the military forces to keep them there. In the meantime placing our trust in God, we must continue the performance of our duties, each and every one of us, so that we may confront this destructive adversary with a nation united, courageous, and consecrated to the preservation of human supremacy on this earth. I thank you.

Davidson Taylor, CBS' supervisor of the broadcast, was summoned from the control room near the end of the Secretary's appeal. A few minutes later, when he returned, he appeared shaken. By now the Martians had swept all opposition aside as they advanced upon New York. Those participating in the broadcast thought it was going well. Taylor, however, had just learned how well. The CBS switchboards were uselessly swamped; a madness was sweeping the country because of the broadcast. Rumors had reached the network of panic injuries, deaths, and suicides. Taylor had been requested to interrupt the show immediately—to issue an announcement by the station about the broadcast.

The broadcast was less than a minute from the station break. The Martians were blanketing New York with poison gas. The music swirled, the "last announcer," Ray Collins, died heroically on the roof of the Broadcasting Building, and the boats in the harbor whistled until all who manned them were dead. As all these sounds died away, an amateur radio operator was heard, reaching weakly into the dark night to an empty world.

> 2X2L calling CQ
> 2X2L calling CQ
> 2X2L calling CQ
> Isn't there anyone on the air?
> Isn't there anyone?

There followed complete silence. Five seconds later, the network announcer broke the spell, shattering the "reality" of the end of the world:

> You are listening to the CBS presentation of Orson Welles and the Mercury Theatre on the Air in an original dramatization of *The War of the Worlds*, by H. G. Wells. The performance will continue after a brief intermission.

According to Houseman, the remainder of the show was well written and sensitively played.

In the last part of the broadcast, the play was clearly identified as a fantasy. The problem was that almost no one heard it. It described the adventures of a lone survivor and his observations on human society. The Martians finally died, but not by man's action. All his defenses had failed. What finally destroyed them was bacteria. The microorganisms of the earth overpowered the conquerors. Finally came the hope of rebuilding a new world.

The broadcast ended with an informal speech by Welles:

> This is Orson Welles, ladies and gentlemen, out of character to assure you that the *War of the Worlds* has no further significance than as the holiday offering it was intended to be. The Mercury Theatre's own radio version of dressing up in a sheet and jumping out of a bush and saying BOO! Starting now, we couldn't soap all your windows and steal all your garden gates, by

tomorrow night...so we did the next best thing. We annihilated the world before your very ears, and utterly destroyed the Columbia Broadcasting System. You will be relieved, I hope, to learn that we didn't mean it, and that both institutions are still open for business. So good-bye everybody and remember, please, for the next day or so, the terrible lesson you learned tonight. That grinning, glowing globular invader of your living room is an inhabitant of the pumpkin patch, and if your doorbell rings and nobody's there, that was NO Martian...it's Halloween.

Also identifying the presentation as fantasy were additional announcements made by CBS immediately following the broadcast. For example, one such announcement was aired right away:

> For those listeners who tuned in to Orson Welles's Mercury Theatre on the air broadcast from 8 to 9 P.M. Eastern Standard Time tonight and did not realize that the program was merely a modernized adaptation of H. G. Wells' famous novel *War of the Worlds*, we are repeating the fact which was made clear four times on the program, that, while the names of some American cities were used, as in all novels and dramatizations, the entire story and all of its incidents were fictitious.

The four announcements CBS referred to occurred (1) at the beginning of the broadcast (when most people were not listening), (2) before the station break, about 8:35 (by this time, most of those who panicked were no longer listening, but fleeing), (3) right after the station break, and (4) at the end of the broadcast. Moreover, the most terrifying part of the broadcast, it should be remembered, came *before* the station break. Those listeners who failed to hear the original announcement therefore had ample opportunity to become frightened.

The Panic. The panic began well before the broadcast had ended. Terrified people all over America prayed and tried frantically, in one way or another, to escape death from the Martians. The reaction was strongest in the New Jersey area (in a single block, more than 20 families rushed out of their houses with wet handkerchiefs and towels over their faces), but people were affected in all sections of the country. Some examples:[9]

> *New York*—Hundreds of people fled their homes. Bus terminals were crowded. One woman telephoned Dixie Bus Terminal for information and spoke impatiently, "hurry please, the world is coming to an end and I have a lot to do."
> *Rhode Island*—Hysterical people swamped the switchboard of the *Providence Journal* for details of the Martian invasion. Officials of the electric company reported that they received many calls urging them to turn off all lights so that the city would be safe from the enemy.

Boston—The *Boston Globe* was swamped with calls from frightened individuals. One woman said she could see the smoke and the fire brought about by the Martian invasion.

Pittsburgh—A man came home in the middle of the broadcast and found his wife in the bathroom with a bottle of poison in her hand and screaming, "I'd rather die this way than that."

Birmingham, Alabama—Many people gathered in churches and prayed. On the campus of a southeastern college—"The girls in the sorority houses and dormitories huddled around their radios trembling and weeping in each other's arms. They separated themselves from their friends only to take their turn at the telephone to make long-distance calls to their parents, saying goodbye for what they thought might be the last time."

Kansas City, Missouri—One telephone informant said that he had loaded all his children into his car, filled it with gasoline, and was going somewhere. "Where is it safe?" he wanted to know. The Kansas City Bureau of the Associated Press received queries on the "meteors" from Los Angeles, Salt Lake City, Beaumont, Texas, and St. Joseph, Missouri.

Concrete, Washington—The town experienced a power failure at the very moment the Martians were supposed to have been interrupting communications across the nation and disrupting the nation's power sources. This created mass hysteria because it appeared to confirm the broadcast.

Newspapers carried stories relating the shock and terror of many citizens for weeks after the broadcast. Around the world, newspaper accounts tried to recreate the atmosphere of terror that spread throughout America that October night.

As we shall show in a later section, several million people heard the broadcast. It has been estimated that about one million of these were frightened. Many of them engaged in panic behavior, a reaction that brought wide criticism to the producers of the show. Welles bore the brunt of most of the initial criticism. Reporters hounded him; outraged citizens threatened him. But the focus eventually shifted to CBS and Mercury Theatre. Legal actions were filed against both seeking compensation for injuries and damages totalling millions of dollars. None of these suits ever went to trial, however; there was no legal precedent for such claims. CBS did choose to settle one claim. A man living in Massachusetts wrote:

> I thought the best thing to do was to go away. So I took three dollars twenty-five cents out of my savings and bought a ticket. After I had gone sixty miles I knew it was a play. Now I don't have money left for the shoes I was saving up for. Will you please have someone send me a pair of black shoes size 9B![10]

Against the advice of its lawyers, CBS sent the shoes.

The casualties turned out to be neither as numerous nor as serious as first thought. One young woman had broken her arm when she fell while running down stairs. The Federal Communications Commission held hearings on the broadcast and adopted a resolution prohibiting the use of "on the spot" news stories in dramatic broadcasts. CBS issued a public apology and promised no more Halloween scares. The incident was then officially closed.

THE RESEARCH

The Office of Radio Research of Princeton University hastily organized a research study following the panic. The group had been formed a year earlier when the Rockefeller Foundation provided the University with funds to assess the influence of radio on listeners in the United States. The occurrence of the great panic suddenly presented it with a rare opportunity. Social scientists could study, for the first time, panic behavior triggered by a mass communication event. Funds for the special investigation were provided through a special grant from the General Education Board.

Although the scope of the investigation was limited in many ways, and the research had a number of methodological problems, the study became one of the classics of mass communication research. The results were reported in *The Invasion From Mars* by Hadley Cantril, written with the assistance of Hazel Gaudet and Herta Herzog. The purpose of the study was to discover the psychological conditions and the situational circumstances that led people to believe that the broadcast drama was real. The result was a sensitive study of the feelings and reactions of people who were badly frightened by the believed arrival of the Martians.

The researchers were trying to answer three basic questions: (1) What was the extent of the panic (i.e., how many listened and how many panicked); (2) Why did this broadcast frighten some people when other fantastic broadcasts did not; and (3) Why did this broadcast frighten some people but not others?

Methods
Because the research questions were so complex, several approaches were employed to seek out the answers. The results obtained by one method could thus be compared with those obtained by another. Such a pluralistic approach to the research was desirable because the phenomena under investigation were of so transient a nature. The following techniques were used: personal interviews, scientific surveys, analysis of newspaper accounts, and an examination of volume of mail. We shall discuss each of these in turn, in the order of their importance for the study.

Personal Interviews. Much of the information contained in Cantril's book was derived from in-depth personal interviews with persons who listened to the broadcast. These interviews began one week after the broadcast and were completed by the time four weeks had elapsed. A total of 135 individuals were interviewed. On these, 107 were selected because the broadcast had badly frightened them; an additional 28 listeners who had not been frightened by the broadcast were interviewed to provide a basis for comparison.

The interviews were limited to the New Jersey vicinity (Princeton's locale) for two reasons: (1) funds were limited, and (2) the researchers wanted to insure that there was proper supervision of this aspect of the research program. According to Cantril:

> Every attempt was made to keep the group representative of the population at large. However, no pretense is made that the group is a proper example of the total population.[11]

In addition, the respondents who had been frightened were identified almost entirely through the personal initiative and inquiry *of the interviewers*. Many more persons were identified than could possibly have been interviewed, given the funding limitations.

Surveys. The results of several different surveys were included in the study. The most significant were: (1) a special survey conducted by CBS the week after the broadcast in which the interviews were taken throughout the country from 920 persons who had listened to the broadcast; and (2) a nationwide survey of several thousand adults conducted by the American Institute of Public Opinion (AIPO) about six weeks after the broadcast. Although the delay was unfortunate, it was also unavoidable. It took that long to obtain sufficient funding to conduct it. The results obtained, however, are extremely valuable because the Institute reached many small communities and homes without telephones that were not regularly sampled by the radio research organizations.

Newspaper Accounts and Mail. Twelve thousand five hundred newspaper clippings that appeared in papers throughout the country for three weeks following the broadcast were analyzed in the study. Analysis indicated continued interest in the broadcast, although the number of articles diminished somewhat at the end of the three weeks.

In addition, analysis of the volume of mail to CBS stations, The Mercury Theatre itself, and to the Federal Communications Commission (FCC) was also undertaken. It was not surprising that huge increases in the volume of mail were reported. Interestingly, most of the letters to the Mercury Theatre in particular and to CBS stations in general were favorable, even congratulatory. However, letters to the FCC, the "watchdog of broadcasting," were generally unfavorable. It seemed that those who wanted their protests taken seriously did not hesitate to communicate with the proper authorities, whereas those who appreciated good drama gave praise where praise was due.

It is clear that even with the study's multifaceted approach, it had many methodological problems. For example, there was almost a haphazard aspect to the selection of subjects for personal interviews. This aspect of the research program was almost totally lacking in rigor. Moreover, the delays of up to four weeks in obtaining the interviews was unfortunate. One of the major scientific surveys also shared this shortcoming.

There was also a validity problem. Many people may have been reluctant to confess their gullibility in an interview after having read newspaper accounts, such as one by Dorothy Thompson, in which she claimed that nothing about the broadcast was in the least credible. Nevertheless, the authors freely admitted the shortcomings of their data-gathering procedures and qualified many of their findings. On the other hand, we must remember that no one anticipated that a panic would occur, and the delays in the research were therefore unavoidable. Although the findings may have limitations, they give us insight and understanding of the reasons why a radio broadcast caused more than a million people to panic.

The Findings
The findings have several dimensions. As we noted earlier, the study sought to determine the size of the audience (including how many were frightened), the unique aspects of the broadcast as a trigger for panic behavior, and why some listeners were frightened while others were not.

The Size of the Audience. The best evidence regarding "who listened" came from the American Institute of Public Opinion poll. It was estimated from their sample that nine million adults heard the broadcast. If children were included, the number would increase to 12 million. The AIPO estimate was, however, much *higher* than that yielded by any other known audience measure. This may be due to the fact that its sample, unlike those of other surveys, included small communities and homes without telephones. Because of the wide discrepancy, Cantril pooled the results of the AIPO poll with the findings of C. E. Hooper, Inc., a commercial research organization that made continuous checks on program popularity. The Hooper figures indicated a listening audience of about four million for the Mercury Theatre broadcast on October 30, 1938. The pooled results yielded a final estimate of six million listeners—admittedly conservative.

How Many Were Frightened. The AIPO survey asked "At the time you were listening, did you think the broadcast was a play or a real news report?" Twenty-eight percent of the respondents thought that it was news, and 70 percent of those who thought it was a news report were frightened or disturbed. Thus,

AIPO estimated that 1.7 million listeners thought the broadcast was a news bulletin and 1.2 million were excited by the news. Even more conservative estimates place the number of people frightened at one million or more. Had the program enjoyed greater popularity, the panic might have been even more widespread, depending upon whether or not they heard the introductory announcements.

Unique Aspects of the Broadcast. What was there about this broadcast that caused it to frighten some people when other fantastic broadcasts did not? Cantril's research indicated that the following five factors were important in distinguishing *War of the Worlds* from other "frightening" programs.

1. The sheer dramatic excellence of the program was an important factor, Dorothy Thompson's remark about its credibility notwithstanding. No one reading the script can deny that the broadcast was so realistic for the first few minutes that it was almost credible, even to relatively sophisticated and well-informed listeners.

2. Radio was an accepted vehicle for important announcements. A large proportion of listeners, particularly those in the lower income and educational groups, had learned to rely more on radio for the news than on newspapers. Almost all of the listeners who had been frightened and were interviewed mentioned somewhere during the course of the interview the great confidence they had in radio. They expected that it would be used for such an important announcement. Listeners had learned to expect that dramas, musical programs, and the like would be interrupted or even cut off in an emergency in order to inform the public. A few examples of the respondents' comments indicate their attitudes toward and reliance on radio.

> We have so much *faith in broadcasting*. In a crisis it has to reach all people. That's what radio is here for.
> I always feel that the *commentators bring the best possible news*. Even after this I still will believe what I hear on the radio.
> It didn't sound like a play the *way it interrupted the music when it started*.

3. The use of the "expert" in the broadcast gave it credibility. In many situations where events and/or ideas are too complicated, or too far removed from one's immediate experience, then only the expert is expected to understand them. The rest of the people must rely on the expert's interpretations. The logical "expert" in the panic broadcast was the astronomer, "Professor Richard Pierson," the chief character in the drama (played by Orson Welles). Other fictitious astronomers were also mentioned: "Professor Farrell of the Mount Jennings Observatory of Chicago," "Professor Morse of MacMillan University in Toronto,"

and "Professor Indellkoffer of the California Astronomical Society."

When the dramatic situation changed, other experts were introduced. "Gen. Montgomery Smith of the State Militia" provided expertise for organized defense. "Mr. Harry McDonald" of the Red Cross, "Capt. Lansing" of the Signal Corps, and the "Secretary of the Interior" all described the terrible conditions and gave orders to evacuate or attack. This technique appeared to have a powerful effect on the listeners.

I believed the broadcast as soon *as I heard the professor from Princeton* and the officials in Washington.

I knew it was an awfully dangerous situation *when all those military men were there and the Secretary of State spoke.*

If so many of these astronomers saw the explosions they must have been real. *They ought to know.*

4. The *use of real places* added a familiar frame of reference to the broadcast. The use of actual towns, city streets and highways, and so on in the broadcast were crucial cues for many people. For example, mention of places well known to them was particularly frightening to listeners in New Jersey and Manhattan. The towns of Grover's Mill, Princeton, and Trenton, New Jersey were all mentioned early in the broadcast. Other familiar places such as Watchung Mountains, Bayonne, the Hutchinson River Parkway, Newark, the Palisades, Times Square, the Pulaski Skyway, and the Holland Tunnel were all familiar to residents of the New York/New Jersey area. Even listeners in other areas of the country recognized many of the names as real.

When he said, "Ladies and Gentlemen, do not use *route number 23*," that made me sure.

I was most inclined to believe the broadcast *when they mentioned places like South Street and the Pulaski Highway.*

If they had mentioned any other places but streets right around here, I would not have been so ready to believe.

5. Tuning in late was a major factor in leading people to believe that the broadcast was real. It seems highly unlikely that a listener would take the broadcast seriously if the opening announcements had been heard. Indeed, data from two separate surveys (CBS, AIPO) indicated that the time a person tuned in was a major factor in determining whether or not the person was frightened by the broadcast. For example, among the questions asked as part of the CBS study were: "At what part of the program did you tune in?" and "Did you realize it was a play or did you think it was a real news broadcast?" Forty-two percent indicated

that they had tuned in late. As Table 3.1 shows, there was a very pronounced tendency for those who tuned in late to accept the broadcast as news, and for those who tuned in at the beginning to take it as a play. Only 20 percent of the persons interviewed who listened from the beginning thought they were hearing a news report.

Why did such a large percentage of the listeners tune in late? We mentioned earlier that Mercury Theatre was competing with the most popular program on the air, Edgar Bergen and Charlie McCarthy. Most listeners heard their first routine and changed the station when an unpopular singer came on the show. Another reason people tuned in late was the contagion that the excitement of the show created. Many who were frightened called friends and relatives who then tuned in. In the AIPO survey, the respondents who tuned in late were asked: "Did someone suggest that you tune in after the program had begun?" Twenty-one percent responded that someone had. In the CBS survey the figure was 19 percent.

Still, there *were* those who tuned in from the beginning yet believed the clearly introduced play to be a news broadcast. Analysis of the data revealed two main reasons such a misinterpretation came about. First, many people who had tuned in to hear the Mercury Theatre play thought that it had been interrupted for special news bulletins. They were familiar with this kind of interruption and had experience with it in the war crisis earlier that October. It was easier to accept the news interruption as irrelevant to the expected play than to infer that it was a part of the play. In the CBS survey, 20 percent listened from the beginning and thought it was a newscast. Of these, nearly two-thirds (61 percent) thought the interruption was authentic. Their comments make this apparent.

> I have heard other programs interrupted in the same way for news broadcasts.
>
> I believed Welles' statement that he was interrupting the program for a news flash.

TABLE 3.1. TIME OF TUNING IN AND INTERPRETATION (CBS SURVEY)

Interpretation	Tuned in		Total Number
	From the Beginning (percent)	After Beginning (percent)	
News	20	63	175
Play	80	37	285
Total percent	100	100	
Total numbers	269	191	460

Source: Hadley Cantril, *The Invasion from Mars* (Princeton: Princeton University Press, 1940), p. 78.

The second major reason for the misunderstanding was that many people simply did not pay attention to the opening announcements. Some people kept their radios turned on and paid attention to them only when something of interest caught their attention. Since the beginning announcements frequently contained station identifications and commercials, many people were probably inattentive. For example, 10 percent of those people who heard it from the beginning said that they had not paid any attention to the announcements.

> My radio had been tuned to the station several hours. I heard loud talking and excitement and became interested.
> My radio was tuned to the station but I wasn't paying attention to it.
> We had company at home and were playing cards while the radio was turned on. I heard a news commentator interrupt the program but at first did not pay much attention to him.
> I started to listen only when the farmer began giving a description of the landing of the tube.

Tuning in late, however, was a much more important factor in determining whether the listener would follow the program as a play or as a news report than was ignoring or misunderstanding the beginning of the show.

Why Some Were Frightened and Some Were Not. In spite of the fact that many persons tuned in to the *War of the Worlds* broadcast late, certainly not all of them believed the show to be news. Even among those who believed the invasion to be real, the patterns of behavior differed significantly. To understand better the varying behavior demonstrated, Cantril and his associates placed the listeners into four categories, identifying why some were frightened while others were not (assuming that all persons at first thought the broadcast was a news report):

1. *Those who checked the internal evidence of the broadcast. (They made successful internal checks.)* The persons in this category did *not* remain frightened throughout the entire broadcast because they were able to discern that the program was fictitious. Some realized that the reports must be false because they sounded so much like science fiction literature.

   > At first I was very interested in the fall of the meteor. It isn't often they find a big one just when it falls. But when it started to unscrew and monsters came out, I said to myself, "They've taken one of those amazing stories and are acting it out. It just couldn't be real. It was just like some of the stories I read in *Amazing Stories* but it was even more exciting."

   Other persons in this category initially believed the broadcast to be news but could not believe the subsequent description of events.

It all sounded perfectly real until people began hopping around too fast. . . . when people moved 20 miles in a couple of minutes I put my tongue in my cheek and figured it was just about the smartest play I'd ever heard.

I kept translating the unbelievable parts into something I could believe until finally I reached the breaking point—I mean my mind just couldn't twist things any more, and somehow I knew it couldn't be true literally, so I just stopped believing and knew it must be a play.

2. *Those who checked the broadcast against other information and learned that it was a play. (They made a successful external check.)* Like the listeners in the first category, these were suspicious of the "news" they were getting. Some thought the reports too incredible to believe; others realized things were moving too quickly. Some listeners checked simply because they thought it was a reasonable thing to do. Mostly, they compared the news on the program with some other information. Many checked to see if other stations were reporting the invasion. Some even looked up the program in the paper.

I tuned in and heard that a meteor had fallen. Then when they talked about monsters, I thought something was the matter. So I looked in the newspaper to see what program was supposed to be on and discovered it was only a play.

3. *Those who tried to check the program against other information but who, for various reasons, continued to believe the broadcast was an authentic news report. (They made unsuccessful external checks.)* These people differed from those in category 2 (those who made successful external checks) in two ways. First, it was difficult to determine why they even wanted to check; they were not seeking evidence to test the authenticity of the reports. They appeared to be frightened individuals who wanted to find out if they were yet in any personal danger. Second, they used ineffective and unreliable checks. For example, the most frequent method of checking was to look out the window or go outdoors. Some telephoned their friends or ran to consult with their neighbors. Whatever "new" information they obtained tended to be used to verify their existing beliefs.

I looked out of the window and everything looked the same as usual so I thought it hadn't reached our section yet.

We looked out of the window and Wyoming Avenue was black with cars. People are rushing away, I figured.

No cars came down my street. "Traffic is jammed on account of the roads being destroyed," I thought.

My husband tried to calm me and said, "If this were really so, it would be on all stations" and he turned to one of the other stations and there was music. I retorted, "Nero fiddled while Rome burned."

We tuned in to another station and heard some church music. I was sure a lot of people were worshipping God while waiting for their death.

4. *Those who made no attempt to check the broadcast or the event.* Many of these people were so frightened they stopped listening, became frenzied, or paralyzed with fear. Cantril subdivided them according to the apparent reasons for their actions.

a. Persons so frightened they never thought of checking.

We were so intent upon listening that we didn't have enough sense to try other hook-ups—we were just so frightened.

b. Persons who adopted an attitude of complete resignation. To them, any attempt to check the broadcast appeared senseless.

I didn't do anything. I just kept listening. I thought if this is the real thing you only die once—why get excited?

The lady from the next floor rushed downstairs, yelling to turn on the radio. I heard the explosion, people from Mars, end of the world. I was very scared and everybody in the room was scared stiff too. There was nothing else to do for everything would be destroyed very soon. If I had had a little bottle of whiskey, I would have had a drink and said, "let it go."

c. Persons who felt that, in light of the crisis situation, immediate action was required.

I couldn't stand it so I turned it off. I don't remember when, but everything was coming closer. My husband wanted to put it back on but I told him we'd better do something instead of just listen, so we started to pack.

d. Listeners who interpreted the situation in such a way that they were not interested in making a check-up.

In some cases the individuals tuned in so late that they missed the most incredible parts of the broadcast and were only aware that some type of conflict was in progress.

I was in my drugstore and my brother phoned and said, "Turn the radio on, a meteor has just fallen." We did and heard gas was coming up South Street. There were a few customers and we all began wondering where it could come from. I was worried about the gas, it was spreading so rapidly but

I was puzzled as to what was actually happening, when I heard aeroplanes I thought another country was attacking us.

I knew it was some Germans trying to gas all of us. When the announcer kept calling them people from Mars I just thought he was ignorant and didn't know yet that Hitler had sent them all.

For other listeners, the events described did not appear to involve *immediate* personal danger.

I was at a party, somebody was fooling around with the radio, and we heard a voice, the Secretary of Interior was talking. We thought it was a normal bulletin because of the conditions abroad. Then the local militia was called so we decided to listen. It sounded real but not like anything to get panicky about. This riot or whatever it was was still a couple of miles away.

Both the personal interviews and the CBS survey indicated that those individuals who were able to make successful checks (either by internal or external tests) remained fairly calm. Those who checked unsuccessfully or not at all tended to become either excited or paralyzed. Thus, there was a very strong relationship between feelings, beliefs, and subsequent behavior.

The researchers found that those people who were frightened by the broadcast were *highly suggestible;* they believed what they heard without making sufficient checks to see if the information was accurate. But some people did not jump to conclusions but instead scrutinized what they heard and then rejected it as news. These people were said to possess *critical ability*. Cantril defined it in the following manner:

By this we mean that they had a capacity to evaluate the stimulus in such a way that they were able to understand its inherent characteristics so they could judge and act appropriately.[12]

Thus, individuals possessing critical ability were able to assess the credibility of the events in the radio play against their knowledge of the world. And there were just too many events in the play that did not conform to their conception of reality.

Unfortunately, although the concept of critical ability was the single most promising "psychological tool" for examining the data, there was no way to measure it directly. However, the researchers hypothesized that it was related to the amount of formal education a person possessed. Education "instills readiness to examine interpretations before accepting them," they argued.[13] Indeed, such a relationship between education and orientation toward the broadcast was found, as shown in Table 3.2. While college graduates were not immune to panic behavior, the response to the broadcast varied in proportion to the amount of education an individual possessed.

TABLE 3.2. EDUCATION AND INTERPRETATION AS NEWS (CBS SURVEY)

Education	Percent Who Thought Program Was News Report	Total Number of Cases
College	28	69
High School	36	257
Grammar School	46	132

Source: Hadley Cantril, *The Invasion from Mars* (Princeton University Press. 1940) p. 112.

Religious Beliefs and Personality Factors. Religiosity was also an important variable in determining how an individual would react to the broadcast. Those with strong religious beliefs were likely to think that the invasion was actually an act of God and that the end of the world was near.

> We just sât and listened. You see we're good Christians and a Providence will take care of us. We're not afraid to die because we're prepared for it.
> At first I didn't think it was the end of the world because I read in the Bible, in Revelations, that the end of the world was coming by fire and I didn't think this was a fire. I thought buildings were being struck and falling down. But then I realized that eventually they might catch on fire so I thought the end was coming.
> The Bible says that the first time the end of the world was by flood and next time it will be by fire and that went through my mind.

Other individuals were found to be particularly susceptible to the broadcast because of personality factors such as (1) emotional insecurity, (2) phobic personality, (3) lack of self-confidence, and (4) fatalism. A person who believes that his life is in the control of somewhat mysterious powers is obviously capable of rationalizing *any* experience as preordained.

> I believe what is to be will be. I didn't pray during the broadcast.
> I just kept listening. I thought if this is the real thing you only die once—why get excited. When the time comes you go and there is no way getting away from it.

Finally, it was discovered in addition that the characteristics of the listening situation could also influence an individual's susceptibility to the broadcast. For example, a person who was told to tune in by a frightened friend would listen under different conditions than someone who tuned in for other reasons. If the person who called or informed the listener was someone in whom he had confidence, the listener would be particularly susceptible to accepting that person's opinion.

> I had just gone to the store to get some last-minute things for my daughter's party. When I came in my son said, "Mother, something has come down from Mars and the world is coming to an end." I said, "Don't be silly." Then my husband said, "It is true." So I started to listen. And really, I heard forty people were killed and there was gas and everybody was choking.

Moreover, the sight and sound of other people (even strangers) who were frightened might increase the emotional tension of an otherwise calm individual and thus reduce that person's critical ability.

> I don't think we would have gotten so excited if those couples hadn't come rushing in the way they did. We were both very calm people, especially my husband, and if we had tuned in ourselves I am sure we would have checked up on the program but they led me to believe it was any station.
>
> When I came out of the telephone booth, the store was filled with people in a rather high state of hysteria. . . . This hysterical group convinced me that something was wrong.

In short, the researchers found that "critical ability" was the most important factor in distinguishing those who panicked from those who did not. However, other factors such as religiosity and personality factors were also important. In fact, critical ability alone, as measured by the amount of formal education, was not a sure preventive of panic behavior. The authors concluded that critical ability may be overpowered by either an individual's own susceptible personality or by emotions generated in a person by an unusual listening situation.

Causal Factors in Extreme Behavior. Recognizing that some people believed the broadcast to be true, why did they become so hysterical? Why did they pray, telephone relatives, drive at dangerous speeds, cry, awaken sleeping children, and flee? Of all the possible modes of reaction they may have followed, why did these particular patterns emerge? The obvious answer is that this was a serious affair. As in all other panics, the well-being of individuals, their safety, or their lives were at stake. The situation was perceived as a real threat.

Social scientists generally agree that a panic occurs when commonly accepted values are threatened and when no possible elimination of that threat is in sight. The invasion by the Martians was a direct threat to life, one's own as well as that of loved ones. Indeed, it was a threat to all other cherished values. Frustration resulted when no directed behavior seemed possible. One could either resign onself to complete annihilation or attempt to escape. One could flee, call upon a higher authority for protection, or seek out someone stronger to destroy the enemy.

If listeners assumed the destruction was inevitable, their choices were limited. They could accept their fate in a number of ways: crying, prayer, gathering the family together. Or they could run. If they believed something could still be done to stop the enemy, they could appeal to stronger powers (e.g., God). But none of these alternatives attacked the problem directly. Nothing was done to remove the cause of the crisis. Panic behavior is characteristically undirected; it is, in terms of the situation, nonfunctional.

In short, the extreme behavior evoked by the broadcast was due to the threat to values that the situation created and the complete inability of the individual to alleviate or control the consequences of the invasion. People could not choose one value over another and thus preserve some; all stood to be lost. All their loved ones, their country, and indeed their world, would by ruined physically, financially, and socially. Believing total ruin imminent, panic was inescapable.

CONCLUSIONS AND IMPLICATIONS

Overall, what were the principal findings and the major conclusions of the Cantril study? What was their importance from the point of view of developing mass communication theory and methodology? Finally, how did this broadcast, its aftermath, and the research project influence the public's perceptions of radio as a medium?

Summary of the Findings

First, at least six million people listened to the program and, of those, at least one million were severely frightened or panicked. Second, there were several important reasons why this particular broadcast frightened many listeners whereas other such "fantastic" broadcasts did not. Among these reasons are:

1. The confidence that the American public had developed in radio. It had become their primary source of news and the public expected that radio would be used to present important announcements.
2. The historical timing. The broadcast came at a time when Americans had endured years of economic insecurity and were facing the imminent threat of another war.
3. The sheer technical brilliance of the show—especially the innovative use of the "on-the-spot reporting" technique and the interviewing of "experts."
4. Tuning in late. Missing the announcement that the broadcast was a dramatic adaptation of the *War of the Worlds* was an important factor.

A third conclusion was that there were many reasons why some individuals panicked while others did not.

1. Those who possessed critical ability were most likely to discover that the broadcast was a play, rather than news.
2. Those with strong religious beliefs were likely to believe that the invasion was real.
3. Personality factors such as emotional insecurity, phobic personality, lack of self-confidence, and fatalism were also important. Those manifesting such traits were more likely to believe that an invasion was taking place.
4. An individual's susceptibility to the broadcast could also be influenced by an unusual listening situation. For example, someone encouraged to tune in by frightened friends would listen under different conditions (expectations) than someone who tuned in the broadcast for other reasons.

Subsequent events made it evident that the social and psychological factors that contributed to the panic were not confined to the United States. A few years later, similar broadcasts of the *War of the Worlds* in Spanish induced panics in two Latin American countries—Chile and Peru. The idea for the Chilean program came from William Steele, a former writer for Mutual Broadcasting's "The Shadow" series, who was then writing for a station in Santiago. Steele set the scene for his adaptation in Puente Alto, fifteen miles south of Santiago. Like Koch, he depicted horrible Martians overrunning the country. "News flashes" reported the Civic Center in Santiago destroyed, the armed forces defeated, and the roads flooded with fleeing refugees. Thousands of people all over Chile were panic-stricken.

At least one death was verified (an electric company employee, Jose Villarroel, died from a heart attack believed to have been brought on by his terrified state of mind). Ample warning had been given the public for this *War of the Worlds* broadcast during the week preceding it, by both radio and the press. It was said to be "all in fun." Announcements were repeated twice during the broadcast warning that it was only a play. Again, as in the United States, many people failed to notice the message. In the aftermath of the broadcast, the indignant Chilean people pressured the station to close and they sought to have Steele suspended. However, no official action was taken.[14]

In Lima, Peru, another similar broadcast also created a panic, although on a much smaller scale because there were fewer radios within the station's broadcast range. However, the aftermath was even more devastating. When the Peruvians discovered they had been tricked and the world was not coming to an end, they decided to put an end to the offending station. They burned it to the ground. Since that time, because broadcasts of *War of the Worlds* have demonstrated such power, there has been a conscious effort to keep the "Martian genie" from escaping its bottle. A broadcaster opens it at his own peril.[15]

The Significance of the Study

The Cantril study has remained important in the history of mass communication for a number of reasons. It was the first study of panic behavior triggered by a mass medium. However, it has theoretical significance beyond that particular focus. The researchers were not trying to develop a theory about the effects of mass communication; they were more narrowly interested in the psychological and sociological factors associated with panic behavior. In retrospect, however, their framework for research in addition to their findings played a part in the evolution of contemporary media theory.

Looking back, it is clear that Cantril shaped his study around what we have called the selective influence perspective based upon individual differences. This perspective is obvious in one of Cantril's major research objectives—determining why some people were frightened or panicked while others were not. The answers to that question were found in the differences in critical ability, which led to selective forms of response to the broadcast. Certain personality factors also played a role (emotional insecurity, phobic personality, lack of self-confidence, and fatalism). Social categories were found to be important. Factors such as religion and education influenced the probability of perceiving the broadcast as news or as a play. Finally, in retrospect, a review of the findings reveals that social relationships were significant influences on the patterns of behavior people selected to cope with the invasion. The activities and perceptions of family, friends, and even strangers contributed to the meaning that the subjects attributed to the broadcast. Thus, although it was by no means clear at the time, the panic study was one of the first challenges to the magic bullet theory. It opened the way to theories stressing selective influences.

Methodologically, no innovative techniques were used in the study. In fact, the techniques that were used were not particularly impressive; indeed, more rigor should have been applied. Yet, given the unexpected nature of the event, and the constraints of time and money, it is remarkable that the research was performed at all with any degree of precision. The logistics of planning and obtaining funding for such a study require enormous investments of time. As a matter of fact, the bureaucracy of research that has developed in the intervening years would probably preclude such an "instant" research effort should another similar event occur.

Perhaps the real significance of the study was the way in which it confirmed public thinking about the effects of the mass media. In short, it reinforced the legacy of fear. October 30, 1938, continues to be remembered as the night American panicked. For many people, the powerful influence of radio had been proven in a most unorthodox manner. Contrary to the unnamed CBS employee's prebroadcast evaluation, the show did "come off." Of that, there can be no doubt.

NOTES AND REFERENCES

1. Hadley Cantril, *The Invasion From Mars: A Study in the Psychology of Panic* (Princeton, N.J.: Princeton University Press, 1940), p.x.
2. Melvin L. De Fleur and Sandra Ball-Rokeach, *Theories of Mass Communication*, 3rd ed. (New York: Longman Inc., 1975), p. 93.
3. Howard Koch, *The Panic Broadcast: Portrait of an Event* (Boston: Little, Brown and Co., 1970), p. 13.
4. John Houseman, "The Men From Mars," *Harper's*, 168:76, 1948.
5. Ibid., p. 76.
6. Ibid., p. 76.
7. This quotation and those that follow (from the original radio script) are presented in full in Hadley Cantril, op. cit., pp. 4–43.
8. Hadley Cantril, op. cit., pp. 10–11.
9. John Houseman, op. cit., pp. 76–77.
10. John Houseman, op. cit., p. 82.
11. Hadley Cantril, op. cit., p. xi.
12. Ibid., pp. 111–112.
13. Ibid., p. 112.
14. "The Men From Mars," *Newsweek*, November 27, 1944, 89.
15. Howard Koch, op. cit.

4

The People's Choice:
The Media in a Political Campaign

The year 1940 was a fateful one for the United States. It represented the end of one era and the beginning of another. It was the last year during which the principal concerns of Americans were the issues associated with the Great Depression of the 1930s, and also the last peacetime year before the United States was plunged into war. The selection of a national leader in 1940, then, was a matter of far graver concern than any of the voters could imagine as the spring approached and the media campaign for the presidency slowly began to gear up. The incumbent was Franklin Roosevelt; the challenger, Wendell Willkie, an almost unknown candidate without prior political experience. Franklin Delano Roosevelt was a very popular president. First elected in 1932, he inherited a country nearly paralyzed by the worst financial crisis in its history. The stock market had crashed late in 1929, and by 1932 banks were on the thin edge of failure all over the country. Unemployment soared as factories closed because people had no money to buy things. Farmers couldn't even give their crops away. People were going hungry, but food was rotting in the fields. It was a democratic depression; the previously well-to-do suffered along with ordinary people who worked with their hands in mines, mills, and farms. Bread lines were long in the cities, and rural people were driven from their farms when their mortgages were foreclosed.

Into this situation came the calm and cultured voice of Franklin Roosevelt, soothing people via the radio, telling them that "all we have to fear is fear itself." He was elected in a landslide, and in his first weeks in office he surrounded himself by a "brain trust" of liberal university professors who helped him design and set into motion a set of sweeping changes and social programs that were labeled the "New Deal" for the American people. These included the Social Security Act of 1935, still our basic welfare legislation; it provided a number of welfare measures, funded on a national basis for the first time in the history of the nation. Many other economic policies, governmental controls, and social programs were added. The country shifted jarringly away from the earlier reliance on unfettered free enterprise and a limited role for government to a profusion of social programs and policies funded by a progressive income tax and policed by a large bureaucracy in Washington.

These changes received great approval from the common people, from whom Roosevelt drew his political strength. The business community deplored them to the point where many people would not even use Roosevelt's name, but simply referred to him disgustedly as "that man in the White House." Nevertheless, he was reelected in 1936 in another landslide. He overwhelmed the hapless Republican candidate, Governor Alfred M. Landon of Kansas, and solidly swept forty-six of the (then) forty-eight states.

But as Roosevelt entered his second term, he began to have serious political difficulties. For one thing, he tried to gain control of the U.S. Supreme Court (which had blocked some of his New Deal measures) by enlarging it considerably with appointees loyal to his administration. It didn't work. In fact, it backfired, and his "court-packing" attempt was a total humiliation. Undaunted, he pressed on with his enlargement of the role of the federal government in regulating and controlling the economy. He succeeded in "ramming through" legislation that provided for public housing, agricultural support programs, and an expansion of the power of organized labor. These were important additions to the earlier New Deal measures.

One major problem of the New Deal changes as a means of restoring prosperity to the country was that they didn't work very well. By 1938, it became clear that the country was sliding back into a recession. Roosevelt responded by initiating what he called "pump priming." He persuaded Congress to spend huge sums for relief programs and public works that would put the unemployed on the payroll. These measures put federal dollars into the pockets of working people, and some recovery resulted, even though the measures were very costly to the taxpayers. The country borrowed to pay its bills—a trend that continues even today.

In consequence, the Republicans began to realize what the limitations to Roosevelt's economic programs were. They began to smell just a hint of the possibility of defeating the Democrats in the next election in 1940. After all, they reasoned, Roosevelt had already been elected twice, and they would face a new candidate. Little did they know that shortly before the Democratic Convention in the summer of 1940, Roosevelt would decide to run for an unprecedented third term! Not suspecting this, the Republicans began to seek a candidate with just the right characteristics that would be needed to rout the Democrats, or at least give them a run for their money.

A new area of intense debate emerged during that time, one that would have great significance for the future. It concerned the role of the United States with respect to the war that had broken out in 1939 in Europe. One large bloc of Americans—mainly conservative Republicans—were "isolationists." They demanded that the country remain completely neutral. In fact, in 1937 they succeeded in getting passed a National Neutrality Act. Roosevelt had signed the measure with misgivings. Later, as the European war intensified and Britain was threatened, he tried various ways to get around this Act, with Lend-Lease programs and other efforts aimed at helping the British while avoiding formal hostilities with Germany. Those who sympathized with the idea of gearing up

America's defenses because the country might be drawn into the war were advocates of "preparedness." The division between these two points of view was substantial, and to a considerable degree paralleled party lines.

The Republicans started with a number of contenders but eventually narrowed their field to three serious candidates for the nomination. One was Thomas Dewey, a young and aggressive District Attorney from New York. He had gained the national spotlight because of his "racket-busting" activities and was acknowledged as an excellent speaker and a shrewd politician. His major shortcomings as a presidential nominee were his lack of experience in an important national office and his youth. At 37, he was so young as a possible president that Harold Ickes, the sharp-tongued Secretary of the Interior, ridiculed his candidacy by declaring that Dewey had "thrown his diaper into the ring."[1]

A formidable candidate was Ohio Senator Robert A. Taft, the son of former President William Howard Taft. He was a bitter opponent of the New Deal and an ardent isolationist. Taft's problem was his somewhat narrow political constituency. He represented the "Old Guard" among Republicans and was an outspoken advocate of a return to the "good old days" of a very limited role for government and a free-enterprise economy unbounded by the measures of the Roosevelt administration.

The "dark horse" was Wendell L. Willkie, a former Indiana farm boy who had risen in the world of business to head a giant public utilities corporation. Curiously, he had never been elected to public office or been appointed to high political position. Yet, it was clear that he was an extraordinarily capable administrator and a man of considerable intelligence and personal charm. To try to gain the nomination he had mounted a very well-financed and energetic campaign among his fellow Republicans. Willkie captured the nomination largely because the Republicans could not agree on anyone else. What finally convinced the delegates was that he had a background that would make him attractive to a broad spectrum of voters. He was not a moss-backed conservative, and he did not take a strong isolationist position. In fact, he was actually a former Democrat and something of a liberal! This caused a great deal of concern among Old Guard Republicans. In fact, it led conservative Senator Jim Watson to tell Willkie as he pushed for the nomination as the Republican presidential candidate, "Well, Wendell, you know that back home in Indiana it's alright if the town whore joins the church, but they don't let her lead the choir the first night."[2] Nevertheless, Willkie finally captured the nomination in the convention on the sixth ballot and went on to confront the mighty Roosevelt.

In many ways it was a David and Goliath battle. Roosevelt had won his party's nomination overwhelmingly on the first ballot, and he had no serious opposition. Roosevelt was deeply entrenched; his name was known and respected throughout the nation; he was a skilled orator who made effective use of radio as a new medium of national politics; and he was a consummate politician who had crushed every previous opponent.

Willkie, on the other hand, was a brilliant and engaging man with a rather touseled and rumpled "down-home" look. He often wrote his own speeches and delivered them somewhat awkwardly at times. But he was a tireless campaigner who hammered skillfully at the significant issues where Roosevelt was weakest. In a short time, he developed a considerable national following, considering the nature of his opponent.

In the end, of course, Roosevelt won decisively. He gained 449 electoral votes to Willkie's 82. The popular vote gave Roosevelt a large margin of nearly five million. Willkie conceded defeat graciously and made a national plea for an end to the internal differences in the nation that had arisen during the campaign. Roosevelt admired him greatly and gave him significant roles and missions that Willkie performed in the national interest. Roosevelt even explored with him the prospects of a joint ticket in 1944. All in all, it was a great election.

THE RESEARCH PROCEDURES

The small book in which the research project on this election was reported is entitled *The People's Choice*, by Lazarsfeld, Berelson, and Gaudet. It has the subtitle, *How the Voter Makes Up His Mind in a Presidential Election*. That subtitle rather succinctly summarizes the main focus of the investigation. More generally, the authors state their objectives in the following terms:

> We are interested here in all those conditions which determine the political behavior of people. Briefly, our problem is this: to discover how and why people decided to vote as they did.[3]

The investigators chose the survey method to find answers to their research question. In fact, the study represents one of the most imaginative uses of survey designs and techniques in the history of social science.

The methodology and techniques of survey research have proven to be one of the most significant contributions of the social sciences to the study of human behavior in the twentieth century. The use of this research tool began with the primitive surveys among mining families in France during the last century and early in the new century with Charles Booth's exhaustive studies of London's poor. However, it was during the 1920s that the basic techniques of modern survey research were finally put together. Sampling theory and applied procedures had been developed by statisticians and had come into use by scientists in many fields. The idea of sampling was combined with systematic interviewing procedures and adapted for use in many kinds of sociological studies. This new approach to social research was so effective that it was quickly adopted by public opinion pollsters, market researchers, and many other professionals interested in assessing the characteristics, behavior, or ideas of large aggregates of people. Combined with procedures for statistical analysis and control, it came to rival the experiment as a major tool of social and behavioral science.

By the time of the election of 1940, the survey method had been highly refined and was little different from what it is today. Its major pitfalls and limitations had become increasingly understood, along with its numerous advantages. As we noted, the study of mass communication and political behavior that was conducted during the presidential election by Paul F. Lazarsfeld and his associates, using the survey method, represents a remarkable appreciation of this research strategy. Their sophisticated study still stands as a monument to good survey research and represents a high point of innovation and precision in the study of the effects of mass communication during a presidential political campaign. The investigators were able to probe deeply into the influence of political propaganda presented by the media as voters pondered their choice of a candidate.

The study was funded by the Rockefeller Foundation, Columbia University's Office of Radio Research, *Life* Magazine, and Elmo Roper, the public opinion analyst. The investigation was on a large scale. It made use of a professional field staff and fifteen locally hired but carefully trained interviewers. Some 3000 households were initially contacted to gain data that would be used in designing the study. Later, repeated interviews would be held with samples of these people. In an era before computers were available, organizing, processing and interpreting the mass of statistical data assembled from thousands of detailed interviews was a formidable task. The first version of the results was not available in published form for four years.

Erie County, Ohio

The researchers had to select a site for their investigation. They reviewed many possibilities and finally settled on a small county in Ohio. In 1940, Erie County had a culturally homogeneous population of about 43,000. Its population size had been stable for about 40 years; its inhabitants were almost all white and almost evenly divided between farming people and those involved in the industrial labor force.

Erie County is located in the northern part of the state on the lake of the same name. It is about halfway between Cleveland and Toledo. The main city, Sandusky, with its population at that time of 25,000, was both the county seat and principal industrial center. There were three newspapers in Sandusky, but many people read the *Cleveland Plain Dealer*. Radio stations from Cleveland and Toledo were received clearly, and all major networks were represented.

Erie County had one additional characteristic that intrigued the investigators considerably. *In every presidential election in the twentieth century, the county had deviated very little from the national voting patterns.* The authors of *The People's Choice* disclaimed this as one of their main reasons for selecting Erie County as the site of their research. However, the county's representative voting patterns were certainly a plus in using the results of the study to interpret the relationship between the media and political behavior on a wider basis. The researchers maintained that Erie County was finally chosen because it was small enough to permit effective supervision of interviewers; free from sectional peculiarities; not dominated by a large urban center; and diverse enough in terms of its rural-urban split to make meaningful comparisons possible.

The Panel Design
In May of 1940, every fourth house in Erie County was visited by an interviewer. The results of these initial contacts permitted the investigators to select some 3000 persons in such a way that they were representative of the county as a whole. The key variables in this determination were age, sex, rural-urban residence, education, nativity, telephone ownership, and automobile ownership.

From these 3000 individuals, four separate stratified samples of 600 persons were drawn. Each of these samples was matched in such a way that all four were like each other and representative of the county as a whole. The four samples were called "panels" because they were used to construct an innovative *panel design.* The purpose of this special research design was to provide effective controls to assess the effects of repeated interviewing. It must be kept in mind that the purpose of the research was to study the formation of voting decisions *over time.* In more specific terms, this meant observing respondents repeatedly between May, at the start of the campaign, through early November, the time of the actual election.

The procedure used to make such repeated observations was a monthly survey, in which the same individuals were interviewed as the campaign progressed. It was an excellent idea because each subject could be interviewed before making a decision for whom to vote, again at the time of that decision, and after the decision had been made. The role of the mass-communicated political propaganda could be related to political behavior at each of these stages. The only problem with repeated observations is that they might be an influence on the very process under study. Perhaps, it was hypothesized, the voter who was interviewed repeatedly over a seven-month span would reach different decisions and see the issues differently than one who was not interviewed, or interviewed only once.

The panel design was an ingenious method for discovering whether, and to what extent, such repeated interviews did influence decisions about the election. The general idea was to use one sample of 600 subjects as the "main panel" to be interviewed every month, from May to November. However,

	May	June	July	August	September	October	November
Time Table			REP. CONVEN.	DEM. CONVEN.		ELECTION	
Interview Number	1	2	3	4	5	6	7
Group	Total	Main Panel 600	Main Panel 600	Main Panel 600	Main Panel 600	Main Panel 600	Main Panel 600
Interviewed	Poll (3000)		Control A 600	Control B 600		Control C 600	

Figure 4.1. Outline of the Panel Design and Schedule of Interviews.
Source: Paul F. Lazarsfeld, Bernard Berelson, and Hazel Gaudet, *The People's Choice* (New York: Columbia University Press, 1948) p. 4.

another panel of 600 (Control A) was to be interviewed during the third month (July). The results of a number of key variables could then be compared to see if the main panel differed, and to what degree, from the main control panel.

As is shown in Figure 4.1, the same thing was done during the fourth month (August) using Control B. Finally, in October, Control C was interviewed along with the main panel. Overall, then, 600 people were under repeated monthly observation with seven interviews between May and November. Three other panels of 600 each were interviewed as controls in July, August, and October, respectively. The final interview with the main panel was just after the election in November.

As it turned out, the interviews with the matched control panels showed few differences from the results obtained with the main panels. In other words, the repeated interviews did not seem to have any notable influence on the behavior of the voters who were studied month after month.[4] This finding laid to rest any suspicions that the interviewing itself changed the decisions or the behavior of the main panel. Although it was an expensive procedure, the additional interviewing with the controls did provide larger numbers of cases on which to base conclusions on many of the issues under study.

The most significant aspect of the panel technique was that a given individual could be followed longitudinally over the time period of the election as he or she became interested in the election, began to pay attention to the media campaign, was influenced by others, reached a decision, possibly wavered or changed sides, and finally voted. The usual one-shot survey cannot provide such data over time. The same is true of an experiment that is particularly difficult to repeat with the same subjects. As the authors put it, the panel design was an effective method for studying a whole list of questions:

What is the effect of social status upon vote? How are people influenced by the party conventions and the nominations? What role does formal propaganda play? How about the press and radio? What of the influence of family and friends? Where do issues come in, and how? Why do some people settle their vote early and some late? In short, how do votes develop? Why do people vote as they do?[5]

Neither the research report of the investigators nor the summary of their work in the present chapter provides full and complete answers to all these questions. Nevertheless, a number of important insights into many of the issues can be summarized.

THE RESULTS

Generally, the findings obtained in this large-scale study can be divided into two broad categories: those that help us in understanding the voters themselves and the forces that influenced their political ideas and behavior, and the role of the mass media political propaganda in helping to shape their voting decisions. The sections that follow present the highlights of what the results revealed.

Assessing Participation in the Election

Political life in the United States was more predictable before World War II than it has been since. Generally, the country had been dominated by the Republican party until Roosevelt won in 1932. After Woodrow Wilson left the White House, a series of Republican presidents—Harding, Coolidge, and Hoover—were all more or less firmly committed to the idea that "the business of America is business." In other words, the route to national prosperity and a more abundant society was held to be through the fostering of private enterprise, limiting the role of government, and avoiding participation in the troubles of foreign nations. It was a conservative philosophy, but for decades it had seemed to work. Until the crash of 1929, the country had experienced rather steady growth.

When the Great Depression shattered the economy, Franklin Roosevelt put together a broad coalition of organized labor, northern blacks, liberal Jews, and a huge base of poor people who had not previously been politically active. With the country reeling from hard times it had not been difficult to pin the blame on Hoover and the Republicans and to formulate and implement his New Deal. He sharply elevated the role of government in regulating business, gave increasing power to organized labor, brought considerable change to the federal income tax structure, and developed a national welfare system. These moves polarized the two parties. Later, his strong sentiments and policies concerning national defense preparedness and sympathy toward aiding Britain further split the two groups. These clear differences in the ideologies and composition of the two parties led the researchers to look for social characteristics of voters that would predispose them to lean toward one candidate or the other.

Social Categories and Voting Predispositions. Following the lead that the social composition of the two parties differed, the hypothesis was formulated that those who intended to vote as Republicans or Democrats would differ in *socioeconomic status*, and that such SES differences would predispose them to vote in one way or the other regardless of who the candidates were. *Religion* provided another such variable. Republicans and those inclined toward their views were more likely to be Protestant, while Catholics were more likely to favor the Democrats. Other variables that would predispose voters in this way were thought to be *rural-urban residence* (with farmers more likely to vote Republican), *occupation* (with blue-collar laborers more likely to be sympathetic toward the Democratic candidate), and *age* (with older people more conservative generally and more likely to lean toward the Republican candidate). Each of these possibilities was examined with care to see how it correlated with claimed party affiliation and an intended vote for the Democratic or Republican candidate.

Generally, the variables were interrelated in a number of complex ways, but the following summary provides an overview of the general picture:

1. Those high in socioeconomic level (SES) were more likely to intend to vote Republican than Democratic.
2. Fewer laborers than white-collar workers intended to vote Republican. (However, if SES level was held constant, occupation seemed to make little difference).
3. Self-identification made a difference. If a person felt that he or she belonged to "the business class" they generally intended to vote Republican. If the self-identification was with "the laboring class" the intention was more likely to be Democratic (regardless of the actual occupation of the person).
4. Religious category was a strong influence on voting intention. At all levels of SES and among all occupations, Catholics leaned toward a Democratic vote and Protestants toward the Republicans.
5. Age was very significant as a predictor of intended voting patterns. Among both Protestants and Catholics, younger people leaned toward the Democrats and the older toward the Republicans.

These complex relationships were painstakingly sorted out and illustrated with bar charts based on simple percentage comparisons. Armed with today's linear models for multivariate analysis, and a computer to do the "slave labor" of computation, a far more efficient analysis would be possible. Nevertheless, the overall finding that emerged was expressed elegantly enough: "Different social characteristics, different votes."[6]

An Index of Political Predisposition. The predisposing factors noted above made it possible to develop for each subject an index of the likelihood of a Democratic or a Republican vote. This was done before knowing how the person actually voted in November, basing the predictions on the hypothesis that the variables would be predictive. Later, three of the factors were found to have provided the greatest predictive value. These were SES, religion, and rural-urban residence. For each person, the researchers constructed an index of political predisposition (IPP) and used this in studying the way in which the subjects reached their voting decisions. The index classified the voters into six categories: (1) Strongly Republican, (2) Moderately Republican, (3) Slightly Republican, (4) Slightly Democratic, (5) Moderately Democratic, and (6) Strongly Democratic. For example, a person was classified in category (1) if he was a rich, Protestant, farmer. At the other end, a person was in category (6) if he was a Catholic laborer living in Sandusky. (Category 7 was combined with 6.) Others were in the intermediate categories, depending on their SES level and their mix of the other critical factors.

This IPP proved to be remarkably well correlated with vote intention.

Figure 4.2. Political Predisposition and Voting Pattern.
Source: Paul F. Lazarsfeld, Bernard Berelson, and Hazel Gaudet, *The People's Choice* (New York: Columbia University, 1948) p. 26.

Figure 4.2 shows the relationship. Clearly, the social composition of the public made a considerable difference. Later, the way in which these predispositions led people to attend and respond to media propaganda in different patterns will be brought out.

The concept of political predisposition based on social categories was to prove valuable in understanding the process by which people initially formed and then solidified their vote intention, even if they did not know themselves what they were going to do initially. The simple fact is that most eventually went in the direction predicted by their IPP category. Their social categories led them to be selective in their exposure to media propaganda and selective in influences from other people. This was clearest for people toward the ends of the scale, but considerably less clear for those subjected to conflicting forces if they were somewhere in the middle categories.

Democratic and Republican Ideas about Public Affairs. Not all voters are aware of the critical issues confronting their nation, even during a presidential election when the issues are receiving heavy attention in the campaign. However, thinking about the issues does make a difference in voting intentions and behavior. Those leaning toward the Republicans or the Democrats had different ideas about social and economic matters in 1940, and the researchers tried carefully to probe these differences in awareness and thinking to see how they influenced vote intention. For example, on such issues as "unemployment," "relief" (welfare), and the "WPA" (a make-work program using federal funds to reduce unemployment), members of both parties conceded a Roosevelt victory to the poor, who after all were the recipients of such measures. However, the Republicans did not feel that these were the kinds of people who should be helped by federal expenditures. Republicans wanted a more favorable climate for business, rather than increased expenditures on social benefits for the needy. On the other hand, more than half of the Democrats felt that a Willkie victory would benefit only business groups and the relatively well-to-do. Republicans tended to deny this and maintain that stimulating business would provide more jobs and consequently a more prosperous nation. In short, both groups tended to see Willkie as a businessman's candidate and Roosevelt as a working man's candidate. Thus, the rich man versus poor man theme was salient during the entire campaign.

The war in Europe also provided ample grounds for political differences. We noted earlier that one large segment of the society was "isolationist" and wanted to stay completely clear of the "mess in Europe." Another part of the population felt that Hitler's and Mussolini's totalitarianism was threatening to overwhelm democracy in Europe and that it was only a matter of time until America would have to become involved. With these isolationist versus interventionist views in the background, Republicans generally opposed the recently passed conscription (draft) bill, and were against increases in military aid to

Britain. Democrats, on the other hand, were behind various measures related to "national preparedness" and efforts to aid Britain. Military participation in the war, however, was not thought by either party to be likely in the near future.

In addition to the domestic economy and national defense, there was a host of other issues on which Democrats and Republicans found themselves on different sides. Roosevelt's third term was one. Farm issues, and policies toward labor were others. The strikingly different personalities of the candidates appealed to different types of voters. Willkie's lack of experience in foreign affairs troubled some; his strong business background attracted others. Roosevelt's boldness in reshaping American government put some people off; his imaginative leadership made a great deal of sense to others.

These were the kinds of issues around which the media campaign was organized. Each of these topics provided the basis for newspaper editorials, radio commentaries, magazine articles, movie newsreels, political speeches, and arguments between friends. They were debated in every setting from dingy barrooms to lofty mansions. And it was these issues that provided the grounds upon which people formed their opinions, reached a decision concerning their vote, decided to remain aloof, shifted from one candidate to another, or remained firm in their resolve.

Before the media campaign could interact with predispositions of the voters, however, their interest in the election had to be stimulated sufficiently so that they would attend. Not everyone was equally interested at the outset. In fact, interest in the election was a function of a number of variables.

Variables Related to Interest in the Election. The social composition of the parties and their opinions about the issues are not the only significant factors that shape a presidential election. The level of interest in the election and the campaign is also critical. Throughout the interviewing program data were collected to try to assess what variables, what categories of people or their personal characteristics, would provide the best index of their interest in the election. As it turned out, the best predictor was the simplest of all: the respondent's self-rating of his or her level of interest. During the interviews the respondents were asked to classify themselves according to their level of interest. In other words, people were asked to indicate whether they had (1) a great deal, (2) moderate, (3) mild, or (4) no interest in the election. These four were later reduced to three by combining moderate and mild. This provided only a crude ordinal measure of level of interest, but the researchers justified the procedure by their findings. Those who claimed the highest level of interest were more familiar with the issues and had clearer opinions than those who claimed less interest. The most interested also participated more in election events, were more likely to attend to political communications and discuss them with others.

Interest was also related to some of the social categories discussed earlier. For example, both a higher SES and educational level were positively correlated with interest. The least interested respondents tended to be the poor and the relatively uneducated. Urban versus rural residence was not a predictor of level of interest, but age certainly was. Regardless of educational level and nearly everything else, it was the older respondents who had the highest level of interest in the election. Finally, men were more interested than women.

Level of interest was a good predictor of actual participation in the voting. As might be suspected, the greatest proportion of nonvoters was found at the lowest level of interest. Figure 4.3 shows the dramatic impact of this variable. It can be added that nonvoting tended to be deliberate rather than accidental or unwitting. In two out of every three cases of nonvoting, the respondents had indicated their intention not to vote early in the campaign. There were, in 1940, factors operating to produce alienation among at least some citizens.

Factors Influencing Voters at the Time of Final Decision

A respondent's level of interest in the campaign was a good indicator of how *early* or *late* he or she reached a final decision concerning which candidate to vote for. Another strong factor at the time of final decision was the degree to which the person was caught in *cross pressures*, or, in other words, conflicts and inconsistencies among the variables that influence vote decision.

Early versus Late Decisions. The more interested people were in the election, the earlier they reached a decision as to how they would vote. This held true regardless of party affiliation or other factors. Nearly two-thirds of the respondents with a "great deal" of interest in the election had already made up their minds by May when the interviewing began (even though the nominees

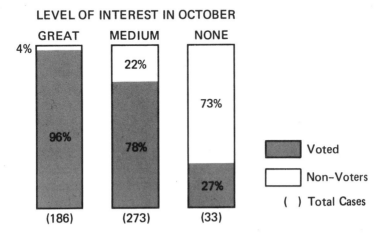

Figure 4.3. Voting and Level of Interest.
Source: Paul F. Lazarsfeld, Bernard Berelson, and Hazel Gaudet, *The People's Choice* (New York: Columbia University Press, 1948) p. 46.

had not yet been selected in their respective conventions). Only one-eighth of such respondents waited until late in the campaign to make their choice. As we will note later, this closing of the mind early in the campaign was an important condition, because it had a strong influence on their mass communication behavior with respect to selecting political propaganda from the media.

On the other side of the coin, those with less interest decided on their candidates much later. This posed some interesting problems for those in charge of the media campaigns. How could these people whose minds remained open be attracted to a particular candidate? One difficulty was that even though they were uncommitted, they were also uninterested. This meant that they paid little attention to political propaganda. At the same time, in a close election their votes could spell the difference between victory and defeat.

Toward the end of the campaign, the pool of such uninterested and undecided potential voters grew smaller and smaller. Campaign managers had to exert their greatest efforts to interest such people in supporting their candidate.

The Problem of Cross Pressures. Earlier, three specific variables were discussed that most sharply differentiated Republicans and Democrats. These were SES, religion, and rural-urban residence. These three factors were the basis of the index of political predisposition (IPP). But what happened when an individual was caught in a conflicting pattern of these variables? For example, if a person is both prosperous and a Catholic, or both poor and a farmer, what is the most likely outcome of the vote decision?

There are many additional ways in which a person can be caught in cross pressures. For example, people who voted for a given party in the previous election have a considerable probability of voting the same way again. Yet, if they are disaffected by their party's new candidate, they are under cross pressure. The family is another potential source of cross pressure. If a person's family is strongly affiliated with one party or the other, the individual is under pressure to vote with them, even if he or she has another preference. Other similar sources of cross pressures are friends or even work associates. All of these together make up a considerable web of potential cross pressures, some stemming from social categories and some from social relationships.

But whatever the source of such cross pressures, one effect was clear. Cross pressures *delayed* the voter's final decision. Among the various sources of cross pressures, the most influential in causing delays was the family. The reluctance of many voters to commit themselves to a particular candidate was often traceable to exactly this kind of difference with family members.

Cross pressures and their associated delays have implications for the media campaign of political propaganda. Voters under cross pressures delay their vote hoping that some event will occur to resolve their indecision. This indecision makes these voters fair game for political managers, who hope to get into their propaganda just the right message to break the indecision and attract the person to their candidate. Toward the end of the campaign, efforts are intensified to attract undecided voters, and these efforts can pay off. Thus, both the potential voter with low interest in the campaign and those under cross pressure become targets of special efforts as the media campaign begins to come to an end.

The overall effects of low interest and cross pressures were very different for different kinds of voters. In other words, the process of delay did not work in the same way for all people. Some remained undecided until the last moment. Others moved tentatively to one candidate but then shifted later to the other. Still others reached a decision, fell back into doubt, went over to the other side, and eventually shifted back to the earlier choice. For the most part, there were three main patterns of changes that described such voters. Some 28 percent were *crystallizers*. They simply delayed reaching a decision until the last minute. These were evenly divided between the parties. Another 15 percent were *waverers*. They started out in May with a clear vote intention. Later in the campaign they slid back into indecision, but later returned to their original choice. Finally, a smaller proportion (8 percent) were *party changers*. They started out with a clear vote intention but eventually deserted to the other candidate. The simplest generalization that emerged from all of these data was that individuals who leave their party and fall into indecision usually return to their first choice. Those who change from one party to another, however, seldom return.

Major Effects of the Media Campaign
One of the main results of the study was to identify three clear patterns of influence of the mass-mediated campaign of political propaganda. These patterns describe the way in which mass-mediated information can play key roles in leading voters to form voting decisions, given their existing pattern of political predispositions. In other words, there is a considerable amount of interaction between the predisposing social characteristics of voters, what they select and use from the political propaganda presented by the media, and their ultimate voting choice. These complex relationships can best be understood by examining three concepts that identify the patterns of influence of the mediated propaganda. These are *activation*, *reinforcement*, and *conversion*.

Activation. Political communications activate latent predispositions. They do so by presenting effective arguments to people who selectively attend to them because they are consistent with their predisposing orientations. This is true both for formal propaganda presented by mass-mediated campaigns and more personal persuasion presented by family members or friends.

Activation refers to the process of making something manifest or observable. In the case of a voter, it refers to bringing the individual to a conscious decision that is consistent with the kinds of predisposing variables identified earlier as making up the IPP. Since about half of the voters had already made up their minds in May, and some never did reach a decision, activation took place only among a limited number of voters. The best estimate places it at about 14 percent among the people studied.

The activation of political predispositions is a process that takes place in stages or steps. These steps identify the relationship between the voter's latent predispositions and political persuasion presented as either media propaganda or personal influences:

1. *Propaganda arouses interest.* We showed earlier that interest was a key variable in reaching a decision to vote. Thus, a rising level of propaganda gets attention and begins to increase interest.
2. *Increased interest brings increased exposure.* This is a circular effect. The more people pay attention, the more interesting the campaign becomes, and this increases their interest even more.
3. *Increased attention causes voter to select information.* As interest and attention increase, the more likely it is that the voter will select information consistent with his or her underlying predispositions. Thus, selective attention reinforces predispositions, which in turn increases selectivity.
4. *Votes crystallize.* The latent becomes manifest. The voter is now aware of the candidate and the candidate's position on the issues. This awareness is highly selective, but it leads to the forming of a decision based on a body of information.

The process of activation is somewhat inconsistent with the concept of the "rational" voter, supposedly the ideal in a democratic society. Such ideal voters would review carefully the issues and the candidates and make a decision on the basis of enlightened self-interest only after learning and assessing all of the facts. Activation, on the other hand, takes place because voters already are strongly predisposed to one party or the other and they crystallize their vote to support that party's candidate. It is hardly a rational model, because the opposition is given little systematic consideration. Nevertheless, activation is one of the principal effects that results from the flow of information during a political campaign.

Reinforcement. More than half of the voters had already consciously selected their candidate before the interviewing began in May. They were not certain who their party would select in the convention, but they intended to vote for him in any case. For those people the propaganda campaign served quite another purpose. Campaign managers have to supply such already-decided voters with a continuing flow of arguments and justifications for remaining right where they are. This is a very important function of the media campaign. We noted that about half of the people interviewed already knew in May for whom they would vote. If such partisans are not kept in line, they could become waverers, or even worse, party changers. As the researchers put it:

> Party propaganda—from his own party—provides an arsenal of political arguments which serve to allay the partisan's doubts and to refute the opposition arguments which he encounters in exposure to media and friends—in short, to secure and stabilize and solidify his vote intention and translate it into an actual vote. A continuing flow of partisan arguments enables him to reinterpret otherwise unsettling events and counter-arguments so that they do not leave him in an uncomfortable state of mental indecision or inconsistency. [7]

Generally, then, reinforcement is far less dramatic than the process of persuading voters to desert their party for the other camp. However, because such a large proportion of the voters are involved, it is far more important. A failure to understand the reinforcement effects of political propaganda could easily cost a candidate the election.

Conversion. When ordinary people think of the influence of political propaganda, they usually have conversion in mind. Through the clever use of words, emotional appeals, or even rational arguments, it is assumed, individuals can be persuaded to desert their candidate and switch sides. But does it really happen? The answer is a highly qualified "yes," but only in a few cases and in particular circumstances. In Erie County, there were people who were converted, but they were few indeed. Only about 8 percent of the voters made a switch.

There are a number of reasons why it is unrealistic to look for large numbers of conversions. For one thing, fully half of the voters never wavered from their early decisions, making them unavailable for conversion attempts. Clear-cut political predispositions anchor another large proportion of voters in their party, even though they remain undecided and undergo the process of activation and eventually reach a decision that is entirely consistent with those predispositions: These voters are not open to conversion. Only those who remained less interested and who were under strong cross pressures were the prospects for conversion when they did reach a tentative decision. In such decisions, their commitments were weak, unsupported by strong interest, ties to a party, or a consistent network of social pressures. The numbers of such people grew smaller and smaller as activation and reinforcement took place, as interest grew stronger, and as cross pressures were resolved. In the final stages, only a handful could be persuaded to switch from an earlier tentative vote decision. For the most part, the authors concluded, the completely open-minded voter who remains undecided until the end, or who switches from one candidate to another because of compelling logic in the discussion of issues, exists only in textbooks on civics.

Overall Effects. The speeches, newspaper editorials, magazine articles, radio talks, and all the rest making up the presidential campaign had three principal effects. They activated the indifferent voter who was predisposed; reinforced the partisan; and converted a few of the doubtful. For Erie County as a whole, the Republicans made gains over their pattern of support in the election that had been held four years earlier. The 1936 election had been a considerable victory for Roosevelt in the county. Basically, his modifications of the American economic and governmental institutions made during his first term were well-received by the electorate. But events since 1936 had, to a degree, dimmed that enthusiasm. The issues of the third term, the slow recovery from the Depression, the war clouds in Europe, and the unknowns of the new welfare state troubled many people in Erie County. For these reasons they had returned in the direction of their basically conservative orientations of the past. Nationwide, of course, the election went overwhelmingly to Roosevelt. However, the conservatives of Erie County decided that their day would come at a later time.

Patterns of Attention to Campaign Propaganda

Those who design and manage presidential campaigns devise detailed, comprehensive, and sophisticated strategies in their efforts to attract the votes of the electorate to their candidate. This was as true in 1940 as it is now. At that time, of course, television was only an experimental device being studied in laboratories and test sites. The media of the campaign were radio, newspapers, and magazines. And, in the case of magazines, the country was still in the era of the general, huge circulation periodical, such as the *Saturday Evening Post.* Some specialty magazines, such as the *Farm Journal*, also played a role.

Whatever the medium, the purpose of political propaganda is to capture the attention, whet the interest, and shape the decisions of voters. As the authors of *The People's Choice* put it, political messages are designed

> ...to corral the timid, lead the willing, and convince the reluctant. Partisan leaders of opinion—the newspaper editor, the columnist, the free-lance writer, the syndicated cartoonist, the radio commentator, and the local sage—all edge into the campaign by placing the weight of their authority behind the cause of their favorite candidate. Propaganda is let loose upon the land to control or inform, to constrain or tease potential voters into the appropriate decision.[8]

In other words, an enormous amount of political information is transmitted by the media at election time. However, the big question is not how much was printed, broadcast, or said, but how many in the audience attended and understood that information. The big question also includes another issue. Was the media exposure more or less evenly spread through the population, or was it concentrated more among some kinds of people?

This last issue is one with considerable theoretical relevance. Early thinking about propaganda was that, like magic bullets, it struck all members of the mass audience equally and created uniform effects among them in a very direct way. This idea was, as we have seen, under considerable question by the time the present research was undertaken. However, the research strategy of *The People's Choice*—in particular the repeated interviewing—permitted the researchers to address fairly directly the question of who attended to a particular medium and with what outcome. It was an opportunity, in other words, to test the major propositions of the magic bullet theory. To be historically accurate, *The People's Choice* researchers did not actually pose their investigation of patterns of media attention in those terms. They simply wanted to know whether every voter received a more or less equal exposure to the media, or whether attention to the campaign was concentrated among a few. And, if the latter were the case, who were they, and what did the exposure do to them? Yet, in retrospect, their study *did* test the magic bullet theory, even if the authors did not specifically set out to do so at the time.

An associated issue under investigation in 1940 was the question of the relative importance of the three major media. Did people attend to radio, the newspapers, or magazines in an equal manner, or was one a dominant source of political information for certain kinds of people? Answers to these several questions were provided as the analysis examined the formation of decisions about choosing a candidate in relation to patterns of attention to mediated propaganda.

The Concentration of Exposure. Who listened and who read? Those were critical questions concerning the outpouring of political information during the election. The answer was that close attention was given to the media propaganda by some but certainly not all. The pattern was dependent upon what medium, what candidate, what issues, and what voters were under consideration. Patterns of attention, in other words, were very *selective*. They were by no means spread evenly among the electorate. For example, during the last twelve days of the campaign, 54 percent of the respondents had attended to at least one political talk on radio; another 51 percent had read at least one front page campaign story in a newspaper; and 26 percent had read a campaign-related article in a magazine. Earlier in the campaign, such material had been ignored by one-half to three-fourths of the population interviewed. But even in the last days of the campaign, only part of the voters attended to any of the material, and a very large proportion ignored the media campaign altogether. In other words, as the campaign moved into its last days, a flood of political material was directed at the voters. But, as the authors put it, "far from drowning any of these people, it did not even get their feet wet."[9]

Who were the people who did attend to the messages? Actually, with remarkable consistency, political propaganda presented by the various media reached the *same* segment of the population. In other words, those who listened to material about the campaign on the radio also tended to read about the same issues in the newspapers and follow the treatments of the topics in magazine stories. Thus, there was a segment of the population that was heavily exposed to the campaign propaganda whereas the remainder gave the same material only little if any attention.

Who were these people who received multiple exposure? The answers to that question have already been suggested in previous analyses of the process by which people arrive at their voting decision. Those who attended most to the media were the highly *interested* voters, those who had *already decided*, and those of *higher SES*. In particular among those categories, it was the more affluent, well-educated, and older males who lived in urban areas.

There are a number of possible explanations for this pattern of concentration of attention among particular kinds of voters. The researchers suggested that such people probably believe that they have an especially large stake in the outcome of the election. Certainly, they tend to be more politically aware, and they have a deeper understanding of the issues. But whatever the explanation of this particular pattern of concentration, it was clear that the propositions of the magic bullet theory concerning uniform patterns of attention and influence from the media were not consistent with the findings. So much for the magic bullet theory!

Radio versus Print. The study of the presidential election provided one of the first large-scale investigations of what was, in 1940, still a relatively new medium of mass communication. Radio was compared with newspapers (and magazines) in terms of their comparative roles in the campaign. No one really understood radio as an instrument of politics. Ten years earlier, only about 40 percent of American homes had radio ownership. By 1940, that figure had risen so rapidly that virtually everyone had a receiver. In fact, the figure in that year was 1.4 sets per household, on the average, in the United States. In a decade, radio had become a giant and had saturated the American population.

But how did this new medium compare with the venerable newspaper? After all, the mass newspaper had been around for a century. Its role in politics was virtually undisputed. In 1940, newspapers were still close to their all-time peak of popularity in American society. Only a decade earlier, Americans had subscribed to daily newspapers at near-record levels of 1.32 per household. In the highest year, 1910, the figure had been 1.36 subscriptions per household; in 1940, the figure was still high at 1.18. This compares to a mere .82 subscriptions per household in 1980.

Some had begun to claim that radio was the medium of the future in politics, and that even in 1940 it was more meaningful than print in the campaign because the audiences could hear the speeches of the candidates and get a feeling for their personal qualities far more than from reading about them.

Others felt that the printed word still retained its authority, and that a mere gadget like radio could never replace the newspaper as a medium for the serious presentation and exchange of political ideas.

The researchers decided to sort out this question—to try to find out to what media people had attended and how much they had been influenced by these media. They proceeded by getting people to identify in very specific terms exactly what newspaper editorials, news stories, or speeches they had read, and how this exposure had influenced their thinking about the issues. They probed into what magazine stories the voters had read, what kinds of information they had learned from such sources, and how this had helped shape their political views. They also had their respondents indicate what particular program they had listened to on the radio—what speeches they had heard, what commentaries, and so forth. By such detailed assessment of the exposure patterns for each medium among various categories of voters, the relative role and comparative significance of newspapers, magazines, and radio could be determined.

As it turned out, radio had played a larger role in the campaign than anyone had suspected. When respondents were asked which media were "helpful" as they were making their decisions, about two-thirds mentioned both radio and newspapers about equally. However, when the voters were asked to indicate which of the media was the "most important" source for political information that played a part in their decisions, radio clearly led (by roughly a 50 percent margin).

Radio was also more heavily used by the Democrats. In both 1936 and 1940, the majority of the nation's newspapers openly supported the Republicans. Presumably this was because of the close ties newspapers had to the business community. Meanwhile, Democrats had turned to radio as an alternative. Roosevelt, in particular, used the medium masterly as a political tool. He often went on the air to explain his programs to the nation. He held periodic "fireside chats" via radio, in which he spoke informally concerning the issues of the day. Because of these "fireside chats," his voice was well known to almost everyone. Willkie, on the other hand, was not an effective radio personality, and this hurt him in the election.

In the final analysis, radio emerged as a medium favored by the Democrats, and newspapers were favored by the Republicans. But in spite of the overwhelming support given by newspapers to the Republican candidate, he lost badly. Radio emerged as a politically potent medium with considerably greater significance than the printed page. It was the beginning of an era in which the personal qualities of the candidates could come under the close scrutiny of the electorate via a medium of telecommunication, bringing the personality of the presidential hopeful to a level of significance not known in earlier times.

It can be added that magazines played a minor role in the election. Some 15 to 25 percent of the respondents obtained political information from magazines. For those individuals, magazines did play a part in shaping their political views and decisions, along with exposure to political propaganda from the other media. In other words, few voters, if any, relied solely on magazines for their information. They used them to supplement information obtained from newspapers and radio.

Personal Influence and the Two-Step Flow

As the interviewing progressed month after month in Erie County, it became increasingly apparent that there were sources of influence on people's political decisions that had not been given sufficient attention when planning the study. The interviewers were discovering that people received a great deal of their information and influence directly from other people! Whenever the respondents were asked to report on their recent exposure to political communications, they mentioned discussions about politics with friends, relatives, or acquaintances much more frequently than exposure to radio or print. Face-to-face discussions were a more important source of political influence than the researchers had anticipated.

The significance of personal influence was not realized until the study was well under way. It was a serendipitous finding that simply emerged as the research was in progress. For that reason, no formal hypotheses had been built into the study to assess this phenomenon. However, once the investigators realized that people were talking to each other extensively about the election, and that these interpersonal exchanges played a key role in leading the voters to their decisions, they quickly revised what they were doing and gathered as much data concerning this interpersonal flow of information and influence as they could.

The hypothesis the investigators developed would have a significant impact on the direction of mass communication research for many years. They called it the "two-step flow of communication." After examining their data they concluded that some individuals among the people they had studied were serving as "opinion leaders." These were people who were heavily exposed to the political campaign to whom others, who had lower levels of exposure, knowledge, and interest, would turn for information and advice. The opinion leaders would pass on to these others information that they had received from first-hand exposure to the media, along with their own special interpretations of what it all meant. Thus, the heavy involvement of people in political discussions led the researchers to suggest that: "ideas often flow *from* radio and print *to* the opinion leaders and *from* them to the less active sections of the population."[10] This was their formal statement of the two-step flow hypothesis.

There were a number of reasons, the researchers pointed out, why personal influence would be particularly effective in helping shape people's decisions—in many cases much more effective than persuasive information presented in more formal media. For example, personal influence from opinion leaders was more likely to reach the undecided and the uninterested voter, both of whom were all but impervious to the political campaign presented via the media. The opinion leaders were also likely to be trusted as nonpurposive sources of information and interpretation. Political propaganda presented by radio and print, on the other hand, is clearly designed to persuade and is therefore not trustworthy. There is also the factor of flexibility. In a casual discussion setting, the person giving another his or her views can be very flexible and counter resistance that might occur—a fact well known by all effective sales people. The factor of reward can be added. When one agrees with or accepts the views or interpretations of another who is trying to "set us straight," a considerable amount of social approval is likely to be forthcoming. It is rewarding to accept personal influence; yet this factor is absent in more formal media presentations. Finally, one seldom mistrusts an intimate source. This may be largely because those who exercise personal influence do it unwittingly. And those whose views are modified may not even realize that this is happening to them. Generally, then, as information moves from the media to the opinion leaders and from them to the less active, the idea that they are engaging in political persuasion or are accepting political influence may never cross their minds.

CONCLUSIONS AND IMPLICATIONS

The People's Choice was one of the most important studies in the history of mass communication research for several reasons. First, it showed how an innovative survey design could be used in longitudinal research. Many important forms of social behavior are processes that take place over time. Typically, researchers study subjects with an experiment or a survey at only one point in that time. Sometimes, to try and get around that limitation they will study different samples of people representing cohorts at different stages in the process, but this has many pitfalls. The panel design used in *The People's Choice* got around those limitations and pitfalls by following the same subjects through the entire process. The design effectively answered the question of which influences were introduced by the repeated assessments. The answer in this case was none. Although there is no guarantee that repeated interviewing will never influence subjects, the panel design continues to be a major procedure used in longitudinal research.

A second major contribution of the research was its insights into the role of political propaganda presented by the media during the campaign. The findings showed clearly that such propaganda activated those with latent predispositions based on social category membership; reinforced those whose decisions were already firmly anchored by the constraints of those category memberships; and even swayed a few to move from one side to the other. The conversion process, however, was shown to be very limited. It occurred mainly among voters who had made a tentative earlier choice to which they were only weakly tied. Such individuals were not much interested in the campaign, and they were under confusing cross pressures from their social category memberships.

These findings on selective influences based on social categories were to prove to be theoretically significant in ways that the researchers of the time could not appreciate. Activation and reinforcement—the principal media effects according to the study—are really quite limited by comparison with the kinds of effects of the media envisioned by the critics of World War I propaganda. The legacy of fear had people believing that clever politicians could use newspapers, or even the new medium of radio, to sway and control the political behavior of the masses at will. The specter that alarmed critics the most was that of clever manipulators controlling the mass society in such a way that democratic nations could be converted to fascism, or even worse, to communism. *The People's Choice*, however, showed that conversion on this scale was extremely unlikely. The effects were not all-powerful, swaying helpless audiences uniformly and directly. They were limited effects linked to the demographic characteristics of the audiences in highly selective ways. Opinion leaders, a small category, were selectively influenced by the media. However, the majority of the people remained little touched by the propaganda from the media. As it turned out, interpersonal channels brought them more influence than the media.

Above all, it was the issue of the "two-step flow" that caught the imagination of a new generation of researchers. The edition of *The People's Choice* that became widely available to the scientific community did not appear until 1948. Following that, research on the interpersonal processes linked to mass communication burgeoned. The two-step flow hypothesis, in other words, opened up a new theoretical vista. Social relationships between people had definitely *not* been thought to be significant in the process of mass communication. Mass society theory, and its mass communication derivative, the magic bullet conceptualization, had stressed a *lack* of social ties between people. Yet, here were research findings from a large-scale study showing that ties between people were one of the most important parts of the mass communication process.

The two-step flow hypothesis emerged serendipitously from the research. But in many ways the hypothesis seems, in retrospect, the study's most important contribution. It certainly called into question most of the assumptions of the magic bullet theory, and it did little to vindicate continued belief in the legacy of fear. But in spite of this, both ideas remained in force among the beliefs of the public regarding the influence of mass communication on people.

Overall, *The People's Choice* remains one of the most sophisticated survey research studies in the history of social science. Its place in the development of mass communication theory is undisputed. It forced communication theorists to reconsider the mass society concept, the powerful influences idea, the role of social category membership, and the significance of interpersonal ties. Few studies in the history of mass communication research have had such an impact.

NOTES AND REFERENCES

1. Arthur M. Schlesinger, Jr., Fred L. Israel, and William P. Hanson, eds., *History of American Presidential Elections, Vol. IV* (New York: Chelsea House Publishers, 1971). See Chapter 1 by Robert E. Burke, "Election of 1940," p. 2923.
2. Ibid., p. 2925.
3. Paul F. Lazarsfeld, Bernard Berelson, and Hazel Gaudet, *The People's Choice* (New York: Columbia University Press, 1948).
4. Ibid., p. 159 (footnote 2).
5. Ibid., pp. 6–7.
6. Ibid., p. 21.
7. Ibid., p. 88.
8. Ibid., p. 120.
9. Ibid., p. 121.
10. Ibid., p. 151.

Experiments on Mass Communication: Persuading the American Soldier in World War II

On Sunday, December 7, 1941, Americans, in near disbelief, heard from their radios that Japanese aircraft had without warning attacked U.S. naval and other military forces at Pearl Harbor. The heavy loss of life and disastrous destruction of ships, aircraft, and Army bases left the nation reeling. Nearly a quarter of a century of peacetime had come to a sudden end.

How could it be? Who were these strange people who came from nowhere to commit such a dastardly deed? The Japanese, in the minds of most Americans—if they thought of them at all—were a rather pathetic little nation of slant-eyed people who made cheap imitations of products developed by more advanced countries. It simply did not seem possible that such people could dare to assault the might of the United States of America! Nevertheless, the forces of the Empire of Japan had blasted most of the U.S. Pacific Fleet to ruined hulks and had humiliated the armed forces of what Americans regarded as the finest nation on earth.

The next day, President Franklin D. Roosevelt in a special joint session of the Congress addressed the country by radio to declare that a state of war existed between the United States and the Empire of Japan. The President called December 7 "a day that will live in infamy." The state of war was extended to include all of the Axis Powers who were allied with Japan.

In the days that followed, Japan's victories at Pearl Harbor were to be repeated in other areas of vital significance to the United States. The Philippines were quickly overrun, and their American defenders were subjected to a terrible "death march" on the Bataan peninsula. The Japanese overran virtually the whole Southwest Pacific, threatening Australia and New Zealand. They even landed on remote parts of Alaska. For the first time the United States was called upon to fight for its very existence against the hostile forces of a foreign enemy.

THE NATION AT WAR

World War II was a conflict with a clear-cut moral purpose. The Axis Powers (Germany, Japan, and Italy) vowed to subdue the world with military might and to dominate it with their various brands of dictatorship and fascism. The Allied Forces, made up of the United States, what was left of the British Empire, and the remnants of various armed forces from countries that had been overrun by the early victories of the enemy, vowed to fight back to an eventual "unconditional surrender" of the Axis nations.

From the point of view of the United States, it was a war with the highest possible justification—a very different situation from more recent conflicts. The Japanese had "stabbed America in the back." In the minds of most citizens, the Japanese were sneaky, cruel, and virtually subhuman. The Germans had overrun helpless people in Europe and violated every treaty that had been forged at the end of World War I. They were widely held to be ruthless, cunning, and brutal. The Italians, on the other hand, were regarded with low esteem—a joke as soldiers, but a bother nevertheless.

All of these attitudes and beliefs were quickly taken up and reinforced by the mass media, by thousands of political speeches, cartoons, posters, and barroom exchanges. Hollywood epics and newspaper editorials portrayed the Germans as "pretty tough," but the Japanese as monkeylike people who should not be taken seriously. Some people maintained that the enemy would be easily defeated and the war brought to an end within a year. But as many a soldier, sailor, and marine found out later in combat, crude stereotypes obscured the fact that the enemy was tough, determined, and thoroughly courageous.

Turning Citizens into Soldiers

For a few weeks after Pearl Harbor, volunteers lined up at the recruiting offices and even scuffled with each other to be among the earliest to enlist. But the rush to get into the fight soon waned, and the less enthusiastic had to be brought in by the Selective Service System—the draft. Actually there was little resistance; to be a "draft dodger" during World War II was considered a disgrace. Even those classified as 4-F (not suitable for military service because of health or occupation essential to the war effort) were all but accused of being cowards. By the war's end, some 15 million Americans, mostly males but a few females, had donned uniforms.

The sheer logistics of locating, sorting, classifying, training, and assigning 15 million people to military duties staggers the imagination. Nevertheless, it was done. Young men and women from every walk of civilian life were transformed from their roles and statuses as bank clerks, secretaries, truck drivers, farmers, and so on, into riflemen, artillerymen, bosuns, sergeants, cooks, signalmen, pilots, navigators, and all of the other specialists that were required by the military services. What is more, it was done in a very short time.

Camps were set up in all parts of the nation, and recruits were quickly brought in for training. Their hair was cut short, and they exchanged their civilian clothes for uniforms. Awkward at first, they soon settled into the routines of training—close order drill, how to use weapons, the intricacies of military life, and the inevitable specialized training required in the complex division of labor of a modern army or navy.

Teaching a recruit such matters as wearing a uniform, how to salute, march, and use weapons is the less difficult part of military training. Beyond that lies the more complex task of shaping his motivation and morale. He has to be taught to hate the enemy and love his country, to be intensely dedicated to his military unit, and to place its survival and welfare above his own. In other words, in developing an effective fighting force it is essential to instill attitudes and loyalties that can provide critical psychological and social supports that sustain the combat soldier when the going gets tough. As a matter of fact, the vast majority of those so trained never saw combat. Nevertheless, they had to be taught to place military goals above their personal convenience and comfort even when the job was boring, seemingly endless, and obviously insignificant. For those who would see combat, indoctrination was needed to prepare them psychologically to confront and defeat a very determined and dangerous enemy. There was simply no other choice.

Turning millions of young civilians into effective teams of military personnel was no easy task. The training was made more difficult by the sheer diversity of American society. Draftees were called into service from every corner of the country. They came from ethnic communities in urban centers, small towns in the midwest, farms in the rural south, and cattle ranches in the far west. Not only were they diverse in regional origin, but they varied greatly in every other respect. They differed in education, income, occupation, religion, political affiliation, and so on. This diversity in social origins meant that the recruits also represented a broad range of individual differences in intelligence, aptitudes, values, skills, and other psychological factors. It was not easy to assess their differences and to assign these human resources to military tasks that they were capable of performing. To do so the Army (and other services) made use of psychologists, sociologists, and other social scientists who developed tests to measure intelligence and other attributes so that the proverbial "square pegs" among the recruits would not wind up in the "round holes" among the tasks that needed to be performed.

The Lessons to be Learned: The *Why We Fight* Films

Another serious problem was the sheer ignorance of the majority of the draftees concerning public affairs. Few of the recruits had any real grasp of the complex international events that had led up to the entry of the United States into the war. They knew well enough that "the Japs were the dirty guys" because they had bombed Pearl Harbor in a sneaky way. They also knew that "the Germans were mean guys" because they had overrun some of the countries of Europe and wanted to take over the world. That was about it! Beyond those simple ideas, the majority had very little knowledge of the political history of the period between the two world wars, the existence or substance of the negotiations between the United States and Japan before Pearl Harbor, or the sequences of events that led to the rise of totalitarian governments in Europe, or the strategies of those governments for world conquest.

Why were they so ignorant of international events? In large part, the United States was isolated from world problems, by both its physical location in the new world and its preoccupation with its own internal affairs. Since the end of World War I, Americans had been focusing their attention on such domestic matters as Prohibition, the Great Depression, the Dust Bowl, and the New Deal. The troubles in Europe and Asia were beyond the interest and comprehension of all but a few of the draftees. Yet, it was essential that the recruits have a good understanding of these events.

The Army was painfully aware of the need to inform its recruits, but how it could be done was another matter. Army leaders saw immediately that they needed a rapid and effective means of teaching soldiers about the nature of the enemy, their allies, and why it was necessary to be there training for war. The use of a series of training films to do the task quickly and for large numbers of trainees seemed a sensible way to get the job done. However, there were no such films, and they would have to be prepared very quickly.

Early in 1942, General George C. Marshall, newly appointed Chief of Staff of the Army, turned to Hollywood to assist in the preparation of the necessary orientation films. Specifically, he sought the aid of Frank Capra, a well-known director. His proposal was simple:

> Now Capra, I want to nail down with you a plan to make a series of documentary, factual information films—the first in our history—that will explain to our boys why we are fighting and the principles for which we are fighting.[1]

Capra wanted to help, but he wasn't certain that he was the right person to do the job. He explained to General Marshall that he lacked the right kind of experience. He had never made documentary films before. General Marshall had a simple answer:

> Capra, I have never been Chief of Staff before. Thousands of young Americans have never had their legs shot off before. Boys are commanding ships today who a year ago had never seen the ocean.[2]

Capra was convinced and began work immediately. In a very short time, he had produced seven 50-minute documentary films, and the Army started making them a part of the training program for its recruits.

> The style of the films was for the most part objective and documentary, with direct quotations, reference to official sources, animated diagrams, cuts from domestic newsreels, and cuts from foreign newsreels and propaganda

films. The visual presentation was drawn together by a running narration which told the story of the war and explained the scenes. While the general tenor of the films was "let the facts speak for themselves," they were not dryly factual. Foreign speech was frequently translated into English with a "foreign accent," "production" shots using actors were employed to tie the documentary material together, the films were scored throughout with background music, and montages and trick photography were used in trying to achieve vivid and dramatic presentation.[3]

Generally, these seven films traced the history of World War II from the rise of fascism in Italy and Germany, and the Japanese in Manchuria in 1931, through America's mobilization for war and participation in the conflict following Pearl Harbor.[4] The title of the series was *Why We Fight*, and the films were seen by hundreds of thousands of Americans as they trained for war. However, only four of these films were used in the research described in the present chapter. The content of these four films can be summarized briefly.

Prelude to War. This first film in the series described the rise of Mussolini and fascism in Italy, the rise of Hitler and Nazism in Germany, and the manner in which a military clique gained control in Japan. It showed the Japanese attack on Manchuria in 1931 and the Italian conquest of Ethiopia in 1935. In contrast, the film showed how the United States had followed a noninterventionist policy and had not prepared for global war. It made clear how the Axis countries had emphasized the growth of aggressive militarism and the massing of armed might. The major theme of the film was that the three Axis countries had joined in a plan to conquer the world and to divide it up to suit themselves. There was no way for the United States to ignore the war, and it had to defend itself; this defense was all the more difficult because of the lack of preparedness.

The Nazis Strike. This film presented a summary of the past military conquests of Germany under Bismarck and Kaiser Wilhelm, indicating that Hitler's aggressions were repeat performances of such behavior. The way in which Hitler had built up his war forces was described and his first acquisitions of territory were shown (the Austrian *Anschluss* and other actions in which Britain tried to appease Hitler by agreeing to his activities). The straw that broke the camel's back was Hitler's attack on Poland, which brought a declaration of war by Britain and France. The Polish campaign was shown in great detail to illustrate the ruthlessness, brutality, and efficiency of the German forces. The major theme of the film was that Hitler could not be appeased and that the Allies had to stop him by declaring war.

Divide and Conquer. This was a sequel to *The Nazis Strike.* It continued to show the strategy of the Nazis. It explained how they overran Denmark and Norway to the north. They were aided in this activity by traitors among the local populations (called quislings, after Vidkun Quisling, a Norwegian Nazi collaborator) and by the failure of Allied efforts to help the Norwegians. To the south, the Nazis invaded the Low Countries (Holland and Belgium) and broke through the French defensive fortresses, which permitted the Germans to move through France and catch Britain in a kind of pincers from both North and South. The theme of the film was that the early defensive strategies relied upon by the Allies were unsuccessful in the face of the strategy and tactics used by the Germans.

The Battle of Britain. This film dealt with Hitler's plan for world conquest, which had succeeded thus far as his forces defeated France and forced the British to evacuate their armies from the beaches at Dunkirk. The next step was to conquer Britain itself. If Hitler had taken over the British Isles and neutralized the British fleet, the United States would have found itself in a very dangerous situation. The film showed how Hitler failed to conquer England because of the tough resistance of the British, both in the air and on the ground. The Royal Air Force stopped the Luftwaffe cold, even after weeks of the latter's relentless bombing and fighter attacks; the British were bombed severely, but they continued their war effort in spite of the attacks. Thus, winning the "Battle of Britain" gave the United States precious time to prepare.

Overview of the Research Mission

Generally, two basic assumptions were made by the War Department concerning the *Why We Fight* films. First, it was assumed that they would do an effective job of teaching the recruits *factual knowledge* about the war, the enemy, and the Allies. Second, it was assumed that such factual knowledge would shape *interpretations* and *opinions* in ways needed to improve acceptance of military roles and the sacrifices necessary to achieve victory.

In more detail, the orientation program using these films had a number of specific objectives that were spelled out in a directive from the office of the Chief of Staff to the Information and Education Division, which was in charge of the orientation program. According to this directive, the films were intended to foster:

1. A firm belief in the right of the cause for which we fight.
2. A realization that we are up against a tough job.
3. A determined confidence in our own ability and the abilities of our comrades and leaders to do the job that has to be done.
4. A feeling of confidence, insofar as is possible under the circumstances, in the integrity and fighting ability of our Allies.
5. A resentment, based on knowledge of the facts, against our enemies who have made it necessary to fight.
6. A belief that through military victory, the political achievement of a better world order is possible.

Each of the films had been designed to achieve these objectives, although every one of the seven *Why We Fight* films told only a part of the story.

The big question, of course, is did the films work? The films seemed great, and common sense implied that showing them to the recruits as part of their training would not only teach them the factual information, but would raise their commitment and morale. Yet, common sense is not always an adequate basis for reaching reliable conclusions. A systematic and objective evaluation was needed to see if these films were in fact reaching their goals. To accomplish this assessment, the task of designing and conducting evaluation studies of the orientation program was assigned to a special unit within the War Department's Information and Education Division.

Early in the war, the Army had taken the precaution of bringing a number of distinguished social and behavioral scientists into the service. These scientists, in consultation with civilian colleagues, assisted the armed services with a variety of problems involving psychological measurement, evaluation of programs, surveys of many kinds, and studies of "morale." Within the Information and Education Division, the Research Branch was composed of the Experimental Section and the Survey Section. These units often cooperated with the Military Training Division of the Army Service Forces. Indeed, the present research represents just such a cooperative venture between the Experimental Section and Training Division.

While there were a number of psychologists and social psychologists involved in the evaluation of the *Why We Fight* series, the main team that planned and conducted the studies for the Army consisted of Frances J. Anderson, John L. Finan, Carl I. Hovland, Irving L. Janis, Arthur A. Lumsdaine, Nathan Macoby, Fred D. Sheffield, and M. Brewster Smith. The report on which the present summary chapter is based was prepared as Volume III in the "American Soldier Series," which was published several years after the war. The authors of the report were Carl I. Hovland, Arthur A. Lumsdaine, and Fred D. Sheffield. Like the others in the longer list above, each went on after the war to become an internationally known psychologist. The remaining sections of the present chapter are devoted to a presentation of the highlights of *Experiments on Mass Communication*, which brought together the results of the film evaluation studies and a number of additional experiments on communication issues. The work touched off a considerable interest, as we will note later, in the experimental study of the persuasion process.[5]

THE FILM EVALUATION STUDIES

A series of experiments were carried out, aimed at assessing the degree to which exposure to the films described above resulted in changes in their audiences. These changes were, broadly speaking, the acquisition of factual information about various aspects of the war and modification in the recruits' interpretations and opinions concerning the six objectives listed earlier.

In designing this research, the experimenters had advantages that had seldom before existed regarding control over their subjects. They could choose where, when, and how many subjects would see a particular film. They did not have to rely on voluntary cooperation in the completion of the questionnaires. They were already in possession of a substantial amount of background information on each subject from Army records, to which they had complete access. The population they were studying had limited variation in terms of age, sex, race, and current residential circumstances. And finally, the costs of the research were not really a consideration. For contemporary scholars struggling with the realities of research among today's populations, such conditions seem close to ideal.

Assessment of *The Battle of Britain*
Somewhat parallel experiments were completed on each of the four films described earlier. The main difference between them was that the research on *The Battle of Britain* assessed the impact of a single film, whereas the remaining experiments studied the cumulative impact of two or more films or made use of alternative research designs.

Objectives. *The Battle of Britain* presented a considerable amount of factual material, but in the list of the Army's six objectives to be achieved it emphasized number four (a feeling of confidence in our allies). The overall purpose of the research itself was to measure both knowledge and opinion orientations among the subjects before they saw the film, to expose them to the film, and then to assess any *change* in knowledge and opinions that had been created by seeing the moving picture.

Various procedures and strategies were used to minimize the influence of other sources of information about topics covered in the movie so that whatever change took place could realistically be regarded as due to exposure to the film. The situation of the subjects, relatively isolated from civilian life, was an aid to the researchers in this respect.

Experimental Procedures. The research was organized around (1) the use of an *experimental group* of subjects that actually saw the film and a *control* group of very similar subjects who did not see the film and (2) the administration of anonymous checklist questionnaires to both groups *before* and *after* the time when the experimental group viewed the film. While such procedures are now common in research, at the time this was a relatively new research strategy in communication studies. This way of conducting such an experiment is called a "before–after design with control group." However, an additional study was done with an "after-only" design, where no "before" measure was used and the control and experimental groups were simply compared after the film was shown to the experimental group.

The measuring instruments for the experiment were constructed with great care, and each item that finally became a part of the questionnaires was carefully pretested to make certain that it could be understood by the subjects and that it gathered the exact information that was needed by the researchers. Such pretesting, item by item, is a hallmark of careful research procedures today. The items finally used in the checklist questionnaires were of two types. These were (1) *fact-quiz* questions, such as those found on a multiple choice test, where the subject selects the correct answer from a list of alternatives, and (2) *opinion* items, either in a multiple choice style, expressing varying opinion positions from which the subject could select that closest to his own, or agree–disagree statements that the subject could endorse or reject as consistent with his own opinions. Some of these opinion items were highly related to the factual information and were quite specific. Other items dealt with broader and more general issues less tied to the facts. The questionnaires also included several personal history items (education, age, and so on) that could be used, along with handwriting, to match the before and after questionnaires of each subject. Finally, there was a need to direct the attention of the subjects away from the idea that they were simply being tested to see what they had obtained from the film. The study was portrayed to the soldiers as a sort of "general opinion survey." For this reason, the questionnaire contained a number of "camouflage" items intended to distract the subjects from perceiving its actual purpose. (Ethical considerations today might raise questions about deception, but it was not a problem for the Army at the time.)

Two such questionnaires were prepared around the content of *The Battle of Britain*. They were intended to be parallel and to cover the same items in essentially the same way. This permitted a "before" and "after" measure to be taken on each subject without using the same measuring instrument, which could have confused the results.

The time interval between seeing the film and responding to the "after" questionnaire was one week. (One segment of the group of subjects was measured nine weeks later to study long-term effects. This will be discussed later.) At one camp, 2100 subjects (half of whom saw the film) were studied in the "before–after with control group" design. In another camp an additional 900 were studied in the same way. Finally, the "after-only with control group" design was used for the study of another 1200 subjects. Overall, this added up to an impressive 4200 subjects, all of whom responded to the questionnaire at least once and half of whom saw the experimental film.

The sampling was done in a practical way by selecting company units rather than individuals. However, considerable effort was made to equate or "match" the experimental groups and the controls. Various background variables on the soldiers were studied well beforehand, and those companies most alike in their distributions of such variables as age, region of birth, and scores on Army tests were paired.

As was mentioned, the questionnaires were presented to the men as a "general opinion survey" to find out "how soldiers felt about various subjects connected with the war." The subjects were assembled in platoon groups (of about 50 men) to fill out the questionnaires in their mess halls under the watchful eyes of trained personnel. Anonymity was assured, and no officers were present.

To distract the men from wondering why they had to respond to the questionnaire twice (in the before–after design) it was explained that "the questionnaire had been revised" on the basis of the earlier results, and it was being studied again. In fact, the second version had REVISED printed in large type at the top. A number of other precautions were taken to avoid suspicion that some other purpose was at stake.

Results. The outcome of the evaluations of the *Battle of Britain* can best be understood by contrasting the responses of the control and experimental, or as we will call it, the "film" group. We noted that various objectives were built into the content of the film, and these were assessed by items in the questionnaire. Simple percentage comparisons show the influence of the film in reaching those objectives. A difference of 6 percent between the control and the film group constitutes a statistically significant result, ruling out chance and implying that the film did have an effect on those who saw it.

Generally, it is convenient to review the findings around four major issues. These define broadly the kinds of effects that the makers of the film hoped to achieve. These effects concern the following questions:

1. Was the film effective in improving *factual knowledge* about military events?
2. Did the content of the film alter the *opinions and interpretations* of viewers regarding several major themes presented in the film?
3. How much did the film improve the *general attitudes* of the soldiers toward their British allies?
4. Was the film a significant factor in improving *overall motivation* among the recruits to fight a tough war?

Each of the above was a complex issue, and only the highlights of the results of the experiment can be presented. Nevertheless, the findings were relatively clear.

First, the film did have a major effect on the acquisition of factual knowledge. Differences between the control and the film groups were consistently large. For example, the questionnaire asked why the Germans "were not successful at bombing British planes on the ground?" The answer given in the film was "because the British kept their planes scattered at the edges of the field." Only 21 percent of the control group checked this answer, whereas 78 percent of the film group got it right. Similarly, other factual items were consistently answered correctly by much larger proportions of the film group.

The effects of the film on opinions and interpretations were also in the direction desired by the designers of the film, but the differences between the control and film groups were not as great as with the factual material. There were four major content themes present in the film about which opinions or interpretations could be altered. Each can be discussed briefly.

One major content theme was that the actual battle of Britain was a major defeat for the Nazis. Many of the soldiers had not previously interpreted the German bombings of England early in the war in this light. The film increased the percentage of soldiers who concluded that the German raids were part of a preparation for invasion and that the Nazis suffered a defeat. For example, one questionnaire item stated that "They heavy bombing attacks on Britain were an attempt by the Nazis to. . ." The key answer provided by the content of the film was "to invade and conquer England." Only 43 percent of the control group checked this, whereas 58 percent of the film group selected this answer. Several similar items showed parallel patterns.

A second content theme in the film was that the British resisted heroically. Items in the questionnaire probed the degree to which the control and film groups differed in their opinions on this issue. A typical item asked "What do you think is the real reason why the Nazis did not invade and conquer Britain after the fall of France?" Only 48 percent of the control group checked the answer provided by the film, "the Nazis tried and would have succeeded except for the determined resistance by the British." By contrast, this answer was selected by 70 percent of those who saw the film.

Two additional content themes in the film produced similar results. More of the film group agreed that the Royal Air Force did a magnificent job than did the control group. And finally, the belief that the British resistance provided other nations time to prepare (the fourth content theme) was held by more of the film group than the control group. Generally, then, the experience of seeing the film did alter the opinions and interpretations of its viewers regarding these four content themes.

The film had less effect on the general attitudes of the soldiers toward the British. In contrast to the clear influence on learning factual information about military events, and in changing opinions concerning the content themes of the film, the viewing experience did not improve general attitudes toward the British allies. This was found in a variety of items where the differences between the control and film groups were consistently negligible. For example, the questionnaire posed the following item: "Do you feel that the British are doing all they can to help win the war?" The difference between the control and the film group in terms of those who answered positively was only 7 percent. A number of other items designed to measure general attitudes toward the British showed even smaller differences between the two groups. On several of these items, two and three percentage points of difference were found. In other words, it could not be concluded that the film had improved attitudes toward the British.

The film was also clearly ineffective in strengthening the overall motivation and morale of its viewers. Major objectives of the film were to increase willingness to serve, encourage attitudes toward demanding unconditional surrender, and deepen resentment of the enemy. To put it simply, the film had no effect at all on these issues. On such items as whether or not the trainees would prefer military duty in the United States, or would like to join the fighting overseas, only 38 percent of the control group wanted to go fight. For the film group—supposedly fired up by the film—the comparable figure was 41 percent, not a significant difference. Similarly, about the same percentage of the control group and the film group thought unconditional surrender was important (control group, 60 percent; film group, 62 percent). Finally, resentment of the enemy, measured by several items, showed differences that ranged from 1 to 4 percent between the two groups. It was not possible to conclude that the film improved motivation or morale. These were very important findings. Their significance to mass communication theory will be made clear.

There were many additional issues probed by analyzing data from the questionnaire. Mainly these issues pertained to checks on whether or not one set of ideas in the film might have adversely affected reactions to some other set of ideas to create a kind of "boomerang" effect. Generally, no significant effects of this kind were located.

The research design used with *The Battle of Britain* was also used with the other three orientation movies that were part of the overall film evaluation studies: *Prelude to War, The Nazis Strike,* and *Divide and Conquer.* However the last two films were shown to the men in combination to test for cumulative effects. Two days were allowed between these showings, and then the combined effects were measured by the questionnaire in the usual way.

The findings of these additional studies need not be presented in detail because they parallel on almost every point those obtained from the evaluation of *The Battle of Britain.* Instead, the implications of the findings from the research on all of these films can be discussed together because of their close similarity.

Implications. The film evaluation studies made use of research procedures such as sampling, control groups, matching, pretesting, and measurement that were the equal of some of the best social science research conducted today. There are few grounds, if any at all, to reject the findings of these experiments as misleading because of methodological or procedural flaws.

The films themselves were produced by the best talent in the nation at the time, and no expense was spared in their production. Even by today's criteria, nearly a half-century later, these films offer a powerful message, in which totalitarian and militaristic forces make brutal war on neighboring nations that had done little to provoke such a conflict. The films portray, in short, a very convincing argument. There are few features of these films, other than color photography, that could be used to improve their technical, dramatic, or persuasive quality.

Given these qualities of the stimulus material and of the assessments of their impact, what can be said about the overall results? Clearly, these films did well in achieving some kinds of results but poorly at gaining other objectives. The authors of *Experiments on Mass Communication* summarized the findings of the film evaluation studies as follows:

1. The *Why We Fight* films had marked effects on the men's knowledge of factual material concerning the events leading up to the war. The fact that the upper limit of effects was so large—as for example in the cases where the correct answer was learned well enough to be remembered a week later by the *majority* of the men—indicates that highly effective presentation methods are possible with this type of film.

2. The films also had some marked effects on opinions where the film specifically covered the factors involved in the particular interpretation, that is, where the opinion item was prepared on the basis of film-content analysis and anticipated opinion change from such analysis. Such opinion changes were, however, less frequent and in general less marked than changes in factual knowledge.

3. The films had only very few effects on opinion items of a more general nature that had been prepared independently of film content but that were considered the criteria for determining the effectiveness of the films in achieving their orientation objectives.

4. The films had no effects on the items prepared for the purpose of measuring effects on the men's motivation to serve as soldiers, which was considered the ultimate objective of the orientation program.[6]

An important issue is *why* these films were so ineffective in achieving their major objectives. As noted above, neither attitudes nor motivations were influenced. Hovland and his colleagues had a number of possible explanations that they explored as best they could. For example, they speculated that information from the civilian mass media about many of the topics and themes treated in the films had reached the recruits before they were drafted (after all, material was used in the films from earlier newsreels). This could have reduced the differences found between control and film groups because a substantial number in each case already had positive attitudes toward the British and at least some motivation to serve. By contrast, neither the control nor the film groups had the factual type of knowledge presented to any great degree, so larger effects could be predicted.

Moreover, motivation to serve and fight in the armed forces is a very complex phenomenon with many dimensions: pressures from one's family, general social norms, fear of death or injury, or prior feelings about the combatants. All could have been factors in the dynamics of change when trying to modify such motivation through the use of persuasive films. There are a number of additional issues about which one can speculate, the amount of time between film and measurement being one of those issues. For example, there may be a "sleeper" effect. That is, even though little change had taken place in the viewers by the time the measurements were made after seeing the film, perhaps much later the film's influences could have been found. Finally, there is the question of the entire configuration of a given subject's values, system of beliefs, and personality traits. These can interact in a dynamic way with new stimulus material to produce one kind of effect or another. However, in spite of rather sophisticated attempts to address some of these issues, no clear answers were obtained as to why these films achieved clear effects in the area of factual knowledge, but failed to do so with respect to attitudes and motivations.

Other Film Studies

In using a film to try to change knowledge, opinions, attitudes, or motivations, it is important to know how the audience itself evaluates the film. That is, do they like the film, find it interesting and objective, or do they dislike it, become bored by it, or believe it to be a biased presentation? Such perceptions on the part of the audience may be closely related to whether or not a given film can achieve the objectives for which it was designed.

The Army researchers made extensive studies of the reactions of the men to various aspects of the orientation films. They were concerned about their level of interest and whether the viewers saw it as "propaganda" designed to manipulate them. The researchers were also concerned as to whether the soldiers saw the movies as Hollywood products, staged with actors and props, or as films of actual events as they happened.

Another significant question about films as media for training or orientation is, how do they compare to the available alternatives? Films like the *Why We Fight* series are obviously very expensive to produce, and the process takes a long time. In contrast, a recorded radio-type program with a lecture, or even filmstrips (which are like projected slides), can be used with narration and are both inexpensive and rapid to produce. Finally, if a film *is* used for training or orientation, what are some ways by which retention of the material presented can be enhanced? For example, having the audience engage in discussion of the content in small groups is one way; having a speaker lead them in a simple review is another. All these questions and issues were under study, and the *Why We Fight* films provided convenient vehicles for trying to find answers. As we will note, however, other kinds of films were also used in these parts of the research program.

Audience Evaluation of Films. Both questionnaires and group interviews were used to try to understand how the recruits themselves evaluated the *Why We Fight* films at the time they saw them. The questionnaires were aimed at three basic issues: Did the men *like* the films? What did they think was the *purpose* of the films? And did they believe that the films gave a *true picture* of the events depicted? For the most part, the men studied were those involved in the film evaluation studies who had seen the film. However, as we will indicate, some additional subjects were included.

In general, the men liked the *Why We Fight* films. They liked some more than others, but fewer than 10 percent gave a negative appraisal on any film (or could give no answer). Those who did not like the films tended to be less educated or to have foreign-born parents from Axis countries.

The *Battle of Britain* study provided more information about the perceived purpose of the film than some of the other films under study. The majority of the men questioned simply saw it as an effort to teach them the facts of the war in an interesting way. Few thought that they were being used as "guinea pigs" or manipulated in some way. A sizeable number did connect the film with its real objective. For example, 27 percent on the questionnaire studies wrote in on the space provided for comments that its purpose was "to raise our morale," "to improve the fighting spirit," or even "to make us want to kill those sons of bitches." Even with this recognition of its manipulative intent, they still tended to like the film.

The majority of those involved in the study saw the *Battle of Britain* as a true picture of what had happened during those days when Britain stood alone (some 65 percent gave such an evaluation). Another 33 percent believed that it gave essentially a true picture even though it was "one-sided" at times. Only a handful (2 percent) said that it did not give a true or honest picture. Similar assessments of the film *The Nazis Strike* yielded results with even larger numbers believing that the film was truthful (some 81 percent), a smaller number feeling that it was basically truthful, if one-sided (18 percent), and only 1 percent who felt that it was "mostly untrue or one-sided."

These audience evaluations are important in trying to sort out the overall effects of the films. The evaluations indicate that there were no glaring problems with the films themselves: By and large the soldiers liked them; they did not see them as untruthful propaganda, and they did not feel improperly manipulated. The reasons for the films' failure to achieve their objectives in the areas of attitudes and morale lie elsewhere.

Group interviews were conducted with 150 men selected so as to be a representative cross section of the recruits under training. These men were not part of the film evaluation experiments discussed earlier but a completely different group. The interviews were conducted in an informal setting after the subjects had seen the film; each interview group discussed the film, and an effort was made to put together a picture of how the men evaluated the film.

About the only additional insights obtained from this approach were that some of the men thought the films had some poor features. For example, in the air combat footage, the same German plane was shown being shot down several times. Some of the men thought that shots of Hitler and his staff planning the assault on England were Hollywood actors (they were not; the footage was genuine). Generally, however, the findings from these group interviews supported those obtained from the questionnaire studies.

A second series of studies of audience evaluation of films did not focus on the *Why We Fight* series, but another separate and rather different series. These were short features, similar to newsreels, shown in conjunction with regular feature films at the base theater. Attendance at these regular entertainment movies was, of course, voluntary. However, those who went to the movies saw a different short feature each week called *The War* as part of the regular program. Each of these short features was made up of five episodes, with the content of each varied every week. However, the same titles for these episodes were used in each issue of *The War*. For example, Issue 5 of *The War* had the following five episodes:

> Episode a: *Finishing School.* This showed training of amphibious (Ranger) troops in invasion tactics such as embarking and disembarking and advancing under live ammunition.
>
> Episode b: *Back Home.* This showed machine tools being produced by a small family shop in Connecticut which was awarded the Navy "E" for contribution to war production.
>
> Episode c: *I Was There.* This featured an Army nurse's eye-witness account of the bombing of Manila and the fall of Corregidor, with action shots to illustrate part of her commentary. The whole story was told in the nurse's voice and was introduced and concluded by shots of the nurse telling her story.
>
> Episode d: *First Birthday.* This documentary reviewed the founding and first year's activities of the Women's Army Corps and depicted the training and duties of WACs.
>
> Episode e: *Snafu.* This was an animated cartoon showing the adventures of a comic character called "Private Snafu," whose complaints about Army routine and duties led to his magically being put in charge of the camp, with disastrous consequences.[7]

Two means of studying evaluations of this type of film were used. Questionnaires filled out by men who had seen the film were used, and a special recording device (called the "program analyzer") was used in the theater itself. This device consisted of a small box for every viewer with two clearly marked buttons. As the viewer watched the film, he pushed down the "like" button if he found the material interesting. If not, he pushed down the "dislike" button. There was no neutral button, but the viewer could refrain from pushing either the like or dislike buttons.

The results from these two approaches show similar patterns. Figure 5.1 summarizes the questionnaire data and Figure 5.2 shows a typical pattern obtained from the use of the program analyzer. The findings are not definitive

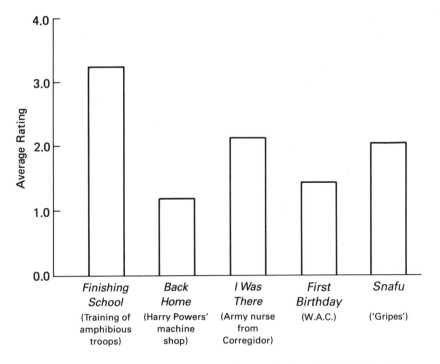

Figure 5.1. Questionnaire Ratings of the Five Episodes in Issue 5 of *The War*. The men were asked to rank the five episodes in the film as "best," "2d best," etc. Ratings for each episode were then scored as follows: "best," 4 points; "2d best," 3 points; "3d best," 2 points; "4th best," 1 point; "worst," 0 points. The values plotted are the average scores for the men whose polygraph records are averaged in Figure 5.2.
Source: Carl I. Hovland, Arthur A. Lumsdaine, and Fred D. Sheffield, *Experiments on Mass Communication* (Princeton, N.J.: Princeton University Press, 1949) p. 110.

because of the limitations on sampling. But, along with supplemental information obtained from written comments on the questionnaires, and after pulling together findings from studying four separate issues of *The War*, the following generalizations seemed to apply:

1. Where the film simply showed someone talking, interest tended to be low.
2. Where real shots of military action were shown, interest was high.
3. Where shots of action were shown with voice-over narration, interest remained high.
4. Repetition of shots seen earlier in the film (as in seeing the same plane shot down) was not well received.
5. Highly realistic material, as opposed to Hollywood versions acted out with props, was much preferred.

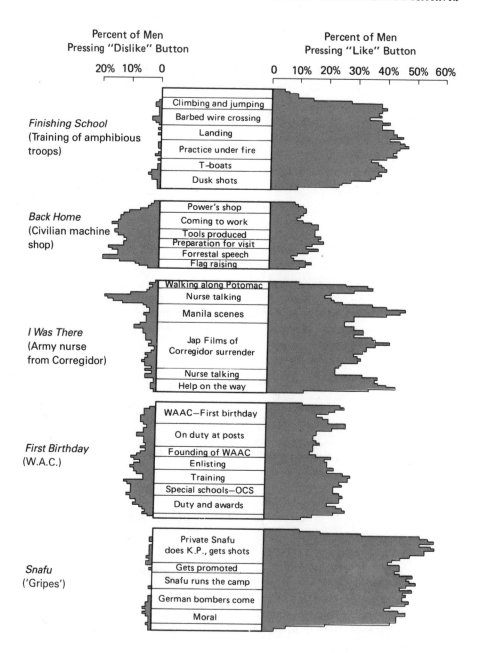

Figure 5.2. Continuous Polygraph Records of the Group "Likes" and "Dislikes" During Showing of Issue 5 of *The War*.
Source: Carl I. Hovland, Arthur A. Lumsdaine, and Fred D. Sheffield, *Experiments on Mass Communication* (Princeton, N.J.: Princeton University Press, 1949) p. 111.

Again, these were tentative conclusions pertaining only to the films studied and should not be regarded as guides to audience evaluations of all kinds of films. Yet, they offer useful hypotheses for studying other types of training films for military personnel.

Alternative Presentations. The relative effectiveness of various media for accomplishing a given objective still merits much research attention. The Army researchers made attempts to probe this issue. They were quite aware that this is a very difficult question to answer, being based on assumptions that the medium may have special properties that themselves can influence change in the audience (i.e., that the "medium is the message" in its own right). However, in spite of the difficulties, the investigators saw such research as possible beginning analyses of any factors that might underly the use of various media for instructional or persuasive purposes.

Among the studies completed, three still appear to be important. One compared a motion picture versus a filmstrip presentation of the same subject; a second compared two types of radio program styles (a "commentator" versus a dramatized "documentary"); and the third compared the technique of having an introductory lecture to a film before seeing it to a review summary of what its salient points were after seeing it. The purpose was to see whether the introduction or the review was the best means of enhancing learning from an instructional film.

Although it may be tempting to conclude that a motion picture with a sound track is obviously a better training device than a filmstrip supplemented with a verbal presentation, the findings did not support such a conclusion. Six companies were matched on the Army's General Classification Test (AGCT) and the educational level that they had achieved. Two were designated as the control group. Two others saw a 43-minute sound film designed to teach map reading. The remaining two companies saw a 50-minute filmstrip presentation on map reading with an accompanying lecture.

After viewing these presentations, the soldiers (plus the control group) responded to a 39-item multiple choice test on the topics covered in the film and the filmstrip. The comparative effectiveness of the two media is shown in Figure 5.3. As it turned out, the film with sound had no inherent advantage over the still pictures of the filmstrip (supplemented with the lecture). The experiment was by no means definitive, but it points to the need for empirical checks on untested assumptions that one medium (e.g., television) automatically has some "greater power" than a simpler medium in all cases.

Of the remaining two studies in this series, the one of most contemporary interest is the comparison of the introductory versus the review lectures on the content of a film as a means of enhancing learning. Films are still widely used in teaching settings, and this issue has not been fully tested in more recent times.

More specifically, the question addressed by the research was the following:

Figure 5.3. Average Test Scores Received by Men in Each Group (N = 253 in each group). *Source*: Carl I. Hovland, Arthur A. Lumsdaine, and Fred D. Sheffield, *Experiments on Mass Communication* (Princeton, N.J.: Princeton University Press, 1949) p. 126.

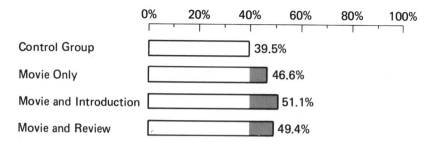

Figure 5.4. Average Test Scores for Each Group (N = 253 in each group). *Source*: Carl I. Hovland, Arthur A. Lumsdaine, and Fred D. Sheffield, *Experiments on Mass Communication* (Princeton, N.J.: Princeton University Press, 1949) p. 143.

In using a film for training purposes, is it better that an instructor provide a preliminary commentary on the major points that will be covered in the film, or is it better to review its salient points after the audience has seen the film? Which approach will most increase learning from the film?

In the Army studies on this issue, four platoons of soldiers were shown the 43-minute film on mapreading after receiving a 20-minute lecture on its main ideas. Another four platoons saw the film first and then had a 20-minute review of its salient points. Care was taken that the persons doing the reviews and preliminary lectures were not greatly different from each other in terms of style or ability. The trainees did not know that they were part of a research effort.

After these presentations, each soldier took a 15-item quiz about the major topics that had been covered in the film. The results of this testing are summarized in Figure 5.4. As can be seen, viewing the movie by itself (as did the control group) improved performance rather considerably. However, both the introductory lecture and the review increased learning even more. The former seemed to have a slight advantage, but the difference was not significant. Results such as these indicate that just "showing a movie" is not the most effective practice in using film as a teaching device. Supplementing the film with an oral presentation before or after the film enhances learning effects.

Films and Intellectual Ability

A complex question concerning the film evaluation research described earlier (the *Why We Fight* series) concerns the degree to which different patterns of effects were observed among different categories of viewers. In the Army studies, the influence of such demographic variables as education, religious affiliation, marital status, intellectual level, and other social categories on the learning of factual material and opinion change was studied wherever possible. Among all these variables, the one most often related to differences in the results was the intellectual ability of the viewer. A brief summary of some of the main findings relating intellectual ability to learning factual material and to opinion change will demonstrate the major points.

Measurement. It was not possible to give the soldiers who saw the *Why We Fight* films, or who served in the control groups, an IQ test. This not only would have been difficult, but would have violated the assurances of anonymity involved in the research. Fortunately, it was not necessary to do this. Two indices of general intellectual ability were readily available. One was the individual's score on the AGCT. A considerable accumulation of research had established that these scores were highly correlated with intelligence test scores. An even simpler index was the level of educational attainment of the soldier. Research had also established the high correlation between amount of schooling completed and IQ test scores. Educational attainment was also, logically enough, highly correlated with AGCT scores. For this reason, the researchers felt confident that they could categorize the men in terms of simple classifications of educational attainment (such as completion of grade school, high school, or college) and use this as a reliable measure of intellectual ability. And, since all subjects in the film evaluation studies had been asked to give their level of educational attainment, the data were already a part of their questionnaire responses.

To determine if seeing a film such as the *Battle of Britain* had different effects on men in these three educational levels, the control and the film groups from the evaluation studies were contrasted. Simple comparisons of the percents in each group who had learned factual information, or whose opinions had been changed, were sufficient, and for the most part, the results showed clear patterns.

Learning Factual Material. It was found, first of all, that even before seeing the films the men with the most education already knew more factual information about the war than those whose educational achievements were lower. For example, on a brief fact quiz, the men in the control groups (who never saw the film) showed very different levels of factual knowledge, depending on their educational level. Only 21.1 percent of those who had completed grade school only could answer all of the items on the fact quiz correctly. The figure for high school men was 28.6 percent and for college men it was 41.8 percent. These figures represent significant differences.

Similar findings were noted in studies of the map-reading film. Before seeing the material, those with higher levels of education *already* knew larger percents of the answers to the multiple choice test on map-reading than those in lower categories (grade school, 26.1 percent; high school, 28.9 percent; and college, 37.1 percent). In other words, intellectual ability, as measured, was a significant indicator of the initial level of factual knowledge commanded by the men, even before they saw any of the films.

But even though those with higher levels of intellectual ability already knew more, they also learned more from the film. A 29-item factual information test was prepared on the *Why We Fight* films. Comparisons were then made of the percents of these items learned, on the average, by the men in each of the three intellectual levels. Substantial differences were found. For example, the grade school men averaged only 16.3 percent on this test after seeing the films. The high school men averaged 36.6 percent, and the college men had 54.2 percent correct. These differences in levels of performance were even more pronounced when only the items of greatest difficulty were taken into account. Clearly, intellectual ability was the key factor in accounting for how much an individual learned from the films.

Opinion Changes. The relationship between intellectual attainment and opinion change presents a more complex picture. A trend was noted for the effects of the films on opinion change to increase with higher intellectual ability. However, in some opinion items, the opposite was found. But another situation was noted in the data that helped to explain what had happened. The more factual material that had to be grasped, especially more difficult material, the more opinion change was seen only among the men of higher intellectual level. The authors considered such changes as "informed opinion." On the other hand, the men of lower intellectual levels often changed their opinion position on the basis of a minimal number of facts or those easier to grasp. This was considered "uninformed opinion." To make matters even more interesting, the findings showed that men of lower intellectual ability were prone to change their opinion on the basis of facts that men of higher intellectual level did not regard as particularly valid.

Implications. Higher learning ability (intellectual level) led to increased levels of initial knowledge. However, it also led to learning more factual material from the film. On opinion change, the more complex the issue and facts concerning it, the more likely that opinion change would be primarily among the more intelligent men. Those of lower ability tended to change their opinions on issues of lesser complexity, less well supported by the facts, and on issues that more intelligent men found difficult to accept. While, as the authors note, these are tentative conclusions based on this research only, it would appear that the less educated are easier to sway with propaganda.

ADDITIONAL EXPERIMENTAL STUDIES

The research findings on films summarized above were obtained for the most part from evaluation studies where the film had been prepared by persons other than the experimenters, and it was introduced in its entirety as the experimental treatment. In these studies, the dependent variable was one or more of the objectives set by the War Department for the film series. Extraneous variables were controlled by a variety of techniques, methodologies, and designs.

Another type of research on the effects of communication on opinion change employs variations in some specific aspect of the message, some characteristic of the audience, or some factor in the communication setting. Generally, such research seeks to find those conditions of the persuasive message, the communicator, the mode of presentation, etc., that will lead to a maximum degree of opinion change. The underlying assumption is that changes in opinion (or attitude, value, belief, and so on) are *keys to changing overt behavior*. After all, mere changes in opinion mean relatively little unless they are linked to changes in action.

The remainder of the present chapter summarizes briefly the results of two (from a set of three) experiments that sought such keys to opinion change. One experiment attempted to see whether opinion change after seeing a persuasive communication was a short-term effect or if it had stable long-term effects. The second experiment assessed a persuasive message that was structured in one of two ways. One structure was one-sided, and presented only arguments in favor of an opinion change under study. The other was essentially the same persuasive message, but some points on the opposite side were also presented in an effort to make the message seem more objective. The goal, of course, was to see which provided a better key to changing opinions in the direction desired by the communicator.

Short-Term versus Long-Term Effects
A significant question in the search for ways to change people's opinions through the use of persuasive communications is whether the effects achieved, if any, will disappear rapidly or persist over a long period. Studies of remembering and forgetting have been made by psychologists for decades. Such research has established that there is a "curve of forgetting" of factual information learned by a subject. The greatest amount of forgetting takes place rather quickly, and then the curve levels off after a few days to decline more slowly. Since opinion changes are based on factual information, the Army

researchers hypothesized that opinion changes would follow a somewhat similar pattern. That is, they expected changes of opinion achieved through persuasive communications to have a relatively short life, with the subject regressing over time to his earlier position.

The study of short-term versus long-term effects was carried out with one of the orientation films—*The Battle of Britain*—because the film was clearly capable of producing effects on both factual knowledge and opinion change. The sample used for this study had already been given their "before" measures as part of the film evaluation studies. In those studies, the subjects took their "after" measures a week after seeing the film. All that was needed was a group of subjects who had seen the film and whose opinions could be measured a relatively long time after seeing the film. It was also necessary, of course, to match the various groups so that any differences in effects could be assigned to the time variable, rather than to differences of some other kind between the two sets of subjects.

The "before–after with control group" design was used for both the short-time subjects and the long-time group. The long-time group was treated in the same manner as the short-time subjects, except that they received their "after" questionnaire *nine weeks* after seeing the film (rather than one week). Table 5.1 shows the general plan.

A clear pattern of forgetting factual material was found. On a ten-item fact quiz based on *The Battle of Britain*, there was a substantial decrement in recalling facts when comparing the short-time and the long-time experimental groups. Over the nine weeks, the long-time groups retained only about 50 percent as many of the fact items as had the short-time group at the end of the first week after seeing the film.

But the main question was the influence of time on opinions. To assess

TABLE 5.1. GENERAL RESEARCH DESIGN FOR COMPARING SHORT-TIME AND LONG-TIME EFFECTS OF SEEING AN ORIENTATION FILM

| | Short-time Groups | | Long-time Groups | |
	Experimental (3 Companies)	Control (3 Companies)	Experimental (2 Companies)	Control (2 Companies)
First week:	"Before" questionnaire	"Before" questionnaire	"Before" questionnaire	"Before" questionnaire
Second week:	Film showing	———	———	———
Third week:	"After" questionnaire	"After" questionnaire		———
Eleventh week:			"After" questionnaire	"After" questionnaire
No. of subjects	450	450	250	250

Source: Carl I. Hovland, Arthur A. Lumsdaine, and Fred D. Sheffield, *Experiments on Mass Communication* (Princeton, N.J.: Princeton University Press, 1949) p. 183.

opinion shifts caused by the film, and to compare the long- and short-time subjects, a 15-item opinion measuring instrument was prepared and used. The results of the comparison revealed some unexpected findings. On approximately a third of the opinion issues, the long-time group showed less change than the short-time group. This was the pattern to be expected from the "curve of forgetting." After all, the underlying factual material had shown a clear pattern of being forgotten. However, on more than half of the 15 opinion issues under study, the long-time group showed a *greater* change than the short-time group. This was not expected. The researchers referred to this kind of outcome as a "sleeper effect." It was difficult to explain, but what had happened was that the subjects had forgotten some of the facts in the film on which their opinions had originally been changed to some degree. Then, freed from the factual basis, the opinions changed even more.

In an attempt to understand this phenomenon better, a number of rather complex analyses of the data were made. The analyses were not particularly enlightening except in one case. There was a high probability of being influenced by the film on a long-time basis if one was *initially predisposed* toward a given opinion change (on a particular topic). Finally, the authors noted that changes in opinion of a general rather than specific nature may show increasing effects with lapse of time. Such general opinions are less firmly anchored to specific facts.

The sleeper effect raises many difficult psychological problems, and the investigators felt that they could not answer them within the context of the data of their studies. The effects of time on opinion change following persuasive communication remains a significant issue around which much research was organized in the years following the Army studies. The problem of initial position on an issue, however, was to prove a valuable key to understanding some of the effects in the next study to be discussed.

Effects of Presenting One versus Both Sides of an Argument

When attempting to change opinions on a controversial topic, is it more effective to present only the materials and arguments supporting the position of the communicator ("one side")? Or is it better to introduce at least some of the opposing arguments ("both sides") to make the persuasive communication look like a balanced treatment of the issues? These were the main questions for a study of the influence of a persuasive message that was used in 1945, toward the end of the war. New draftees were still being trained even though the European war was clearly about to end. The grim facts were that the war in the Pacific was seen likely to continue for two years or more. Although American forces had defeated the Japanese in a number of bitterly fought assaults on island bases, the main body of the Japanese Army had remained at home, anticipating a major invasion attempt. It was estimated that if this were to take place, the Americans would probably suffer hundreds of thousands of casualties. In fact, the war could drag on for years. The Japanese had reserved supplies at home in spite of the heavy bombings of major cities. Each island was a fortress. And there was the vast Pacific to cross: the Americans would have to bring troops and supplies over thousands of miles of ocean. Even the high-level planners in the War Department did not know of the atom bomb that made the assault on Japan unnecessary. This closely guarded secret weapon was known only to a handful at Los Alamos, to the President and his staff, and to a few select people in the military. Thus, the War Department issued directives to begin preparing *all* troops to anticipate a long war. A factor complicating this need was that, with Italy out of the war and Germany clearly about to collapse, the majority of the soldiers felt that the war was about to end. This posed a potential morale problem of serious proportions. The troops *had* to be made to understand and believe that there were still tough years ahead and that there was no choice but to carry on.

Under the new directives, the social scientists of the Experimental Section set about to study the most effective ways to persuade trainees that it would be a long and difficult war in the Pacific. The keys to such persuasion were badly needed. For this reason, the social scientists moved away from films made in Hollywood and prepared their own persuasive messages so that they could build in various message factors in a search for those keys. Fortunately for hundreds of thousands of American young men, the atom bomb *was* used, and the war came to a speedy end. This aspect of the bomb's use tends to be overlooked today. In any case, if it had not been used, it is likely that this phase of the research program would have been greatly extended.

Included in the routines of the training camp was a weekly "orientation hour" that had been used for soldiers to see films, fill out questionnaires, participate in discussions, and so on. This tradition made it possible to use the same general approach for the new research program as had been used earlier with the *Why We Fight* film evaluations.

Since there was no time to prepare films, the more rapid and flexible medium of radio was used. The Armed Forces Radio Service prepared recorded materials according to the specifications of the researchers. The new research program began with a study organized around the issue posed at the beginning of the present section. Would a one-sided radio talk be more effective in changing the opinions of the soldiers concerning the probable length of the war in the Pacific, or would it be more effective to use a radio talk that presented at least some of the arguments on both sides (with the weight of arguments still on the side of a long war)?

Some careful preliminary work was done before designing the two radio programs. Interviews were held with 200 men to see how long they thought that the Pacific war would last and why they felt the way they did. What, in other words, were the counterarguments to the position that the war would be lengthy? This preliminary work paid off, because those counterarguments could be carefully rebutted by material included in the radio messages.

The two transcripts were prepared as a commentator's analysis of the Pacific war. The one-side presentation (about 15 minutes in length) marshalled all the factual information and arguments supporting the conclusion that the war would last at least two more years. The both-sides presentation had essentially the same material, but an additional four minutes of arguments on the other side were included early in the message. These were then carefully rebutted. Overall, the program as a whole supported the conclusion that the war would last at least two more years.

The "before–after with control group" design was used to assess the results. Considerable effort was made to obscure the idea that there was an experiment going on or that the men were being tested in some way. The before and after measurements took place in very different locations for very different announced purposes. Furthermore, in each case the central items were embedded in larger questionnaires addressed to different purposes. This camouflaging of the experiment within other important activities appears to have been entirely successful.

As in previous experiments, the subjects were selected in group units. A total of 24 platoons were used in all; 625 men were involved, with 214 in each of the two experimental groups and 197 in the control group. The after measures were made one week after the men in the experimental groups heard the radio programs. Once again, anonymity was assured, but it was possible to match the before and after questionnaires with the use of background data and handwriting.

When the results were first reviewed it appeared that the two forms of the persuasive message had not achieved different results. The opinions on the length of the war were compared for both experimental groups (one side versus both sides) by calculating the percent of men from each treatment who thought that the war would last more than a year and a half. These differences could then be compared to those found for the two measures of the control group. The results are shown in Table 5.2. Thus, it appeared that both programs were capable of changing the opinions of the men concerning the length of the war.

A different pattern of results became evident when the initial opinions of the men were taken into account. For those who were initially *opposed* to the conclusion that it would be a lengthy war, the one-side program had some effect (36 percent extended their estimates). But for such men the both-sides program had a much greater effect (48 percent extended their estimate). This is a difference of 12 percent. On the opposite side, the effects were even more striking. For those who initially *favored* the opinion that the war would be longer, 52 percent extended their estimates after hearing the one-side radio commentary. But when these initially favorable men heard the both-sides program, only 23 percent extended their estimate. This is a difference of 19 percent and in the opposite direction! Clearly, initial position on the issue seemed to be one of the keys concerning the effectiveness of a persuasive message.

TABLE 5.2. OVERALL EFFECTS OF THE TWO PROGRAMS ON DISTRIBUTION OF
ESTIMATED LENGTH OF WAR

	Percentage Estimating a War of More Than One-And-One-Half Years		
	Experimental groups		
	Program I "One Side"	Program II "Both Sides"	Control Group
Before	37%	38%	36%
After	59	59	34
Difference	22%	21%	−2%
Probability	<.01	<.01	

Source: Carl I. Hovland, Arthur A. Lumsdaine, and Fred D. Sheffield, *Experiments on Mass Communication*
(Princeton, N.J.: Princeton University Press, 1949) p. 210.

Intellectual ability proved to be another important key to the results.
A striking set of differences was found when comparing men of different
educational attainment levels (used as an index of intellectual ability). Briefly
summarized, the two-sides program was more effective with those of at least
high school level (49 percent changed to a long war estimate). The one-side
program produced a change of 35 percent in this category. Exactly the opposite
was found for men with limited schooling. For those with only grade school or
less, the one-side program persuaded 46 percent to extend their estimates. The
two-sides program brought only 31 percent of this category to make such an
opinion change.

When both initial position and intellectual level were considered, even
greater differences were noted. For example, among those of lower education
who initially favored a longer estimate, the one-side program brought an
increased estimate of the war's length among 64 percent. This result can be
compared to the effects of the both-sides program on the same type of men.
Here, estimates of the length of the war actually *decreased!* It appears that the
two-sides program confused these poorly educated men and created an effect in
the opposite direction from that desired by the communicator. For other
combinations of initial position and intellectual ability, the differences were not
dramatic.

CONCLUSIONS AND IMPLICATIONS

The various research programs described in *Experiments on Mass Communication*
constitute a remarkable effort to bring the research expertise of the social
psychologist and other social scientists to the practical problems imposed by the
urgencies of a national crisis. The researchers, drawn into the war effort from
the academic world, were able to make a significant contribution to the

practical problems of designing and testing orientation, teaching, and persuasive communication. But perhaps their most significant contribution was that they uncovered significant issues that would be explored by communication researchers in the decades that followed the war.

The film evaluation studies showed that this form of communication could teach factual material effectively to large numbers of people in a short time. The studies also showed that it was possible to alter opinions and interpretations of those facts and that at least some of these opinions would remain stable through time. Yet, it was clear that the films did not create more general effects on broader attitudes and motivations. In other words, the effects of the films were *clearly limited.* Such communications were not the all-powerful shapers of the psychic structures of their audiences that had been assumed by the magic bullet theory of prior decades. The findings from *Experiments on Mass Communication* led clearly toward a "limited effects" hypothesis concerning the short-term influences of a single communication on its audiences, rather than a "powerful effects" interpretation.

From the standpoint of research methods, the film evaluation studies and the other research programs reported set new standards for communication research. The "before–after with control group" design was not new to social science, but it had not been used so effectively before in communication research. It became a standard. The meticulous care taken in studying the *Why We Fight* films posed other models for later researchers. The investigators carefully analyzed the content of each film and developed their questionnaires around their findings. They took numerous precautions to pretest and fine-tune their instruments. They carefully disguised what they were doing so that their subjects would not modify their behavior according to some conception of the demands of the experiment. They matched groups, used controls, and camouflaged their tests and assessments in larger survey instruments. Finally, they carefully sorted through every set of results so that they understood as fully as possible what they had found and why. Of course their lack of concern over costs and their almost complete control over their subjects made this an almost unique situation that would be hard to duplicate in civilian life.

The results of their experiments supported the perspective that the effects of mass communication are strongly influenced by *individual differences* among the members of the audience. Individual differences led to selective perception, interpretation, and change. Such factors as the initial position of the subject were found to be very important in understanding the results. Similarly, there were differential influences that were related to the *social categories* (e.g., educational attainment) of the audience. Curiously, however, the researchers did not look into the *social relationships* that prevailed among their subjects as a source of influences on their results. Research on the role of the mass media in an election campaign was uncovering such influences, but the results of that work were not available to the Army researchers at the time.

Perhaps most of all, the Army research on how to persuade the American soldier represents a significant turning point in the study of mass communication. It can be seen in retrospect as the end of an era when the assumptions of the magic bullet theory were still thought to be viable. In its place, and in many ways as a result of these experiments, a new search began—a search for the "magic keys" of persuasion. The basic assumptions of the magic keys theory of persuasive communication are closely related to what DeFleur has referred to as the "psychodynamic approach" to persuasion.[8] It is assumed that there is some set of characteristics that can be built into the message that will modify the structure or functioning of the cognitive/emotional processes within the individual. These in turn will lead to changes in decisions and subsequent patterns of overt action, if all goes well, in the direction desired by the communicator. Thus, it is important to discover whether a one-side or a two-side form of a communication will alter opinions more effectively. If opinion is altered, it can be assumed that some form of action will then be altered. The authors of *Experiments on Mass Communication* fully believed that there was a regular relationship between attitude and opinion states and forms of overt action—a set of assumptions that does not seem so attractive today.[9]

But at the time, when researchers were undisturbed by the thought that opinions and attitudes might *not* be related to overt behavior, the magic keys approach to communication research appeared to hold great promise. In fact, it became the dominant perspective on research on persuasive communication for many years to follow:

> Untold numbers of studies have tried to identify ways in which we can persuade people to view some perceptual object differently—and thereby cause them to act toward that object in modified ways. If only the right combination of words, message structure, emotional appeals, type of communicator, or mode of presentation can be found (so the vision goes) then people's subjective orientations can be reshaped and their patterns of overt behavior can be influenced.[10]

So the search for the magic keys began in earnest. It was the ultimate idea of pragmatic application of social and behavioral science. Find the ways to persuade people to buy, vote, give, accept military training cheerfully, and so on, and the world will beat a pathway to the door of social science. Unfortunately, as will be seen in later chapters, the search for the magic keys, like the search for the Philosopher's Stone, has had less than spectacular results.

NOTES AND REFERENCES

1. Frank Capra, *The Name Above the Title: An Autobiography* (New York: The Macmillan Company, 1971), p. 327.
2. Ibid., p. 237.
3. Carl I. Hovland, Arthur A. Lumsdaine, and Fred D. Sheffield, *Experiments on Mass Communication* (Princeton, N. J.: Princeton University Press, 1949), p. 22.
4. For a detailed analysis of the films' techniques and content, see Paul Rotha, *The Film Till Now* (New York: Funk and Wagnalls, 1949), p. 462.
5. Carl I. Hovland, et al., op. cit.
6. Ibid., pp. 64–65.
7. Ibid., p. 215.
8. Melvin L. De Fleur, *Theories of Mass Communication* (New York: David McKay, 1970), p. 141; see also 4th edition, 1982, p. 218.
9. Melvin L. De Fleur, op. cit., pp. 247–248; see also H. Schuman and P. Johnson, "Attitudes and Behavior" in A. Inkeles, J. Coleman, and N. Smelser, eds., *Annual Review of Sociology*, (Palo Alto, Calif.: Annual Review, Inc., 1976).
10. Timothy G. Plax and Melvin L. De Fleur, "Communication, Attitudes, and Behavior: An Axiomatic Theory with Implications for Persuasion Research," paper presented at the annual meeting of the Western Speech Communication Association, Portland, Oregon, 1980.

6

Communication and Persuasion:
The Search for the Magic Keys

World War II was finally over. Through that brutal struggle the world—and America—was changed forever. Before the war, the nation had remained somewhat isolated; its concerns had been mainly with its own affairs. However, by the end of the war it had been thrust into global responsibilities for which its people were ill-prepared. Yet they responded both ideologically and militarily; the nation rose to the challenge and prevailed against formidable odds. The United States had become the most powerful nation on the earth and the unquestioned leader of the "Free World."

The war years also had a profound impact on the American national consciousness. Americans had come to nurture an almost boundless faith in their ability to solve the world's problems. Beginning as a marked underdog, they had martialed their industrial and military might to crush the powerful forces of fascism. Once that was accomplished, and the war over, the United States set out to solve the problems of its former enemies. It helped them to rebuild their ravaged countries and economies, an act of generosity unprecedented in the world's history.

Perhaps the greatest victory of the war was America's conquest of the atom. It was an amazing feat; science won the battle by splitting the atom. This accomplishment brought the role of science a new significance in modern life. Although atomic power had been developed for use as a weapon, many thoughtful people saw in it a bright vision for the future—unlimited power for peaceful purposes.

Thus, it was science that emerged from the war as the great hope of mankind. And science dedicated to basic research seemed the most important kind. Once new principles were uncovered, they could then be used by pragmatic, innovative Americans to make a better world for everyone. That postwar dream fired the imagination of all scientists—and social scientists were no exception.

There was much work to be done by social and behavioral scientists. The world was still filled with prejudice, discrimination, and bigotry. And now that nuclear weapons were a reality, the task of improving relationships between peoples seemed more urgent than ever. Badly needed, for example, was a better understanding of how people's beliefs, attitudes, and behavior could be modified in socially approved ways through carefully designed persuasive communication. If basic research into the "laws" of persuasion could be successful, then such knowledge could be used to achieve many prosocial goals. It seemed clear enough from earlier research on communication, such as that done by the Army researchers in training camps during the war, that there were underlying regularities waiting to be discovered by careful scientific research. Once those keys to the communication-persuasion relationship were available, they could be used to unlock the mysteries of how opinions and attitudes could be modified. Then it would be possible to change overt behavior patterns in socially desirable ways. Thus, such keys were critical in order to improve the human condition.

This mission held great appeal to social psychologists such as Carl Hovland, who had been one of the principal researchers in the Army's investigations of the persuasive use of films. Prior to the war, Hovland had been a "rising star" in experimental psychology at Yale, but the demands of the war altered the direction of his career. While the Army research involved the investigation of "practical" problems, Hovland could see the implications of that research for building a systematic theory of persuasion. Thus, the seeds of a new program of scientific research were planted and took root in Hovland's wartime experience. During the war, he had worked with an outstanding group of social scientists, including Irvin Janis, Arthur Lumsdaine, Fred Sheffield, Nathan Macoby, and M. Brewster Smith. When he returned to Yale at the end of the war, he took Janis, Lumsdaine, and Sheffield with him. Together they founded a broad-based research program drawing on scholars and theories from several disciplines.

THE RESEARCH PROGRAM

Between 1946 and 1961, the Yale Program of Research on Communication and Attitude Change conducted more than 50 experiments that produced a considerable body of published results. Hovland remained the driving force behind the research during the entire period. The theoretical bases as well as the framework for the program's experiments were outlined in *Communication and Persuasion* (1953), the first major book to emerge from the research program.[1] *Communication and Persuasion* reports the results of a number of investigations of the ways in which opinions and beliefs are modified by persuasive communications. Funded by the Rockefeller Foundation, the work involved the efforts of some 30 social scientists—mainly psychologists, but including sociologists, anthropologists, and political scientists.

It should be noted that the Yale Program did not actually study mass communication or actual media campaigns. It made use of experiments in a variety of settings. The research dealt with more intimate, interpersonal channels of communication, such as live speeches and illustrated lectures. A few of the studies did use recorded speeches and written passages, but they were not used to stimulate mass communication situations. Nevertheless, many scholars of the time felt that the laws of persuasion would operate similarly in both the experimental and real-life situations and that uncovering the keys to the process in the laboratory would also lead to an understanding of their operation in mass communication persuasion.

The project focused on several areas thought to be important to the persuasion process. These areas were generated by the researchers' definition of communication. They defined communication in terms of stimuli that create changes in the responses of people. More specifically, they defined communication as "the process by which an individual (the communicator) transmits stimuli (usually verbal) to modify the behavior of other individuals (the audience)."[2] This stimulus-response definition was characteristic of the way in which the process of communication was viewed at the time. Harold D. Lasswell had formulated a well-known statement that indicated that the proper study of the act of communication was to look at *who* said *what* to *whom* over what *channel* with what *effect*.[3] Thus, the main categories of analysis were: (1) the communicator, (2) the content of the communication, (3) the audience, and (4) the actual responses made by the audience. Selected topics, such as communicator credibility and group conformity effects, were then studied in each of these categories.

There are several reasons why most of the research reported in *Communication and Persuasion* was conducted in controlled experimental settings. For one, most of the researchers had backgrounds in experimental psychology. They were therefore familiar with and had confidence in experimental methods. More importantly, the researchers were searching for causal regularities—the "laws" of persuasion. They believed that in this search it was necessary to use methods that they thought would allow for causal interpretations of their data.

The nature of the experimental situation was basically the same throughout the various studies. Messages were constructed for the project, then tested under specially defined circumstances where the effects of various factors influencing persuasion could be isolated. The communication was one-way. No verbal interaction was allowed between the audience and the communicator; in addition, interaction was restricted among audience members during the experimental sessions. Moreover, the subjects were part of a "captive" audience (i.e., they were not allowed to leave the sessions once they had begun). The topics presented in the studies were carefully chosen: they were selected on the basis of their relative neutrality, in other words, "to arouse little motivation for either suppression or distortion."[4] Finally, standard methodological precautions were taken throughout the studies. These precautions included careful attention to questionnaire construction; independent test administrators; assurances of anonymity; and so on. In general, the research techniques used in the project were rigorous, and attention to detail appeared complete.

Assumptions About the Nature of Opinion and Attitude Change

Hovland and his associates measured persuasion in terms of the amount of attitude and opinion change. They viewed attitudes and opinions as intimately related, yet analytically distinct. The term "opinion" was used in a very general sense by the authors. It referred to "interpretations, expectations, and evaluations." For example, this term included beliefs about the intentions of others, anticipations of future events, or appraisals of the consequences of alternate courses of action. While *opinion* was used to refer to a broad class of anticipations, *attitude* was more exclusive; it was reserved only for explicit responses approaching or avoiding some object, person, group, or symbol. In other words, attitudes possessed "drive value."

Another factor that distinguished an attitude from an opinion was that opinions could always be verbalized and attitudes need not be: an attitude might be unconscious. However, the researchers' formulation includes a high degree of interaction between attitudes and opinions. A change in general approach and avoidance orientations (attitudes) might affect a person's expectations (opinions) on a number of related issues. A more important aspect of this interaction for the research reported in *Communication and Persuasion* was that change in a person's general attitude might result from changes in opinion. Hovland, Janis, and Kelley assumed that attitudes were mediated by verbal beliefs, expectations, and judgments and that one of the primary ways in which communications could change attitudes was to change those verbal responses (opinions).

Some important methodological problems arose out of this conceptualization of opinions and attitudes. When the authors said that opinions could be verbalized and were "implicit responses" they meant that they were the verbal answers a person gives in inner speech. They were thus to be distinguished from overt verbal responses, the answers to those questions as expressed to others. Typically, the overt and covert answers are identical, but they need not be—especially if external constraints (e.g., social pressure) hinder their free expression. Thus, the methodological problem in the context of this research was: How do you observe changes in the implicit responses? Hovland, Janis, and Kelley resolved this problem by assuming that under certain conditions (which they tried to arrange) the overt verbalizations approximated the implicit verbal responses. Thus, they elicited verbal responses to questionnaire items, where the questions they used were designed and administered to minimize distorted responses to the items.

Another methodological problem that confronted the authors was whether they were measuring real opinion change rather than simply change in response to the question items. They handled this problem by using a series of items that approached the subject matter from a number of points of view. In addition, they used stimuli (e.g., language) similar to those found in everyday situations. The ultimate justification for the questionnaires, in their eyes, was their utility.

The questionnaires allowed the investigators to observe consistent relationships between communicated stimuli and changes in verbal responses. The researchers checked the validity of these relationships by comparing them with observations from other studies. In addition, they also checked the relationships by examining behavioral data concerning changes in voting, buying products, and contributing to charities.

The Theoretical Model

The researchers assumed that attitudes and opinions were enduring. That is, they assumed that a particular attitude or opinion would persist unless the individual underwent some new learning experience. And, in fact, the theoretical framework presented by Hovland, Janis, and Kelley was a learning model—in essence, a stimulus-response model.

In the learning of new attitudes, Hovland and his associates believed that three variables were important: attention, comprehension, and acceptance. The first of these factors, *attention*, recognizes the fact that not all message stimuli that a person encounters are noticed. Driving down a highway littered with billboards, for example, you may notice only a fraction of the persuasive messages that you pass. Lacking your attention, the attempted persuasion will not be successful. But even when an appeal is noticed, it might not be effective. The second factor posited by Hovland and his colleagues, *comprehension*, recognizes the fact that some messages may be too complex and too ambiguous for their intended audience to understand. Thus, a highly complex treatise on the balance-of-payments deficit, for example, may be totally ineffective in persuading the economic novice to vote for or against the passage of a particular bill. Finally, a person must decide to accept the communication before any real attitude change takes place. The degree of *acceptance* is largely related to the incentives that are offered. The message may provide arguments or reasons for accepting the advocated point of view, or it may engender expectations of rewards or other pleasant experiences. For example, a billboard on the highway may tell you that a nationally known restaurant is only minutes off the highway, thus promising you something better than you had planned at the next truck stop. Stimulus-response theories regard this assumption as basic— attitudes are changed only if the incentives for making a new response are greater than the incentives for making the old response. In short, the theoretical model of Hovland and his associates suggests the following steps in the process of changing attitudes or opinions:

1. A recommended opinion (the stimulus) is presented.
2. Assuming that the subjects have paid attention to and understood the message, the audience responds or reacts. That is, they think about their initial opinions and also about the recommended opinion.
3. The subjects will change their attitudes if incentives (rewards) for

making a new response are greater than the incentives for making the old response.

Overall, the research discussed in *Communication and Persuasion* could be described in terms of three of its principal characteristics. First, it was primarily concerned with theoretical issues and basic research; its main purpose was to discover the "laws" of persuasion. Second, the principal theoretical approach used was a version of stimulus-response learning theory in which it was assumed that attitudes (and opinions) could be changed *only if* the incentives for change are greater than the incentive for stability. Third, the methodological emphasis was on controlled experimental research.

THE EXPERIMENTS AND THEIR FINDINGS

Both the experiments and their findings were numerous, complex, and were discussed in detail by the authors. There were far too many studies to review each separately. For the sake of simplicity, only the major ideas in each of the four categories (communicator, content, audience, response) will be discussed. A representative study in each category will also be presented.

Characteristics of the Communicator

The first area discussed in *Communication and Persuasion* was that of the communicator's credibility. It was assumed by the researchers that the effectiveness of a communication depended to a considerable extent upon who delivered it. Government agencies, for example, take great pains to have their statements to Congress presented by the most acceptable advocate. Even backyard gossips liberally sprinkle the names of respectable sources throughout their rumors. How often, for example, have you heard "it came from a good source" attached to a rumor?

Hovland and his associates were particularly interested in how differences in the credibility of the communicator would affect: (1) the way in which the presentation and the content of the presentation would be perceived and evaluated by members of the audience, and (2) the degree to which the attitudes and opinions of the audience members would be modified. The researchers limited their investigation to the influence of the following two factors: (1) "expertness" or "the extent to which the communicator is perceived to be a source of valid assertions"[5] and (2) "trustworthiness" or "the degree of confidence in the communicator's intent to communicate the assertions he considers most valid."[6] It would appear to be obvious that "expertness" of the sources is an important factor. For example, previous research had found that the credibility of an advertisement appears to be related to some extent to the reputation of the particular magazine in which it appeared. As an example of this, consider your own reaction when you read a sensational news story. Does it make any difference to you whether the story appeared in *The New York Times* or in *The National Enquirer?*

Trustworthiness also appeared to be an important factor from previous research. For example, in Chapter 5, it was indicated that men who viewed the film *The Battle of Britain* and thought it was "propaganda" showed less opinion change in the direction advocated by the film than did those who viewed the film and thought it simply "information." Again, in everyday life we often wonder about people's "ulterior motives." If we perceive a person as having a definite *intention* to persuade us, the likelihood is increased that this source will be perceived as an individual with something to gain by our persuasion; therefore, that person is less worthy of trust.

To test the effects of variations in expertness and trustworthiness, Hovland and Weiss designed an experiment that consisted of presenting an identical communication to two groups. Four different topics were used. Table 6.1 lists the topics of the articles and the sources to whom they were attributed. In one group, the articles were attributed to *high-credibility* sources and in the other they were attributed to *low-credibility* sources.

TABLE 6.1. THE TOPICS OF FOUR PERSUASIVE COMMUNICATIONS AND THE SOURCES TO WHOM THEY WERE ATTRIBUTED

	High-Credibility Source	Low-Credibility Source
A. *Antihistamine Drugs:* Should the antihistamine drugs continue to be sold without a doctor's prescription?	*New England Journal of Biology and Medicine*	Magazine A (A mass circulation monthly pictorial magazine)
B. *Atomic Submarines:* Can a practicable atomic-powered submarine be built at the present time?	J. Robert Oppenheimer	*Pravda*
C. *The Steel Shortage:* Is the steel industry to blame for the current shortage of steel?	*Bulletin of National Resources Planning Board*	Writer A (An antilabor, "rightist" newspaper columnist)
D. *The Future of Movie Theaters:* As a result of TV, will there be a decrease in the number of movie theaters in operation by 1955?	*Fortune* magazine	Writer B (A woman movie-gossip columnist)

Source: Carl I. Hovland, Irving L. Janis, and Harold H. Kelly, *Communication and Persuasion* (New Haven, Conn.: Yale University Press, 1953) p. 28.

Both affirmative and negative versions of each topic were employed. Opinion questionnaires were administered before, immediately after, and a month after the communication. In the questionnaire given before the communication, college students were asked to judge the trustworthiness of a long list of sources, including those used in the study. Analysis of these judgments showed that the sources that the researchers felt had high credibility did, in fact, have high credibility; that is, they were judged so by the subjects. The same was true for the low-credibility sources: they were judged by the students to be low in trustworthiness. The subjects were then given the articles to read. Each student received a booklet containing one article on each of the four topics; the name of the source was given at the end of each article. Then, another questionnaire was administered immediately following this reading, asking for their opinions and evaluations of the article.

The results of the experiment showed that differences in initial attitude toward the source influenced evaluation of the presentations. Even though the communications judged were identical in content, the presentations were considered to be "less fair" and the conclusions "less justified" when the source was of low credibility. (See Table 6.2).

Table 6.3 displays the effects of source credibility on opinion change in these subjects, taken immediately after the exposure. Opinion change in the

TABLE 6.2. THE EFFECTS OF HIGH- AND LOW-CREDIBILITY SOURCES ON EVALUATIONS OF FAIRNESS AND JUSTIFIABILITY OF IDENTICAL COMMUNICATIONS

	A. Percent considering author "fair" in his presentation			
	High-Credibility Source		**Low-Credibility Source**	
Topic	**N***	**Percent**	**N**	**Percent**
Antihistamines	31	64.5	27	59.3
Atomic Submarines	25	96.0	36	69.4
Steel Shortage	37	24.3	26	19.2
Future of Movies	29	93.1	33	63.7
Mean		65.6		54.9

	B. Percent considering author's conclusion "justified" by the facts			
	High-Credibility Source		**Low-Credibility Source**	
Topic	**N**	**Percent**	**N**	**Percent**
Antihistamines	31	67.7	27	51.8
Atomic Submarines	25	80.0	36	44.4
Steel Shortage	37	32.4	26	26.9
Future of Movies	29	58.6	33	42.4
Mean		58.2		41.8

*N = number of cases used.
Source: Carl I. Hovland, Irving L. Janis, and Harold H. Kelly, *Communication and Persuasion* (New Haven, Conn.: Yale University Press, 1953) p. 29.

TABLE 6.3. NET CHANGES OF OPINION IN DIRECTION OF COMMUNICATION FOR SOURCES CLASSIFIED BY EXPERIMENTERS AS HIGH OR LOW CREDIBILITY*

| | Net Percentage of Cases in Which Subjects Changed Opinion in Direction of Communication | | | |
| | *High-Credibility Sources* | | *Low-Credibility Sources* | |
Topic	N	Percent	N	Percent
Antihistamines	31	22.6	30	13.3
Atomic Submarines	25	36.0	36	0.0
Steel Shortage	35	22.9	26	−3.8
Future of Movies	31	12.9	30	16.7
Mean		23.0		6.6
Difference			16.4	
p			< .01	

* Net changes = positive changes *minus* negative changes. Cf. [18] pp. 302–305 for a discussion of the use of this measure.
Source: Carl I. Hovland, Irving L. Janis, and Harold H. Kelley, *Communication and Persuasion* (New Haven, Conn.: Yale University Press, 1953) p. 30.

direction advocated by the communication occurred significantly more often when the communication originated from a high-credibility source than when it originated from a low-credibility source. More specifically, the expected difference was obtained on three of the four topics, the exception being the one that discussed the future of movies.

However, the researchers obtained additional data on these opinion changes four weeks later, and the differences between the effectiveness of the high-credibility and low-credibility sources had disappeared. This resulted from both (1) a decreased acceptance of the point of view advocated by the high-credibility source, and (2) an increased acceptance of the position advocated by the low-credibility sources. Of course, the first could be attributed to forgetting the content. However, the second suggested that the negative effects of the untrustworthy source wore off and permitted the arguments presented in the communication to produce a delayed positive effect, known as the "sleeper effect" (discussed in Chapters 2 and 5). Thus, the researchers concluded that the effect of the source is maximal at the time of communication but decreases with the passage of time more rapidly than the effects of the content.

Based upon this evidence and the results derived from follow-up studies, the researchers concluded:

1. When a communication was attributed to a low-credibility source, it was considered to be more biased and unfair in its presentation than when it was attributed to a high-credibility source.
2. High-credibility sources had a considerably greater immediate effect on audience opinion than did low-credibility sources. However, after a few weeks, the positive effects of high-credibility sources and the negative

effects of low-credibility sources tended to disappear. There were no differences between the two sources in either subject evaluations of the presentation or in their acceptance of the conclusions that each source advocated.

3. The immediate effects on opinion were not the result of differences in either the amount of attention the audience paid to the communicator or of the audience's comprehension of the presentation. Tests taken of the amount of information retained by the audience revealed that the audience learned what was said equally well, no matter what the perceived credibility of the communication. Variations in source credibility thus influence primarily the motivation of the audience to accept the conclusions which were advocated.

The Content and Structure of the Message

The study of the effects of the content in a communication on persuasion was broken down into two areas: (1) motivating appeals and (2) the organization of persuasive arguments. Motivating appeals were defined as "stimuli which operate as appeals that arouse motives to accept recommended opinions."[7] Hovland, Janis, and Kelley discuss three major classes of such incentives: (1) substantiating arguments, (2) positive appeals, and (3) negative appeals. Substantiating arguments tend to lead the audience to believe that the conclusion advocated in the presentation is true or correct. Positive appeals emphasize the rewards of accepting those conclusions, whereas negative appeals (including fear-arousing content) depict the unpleasant consequences of not accepting that conclusion. The researchers present evidence involving only negative, fear-arousing appeals.

Fear Appeals. Research into fear-arousing appeals was designed to investigate factors that determine the degree to which threat appeals are effective or ineffective in producing opinion change. Research in this area focused on two problems: (1) identifying content stimuli that were effective in arousing fear or threat and then (2) determining how they facilitated or interfered with the overall effectiveness of the communication.

The researchers assumed that any intensely disturbing emotion, such as fear, guilt, anger, and so on, has the functional properties of a drive. In other words, these emotions provide motivation for some kind of behavior. A successful fear appeal arouses, then relieves, emotional tension. The tension is removed through the presentation of new opinions for acceptance that provide solutions to the problem. Specifically, the actual persuasion process using fear appeal involves the following steps:

1. The individual is first exposed to relatively neutral content, which defines the topic of communication.

2. Threat statements follow, which are interpreted as referring to a genuine danger and which evoke anticipations such as "This might happen to me."

3. As these anticipations are mentally rehearsed, the individual experiences a marked increase in emotional tension.

4. While in a state of high emotional tension, the individual is exposed to other statements in the communication that make assertions about ways of averting the threat. That is, the threat can or should be avoided by performing the recommended action or by adopting the recommended attitude.

5. As the reassuring recommendation is mentally rehearsed, emotional tension subsides.

6. The reduction of emotional tension operates as a reinforcement of the reassuring recommendation, and thus this new response will tend to occur on subsequent occasions, when similar stimuli are present.

As part of the research program, Janis and Feshbach tested the above model of fear-arousing communication. Using the entire senior class of a large Connecticut high school as subjects, they presented a 15-minute lecture to four randomly assigned groups. Three of those groups saw lectures concerning dental hygiene; each of the lectures contained essentially the same information about the causes and prevention of tooth decay. However, each group was given a separate form of lecture containing a different amount of threat or fear-arousing material. Form 1 contained a "strong" appeal, emphasizing the painful consequences of tooth decay and gum disease. Cancer and blindness were even mentioned as possible consequences of such dental neglect. Form 2 presented a "moderate" appeal in which dangers were described in a milder, more factual manner. This appeal, at its worst, emphasized mouth infections, sore swollen gums, and tooth decay. Form 3, on the other hand, presented a "minimal" appeal that contained few references to the consequences of tooth neglect, although "cavities" were mentioned several times as were "decayed teeth." The fourth group, the control group, was given a nonthreatening lecture on the human eye. Measures were taken before and after the lectures. These included: (1) a measure of each subject's feelings about the possibilities of tooth decay, taken before and after the lecture; (2) a measure of emotional arousal taken immediately after the lecture; and (3) a measure of each subject's conformity with prescribed dental practices, taken one week before and one week after the lecture.

Overall, the lectures did elicit the anxiety that was predicted. As Table 6.4 indicates, all three forms of the presentation produced different amounts of emotional arousal, with the amount of arousal positively correlated with the amount of threat presented. Specifically, the strong appeal produced greater emotional tension than did the moderate appeal, which in turn, produced

TABLE 6.4. PERCENT OF SUBJECTS REPORTING FEELINGS OF WORRY OR CONCERN EVOKED DURING THE DENTAL HYGIENE COMMUNICATION

Questionnaire Responses	Experimental Groups		
	Exposed to Strong Appeal (N = 50)	Exposed to Moderate Appeal (N = 50)	Exposed to Minimal Appeal (N = 50)
1. Felt worried—a "few times" or "many times"—about own mouth condition	74	60	48
2. Felt "somewhat" or "very" worried about improper care of own teeth	66	36	34
3. Thought about condition of own teeth "most of the time"	42	34	22

Source: Carl I. Hovland, Irving L. Janis, and Harold H. Kelley, *Communication and Persuasion* (New Haven, Conn.: Yale University Press, 1953) p. 70.

greater tension than did the minimal appeal. Additionally, there was a marked increase in worrying about the possibility of tooth decay after the lecture, which again correlated positively with the amount of threat. This led Janis and Feshbach to conclude that content factors that increase the meaningfulness of a threat (i.e., elaborating on the consequences and relating them to the audience) tend to increase the level of emotional arousal.

Furthermore, it was found that fear appeals did increase conformity with recommended practices. However, the results were surprising, to say the least. It was the minimal appeal (not the strongest appeal) that produced the greatest changes in conformity with the communicator's recommendations! (See Table 6.5.) In fact, the group exposed to the strong threat failed to differ significantly from the control group. Overall, Hovland, Janis, and Kelley concluded that a minimal amount of fear appeal is the most effective in terms of persuasion. Moderate and strong appeals may be effective in arousing interest and a high degree of emotional tension, but decrease the overall effectiveness of the presentation by evoking some form of interference. For example, when a communication arouses intense feelings of anxiety, individuals will sometimes fail to pay attention to what is being said and miss the intended message. Other individuals, when exposed to anxiety-producing communications may react to the unpleasant experience by becoming aggressive toward the communicator and rejecting his/her statements. In short, high levels of anxiety can interfere with the person attending to, comprehending or accepting the communication.

Message Organization. Whether or not a persuasive communication is effective depends not only on the nature of the motivating appeals used, but also upon the organization of the arguments used in support of the position

TABLE 6.5. EFFECT OF THE ILLUSTRATED TALK ON CONFORMITY TO DENTAL HYGIENE RECOMMENDATIONS

	Group			
Type of Change	*Strong* *(N = 50)*	*Moderate* *(N = 50)*	*Minimal* *(N = 50)*	*Control* *(N = 50)*
Increased conformity	28%	44%	50%	22%
Decreased conformity	20	22	14	22
No change	52	34	36	56
Total	100	100	100	100
Net change in conformity	+8%	+22%	+36%	0%
Reliability of Differences	Critical Ratio		Probability Value	
Control vs. minimal	2.54		<.01	
Control vs. moderate	1.50		.07	
Control vs. strong	0.59		.28	
Strong vs. moderate	0.95		.17	
Strong vs. minimal	1.96		.03	
Moderate vs. minimal	0.93		.18	

Source: Carl I. Hovland, Irving L. Janis, and Harold H. Kelley, *Communication and Persuasion* (New Haven, Conn.: Yale University Press, 1953) p. 80.

advocated. Typical problems discussed under this topic include: (1) whether or not a conclusion should be explicitly stated, (2) whether or not both sides of an argument should be presented, and (3) if both sides are to be presented, which one should be presented first.

Overall, the results of the studies on these topics were rather predictable and in line with the findings of earlier research. For example, Hovland and Mandell performed a study to test the relative effectiveness of either explicitly drawing a conclusion or leaving it implicit. The topic used was "Devaluation of Currency." The communication was tape-recorded and presented as a transcription from a radio program called "Education for Americans." All subjects (college students) heard the identical communication, but for half of them the part containing the explicit conclusion drawn was omitted. It was found that much more opinion change occurred when the conclusion was explicitly drawn by the communicator. However, the researchers cautioned that the intelligence and the degree of sophistication of the members of the audience, in terms of the issue being presented, are important factors in the relative effectiveness of other methods of presentation. Thus, with a sophisticated audience, it might be more effective to leave the conclusion implicit.

Another issue that relates to the organization of persuasive messages is the question of one-sided communications versus two-sided communications. For example, if you are arguing in favor of reduced television time for children, should you present only arguments that are favorable to your position, or should you acknowledge and attempt to refute an opposing viewpoint? The issue, of course, had been dealt with in the film research discussed in Chapter 5. In that work, Hovland, Lumsdaine, and Sheffield argued that, on the whole, there was no difference between a one-sided and a two-sided presentation in terms of opinion change. However, few answers are "all or none," and Hovland et al. did find some differences when special conditions were considered (see Chapter 5).

One study in this present research program that provided some interesting results was one conducted by Lumsdaine and Janis. They considered the effectiveness of a one-sided message versus a two-sided message. Their special interest, however, was which of these two types of messages would be most likely to prepare an audience to resist influences of subsequent counter-propaganda. Their subjects were high school students with whom they used two different versions of a recorded radio program. In both versions, the commentator presented the view that the U.S.S.R. would not be able to produce A-bombs in quantity for at least five years. One group, however, received a one-sided version and were presented only arguments that supported the speaker's position. (They were told, for example, that Soviet scientists had not yet discovered all the crucial secrets and that even after acquiring all the know-how, the U.S.S.R. still did not have sufficient industrial potential to produce the bombs in quantity.)

The second group received a two-sided version that contained all of the arguments in the first group's presentation, reached the same conclusion, but also discussed the main arguments on the other side of the question. (For example, they were given the additional information that the U.S.S.R. had many first-rate atomic scientists and that Soviet industries had made a tremendous recovery since the war.) A week later, half of the subjects in each group were given a second communication in which another speaker advocated a position opposite the one presented in the original communication. That is, he argued that the U.S.S.R. had probably already developed the A-bomb and that within two years would be producing it in large quantities. The main question used to measure the effects of the communication was: "About how long from now do you think it will be before the Russians are really producing *large numbers* of atomic bombs?"[8] Questionnaires were filled out several weeks before the presentations and after the presentations. The results showed that when there was no subsequent exposure to counterpropaganda, the two versions were equally effective in changing opinions. However, when there *was* subsequent exposure to counterpropaganda, the two-sided version was more effective in producing sustained opinion change. The researchers concluded that when the two-sided presentation was used, the listeners were led to accept the recommended opinion; they had already taken into account the opposing arguments, and thus had a basis for either ignoring or discounting contra-dictory arguments. This process of inducing resistance to later persuasive attempts was labelled "innoculation." (This became an important concept in the study of attitude change.)

The last major issue considered in message organization was the old "primacy versus recency" debate. In other words, when there are occasions in which it is most effective to present both sides of an argument, which side should be presented first for maximum impact? Will the side presented first or the side presented last be the more persuasive? After reviewing the existing research, Hovland et al. concluded: "It is doubtful it will ever be meaning(ful) to postulate a Law of Primacy in social psychology."[9] This issue, in other words, was one which Hovland thought best laid to rest. In short, then, the most effective message is one in which a conclusion is explicitly drawn and both sides of the argument presented; the order of presentation does not really make a difference.

The Audience

The audience was first studied in two ways. The researchers examined the effects of group membership and group conformity on the acceptance of persuasive communications. In addition, personality factors and their effects upon persuasibility were examined.

Effects of Group Membership. Hovland, et al. argued that individuals' conforming tendencies stem from membership in groups. These tendencies are based upon knowledge of what behavior is expected of them by other members and upon the individual's motivation to live up to those expectations. Thus, group norms often interfere with the effectiveness of persuasive communications because they tend to make the individual resist change. The researchers were therefore particularly interested in "counternorm communications," that is, in messages that argue in direct opposition to group norms.

Previous research had shown that the more highly a person valued his membership in a group, the more closely his attitudes and opinion conformed to the consensus within that group. From this, Kelley and Volkhart hypothesized that individuals who highly value their membership in a group will be less influenced by communications contrary to the group's norms than will those who do not value membership as much. That is, opinion change will be inversely related to the degree to which the person values group membership.

In testing this hypothesis, they experimented with twelve troops of Boy Scouts from a large New England industrial community. The boys filled out a questionnaire in which they were asked how highly they valued their membership in the troop and what their attitudes toward woodcraft were. These attitudes were compared with attitudes about other, more urban activities. A week later, the boys were presented with a speech in which a non-Scout adult criticized woodcraft activities and suggested that the Scouts would be better off learning about the city. Finally, each group was divided in half and everyone filled out the questionnaire again. Half of each group was told that their answers would be kept secret (private condition), while the other half was told that their responses would probably be made known to the rest of the group (public condition).

The results of this experiment at least partially confirmed Kelley and Volkhart's hypothesis. That is, when the opinions were expressed privately, the boys who most valued their scout membership were the least influenced by the communication. However, in the public condition the results were inconsistent and no definite pattern could be identified. Overall, however, the authors argued that the findings did support the general hypothesis that persons who were strongly motivated to remain members of the group would be the most resistant to communications that presented recommendations contrary to the standards of the group.

Personality Factors in Persuasibility. The authors argued that the effects of a communication are partly dependent upon the charactertistics of individual members of the audience. Thus, taking account of personality characteristics should improve predictions concerning the way in which a given type of audience (or a given individual within the audience) will respond. Therefore, the researchers believed that investigations of personality factors were necessary if they were to discover the elusive "laws" and thus be able to predict the degree to which a persuasive communication will succeed in changing beliefs and attitudes.

Hovland and his associates discussed two general types of personality factors: intellectual abilities and "motive factors." Intellectual abilities are significant because they determine the way an individual attends to, interprets, and assimilates the many communications to which a person is constantly exposed. However, Hovland and his associates believed that for those individuals who possess "at least a certain minimum of essential intellectual abilities," "motive factors" are probably more important determinants of individual differences in persuasibility. Motive factors are said to involve "predominant personality needs, emotional disturbances, defense mechanisms, frustration tolerance, thresholds of excitability, etc., which may facilitate or interfere with a person's responsiveness to many different types of persuasive communications."

The authors concluded, in regard to the relation between intellectual ability and persuasibility, that it was a complex matter. On the one hand, it is *easier* to persuade individuals with high intelligence than those low in intellectual ability. This is because the former have more ability to draw valid inferences when exposed to persuasive communications that rely primarily on impressive logical arguments. At the same time, those with high intellectual ability are also more likely to be critical of the arguments presented. They will therefore be *less likely* to be influenced than those with low intellectual ability when they are exposed to persuasive communications which rely primarily on unsupported generalities or upon false, illogical, irrelevant argumentation. The researchers hypothesized that there would be an interplay between intellectual factors and motive factors. Mental ability alone would be insufficient data when predicting the influence of individual differences on persuasibility. Some individuals, the researchers hypothesized, had personality needs that inclined them to be highly gullible. What motive factors, then, do make for indiscriminate acceptance of persuasive communications? Janis attempted to link personality characteristics to susceptibility to persuasion. The experiment measured opinion change in 78 male college students. Each student was exposed to the same set of three persuasive communications. In addition, the researchers obtained information about the personality characteristics of the subjects. Thus, it was possible to examine the relationship between opinion changes and personality factors.

The students were given a series of written communications similar to magazine articles or news commentaries or editorials. These materials provided a series of factual statements in an attempt to convince the audience that a particular belief or expectation was the correct one. Because the communications were in simple language, it is probable that all of the student subjects had the minimal skills necessary for absorbing the message.

Each subject was exposed to the communications in a standard way. The subject had to read all three communications; in addition, he had to present one of them orally, then listen to oral presentations of the other two. The subjects' initial opinions on these issues were obtained through an opinion questionnaire administered approximately four weeks earlier. The key items in the questionnaire for this study focused directly on the issues dealt with in the communications. There were: (1) the number of movie theaters in business in three years, (2) the amount of meat available to the population of the United States in two years, and (3) the length of time before a cure for the common cold is discovered. No one in this original survey gave estimates that were anywhere as low as the ones advocated by the communication. After exposure to the communications, questionnaires containing these three items were administered to each subject again. Approximately two-thirds of the subjects lowered their estimates; they changed in the direction advocated by the communication to which they had been exposed.

Janis then divided the subjects into categories on the basis of the degree of change they exhibited: high, moderate, and low persuasibility. The "high" category contained 32 cases; all these individuals had been influenced by all three communications. Another 21 cases were classified as "moderate"; they were influenced by two of the communications. The "low" category was composed of the 25 cases in which the individuals were influenced by one or none of the persuasive communications. The three groups were then compared with respect to personality characteristics.

Personality data were obtained from two independent sources. Janis obtained detailed clinical reports for 16 of the subjects who had received psychiatric counseling. In addition, he administered a personality inventory to all 78 subjects at the time they completed the precommunication questionnaire. Both sets of data indicated that there were marked differences between the men who were highly influenced and those who were relatively uninfluenced by the persuasive communications. Those who were highly influenced possessed low levels of self-esteem. They expressed feelings of social inadequacy; for example, they showed concern about feelings of shyness, lack of confidence in their conversational abilities, high concern about the possibility that friends may have a low opinion of them, and uneasiness at social gatherings. Moreover, this group was also described as "aggressively inhibited." In other words, they rarely criticized others, rarely felt angry toward anyone, rarely felt like resisting the demands of others, and felt a lack of resentment when deceived by others. In addition, the group was also highly characterized by depression. They often reported feeling "blue," "unhappy," and "discouraged." In short, then, the study found that high persuasibility was associated with feelings of social inadequacy, inhibition of aggression, and depression, in addition to general levels of low self-esteem.

Up to this point, we have been discussing personality factors associated with persons who are relatively easy to persuade. The researchers did, however, discover three distinct personality traits associated with those who are difficult to persuade. These traits were: persistent aggressiveness toward others, social withdrawal tendencies, and acute psychoneurotic complaints. Persons who openly expressed hostility and displayed overt aggression toward others in everyday life were found to be relatively unaffected by persuasive communications. Moreover, socially withdrawn persons, those extremely indifferent toward others, were typically resistant to change. This was also true of persons displaying acute psychoneurotic symptoms—notably, obsessional ideas, hypochondriacal complaints, insomnia, and work inhibitions. The author hypothesized that these symptoms interfere with the person's attention, comprehension, and acceptance, thereby explaining why such individuals are difficult to influence.

While in this chapter we have categorized the research presented in *Communication and Persuasion* as focusing on the communicator, the communication, and the audience, all the studies in Hovland et al.'s book examined the *effects* of communications. Thus, all of the studies were implicitly concerned with the responses of the audience. Some, however, examined special aspects of the audience's response to communications.

Audience Response Patterns

The two issues that the Yale Program focused upon in its analysis of response factors were: active versus passive participation by the subject and the duration of the effects of the communication. More specifically, does active participation by individuals have any effect on attitude or opinion acquisition or change? Is attitude or opinion change brought about by persuasive communications typically long-term or short-term change?

Active versus Passive Participation. In everyday life, most people occupy several roles, such as mother, wife, lawyer, community leader. When fulfilling some of the behavior required by these roles, some individuals may find themselves expected to express ideas that are not necessarily in accord with their private beliefs. What happens to an individual's private opinion when this person is induced to assert what has been said in a communication as though it represented his/her own opinion? This is a question that the researchers sought to answer. Janis and King compared the opinion change of two groups: "active participants" and "passive controls." In one group, subjects were induced to play a role that required them to deliver a persuasive communication to others; in the other group, the subjects were required only to read and listen to the same communication. The experiment was conducted in a series of small group meetings involving male college students. Each student was given an "oral speaking test." In the process, they were exposed to three different communications. The purpose of the study was supposed to be to assess their ability to speak effectively in a group conference. At the end of the session, ratings were obtained from each subject on each speaker's performance. In addition, the subjects answered a series of questions concerning their interest in, and their opinions on the various topics covered. The subjects were told that this information was necessary in order to study agreement among different judges. The researchers compared each subject's postcommunication answers with those he had given in a general opinion survey approximately four weeks earlier. They were thus able to detect opinion changes produced by the communications.

Subjects were asked to give an informal talk in each of the experimental sessions. The talk was based upon a prepared outline provided by the researchers. Each active participant was instructed to play the role of a sincere advocate of the point of view he was presenting. The others listened to this talk and read the outline as he spoke. Each subject delivered a talk in turn, while the other two were passively exposed to the communication. None of the subjects knew which topic he would speak on in advance, in order to prevent selective attention effects.

In each communication the speaker talked about a controversial issue involving future events. In all cases the communication took an extreme position. While the arguments were highly relevant, they were also highly biased; they emphasized evidence that supported only one side of the issue. Communication A predicted that two out of three movie theaters would be forced out of business in the next three years because of the intense competition of television and other recent events. The essence of Communication B was that within the next two years the availability of meat to the civilian population of the United States would decline to 50 percent of its present level. Communication C argued that a completely effective cure for the common cold was very close to development; it would probably be available in the next year or so.

The results indicated that active participation (in the experiment role playing) was a much more effective way of changing opinions than passive participation (merely listening to and reading the outline). Additional studies of this topic in the research program yielded similar results. All confirmed the importance of active participation in bringing about opinion change.

Duration of Opinion Change. All the studies in the Yale Program focused to some degree on the duration of opinion change, many issues relevant to this topic have already been discussed. The researchers raised two questions when they addressed this topic: (1) What are the factors dealing with learning and remembering the content of a communication, and (2) What are the factors dealing with the persistence of acceptance of the communicator's conclusions?

Research on the learning and retention of content delineated several important factors. In general, it was found that the meaningfulness of the content will influence retention. That is, the more vivid and the more emotional the material, the better the retention. Also, the more completely the material is initially learned, the longer it will be remembered. Moreover, the type of retention required was found to be an important factor. Specifically, the rate of forgetting depended upon the criteria used to evaluate retention. For example, simple recognition was easier than total recall. Finally, it was found that the motivation of the audience will influence both the quality and quantity of retention. That is, "unpleasant" material tended to be forgotten more rapidly than "pleasant" material.

In terms of the retention of opinion change, or acceptance of the communicator's conclusions, the researchers reviewed a previous study that provided insight. Hovland and Weiss, in a study described earlier, found that a "high-credibility" source was initially more successful in producing opinion change than was a "low-credibility" source. However, after four weeks, differences between the sources' respective success ratios had disappeared. This was due to increased acceptance of the low-credibility source and decreased acceptance of the high-credibility source (the sleeper effect). While forgetting could account for the decreased acceptance of the high-credibility source, it could not explain the delayed opinion change in a positive direction. The researchers hypothesized that a dissociation between the communication and the communicator might be producing the sleeper effect. In other words, arguments and conclusions were being recalled without associating them with the source.

Kelman and Hovland therefore conducted a study to find out what would happen if the subjects were reminded of the source at a later testing. They used a total of 330 high school seniors as subjects during regular class periods. The subjects were asked to listen to a recording of an educational radio program and judge its educational value. During the program, a guest speaker gave a talk favoring extreme leniency in the treatment of juvenile delinquents. Three different versions of the introduction to the speaker were used in the experiment. In the positive version, he was identified as a juvenile court judge—well-trained and well-informed. In a neutral version, he was identified as a member of the studio audience, chosen at random. No additional information was given concerning him. In the negative version, he was again presented as coming from the studio audience, but it was also divulged that he had been delinquent in his youth and that he was presently free on bail after an arrest for peddling dope.

After hearing the speech, each group completed an opinion questionnaire concerning juvenile delinquency. Three weeks later, all three groups completed the same questionnaire, except that *half* of each group heard the same introduction again (a "reinstatement of the source"). Initially, the positive communicator had the greatest effect and the negative communicator the smallest effect. When the source was not reinstated, there was a decline in agreement with the positive speaker and an increase in agreement with the negative speaker, just as in the Hovland and Weiss study. When the source was reinstated, however, the extent of agreement with the positive communicator increased and agreement with the negative source decreased. The effects produced by the reinstated sources were approximately equal to those that were produced by the original communication. Kelman and Hovland concluded that overall, with the passage of time, the content of a statement is less likely to be associated spontaneously with the source. That is, people often remember *what* was said without recalling *who* said it.

In general, the two most common results concerning retention effects were: (1) An individual may be exposed to a communication and accept the communicator's point of view (at the time), but after a period of time revert to his/her previously held attitude. (2) An individual may at first reject the communicator's point of view but after a time "come around" to the communicator's position. Of the two, the first was the more common.

CONCLUSIONS AND IMPLICATIONS

Overall, what were the principal findings and the major conclusions of the *Communication and Persuasion* studies? Moreover, what was their importance from the point of view of developing the theory and the methodology of mass communication? Finally, what did the researchers find regarding the "magic keys" to persuasion? Do we know, from their work, the right combination of words, message structure, emotional appeals, type of communicator, and so on, to change people's attitudes and opinions? These questions need careful review.

In summary, the many separate but related studies of the Yale Communication Research Program can be categorized as focusing on the communicator, the message, the audience, and the audience's responses to persuasive communications. In terms of the communicator, the program found that source credibility was an important factor in obtaining immediate opinion change. Low-credibility sources were seen as more biased and more unfair than were high-credibility sources. The researchers also found that the effects of the communicator's credibility diminish over time, because members of the audience tend to dissociate the message from the communicator. However, these credibility effects can be reinstated simply by reminding the audience *who* said *what*. Overall, however, most of the opinion change obtained was short-term rather than long-term. Thus, while it is not difficult to change opinion *immediately* after a persuasive communication, when the change is measured a month later, the audience often has "reverted" to its original opinion.

The content and structure of the message were also found to have important effects. Threatening or fear-arousing materials were shown to arouse emotional tension and to produce opinion change, if used in the proper amounts. It was necessary to be careful not to evoke so much fear that high levels of anxiety resulted, since such intense feelings of anxiety can interfere with the individual's acceptance of the communication. In terms of structure, communications should generally state their conclusions explicitly, unless the audience is intelligent and sophisticated. Moreover, both sides of an issue should be included if it is likely that the audience will be exposed to subsequent counterpropaganda.

The studies of the audience provided some interesting, if not always conclusive, results. For example, the studies found that people who value their membership in groups highly will be least affected by communications that advocate positions counter to the norms of the group. Personality factors were also examined, and it was discovered that persons who have low self-esteem are easily influenced. In addition, people who are aggressive toward others and who have psychoneurotic tendencies are very difficult to influence.

Finally, the research into response factors indicated that active participation in the communication, such as having to deliver a speech and argue one side of a question, changes opinions in the direction argued more effectively than does passive participation such as reading the speech or listening to it.

There are several reasons why *Communication and Persuasion* is an important study in the history of communication research. Even though the research did not focus on mass media, it led to a greater understanding of the process of persuasion—a truly significant issue in mass communication. Its studies led to a better understanding of the many facets of persuasion, such as the nature of credibility, "innoculation" against propaganda, the nature of fear appeals, group allegiance, the "sleeper effect," and audience participation. And this new understanding was just a beginning; media researchers have followed these leads ever since. It does not matter that the findings reported in *Communication and Persuasion* did not always hold up in subsequent studies. These studies were the seeds from which sprouted a veritable garden of research, sinking its roots in the firm soil prepared by Hovland and his associates. The (inverse relationship) results obtained with the fear appeals, for example, have not always been confirmed in later studies. Indeed, it has been found that the greater the fear, the greater the opinion change.[10] That is, there is often greater attitude/opinion change following high-intensity fear appeals. Moreover, advertising and public service agencies have been influenced in the content of their commercials and public service announcements by this work. For example, recall the last American Cancer Society TV "spot" announcement you saw.

The Yale Program studies were innovative methodologically. They introduced many refinements in the use of the methods of experimental psychology applied to the study of the effects of communications. The project provided for experiments with "strategic variations" to test for and isolate the effects of relevant variables. Some researchers, however, have questioned the use of experimental methodology by itself to study persuasion. They have raised the often repeated objection: Can research conducted under artificial conditions be generalized to more natural conditions? The researchers in the Yale Program obviously felt that this could be done. As mentioned earlier, they felt that experimental research was essential to the formulation of a theory in which basic "laws" could be postulated. These "laws" would then allow social scientists to make valid predictions about future events. This, they thought, was the real goal of any kind of research. Thus, they argued that not only was the experimental method a valid one in this context, but that it was also basic to understanding. It is important for us to remember, however, that the results obtained in any experiment are not, in and of themselves, conclusive. They should not be taken as "the answer." Their potential validity lies in replication and in the integration of the findings with data from other sources (e.g., survey generalizations, field observations, etc.). Even Carl Hovland, in later years, came to recognize the importance of survey data:

> I should like to stress...the mutual importance of the two approaches to the problem of communication effectiveness. Neither is a royal road to wisdom, but each represents an important emphasis. The challenge of future work is one of fruitfully combining their virtues so that we may develop a social psychology of communication with the conceptual breadth provided by correlational study of process and with the rigorous but more delimited methodology of the experiment.

However, in spite of its drawbacks, the use of the experimental design has had profound and lasting influence on the conduct of communication research. That influence continues today.

The theoretical model used in this study was a version of learning theory that assumed that attitudes and opinions could be changed by persuasive communications only if the incentives for change were greater than the incentives for stability. However, before an individual could be influenced by a persuasive communication, he or she must first attend to it and accept it. The researchers were looking for the "keys" to this process. What kind of communicator was most effective? What was the best way to design and structure a message? And what role did personality factors and group allegiances play? Obviously, the general theoretical approach was that of *selective influence*, based upon individual differences. Other theories of selective influence, such as those based upon social categories and social relationships were not pertinent to this research program. The subjects, for the most part, fell into one major social category: students. Most were college students, but some were high school students. In addition, the researchers did not look into the *social* relationships that prevailed among their subjects as a source of influence.

The researchers began with the hope of discovering basic "laws" of persuasion. The idea was that once those keys to the communication-persuasion process were available, they could unlock the mysteries of many social doors. With the possession of these magic keys, we would be able to modify opinions, attitudes, and, theoretically, behavior; we could then reduce prejudice and discrimination, and improve relationships among human beings. In light of the advancement of the "hard" sciences, obtaining this knowledge seemed urgent.

But did these researchers find the magic keys? Not really! Certainly, new findings resulted from the experiments. We remain uncertain whether experiments portray the "real world," but we gained information about the characteristics of an effective communicator; we learned how to "innoculate" subjects from later propaganda; we learned that active participation is more effective than passive. Overall, we learned a great deal concerning immediate or *short-term* opinion change. But we did not learn how to modify opinions and attitudes permanently, or even for as long as three or four weeks. How could we accomplish some of our real world goals—such as reduction of prejudice—when opinions and attitudes apparently tend to revert to the *status quo ante?* Certainly, the new information seemed useful to some people, such as advertising consultants. Armed with it, they may have persuaded more of us to buy products that we ordinarily would not have purchased and didn't know we needed. But this information did not dramatically improve our social world—not as we had hoped. However, Hovland and the other researchers at the Yale Communication Program did not give up on the search for the magic keys. *Communication and Persuasion* was only a start. For years to come, the search would continue. Carl Hovland led the way; a host of others followed.

NOTES AND REFERENCES

1. Two other books, *The Order of Presentation in Persuasion* (1957) and *Personality and Persuasibility* (1959), refined and extended some of the findings presented in *Communication and Persuasion*.

2. Carl Hovland, Irving Janis, and Harold H. Kelley, *Communication and Persuasion* (New Haven: Yale University Press, 1953), p. 12.

3. Harold D. Lasswell, "The Structure and Function of Communication in Society," in *The Communication of Ideas,* ed. by Lyman Bryson (New York: Harper & Brothers, 1948), pp. 37–51.

4. Carl Hovland et al, op. cit., p. 9.

5. Ibid., p. 21.

6. Ibid., p. 21.

7. Ibid., p. 56.

8. Ibid., p. 109.

9. Ibid., p. 9.

10. See, for example, K. L. Higbee, "Fifteen years of fear arousal: Research on threat appeals: 1953–1968, *Pyschological Bulletin*, 1969, 72, 426–444. See also H. Leventhal, "Findings and theory in the study of fear communications." In L. Berkowitz, ed., *Advances in Experimental Social Psychology* (Vol. 5), (New York: Academic Press, 1970), pp. 119–186.

7

Personal Influence:
The Two-Step Flow of Communication

The decade following World War II was an extraordinarily active period for research on the effects of mass communication. Carl Hovland and his associates followed up the Army studies by conducting experiments on communication issues. The Erie County study of the 1940 presidential campaign had uncovered the possible significance of social ties among members of the audience in the second stage of the "two-step" flow. Other researchers were turning their attention to other media, such as airborne leaflets and comic books (to be discussed in chapters to follow). All of these studies were pressing forward vigorously the task of discovering the principles, processes, and influences of mass communication. This enthusiastic curiosity was aided by a growth in sophistication of the research methods available to social scientists. Although the computer was not yet at hand for academic researchers, statistical procedures were highly developed, and the electric calculating machines of the day permitted the analysis of relatively large data sets.

Controversies raged in both academic and political circles regarding the implications of our society's expanding ability to communicate on a mass scale with its citizens. For some, the escalating technology of the media seemed to hold high promise for improving both society and the human condition. Mass communication could save democracy, some said, because the media had the capacity to create informed public opinion. The media could become a kind of mass society version of the "town meeting," where citizens would have increasing access to accurate and complete accounts of the events, issues, and problems that required their attention and decisions. The growing power of the mass media to enlighten people, in other words, would make possible that expansion of the human consciousness forecast by Charles Horton Cooley at the beginning of the century.[1] Although newspapers were the only mass medium of his time, he felt that the huge increase in access to information that they provided for ordinary people had brought mankind to the dawn of a new era of enlightenment.

For others, the media continued to loom as menacing agents that threatened the destruction of democracy. The expansion of the media from print, to film, to broadcasting, seemed only to make it easier to shape and control the ideas of people who were becoming increasingly defenseless against media suggestions. In a society thought to be characterized by increasing urbanization, industrialization, and modernization, the original magic bullet theory, linked with the related conception of mass societal organization (Chapter 1), seemed to provide a clear basis for concern about the effects of the media. The legacy of fear, in other words, appeared to many citizens to be increasingly justified as the media continued to expand.

As research on mass communication intensified, however, communication scholars were forced to reassess their thinking. The problem was that the powerful effects that had been attributed to the media—both good and bad—simply did not seem to be there. The earliest large-scale research, such as the Payne Fund studies (Chapter 2) and the investigation of the *War of the Worlds* broadcast (Chapter 3) had seemed to support the conclusion that the media had immediate, powerful, and direct influences on their audiences. But subsequent studies, with more careful research designs, controls, and measurements, showed far less dramatic effects. The idea that the media controlled people's beliefs, attitudes, and behavior was not being supported by the accumulating evidence. This was not only true of the large-scale studies reviewed in the present book, but of the hundreds of smaller efforts that were increasingly appearing in the research journals.

In his well-known book summarizing the findings in the entire field of mass communication studies that had accumulated up until about 1958, Joseph Klapper maintained that the main conclusions were approximately the following:[2]

1. The media appear to have *less* power than the average citizen has assumed (then or now). No case can be made for simple cause–effect relationships between a person's paying attention to some message conveyed by the mass media and his or her beliefs, attitudes, or behavior.
2. Many studies have found that the messages conveyed by the media do have effects on their audiences, but these effects are relatively *minor.*
3. The conditions under which these messages have effects on their audiences are far *more complex* than had been suspected by social scientists who first studied the media.

Replacing the hypothesis of powerful and immediate effects was not an easy matter, or one that took place overnight. For one thing, the public was deeply committed to the kind of thinking represented by the magic bullet theory. And, as we will show in Chapter 9, a very popular book by a well-known psychiatrist, who claimed that he had clearly demonstrated the powerful influences of one medium (comic books), strongly reinforced among the public the old idea that mass communication could achieve dreadful effects. Thus, by the early 1950s the study of mass communication was proceeding with vigor, but for social scientists the findings seemed to demand new approaches to further investigation of the mass communication process.

Increasingly, research became designed not to demonstrate the awesome power of mass communication but to trace more subtle and complex patterns of its influence. The research community, if not the public, clearly believed that a hypothesis of minimal effects was closer to reality. To some communication scientists this was a source of disappointment and frustration. One prominent researcher even decided that studying the media was no longer worthwhile and declared the field to be dead.[3] Many others, however, remained excited by media research and designed numerous innovative studies of the more subtle and indirect influences of mass communication.

One important large-scale study of indirect influences of the mass media was actually a follow-up of the research reported in Chapter 4, on the impact of a mass-communicated presidential campaign. The new effort probed into the nature of opinion leaders and the kinds of influences they had on their followers. It focused on, in other words, those who were involved in the second stage of the two-step flow of communication. The research was actually planned in 1944, and its field work was started in 1945. However, its data analyses and final report were not completed for a decade. Its findings were finally published in 1955 by Elihu Katz and Paul F. Lazarsfeld, in their book *Personal Influence: The Part Played by People in the Flow of Mass Communication*. It is with this research that the present chapter is principally concerned. The book was much more than simply a research report; it was an effort to interpret the authors' research within a framework of conceptual schemes, theoretical issues, and research findings drawn broadly from the scientific study of small groups.

THE PART PLAYED BY PEOPLE: THE NEED FOR A NEW APPROACH

With the recognition that the process of mass communication was far more complex than anyone had previously thought, researchers from several disciplines sought to find the many factors that played a part in shaping what happened between media and mass. The Hovland team of social psychologists was convinced that the keys were in such factors as message structure, which could interact with individual differences in personality factors, including attitudes, emotions, credibility or other variables that influenced perception, remembering, or motivation to respond. The sociologists who had uncovered the two-step flow process felt that a more promising focus of research would be on the close personal groups that Cooley, at the beginning of the century, had labeled *primary groups*.[4] Katz and Lazarsfeld reviewed this concept in some detail.

Actually, the idea that primary groups might play an important role in the process of mass communication was an almost radical departure from earlier thinking about the media. We showed in Chapter 1 that the first rather simplistic stimulus–response theories dealing with the influences of mass communication in modern life were premised on assumptions about "mass" society, with its emphasis on individuality, loss of meaningful interpersonal ties, and a reduction of informal social controls. Yet, at the heart of the two-step flow idea is the assumption that very opposite kinds of variables might be important. The two-step flow concept presumed a movement of information through interpersonal networks, from the media to people and from there to other people, rather than directly from media to mass.

It seemed to follow, then, that a member of the audience of mass communication was not an impersonal individual without effective social ties to others. More likely, the audience member was in some way *influenced* by his or her ties with others in the interpretation of mass media messages and in making decisions whether to act one way or another on the basis of such messages.

Preliminary evidence from Paul Lazarsfeld et al.'s *The People's Choice* clearly suggested that it was one's family and peers that were the most important in the secondary stage of the two-step flow. In other words, the primary group was an obvious and logical focus for research aimed at better understanding the movement of messages from media to audiences via the two-step flow.

The "Rediscovery" of the Primary Group

As soon as it became apparent that close social ties played a part in the flow of information from media to mass, it seemed in retrospect that communication researchers should have started with such a model in the first place. The problem was that the theory of mass society led inevitably to assumptions that people in modern social life were isolated and individualistic. But as research on contemporary populations and social systems progressed, it had become increasingly apparent that the theory of mass society was not a very accurate model. Over and over, the important role of close personal ties in modern life was being uncovered in major research studies on social behavior.

The primary group, in other words, was *rediscovered* in modern urban society. The term "rediscovery" is appropriate because the concept became important shortly after the turn of the century with the work of social psychologists who were concerned with the process of socialization. The primary group was seen as a very important source from which people derived their "human nature." This was at a time when the famous *nature* versus *nurture* debates sought to settle whether personality was mainly a product of inherited factors or was heavily influenced by learning in social settings. The result of those debates was that older theories of human nature based on such biological factors as "instinct" became increasingly obsolete to many social scientists. The influence of learning from social and cultural sources became correspondingly more predominant in theories of human socialization.

But while students of socialization had given primary group interaction a central place in their thinking, this idea did not carry over into the accounts of those who were examining other kinds of social processes. Mass society thinking, in other words, continued to dominate the conceptual formulations of most social scientists. Then, starting in the early 1930s, a series of studies, one after the other, began to find that primary social relationships were a significant factor in the way people behaved. A very brief summary of several of these "rediscoveries" of the primary group will place the issue in perspective. Such a perspective is important in understanding the new directions in mass communication research represented by the *Personal Influence* project.

The classic rediscovery of the primary group as a set of influences that helps us understand life in modern society emerged as a central theme in the work of Rothlisberger and Dixon.[5] Theirs was a study of worker productivity in a factory that made parts for the Western Electric Company. Called the Hawthorne studies (after the name of the plant), the research showed that the so-called "piece rate" system for motivating greater worker productivity was often ineffective because workers had strong personal ties to each other. They did not act in an individualistic manner to maximize their own rewards but regulated their output in conjunction with the norms and expectations of their fellow workers with whom they had close personal ties.

In the late 1930s, social scientists studying the patterning of social relationships in American communities found that clique structures (e.g., primary groups) played a key role in placing people socially in one level or another.[6] In fact, in determining patterns of social stratification, cliques turned out to be second only to the family in importance.

Finally, during World War II, research on American soldiers and their willingness to fight revealed that combat motivation was associated with attachment to a close personal group.[7] Primary groups, in other words, emerged within the framework of a large, formally organized social structure (the Army) and determined to a considerable degree the willingness of individuals to carry out their roles in an effective manner. Soldiers would fight tenaciously if it meant protecting the lives of their buddies. Such factors as hatred of the enemy or broad ideological values counted for relatively little on the actual field of battle.

The Contribution of Small Groups Research

What did all of this mean for the investigation being summarized in the present chapter? One implication was that the development of theories about the nature of mass communication needed to rest upon the assumption that small intimate groups have a profound influence on nearly every aspect of social life—including the activities engaged in by people involved in the flow of information from media to mass. Once this assumption was made, it opened much broader vistas for conceptualizing the *process* of mass communication. It meant that the accumulated findings of social and behavioral science research concerning the nature and functioning of small groups became a fertile source for insights into how people could be expected to act in a mass communication setting. The research findings provided concepts and generalizations about how people could be expected to act and interact as they perceived messages from the media, told those messages to others, received influences from others whom they trusted, and eventually made some form of response to media content.

By the time the Katz and Lazarsfeld study of opinion leaders and their influences was first begun, small-groups research was off to a good start. By the time the research report was written a decade later, the accumulated findings of the social sciences regarding the nature and functioning of small groups was impressive indeed. In *Personal Influence*, the authors presented a detailed summary of the relationship between their study of opinion leaders and a host of factors to which their research objectives were related. For the most part, this work was an *ex post facto* analysis. Such an "after the fact" strategy is often criticized because the research is conducted first without the organizing framework of a strong conceptual basis, which comes later when the theoretical implications are sorted out against the findings of previous studies or interpretations. Nevertheless, the authors' analyses did illustrate the broader base of evidence, regarding the primary group and the functioning of close interpersonal ties, that needs to be taken into account in the study of the two-step flow of communication. The authors discussed how opinions and attitudes within such groups tend to be shared. Dozens of studies were summarized to show that people tend to conform to the norms and expectations of such groups and that numerous benefits result from such conformity.

Small Groups and Meaning Theory. As an illustration of the significance of the study of small groups in general to the development of theory in mass communication, the authors pointed to the functions of such groups in providing *meanings* for their members regarding ambiguous situations for which individuals do not have an adequate or standard interpretive framework. During the 1940s, Kurt Lewin, a well-known social psychologist, and his followers studied the processes by which a "social reality" is created in small group settings:

> Experiments dealing with memory and group pressure on the individual show that what exists as "reality" for the individual is to a high degree determined by what is socially accepted as reality. This holds even in the field of physical fact: to the South Sea Islanders the world may be flat; to the European it is round. "Reality," therefore, is not an absolute. It differs with the group to which the individual belongs.[8]

It is through social processes that we develop meanings for the words and labels that make up our language. Few people can have, or even want to have, personal and direct experience with every aspect of reality for which we have a label (e.g., "death in the electric chair"). Nevertheless, we collectively construct a socially derived reality that we share and use to provide meaning to such labels.

Although these authors did not extend their ideas to the mass media, it has become clear today that the mass media, as well as small groups, are an important part of the social processes of communication by which we collectively develop social constructions of reality. This idea is at the heart of what De Fleur has called the *meaning theory* of the effects of the mass media.[9]

The significance of the social reality function of small groups for Katz's and Lazarsfeld's research on personal influence was explained by them: In a presidential election the media provide confusing and often contradictory facts about the issues and candidates; yet, the individual must choose between one or the other, even in this ambiguous situation. He or she can turn to members of the primary group for interpretations, which then become "reality."

Values and the Reference Function. The values shared in small groups are another source that draws people to the groups as sources of influence and interpretation. Research had shown that people with similar values tended to be drawn toward each other and to form close-knit groups. When people are in a system of close and interdependent interaction with one another, they tend to demand a high degree of conformity of each other. Thus, the primary group becomes a "reference group" to whom its members turn for interpretations, advice, and influences as they shape their responses to the external world. An important part of that external world is what they encounter, or think that they encounter, in mass communication.

Many other aspects and functions of small groups in daily life are discussed in *The People's Choice*. Indeed, the first half of the work is a rich source of ideas of how mass communication behavior is linked to other important social processes and activities:

> The whole moral of these chapters is that knowledge of an individual's interpersonal environment is basic to an understanding of his exposure and reactions to the mass media. Thus, planning for future research on the short-run influencing effects of the mass media must build, first, on the systematic investigation of the everyday processes which influence people and, secondly, on the study of the points of contact between those everyday influences and the mass media.[10]

To this, most researchers even today would say "amen." Unfortunately, too few have chosen to follow the path pointed out by Katz and Lazarsfeld nearly thirty years ago.

THE DECATUR STUDY OF OPINION LEADERS

Leadership comes in many forms. Most visible are official leaders that head formally organized groups—corporations, labor unions, schools, government, clubs, banks, and so on. The leaders are easily identified in any community by their official positions of power and authority. The decisions of these leaders can clearly have an impact on the ebb and flow of the vital social and economic political processes of community life.

But another kind of leadership is far less visible. It is informal and often unwitting. It takes place when people turn to others at their same social level whom they know and trust. They do this because they need advice or interpretations to try to make sense out of some complex situation confronting them. They need to understand the dimensions of the reality before them, so that they can make sensible decisions and act in their own best interests. The others they select as leaders in this process are people like themselves but whom they feel command some special expertise, or possess some special wisdom, regarding the topic about which a decision must be made. When ordinary people make decisions on such matters as to what to believe, purchase, join, avoid, support, like, or dislike, they turn to *opinion leaders* for advice. Often, the opinion leaders' personal influence is both given and received without either party consciously recognizing it as such.

It is this type of informal personal influence that was under investigation in what has come to be called the Decatur Study (after the community in which it was done). As we noted earlier, the research was designed to follow up more systematically the idea of the two-step flow of communication, first noted in the study of the 1940 presidential election in Erie County, Ohio. The research was conducted under the auspices of the Bureau of Applied Social Research of Columbia University. Financial support for the project was supplied by Mcfadden Publications, Inc. (presumably because of its potential implications for advertisers) and the Roper polling organization (presumably because of its implications for understanding the process of opinion formation).

The study focused on the role of opinion leaders as they influenced others in four areas of decision making in day-to-day life. These were (1) *marketing* (where choices must be made regarding foods, household products, and small consumer items); (2) the world of *fashion* (where choices must be made concerning clothing, hair styles, and cosmetics); (3) *public affairs* (a potentially confusing arena of political and social issues in the news, civic activities, and national and local events); and (4) the selection of *movies* to see (again, a multiplicity of choices). In other words, the problem was to determine who influenced whom in these areas where decisions often have to be made, but where there are many potential choices and few clear definitions of objective reality.

The Research Procedures

To locate instances of personal influence regarding these four topics, the research procedures included selecting a suitable community to study, drawing a sample of people to interview (on two separate occasions, once in June and once in August), identifying leaders and followers, and studying the characteristics of each. A fairly unique feature of the research plan was the intention to trace out who had, in a face-to-face manner, influenced whom. In other words the researchers wanted to study opinion leaders who were in actual contact with recipients of their influence on a day-to-day basis. It was not their intention to study persons who might be influential by virtue of their prominent position in the social, political, or business life of the city.

Selecting the Research Site. The financial resources available for the investigation played a key role in dictating the size of the community to be studied. The plan was to maintain a ratio of no fewer than one interview to every twenty homes in the city. Since 800 interviews were anticipated, this indicated a community with a population of approximately 60,000. The Middle West was chosen as a region within which to locate such a community, on the grounds that this part of the country was generally less characterized by sectional peculiarities. The problem, therefore, was to locate the most "typical" communities in the Middle West which were of the required population size.

First, all cities in the range 50,000 to 80,000 located in Ohio, Michigan, Indiana, Illinois, Wisconsin, Iowa, and Kansas were listed for detailed demographic, social, and economic analysis. This search yielded 28 cities. From these, all that were suburban communities dominated by a large city were eliminated. This left 18 potential sites. For each of these, data were assembled on 36 indices relevant to the problem under study. These indices provided key information on population composition, economic status, commercial activities, mass communication usage patterns, and the general quality of community life.

With all of this information at hand it was possible to reduce the list to three cities that deviated the least from the central tendencies (Decatur, Illinois; Terre Haute, Indiana; and Springfield, Indiana). Of the three, Decatur was judged to be the most consistently typical in the clusters of variables thought to be potentially significant to the research goals. As such it was chosen as the site for the research.[11]

The Sample. The authors of *Personal Influence* provide relatively little information about the actual procedures used to develop their original sample. In fact, they provide only the following paragraph:

> Within Decatur, the sample to be interviewed was drawn according to usual probability methods and nothing special need be said about it. Within each household, women residents (not domestic help) age 16 and over were interviewed alternating on successive interviews between older and younger women whenever more than two women occupied the same household.[12]

Elsewhere (p. 335) they indicate that a sample size of 800 was dictated by their financial resources. It is not clear, however, whether this sample size was actually achieved in their first round of interviews (in June) or not. However, it should be kept in mind that the final assembly of data was not simply a compilation of results from a single social survey. As will be made clear, the researchers sought to apply *sociometric* methods to their research by tracing out who claimed to have influenced whom concerning the four topics discussed above.

The Problem of Defining and Locating Personal Influence

This was a pioneering study into a largely unknown territory. Very little was known at the time about what kinds of people influenced others on an informal basis. Therefore, no clear guidelines were available *a priori* concerning the best means to identify informal influentials or to gather quantitative information on instances of opinion leadership. Consequently, several approaches were tried.

Alternative Approaches. Four different strategies were tried to locate opinion leaders and instances of personal influence. One technique was an attempt to identify "generally influential" people who gave advice or interpretations to others on a range of topics. The question was whether opinion leadership was *specific* to a particular topic, or whether people turned to the same individuals more generally. There was some limited evidence that there were general influentials. For example, in the initial interviews, respondents were asked if they regularly turned to a particular person for advice concerning public affairs (a rather general topic). Specifically, the question was asked: "Do you know anyone around here who keeps up with the news and whom you can trust to let you know what is really going on?" About half of the women studied could identify such a person. This varied considerably with age and education. Older, better educated women were more able to identify such a generally influential person. Younger women with less education often could not. Even so, the "generally influential" individuals were for the most part the *husbands* for the married women, *male parents* for the unmarried, and *male friends* for the once married. In fact, women of all categories tended strongly to nominate males as individuals of general competence in public affairs rather than females (about two to one). In any case, this particular strategy was not judged to be especially fruitful for the study of opinion leaders.

Another strategy for defining and locating opinion leaders focused on "specific influentials." This procedure was based on information provided by the two separate interviews with the 800 respondents, in June and again in August. Again using the area of public affairs as an illustration, the women's opinions on nine specific topics of current interest were recorded during the first interview. On the second interview, any *changes* in those opinions were noted. Once these changes had been verified, careful probing was undertaken to determine with whom the respondents had discussed these issues, and if those discussions had been influential in modifying their opinions. This proved to be a fruitful strategy, and some 619 verified opinion changes were identified. The "specific influentials" who had played a key role in each change were nominated by the respondents, providing both empirical instances of personal influence and the names of the opinion leaders. Again, family relationships were paramount, and males played a predominant role.

The third technique tried for studying opinion leadership was a somewhat less complicated effort to identify the "everyday contacts" of the respondents—people with whom they usually talked things over, regardless of the direction of influence. This approach was not particularly fruitful because only about half of the women could identify someone with whom they usually talked things over. Those that did usually nominated a member of their family.

The final technique tried for identifying opinion leaders was *self-designation*. This procedure was the one actually used to generate the main body of data that made up the research report. Self-designation means that the women interviewed were asked whether they had recently been influential to others. This line of questioning was used in both the first and second interviews. For example, the following question was posed for each respondent: "Have you recently been asked for your advice about (one of the four main topics: marketing, fashions, movies, or public affairs)?" If the respondent answered "yes," detailed information was collected regarding who asked for advice, about what, and so forth. In other words, the respondent was asked to identify the exact individual, by name and address, with whom the interaction took place. In this way, instances of opinion leadership were identified both in terms of the persons involved, the direction of the process, and the topic of influence.

The obvious problem with self-designation as a means of identifying and studying opinion leaders and their influence is that it views the process from only one end. There is, in other words, a problem of *validity*. If a person claims to have talked to and influenced another, how can such a claim be verified? Because the researchers had asked their respondents for the names and addresses of those whom they claimed to have influenced, one possible means of verification was to go to those designated and ask for confirmation. In fact, the investigators did obtain some 1549 designations of persons who had sought advice from 693 of their 800 respondents. The intention was to contact all of those designated in order to view the influence process from their end. Unfortunately, many were unavailable during the study period (out of town, and so on). However, some 634 were contacted. Of these, two-thirds confirmed the contact and the topic of the conversation. A fourth could not recall the claimed contact. Between nine and ten percent denied that the conversation ever took place! Overall, then, the question of validity was never answered in a rigorous manner, but at least some confirmations were made, and the researchers were satisfied that self-designation was a realistic strategy for the study of personal influence. The main subjects for the analysis, then, were the 693 "self-detected" opinion leaders.

After looking at all of the types mentioned—the generally influential, specific influentials, everyday contacts, and self-designations, the researchers narrowed their conceptualization of opinion leadership and personal influence. Opinion leaders are people recognized by their peers as having some special competence in a particular subject. People turn to opinion leaders for advice about a specific topic, but usually do not seek them out for their opinions on a range of issues. Personal influence, then, takes place between people in face-to-face settings and concerning rather specific topics.

Opinion Leadership versus Other Influences. A major difficulty in studying the impact of opinion leadership on decisions is to sort it out from other sources of influence. For example, we are all influenced to an unknown degree by mass media advertising in our purchasing consumer goods, household products, or even food at the supermarket. For women, salespeople may play an influential role in the purchase of cosmetics or fashionable clothing. Newspaper ads for movies may be a factor for all of us in selecting a film to attend. In other words, opinion leadership is only one influence in a context of many. Identifying which influence played a predominant role in any particular decision may not always be possible, even for the person who made the choice.

Still, most people can recall whether or not they talked to someone else about a new brand of household cleaner, a new nail polish, or the merits of a particular movie before attending it. They can also assess to a reasonably accurate degree the extent to which these contacts influenced them to adopt the product in question.

The reseachers made an extensive study of the comparative impact on such decisions by personal contacts versus media advertising and salespeople. In the area of marketing, for example, personal contacts with opinion leaders were substantially more effective in prompting marketing shifts than were advertisements in newspapers, radio, or magazines. Salespeople played an even smaller role. But for selecting a motion picture, newspaper ads had a much greater effect than personal contacts. In the world of fashion, by contrast, personal influence played an especially powerful role, although salespeople and magazine ads were also important.

Generally, in the areas of marketing, fashions, and movie selection, the impact of personal influence on people's decisions to change patterns of use, or to adopt something new, was greater than that of the formal media. There were many exceptions to this generalization, and there are undoubtedly many reasons why this tendency was found. Also, opinion leadership does not occur in a vacuum. A person may be exposed to media advertising, the blandishments of salespeople, *and* personal influence from a trusted source. Nevertheless, the data clearly supported the conclusion that opinion leaders were one of the more powerful influences on people's decisions in the marketplace of either consumer products and services or of ideas.

The Characteristics of Opinion Leaders

Who were these 693 "self-detected" opinion leaders?[13] That is, how did they fit into the social life of Decatur? The researchers identified three significant dimensions in the lives of their respondents that were related to the opinion leader role. These factors played a central part in determining *if* a woman was likely to influence others, and if so, with respect to *what*. These dimensions were: (1) position in the "life cycle," (2) position on the community's socioeconomic ladder, and (3) the extent of the individual's social contacts. These three factors provided a convenient framework within which to describe and analyze the flow of interpersonal influence concerning the four topics under study.

Position in the Life Cycle. The classifications used to describe this dimension identify clusters of variables that change as the individual moves from one position to another. For example, younger, unmarried women have greater knowledge concerning fashionable clothing, hairstyles, and cosmetics than those whose lives are more centered on homemaking and raising children. By contrast with both groups, older women, whose children have grown, and who have a wide circle of contacts within the community, can be expected to know more of public affairs and community issues. Position in the life cycle, in other words, raises the probability of being knowledgeable about some topics but not others. Familiarity with a topic, and possession of the skills to deal with it effectively, are the foundations of the capacity to exercise personal leadership and be perceived as an effective opinion leader.

The investigators identified four life cycle classifications into which they could categorize the opinion leaders identified in their sample (see Table 7.1).

Socioeconomic Status. People at distinctive levels in a community are characterized by differences in education, prestige, and income. These may be important factors in determining whether or not they will be sought out as sources for interpretation and advice. An important question for this research on opinion leaders was whether personal influence travels up, down, or laterally among such community social strata. To address this issue, the researchers divided their sample into three categories—high, middle, and low status—with about one-third in each. This was done on the basis of years of education, and amount of rent paid (as an indicator of economic level).[14]

Social Contacts. The woman with limited social contacts has few opportunities to exercise personal influence. The one who regularly interacts with many people will have more opportunities to serve as an opinion leader. To test this

TABLE 7.1. DISTRIBUTION OF LIFE CYCLE TYPES IN THE SAMPLE

Girls (single women, under 35)	12%
Small Family Wives (married, under 45, with one or no children)	26
Large Family Wives (married, under 45, with two or more children)	25
Matrons (married, over 45, most of whose children are older than 15)	37
	100%
	N = 693

Source: Elihu Katz and Paul F. Lazarsfeld, *Personal Influence* (Glencoe, Ill.: The Free Press of Glencoe, 1955) p. 225.

TABLE 7.2. DISTRIBUTION OF SAMPLE BY SOCIAL ACTIVITY

		Number of Friendships	
		high	*low*
Number of } organizations }	high	27%	14%
	low	31%	28%

Source: Elihu Katz and Paul F. Lazarsfeld, *Personal Influence* (Glencoe, Ill.: The Free Press of Glencoe, 1955) p. 228.

idea, the researchers constructed a simple index of *gregariousness*. It was based on: (1) the number of persons in the community the subject claimed to be "friendly with and talk with fairly often" and (2) the number of organizations and clubs to which she belonged.[15]

Information on these kinds of social contacts provided a relatively simple classification pattern. A subject who claimed seven or more friends and belonged to at least one organization was placed in the high category. At the other end, a subject with no organization memberships and few friends were placed in the low category. These subjects were then cross-classified into the four categories shown in Table 7.2.

These three factors, life cycle, socioeconomic status, and gregariousness, were found to be related in many complex ways among the women in the sample. Summarized briefly, the more important of these relationships were as follows:

1. High gregariousness increases with life cycle progression.
2. Girls (as defined by the authors) tend to score medium in gregariousness. They belong to fewer organizations but have many friends.
3. Lower socioeconomic status women tend to be low in gregariousness.

The significance of these three factors appears to lie in their power, either singly or in combination, to shape a woman's interest in certain life areas. They place her at different points in the social structure and limit or expand her contact with others in the community.

THE FINDINGS

The four topics of personal influence chosen for study were everyday concerns in the life of Decatur: what to buy for the family, how to select from the world of fashions, what movie choices to make, and what to believe or decide regarding public events and issues. The three characteristics discussed in the previous section were used as a framework to follow the flow of personal influence from different types of opinion leaders to those who sought their advice and interpretation on these four topics.

Marketing Leaders

The researchers found that the women in their sample often consulted each other for opinions about new products, the quality of different brands, and shopping economies. In fact, about half of the respondents interviewed in the June and August efforts reported making some kind of change from a product or brand that they had regularly used to something new. Opportunities for personal influence in this area were abundant. The task was to study how this influence flowed from one type of person to another. The analysis of who influenced whom in marketing decisions was made in terms of social status, life cycle, and gregariousness, in that order.

The Horizontal Flow of Marketing Leadership. There was little reason to assume that higher social status women were more skilled at marketing. A "trickle down" effect was a possibility, with higher prestige making advice seem more significant. However, an examination of the proportion of the women at each status level who claimed to have provided marketing advice did not support the trickle down concept. Marketing opinion leaders were found more or less equally at all status levels: Among the high social status women, some 27 percent claimed to have given marketing advice. The figures for middle and low social status respondents were 24 and 21 percent respectively (differences not statistically significant). In other words, high status did not seem to increase a woman's chances to serve as an opinion leader in any significant way. Generally, according to the authors, the flow of marketing influence was *horizontal*. They explained it in the following terms:

> . . . it is more reasonable to expect that marketing influence is confined within the boundaries of each of the several social strata than it is [to assume] a random exchange conducted without regard for status differences. Seeking out a woman of like status for advice means seeking out a woman with similar budgetary problems and limitations. That is one major reason why we may expect that traffic in marketing is a status-bound activity. Secondly, since stores and shopping centers are likely to cater somewhat more to women of one status than another—by design or because of location or the

like—women are more likely to encounter status peers during their marketing activities than to encounter status unequals.[16]

This generalization was confirmed in some degree by comparing the status levels of both the giver of advice and the receiver in those cases where both could be established. Unfortunately, such information was available for less than half of the cases where follow-up interviews were attempted to verify the self-designations of opinion leaders (see p. 173). Although these data have many limitations, they appear to show that "influences turn to influentials of their own status level much more often than they turn to those of other statuses."[17] Where crossovers in status levels did occur, they were just as likely to go up as down. In short, personal influence in marketing appears to take place horizontally, in other words, between people at the same general status level.

Life Cycle and Marketing Leadership. The researchers anticipated that position in the life cycle would be an especially important factor in marketing leadership. Unmarried, younger women with no children would be unlikely sources for consultation about products related to family meal preparation, child rearing, or household domestic tasks. Older women, most of whose children had grown, might have had years of experience in marketing. However, their current responsibilities are more limited. Therefore, they were not expected to be the dominant category. The category with the heaviest current responsibilities and daily experience in marketing matters would be *large family wives*, and the data strongly supported the speculation that they would be most sought for advice. In fact, 38 percent of the large family wives claimed that they had served as marketing opinion leaders. The comparable figures were 23 percent for small family wives, 20 percent for girls, and 16 percent for matrons.

A second question is whether these large family wives mainly influenced each other, or whether their personal influence flowed disproportionately to the other categories. The study provided only limited data on this issue. The authors were able to conclude only that women of age 25–44 seemed to influence women somewhat younger or somewhat older than themselves. This included both small and large family wives. While not conclusive by any means, such information offers minor support for the conclusion that active homemakers offered marketing influence disproportionately to younger single women and older matrons.

Gregariousness and Marketing. Here the findings were very clear. At all status levels and in all life cycle positions, the women with more social contacts were the most influential in marketing. Among those classified as high in gregariousness, 33 percent had offered marketing advice. The corresponding figures for the other categories were 25 percent for those of medium gregariousness and 13 percent for those classified as low. These are statistically significant differences and they imply a clear positive relationship between gregariousness and marketing leadership.

Fashion Leaders

Fashion is an area of constant change. Keeping up with change in just the right sequence is the essence of being fashionable. Some two-thirds of the women in the sample had made some sort of change in fashion between their two major interviews. The problem was to discover what the role of opinion leaders of various kinds had been in influencing those changes.

Fashions and the Life Cycle Position. The factor that proved to be most important in fashions was life cycle position, the same factor that had played a central role in marketing. In fashions, however, it was the "girls" who provided the greatest amount of influence. In terms of the four life cycle categories, there were considerable differences in the proportions who claimed to have offered advice to others on fashions (see Table 7.3). Clearly, fashion leadership declined with each step in the life cycle. The authors explained this progression in terms of a rather traditional interpretation of women's roles:

> According to this view, marriage, as the realization of one goal of fashion participation, would be associated with a decrease in fashion activities and leadership; motherhood, as a competing interest and activity, would also be accompanied by a further decrease in such fashion leadership; and matronhood, which for most women involves a withdrawal from youth-oriented competitiveness, should be associated with least fashion advice giving.[18]

In other words, the authors saw attention to fashion as a means of catching a man. Once a male was landed, however, women were likely to increasingly forget fashion matters and concentrate more on their children. Later, they would lose even the little interest they might have left. This is obviously a very old-fashioned view by today's standards.

Whatever the reasons, the younger single women were the most active as

TABLE 7.3. PERCENT WHO OFFERED FASHION INFLUENCE BY LIFE CYCLE POSITION

Girls	48%
Small Family Wives	31
Large Family Wives	18
Matrons	14

Source: Elihu Katz and Paul F. Lazarsfeld, *Personal Influence* (Glencoe, Ill.: The Free Press of Glencoe, 1955) p. 248.

opinion leaders in the area of fashion. The "girls" were well ahead of the others in such matters as cosmetics, hairstyles, and fashionable clothing. They had made more purchases and showed a considerably greater propensity to change. They were also the greatest "exporters" of fashion advice. That is, they not only talked to each other about fashion matters but were the strongest influences on the other categories of women.

Gregariousness and Fashion Leadership. As was the case in marketing, gregariousness was an important factor in fashion leadership. In fact, there was a very similar pattern of positive association between gregariousness and influence. For the high category on gregariousness, 29 percent claimed to have offered fashion advice. The corresponding figures for the medium and low categories were 23 percent and 15 percent respectively. These different rates appear to have occurred for much the same reason in fashions as they did in marketing: The socially active have more opportunities to offer advice to a broader range of recipients. Also, gregarious women at all social levels and in all life cycle positions were more *interested* in fashion matters than their more reclusive counterparts. Presumably, then, there is a link between more intensive social activity and more intensive interest in fashion, leading to offering more advice, regardless of other life circumstances.

Status and Fashions. Most people assume a relationship between being fashionable and being high in socioeconomic status. The stereotype of the wealthy and glamorous woman is well established in our culture. This, however, was not what the investigators had in mind when they probed into a possible link between social status in Decatur and serving as a source of advice on fashions. They anticipated that there would be a positive relationship between the two variables, but not a concentration of leadership at the top.

What they discovered was that there was no such concentration. There were as many fashion leaders among the women of middle status as among those at the high level. On the other hand, women low in status played a much more minor role in distributing fashion advice. For examples, among those in the high category, 26 percent claimed to have served as sources for influence on fashions. The middle category claimed the same figure, 26 percent. Only 16 percent of those in the low category claimed to have offered personal influence on fashions.

To summarize the flow of fashion influence, it is dependent most of all on life cycle position. The younger, single women were much more active as fashion opinion leaders. Gregariousness was also important. Status made little difference, unless one was low in this factor. It was the young, socially active women with high status that had the most influence. Older women who were less active socially and of low status had virtually no influence on fashion at all.

Public Affairs Leaders

Katz and Lazarsfeld made their analysis of public affairs opinion leaders on the basis of several assumptions about the role of women in such matters:

> Without endangering their self-respect or the respect of others, women can, to a greater extent than men, get through life without participating in, or having opinions about, public affairs. Much more often than men, women express ignorance about current national and local events and issues; they talk less about these matters, and, when asked directly about their interest in politics and specific political events, they claim less interest than men.[19]

In other words, women of the time tended to be seen but not heard! Obviously, times have changed, but these conditions appear to have been present in Decatur at the time of the study in the immediate postwar years. Thus, findings in this area need to be interpreted within such a framework. In any case, the three factors—social status, gregariousness, and life cycle position—once again provided the principal framework for analysis.

Status and Public Affairs Leadership. The investigators reasoned that the factors that would lead their subjects to participate actively in the arena of public affairs would be contacts with politically active people (mainly males), level of education, and enough leisure time to pursue extrahousehold activities. These are obviously associated with high social status in a community like Decatur. For this reason, the researchers hypothesized that there would be a positive association between socioeconomic status and opinion leadership in the area of public affairs.

Their prediction was clearly supported. First, there were fewer women who were opinion leaders in public affairs than in the other areas studied, and those women tended to be concentrated in the high social status level. Among high status women, 19 percent claimed to have provided personal influence on some aspect of public affairs. For the middle and low status categories, the figures were 12 percent and 6 percent, respectively.

Following up their assumption that women were generally inactive in public affairs, the authors asked women who had been influenced to identify their sources of influence. Generally, the answer that they received was *men:*

> Unlike marketing and fashions, the public affairs arena is one in which men play an important role in influencing opinions and attitudes. Almost two-thirds of the persons named by the respondents as having influenced their opinion changes were men.[20]

These influences from men were likely to come from members of the family. In other words, husbands and fathers were the principal public affairs influentials for these subjects, rather than other women.

Gregariousness and Public Affairs Leadership. There is little doubt that women who have numerous social contacts offer more advice on public affairs than those who are less gregarious. Among those classified as high on this factor, 20 percent claimed to have offered personal influence on some aspect of public affairs. Among the medium category, the figure was 11 percent, and among those low in gregariousness, only 4 percent claimed to have been influential.

Gregariousness and status level were found to be associated, and both were factors in predicting opinion leadership. However, statistically controlling for gregariousness in the analysis did not account for the variations in the proportion of public affairs leadership at each status level. In other words, gregariousness and status were independent variables, but gregariousness was the more important.

Life Cycle Position and Public Affairs. The authors noted that women who are busy with housekeeping and child rearing may not be active in public affairs. This would suggest a dominant role for the "girls." On the other hand, younger people generally take less interest in public affairs than those who are more mature. This meant that there were contradictory factors at work, making prediction difficult.

The data showed a rather weak association between life cycle stage and public affairs leadership. The proportion who claimed to have influenced others on public issues declined somewhat with each stage: For girls, the figure was 17 percent; small family wives, 13 percent; large family wives, 10 percent; and matrons, 8 percent. Such a trend suggests an inverse relationship between age (and life cycle stage) and informal influence in public affairs.

In summarizing the flow of influence on public affairs, the authors noted the following: The public affairs leaders among these women were different from those who were influential in marketing or fashions. Life cycle was somewhat less important. On the other hand, social status, which is almost unimportant in marketing leadership, and which is only marginally related to fashions, is a key factor here. Gregariousness is also related to being influential. Generally, the most influential women were the better educated and more affluent, who had many social contacts in the community. Even so, most personal influence on public affairs issues came from men.

Movie Selection Leaders

At the time the data were gathered, Americans went to the movies far more often than they do now. Television had not yet entered every home. Some 60 percent of the respondents said that they went to the movies at least once a month. The analysis of personal influence on movie selections was confined to this segment of the total sample.

From their earliest days, movies have had a special appeal to youth. This was certainly true in Decatur: Among the youngest category of subjects, those under 25, two-thirds went to the movies once a week or more! About half of those 25–34 went to the movies once a week or more. For those 35–44 the figure was about one-third. Among those 45 or older, less than a fifth went that often. In other words, moviegoing was clearly related to age and it was far more popular than it is now.

These data led the investigators to anticipate that it would be the younger women in their sample, the girls, who would be highest in opinion leadership in movie selection. We will see that this was clearly the case. However, gregariousness and socioeconomic status offered further guides to understanding the findings.

The "Youth Culture" and Movie Leadership. The influence of life cycle position on this form of opinion leadership was especially clear. This reflects the central role of motion pictures in the lives of the young people of the time. Among the girls, 58 percent claimed to have influenced others on movie choices, a very high figure. For small family wives the figure was 23 percent; large family wives, 27 percent; and for matrons, 16 percent. For the single women, then, movies with friends were an important form of recreation and dating.

Movie Leadership and Gregariousness. Here, a pattern emerged that was rather distinct from those of other areas. It was not those with the largest number of social contacts that were most influential. There was no clear relationship between gregariousness and personal influence on movie choices. Those subjects classified as medium in gregariousness claimed to have provided the most opinion leadership (32 percent) on movie selections. Those who were high and low were quite similar, with 26 percent and 24 percent, respectively.

The investigators tried to interpret these findings by noting that going to the movies is an activity that is almost always shared by others. People go to the movies with friends and members of their families but seldom alone. The selection of a movie takes place within a complex social process involving other people, namely family and friends. Whether one belongs to clubs and has a wide circle of acquaintances may make little difference on how a motion picture is selected.

Socioeconomic Status and Movie Influence. As in the case of gregariousness, status did not seem to be a factor in providing personal influence on movie selection. This was probably the case because people at all levels in Decatur went to the movies rather frequently. About 25 percent of the women at each level claimed that they had offered advice to others regarding a movie. Within each of the status levels, however, it was the young unmarried women who played the dominant role.

In summary, moviegoing in Decatur was an important part of the youth culture. At all status levels and among shy as well as socially active people it was the young single individuals who gave the most advice.

CONCLUSIONS AND IMPLICATIONS

The two-step flow hypothesis, first identified as a result of the study of the 1940 presidential election, provided an important turning point in the development of theory and research in mass communication. The hypothesis as first formulated said merely that "ideas often flow *from* radio and print *to* opinion leaders and *from* them to less active sections of the population."[21] In retrospect this seems like a simple idea; yet it was overlooked for decades. However, when attention was finally focused on this secondary movement of information and influence through interpersonal networks among members of the audience, it changed thinking about the process of mass communication forever. No longer could mass communication be thought of solely in terms of a stimulus–response framework in which the media were on one side and members of the audience on the other, with little in between.

This new way of thinking was badly needed at the time. The accumulated findings of mass communication research at the time of the Decatur study were not providing support for the idea of simple, immediate, and direct effects that were produced by stimulation from mass-communicated messages. It was time to look for more indirect effects that were produced over a longer span of time by more complex processes. It was *Personal Influence* that opened up this avenue of research. It tried to explore "the part played by people" in the social flow of information and influence from media to mass.

The Decatur study can be faulted on many grounds if the standards of contemporary research are imposed. Its measurements, statistical analyses, sampling techniques, and verification procedures have clear limitations, to say the least. In addition, the goals of the research were never made clear from a conceptual point of view. For example, although much was made of the "flow" idea, the study did not trace the actual movement of ideas from the media to those who were identified as opinion leaders and on to the individuals that they influenced. The authors appear to have set out to do this but they had to give up (mainly for lack of resources). Thus, when one woman in their sample claimed to have influenced another about nail polish, canned soup, or an issue in the community, it is not at all clear that this actually represented some type of flow from a mass medium to an audience. The strategy of interviewing in April, then returning some months later to look for changes, was not adequate to the task. The researchers should have focused on specific media content (e.g., advertising messages or public affairs presentations) and then traced them from opinion leaders through interpersonal networks to study the two-step flow as it actually took place.

In spite of these criticisms, based on 20/20 hindsight, the Decatur study is one of the milestones in mass communication research. Earlier research had concentrated on individual differences characterizing the people who made up the audiences for mass communication and how those differences shaped their psychological and overt responses to the media. A little later, there was a shift to the study of social category memberships among members of the audience, and how these influenced patterns of attention and response. *Personal Influence* represented the first clear and intensive focus on social relationships and their role in the mass communication process. The ties between people were seen as the most important factors, rather than the structure of the message stimulus, the perceived characteristics of the communicator, or the psychological make-up of the receiver, in significantly shaping the mass communication process.

We noted earlier that in its analysis of the findings from small-groups research of the time, the research report clearly identified the meaning functions of primary groups, an idea which is an important part of the meaning theory of mass media portrayals (Chapter 1) that has only recently moved to center stage in thinking about media effects.[22] More important, the Decatur Study, and the two-step flow idea generally, set off significant new directions of research in the adoption of innovation, the diffusion of the news, and the study of distortions in interpersonal communication.

Perhaps most important of all, the influences of the media studied in *Personal Influence* seem a far cry from the powerful effects feared by those who saw the media as the ultimate agents of evil—or for that matter the powerful effects of those who thought the media would be the means of salvation of modern democracy. The influences investigated were minor, difficult to detect, and completely nonthreatening. The study not only failed to confirm the validity of the legacy of fear, it went a long way toward making the idea look quite unrealistic.

NOTES AND REFERENCES

1. Charles Horton Cooley, *Social Organization* (New York: Charles Scribners and Sons, 1909), pp. 80–90.
2. Joseph T. Klapper, *The Effects of the Mass Media* (Glencoe, Ill.: The Free Press of Glencoe, 1960).
3. Bernard Berelson, "The State of Communication Research," *Public Opinion Quarterly*, 1, 23, Spring 1959, 1–17.
4. Charles Horton Cooley, op. cit., pp. 23–31.
5. Fritz J. Rothlisberger and William J. Dickson, *Management and the Worker* (Cambridge, Mass.: Harvard University Press, 1939). See also: Elton Mayo, *Human Problems in an Industrial Civilization* (New York: The Viking Press, 1966); first published in 1933.
6. W. Lloyd Warner and Paul S. Lunt, *The Social Life of a Modern Community*, Vol. I, Yankee City Series (New Haven: Yale University Press, 1941).

7. Samuel A. Stauffer et al., *The American Soldier: Studies in Social Psychology in World War Two*, Vols. I and II (Princeton, N.J.: Princeton University Press, 1948).

8. Kurt Lewin and Paul Grabbe, "Conduct, Knowledge, and Acceptance of New Values," *Journal of Social Issues*, Vol 1, No. 3, 1948, 53–64.

9. Melvin L. De Fleur and Everette E. Dennis, *Understanding Mass Communication* (Boston: Houghton Mifflin, 1981).

10. Elihu Katz and Paul F. Lazarsfeld, *Personal Influence: The Part Played by People in the Flow of Mass Communication* (Glencoe, Ill.: The Free Press of Glencoe, 1955), p. 133.

11. Ibid., p. 137.

12. Ibid., pp. 335–338.

13. The exact number of the original interviewees who served as opinion leaders is a bit difficult to pin down. The figure 693 is the largest N of any of the tables appearing in the analysis (p. 225). In other places different and smaller Ns are given.

14. No indication was given as to how home owners, who pay no rent, were handled.

15. Ibid., p. 227.

16. Ibid., p. 236.

17. Ibid.

18. Ibid., p. 248.

19. Ibid., p. 271.

20. Ibid., p. 276.

21. Paul F. Lazarsfeld, Bernard Berelson, and Hazel Gaudet, *The People's Choice* (New York: Columbia University Press, 1948), p. 151. This is an earlier report than the one cited in Chapter 4.

22. Katz and Lazarsfeld, op cit., pp. 53–56.

8

Project Revere: The Quality and Pathways of Message Diffusion

As the 1950s began, it became increasingly clear that World War II had not resolved the major political differences among the powerful nations of the world. If anything, the defeat of Germany and Japan had simply moved forward in time the point at which the political philosophies of the Soviet Union and China would confront those of the United States and its allies in a global struggle for power, even though they had all fought together to defeat the Axis powers. In the end it led to the cold war and the possibility of nuclear holocaust. Thus, the first half of the twentieth century ended with an uneasy confrontation between democracy, communism, and the remnants of fascism. But for the ordinary people in the United States there was no such global perspective—only a frustrated feeling of *déjà vu* as once more American soldiers battled an Asian enemy.

The Korean conflict was very different from World War II in a number of respects. It had not caught the nation off guard and unprepared militarily. The United States had a large fleet left over from the earlier war. It had an adequate number of well-trained combat divisions equipped with modern weapons. Above all, it had a large and aggressive Air Force. The country had emerged from the second world war as the most powerful nation on earth, and it took on a peacekeeping mission that was worldwide in scope. Its so-called containment policy, forged by John Foster Dulles, was to keep the Soviet Union and China, as well as their satellite countries, surrounded by coalitions of allied forces. Therefore, when North Korea invaded South Korea and challenged that policy, President Truman felt that intervention was essential.

But whatever their causes or labels, wars are not won by force of arms alone. In every war, ancient or modern, the beliefs, attitudes, and loyalties of the participants—whether military or civilian—have had a critical role in the outcome. Such factors have strong influences on motivations, decisions, and actions that can sometimes shape victory or defeat. Military leaders understand these issues very well, and they try to use whatever persuasive communications they can to shape people's behavior to the best advantage. The use of propaganda in wartime can be clumsy and a waste of time. However, if on occasion propaganda can reduce the efficiency of the enemy by only a fraction of 1 percent, it can be effective. Under the right circumstances, the right message delivered to the right people at the right time can profoundly alter the course of a conflict.

It was for these reasons that the American forces in Korea were highly interested in communicating with civilian as well as military groups in enemy territory. In fact, they used every opportunity to deliver a great variety of messages to North Korean communities, military units, and rural populations. Most of these messages were designed to bring to a target population information that could serve as the basis for changes in beliefs, modifications of opinions and attitudes, reductions in motivations, and a weakening of loyalties.

Most of the time it didn't work! For one thing, when one is trying to communicate on a large scale with an enemy population, there are a limited number of ways to do so. Obviously, one has no access to the usual mass media. Under such closed conditions, one alternative is to broadcast to the relevant population from the outside and hope that someone is listening. But this can be very ineffective where people have few receivers, where those receivers that exist must be operated clandestinely, or where there is little motivation on the part of potential listeners to tune in. All these conditions prevailed in North Korea. About the only medium left under such circumstances is the airborne leaflet.

LEAFLETS AS A MEDIUM OF LAST RESORT

Leaflets are pieces of paper containing print, photographs, or drawings. They are a primitive device for communicating to people, but if they can be delivered in large numbers with messages that can be readily understood by the recipients, they can provide a significant channel for communication. Leaflets have been used ever since the printing press has been around. They have a long history in politics as well as in war. They remain a significant medium in countries that control their media as a means of limiting dissent, and they are being used every day in countries around the world for a variety of reasons and causes, especially where power and authority are being challenged.

American forces distributed about three million leaflets during World War I. This figure rose to about three *billion* during World War II. Additional billions were used during the Korean conflict. They have been used in all subsquent military operations. One of their more effective uses in wartime settings has been in the form of "surrender passes" for enemy troops who want to give up but are afraid of being killed. The official-looking "passes" delivered over enemy areas in large numbers can be effective, on occasion, in triggering surrenders. Leaflets have had other successes. In 1945, airborne leaflets delivered on a massive scale to the Japanese population, in conjunction with both conventional and atomic bombing, probably shortened that war somewhat by convincing people that further resistance was unrealistic. In spite of their occasional successes, leaflets have clear limitations. If other more usual ways of communicating are available, almost any other medium would probably be more efficient. Still, when other channels are *not* available, as in wartime or during periods of political repression, this primitive device may be the only means by which information can be delivered to large numbers of people.

A major problem with leaflets as a medium is that their limitations and capacities are poorly understood. Almost no scientific research has been done on their effectiveness as a communication medium. Controlled studies of communication to hostile populations are not possible during wartime. Impressions of their effectiveness can sometimes be gained by interviewing prisoners who have seen propaganda leaflets or who have used surrender passes. However, these impressions are limited at best. What is needed is more systematic information about who will pick up leaflets, under what conditions, who will read them, pass on their messages to others, or comply with requests for action. These questions need to be answered not only for war, but under more peaceful conditions. Generalizations are needed about how leaflets can be used to provide vital information in *any* situation where the normal channels of communication are not available.

With this lack of knowledge in mind, the U.S. Air Force made a decision to learn more about the communication efficiency of airborne leaflets as a mass medium. It sought a research contractor who would design and conduct investigations into the use of airborne leaflets as a means of communicating simple messages to civilian populations: a contractor who would not necessarily answer all possible questions about leaflets when used under all possible circumstances, but who would at least provide a beginning point, seeking basic generalizations about the advantages, capacities, and limitations of leaflets when studied under controlled conditions.

Responding to this challenge was a group of sociologists at the University of Washington under the leadership of Stuart C. Dodd. This group agreed to make the studies over a three-year period. The overall program was called *Project Revere* (after the well-known American patriot). It is a series of studies conducted between 1951 and 1953. The series had the common purpose of investigating some aspect of the problem of disseminating information by airborne leaflets, including the spread of information from these printed sources by word-of-mouth to other segments of the population who did not directly see them first hand.

PROJECT REVERE

The climate of opinion on American campuses during the early 1950s concerning the merits of the military establishment, and the wisdom of responding to its research needs, was far different from the case during the Vietnam years. In the early 1950s, large numbers of World War II veterans were in school because of the G.I. Bill. Many were working on graduate degrees. These young scholars respected the military services, thought that they were important, and felt it was patriotic to assist them. It was in this climate of opinion that Project Revere was designed and conducted. Those responsible for specific studies in the series had all seen active service in the Navy, Army, or Marines. The military-related research appeared to them an opportunity to conduct studies on complex communication issues and to help their country at the same time.

The Air Force laid down few restrictions on what should be done and their emphasis was on basic research rather than practical problems or wartime applications. The fact is, the Air Force left it to the research team to formulate the problem, design the means of addressing it, and sort out the implications of the findings. The only requirement was that the researchers try to find out more about leaflets as a device for communication. In an era before large-scale federal government grants became widely available, the third of a million (1950s) dollars allocated to the research provided an almost unprecedented opportunity. The researchers noted this at the time:

> To social scientists characteristically working on meager budgets it seems somewhat incredible that a group of researchers would have placed at its disposal almost unlimited funds for the purpose of deliberately conducting research into basic problems of communication without the insistence that practical problems were of importance. Yet, this is the context within which the present research was carried out. The United States Air Force felt that a truly practical research program into communication problems would be one that had long range aims. They recognized that the development of a full understanding of communication procedures requires first of all a good understanding of fundamentals.[1]

The research program was complex and included many separate studies. These investigations were completed in settings that included towns, grade schools, universities, colleges, large urban centers, housing projects, boys' camps, small groups, and communities struck by disaster. The central objective in these wide-ranging investigations was to gain knowledge about the leaflet as a medium of communication.

Leaflets can be delivered in a number of ways, openly or clandestinely, depending on the situation of the area. Most frequently in modern times large-scale leaflet operations have depended upon distribution from aircraft. Airborne delivery is, of course, a chancy proposition at best. In addition to the vagaries of the elements—wind, weather, terrain—it is difficult to predict who will pick up a leaflet and what they will do with it once they have it. With luck, the leaflet will arrive at the relevant site in good condition, be picked up by a member of the intended audience, read, and passed on to other appropriate individuals. With even more luck, this will stimulate some form of desired action.

Sometimes the process works; usually it does not. In some respects, this is a problem with all mass-communicated messages. Newspapers, magazines, film producers, and broadcasting stations have only limited control over their intended audiences. Exactly who will receive what and how this will influence them remain questions for every attempt at communication, no matter what the medium. The unknowns, however, seem far greater for leaflets than for other kinds of media.

The only advantages that leaflets have over other media were noted earlier. They can be distributed to target populations under circumstances where other media do not exist, are inoperative, or are forbidden. And in spite of their small size, they do provide a permanent record that can be read or reviewed in secret and at the reader's own pace. With the use of pictures, maps, cartoons, diagrams, or symbols of authority, a leaflet can deliver both verbal and nonverbal messages in a relatively straightforward manner.

Under some circumstances, leaflets can stimulate significant action. For example, under wartime conditions leaflets have been used to warn civilian populations of forthcoming heavy bombing raids on particular targets. This has sometimes resulted in mass evacuations, with consequent disruption of the enemy's transportation routes and production facilities. In nonwar settings, leaflets can be used as an emergency medium to warn people of hazards, provide directions, indicate safe evacuation routes, or indicate that help is on the way. In a situation of political repression or occupation by hostile forces, even crudely printed leaflets delivered by any means possible can provide a last-resort medium of communication. In spite of their simplicity, then, leaflets can be a significant mass medium under certain conditions.

The use of leaflets in Project Revere was in the context of civilian populations and their role in emergency conditions. No attempt was made to use leaflets to communicate propaganda messages in the usual meaning of that term, or to use them under the stress of wartime, or during politically disruptive conditions.

The Coffee Slogan Experiment

The investigators quickly became aware that research on the spread of a message through a population via leaflets involved the study of two distinct processes. The first was getting the message designed, printed, and delivered into the hands of at least some segment of the intended audience. The delivery would presumably ensure that at least some part of the relevant population had read and understood the message. The second process was to get the initial receivers not only to read the message but to give leaflets to others, or at least to *tell* others what they had learned: to get the initial receivers, in other words, to pass on the message by word-of-mouth. Broadly speaking, these two processes can be thought of as *message delivery* (to the target population) and *interpersonal message diffusion* (through the target population).

To provide initial information on message delivery, 55,000 airborne leaflets were dropped on Salt Lake City, Utah. Both face-to-face and telephone interviews were conducted in the drop zones to determine what kinds of people and how many had received a leaflet and if they had understood its message. A mail-back postcard questionnaire was attached to each leaflet. The purpose was to try out the mail-back request to see how compliance was related to a list of social and demographic factors. A similar but much larger study was then conducted in Birmingham, Alabama, where 326,000 airborne leaflets were dropped. The purpose here was to study the mail-back procedure more closely and to try to gain further information on what kinds of people would learn the message, pass on a leaflet to others, or mail back a completed postcard questionnaire.

While much was learned in these preliminary studies about dropping leaflets and assessing the degree to which people obtained information from them, it became increasingly apparent that getting subjects to pass on messages by word-of-mouth was entirely another matter. Generally, it appeared, people would do so only under rather special circumstances that provided adequate motivation. In fact, it became increasingly vexing and frustrating for the researchers as attempt after attempt failed to get people to pass on oral messages.

After a number of abortive attempts to stimulate spontaneous oral message transmission through several different kinds of groups, it was realized that special efforts would be needed to get some sort of message started through an actual community so that its routes by word-of-mouth could be traced. To achieve this objective, and to generate the data needed to identify and study the problems and dimensions of person-to-person message diffusion in a natural (community) setting, a rather elaborate experiment was conceived. The purpose of this unusual experiment was to stimulate a high level of social transmission of a simple message through a community, strongly motivating its residents to pass it on. This would make it possible to study the message's speed, accuracy, and extent of penetration as it spread through the community's word-of-mouth networks.

Stimulating Interpersonal Diffusion. A small and relatively isolated rural community in western Washington State was chosen as the research site. It was a town of just over 1,000 inhabitants, with 249 dwellings included in its city limits and immediate environs. The community was carefully mapped, with the location of every dwelling and place of business plotted. The immediate goals were to start a short message with a sample of the residents, to motivate them strongly to pass the message on to others, and to encourage those who did *not* know the message to learn it. The research team planned to return several days later and interview every household in town. The long-range goal was a detailed study of the social routing through which the message had travelled as it diffused through the community. In other words, the experiment would permit a study of the extent, speed, accuracy, and directions taken by a message started with a limited number of people and spread solely via interpersonal diffusion.[2]

A major problem was to design a simple message that could easily be spread and that could later be traced as it moved from person to person. Another problem was to provide some sort of "cover" for the experiment so that the community residents would see what they were doing as natural and not as part of some study of "human guinea pigs." There was also the problem of motivation; an effective reward had to be attached to the acts of learning the message and passing it on to others.

A happy, if unusual, solution was found to this set of problems. A wholesale coffee distributing company was located that wanted to promote its house brand, called *Gold Shield Coffee*. The company was intrigued with the idea of working with the researchers on the message experiment. Its directors agreed to donate several hundred pounds of their product as rewards in exchange for the advertising exposure they would receive. The researchers and company officials made up a simple six-word slogan: "Gold Shield Coffee; Good as Gold!" This was the message to be passed along.

To stimulate people to learn this message and pass it on to others, the investigators and their interviewer team posed as representatives of the coffee company. They called upon a carefully selected sample of the households in the community, representing 17 percent of the dwellings. Each subject interviewed at these households was given a free pound of coffee and was informed that the company was "trying out a new advertising slogan to see how it would catch on." Each recipient of the coffee read the six-word slogan from a printed card and then repeated it back. These respondents were to serve as "starters" of the message. They were told that the "advertising team" would return in three days with additional coffee to call on *every household in town*. Those that knew the slogan, the interviewers made clear, would receive a free pound of coffee. This would include the starters who were originally taught the slogan, provided that they could remember it three days later.

The coffee reward and the advertising cover turned out to be fortuitous selections. The price of the product had risen sharply about a month before the experiment, and many people in the area were deploring the situation. The free pound of coffee was gratefully received, and the prospect of an additional gift three days later was keenly anticipated. This advertising venture seemed to make sense to the subjects. They had long since become accustomed to both free samples and the sometimes curious antics of the advertising world. The entire community seemed eager to spread the slogan. (Indeed, in many cases while the interviewer was departing the front door of a dwelling the householder could be seen running out the back door to spread the word to a neighbor.)

Nevertheless, the investigators were determined to use every means to get people to pass on the message to others, and accordingly they had prepared an additional way of stimulating interest and providing motivation to spread the message. Late in the day of the first interview, 30,000 airborne leaflets were distributed evenly over the community by a low-flying light plane (with official clearance). These leaflets informed the members of the community about the slogan-spreading venture (but did not reveal the slogan itself). They pointed out that "one out of every five housewives in town already knew the message." The reader was informed that the "advertisers" would return in three days to every household, and that a free pound of coffee would be awarded at each dwelling where the slogan was known. (It should be noted that the news media serving this community had agreed to avoid mentioning the study until after it was completed. This cooperation was excellent.)

With these steps completed, the community was left to its own devices for a three-day period. During this time, the people of the town became very active in spreading the message. The leaflets were widely picked up and distributed, raising curiosity about the mysterious message. The starters were in a position to reward others by passing on the slogan, and they did so with enthusiasm. When the researchers returned three days after the initial contacts, they found an eager community waiting to tell them the message and get their reward. Often, the interviewer was confronted in the street before he or she could even call on the householder. After it was over, it was found that some 84 percent of those interviewed had a recognizable version of the original slogan. A number of others reported incorrect or badly garbled slogans, but they received coffee in any case. In fact, several hundred pounds were given away. The householders were pleased with their rewards; the coffee company was delighted with the relatively inexpensive product exposure; and the Project Revere researchers obtained their badly needed data.

Tracing the Social Pathways. The interpersonal networks through which the slogan spread were carefully traced. This was possible, if laborious, through the use of the aerial photographs, the maps of the dwelling places, the questionnaire data, and the addresses of the respondents. A person who received the message from a starter was identified as being in the *first remove* (from the starter); one who was two stages away from a starter was in the second remove, and so forth. By this means a total of 92 interpersonal networks were reconstructed. (There were 64 two-stage networks; 18 had three stages; there were 5 with four stages; 2 with five stages; and finally, one complex network involved 18 people and six stages.) These networks represented first tellings only; many people in town told the slogan to people who already knew. Overall, during the three-day period, the message travelled repeatedly through the social structure—up, down, and sideways. The only people who *didn't* know the message were social recluses, people who had been out of town, and a few who were retarded, senile, or too ill to be involved.

The Patterns of Message Distortion

It should be emphasized that a major reason for choosing a simple six-word slogan with most words of one syllable was to minimize distortion as the message moved from person to person. One goal in studying the data was to reconstruct the curve showing the proportion of the population which knew the slogan at different points in time. Thus, it was anticipated that distortion of the message would pose few problems, and people who knew the message could easily be distinguished from those who did not.

In spite of these hopes, many inaccuracies crept into the message as it moved along the interpersonal networks of the community. In fact, it soon became apparent that message distortion was a major problem and that the emerging patterns of distortion resembled closely those that had been identified by students of the "rumor" process, for instance, by Barlett in the 1930s and Allport and Postman in the 1940s.[3] In other words, as the number of stages or removes through which the information passed became greater, the message became less and less like the original. It became noticeably shorter; extraneous words crept in; new ideas replaced the original content; and contents from the surrounding culture of the subjects were incorporated. These changes constitute the *embedding pattern* that has been widely found in laboratory-type studies of serial message retelling.[4] The key concepts in these studies are *leveling, sharpening*, and *assimilation*. These patterns described the distortions that occurred in the slogan unusually well.

Leveling. The six-word slogan was frequently shortened as it passed from person to person. Figure 8.1 shows that a fairly high degree of accuracy was retained through the first two removes from the starter. After that, the message deteriorated; the number of words declined sharply. These results raised serious doubts about the accuracy of interpersonal networks as communication channels. Due to the short message that the starters received, and the fact that they were carefully taught its content, the pattern of leveling in this community experiment was not as dramatic as those obtained from laboratory experiments that provide the starters with a wealth of detail, a long message taxing the memory, and freedom to construct the meaning as the individual starter sees fit. Even so, the simple message was leveled to a considerable degree.

Sharpening. Sharpening in rumor experiments occurs when certain details of a message are retained and emphasized as the message is passed along. These details then become the central core of the surviving message in serial retelling. Two somewhat different types of sharpening were noted in the respondents' versions of the six-word slogan. The first can be called *sharpening by selection.* This pattern of message distortion is what Allport and Postman referred to when they defined sharpening as "the selective perception, retention and

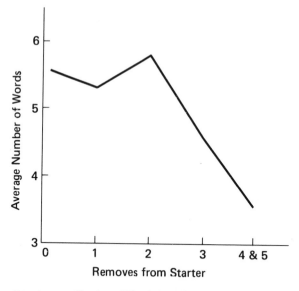

Figure 8.1. Leveling: Average Number of Words from Original Slogan Reported by Each Remove from the Starters.
Source: Melvin L. De Fleur, "Mass Communication and the Study of Rumour," *Sociological Inquiry* 32, 1, Winter 1962, p. 63.

reporting of a limited number of details from a larger context."[5] In the present situation, it means that certain words in the original slogan were retained to become its central ideas whereas others were selectively dropped out as the message moved from person to person. Specifically, the last three words of the slogan, "Good as Gold," tended to survive the retelling process better than the first three. The words "Gold Shield Coffee" frequently dropped out during the leveling process as the number of removes increased. In addition, another form of sharpening identified as selective emphasis was given to certain parts of the message. This was termed *sharpening by intensification*. It is illustrated by the fact that some respondents in their enthusiasm intensified the basic idea of the slogan and reported that (the coffee) was "better than gold," "finer than gold," "pure gold," or even a "pot of gold."

The sharpening pattern, then, was one where the last half of the slogan tended to survive, and in some instances to become intensified by exaggeration as the message diffused through the interpersonal networks. The brand name of the product, and the word "coffee" itself, were both essential to the original idea of the slogan. Nevertheless, they were frequently omitted as the message moved along its social pathways.

Assimilation. Investigators of rumors in laboratory settings have uniformly noted that messages undergoing serial retelling tend to become distorted in accord with the interests, attitudes, cultural norms, or stereotyped expectations of the subjects. Collectively, such forms of distortion are referred to as "assimilation." In other words, extraneous meanings or content are assimilated into the message as it is passed along. The instances of assimilation that occurred in the slogan study were essentially of three types. First, many respondents introduced a word or two into their version of the slogan to make it conform more closely to their verbal habits or to common modes of English speech. Thus, words such as "is as," "it's as," or "is just as" were variants of this practice of adding words to the middle of the slogan. This type of *linguistic* assimilation is frequently found in laboratory studies of serial retelling. For the most part, the proportion of respondents distorting the message in this minor way increased during the first two removes and declined sharply when the slogan became much shorter in the later removes (where such extra words were not relevant).

A second, and more important, type of assimilation is illustrated by respondents who altered the slogan conceptually by substituting or incorporating ideas that they obtained from the culture around them. For example, one person reported that the message was "The coffee that is good to the last drop" (the slogan of another brand). Another individual reported that the message was "The coffee that is *so* good" (an advertising claim of yet another brand). Another form of such *conceptual* assimilation occurred when respondents incorporated into their versions of the slogan ideas commonly associated with the word "gold". Such words as "pot," and "pure" are frequently used in connection with the term "gold" and were thus assimilated to the concept. This type of distortion appeared to be more frequent in later removes.

Finally, another source of distortion was called *assimilation to logical source*. While not strictly a change in message content, it is illustrated by respondents who claimed to have obtained the slogan via the regular mass media, or from some other source. Several persons claimed to have heard it on the radio. Others mentioned newspapers or television. One person reported reading it on a can of coffee. These claims were, of course, without foundation. The only possible source for learning the slogan was other people in the community.

What did these findings imply for the study of leaflets as a means of communicating to large numbers of people? While the results were in no way definitive, they indicated that even a very brief message, diffused under motivational conditions stressing accuracy, became substantially distorted as it moved from person to person. The resulting embedding pattern included leveling, sharpening, and assimilation in a manner closely resembling results obtained from typical laboratory research on rumoring. If the results of this community diffusion experiment can be interpreted as a reasonable guide to what can be expected to happen to information as it moves through the interpersonal networks involved in the "two-step flow" of communication (from a mass medium to a secondary audience), then several implications follow. Those people who are informed by others, as opposed to those who receive direct exposure to the medium, are likely to be poorly informed indeed. The farther they are removed from the person who had direct contact with the medium, the more inaccurate the information they receive is likely to be. The individual at the end of a chain of tellers and retellers is likely to receive a version of the message that is substantially shorter, and which has been selectively edited and distorted in accord with prevailing verbal habits, cultural themes, and stereotypes.

When mass communication depends heavily upon word-of-mouth diffusion to extend its range of contact, a low degree of fidelity to the original content is likely to prevail. These truncated or highly distorted messages are likely to be of limited utility in attempts to achieve propaganda goals or even to transmit simple instructions in times of emergency. What this social diffusion experiment told the researchers of Project Revere was the *first-hand contact with the medium itself is essential in achieving accurate communication*. It was for this reason that further experiments were deemed necessary to find the most effective way to get leaflets directly into the hands of their intended recipients. In other words, interpersonal message diffusion was undoubtedly important, but direct message delivery—getting a leaflet to its intended audience member was even more important.

THE REPETITION EXPERIMENT

A major experiment was designed to try to determine how to use leaflets efficiently. Stated simply, how many leaflets per person in the intended audience does it take to insure that the message will be learned by a given percent of the recipients? Obviously, using too few would not result in a satisfactory level of communication. On the other hand, oversaturation might have various negative effects and achieve less in getting the message across than an optimum number. Although in the Project Revere research this issue was studied in the context of airborne leaflets, it is clearly a problem with many kinds of communications. For example, how often should an advertising message be repeated in order to maximize its influence on a given category of consumers? How often should a charity appeal be presented; or how frequently should an idea be presented in an educational setting? There are obviously a host of other considerations in these questions; the personality characteristics of the receivers, their cultural milieux, and the relationship between the factors and the content of the message remain paramount. But no message, no matter how closely related to the interests, values, and motivations of its audience, can achieve its effect if it is not perceived accurately and fully by the largest proportion of its intended recipients.

Instead of proceeding by trial and error blindly to study the question of message repetition versus level of response, the Project Revere researchers felt that it would be better to develop a *formal theory*. It was hoped that a formal theory would predict the relationship between the frequency of message presentation and the proportion of the intended audience who would learn its content.

The basis for a formal theory was found in the much-studied relationships between stimulus intensity and response from the field of classical psychophysics. Work on this problem began during the mid-nineteenth century. The purpose was to understand the relationship between the external world of stimuli and the internal or subjective world of sensations. For the purposes of developing the needed theory, it was postulated that any message transmitted over any medium can be regarded as a *stimulus* intended to elicit some form of desired *response*. This stimulation can be presented to a responding audience in varying intensities, either by presenting it more frequently or in greater volume. In the case of leaflets, increasing the sheer number dropped on a given group can be regarded as one method of increasing the intensity of stimulation toward the desired response of knowing the message or taking some action proposed by it. The development of an equation, a formally derived hypothesis, stating this relationship between communication stimulus intensity and amount of group response was the next step.

Stimulus Intensity versus Response

There had been little systematic investigation dealing with quantitative stimulus–response relationships in leaflet communication. Hertz had summarized problems of measuring response to propaganda leaflets during wartime, but this literature was of little help.[6] A review of literature for the twenty-five years prior to Project Revere revealed a few studies of other media where variations in stimulus intensity were studied in relation to response, but most of these dealt with advertising messages and were characterized by contradictory findings.[7] In other words, it was necessary to begin from scratch.

Any discussion of stimulus intensity and response automatically brings to mind the sensory psychology studies of the last century, which resulted in the much-tested Weber's Law. A voluminous literature was available on this generalization concerning variations in sensations that result from quantitative alterations in the intensity of stimulation. Weber's Law is an equation (actually developed by Fechner) relating magnitudes of response—used as an index of sensation—to various magnitudes of stimulus intensity. Fechner wrote the *fundamentalformal*, the basic equation, after integration, in the following form:

$$R = a \log_e S + b$$

The equation can be explained rather simply: S is the level of stimulus intensity, whereas a and b are constants of proportionality and integration respectively. Even if one is not familiar with mathematical representations, the idea is not very complex. The equation describes a *curve* showing that when stimulus intensity (S) is increased by a given amount, the response of the subject (R) will also increase by a regular and predictable amount. The pattern of the curve is one of *diminishing returns*, and this shape is set by the other terms in the equation. What it all boils down to is that doubling the intensity of a stimulus will not double the sensation felt by the subject (measured by some form of response). In fact, as stimulus intensity is increased, it takes larger and larger increases to elicit increasingly smaller increments of sensation (response). This relationship has been supported by numerous experimental studies conducted over many decades.

This psychophysical formulation was used as a basis for developing a parallel "law" (actually a formal hypothesis) to describe the relationship between stimulus intensity and response in leaflet communication. In other words, the more leaflets that are dropped on a community, the greater will be the response of learning the message. However, this was expected to occur in a pattern of diminishing returns. In other words, the increments in response, when one increased the number of leaflets per person in the target population, were expected to become smaller and smaller as ever larger numbers of leaflets were used for each inhabitant. This general idea was tested in a preliminary study that used varying ratios of leaflets per person.

The Pilot Study. An investigation was conducted to test the diminishing returns idea and to train the research team. Four small communities were used (populations ranged between 969 and 1175). These communities were carefully selected for their similarity. All had the same type of economic base, none were satellites of an urban area, and all had similar population compositions. A ratio of one leaflet per person was used on one community, four per person on two others, and sixteen to one on the other community. This provided three points along a possible curve, showing what proportion of the population in each community had learned the message.

The experiment was carried out in cooperation with the Washington State Office of Civil Defense, and the leaflets stated that "One visit from an enemy bomber could send evacuees pouring into your town!" It went on to ask recipients to consider, if such a disaster occurred, "how many refugees they could take into their home." The leaflet was signed by the State Civil Defense Director, and it indicated that a Civil Defense representative would soon call at each home in the community to get their answers. The "representatives" were, of course, interviewers from the Project Revere team. Careful preparations had been made with aerial photographs and maps for each community, and interviews were conducted at every household. Once again, local media cooperated by refraining from mentioning the leaflet drop. The study was a training exercise for the larger experiment to come, but a considerable amount of useful data were obtained on interpersonal diffusion, time-growth patterns of the message, and other issues.

The civil defense theme provided an excellent cover for the experiment. The civil defense authorities were delighted with the information the researchers provided and the townspeople found it to be a realistic issue, much on the minds of people during the time.

The data showed that using one leaflet per person resulted in 18 percent of the residents learning the message by the end of the first day. A four-fold increase of the ratio of leaflets per person (four for each inhabitant) nearly doubled the proportion who learned the message: 32 percent. Another four-fold increase, 16 leaflets per person, resulted in 55 percent of the population learning the message. When plotted on a simple graph these three figures imply a curve of diminishing returns. Clearly, however, three points are insufficient to test the idea that this regularity will hold over a large number of cases. Nevertheless, the results of this pilot study were most encouraging, and the investigators decided to plan and conduct a more definitive test of the diminishing returns relationship. The first task in planning the study was to develop the hypothesis into a statement of greater precision.

Formalizing the Hypothesis. In the discussion below, the manner in which the formalized diminishing returns hypothesis was derived in equation form is explained. For the reader who is not familiar with this type of mathematics, it is not essential to follow the formal derivation to understand the experiment and its results. The present section provides a verbal explanation of what the formal hypothesis was about. The mathematical derivation is presented in the section that follows. In nonmathematical terms, then, the general idea was to come up with an equation that described a curve of diminishing returns predicting how much communication would take place with the use of a given level of stimulus intensity (in this case, a given ratio of leaflets per person). Even if one does not follow the mathematics, it is important to see that it is possible: (1) to begin with a specific set of assumptions, (2) to translate these into a formal mathematical statement, and then (3) to derive a testable hypothesis. Such a hypothesis has the advantage of specifying in the clearest possible terms the kinds of data that are needed for the test and the design of the experiment that will be required. We can assume that a community consists of many individuals interacting. We will further assume that the relationship between the intensity of a communication stimulus and the collective response of such a "subject" will show some similarity to the diminishing returns pattern described by Weber's Law. (The pilot study data seemed to suggest that such an assumption had merit.)

A range of stimulus intensities is needed against which to check the corresponding degrees of response that are to be elicited. But the same subject (community) cannot be used over and over because each succeeding leaflet presentation and response measurement would contaminate the experimental situation for the next. An experimental design is required in which a number of communities, selected carefully for their similarity, are exposed to different degrees of message stimulus intensity and in which comparable measures of response are obtained from each.

Given these circumstances, one can define a set of stimulus intensities that start at some arbitrary lower limit and increase by some power, say *two*, by doubling each preceding intensity. A suitable set of intensities for the leaflet experiment would be to begin with one leaflet for every four people. This can be doubled to one for every two people, redoubled to one per person, two per person, and so on. If this is carried through eight steps of doubling and redoubling, the following set of leaflet intensities would be obtained: 1/4, 1/2, 1/1, 2/1, 4/1, 8/1,16/1, and 32/1.

Given such a range of stimulus intensities, response measures must also be specified. These can be defined as the proportion of a community's population that performs an observable act as a result of the message stimulation. This act could be learning the message, of course, but it could also be some other form of response such as passing a leaflet on to others or filling out and mailing back a postcard questionnaire attached to the leaflet.

With these measures of stimulus intensity and response defined, we can state the hypothesis (in verbal terms) that the increase in response from one community to the next—where the next higher intensity is used—will be directly proportional to the change in stimulus intensity and inversely proportional to the previous stimulus intensity. We are stating, in effect, that a version of Weber's Law will hold not only for individual stimulation but for the collective case when a community is stimulated to give some form of response, even though that response may depend upon social processes and the individual actions of many persons in the collectivity. (At this point nonmathematical readers may wish to turn to the section on Experimental Procedures on p. 204.)

Deriving the Equation. To formulate our hypothesis into an expression suitable for testing, let p denote the proportion of the population who respond as defined, and r denote the measure of stimulus intensity. With a constant of proportionality, a, the above diminishing returns hypothesis can be stated in mathematical form as:

$$\Delta p = \frac{a\Delta r}{r} \qquad [1]$$

Since stimulus intensity increases in powers of two in the series of leaflet ratios chosen, the above can be written:[8]

$$p_{i+1} - p_i = a \qquad [2]$$

The solution to equation [2] can now be written as:[9]

$$p_{i+1} = p_i + ia \qquad [3]$$

However, for the present development it will help to express p in terms of r, rather than in terms of i. Thus, for i equal to or greater than 1, $r_i = 2^{i-3}$, which may be written as:

$$i = 3 + \log_2 r_i \qquad [4]$$

We may put this into equation [3] to get:

$$p_{i+1} = p_1 + (3 + \log_2 r_i)a = a \log_2 r_i + 3a + p_1 \qquad [5]$$

Equation [5] expressed p_{i+1} in terms of r_i, but it is more desirable to express p_{i+1} in terms of r_{i+1}. This may be accomplished by recalling that each stimulus intensity will be just one-half the next greater one. That is to say, $r_i = \frac{1}{2}r_{i+1}$, and with this we can now write:

$$\log_2 r_i = \log_2 \frac{r_{i+1}}{2} = \log_2 r_{i+1} - \log_2 2 = \log_2 r_{i+1} - 1 \qquad [6]$$

If we put this result into [5] we get:

$$p_{i+1} = a \log_2 r_{i+1} + 3a + p_1 = a \log_2 r_{i+1} - a + 3a + p_1 \qquad [7]$$

This gives a prediction of the extent of response for the (r_{i+1})th stimulus intensity. This can be labeled the typical case and designated as the ith case, rather than the $(i + 1)$th, allowing for the simplification:

$$p_i = a \log_2 r_i + (2a + p_i) \text{ valid for all } i \geqslant 1 \qquad [8]$$

The expression we are seeking comes out when equation [8] is further simplified by letting $2a + p_i = b$. Thus, we get the formal hypothesis:

$$p_i = a \log_2 r_i + b \qquad [9]$$

It can be noted how similar this is to Weber's Law. As we noted on page 218, Fechner integrated his *fundamentalformal* to the expression:

$$R = a \log_e S + b$$

This similarity of form is to be expected. However, equation [9], our formal hypothesis, avoids the assumptions involved in infinitesimal calculus (which would be difficult to justify in this case) and was derived from a different equation. In any case, equation [9] predicts values of response level for the communities that will get each leaflet ratio in the doubling and redoubling series defined earlier.

Ordinary statistical methods can be used to evaluate the differences between the predicted values and the values actually obtained from conducting the experiment. In the present case, chi-square provides a simple procedure for evaluating the goodness of fit between the observed and theoretical data. Note that equation [9] is not confined to leaflet communication specifically. It can be advanced as a testable hypothesis for any medium where measures of stimulus intensity and a level of community response can be obtained.

Experimental Procedures

To test the formal hypothesis stated in equation [9], a rather elaborate experiment was designed around the series of leaflet ratios indicated earlier (p. 202). Eight small communities in western Washington State were chosen as sites for the test. Each was to receive a different leaflet ratio, and interviewing in each town would determine the proportion of the population who had learned the message (or made some other response) within a specified period of time. The actual results obtained can be compared to the theoretical proportions predicted by equation [9].

The communities were selected to be as much alike as possible. Their populations ranged between 1015 and 1800. They were relatively stable; all had similar climates and economic bases (lumbering and agriculture); and none was a suburb or bedroom community for a large city.

These eight "subjects" were assigned "treatments" by an elementary randomization procedure. These treatments were, of course, the leaflet drops, using the different ratios described earlier. Table 8.1 shows the ratio assigned to each community.

As in earlier Project Revere experiments, extensive preparations were completed before the leaflets were dropped. Town authorities were contacted; the cooperation of relevant news media was solicited; maps and aerial photographs were prepared; reconnaisance flights were made over the community to plan the best drop patterns; questionnaires were pretested; and interviewers were carefully trained. All went well. The nine newspapers, three radio

TABLE 8.1. RATIOS OF LEAFLETS PER PERSON ASSIGNED TO THE EIGHT TOWNS

Leaflets per person	Town	Population	Total Number of Leaflets
1/4	Orting	1,299	325
1/2	Sequim	1,096	548
1/1	Poulsbo	1,306	1,306
2/1	Oak Harbor	1,475	2,950
4/1	Ferndale	1,015	4,060
8/1	Arlington	1,800	14,400
16/1	Darrington	1,052	16,832
32/1	McCleary	1,175	37,600
			78,021

Source: Melvin L. De Fleur, "A Mass Communication Model of Stimulus Response Relationships: An Experiment in Leaflet Message Diffusion," *Sociometry* 19, 1, March 1956, p. 18.

stations, and one TV station serving the area agreed to the plan. Town officials were most cooperative. The interviewer teams had been thoroughly briefed, and all other details had been taken into account.

The leaflet used was a simple one. It combined the civil defense theme used in the pilot study with the mail-back postcard questionnaire developed in earlier research. The leaflet informed the reader that:

> One raid from an enemy bomber could paralyze radios, telephones, newspapers. *In such a disaster*...leaflets like this could be dropped from airplanes to give official instructions. *You* are part of this scientific test to find out how effective leaflets are for spreading vital information to everyone.

The reverse side of the leaflet contained an appeal to "Be a Modern Paul Revere" and pass on extra leaflets to others to "help spread the word." It also asked the recipient to fill out and mail the (self-addressed and postage-free) questionnaire attached to the leaflet in the form of a small postcard. The purpose of the postcard was to provide a measure of *compliance* with the request for a specific action.

All leaflet drops occurred on a Wednesday, commencing promptly at noon in each community. Skilled crews made sure that the leaflets were spread evenly over each site. Three days later, beginning at 9 A.M., face-to-face interviews were conducted in every other household in each community. (Previous Revere studies had shown that three days were ample for the message to spread.) The exact person in the household to interview was selected by a special method (often used by the U.S. Census).[10] The data-gathering was designed to determine if the respondents had learned the message, and if so, *how* they learned (via social diffusion or directly from a leaflet); *when* they learned; and what subsequent *action* they had taken on the basis of the requests on the leaflet. Cooperation by the townspeople was excellent in every respect. After the experiment was concluded, local news media described the leaflet drops and their purposes.

The Hypotheses versus the Data

To determine if a given respondent knew the message on the leaflets, his or her verbatim reply to the question "What did the leaflet say?" was carefully recorded by the interviewers. These replies were then independently reviewed by two judges who used previously established criteria to make their decisions as to whether or not a subject should be classified as a "knower" or a "non-knower." The procedure worked well, and interjudge reliability was $r = .94$.

The proportion of those interviewed who were classified as "knowers" was plotted by leaflet ratio as shown in Figure 8.2. By the method of least squares, the curve described by equation [9] was fit through the resulting points. This means simply that the curve predicted by the theory (equation [9]) goes through the observable data points in a manner that minimizes the distance between the empirical data and the points predicted by the curve. The whole idea is shown graphically in Figure 8.2.

By using chi-square to compare how much the observed data differed from the predictions provided by the hypothesis (equation [9]), a test of good fit was provided. Visual examination of the graph shows that the fit of the theoretical curve to the observed data was, on the whole, quite good. The probability value associated with chi-square indicates that the observed and the hypothesized (theoretical) percents do not differ significantly. The differences between observed and theoretical values could easily have occurred by chance in a universe of such data described by the model. Stated more simply, the curve apparently fits the data, and the outcome supports the formal hypothesis.

A similar test of equation [9] was made with the data shown in Figure 8.3, obtained from the leaflet postcards that were mailed back. In this case, the curve fits the data pretty well, except in the case of the town that received eight leaflets per person. Here, the mail-back compliance was especially high. It was discovered that in this particular community an active voluntary civil defense group took it upon themselves to see that the "civil defense test" was a success, and these public-spirited citizens made sure that as many people as possible completed the questionnaire and mailed back the postcard. Aside from this

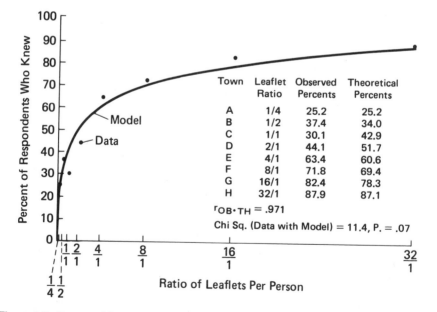

Town	Leaflet Ratio	Observed Percents	Theoretical Percents
A	1/4	25.2	25.2
B	1/2	37.4	34.0
C	1/1	30.1	42.9
D	2/1	44.1	51.7
E	4/1	63.4	60.6
F	8/1	71.8	69.4
G	16/1	82.4	78.3
H	32/1	87.9	87.1

$r_{OB \cdot TH} = .971$

Chi Sq. (Data with Model) = 11.4, P. = .07

Figure 8.2. Percent of Respondents Who Knew Message for Each Leaflet Ratio.
Source: Melvin L. De Fleur, "A Mass Communication Model of Stimulus Response Relationships: An Experiment in Message Diffusion," *Sociometry* 19, 1, March 1956, pp. 21–22.

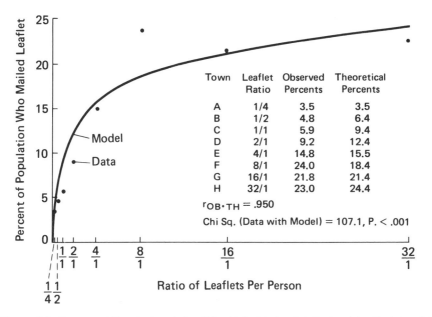

Figure 8.3. Percent of Town's Population Who Mailed in Leaflet Postcard for Each Leaflet Ratio.
Source: Melvin L. De Fleur, "A Mass Communication Model of Stimulus Response Relationships: An Experiment in Message Diffusion," *Sociometry* 19, *1*, March 1956, pp. 21–22.

understandable aberration, however, the formal hypothesis seemed to predict this form of compliance behavior rather well.

The conclusion of this study was that the formalized hypothesis (equation [9]) provided a good description of the relationship between the specified stimulus intensity measures and the amount of communication that took place. With the exception of the one deviant case with the active civil defense group, the formal hypothesis also did well in describing the relationship between stimulus intensity and compliance. This version of Weber's Law, in other words, seemed to apply in this communication setting.

Message Diffusion and the Social Structure

The results of the stimulus intensity experiment indicated clearly that the frequency or redundancy with which a message is presented to a target audience is a vital factor in determining the eventual level of communicative and compliance outcome. But a message brought to the attention of the audience will also travel through social channels, as was demonstrated in the coffee slogan experiment. The significance of social diffusion had originally been suggested by *The People's Choice* research (see Chapter 4), which resulted in the discovery of the "two-step flow" of communication. However, at the time of the Revere studies, little was known of the pathways through the social structure which a message would follow as message diffusion took place. The eight-community experiment not only provided data on the Weber's Law hypothesis, it yielded abundant information on what kind of people passed on the message to what other kind of people. In other words, it was possible to sort out the social itinerary followed by the information as it moved through interpersonal networks.

One clear pattern that became apparent was that in a situation of relative *scarcity*, with fewer leaflets available per person, a larger proportion of those receiving the message learned it through social means. When leaflets were relatively *abundant*, on the other hand, that proportion dropped and more people learned by direct contact with a leaflet. For example, among those classified as "knowers" of the message in those four communities with lowest ratios of leaflets per person, 62.9 percent learned by social means. In the four communities with the highest leaflet ratios, the comparable figure was 47.8 percent (a significant difference). It should not be forgotten, however, that in absolute numbers there were considerably larger numbers of knowers in the high-ratio communities. The implications of this pattern are of pragmatic interest in that learning by social means tends to result in relatively inaccurate communication. Therefore, if the intent of the communicator is to reach as many people as possible, high redundancy (stimulus intensity) is required.

The knowers of the message were not evenly distributed throughout the various social categories and subgroups in any of the communities. Under both high and low stimulus intensity conditions, both *age* and *family size* were significantly related to the probability of learning the message. Children were more likely to know the message than were adults; and adults from large families were more likely to know the message than adults from small families. This suggests that an important aspect of the dynamics of social diffusion (at least in this research) was that a flow of information took place *from children to adults*. More specifically, this flow tended to be from children to their parents. (An analysis of differences by sex showed no significant patterns). Children, then, were more active in picking up the leaflets, learning their content, passing on the message to others, and passing on leaflets to adults in particular.

Further analyses showed that family and friendship ties were important in the process of social diffusion. Among adults, transmitting or receiving the message by any means tended to take place more within the family than among neighbors, acquaintances, or strangers. This was not the case with children, who both learned and transmitted the message more with others outside the family. This was especially true in the case of oral transmission, as opposed to passing on a leaflet. Table 8.2 summarizes the relevant data.

How can we interpret these findings concerning the penetration of this particular message into the social structure of the communities involved? The

TABLE 8.2. THE FLOW OF INFORMATION FROM VARIOUS CATEGORIES OF LEAFLET RECEIVERS TO CHILDREN AND ADULTS

Identity of Message Transmitter	Age Status of Message Receiver							
	Pass-on Diffusion				Oral Diffusion			
	Adults		Children		Adults		Children	
	N	%	N	%	N	%	N	%
Family member	142	49.8	12	22.7	21	35.6	1	3.7
Neighbor	61	21.4	13	24.5	17	28.8	3	11.1
Acquaintance	75	26.3	28	52.8	21	35.6	23	85.2
Stranger	7	2.5	0	0.0	0	0.0	0	0.0
Total	285	100.0	53	100.0	59	100.0	27	100.0

Pass-on: For 3df, $X^2 = 19.0$, $P < .001$.
Oral: For 2df, $X^2 = 18.2$, $P < .001$.

Source: Melvin L. De Fleur and Otto N. Larsen, *The Flow of Information* (New York: Harper and Brothers, 1958) p. 178.

following generalizations describe what happened: The leaflets appeared to have a special appeal to children, who picked them up, told other children, or passed on leaflets to their friends, parents, adult neighbors, or acquaintances. This in turn appeared to lead adults to discuss the leaflets and their message with other adults, or to take the requested action and comply by mailing back the postcard. Thus, children were, in a sense, *neutral transmitters* of the oral message, or of the leaflets. The principal role of children, then, was to obtain leaflets, bring them home, pass on the message to others, and thus stimulate action by adults.

CONCLUSIONS AND IMPLICATIONS

The airborne leaflet is obviously a highly specialized medium of communication. As was pointed out, its significance today is as a medium of last resort—as a means by which audiences can be reached during emergencies, wartime, or times of political repression when no alternative channels remain open. Sadly, such situations are as frequent in contemporary times as they were in earlier periods. However, because of the unique qualities of leaflets as a medium, it is appropriate to raise questions about the "generalizability" of the Revere findings to other media and other situations. Would they apply, say, to newspapers, radio, comic books, or television? In addressing this question, one can focus on the differences among these media and wonder if they share *any* common principles. Each conveys its message in a different manner, is attended to as a result of different needs and for varying gratifications. Yet, in spite of these differences, even a moment's reflection confirms that there *are* common principles underlying the process of communication when any of these media are used. Each involves an attempt on the part of communicators to achieve some form of change in their intended audiences. Each depends upon processes of perception and learning. And each is dependent upon the cultural rules of language usage to bring about some paralleling between the intended meanings of the communicator and the interpretations of the recipient.

Beyond these considerations is the fact that communication by any medium includes the two major stages through which information flows from media to audiences, first described as the "two-step flow of communication" in *The People's Choice*. This work became available to the academic community at large in 1948. By the time Project Revere began some three years later, little was known about this form of secondary communication other than the fact that it had been discovered somewhat serendipitously in the Erie County study. Later research on the two-step flow helped fill this gap. It focused on the *people* involved and the *roles* that they played in this form of interpersonal transmission of information and influence. Thus, studies of "opinion leaders" were undertaken, including studies of who their followers were and what topics were involved in such influence (see Chapter 7). In contrast, the Revere studies concentrated on the *quality of the information* that was spread by word-of-mouth through interpersonal networks.

The most significant conclusion from such studies as the coffee slogan experiment was that the person-to-person flow of information resulted in message incompleteness, inaccuracy, and distortion. The implications of this were considerable: The Revere study showed the applicability of the *embedding pattern*, found earlier by social psychologists who had studied "rumoring" by use of the serial retelling strategy, to the word-of-mouth movement of information in the two-step flow. The complex processes of levelling, sharpening, and assimilation were found in the social diffusion of a message through a community. In other words, considerable doubt is cast on the importance of the secondary stage of the two-step flow as a process by which the meanings intended by a mass communicator can be paralleled in the interpretations of the audience toward whom the communication is directed. This issue is even more serious when it is recalled that the message under study was only six words and included only one word of more than one syllable!

The problems posed by the Revere research on message distortion also have a bearing on another line of research that became popular during the mid-1950s and later. The interpersonal diffusion of the news began to be studied intensively by researchers in journalism and communication. Dozens of studies traced time patterns in the spread of important news stories (e.g., Senator Taft's death, Alaska statehood, the Kennedy assassination) as they moved from the media to the secondary stage of the two-step flow. Such time patterns were investigated as part of the Revere studies and were among seven doctoral dissertations and numerous articles in professional journals that appeared during or immediately following the project.[11] However, the significant factor here is that when the news is transmitted from person to person it is likely to be badly distorted, no matter how fast or slow it moves, or how extensively it penetrates the population by word-of-mouth.

If social diffusion is not accurate and reliable, the importance of *direct* contact with the medium by every member of the audience is obvious. At least this was clearly the case with the relatively simple medium used in the Revere studies. This need for direct contact meant that it was important to understand the stimulus intensity issue. How often should the message be presented, with what level of redundancy, to insure that a given level of the intended audience *would* have direct contact with the message? The formal hypothesis based on Weber's Law was an attempt to answer this question. The answers found and the diminishing returns relationship that emerged from the study may have been less important than the opportunity to conduct such research at a level of considerable precision. The mathematical model and its derivation were at a level of formal theory construction not often found in mass communication research, at least up to that time. The large-scale investigation, with eight separate communities carefully surveyed, and with the entire effort aimed at supporting or rejecting a formal mathematical model, was also unusual for the time. In fact, it is not at all clear that research in mass communication has increased its level of precision and theory construction beyond that achieved in Project Revere, even at present.

NOTES AND REFERENCES

1. Melvin L. De Fleur and Otto N. Larsen, *The Flow of Information* (New York: Harper and Brothers, 1948), p. xiv. (This book reports a number of the Project Revere studies.)
2. Melvin L. De Fleur, "Mass Communication and the Study of Rumor," *Sociological Inquiry*, 32, 1, Winter, 1962, 51–70.
3. F. C. Bartlett, *Remembering* (Cambridge, England: Cambridge University Press, 1932); Gordon W. Allport and Leo Postman, *The Psychology of Rumor* (New York: Henry Holt and Company, 1947).
4. Allport and Postman, ibid., pp. 75–115.
5. Ibid., p. 86.
6. Martin F. Herz, "Some Psychological Lessons from Leaflet Propaganda in World War II," *Opinion Quarterly*, 13, 1949, 471–486.
7. Melvin L. De Fleur, "A Mass Communication Model of Stimulus–Response Relationships: An Experiment in Leaflet Message Diffusion," *Sociometry*, 19, 1, 1956, 12–25. (See footnote 3 in this article.)
8. That is, if i denotes the ith increase in stimulus intensity, then $r = 2^{i-3}$ because the lowest intensity ratio in the proposed set was $\frac{1}{4}$ or 2^{-2}; in the next higher, $r = \frac{1}{2}$ or 2^{-1}; and so on through the fourth, $r = 2$, the sixth, $r = 2^3$, etc. In the ith

increase, then $r = 2^{i-3}$; and since $\Delta r = r_{i+1} - r_i = 2^{i-3}$ also, then Δr must equal r. This being the case, $\Delta r/r = 1$, yielding equation (2).

9. The expression p_{i+1} merely denotes the response of the community receiving the $(i + 1)$th stimulus intensity. But, if $p_{i+1} = p_i + a$, then it also equals $p_{i-1} + 2a$, $p_{i-2} + 3a$, and so on. By continuing this process we could express p_{i+1} in terms of p_1 plus a certain number of a's. If we want to express p_{i+1} in terms of p_i, it is obvious that one must be added to the subscript of the latter, and it will also be noted that this is precisely the number of a's which must be added to a p to get p_{i+1}. In general, the number of a's which must be added to a given p to get p_{i+1} is the same as the difference between their subscripts. Thus to p_{i_1} we must add ia's to get p_{i+1}. This situation is summarized in equation (3).

10. Leslie A. Kish, "A Procedure for Objective Respondent Selection within the Household," *Journal of the American Statistical Association*, 44, 1949, 380–387.

11. See pp. 285–293 in *The Flow of Information* for a list of publications and dissertations resulting from Project Revere studies, with special reference to the work of Willian Catton, Melvin De Fleur, Richard Hill, Otto Larsen, Ørjar Øyen, and Gordon Shaw.

9

Seduction of the Innocent:
The Great Comic Book Scare

By 1954, most communication researchers and other social scientists had become complacent in regard to the issues concerning media effects. They considered the matter more or less settled. After all, a number of careful studies, including the milestones presented in Chapters 4, 5, and 6, had indicated that the media had neither dramatic nor dangerous effects. Because the effects of the media had been shown to be so slight, at least some scholars thought that there was no longer any pressing reason even to continue studying them.

These claims about the innocuous nature of media effects were not un-challenged, however. A loud objection was raised by Dr. Frederic Wertham, a noted New York psychiatrist. He claimed that one form of mass communication had practically taken over the minds of our children—silently, very quickly, and without the knowledge of their parents. The villain he referred to was "comic books," and there was, he thought, "nothing funny" about them. Instead, he argued, at their worst they were turning children into dangerous juvenile delinquents; at best, they were giving the children who read them a distorted view of the world.

A few social scientists agreed with Wertham; others disagreed and debated the issue with him in scientific circles; the great majority of social scientists, however, simply ignored him. Not to be denied, Wertham found another audience for his work; he took his argument to the people—to the parents of America. He published articles in widely read popular magazines such as *Ladies' Home Journal* and *Reader's Digest*. He presented his views on radio and television shows. Wertham thus effectively used other media to condemn comic books. And he succeeded in resurrecting the legacy of fear, at least in the public's mind.

COMIC MAGAZINES AS A CONTROVERSIAL MEDIUM

Comic magazines are offspring of the newspaper comic strips—the "funny papers"—which have a colorful history of their own. They developed during the 1890s when Joseph Pulitzer's *New York World* and William Randolph Hearst's *New York Journal* went all out to lure sensation-hungry readers for their newspapers. Both published lurid stories of murders, scandals involving the rich, tragedies, and disasters. It was said that when news was scarce, neither Pulitzer nor Hearst hesitated to manufacture it. The two newspapers are credited with playing a major role in pushing the country into the Spanish-American War in 1898. They played up atrocities—real and imagined—by the Spanish in Cuba and whipped up a patriotic fervor against Spain in the United States.

In 1896, a cocky, lovable urchin had quietly begun to entertain readers of the *World* in comic drawings. These were single panels; the comic "strips" would come later. The street kid, who wore a garment resembling a nightgown, began appearing in a bright yellow gown. Suddenly, "The Yellow Kid," the creation of artist Richard Outcault, had boosted the circulation of the *World* ahead of that of the rival *Journal* in their frantic battle for readers. Hearst counterattacked; he hired Outcault away from Pulitzer and began publishing his own comic strip supplement in color. Pulitzer answered this challenge by obtaining the copyright to "The Yellow Kid" and assigning another artist to depict the child's adventures. "The Yellow Kid," however, became immortal; from that strip derives the term "yellow journalism," an epithet used to describe the Pulitzer/Hearst brand of sensationalism in the handling of the news.[1]

Hearst began publishing the first authentic comic strip in 1897, "The Katzenjammer Kids." The strip used a row of panels and dialogue enclosed in balloons to tell the story of two troublesome children and their harried mother and father. The strip set the style for comic strips and was soon followed by others such as "Happy Hooligan," "Little Nemo," and "Mutt and Jeff." The development of the major newspaper syndicates during the early 1900s, including Hearst's International News Service, King Features, United Features, and the Chicago Tribune Syndicate, made it possible to distribute an artist's work throughout the country in scores of newspapers each day. Among the most popular of these syndicated strips were "Bringing Up Father," "Little Orphan Annie," and "Buster Brown," another creation of Outcault, the developer of the original "Yellow Kid."[2] During the 1930s, such syndicated comic strips helped millions of Americans to forget temporarily the hard times of the Depression years. It was in this period that such all-time favorite comic characters as "Buck Rogers," "Superman," and "Tarzan" came into their own.

Comic magazines first appeared in the middle 1930s. A New York company, the Eastern Color Printing Company, which already printed Sunday newspaper comic supplements, conceived the idea of printing the comics in book form. They successfully published "Funnies on Parade" and followed it with "Famous Funnies." "Famous Funnies" was distributed through variety stores and proved to be so popular that the publishers began issuing it on a monthly basis. Once the marketability of the comic magazine had been established, many famous comic strip characters began to appear in such publications. "Superman," "Tarzan," "Buck Rogers," and other "action" comics were particularly popular before the outbreak of World War II. They contributed heavily to the success of the comic magazine. And successful they were. In 1941, 10 million copies were being sold a month, and by 1947, the figure had risen to 60 million a month.[3] In 1950, a Fawcett Comics Group advertisement was headlined in true comic book style: "The comic books bought each month laid end to end would reach ⅕th the space from the earth to the moon." Comic books had truly arrived—quickly, quietly, and almost unnoticed. The tranquility of the industry was soon disrupted, however. Dr. Wertham brought controversy to the industry and altered the silent acceptance that comic books had enjoyed.

Dr. Wertham was not the first, nor the only professional, to express concern about the effects of comic book reading. However, most of the discussion and disagreement that occurred before his public attack on comic books might be described as a civil war between opposing groups of psychiatrists. The leading critics of comic books, as well as their defenders, were psychiatrists.[4] The critics argued that comic books were "the opium of the nursery" and that they led individual children, who were held spellbound by the crime and horror stories, straight onto the road to crime. Even those children who were not led to criminal behavior were damaged because they were introduced to the comic book world, which they accepted as real. The fears of this group of critics were epitomized by the little boy who got a Superman cape for his birthday, wrapped it around himself, and sprang out the window of his apartment house to his death.[5] The defenders, on the other hand, claimed that the comics provided a healthy outlet for the child's violence-play and for his aggressive fantasies. Since children had to suppress this violence and aggressiveness in the presence of adults, both at home and in school, the comics provided a harmless outlet for those forces in their personalities. Comic books and horror stories, they reasoned, were the child's "aspirin and penicillin" for overcoming the painful experience of growing up in a peaceful adult world. This was of course, a simple restatement of the widely known catharsis theory.

This debate about comic books was waged largely within the confines of the profession of psychiatry, although some of the more active defenders of the comics were also retained as "advisors" by comic book publishers and received lucrative fees for this service. Cynical critics claimed that these "advisors" received their money largely for having their names displayed on the comic books. This, they claimed, amounted to nothing more than a public relations campaign for parents.

Wertham began his public attack on comic magazines in 1948, when he published no fewer than five articles in both professional journals and popular magazines. His position was also stated in some detail in an article written by Judith Crist for *Collier's* magazine. It appeared on March 27, 1948, and was entitled "Horror in the Nursery." The next year, another manuscript entitled "What are Comic Books?" (a study course for parents) was published by the

National Parent Teacher Magazine. In addition, another article appeared in the *Ladies' Home Journal* under the title "What Parents Don't Know About Comic Books."

Reactions to Wetham's writings by social scientists were mixed. Some vigorously agreed with his conclusions. Others, including the noted sociologist Frederic Thrasher, hotly disagreed.[6] Thrasher, an expert on juvenile delinquency, correctly pointed out that delinquency is a complex phenomenon that cannot be attributed solely to any single cause—whether it be poverty or the media. However, Thrasher's rebuttal was published in a professional journal (*Journal of Educational Sociology*) and was therefore not widely read outside the discipline of sociology.

The public took Wertham's arguments much more seriously. After all, he *was* a well-known psychiatrist, and his credentials were impressive. He was Senior Psychiatrist for the Department of Hospitals in New York City (1932–1952). He directed the mental hygiene clinics at both Bellevue Hospital and Queens Hospital Center, and he was in change of the Court of General Sessions Psychiatric Clinic. For more than twenty-five years, Dr. Wertham had been giving expert opinion in medico-legal cases, and his advice had been sought by defense counsels, district attorneys, judges, and legislators. His views had been discussed before the Supreme Court of the United States. Moreover, he had published many books, including a well-known textbook that was used all over the world, *The Brain as an Organ.*

The most complete treatise on Wertham's position concerning the effects of comic books was published in 1954, under the title *Seduction of the Innocent.* The book received a great deal of attention, both praise and criticism. A condensed version of it was published in *Reader's Digest* under the title "Blueprints for Delinquency," and the book itself was available as a Book-of-the-Month selection in June 1954, as well as for participants in the Reader's Digest Book Club. By publishing in such a forum, Wertham was able to reach the public and to influence a great many people. It is the ideas and findings reported in *Seduction of the Innocent* to which we now turn.

THE RESEARCH PROCEDURES

Wertham's foremost concern was to discover the effects that comic books had on the attitudes and behavior of children. While he studied *all* varieties of comic books, he concentrated on "crime comic books." Crime comics were "those comic books that depict crime whether the setting is urban, western, science-fiction, jungle, adventure, or the realm of superman, horror or supernatural beings."[7] Wertham felt that *all comic books* had undesirable effects (even "Donald Duck"), but he believed that the crime comics were particularly insidious because they had the most virulent effects. Moreover, he made it clear that he was concerned *only* with *comic books* in the study and *not* with *newspaper comic strips*, because he felt that there were fundamental differences between the two types of comics. In the first place, they had different readerships. Comic books were read mostly by children, whereas comic strips had a predominantly adult audience. In addition, the strips that appeared in the newspapers were subject to the strict censorship guidelines of the newspapers's editors and publishers. Those editors sometimes rejected undesirable detail in the strips, or even failed to print whole sequences of the strips. In contrast, no such institutional censorship existed for comic books. No outside agency examined their content for appropriateness or for good taste. Wertham pointed out that even when comic strips were reprinted as comic books they lacked the controls of censorship that existed when they were intended for adults. The publisher enjoyed complete license to print whatever he wanted. He could, and sometimes did, add a semipornographic story for the children, and perhaps a gory cover—things from which censorship protected the adult comic strip readers.

The overall methodology of the project consisted of qualitative content analysis of comic books and clinical case studies of children along with the use of psychological testing. Wertham examined thousands of comic books in order to determine the manner in which life, violence, sex, and different groups of people were portrayed. He felt that it was important to describe the contents of comic magazines because he believed that very few adults had any idea what kinds of material they contained. Indeed, he believed that many professionals dealing with child care knew nothing about comic books. Of course, almost everyone knew that children read those little books; they knew about the funny animal stories that children liked to read. Comic books, they assumed, were just reprints of comic strips from newspapers—"like 'Bringing Up Father,' you know"—or other such humorous sequences. Because of this ignorance, Wertham felt that it was necessary to have an adequate description of the contents of comic magazines.

Clinical Research

Because Wertham was a psychiatrist, it is not particularly surprising that case histories were employed. The project reportedly studied a large cross section of children: This included children from well-to-do families, children from the middle class, and children from the lowest rung of the socioeconomic ladder. Yet, his sample had some unique characteristics: All the children were seen in mental hygiene clinics. The children who were studied were referred to Wertham by all kinds of public and private child care agencies. Some of them had come to the attention of the juvenile section of the Police Bureau, or to the Children's Court; some were seen in the course of private practice. Some of the children were confined for observation in psychiatric wards for adolescents, while others were confined for physical diseases in pediatric wards or were seen in pediatric clinics. Wertham described a large proportion of these children as being "normal"—children who came to his attention for some social reason. In fact, he pointed out, the sample included some children of superior intelligence who were candidates for scholarships. The upper limit for the age of children included in the study was sixteen; Wertham, however, did not adhere to this limit rigidly. He obtained at least some data from older teenagers and from adults who provided information about their earlier comic-book-reading stage.

It was pointed out that the reasons given why these subjects were brought to the attention of physicians, psychiatrists, psychologists, or social workers usually did not include any reference to comic books. There were, however, a few cases where the reading of comic books was part of the complaint about the child. In these cases, the main complaint was referred to as the "extreme avidity" of their comic book reading. Such children took the comic books to bed with them; they walked along the street on the way to school reading them; they read them in school; and they took them on outings and on vacations. Overall, these children gave an abnormal amount of attention to the comics.

Routine psychiatric examinations were also given to all of the children. A history of the child's development was taken from his or her parents or from those with whom the child lived. As much information about each child was gathered as was possible; Wertham explained:

> Whenever possible, social workers studied the child's social environment, obtained school reports, interviewed teachers, and relayed information from other agencies who had contact with the child or his family. In the same way, pertinent information was obtained from hospitals, private doctors and clergymen. In cases where the courts were involved, probation reports were added to the record or probation officers interviewed.[8]

In cases where children indicated that they belonged to gangs, an attempt was made to talk with other members of the gang. Moreover, an attempt was made to determine the recreational influences to which children were exposed: games, community centers, radio, television, books. It was in that setting and with that perspective that Wertham, with the help of his associates, attempted to ascertain the influence of comic books on children.

Psychological Testing

Several psychological tests were administered since Wertham did not believe that any one test, however valid, was sufficient to make a judgment about children. The *Rorschach*, popularly known as the "ink-blot" test, was routinely used. The test consisted of a series of ten ink-blot pictures; the subject was asked what he or she saw in them. Wertham had been one of the first psychiatrists in the United States to use the Rorschach and he had more than twenty years' experience with it. He noted, from previous research findings, that children often see forms that adults usually do not see. These forms often turned out to be, he argued, related to things that the children had seen in comic books, especially weird and horror comics (e.g., ghost forms, fantastic hands). Wertham cautioned that such forms were likely to be misinterpreted by psychologists as meaning complex-determined anxieties and phobias, whereas actually they were just reminiscences from comic-book illustrations.

The *Thematic Apperception Test* (TAT) was also regularly used. In this test, the child was shown a series of pictures depicting various scenes and then asked to tell stories about them. Sometimes, Wertham found children who were preoccupied with stories of murder and violence. He claimed that this kind of preoccupation occurred much more frequently among avid crime-comics readers than among other children.

The *Mosaic Test* was also routinely used. Here, the children had a choice of a large number of mosaic pieces of different colors and shapes. They were asked to put them on a tray and make any design they wished. Wertham indicated that the Mosaic Test was:

> . . . very useful in a diagnosis for ruling out. . . psychotic conditions, even inconspicuous or incipient ones. These tests revealed in a large series of cases that there is nothing intrinsically abnormal about those children who either became very addicted to reading crime comics or are influenced by such reading to delinquent acts. As a matter of fact, the Mosaic Test—in conjunction with clinical findings—indicated or confirmed the finding that those children who suffer from any really serious intrinsic psychopathological condition, including those with psychoses, are less influenced by comic-book reading.[9]

Intelligence tests and *aptitude tests* were also frequently used. Tests for reading ability were considered to be of crucial importance, because the effects of comic book reading on children's ability to read was a special research question. The *Association Test* was also found to be useful. Wertham believed that word associations could reveal preoccupations and fantasies that cannot be obtained on a conscious level, and certainly not by questioning. Moreover, he claimed that in cases where children were accused of serious delinquencies, the Association Test functioned as a "lie detector" test and could help reconstruct what had actually happened. For example, a ten-year-old boy was referred to Wertham because he had been accused of drowning a younger boy. Another boy had witnessed the act, but the subject denied doing it. The authorities felt, therefore, that it was one boy's word against another's. The Association Test showed a definite blocking to key words—such as drowning, water, little boy, and pushing. Wertham believed the boy to be guilty primarily on the basis of this evidence. The subject also happened to be an avid comic book reader.

Briefly, then, the three major approaches used to study the effects of comic book reading were: (1) content analyses, (2) case histories, and (3) psychological tests.

THE FINDINGS

The major findings can be best summarized by examining two topics: (1) the types and content of crime comics and (2) the effects of crime comics.

Types and Content of Crime Comics

As indicated earlier, crime comics as a category were of particular interest to Wertham. He found a great deal of violence in this type of comic book. His argument was clear: "It is violence for violence's sake. The plot: killing. The motive: to kill. The characterization: killed."[10] Of particular concern to Wertham was the apparent increase in the popularity of such comics. For example, in 1946–47, crime comics comprised about one-tenth of the total of all comic books sold. By 1948–49, however, they had increased to one-third of the total, and by 1949–50, they made up over one-half of the industry's output. In 1954, the vast majority of all comic books published were crime comics. Wertham felt that this was an ominous trend. He also pointed out that it was necessary to distinguish between the number of comic books printed, published or sold and the number actually read. The last item, the pass-on circulation, he considered particularly important. Many comic books are traded for others after they are sold; others are resold for lower prices. Readership, therefore, may vastly exceed sales. Wertham found that *every imaginable* kind of crime was described *in detail* in the comic books. "If one were to set out to show children how to steal, rob, lie, cheat, assault, and break into houses, no better method could be devised."[11] Furthermore, besides presenting the details of how to commit crimes, he found that the comics also instructed the children how to conceal evidence and how to evade detection. For example, some comic books gave instructions about how to commit robberies. While a child might not attempt a robbery, it is easy and natural, he argued, to translate this crime into a minor key—stealing from a department store instead of breaking into a bank. Other comic books were found to illustrate how a youngster might murder for profit. One book gave a price list for harming people (1954 prices)!

Eyes blackened	$ 4.00
Arm or leg broken	10.00
Whole job	100.00 and up

Other comic books described how to set fires by methods too numerous to list. Some described car thefts in very complete detail. And, of course, all kinds of thefts were described. One frequent depiction was how to steal a woman's pocketbook. According to the stories it could be done skillfully and peacefully —but if that did not work, "just hit them over the head." In addition, numerous "minor" incidents were discussed; skipping school was often described as the "smart" thing to do.

It was also discovered that the comic books often described real crimes that had previously been featured in the newspapers. However, they added many juicy details. In adapting the news story to comic books, the following points were found to be stressed: the daring and success of the criminals; brutal acts shown in detail; sordid details emphasized; and, sexual episodes, if present, featured. An example of this type of story adaptation occurred in 1952. A major newspaper story appeared about three men who escaped from a penitentiary. The story was used by a popular crime comic with descriptive details added. The men stole cars, evaded police, kidnapped people, held up a bank, and were finally caught in New York, where they had been living with three women. In the comic book, the prison break was described as a heroic feat. It was also shown to be easy to steal cars. One of the criminals boasted to a little boy that he had killed 15 or 16 people, "I lost count." Moreover, pictures of half-nude women were featured. There were in this comic book, overall, 76 pictures of exploits by the criminals; in the 77th picture, the police take over with a cheap wisecrack. In other words, crime, violence, and sex were glamorized until the last picture. In that last picture, the action was dull. To Wertham, this finding was typical of all the crime comics he examined. Clearly, crime *does pay*—until the last picture or two.

These crime comics came in many forms; cops-and-robbers dramas were only one type. The vast majority of "westerns," for example, were found to fit into this category. They often described all kinds of crime in vivid detail. One popular western showed a close-up of a dying man with blood streaming from his mouth. The general philosophy expressed by this type of comic was "Since when do we worry about killin' people."

Jungle, horror, and interplanetary comics were a special category of crime comics. Wertham described jungle comics in the following manner:

> Jungle comics specialize in torture, bloodshed and lust in an exotic setting. Daggers, claws, guns, wild animals, well or over-developed girls in brassieres and as little else as possible, dark skinned "natives"; fires, stakes, posts, chains, ropes, big-chested and heavily muscled Nordic he-men dominate the stage. They contain such details as white men banging natives around; a close-up view of the branded breast of a girl; a girl about to be blinded.[12]

While the white people in the jungle books were blonde, athletic, and shapely, the natives were depicted as somewhere between apes and human beings. The dark-skinned people, in short, were characterized as subhuman, while the white people were portrayed as heroes. In addition, amidst all the violence among the slaves, apes, and human beings, the books included big pictures of lush girls, "as nude as the Post Office permitted." The impression of sex plus violence was definite, even to an adult. In the jungle books, the jungle was not a place but a state of mind. And this state of mind was easily transposed to other locales. For example, it was present in outer space in the interplanetary and science-fiction comics. Women were similarly dressed and roughly treated. The torture, however, was more refined. If someone's eye was to be blinded, it was done with some advanced scientific equipment rather than by simply gouging it out.

The "Superman-Batman-Wonder Woman" comics were another variety of crime comics. In this form, a distinction was usually drawn between super-people and sub-people. The latter were usually foreigners. Prejudice against foreigners was a recurrent theme, as the following example demonstrates. A scientist was shown addressing a meeting:

Scientist:	So, my fellow Americans, it is time to give America back to Americans. Don't let foreigners take your jobs!
Member of Audience:	He's right!
Another Applauds:	YEAHHH!

To Wertham, the most dangerous aspect of the superman type of comic book was that these books "present our world in a kind of fascist setting of violence and hate and destruction."[13] They placed too much emphasis on a fascist society and overlooked democratic ideals. In addition to the supermen and superwomen comics, there were superanimal magazines such as "Super Duck." There were also superchildren such as "Superboy." Superboy could slice a tree like a cake, melt glass by looking at it, defeat powerful enemies, and even rewrite American history. For example, in one story he saved the life of George Washington and was even responsible for getting him elected President. Washington was also shown to be crossing the Delaware River with Superboy guiding the boat through the ice floes. It was really Superboy who crossed the Delaware, Washington was simply in the boat!

The love/confession was another type of crime comic. Representative titles included "Intimate Love," "My Desire," "My Love Life," and "Love Scandals." They were merely crime stories with a seasoning of love added. In one of these love comics, a demonstration was given of how to steal a "very expensive gown, Paris original" from a department store.

> "I'll slip it on in the dressing room. They won't notice me!" "I'll put it in that box and walk out, while the saleslady is busy with someone else...I walked out, trying to keep calm, trying to look and act natural...Nobody has seen me! Ohh! If I can only reach the door!"

The love-confession comics were often very sexy, specializing in highly accented and protruding breasts. They were better known among adolescent boys as "headlight comics." One story, "I was a Spoiled Brat," began with a big picture of an attractive girl looking at herself in the mirror and baring herself considerably. A dash of violence was supplied by hit-and-run driving and by her father's death from a heart attack when he heard about his daughter's wild life. Overall the love comics were found to portray a false picture of love and life.

In summary, the main types of crime comics were: (1) cops-and-robbers comics, (2) jungle comics, (3) supermen comics, and (4) love-confession comics. All of these mixed violence with sex to varying degrees and often added a little sadism as well.

The Effects of Crime Comics

The major concern of this reseach was the effect that crime comic books had on children. It was discovered, for example, that the "average child" spent two or three hours a day reading comic books. Some, of course, spent much more time involved in such activity. "How," Wertham asked, "can you get a total picture of the child when you leave out entirely what occupies him two or three hours a day?" Ultimately, he felt, reading comics was a "social problem" because the effects of such reading would have repercussions for all of society. Overall, three major effects were attributed to reading comic books in the Wertham study: (1) Comic books contributed to the increase in juvenile delinquency; (2) They presented children with a distorted and dangerous view of life; and (3) They contributed to reading problems. Each effect will be discussed in turn.

Design for Delinquency. While crime comics were certainly not the only cause of delinquency, Wertham believed them to be a major one in many cases, particularly cases involving serious delinquencies. Up to the beginning of the comic book era, he reasoned, there were hardly any serious crimes, such as murder, committed by children under twelve years of age. Yet, in the 1950s he saw younger and younger children committing more and more serious and violent crimes. Indeed, in 1953, *The New York Times* commented in an editorial, "It is difficult to think of children as burglars, gangsters, drug addicts, or murderers. Such has become the reality, however."[14]

The modern and more serious forms of delinquency involved knowledge of technique. As previously illustrated, the crime comics certainly provided this knowledge. Moreover, by showing the techniques, the comic books also suggested the context. The moral lesson provided was that "innocence doesn't pay." Indeed, many delinquents claimed that they had gotten their criminal ideas from the comics as illustrated in the following quotes:

> I got my bad ideas from the comics; stabbing, robbing, stealing guns and all that stuff. In a comic book I read two kids rob a store and steal guns and

get away and grow up to be bank robbers. So I did the same thing—only I didn't grow up to be a bank robber—yet!

I read about a perfect robbery and used parts of it. This was in a crime comic magazine and it said these three men were still at large and didn't get caught, so I figured I could pull the same stuff.

Throughout Wertham's book, there are repeated instances where children imitated violent acts found in crime comics. The following examples illustrate Wertham's claim that "there is a significant correlation between crime comics reading and the more serious forms of juvenile delinquency."

Three boys, six to eight years old, took a boy of seven, hanged him nude from a tree, his hands tied behind him; then they burned him with matches. Probation officers who investigated found that they were reenacting a comic book plot.

A boy of eleven killed a woman in a holdup. When arrested, he was found surrounded by comic books. His twenty-one-year-old brother said: "If you want the cause of all this, here it is: It's these rotten comic books. Cut them out and things like this wouldn't happen."

A boy of twelve and his eight-year-old sister tried to kill a boy of six. They knocked teeth out, stabbed through his hands with a pocket knife, choked him, kicked him, and jumped on him. Both brother and sister were avid comic book readers.

A ten-year-old boy hit a fourteen-month-old baby over the head with a brick, washed the blood off the brick and then threw the baby into the river. He claimed to have gotten the idea from comic books.

When a well-to-do surgeon received an extortion note demanding $50,000 and threatening harm to his young daughter, experts deduced that the note was the work of an "adult male psychopath under emotional strain." As it turned out, it was a fourteen-year-old girl reenacting a comic book plot.

All of these examples are obviously extreme cases. Wertham pointed out that many children who read comic books do not become delinquent; nevertheless, they have been adversely affected by them. When a constant barrage of crime and violence is leveled at young children, he argued, it leads them inevitably to preoccupation with these subjects and subsequently to psychological maladjustment. For example, one frequent theme running throughout many crime comics was that of hanging. So it was not surprising to Wertham that he found many cases of children hanging themselves. Often found beneath the child was an open comic book luridly describing and depicting a hanging. Wertham felt that such cases basically involved the processes of imitation and experimentation in childhood. Even "normal" children imitate, but children who see hanging scenes frequently are more likely to become preoccupied with such behavior. They are thus more likely to "try it out."

In general, Wertham concluded that crime comics were a major factor in delinquency causation, albeit not usually the only factor. Moreover, crime comics often led to psychological maladjustments and preoccupation with crime and violence.

Distorted Perception of Reality. Wertham argued that crime comics altered children's perceptions of reality. A daily dosage of crime, violence and cruelty would often convince the child that this was what the world was really like. Quite often, this view of the world was reinforced in the comic-book reader by the placement of an insert below the book's title. It read: "Every word is true." On the cover of one book bearing this inscription was the picture of a car speeding away. Two men were tied by their feet to the rear bumper and lay face down. One of the men's hands was tied behind his back and the lower part of his face was dragging on the road. The other man's hands were not tied, but his arms were stretched out. The text, enclosed in balloons, indicated that the men in the car were talking.

> "A couple more miles oughta do th' trick!"
> "It better! These #-**@# GRAVEL ROADS are tough on tires!" "But ya gotta admit, there's nothing like'em for ERASING FACES!"[15]

Next to these balloons is a huge leering face, eyes wide, gloating, and a mouth showing upper and lower teeth in a big grin.

> "Superb! Even Big Phil will admire this job—if he lives long enough to identify the MEAT!"

Every word true? That was the claim made on the cover! Not surprisingly, this sort of crime adventure was found to affect children's views about punishment. The reply was frequently that it served the criminal right, whatever the punishment. "He got caught, didn't he?" That was the real crime for these children. The children did not have faith in society's notions of justice. To them, law enforcement officials were no different from the criminals. Whichever side was the strongest, had the most men, would win. "In many subtle and not so subtle forms, the lynch spirit was taught as the moral lesson."[16]

Many children thought that lynching was acceptable behavior and pointed to examples from comic books. In one story, the townspeople get together, hanged the criminal, and finally shot and killed him. The lesson is in the last sentence: "The story of Lee Gillon proves that fearless people banded together will always see that justice triumphs."

It was the superman type of comic book in which the theme of taking punishment, or rather revenge, into one's own hands was most insidiously pursued. This superman ideology ran throughout the stories and can best be summarized as: "the stronger dominates the smaller and weaker."[17] Children often developed what Wertham referred to as the "superman conceit" from reading this type of material. The superman conceit gave children the feeling that ruthless go-getting, based upon physical strength or the power of weapons or machines was the desirable way to behave. Such children expressed a wish for overwhelming physical strength, domination, power, ruthlessness, and emancipation from the morals of the community. As an example of this, Wertham pointed to the "superman-speed-fantasy" in girls. One teenage girl told him that she would go out only with boys who would not let other cars pass them on the road. This was her idea of proper male behavior. Moreover, this girl, along with many others, got this idea from the comics. Wertham believed that children had been poisoned by this "endless repetition" of superman stories. Such stories, he felt, undermined the authority and dignity of ordinary men and women who tried to teach their children community morals and rules of conduct.

Crime comics were also found to interfere with the development of the superego, or conscience, in children. The development of the conscience takes place, Wertham argued, not only on the basis of identification with parents but also with successive parent substitutes. Both the parents and the substitutes represent group demands and are symbols of group responsibilities. "In this sphere, comic books are most pernicious. They expose children's minds to an endless stream of prejudice-producing images." Wertham continues:

> If I were to make the briefest summary of what children have told us about how different people are represented to them in the lore of crime comics, it would be that there are two kinds of people: on the one hand is a tall, blonde, regular-featured man sometimes disguised as a superman (or superman disguised as a man) and the pretty young blonde with the super-breast. On the other hand are the inferior people: natives, primitives, savages, "ape men," Negroes, Jews, Indians, Italians, Slavs, Chinese, and Japanese. Immigrants of every description, people with irregular features, swarthy skins, physical deformities, Oriental features. In some crime comics the first class sometimes wears some kind of superman uniform, while the second class is in mufti. The brunt of this imputed inferiority in whole groups of people is directed against colored people and "foreign born."[18]

Wertham found that children as young as four years old could acquire prejudice from comic books and that six- or seven-year-olds were quite articulate about expressing their contempt for minority groups. Obviously, many of these distorted stereotypes were acquired at home, or in the street. However, they were reinforced by comic book reading. Wertham explained that when a child was shown a comic book that he or she had not read and was asked to "pick out the bad man," the child unhesitatingly picked out bad types according to the stereotyped conception of racial and ethnic prejudice.

Another prejudice-producing situation found in many of the comic books involved the depiction of dark-skinned people in rape-like situations with white women. One picture, which showed a woman nailed by her wrists to trees, with blood flowing from the wounds, could easily have been taken directly from the pages of an illustrated edition of the life of the Marquis de Sade. In another comic, this type of editorial viciousness was carried to the extreme by portraying a white woman being overpowered by dark-skinned people who had tails. Another book showed the hero throwing bombs at a black-skinned individual from his airplane. The hero yelled: "BOMBS AND BUMS AWAY!"

The comic books, moreover, often made a distinction between white and nonwhite females. Pictures of white women with completely bared breasts were taboo while such pictures of dark-skinned women were permitted. Indeed, only brown or black-skinned females had their breasts fully exposed. Wertham thought that this was one of the most sinister methods of suggesting that races are fundamentally different in regard to moral values, and that one is inferior to the other. This, he argued, is where a psychiatric question becomes a social one.[19]

False stereotypes of race prejudice were also found to exist in the "love comics." Children were usually able to pick out unsatisfactory lovers just by their looks. War comics, where war is the setting, also promoted race hatred. For example, Americans were always shown to be good looking with regular features, while people of Asia were depicted as cruel, grimacing, and toothy creatures, often with an unnatural yellow color.

These comics tended to engender two overall attitudes in children: *Either* they viewed themselves as some sort of supermen or superior human being, with the attendant prejudices against those who were subhuman (i.e., members of minority groups), *or* they viewed themselves as really being "submen" and thus were receptive to the blandishments of "strong men," men who would solve all of their social problems for them by the use of force.

Another area where reality was distorted and unhealthy stereotypes were promoted was the depiction of women. Wertham found that women were usually portrayed in one of two ways: *Either* they were scantily dressed *superwomen* flying through the air and outsmarting hostile natives and wicked men, *or* they were *possessions of men*, with no value other than to be sexually used, pushed around, and sadistically abused. Indeed, he claimed, in no other literature for children was the image of womanhood so degraded. Where else, for example, in children's literature besides the comics, would one find a woman called (and treated as) a "fat slut"? In addition, the activities which women shared with men were exclusively related to sex, force, and violence.

The superwoman comics were found to be very popular among delinquent and maladjusted girls. "Wonder Woman," for example, was a horror type. She was physically very powerful, tortured men, and had her own female following.

Overall, she was a very frightening figure—and she was created by a child psychologist who argued that it was necessary to create a female character who was alluring and at the same time had the strength of Superman, because "Who wants to be a girl?" To Wertham that was just the point. Not even girls wanted to be girls when they were portrayed as second class citizens.

Not only did the children receive a false concept of womanhood from reading comic books, they also received a false concept of "love." They associated love with brutality, murder, and robbery. For example, one teenage boy discussed the comic book, "Crimes by Women," with Wertham.

> There is one that is sexy! Her headlights are showing *plenty!* She has a smoking gun in her hand as though she had already shot somebody. When you see a girl and you see her headlights and she is beaten up, that makes you hot and bothered. If she will take a beating from a man she will take anything from him.

Another boy, described as a twelve-year-old sex delinquent also discussed his comic book reading with Wertham.

> In the comic book sometimes the men threaten the girls. They beat them with their hands. They tie them around to a chair and then they beat them. When I read such a book I don't get sexually excited all the time, only when they tie them up.

The keynote of the comic books' sexual message was the mixture of sensuality with cruelty. And children were given this message from a tender age. This cultivated, to Wertham, a special kind of perversion, *sadism.* Sadism was defined as "the gratification of sexual feeling by the infliction of or sight of pain." Very young children were especially likely to become confused by a sadistic interpretation of sex, as illustrated in the following example.

> Ronnie, a six-year-old comic book addict attending the clinic, often played with a boy a year or so older who lived downstairs in the same house. One day this playmate took a little girl into his room and proceeded to take off the girl's clothes. Ronnie watched a bit, then ran upstairs excitedly, told his mother all about what he had seen and asked her, "What's he going to do—choke her?"[20]

Graphic descriptions of sexual flagellation of the buttocks were also found in many of the comic books. This sort of illustration, Wertham pointed out, was frowned upon by the Post Office if it occurred in adult books. However, in many children's comic books such erotic scenes were described in detail. Indeed, beatings and brutality were common fare in many comic books. For example, one "typical" book showed the villain (a foreigner) with a half-nude girl in his power. As an appetizer, she is hit in the face. Then she is told:

> I know that you shall love me and shall be loyal after you have taken a dozen or so lashes across your beautiful back.

She is then taken to the cellar, bound by the wrists to a tall post, her breasts conspicuously drawn, where she pleads for mercy. The man stands behind her with a coiled whip in his hand. . . .

Some comic books were found to describe sexual sadism with its morbid psychological refinements. One book, for example, showed a villain making love to a married woman. Her husband, whose leg had been injured by the lover, had to look on helplessly. The villain kisses and fondles the woman, all the while taunting the husband. The result is that the woman becomes sexually excited by this perverse situation. Wertham asked: What kind of message does this story communicate to children?

The drawing of blood from a woman's veins in order to completely overpower her was another morbid fantasy often found in the comic books. According to Wertham, such fully described and depicted perversity was to be found only in one place besides these children's comic books—in the forbidden pages of de Sade himself.

"High heel" literature appeared frequently in the children's comics. This type of literature dealt with the erotic character that high heels have for certain males; often such material appears in pornographic or semipornographic literature for adults. It is well known that some men have a fetish for high-heeled shoes; they collect them for erotic pleasure. Such fetishes, however, are often learned during childhood and adolescence; Wertham argued that one source for such learning was the ordinary comic book. Indeed, exaggeratedly high heels were often portrayed in comic books. This type of picture, showing only legs and extremely high heels, was a repeated motif in many different kinds of comic books. Several boys told Wertham that they collected this type of comic illustration and used them to fantasize and for masturbation. One nineteen-year-old described his high-heel fantasy in the following manner:

> I think of girls twisting their heels on my chest and face. My first complete sexual stimulation came from such comic book scenes at the age of about ten or eleven.

Overall, Wertham concluded, the only difference between surreptitious pornographic literature intended for adults and children's comic books was that in the first it was a question of *attracting* perverts, in the other it was a process of *making* perverts. Moreover, all types of crime comics portrayed a link among love, sex, violence, and brutality.

Many of the "love" comics were written to appeal to females. Like other types of crime comics, they played up the angle that what was depicted was real life. "These girls are real people with real problems and real dramatic confessions," states a typical issue. What is it, then, that these real girls wanted? Again the message is clear. "More than anything in the world I wanted glamor, money, adventure...." What were the typical problems these "real" girls faced? the titles of their stories give the answer.

FALLEN WOMAN
RUNAWAY PASSION
PRICE OF PRIDE
FORBIDDEN LOVE
MY FOOLISH MISTAKE
MUST I REVEAL MY PAST?

Wertham believed that crime comics, especially the love-confession variety, played a role in laying the groundwork for childhood prostitution, which he reported to be on the increase. He used the following example to support this argument.

Annie, aged ten, engaged in sex play with men for which she received money. Like most children she was very suggestible. From comic books she absorbed fantasies of violence and sex....

I fooled around with men, young men and old men. They gave me a dollar. I don't have my period yet. They just took down my pants. I meet the men on the docks. They did it in a shady house, a house that has all kinds of tools in it—hammers. I went over there four times a week. I don't like it. Girls don't like it. I did it for the money. Sometimes I would get half a dollar, sometimes a quarter. Some men don't give you anything. Cheap, ain't they!

This girl read about twenty comic books a day. She read some of them three and four times over.

In his investigations, Wertham found that there were a number of obscure stores where children would congregate, usually in back rooms, to read and buy secondhand comic books. As a rule, the proprietors allowed the children to spend a lot of time in their establishments and to pore over the comic books. In parts of some cities, men "hung around" these stores, which sometimes were the foci of childhood prostitution. Evidently, he argued, the books prepared the little girls quite well for prostitution. In addition, they also apparently prepared little boys for childhood homosexual prostitution. For example, Charles, a twelve-year-old, regularly engaged in prostitution. He did not play hooky, but followed the occupation after school hours. He reported:

> I meet the men in office places or places of business. They give me a dollar or fifty cents. I wondered how they'd be so generous. Some men are about thirty-five.

Wertham attributed Charles' behavior to moral confusion, which he believed was caused by the child's avid reading of crime comics such as "Gangbusters" and "True Comics."

The comic books also allegedly contributed to homosexuality in other ways. For example, many preadolescent boys pass through a psychological phase of disdainment toward girls. To Wertham, some comic books tended to fixate that attitude and to instill the idea that "girls are good only for being banged around or used as decoys." He felt that homoerotic attitudes were promoted by presenting women in an antierotic light. Women were shown as masculine, bad, violent, and witchlike. At the same time, the young male heroes were often presented with pronounced erotic overtones. Wertham pointed out that many adolescents experience vague fears that they might be homosexual but that they often have no one in whom they feel they can confide. He reported finding the following sequence of events in a number of cases. A boy becomes addicted to homoerotic comic books at an early age. Both during and after reading these comics, the boy indulged in fantasies, which were severely repressed. Subsequent life experiences regarding homosexuality produced feelings of doubt, shame, guilt and eventual sexual malorientation.

Some years earlier, around 1950, a California psychiatrist had argued that the Batman and Robin stories were psychologically homosexual. Wertham's research confirmed this finding and he argued·

> Only someone ignorant of the fundamentals of psychiatry and of the psychopathology of sex can fail to realize a subtle atmosphere of homoerotism which pervades the adventures of the mature "Batman" and his young friend "Robin."[21]

In comic books of the Batman type, homosexual relationships were depicted to children before they could even read. The mature "Batman" and the young "Robin" shared adventure after adventure. They constantly rescued each other from violent attacks by an unending variety of enemies. The feeling was conveyed that the men must stick together because there were so many villainous creatures who must be exterminated. At home, they led an idyllic life as Bruce Wayne and "Dick" Grayson. They lived in a beautiful home, with gorgeous flowers in large vases, and a butler—Alfred. Often, they were shown in a romantic setting, such as sitting together on a couch in front of the fireplace. Robin (Dick) was a handsome boy with tremendous energy, and he was devoted to Bruce Wayne (Batman). He often stood with his legs spread, the genital region discreetly evident.

It was also significant that in the Batman–Robin stories there were almost no decent, attractive, successful women. A typical female character was "Catwoman," who was vicious and used a whip. The atmosphere was homosexual and antifeminine. If a girl was good-looking, she was undoubtedly the villainess. If she was after Bruce Wayne, she would have no chance against Dick.

In his research, Wertham found that a number of treated homosexuals avidly read Batman stories. One young homosexual stated that he began reading the Batman and Robin stories at the age of eight. He gave the following account:

> At the age of ten or eleven, I found my sexual liking, my sexual desires, in comic books. I think I put myself in the position of Robin. I did want to have relations with Batman....I remember the first time I came across the page mentioning the "secret bat cave." The thought of Batman and Robin living together and possibly having sex relations came to my mind. You can almost connect yourself with the people....I felt I'd like to be loved by someone like Batman or Superman.

Another young homosexual was being treated by Wertham for more than his homosexuality. He and a companion had used a knife to force an eight-year-old boy to undress and have sex with them. Like many other homoerotically inclined children, he was a special devotee of Batman.

> Sometimes I read them [Batman comics] over and over again. They show off a lot. They live together. It could be that Batman did something with Robin like I did with the younger boy.

However, homosexuality was not only suggested to the male readers of Batman-type comics. The Lesbian counterpart of Batman was found in the stories of "Wonder Woman" and "Black Cat." Whereas Batman was antifeminine, the attractive Wonder Woman and her counterparts were definitely antimasculine. Like Batman, Wonder Woman had her own following—young girls who were constantly threatened. The stories included mutual rescues and fantasies. Her followers were the "Holiday Girls"; Wertham saw the holiday girls as the gay party girls, or more simply, the gay girls. In one typical story, one character involved in an adventure with Wonder Woman repeatedly referred to "those wicked men." It was clear that the "Wonder Woman" stories were amazingly similar to the Batman ones, except that where Batman was antifeminine Wonder Woman was antimasculine.

In summary, Wertham found that the various types of crime comics influenced children's perceptions of reality in many ways—including the following:

1. They led children to believe that violence is a normal and commonplace aspect of everyday life.
2. They instilled in the children prejudice toward minority groups.
3. They portrayed women as either evil or as second-class citizens.
4. They gave children sexually deviant ideas which sometimes resulted in deviant sexual practices, or guilt about such fantasies.

Retooling for Illiteracy. Reading difficulties among children were reported to be increasing. Wertham argued that comic books were an important cause of this increase. He found that a very large proportion of children who could not read well habitually "read" comic books. Moreover, a very high percentage of the worst readers were comic book addicts who spent a great deal of time "reading" comic books. Actually, they were not readers but gazers. That is, they looked at the pictures and managed to pick up a word here and there. They were, in fact, bookworms without books.

The comic books were found to have a negative influence on reading in a number of ways. First, comic book readers were handicapped in vocabulary building because the emphasis in the comics was on the visual image and not on the written word. Children often knew all that they should not know about torture, but were unable to read or spell the word. One detrimental effect comics have is that they hinder the development of fluent left-to-right eye movement necessary for good reading. Reading scattered messages in balloons does not allow for sufficient practice in mastering the skills required for consistent good reading. Moreoever, the spelling in the comic books was often incorrect. "The Case of the Psycopathic (sic) Lady" was not good for children in either content or spelling. The style and language of the comic books' writing was also extremely poor. Editorial comments were hardly better than the text. Consider the example of "cosmic correspondence":

> Greetings, humanoids! Drag over a cyclotron and crawl in! (If we'da known you were coming, we'da baked an isotope!)

Furthermore, the comics had many words that are not words at all. For example, there may be a series of six pictures with violent scenes and no language, just sounds which have no correct spelling. Some of the most common "words" found in the comics were:

OWW	THUNK
ARGHH	YEOW
OOOHHH	UNGH
GLURG	AANGH
UGH	ARRGG
GLHELP	GLUG-UGH

Some of the children called these words "basic American."

The comic books also influenced the creative abilities of the children. Whereas good reading stimulated them to imaginative writing, the comic book influence directed their natural gifts to a cheap whip-the-girl, beat-the-dark-skinned-native mentality.

Overall, Wertham argued that his research offered conclusive proof that comic book reading and reading difficulties went hand-in-hand and that comic books were a causal and reinforcing factor in children's reading disorders. Since reading difficulties were obviously related to failure in school, Wertham also noted the relationship between failure in school and delinquent behavior. (Indeed, even in the 1980s, failure in school remains the *single* best predictor of juvenile delinquency.)

Advertising in Comic Books: Bumps and Bulges

The types of advertisements present in comic books in addition to their actual and potential effects on children were also examined. Wertham argued that it is typical for teenagers and preteens to be very conscious and concerned with their appearance. Comic book advertisements, he claimed, exploited these worries and anxieties with scare tactics that caused many normal boys and girls much grief. Many of the most pernicious ads fell into one of the following categories: "breast ads," "fat ads," "skinny ads," "skin condition ads," "he-man ads," and "weapons ads." Each will be discussed and illustrative examples provided.

Breast Advertisements. It is, of course, not unusual for girls to be sensitive about their breasts before and during adolescence. Comic book reading itself could promote this fear through the portrayals of characters with shapely, protruding breasts. The breast advertisements, however, were found to create "sexual hypochondriasis" by promising help for "problem bosoms," "NO MATTER WHAT SHAPE BOSOM YOU HAVE." For example, a typical full-page advertisement addressed to young girls in a popular comic book had photographs of two girls. One girl had average breasts, while the other had markedly protruding comic-book-style breasts. The caption read: DO MEN CHOOSE MARY OR ALICE?

> When Tom H ＿＿ met Mary W ＿＿ and Alice B ＿＿, folks wondered who the lucky girl would be. Both girls were pretty and charming and grand fun, and enjoyed the same interests Tom did. But somehow it was Alice whose lips Tom bent to in the moonlight. . . . it was Alice whose "I do" rose breathlessly at the altar. . . .
>
> Tom's choice was not surprising. For it is the woman with a beautiful, alluring bust contour who most often wins the admiration, popularity and affection every woman desires. And there can be no COMPLETE feminine beauty without a warmly rounded, lovely bust contour, symbol of woman

eternal. Look through history. Look around you today. It is the woman with
the graceful, appealing figure lines who enjoys social and romantic triumph.
Yes, there are many lovely Marys whose wit, charm and friendliness cannot
compete with the natural law of man's attraction to beauty fulfilled *completely*.

The _____ Ritual _____ may be able to improve the handicap of
unappealing figure lines...which may mean the difference between
loneliness and thrilling romantic fulfillment! Formerly $2.00.... Don't let
skepticism or discouragement deny you the opportunity for happiness....
Be fair to yourself, to your future as a *woman*.

It was common for this type of advertisement to display "Before" and "After"
photographs. The "Before" looked like an average girl; the "After" had
noticeably pointed, protruding breasts. Many of these advertisements were
directed to growing girls whose busts were just starting to develop and led off
with screamers such as "SMALL BUST." Wertham believed that such
advertisements caused feelings of inferiority in many young girls and that some
carried this emotional burden with them throughout their lives. He cited many
clinical cases to support his conclusions.

Weight Advertisements. Depending upon their type of body build, many
adolescents pass through phases of growth when they are likely to be either too
"chubby" or too "skinny." Comic book advertisements played on this type of
fear—all for the sake of increasing their profits. Some typical "fat" captions
included the following:

> Don't suffer humiliation and ridicule by Being FAT!
> You have nothing to lose but Weight!
> RESTORE the RIGHT CURVES in the Right Places!
> How an Unhappy Fat Girl Became a Happy Slim Girl!

Of course, those adolescent girls who pass through a slender growth phase are
not forgotten.

> Skinny Girls and NOT glamor Girls!
> Ashamed of your skinny, scrawny figure?
> SKINNY GIRLS DON'T HAVE OOMPH!

The boys were not ignored in the weight ads, although the slant was toward
body-building.

> Hey SKINNY! Yer ribs are Showing!

Another full-page advertisement illustrated with photos of muscular men
declared:

> From a SKINNY WEAKLING to a MIGHTY MAN. . . .
> I Gained 53 lbs. of MIGHTY MUSCLE. 6½ inches on my CHEST; 3 inches on each ARM. You can do it in 10 minutes a day!

Other advertisements tended to make boys feel ashamed of their bodies.

> How to make your Body Bring you FAME instead of SHAME! Are you Skinny? Weak? Flabby? . . . I know what it means to have the kind of body that people pity! . . . I don't care how old or young you are or how ashamed of your present physical condition. . . I can shoot new strength into your old backbone. . . help you cram your body so full of pep, vigor and vitality, that you won't feel there's even standing room left for weakness and that lazy feeling!

Skin Advertisements. Another prime target for scare advertisements was skin condition. It was, of course, also not unusual for acne, pimples, and blackheads to trouble teenagers and for them to be a major source of concern. Wertham argued that the comic book ads aggravated this concern and intensified feelings of anxiety and inferiority. They could make boys and girls self-conscious about even the slightest blemish; more importantly, the ads promised an instant, miraculous cure.

One full-page advertisement began with this dialogue:

> Ask your friend Tom.
> Tom, why don't Sis and I get invited to proms and parties?
> Frankly, Jim, it's those ugly blackheads.

Then follows the indoctrination with its attendant fear and shame:

> What a "black mark" is the blackhead. . .according to men and girls popular enough to be choosy about dates! "Nobody's dreamboat!" "Nobody's date bait!" And that's not all that's said about those who are careless about blackheads. But blackheads ARE ugly! Blackheads ARE grimy! And they DON'T look good in close-ups.
>
> So can you blame the fellow who says, "Sure I meet lots of girls who look cute at first glance. But if, on the second glance I see dingy black—it's *good night!*"
>
> Or can you blame the girl who confesses, "I hate to go out with a fellow who has blackheads, if he's careless about that you're sure he'll embarrass you in other ways, too!
>
> But you—are YOUR ears burning? Well, you've company, and, sad to say, good company. There are lots of otherwise attractive fellows and girls who could date anyone they like if they'd only realize how offensive blackheads are and how easily and quickly they could get rid of them, if they *want* to!. . . The "he-man" who is also clean-cut, will get the breaks

wherever he is!. . . . Even cute girls get careless. . .so don't take chances, cute though you may be!

Wertham found that some children became so excessively stressed by acne and the repeated failure of comic-book cures that they withdrew socially, to the extent that they were diagnosed as schizophrenic.

Weapons Advertisements. Weapons of all kinds were attractively advertised, particularly guns and knives. While some were real (e.g., a .22 caliber rifle) the majority were toys. A typical advertisement contains a big picture of a gun:

> Amazing New Gun! Shoots like a real gun.

An accompanying sequence teaches how the gun could be used to threaten people:

> You fooled us, kid, I thought that gun was a real one!

Knives of different types were also advertised in the comic books in a glamorous fashion.

> FLINGS OPEN FAST. BIG SIZE!
> ONLY $1.65
> Whittle your enemies down to size.

Peeping Toms and Human Relations. Wertham also discussed a variety of other advertisements, including those for telescopes and "human relations ads." He was particularly concerned with the telescope ads because he had treated a number of youths after they had been arrested as "peeping Toms." Most of them had looked in windows trying to see women undressing. Many of the boys claimed to have gotten the idea from "peeping Tom ads" in the comics. One telescope ad, for example, offered:

> Real power and up-close clear view! A 1000 thrills are yours with this powerful imported telescope. Enjoy Life!. . .Bring some scenes so close you feel you can touch them!

Another advertisement for binoculars made the following claim:

> You'll get the thrill of a lifetime when you take your first look through these powerful binoculars. It's positively amazing how well you can see. . . You'll be able to see people. . .from a distance and watch what they're doing when they can't see you. Enjoy front row seats from way back!

Other ads explicitly point out that you could even look into "neighbor's" homes.

"Human relations" ads included courses for boys on how to get along with girls.

> It's easy to win her! Women are funny—put psychology to work. No more clumsy mistakes for *you* . . . Don't be a Faux Pas! [sic]

Of course there were also courses for girls on how to handle boys.

Wertham concluded that the comic book stories and the advertisements they contained complemented each other. He argued:

> Comic book stories teach violence, the advertisements provide the weapons. The stories instill a wish to be a superman, the advertisements promise to supply the means for becoming one. Comic-book heroines have super-figures; the comic-book advertisements promise to develop them. The stories display the wounds, the advertisements supply the knives. The stories feature scantily clad girls; the advertisements outfit peeping toms.[22]

In summary, Wertham concluded that comic books had the following effects:[23]

1. The comic book format is an invitation to illiteracy.
2. Crime comic books create an atmosphere of cruelty and deceit.
3. They create a readiness for temptation.
4. They stimulate unwholesome fantasies.
5. They suggest criminal or sexually abnormal ideas.
6. They furnish the rationalization for these ideas which may be ethically even more harmful than the impulse.
7. They suggest the forms delinquency may take and supply the details of technique.
8. They may tip the scales toward maladjustment or delinquency.
9. Overall, crime comics are an agent with harmful potential. They bring about a mass conditioning of children, with different effects in individual cases.

Wertham further cautioned that even children who did not read comic books could have been influenced by them indirectly through contact with children who were comic book readers (the two-step flow of communication concept). He argued:

> Frequently the influence of comic books is not exerted directly, but comes through other children. The influence of children on children is generally underestimated. Parents have sometimes told me that what I have said about

comic books may be true, but that doesn't affect *their* children because they do not read such trash. One of my answers to this is generally, "Don't you think your child will later on, either in school or other places, meet other children who have been steeped in comics and have absorbed their attitudes concerning sex, violence, women, money, races and other subjects that make up social life?"[24]

CONCLUSIONS AND IMPLICATIONS

If nothing more, *Seduction of the Innocent* is an important work because of the attention and controversy its claims brought to the comic book industry. Indeed, that attention nearly destroyed the industry! Before we discuss the social significance of this milestone, however, we shall briefly examine its theoretical and methodological importance.

Wertham's research was theoretically inconsistent. At times he clearly specified a theory of selective influence, based upon individual differences. This was evident in his statements that comic books did not affect all children in the same way. Despite this disclaimer, his *real* message came through that comic books did have relatively uniform effects. Children were helpless victims who could not resist the comic books' messages. This was clearly a version of the old magic bullet theory. Indeed, reduced to its simplest terms, Wertham's argument was that (1) comic books were read by a large number of children; (2) since a large component of the comic diet consisted of crime, violence, horror, and sex, (3) children who read the comics were necessarily stimulated to the performance of delinquent acts, cruelty, violence, and undersirable sexual behavior. At the same time Wertham told us that comic books *did* uniformly affect all children, and that they *did not* uniformly affect all children. It appears that he believed the first but felt that it was necessary to acknowledge the second to appear "scientific."

In some discussions (such as those concerning the portrayals of women, blacks, foreigners, and Jews) he anticipated the conclusions of contemporary meaning theory (Chapter 1). Some researchers thought that this was the most important aspect of Wertham's investigation. One researcher, for example, in commenting on the crime comics argued: "The real point is not that the children will tend to resort to violence themselves; it is rather that they begin to *accept* violence, when practiced by others, as 'normal.'"[25] However, in the final analysis, Wertham gave much more coverage and much more attention to what the comics made children "do" rather than to the meaning of all that was done.

The conclusions of *Seduction of the Innocent* may be criticized on many grounds, but the major weakness of Wertham's position is that it is not supported by scientifically gathered research data. The findings are said to be the result of seven years of study conducted by him and eleven other psychiatrists and social workers at the Lafargue Clinic. The claim was made that numerous children, both delinquent and nondelinquent, were studied and that the results of these studies led to the conclusion that the effect of comic books is "definitely and completely harmful."

Wertham claimed to have studied the content of comic books and found that the content of the comics was almost universally one of crime, violence, horror, emphasizing of sexual characteristics, and so on. Of the millions of comic books that Wertham claimed dealt with crime and brutality, he rested his case on the selection of extreme and offensive examples that he made no attempt to prove were typical. No systematic inventory of comic book content was presented, such as that compiled by Edgar Dale for the movies in the 1920s. (See Chapter 2.) Without such an inventory, the conjectures are biased, unreliable, and useless.

Wertham gave the reader numerous examples of comic-book art. One writer even commented that "the most impressive part of the book is its illustration."[26] For example, there was a picture of a baseball game in which the ball was a man's head with one eye dangling from the socket; the bat was a severed leg; the catcher wore a dismembered torso as a chest protector; the baselines were marked with stretched-out intestines; the bases were marked with lungs, liver, and heart; the rosin bag was the dead man's stomach; and the umpire dusted off home plate with the scalp. Another illustration, a comic book cover, was a close-up of a hanged man, tongue protruding, eyeballs turned back, and the break in the neck clearly drawn. Wertham supplied his readers with 35 such "juicy" pictures, pictures that emphasized violence, sex, or both.

Were these scenes representative of comic book illustrations? Although Wertham argued they were, he did not provide systematic evidence to support the argument. His major claims concerning the effects of comics on children rested on selected and often extreme cases of children's deviant behavior where comics were said to have played an important role in producing that delinquency. Although he claimed that he and his associates had studied thousands of children, normal and delinquent, rich and poor, gifted and mediocre, he presented no statistical summary of his investigation. He claimed to have used nondelinquent control groups, but he did not describe these controls, how they were set up, or how they were equated with his experimental groups of delinquents and maladjusted children in order to assess the difference, if any, between the groups resulting from comic book reading and influence. He told us nothing about the specific interviewing techniques used, so we do not know if the interviewers used "leading" questions. In short, his methodology was clinical and speculative, but by no means scientific.

Moreover, Dr. Wertham pursued his argument with a humorless dedication that tended to place all evidence on the same level. Discussing "Superman," he suggested that it would not take much to change the "S" on that chest to "SS" (a reference to the Storm Troopers of Nazi Germany). He told us, with a straight face, of a little boy who, when asked what he wanted to be when he grew up, replied, "I want to be a sex maniac!" (This comment became a chapter title.) He reported the case of a twelve-year-old boy who had misbehaved with his sister and threatened to break her arm if she told anyone. "This is not the kind of thing that boys used to tell their sisters," Dr. Wertham informed us. Dr. Wertham, in effect, took at face value anything children told him, either as evidence of the harmful effects of the comic books ("I think sex all boils down to anxiety," one boy told him; Wertham's response was to indicate that the boy could not have gotten that from anywhere but the comics) or as direct support for his own views. For example, he quoted approvingly a fourteen-year-old boy's analysis of the economic motives that prompted psychiatrists to endorse comic books. It would have been a very dull child, indeed, who attended Dr. Wertham's clinic and did not discover very quickly that most of his or her problem behavior could be explained in terms of the comic books.[27]

Many of Wertham's critics argued that he did not distinguish between "good" and "bad" comic books. Perhaps he was able to ignore this distinction because so many readers found it hard to conceive of what a "good" comic book might be. Yet, in terms of their potential effects, there could be a significant difference between "Donald Duck" or "The Lone Ranger" on one hand, and the comic book from which Dr. Wertham took the picture of the baseball game played with the disconnected parts of a human body. As one observer commented:

> If the Lone Ranger (type of comics) are bad, they are bad in a different way and on different level. They are crude, unimaginative, banal, vulgar, ultimately corrupting. They are also, as Dr. Wertham claims, violent—but always within certain limits. Perhaps the worst thing they do is to meet the juvenile imagination on its crudest level and offer it an immediate and stereotyped satisfaction.[28]

While this is bad enough, surely it is better (or different) than present raw violence and/or sex.

In critiquing *Seduction of the Innocent*, it· should also be noted that Dr. Wertham presented a picture of society and human nature that is not unlike that found in the comic book. His world, like the world of the comic books, was one where the logic of personal interest was inexorable. *Seduction of the Innocent*, as its title and illustrations suggest, is a kind of crime comic book for parents. The book has the same simple conception of motives, the same sense of overhanging doom, the same melodramatic emphasis on pathology, and the same direct and immediate relation between cause and effect. If a juvenile delinquent were found in possession of comic books, the comic books produced the crime. If a publisher of comic books retained a psychiatrist to advise him on the suitability of the content of his publications, it followed that the arrangement was a dishonest one. If no comic book publisher was prosecuted under the laws against contributing to the delinquency of minors, it was not that the laws were not applicable. It was because "no district attorney, no judge, no complainant ever had the courage to make a complaint."[29] In the same vein, Wertham informed us:

> Crime comic book writers should not be blamed for comic books. They are not free men. They are often. . .very critical of comics. In every letter I have received from a writer, stress is laid on requests to keep his identity a secret. They are told what to do and they do it—*or else* (emphasis added).[30]

What, perchance, did Dr. Wertham mean by that ominous "or else?" Will the recalcitrant writer be dragged face down over a gravel road in true comic book fashion? Surely not! At *worst*, they faced only the mundane possibility of losing their jobs.

Despite all the criticism leveled at *Seduction of the Innocent*, it was still important in the history of communication research. It is true that we can criticize its methodology, logic, conclusions, and so on. But the book had a tremendous impact on the public's perception of the power of the media. In short, this work reinforced the legacy of fear. As previously discussed, Wertham took his argument to the people in popular forums like *Ladies' Home Journal* and *Reader's Digest*—and a great number of them listened and believed. In many ways, his writings can be said to have sparked the flame that led to Senate hearings, conducted by Senator Kefauver, on the relationship between "juvenile delinquency and comic books." The added publicity focused on comic books because of the hearings spelled doom for the publishers of the most violent and sexually blatant comic books. But a stigma was also placed on the "good" comic books, and their circulation began to decline. Other factors, such as the rise of television, contributed to this decline. But Dr. Wertham had had an effect, because in the end, most people agreed! Whatever else they might be—comic books were *not* funny.

NOTES AND REFERENCES

1. For a discussion of this topic, see James P. Wood, "Magazine Publishing Today" in *Mass Media and Communication*, ed. by Charles Steinberg (New York: Hastings House, 1966), pp. 182–183. Also see Melvin De Fleur and Everette Dennis, *Understanding Mass Communication* (Boston: Houghton Mifflin, 1981). See Chapter 2.

2. Norbert Muhlen, "Comic Books and Other Horrors: Prep School for Totalitarian Society?" *Commentary*, Jan. 1949, 80–87.

3. Ibid., p. 81.

4. Ibid., pp. 80–87.
5. Ibid.
6. Frederic M. Thrasher, "The Comics and Delinquency: Cause or Scapegoat," *The Journal of Educational Sociology* 23 (1): 195–205, Sept. 1949.
7. Frederic Wertham, *Seduction of the Innocent* (New York: Rinehart, 1954), p. vi.
8. Ibid., p. 52.
9. Ibid., pp. 57–58.
10. Ibid., p. 111.
11. Ibid., p. 157.
12. Ibid., p. 31.
13. Ibid., p. 34.
14. Ibid., p. 156.
15. Ibid., p. 164.
16. Ibid., p. 96.
17. Ibid., p. 88.
18. Ibid., p. 101.
19. Ibid., p. 105.
20. Ibid., p. 179.
21. Ibid., pp. 189–190.
22. Ibid., p. 217.
23. Ibid., p. 118.
24. Ibid., p. 108.
25. Norbert Muhlen, op. cit., p. 86.
26. Robert Warshow, "Paul, the Horror Comics, and Dr. Wertham," in *Mass Culture*, ed. by Bernard Rosenberg and David White (New York: The Free Press, 1957), pp. 199–211.
27. Ibid.
28. Ibid., p. 207.
29. Frederic Wertham, op. cit.
30. Ibid.

10

Television in the Lives of Our Children: The Early Years

When the movies grew rapidly as a mass medium early in the century, one of the first concerns of the American public was their impact on children. In some ways, the mushrooming growth of television in the immediate postwar years followed a similar pattern. However, its adoption by the public was even more rapid, almost catching everyone by surprise. Suddenly, there was a remarkable new box in everyone's living room, with moving pictures as well as sound. The incredibly rapid pace of the adoption of this device, as well as peoples' growing alarm over its possible effects on the young were factors that helped shape the earliest research directions designed to discover television's role in the expanding system of mass communication.

The television industry exploded across the American landscape during the 1950s; no other mass medium had ever grown so quickly. The extent of this expansion becomes evident when we consider a few facts. In 1948, there were fewer than 100,000 television sets in the United States; one year later, a million sets were in use in American homes—and that was only the beginning! Indeed, by 1959, more than 50 million television sets had been placed in American homes, and approximately 88 percent of U.S. households were the proud owners of television receivers. This was a dramatic turnaround from the beginning of the decade, when only about 6 percent of American households had even one set. Thus, in less than a decade, television had become a pervasive aspect of American life. [1]

Possession of a TV set quickly became a status symbol in the early years of television's diffusion through the American population. Families who could ill afford such a luxury sometimes cut corners on necessities in order to purchase one. Many acquired their sets through installment purchases—the "easy payment plan." In some cases, the urge to own a television and to be identified as an owner was so strong that families were said to have bought and installed antennas in conspicuous locations long before they purchased the sets to hook up and watch. This emergence of television as a status symbol led to occasional public outrage when it was discovered that some people receiving public welfare or other forms of relief possessed sets. Apparently the experiences of those who had lived through the Depression years had been forgotten; at that time, radio sets were welcomed as extremely comforting to people trapped in trying economic circumstances (see Chapter 3).

Television sets might have become a common household item even sooner if it had not been for the intervention of World War II. The technology of television broadcasting had been developed during the 1920s and 1930s, and by 1939, network television broadcasts were already being made in the United States. The World's Fair that year featured demonstrations of that latest scientific marvel, television. President Hoover had experimented with broadcasts, and President Roosevelt even delivered a speech over the new communication medium. The speech's broadcast audience, however, consisted of only a handful of people because commercial manufacturers had not yet begun to mass-produce sets. The Federal Communications Commission approved home television in 1941, on the eve of America's entry into World War II, and the communications industry had already begun to work out plans for its development. At that time, there were approximately 5,000 sets in private hands, mostly around New York City, and several small private stations were broadcasting regularly for two or three hours a day.[2]

World War II, however, abruptly altered this development and postponed the general availability of television until the war had ended. This hindrance to commercial development may account, in some respects, for the extremely rapid growth in both television broadcasting and manufacturing when the country returned to a peacetime economy. For one thing, communications executives had the plans well laid for their expansion into television. In addition, electronics manufacturers had developed new techniques of production during the war that aided the industry in overcoming the problems of mass-producing television receivers. Besides all this, the prewar economic depression had finally ended. In fact, wartime rationing had created an immense pent-up demand for consumer goods and services. Americans, with jobs and money in their pockets, went on a buying spree. With minor fluctuations, the United States entered a period of unprecedented economic growth that was uninterrupted for more than two decades. With this prosperity came an increase in the purchasing power of the average citizen. The purchasing power of the average American family rose to the point that television ownership was within the means of all but the poorest.[3]

By 1960, 150 million Americans had acquired sets and rearranged their lives to accommodate the schedule of television programs presented on their living room screens. This rearrangement appeared to be most striking in homes with children; such homes were more than twice as likely to have a set than homes which did not have children. Television had become the single greatest source of national entertainment; it had displaced radio, comic books, playmates, and babysitters by a wide margin. However, the public knew very little about the effects of this new medium; the legacy of fear persisted among many Americans and there was growing concern about what television might be doing to America's children. Would the new medium stunt or stimulate the mental growth of children? Was it going to create armies of juvenile delinquents? Would it turn children into passive robots incapable of intellectual creativity? Would it propel children into an adult world of sex, liquor, and violence for which they were unprepared? American parents were deeply concerned about such effects on this crucial segment of the population—from toddlers to teenagers.

The few research projects that dealt with the effects of television in the early 1950s provided no assurances to allay the fears of the public. A series of surveys by the National Association of Educational Broadcasters in 1951 discovered that crime and horror stories comprised 10 percent of the programming time in four American cities.[4] While by today's standards this might appear to be a small proportion of the shows, at the time it appeared to be excessive. Other investigations by social scientists revealed that watching television had reduced the amount of time that children spent playing—both indoors and outdoors. Viewing also reduced the amount of time that children devoted to helping out with household chores, such as cooking and cleaning. Children who watched television also spent less time listening to the radio, going to movies, and reading books.[5] Television viewing cut into all of the activities of daily life. No one knew, however, whether television could change attitudes or values. It was unknown whether television could create passivity or aggression, or whether it would enlarge or limit children's intellectual boundaries. Exactly what *was* happening to the tender minds tuned in to the electronic Pied Piper? Clearly, more research was needed to find out television's effects, particularly research focusing on children. In this setting, Professors Wilbur Schramm, Jack Lyle, and Edwin Parker undertook the first large-scale investigation of the relationship between television and children in North America. It is to that investigation that we now turn.

THE RESEARCH PROGRAM

The results of the first major study of the effects of television on North American children were reported in *Television in the Lives of Our Children*. It presented the findings and conclusions from eleven investigations carried out between 1958 and 1960, in ten communities in the United States and Canada. The focus of the project was on the *uses and functions* of television for various categories of children, rather than simply on a straightforward analysis of "effects." The authors believed that the term "effects" was misleading in that:

> . . . it suggests that television "does something" to children. The connotation is that television is the actor; the children are acted upon. Children are thus made to seem relatively inert; television relatively active. Children are sitting victims; television bites them.[6]

Schramm and his colleagues argued that nothing could be further from the truth. Children were not, they emphasized, passive entities being acted upon by television. To the contrary, children were *active agents* who selected material from television that best fit their interests and needs. It was children who used television, not television that used children.

According to Schramm, Lyle, and Parker, children used television to satisfy some need. They drew an analogy between television and a "great shiny cafeteria." From television, as from a cafeteria, children selected only what they wanted at the moment. It was conceded that television's bill of fare contained many dishes heavy in fantasy, that there were large slices of violence and that there was less variety in the menu than some of the patrons might prefer at any one time. But, like the cafeteria, children took and ate only what they wanted from television. Thus, it was argued that in order to understand television's effects, it was necessary to understand a great deal about the lives of children. We needed to know what it was in their lives which made them reach out for a particular experience on television. Only then could we know how their lives interacted with and were influenced by television. This was exactly what they proposed to do.

Research Design and Methodology

As previously noted, Schramm and his associates conducted eleven separate studies between 1958 and 1960. The first study was funded by the San Francisco school system to gain information about the use of television by children in grades one through six. On the basis of the results obtained in the first study, subsequent funding for additional studies was provided, mainly by the National Educational Television and Radio Center. The scope of these studies is briefly summarized below:

Study 1: San Francisco, 1958–1959
In the initial study, the researchers used a total of 2688 children chosen to serve as representatives of grades one through six, and of the eighth, tenth and twelfth grades of the public school system. Some of the children were interviewed directly. Many of them, however, completed questionnaires and tests administered in their classrooms. Several hundred students kept diaries. In addition, data were obtained on some of the younger children through questionnaires completed by their parents. The study also included data from questionnaires completed by 1030 parents, in which they described and reacted to their children's television behavior. The information gathered on each child varied somewhat according to the age of the child, but the researchers tried to learn as much as possible about each child's mass media behavior. Schramm and his associates were interested in what children used the different media for, and what the media meant to them. In addition, they examined what the children knew about public affairs, science, popular and fine art, and other parts of the world. They also learned something about the

children's family lives and their relations with children their own age. The research included measures of some of their psychological characteristics, their mental ability, the use they were making of it in school, and so on. In addition to all of this information gathered directly from the children and their parents, the researchers also talked to teachers, school officials, and other knowledgeable persons.

Study 2: San Francisco, 1958

Interviews were conducted with 188 *entire families, as families*. The researchers talked to the parents and the children together so that the subjects could check up on one another and also so that the researchers could observe their interactions. The families were asked chiefly about the use of the media different members of the family made, and what part the media played in family life. In all, 188 mothers, 187 fathers, and 502 children were interviewed.

Studies 3–7: Rocky Mountain Communities, 1959

The entire sixth and tenth grades, or where necessary an adequate sample of them, were interviewed in five communities in the Rocky Mountain area of the United States. In three of these communities, the researchers also included the first grade. In most respects, the information sought about each child paralleled that which had been obtained in San Francisco, although the questionnaires had been expanded and sharpened as the work progressed. In the case of the three first grade cohorts, for example, the researchers administered vocabulary tests to the children. The total sample from the five towns was 1708 children and 284 parents. As before, local teachers and officials were also consulted as a check on the information.

Studies 8–9: Canada, 1959

Two communities in Canada were studied which were comparable to each other in most respects, except that one of them did not have television. Data were gathered in each community from the first, sixth, and tenth grades using the same materials developed for the Rocky Mountain towns, except that the materials had been improved through use, and somewhat expanded to take into account special characteristics of Canadian mass communication. Again, the first grades were given vocabulary tests. In all, 913 children and 269 parents were interviewed, and as before, the researchers consulted with local teachers and officials.

Study 10: American Suburb

The researchers examined in detail the television behavior, program choice, and time allocations of all of the elementary school children in one school. Data were gathered on a total of 474 children. Again, parents and teachers were consulted.

Study 11: Denver, 1960

This final study examined 204 students in the tenth grade in order to test several hypotheses developed from the results of the previous studies. The information obtained here dealt with the students' media behavior in relation to mental ability and social norms.

To summarize, a total of eleven studies were conducted. Overall, the researchers collected data from 5991 students, 1958 parents, and from several hundred teachers, officials, and other knowledgeable persons in ten communities in the United States and Canada. These communities were chosen to be representative of North America and included isolated areas, metropolitan areas, cities, and towns of various sizes. The sample also included industrial, agricultural, and residential communities, and the level of the development of local television ran the gamut then existing in North America—from no television to highly developed, multistation broadcast areas.

The Functions of Television

Schramm, Lyle, and Parker offered their readers an explanation of why children watched television. They began with the functionalist assumption that every item in a culture exists because it is useful for the members of that culture. Therefore, they reasoned, television viewing must be useful to children. And for it to be useful, it must be meeting certain needs, and it must be the *best* way of meeting those needs among the known and available alternatives. What were those needs? The authors posited three primary reasons why children watched television: (1) for entertainment, (2) for information, and/or (3) because of its social utility. Each of these reasons will be discussed below.

Entertainment. The most important and most obvious reason why children watched television was to enjoy the passive pleasure of being entertained. They enjoyed escaping from real-life problems and from boredom, and the children enjoyed identifying with exciting and attractive people. And television programming was aimed more at escaping problems than it was at solving them. Watching television is an essentially passive behavior; it is something that the children surrendered themselves to; it is something that they did not have to work for or think about.

Information. Most children, when questioned, acknowledged that they learned from television. In many ways the medium served them as had the movies, as reported in Blumer's study (Chapter 2). Girls said that they learned something about personal grooming—how to wear their hair, how to walk and talk, how to choose clothes—by observing the well-groomed mannequins on television. They also learned some of the details of contemporary manners and customs; for example, whether passengers are expected to tip the stewardess on an airplane. Some of the boys said that they learned how other young men dressed in New York or California. Others said that they learned a great deal by watching the performances of good athletes. More than one parent told of a child who learned to swing a baseball bat by watching professional stars on television, and as a result became playground sensations until they began to imitate their young friends instead of the television performers. Typical comments children made about television were: "It helps me to know how other kinds of people live"; or "The news is more real when you have seen where it happens." Many children said that television helped them in school by giving them ideas for themes or topics to discuss.

Social Utility. Another attraction television had for children was its social utility. An example of this utility is that, among teenagers, watching television became a social occasion. It provided a handy excuse for boys and girls to enjoy each other's company; it gave them something convenient and inexpensive to do on dates; and it furnished them with a ready-made excuse for sitting close together. In addition, even when they did not watch television in the company of their peers, the previous evening's programs provided a common ground for conversations at school and on dates. If teenagers were not able to discuss these programs, they became out of step with their peers. Hence, watching television had a direct utility in their social lives.

Schramm, Lyle, and Parker reported that some children appeared to be quite compulsive about television. Such children were vaguely ill-at-ease when they missed a favorite program, or when their set was broken, or when some program or performer they particularly liked was off the air. Some children felt uneasy when they were away from television on a summer vacation. When asked to explain this feeling, one girl responded, "It's just as if they were your friends or your family. You miss them when you don't see them." Some children explained that they felt they were missing something, that they were out of step and were not in touch with what their peers were doing. It is evident, then, that watching television was functional for these children beyond the specific benefits of learning and entertainment.

The authors reasoned that any particular TV program might serve all three purposes for a child. A crime program, for example, would be likely to entertain many children. At the same time, however, it might teach some children specific skills and convey information about "what the world is like." In addition, the program provides the child with something to share and discuss the next day. It should be noted, however, that different children might view the same program in different ways. To one child, a news story about a murder trial might be a "whodunit" entertainment program. To another, it might be a commentary on conditions in the real world. For a third child, it could provide a way of learning how to commit murder. The message the child receives from the television show can thus depend upon what the child brings to the TV set—that is, it depends upon the child's personal, social, and psychological characteristics.

Overall, the authors considered the use of television for entertainment and for information to be the most important uses. They argued that the chief needs for which children went to television were the needs for both *fantasy* and *reality* experiences. The authors distinguished between fantasy content and reality content in the following manner:[7]

Fantasy Content:	*Reality Content:*
invites the viewer to take leave of his problems in the real world;	constantly refers the viewer to the problems of the real world;
invites surrender, relaxation, passivity;	invites alertness, effort, activity;
invites emotion;	invites cognition;
works chiefly through abrogating the rules of the real world;	works chiefly through realistic materials and situations;
acts to remove, at least temporarily, threat and anxiety, and offers wish-fulfillment;	tends to make viewer even more aware of threat, perhaps more anxious, in return for better view of the problem;
offers pleasure.	offers enlightenment.

It was thought that the predominant needs that television met for children were fantasy needs rather than reality needs.

THE FINDINGS

The more quantitative and detailed findings of these eleven studies are too numerous and varied to be discussed in any detail. They can, however, be placed into five general categories: (1) how and when children used television, (2) children's learning from television, (3) reality-seeking and social norms, (4) television and social relationships, and (5) the effects of television. Each of these sets of findings will be discussed in turn.

How and When Children Used Television

The first direct experience that a child had with television typically came at age two, although it could not be said that most of the children were "users" at that age. Typically, such children "dropped in" on a program that someone else was watching. Soon after they began to explore the world of television, and by the age of three, many children were making regular use of the medium. In fact, when asked, they were able to name their favorite programs. Figure 10.1 represents graphically the percentage of children using television between the ages of two and nine.

As can be seen, 37 percent of the three-year-old children were regular viewers, compared to 82 percent of the five-year-olds, 91 percent of those age six, and 96 percent of the nine-year-olds. Thus, by their ninth birthday, only 4 percent of the children could be considered nonusers!

But how much *time* did these children spend in front of the television set? The "average" three-year-old spent about 45 minutes a day watching television.

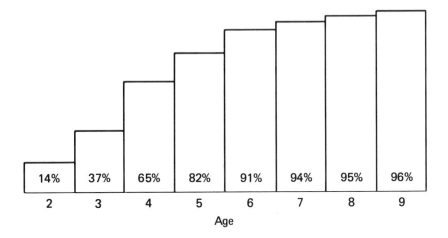

| 14% | 37% | 65% | 82% | 91% | 94% | 95% | 96% |
| 2 | 3 | 4 | 5 | 6 | 7 | 8 | 9 |

Age

Figure 10.1. The Beginnings of Television Use; Percent of Children Using It by Age. *Source:* Wilbur Schramm, Jack Lyle, and Edwin B. Parker, *Television in the Lives of Our Children* (Stanford, Calif.: Stanford University Press, 1961) p. 27.

By the age of five, however, viewing time had increased to a little more than two hours per day. Between their sixth and tenth birthdays, children's viewing time slowly increased to about two and one-half hours each day. When the children reached eleven or twelve, viewing time suddenly jumped to three or four hours daily; at this point, however, it began a slow, steady decline that continued throughout adolescence. It should be noted that these figures were for weekdays. Weekend viewing averages were higher, ranging from half-an-hour to an hour longer. In addition, the authors cautioned that their figures were conservative. Yet they also noted the cumulative situation: They observed that "from ages three through sixteen children spend *more total time* on television than on school. In fact, they are likely to devote more time to television than to any other activity except sleep."[8] (Emphasis added.)

We have indicated that age was an important factor in determining overall viewing time, and that the heaviest period of children's viewing usually came sometime between the ages of 11 and 13. But other factors, especially mental ability and social class background, were also important in determining the viewing habits of children.

The relationship between mental ability, as measured by IQ, and viewing time presented a rather dramatic picture. In the early school years, the children with high IQ scores tended to engage in high levels of television viewing. However, sometime between the tenth and thirteenth years a notable change occurred. The more intelligent children deserted the ranks of heavy viewers. The authors presented interesting data regarding this generalization. In the Rocky Mountain towns, for example, there was no relationship between IQ scores and viewing time among sixth grade students. However, by the time the children had reached the tenth grade, most of the low IQ children had become high viewers, whereas most of the high IQ scorers had become low viewers. The data presented in Figure 10.2 illustrate these findings.

The chart shows that the percentage of light viewers increased generally between the sixth and tenth grades, but the chief increase was among those in the high IQ group. Data from the other regions paralleled the conditions in the Rocky Mountain towns.

Why did the brighter children stop watching so frequently? Schramm and his associates found that television no longer presented a challenge to those children. Most of them were finding greater rewards in the print media and in social and school activities.

Social class background was also found to be important in determining the amount of time spent viewing. Children of well-educated parents tended to watch less than other children, following the example set by their parents. Children of working-class parents, however, were likely to watch more. The authors speculated that this difference in viewing time between social classes could be attributed to a difference in class norms. The middle class norms of work, activity, and self-betterment influenced the viewing patterns of the middle class youngsters by giving them incentives to engage in other activities, thereby reducing the time available for viewing.

Schramm, Lyle, and Parker did indicate a note of caution, however. They pointed out that these general patterns did have exceptions and that there were

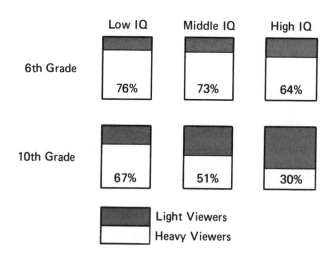

Figure 10.2. Percent of Children Who Are Heavy Viewers of Television, by Grade and Mental Level.
Source: Wilbur Schramm, Jack Lyle, and Edwin B. Parker, *Television in the Lives of Our Children* (Stanford, Calif.:Stanford University Press, 1961) p. 34.

enough exceptions to lead them to believe that some of the most important factors in determining viewing habits must have been missing from their list. They felt that there was something beyond age, intelligence, and family that was affecting the children's viewing patterns. They believed that the missing elements were the child's social relationships and some of his or her personal characteristics.

Social relationships were indeed found to influence a child's use of television. The researchers discovered that children who had unsatisfactory relationships with their families, and/or with their peer groups, tended to retreat from those social interactions into television viewing. When watching television, they could leave real-life problems behind them, at least for a time, and possibly reduce the tension in their lives. The more conflict there was in these children's lives, the more they watched television. It was evident, then, that problems with either the family or the peer group were clearly related to escapist fantasy seeking, and that children with such problems turned to television to escape

What Children Watched. Typically, the first programs that most children identified as their favorites were programs that the broadcasters referred to as "children's programs." The central characters of such programs were usually animals, animated characters, or puppets (e.g., Donald Duck, Huckleberry Hound, Howdy Doody, Rin Tin Tin), although sometimes the children themselves took the role of the sympathetic character. The programs were presented in story form and were full of action, often with a heavy component of slapstick humor. Such programs were traditionally aired in the late afternoon, after school, or on Saturday morning. Programs of this type monopolized the viewing time of preschool children, and their dominance persisted well into the elementary school years, although often in somewhat more mature forms such as "Lassie." By the time the child was well settled in school, however, a new lineup of favorite programs had been etablished. These consisted of a number of program types created especially for children but modelled after adult programs: children's variety shows, children's adventure programs, children's science fiction, and children's westerns. The Walt Disney programs are examples of the "children's variety shows." The format varied widely, offering cartoons, adventure stories, legends, history, and nature stories; many programs contained a mixture of presentations. The authors offered "Zorro" as an example of "children's adventure programs." In these stories, the tale is told of a simple, strong, "good" hero. This hero is the master of his own fate in spite of the perils he faces in his adventures. The children's "science fiction" and "western" programs were both costume dramas—one set in the future and the other in the past or near past. The stories and characters were uncomplicated and featured adventure and excitement.

Such programs dominated the children's early school years, but soon two new types of program became increasingly important in their viewing—the crime program and the situation comedy. The crime programs were only a short step from the adventure sagas, where the hero righted wrongs by his own strength, skill, and daring. The detective also solved crimes through the use of skill, strength, and daring. Although these programs were generally scheduled during the "adult" programming hours, children usually began watching them in their early school years. The programs' largest juvenile audience, however, was teenagers.

As the children entered adolescence, another type of program became important in their viewing, the popular music variety show. The girls discovered these programs earlier, and watched them faithfully, but such programming eventually became part of most teenagers' viewing. At this point, we have almost the entire line-up of programs watched during the teen years. The crime dramas became more absorbing, and the children's westerns were replaced by adult westerns such as "Gunsmoke." Programs like "Disneyland," "Zorro," and "Superman" faded in popularity. Much of the teenager's viewing time was now spent watching crime dramas and popular music shows. By now, little time was devoted to traditional "children's" programs. Interest in public affairs programming came late in this hierarchy. In fact, any use of media other than for entertainment was unusual. Figure 10.3 summarizes the general pattern that Schramm and his associates described in the growth of the

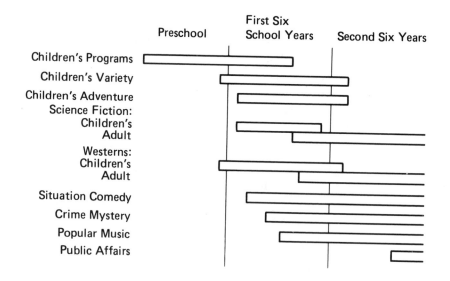

Figure 10.3. Periods in Childhood and Youth When Different Program Types Are Most Important.
Source: Wilbur Schramm, Jack Lyle, and Edwin B. Parker, *Television in the Lives of Our Children* (Stanford, Calif.: Stanford University Press, 1961) p. 39.

children's program diet. As can be seen, the children learned to watch adult programs very quickly. For example, by the time the children were in the first grade, they were already devoting 40 percent of their viewing time to the kinds of programs that most viewers would term "adult." Moreover, sixth grade children were devoting 79 percent of their viewing time to adult programs and were watching nearly five times as many adult programs as children's programs. This finding led the authors to caution that "networks which believe that they are producing programs for adults might do well to take another look at the age of their audience."[9]

Predicting Children's Taste in Programming. It should be made clear that not all children preferred to watch the same types of shows. What were the factors associated with different program preferences? From our previous discussion, it is evident that one important factor was the age of the child. If it was known that one child was nine and another fourteen, other things being equal, it was possible to predict that there would be certain differences in program preferences between them. For example, the younger child would be likely to prefer more traditional children's programs, such as Walt Disney, whereas the older child would likely have more interest in popular music shows and crime dramas. Another important factor was the child's sex. Differences in program preferences between boys and girls were apparent even as early as the first grade. Little girls preferred popular music shows, whereas boys preferred westerns and adventure programs. This pattern continued throughout the school years—girls preferred "feminine" programs built around marriage and romance (e.g., situation comedies, popular music) and boys preferred "masculine" programs of excitement and adventure. The authors offered one explanation for these differences: Girls developed an interest in adolescent and adult roles at an earlier age than did boys.

Mental ability was again found to be an important factor. Schramm, Lyle, and Parker found that brighter children tried different things earlier. They began watching television earlier and more frequently; then they took the "hard steps" to serious programming sooner, such as watching news programs, educational shows, and documentaries. It was found, for example, that about twice as many of the brighter eighth grade students were watching television coverage of the 1958 Congressional elections, when compared to lower intelligence groups. Moreover, of those who viewed this program, it was the brighter ones who most enjoyed it. The high-IQ scorers were also the ones who were chiefly able to identify faces that had appeared on television for public affairs reasons rather than for entertainment reasons. These patterns of viewing news programs, public affairs commentary, and so on began earlier with the brighter children. They were the first of their age group to turn away from the western and situation comedy shows.

In general, the brighter teenagers were being attracted away from television. Homework and their social lives kept them busier and they had less time for television. In addition, they were becoming more critical and discriminating in their choices of programming, abandoning those offerings which seemed to have less durable value for them. Both the high-IQ scorers and the low-IQ scorers were settling into adult viewing patterns. Thus, the high-IQ category used television less often and more selectively, and turned to print media for much of their serious informational needs. The lower-IQ group, on the other hand, tended to use television more and printed media less. As their teenage behavior suggested, they used television heavily for crime mysteries, situation comedies, westerns, comedy, variety, and popular music programs. In short, sex, age, and mental ability were found to be related to program preference.

Attitudes Toward Television. It is not surprising that Schramm and his associates found that most children regarded television with both affection and respect. What is surprising was that they were not alone. Their parents also showed similar attitudes toward television. When the authors conducted interviews in San Francisco with 188 families, each questioned together as a family unit, they asked each member of the family which of the media they would miss the most if they had to do without it. The overwhelming response was television—for the whole family. Overall, television was the most likely to be missed by parents and children alike; and television was the medium mentioned most frequently at every age, even though its relative importance declined during adolescence.

The children were generally enamored of television. When asked, they could find nothing they would change in its content, except that they wanted *more of the same*. Preteen girls, for example, requested more popular music shows and family situations. Boys in the same age group wanted more war stories, sports, crime shows, and more comedy. It was not until the children reached the late high school years that they became critical of television, and even then it was chiefly the brighter children. Those older children who were critical did not have major complaints. Some thought that there were too many commercials; others thought that some television personalities were unpleasant; and a few thought that programming was too repetitive, that it was all the same.

When it came to the parents, however, it was a different story. Overall, they had definite ideas about changes they wanted. Most of them were clearly concerned about the amount of crime and violence on television. This was especially true for the better-educated parents with white-collar jobs. When parents from blue-collar families expressed concern, they tended to be more disturbed about sexual content in programming. In general, however, blue-collar parents were much more likely to express gratitude for television—it kept their children "out of mischief," "off the streets," or was an inexpensive babysitter.

Incidental Learning from Television

The authors argued that most of a child's learning from television was incidental learning. Such learning was defined as "learning that takes place when a viewer goes to television for entertainment and stores up certain items of information without seeking them."[10] In their view, children learned while being entertained; however, the children usually did not seek out television strictly for informational purposes.

A number of conditions were found to be important in determining when incidental learning took place. These included the child's ability to learn, the child's needs at the moment, and what the child paid attention to. The ability to learn was looked upon pretty much as a matter of intelligence. The authors stated that "bright" children learned more from television. Indeed, such children learned more in any learning situation. Other factors, related to attention and needs, were found to be important. For example, children were more likely to pay attention to and learn some particular behavior if it was new to them. The authors discussed, as an example, the impact of a Hopalong Cassidy film in one of their studies. The show produced a considerable amount of learning on the part of younger children, but had very little impact on the older ones. The difference between the two groups was accounted for by the fact that the film was a new kind of experience for the young children, but "old stuff" to the older ones. Because the older children had seen such films many times before, this one did not command their close attention, an effect of familiarity. As children become more familiar with the subject matter, they learn to sort out the material. They note familiar things and set up a pattern of expectation which keeps them from having to pay too much attention to them. In any event, it is the new things, the ones that are not too familiar to them, which they single out for their attention and storage.

On the basis of this familiarity principle, Schramm and his associates posited that the greatest amount of learning from television occurs between the ages of three and eight, when most of the experiences are new to the children. At those ages, those experiences would be especially absorbing to the child. There is, however, another reason why television is an especially effective agent of incidental learning when the child is young. The reason is television seems very real to them. A number of observers have commented that mass media content had greater impact on children if they believed that it had "really happened." The younger children are more likely to think that the events taking place on the picture tube in front of them are real.

The amount of identification that a child has with a television character is another factor that affects the amount of incidental learning that takes place. All parents have observed their children galloping imaginary horses, or seen them acting out an adventure the way their favorite hero would play it. Girls copy the current romantic heroines—mimicking their entrances, their mannerisms, and their seductive manner in love scenes. Many researchers have written about children's identification with characters. "There is no doubt that a child can more easily store up behaviors and beliefs which he has imaginatively shared with a character with whom he identifies."[11]

A child is also more likely to pick out and remember something from an entertainment program if it is clearly useful to him or her. In this respect the child's needs become important. A girl, for example, is more likely to remember an attractive hairdo, whereas a boy is more likely to remember the techniques a third baseman used when he charged a bunt. If the child notices something he or she can tell to friends, then there is ample reason to remember it—especially if it can evoke laughter. Such "little bonuses" occur all the time in the course of entertainment. Something comes to the child's attention as the program progresses, he or she sees a use for it, and stores it away for the future.

In addition, there is reason to believe that the child will more likely learn and use something when he or she thinks that it will work. When a television character fails at something, it is unlikely that the child will try it. But if the behavior appears to be both rewarding and socially feasible, there is more incentive for the child to store it away and then try it when the proper occasion arises.

Schramm and his associates believed that watching television contributed to a fast start in learning but that the advantage children gained did not last. They felt that children who viewed TV would start school with larger vocabularies than nonviewing children of the same age. Likewise, the authors argued, child viewers would be more familiar with wider worlds and know more (at an earlier age) than nonviewers about adult life, sex, crime, and social problems. In order to test these hypotheses, however, the researchers had to compare two Canadian communities because they could not find an American community that did not have television. As expected, they found that first grade children with television had higher vocabulary scores than similar children living in a community without television. By the sixth grade, however, the difference disappeared. Thus, the advantage gained from watching television did not last. It came as no surprise that IQ scores again emerged as an important factor. Remember our earlier discussions, which revealed that brighter children watched more television during their early years but then deserted the ranks of heavy viewers as they grew older. Such factors interact with exposure to television and must be taken into account when we observe that the advantages of television viewing disappear. The authors referred to this interaction pattern as the "principle of maturation." According to this principle, when children mature to a certain point television becomes less attractive and rewarding to them. As a result, they increase the attention they pay to reality-oriented media material, or "material which is at least as useful for its information content as for its entertainment content, if not more so."[12]

Social Norms and Social Relationships

The maturation principle held true for most children, but not for all. While most children decreased their television viewing time considerably during their high school years, others decreased their viewing only slightly, or not at all. Why did this happen? First of all, the pattern of fantasy-seeking and reality-seeking differentiated the children's media behavior more than anything else. Those children who were seeking knowledge or information turned more of their media attention to newspapers, quality magazines, and books. On the other hand, those children who primarily sought entertainment and fantasy/escape remained high users of television fantasy, as well as other media with high fantasy components (e.g., comic books).

The Importance of Social Norms. To understand why these patterns of reality-seeking and fantasy-seeking emerged, the researchers divided children into four groups according to the amount of their use of television, books, and magazines. The first group was fantasy-oriented; it was composed of children who were high users of television and low users of print media. The second group, on the other hand, was reality-oriented; it was composed of children who were high users of print and low users of television. The third group was referred to as the "high users" group. It consisted of children with high use levels for both print and television. The fourth group, the "low users" group, consisted of children who were low users of both print and television. In the sixth grade, membership in the reality-oriented group was very small, but by the tenth grade it had grown a great deal. Children who were members of this group differed from the members of the other groups. They had internalized the norms of the upwardly mobile middle class—norms of activity, self-betterment, and deferred gratification. At the beginning of adolescence there was a turning point for a considerable number of children. They left the universal pleasure norm of their childhood for these middle class norms. It was those children, if their mental abilities were sufficient, who became the chief users of print media and educational television. They were also the viewers more likely to select reality programs from commercial television. Social norms, then, had a great deal to do with what kind of use the child made of television.

Television and Social Relationships. Another factor that determined how a child used television was social relationships. In general, it was found that children who had unsatisfactory relationships with their families or peer groups tended to retreat to television where they could escape from their real-life problems. However, when we examine some other variables, the relationship is no longer so simple. For example, when children of high intelligence and high social status encountered problems in their social relations, the amount of television they used went up, as expected. Such children turned to television for fantasy and escape, rather than seeking reality in print media, as would be expected from them if their social relationships were satisfactory. But when children of low intelligence and low social status faced similar problems in their social relations, the result was not more use of television. If anything changed, there was less use of television.

The quality of the child's home and peer-group relationships did help to determine the amount of television he or she saw, but also much more. The child who came to television filled with aggression because of the frustrations of these poor social relationships was likely to seek out and remember the violent content of television. The authors concluded that if the child sought violence in answer to his or her own social needs, then he or she was likely to remember and resurrect such violence when real-life needs called for aggression. "In other words, parents, friends, schools have it in their power to make a significant contribution to the healthfulness of a child's use of television by giving him a warm and loving home, and helping him to normal and satisfying friendships with children his own age."[13]

The Effects of Television

The relationship between television and a child can be understood only in terms of the characteristics of both. We have already discussed what a child brings to television (i.e., IQ, social norms, social relationships, and the needs and experiences for which age and sex are partial indicators). Now we turn to the question of what television brings to the child. To examine this, the authors monitored and analyzed a week of television in late October 1960, from 4 P.M. to 9 P.M., Monday through Friday. Figure 10.4 summarizes their findings. It can be seen that commercial television brought to children fast moving, exciting fantasy, with broad humor and a considerable amount of romantic interest. The authors considered the content to be "extremely violent." Shootings and sluggings were frequent; in fact, more than half the program hours consisted of programs in which violence played an important part. The authors, it should be pointed out, did not take all of the violence seriously.

For example, the cartoons and slapstick films they deemed were intended to be funny, rather than exciting, were disregarded in the analysis. Nevertheless, in the hundred hours analyzed there appeared:

12 murders
16 major gunfights
21 persons shot (apparently not fatally)
21 other violent incidents with guns (ranging from shooting at but missing persons, to shooting up a town)
37 hand-to-hand fights (15 fist fights, 15 incidents in which one person slugged another, an attempted murder with a pitchfork, 2 stranglings, a fight in the water, a case in which a woman was gagged and tied to a bed, etc.)

One stabbing in the back with a butcher knife
Four attempted suicides, three successful
Four people falling or pushed over cliffs
Two cars running over cliffs
Two attempts made in automobiles to run over persons on the sidewalk
A psychotic loose and raving in a flying airliner
Two mob scenes, in one of which the mob hangs the wrong man
A horse trampling a man under its hooves
A great deal of miscellaneous violence, including a plane fight, a hired killer
  stalking his prey, two robberies, a pickpocket at work, a woman killed by
  falling from a train, a tidal wave, an earthquake, and a guillotining.

This picture of the adult world was heavy in violence, light in intellectual exchange, and deeply concerned with crime. Half of the characters in the stories were either involved in enforcing the law, breaking it, or both. There were sixteen detectives, sixteen sheriffs, nine police officers, and an assortment of other law enforcement officials. In general, the detectives were more successful than the sheriffs, and the sheriffs were more successful than the police. But despite the presence of all these lawmen, a large part of the crime detection and enforcement had to be carried out by amateurs with steely nerves and a quick draw.

The picture presented of family life was mixed. In some programs, a

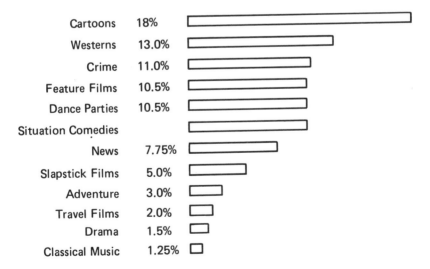

Cartoons	18%	
Westerns	13.0%	
Crime	11.0%	
Feature Films	10.5%	
Dance Parties	10.5%	
Situation Comedies		
News	7.75%	
Slapstick Films	5.0%	
Adventure	3.0%	
Travel Films	2.0%	
Drama	1.5%	
Classical Music	1.25%	

Figure 10.4. Content of Commercial Television Over 1.0 Percent During the "Children's Hour"—4 to 9 P.M. Monday through Friday, late October, 1960.
Source: Wilbur Schramm, Jack Lyle, and Edwin B. Parker, *Television in the Lives of Our Children* (Stanford, Calif.: Stanford University Press, 1961) p. 138.

tolerant, good-humored relationship was shown among the members of the family. Other programs showed conflict, screaming, distrust and violence within the family. Little attention was paid to how the characters earned a living, so the child seeking career information got little instruction from commercial television fare—that is, unless he or she wanted to be a "private eye," a western sheriff, or a crook. On the other hand, some of the programs, particularly situation plays, went out of their way to offer morals to their stories. Typical examples are: "Don't undervalue your real friends"; "What comes easy, goes easy"; "Don't always believe what you hear."

What kind of variety was there for the child to choose from? About 22 percent of the time a child could have found a reality program other than news somewhere on the four available commercial stations. But for more than half the time, the choice was strictly among different types of fantasy: for example, two crime shows, a cartoon, or a western. This, then, is what television brought to the child.

Television's effects are the result of an interactive process between the characteristics of television and the characteristics of its users. Different children could watch the same television content and the effects could be different. For example, the authors discussed a study done by Fritz Redl, who compared the reactions of disturbed children and normal children to selected TV fare. He found that "ordinary" children would avoid extremely violent and frightening television content. Such was not the case, however, with the problem children. They sought to avoid the "nice" and "sweet" programs that showed loving parents and warm friendly relationships. Those kinds of programs, the researcher argued, were likely to cause the disturbed children to lie awake or to have bad dreams because they reminded the children of what was lacking in their own lives. From this evidence, Schramm, Lyle, and Parker concluded: "Thus what would have been soothing (or at least innocuous) for most children was traumatic for these children because of their particular needs and background."[14]

The authors then presented their "inventory" of the effects of television. They felt that they could now discuss the nature of these effects because they had studied the ways in which television entered the life of the child. They placed these effects in the following categories: (1) physical effects, (2) emotional effects, (3) cognitive effects, and (4) behavioral effects. We will briefly discuss what they concluded about each of these effects.

Physical Effects. The authors found that the physical effects of television were not very important. Television caused no special eyestrain (when compared to reading) *if* the children viewed under the proper conditions. On the other hand, eyestrain was likely to occur if the child sat too close to the set, looked up at it, and/or viewed it in a dark room. In addition, the authors found little evidence of any serious loss of sleep as a result of television viewing. The average difference in bedtimes between TV and nonTV homes was fifteen minutes later for those who watched TV.

Emotional Effects. Television's emotional effects were less innocuous. A television program frightened almost all of the children at one time or another. What chiefly disturbed the children were situations where harm threatened some character or animal with whom they identified. It was particularly acute when the harm involved cutting or stepping into a trap—that is, nonritual violence. The children were frightened when they viewed such violent and stressful programs at too early an age, and many became particularly frightened when they viewed television alone or in a dark room.

In general, the children liked and sought excitement, on the television as well as in real life. However, they did not like the excitement to spill too far over into fear. Children engage in "thrill play" because they seek such excitement, and it has a parallel in television. The authors raised serious questions, however, about the possible effect of the high level of excitement in television, a level that they saw as rising. They questioned what the effects of this excitement would be on the children's perceptions of reality. Would it take the edge off the actual experience and lead children to demand something of real life that it cannot give to them? The authors saw signs that this was happening, but felt that the answer could be found only through long-term research.

Cognitive Effects. Television probably helped some children more than others to grow into better-informed adults. It specifically helped those children who chose some of the reality experiences of television. Those children heard important people discuss current issues; they watched demonstrations of the arts and of science. They were "on the scene" in foreign places and observed great events. On the other hand, television was more effective, in all probability, in stimulating interest in the children and contributing to already existing interest, rather than in stimulating creativity or activity. There were cases where television did stimulate some children to read books that had a relation to some program. However, the authors cautioned that the most frequent kinds of activities resulting from TV viewing were either mimicking fads (such as wearing the Davy Crockett hat) or involved adopting details which fit into an already existing interest—for example, a boy who changes his batting stance following the viewing of a major league game on television.

Some people had hoped that television would raise the level of children's tastes; they wanted television to bring more "highbrow" culture into their lives. There was little sign that this had happened, however. Indeed, there were indications that it was creating a level of taste in children based upon its own common denominator. The authors were particularly disturbed by their finding that children learned to like the programs available to them, even though they would not ordinarily have selected them. Equally disturbing was television's treatment of adult life. They found that television was portraying a "markedly erroneous" picture of adult life. This, they reasoned, was not a positive contribution to the child's socialization process and might require some very tough adjustments later in life. Moreover, such portrayals of life, especially the depiction of sexual behavior and violence, could lead to "premature aging" and even cause children to fear the process of growing up.

Behavioral Effects. The possible behavioral effects of television were the ones that had caused the most concern to both parents and researchers, yet the authors indicated that they were in almost every case controllable through the nontelevision life of the child. The authors addressed the question of whether or not television viewing made children too passive. They concluded that in *some cases* it did and suggested that long-term studies were needed to determine the magnitude and lasting quality of such effects. They also argued that "the way to avoid an excessive passivity in our children is not to give them television as a mother substitute early in life; rather to make them feel loved and wanted at home, and so far as possible to surround them with friends and activities."[15]

The most common and most feared charge leveled against television was that it taught delinquency and violent behavior. The authors argued that it was a contributory cause in some cases. For example, some children confused the rules of the fantasy world with the rules of the real world. The authors explained that a child who wanted to put the ground glass in the stew to see if it worked as on the TV program was merely experimenting in the real world with the tools of the fantasy world. They found too that children who brought aggression to television were more likely to remember aggressive acts portrayed there. The children wanted to be like the successful characters, whether those characters were good or bad. The authors cautioned, however, that little delinquency could be traced directly to television. "Delinquency is a complex behavior growing usually out of a number of roots, the chief one usually being some great lack in the child's life—often a broken home, or a feeling of rejection by parents or peer groups. Television is at best a contributing cause."[16] Schramm, Lyle, and Parker concluded that overall the effects of television pointed as much to the parents as to television. Parents who provided their children with warm, secure relationships and an interesting home life had little to fear from television.

CONCLUSIONS AND IMPLICATIONS

Television in the Lives of Our Children was the first major North American study investigating the effects of television on children and the only large-scale investigation available on that subject until the Surgeon General's Report on Television and Social Behavior in 1972 (see Chapter 12). The basic strength of this milestone is the exhaustive research upon which its findings were based. In many ways it resembled the earlier movie study (Chapter 2). As we have seen, the authors' investigations and findings included a fascinating comparison of children in communities with television and without it, an analysis of the influence of fantasy and reality in the content of programs, a detailed discussion of what children learned from television and the conditions under which they learned it, figures bearing upon homework habits and bedtime hours, a report on the program choices of children, and an exploration of the potential physical, emotional, cognitive, and behavioral problems among children that might result from viewing television. It explained in detail that children exhibited several different patterns in their use of television—patterns that changed as the children grew older. Thus, there were considerable differences among the children in their use of television and these differences were not simply the result of age but also varied in accordance with the child's sex, mental ability as measured by IQ, social class background, and the quality of each child's social relations, both with parents and/or with peer group(s). Moreover, the authors found considerable interaction among these five factors. For example, socio-economic class and social relations appeared to interact. On the one hand, middle class children who were frustrated by their parents were likely to watch television more than their middle class peers, other things being equal. In addition, they watched television for its fantasy experiences. On the other hand, working class children who were similarly frustrated by their parents were likely to watch television less than their peers. Thus, differences in social class background altered the children's reaction to difficulties in their social relations.

Schramm, Lyle, and Parker suggested, by their very choice of title, that their approach to communication research focused more on the *uses* and *gratifications* of television for various categories of children rather than on actual direct effects. (The uses and gratifications approach, it might be noted, gained increased popularity in the 1970s and 1980s; see Chapter 13.) Indeed, a *leitmotif* that reappears repeatedly in their discussions is: "in order to understand television's impact and effect on children, we have first to get away from the unrealistic concept of what television does to children and substitute the concept of what children do with television."[17]

The authors did note, however, that it was the possible behavioral effects of television that had aroused the most concern in the public. Was television harmful to children? Was TV turning children into delinquents? Or, conversely, was it making them too passive? Schramm and his associates pulled their findings together in the following widely quoted but less-than-precise statement:

> For *some* children, under *some* conditions, *some* television is harmful. For *other* children under the same conditions, or for the same children under *other*

conditions, it may be beneficial. For *most* children, under *most* conditions, most television is probably neither harmful nor particularly beneficial.[18]

They also reassured us, more than once, that if a child was given love, security, and healthful activities in his or her nontelevision hours, then there was little chance that television would have negative effects on the child. This assumed, of course, that the child was a normal middle class child who had been properly socialized into the Protestant Ethic. Their statements should have been quite comforting, however, to middle class parents, the principal audience of the book.

Theoretically the research was very diverse; the authors used several theories of selective influence. For example, when they stressed the importance of mental ability in determining the effects of television, they implied a theory of selective influence based upon *individual differences*. The major emphasis of the work, however, was on theories of selective influence based upon *social categories* and *social relationships*. Social categories such as age, sex, and social class all played a role in determining the ways in which children used television, and therefore determined how children were influenced by viewing this newest medium. Social relationships, however, were found to be crucial in determining the influence of TV on children. Poor family relationships and/or poor peer group relationships could send a bright middle class child to the tube for fantasy/escape experiences. In many ways, then, social relationships took precedence over social categories in determining the influence of television on children.

The authors anticipated the main tenet of contemporary meaning theory when they discussed the ways in which television could modify children's perceptions of the world. This influence, however, was mediated through such factors as IQ, age, sex, social class, and social relations.

There were some methodological problems with this research, although such a statement could be made of practically any large-scale project. Part of the difficulty seemed to lie in the basic design of the research. Schramm, Lyle, and Parker conducted cross-sectional surveys in several communities, but with a variety of goals in mind. Thus, their findings were not always comparable. In spite of this, the authors attempted to make cross-community comparisons, and the validity of some of their conclusions can be questioned. Overall, this problem points out the difficulty of executing research designs under ever-changing conditions. It should also be noted, however, that this piecemeal approach to planning the research also had a definite advantage, an aspect of the problem that the authors fully utilized. They analyzed the early studies first, then built new measures into the subsequent inquiries to test hypotheses formulated from the results of the earlier segments of the research. This approach allowed them to make the theoretical generalizations more refined than would otherwise have been possible. Thus, we can see that a tradeoff must sometimes be made to achieve research ends. In this case, the researchers traded complete comparability among the various communities surveyed for increased theoretical depth of analysis and for hypothesis testing.

One problem that could have been more easily addressed is the sophistication of the data analysis: it was much too simple. The parts written for general audiences were presented in simple, understandable terms, but the sections of the book intended for more technically sophisticated readers generally did not go beyond simple tabular presentations (although more detailed) of the categories and frequencies of the occurrence. An example of such simplicity is the frequent mention of interaction effects among certain variables (e.g., age, IQ, social class, etc.). Yet these interaction effects were neither systematically investigated in the authors' analyses of the data, nor were they spelled out in any great detail: we were simply informed that there was interaction among the variables.

Beyond the questions about data analysis techniques, however, is a deeper theoretical problem. Schramm, Lyle, and Parker consistently made many arguments and drew conclusions about developmental changes in children based upon cross-sectional data. The authors did *not* examine the changes in a group of children over time. Instead, they compared differences among various age-groups surveyed during the same time period and inferred that changes in the young children by the time they reached the age of the older ones would account for the differences. Strictly speaking, these inferences are not appropriate. In order to make such generalizations, they needed longitudinal data—measures of the same, or comparable groups, over time. The authors never cautioned the readers about this; they accepted the differences as developmental differences. In fact, they *assumed* a "maturation effect" rather than discovered it.

Another difficulty in evaluating this research is the authors' desire to go beyond their own data and to present a total picture of the state of the knowledge in the field. In effect, the book becomes, in its conclusions, self-contradictory. At times, the writers appeared to place great importance on the role of television in the lives of children. They informed us that television occupied more time in the first sixteen years of the child's life than anything except sleep. They also indicated that it played a "major part in socializing children" and that it was the "greatest source of common experience in the lives of children." In addition, they believed that television distracted children from the "solution of real-life problems." Yet, in spite of these statements, they also concluded that for most children "television is probably neither harmful nor particularly beneficial." In a similar vein, they argued that television played at most a reinforcing role rather than an initiatory role in the various social ills that popular discussion had linked with it.

In short, some children could be "damned" by exposure to television. Those who could be "saved" were those who enjoyed the WASP world of love, security, and middle class values. These were the simple solutions to the potential problems of television.

Considering the authors' often quoted final conclusion about the effects of television ("*some* children *some* of the time," etc.) it was not surprising that many researchers interpreted this work as supporting the minimal-effects hypothesis. Yet the public was not satisfied. Perhaps it was the conflicting conclusions that bothered many people. How could something that occupied so much of their children's time and was so important in their socialization be so innocuous? Perhaps, also, some had not forgotten Dr. Wertham's heavy-handed argument against comic books (see Chapter 9). Indeed, television was said by Schramm, Lyle, and Parker to be fulfilling the fantasy needs of children that comic books once fulfilled—and doing it *even better*. In any event, the legacy of fear remained alive because in reality the "big" questions about television and its effects on children remained unresolved.

NOTES AND REFERENCES

1. Wilbur Schramm, Jack Lyle, and Edwin Parker, *Television in the Lives of Our Children* (Palo Alto, Calif.: Stanford University Press, 1961), pp. 11–12.
2. Melvin L. DeFleur and Sandra Ball-Rokeach, *Theories of Mass Communication*, 3rd ed. (New York: McKay 1975), pp. 97–99.
3. Ibid.
4. Eli A. Rubinstein, "Television Violence: A Historical Perspective," in *Children and the Faces of Television*, ed. by Eli A. Rubinstein (New York: Academic Press, 1981), p. 114.
5. Eleanor E. Maccoby, "Television: Its Impact on School Children," *Public Opinion Quarterly*, 15 (1951), 421–444, also Paul I. Lyness, "The Place of the Mass Media in the Lives of Boys and Girls," *Journalism Quarterly*, 29, 1952, 43–54.
6. Wilbur Schramm, Jack Lyle, and Edwin Parker, op. cit., p. 1.
7. Ibid., pp. 63–64.
8. Ibid., p. 30.
9. Ibid., p. 95.
10. Ibid., p. 75.
11. Ibid., p. 78.
12. Ibid., p. 98.
13. Ibid., p. 173.
14. Ibid., p. 143.
15. Ibid., p. 174.
16. Ibid.
17. Ibid., p. 169.
18. Ibid., p. 13.

Violence and the Media:
The Turbulent Sixties

America was bitterly divided in the late 1960s. The social fabric that had bound its people together was being ripped apart by forces that seemed to be uncontrollable on two fronts: The first divisive issue was an increasingly unpopular foreign war; the other was occurring in the streets of America's cities. Many citizens voiced their concern about the justifiability of the United States' involvement in the Vietnam conflict, but people also saw escalating violence at home. They feared rising crime, inner-city riots, campus disturbances, and other forms of civil unrest. In June 1968, President Johnson, in response to concerns about domestic violence and the recent assassinations of Martin Luther King, Jr, and Robert Kennedy, created, by executive order, the National Commission on the Causes and Prevention of Violence. The Commission was charged with investigating violence in America and making recommendations to the President for action. It was to examine "the causes and prevention of lawless acts of violence...the causes of disrespect for law and order, of disrespect for public officials...of violent disruptions of public order by individuals and groups,"[1] and other related matters the President might place before it.

Despite the often violent history of the United States, this domestic turmoil was relatively recent. Indeed, in 1960, sociologist Daniel Bell had commented about America in the 1940s and 1950s:

> A sober look at the problem shows that there is probably less crime today in the United States than existed a hundred, or fifty, or even twenty-five years ago, and that today the United States is a more lawful and safe country than popular opinion imagines.[2]

The country could not understand what had changed this relative tranquility.

The 1960s were years of sometimes violent street demonstrations for a variety of causes. Included among these causes were civil rights, inner-city despair, student activism, and the antiwar movement. Hundreds of people were killed in these confrontations, thousands were injured, and large-scale property damage was inflicted by vandals, looters, and arsonists.[3] In addition, the incidence of crimes unrelated to such disorders soared. The FBI recorded a 100 percent increase in reported violent crimes between 1958 and 1968. Four major political assassinations took place, and the new crime of skyjacking literally took off with the times. The first skyjacking (more accurately, air piracy) that involved an American carrier took place on May 1, 1961, when a National Airlines aircraft was diverted to Cuba. Thereafter, such incidents occurred on the average of once a month until 1968, when security systems became widespread. In most cases, the incidents involved persons who wanted to be flown out of the United States, usually to Cuba.[4]

The rising tide of the civil rights movement had begun to crest at the beginning of the decade. The pattern of response that this movement met was a prelude to much of what would later occur—nonviolent militant protest was followed by backlash, with the conflict finally forcing federal intervention when local officials were unable or unwilling to provide effective, equitable protection for the demonstrators. The new President, Democrat John F. Kennedy, had been elected in an extremely close contest in 1960. He had overcome much latent anti-Catholic prejudice to reach the presidency, and he sympathized with the civil rights movement and took an interest in its goals. But, as a close advisor, journalist Ted Sorenson observed, "John Kennedy did not start the civil rights movement and nothing he could have done could have stopped it."[5]

A new era of "confrontation politics" had arrived on the American scene. Civil rights activists held marches, rallies, vigils, "freedom rides," "sit-ins," and "lie-downs"—often provoking violent reactions. In 1961, James Farmer led a group of followers on a historic journey from Washington, D.C. to New Orleans by bus. Their objective was to force integration of the transportation system, and they focused their attention on segregated bus stations. In Rock Hill, North Carolina, the bus was attacked; in Anniston, Alabama, its tires were slashed. Finally, in Birmingham the passengers were dragged from the bus into an alley and beaten. The group finally arrived in New Orleans, but they came by air. However, they arrived triumphant; they had faced and defeated the lion in its den. Similar confrontations with segregationists, varying in size, occurred all over the South, with consistent gains for the movement. In August, 1963, three hundred thousand people joined Martin Luther King, Jr. in Washington, D.C. in a march for equality and freedom for all—and shared in his dream for democracy.

Political assassinations were a significant factor in the violence of the 1960s. The first jolted the nation on November 22, 1963. President Kennedy was shot as he visited Dallas, Texas. The vibrant young President had been struck down, and the effects were profound in all walks of life. Few who witnessed the funeral, either in person, or on television, have forgotten the sights and sounds of the funeral procession—the flag-draped coffin, the riderless horse symbolic of the fallen leader, and the ceaseless deliberate cadence of the drums as the procession moved to Arlington Cemetery. Other prominent men also fell at the hands of assassins: Malcolm X, a black nationalist leader was killed by gunfire in New York in 1965; Martin Luther King, Jr. was ambushed in Memphis in April 1968; and finally, Robert Kenndey was shot in California in June 1968, as he sought the presidency. It seemed that no one in public life was safe from such attack.

Late in the summer of 1964, riots broke out in two black sections of New York: Harlem and Bedford-Stuyvesant. Six days of burning and looting followed. Similar riots and disorders occurred in over 100 cities during the summers of 1965, 1966, and 1967. Thirty-four people died in the Watts section of Los Angeles in August 1965, during a six-day riot. There were riots in Watts again the next summer, as well as in St. Louis, Chicago, Atlanta, and several other cities. In 1967, Newark and Detroit had major riots and several other cities had disturbances attributed to racial grievances. Riots followed the assassination of Martin Luther King, Jr., in 1968.[6] Not only were lives lost, but the destruction of property and the cost to the nation were almost beyond calculation.

Campus protests for student rights and against the war in Vietnam also led to violent confrontations. Protesters at Columbia University and the University of California at Berkeley, led by the militant Students for a Democratic Society (SDS), were particularly effective in drawing attention to their grievances. A wave of bombings and other terrorist acts occurred during the later years of the 1960s, as disaffected groups adopted violent tactics. Groups like the Black Panthers and the Weathermen (a radical faction of the SDS) emerged to carry on the fight. They preached the use of violence in the service of their causes. Protests against the Vietnam war were particularly violent during and after the Democratic Convention in Chicago in August 1968.

While such riots, violent demonstrations, and militant organizations accounted for only a small part of the nation's overall crime, they attracted a great deal of attention and generated considerable public concern. They were responsible for the enactment of tough anticrime legislation and for a number of police crackdowns. In late June 1968, shortly after President Johnson had created the Violence Commission, Congress passed and sent to him the Omnibus Crime Control and Safe Streets Act of 1968. In spite of his reservations about some of its provisions, Johnson signed it into law. The act was a policeman's program, toughening federal laws, and establishing the Law Enforcement Assistance Administration to provide support for state and local jurisdictions. The government was waging a war on crime.

Besides these new legislative measures, the government also sought to understand the root causes of crime during the 1960s. It searched for ways to deal with the problems of crime through a number of special commissions created to examine particular problems. In November 1963, the President's Commission on Narcotics and Drug Abuse proposed a strategy to control drug traffic and give treatment to drug abusers. The recommendations contained in their report provided the basis for most subsequent drug control measures taken by the federal government.[7] In February 1967, the President's Commission on

Law Enforcement and the Administration of Justice submitted more than 200 recommendations that urged sweeping and costly changes in criminal administration. In February 1968, the President's National Advisory Commission on Civil Disorders, created following the Detroit and Newark riots, warned that America "is moving toward two societies, one black, one white—separate and unequal."[8] The report, which followed a seven-month study, placed much of the responsibility for the riots on a century of white racism and neglect. The Commission felt that the deepening racial division was not inevitable, however, and that it could be reversed with a "massive and sustained" national commitment to act. Among the recommendations were sweeping reforms in federal and local law enforcement, welfare programs, employment, housing, education, and the news media. The Commission indicated that implementation of these recommendations would be expensive, but worth the price.

The final such report of the decade, *To Establish Justice, To Insure Domestic Tranquility*, was submitted by the National Commission on the Causes and Prevention of Violence in December 1969. The commission concluded after a year and a half of study that the time had come to reorder national priorities and make a greater investment of resources in the fulfillment of two of the national purposes of the Constitution—establishing justice and insuring domestic tranquility. They concluded that the cures to America's predicament of violence had to be based on two things—doubling the investment currently being made in the criminal justice system and restructuring urban life. Like the recommendations made by previous commissions, these measures could not be undertaken cheaply.

In addition to its final report, the Violence Commission issued a 15-volume series of reports from its seven task forces and five investigatory study teams. One of these reports, *Violence and the Media*, edited by Robert K. Baker and Sandra J. Ball, has become a landmark in the study of mass communication and was indicative of the growing concern that the public had about the relationship between violence portrayed by the media and violence in everyday life. We now turn to an examination of the contents of that volume.

THE MEDIA TASK FORCE REPORT

Violence and the Media is a massive work. It contains more than 600 pages, including 19 substantive chapters and 18 technical appendices. The editors divided the volume into three parts: (I) An Historical Perspective, (II) The News Media, and (III) Television Entertainment and Violence. Parts I and II contain the first nine chapters and seven appendices; the material in this part of the volume provides the groundwork and background for the Task Force-sponsored research and interpretation discussed in Part III. The volume builds upon the work done by other commissions and by individual scholars. It is well-conceived and presented in an understandable manner by a well-qualified staff and a number of special consultants, many of whom were among the leading researchers in the field.

Part I of the Task Force Report contains a summary of the philosophical and historical antecedents that underlie the American tradition of free speech, particularly as it is embodied in First Amendment rights. In Part II, the authors discuss the development, structure, and functions of the contemporary mass media. Among the topics discussed are the functions and credibility of the media, issues about access to the media, media coverage of civil disorders, and media practices and values. The report then draws a number of conclusions and makes recommendations to the government, to the media, and to the public. While limitations of space do not permit full discussion of all of the material presented in these first nine chapters, it is important that we know and understand the perspectives from which the Task Force research was undertaken.

Perspectives on the Study

The Task Force Report noted that much of our heritage regarding free expression stems from the struggle of the press against censorship and regulation. However, even though the press has functioned as reporter and critic for other social institutions, it has shown a marked reluctance to undertake self-analysis and criticism. Because of this reluctance, the Task Force rejected the argument that the government should not be involved in the study of the mass media. It is important, they argued, that we understand what forces shape the media, because the media touch the lives of Americans in ways that are both complex and intimate. Clearly, the Task Force felt that commercial pressures on the businesses that make up the communications industry did not insure that, in the course of their doing business, the public interest was served. Thus, charges of infringement of free speech and of possible "chilling effects" which might result from government inquiry into media operations and practices did not deny government access to the information it needed to make reasoned judgments about the structure, functions, and possible regulation of the media. In the Task Force's view, it was more likely that public officials would be responsive to citizen need for access to the media channels than that the self-perpetuating corporate management of those media would answer this need. Such corporations already had acquired a highly concentrated ownership of those channels. As the Task Force observed:

> Clearly, then, the media merit study by anyone who would know more about the structure of American society. But when violence becomes the issue, the study is obligatory. For much of what we know of violence in all its forms we understand as observers and students of the mass media, not as participants.[9]

Since the influences of the media are so extensive, it is imperative that we understand how they are doing their job of informing the public. Because of their importance in shaping the public's knowledge and opinions of public affairs, the report focused its attention on media news functions.

Mass Media and the News

When the Task Force turned to the functioning of the news media in American society, it focused particularly on the media's role in intergroup communication and the solution of social problems, particularly media effects on violence. The report, while highly critical of the practices and procedures of the news media, concluded that the news media could be an effective agent in reducing violence if they provided a true marketplace of ideas in which there was enhanced communication between groups. In addition, if they provided increased access to the media by minorities, there might be fewer confrontations that could produce violence in order to gain attention. The Task Force felt that the increased level of violence was due, at least in part, to the slow response of American institutions to demands for social change, and that an important part of this slow response was the failure of the news media to provide routine and peaceful access to new and different points of view. In its opinion, too many news organizations feared social ideas and social action. In addition, because of the failure by the media to report adequately the conditions underlying social protest, the solutions that the media did offer to social problems, and because of their "action-oriented" approach to the coverage of conflict, the media themselves contributed to the widespread use of confrontation in the pursuit of social change.

The report concedes that some groups use violence to exploit press coverage, but such acts were not as common as popularly believed. Besides, the report maintained, violence was not necessary for a group to gain access— dramatizing the conflict was enough to focus attention on the issues. The message was not lost because of the media's tendency to focus on the violence rather than the issues that produced it. The Task Force also endorsed the Kerner Commission's criticisms of the media's handling of civil disturbances. In short, the report called upon the news media to provide the public with the information necessary to have effective democratic action. Journalists, it was felt, needed to reexamine their ways of doing things in order to see if the old ways met modern needs. New approaches were necessary; more emphasis was needed on analysis, opinion, and possible solutions to the problems, once the initial events had been reported. Thus, the news media, in pursuit of these goals, should try to provide a wide variety of such material as a matter of editorial policy. This material should include the full scope of approaches to the subject and should present the views of a wide variety of people. Both experts and nonexperts should cover the entire spectrum of opinion.

THE RESEARCH FINDINGS

The third part of *Violence and the Media* is concerned primarily with television entertainment and the issue of violence. It contains a large number of papers, written by well-known experts in the field, that summarize past research dealing with the subject of violence and the mass media. The most significant presentation in this portion of the volume, however, is the section covering the new research that was prepared especially for the Media Task Force. Specifically, this new research consisted of: (1) a content analysis of portrayals of violence in prime-time television programs and (2) a nationwide survey of the actual violent experiences of Americans. Once these studies had been completed, a comparison of the two worlds of violence—television portrayals versus real-world experiences—could be undertaken and the accuracy of the media ascertained.

The Content Analysis

The Media Task Force was concerned not only with the quantity of violence on television entertainment but also its quality. In other words, how was violence portrayed? Who killed? Who was killed? Were the killings shown to be justified or unjustified? Were the aggressors in these situations rewarded or punished? The Media Task Force considered these inquiries and others to be important in addressing the issue of how violence was portrayed on television. To answer such questions, they contracted with Professor George Gerbner and his staff at the Annenberg School of Communication to do the content analysis. Gerbner, it should be noted, was then and remains a well-known expert both on the research technique of content analysis and the general area of the study of media effects.

The Annenberg/Gerbner content analysis of the television world of violence examined the entertainment programs during prime time viewing hours (4 to 10 P.M.) and Saturday morning viewing hours (8 to 11 A.M.) during the weeks of October 1–7, 1967 and 1968. The analyses were conducted by pairs of trained coders who viewed videotapes of the programs that had been supplied by the networks. A standard recording instrument for analyzing acts of violence was used by all analysts.

Gerbner and his staff had been given an important research goal: "To provide an objective and reliable analysis from which the Task Force could deduce the messages about violence which were communicated to the audience."[10] Since different individuals may perceive different messages from the same content, effects cannot be inferred directly from that content. However, knowledge of the content is a necessary starting point in the study of media effects. If certain messages are repeated over and over again, it was argued, they might be influencing a significant portion of the audience.

Since people do not agree on the boundaries of what constitutes violent behavior, it was obviously important that one and only one definition of violence be used in the content analysis. For example, while most people would agree that killing is an act of violence, many might not extend the concept to include verbal assaults. Therefore violence was defined, in the Gerbner research, simply as "the overt expression of force intended to hurt or kill."[11] The Annenberg staff undertook the study with the understanding that they would produce a "bare bones" report; that is, they were to provide a report that contained little interpretation of the data. Later, the Media Task Force itself examined these data and provided further analysis and interpretation. Thus, the Task Force's treatment of the content analysis can be further divided into three sections: (1) the extent or quantity of violence on television, (2) the qualitative characteristics of television violence, and (3) the Task Force interpretation of the content analysis.

Extent of Violence. It was found that generally the network entertainment presented in 1967 and 1968 was filled with violence. Approximately 80 percent of all programs contained one or more violent incidents—for both years (see Table 11.1).

Furthermore, the total amount of violent programming on the three networks did not decrease between 1967 and 1968. The highest percentage of violent programs (90.9 percent) was broadcast by ABC in 1968, and that network had ranked second highest in 1967 (88.6 percent). If a person who watched ABC wanted to avoid programs containing violence, it would have been difficult in 1967, but more so in 1968. CBS, on the other hand, had the lowest percentage of programs that contained violence in both years, although the percentage increased from 1967 to 1968. Even though their programming ranked lowest in violence among the networks, a regular CBS viewer would have experienced difficulty finding programs that did not contain violence. NBC programming was the only network programming to register a decline from 1967 to 1968, from 89.7 percent of their programs to 80 percent.

TABLE 11.1. PROGRAMS CONTAINING VIOLENCE (PERCENT OF TOTAL PROGRAMS PRESENTED)*

	All Networks		ABC		CBS		NBC	
	N	*Percent*	*N*	*Percent*	*N*	*Percent*	*N*	*Percent*
1967	(78)	81.3	(31)	88.6	(21)	65.6	(26)	89.7
1968	(71)	81.6	(20)	90.9	(27)	77.1	(24)	80.0
Total	(149)	81.4	(51)	89.5	(48)	71.6	(50)	84.7

*N = Number of violent programs

Source: Robert Baker and Sandra Ball, eds., *Violence and the Media* (Washington, D.C.: Government Printing Office, 1969) p. 327.

Nevertheless, a regular viewer of NBC programs who wanted to avoid violent programming during the prime-time hours was in a position comparable to the viewers of CBS and ABC.

On the other hand, if persons sought out violent programs, as was entirely possible, they probably would have been able to find them during all of prime-time television. In short, those who wished to avoid violent programming had an almost impossible task, while those who desired violence had little trouble finding it.

The researchers recognized that various types of programs would probably contain different kinds of violence and varying levels of violence; in some programs violent acts would appear more frequently than in others and might also be more brutal in nature. For the purposes of this research, the investigators classified each of the entertainment programs into one of three categories: (1) crime-western-adventure-style programs, (2) comedy-tone programs, and (3) cartoon-format programs. As we might expect, the crime-type programs were the most likely (96.6 percent) to contain violent incidents. Cartoon shows, however, followed closely (93.5 percent), whereas comedies were the least violent. Nevertheless, 66.3 percent of all comedies contained violence during the two years analyzed. Thus, the researchers concluded that not only was violence prevalent in crime-style programs and cartoons, but "violence plays a significant role in television comedy."[12]

Overall, the researchers examined 183 programs. The analysis of these programs included some 455 major characters—more than half of whom (241) were violent. In addition, a total of 1215 separate violent encounters were recorded! It was clear that violent content was easy to find in the programs and extremely difficult to avoid.

The Qualitative World of Television Violence. Most of the violent episodes were portrayed as serious in intent, rather than as "funny." Humorous intent (slapstick, sham, etc.) was apparent in only two out of every ten violent acts. Violent acts were usually performed at close range, and more often than not, a weapon was used to inflict the pain. Typical weapons ran the gamut from knives and handguns to machine guns and explosives to elaborate devices for mass destruction. Portrayals of violence between members of the same family were rare (2 percent); more than half of the time, violence occurred between or among strangers.

The violence shown, however, produced little visible pain, and the gory details of physical injury (such as blood gushing from a wound) were shown in only 14 percent of all programs. In addition, the violence generally took an entrepreneurial form; in other words, it was undertaken in pursuit of some self-interest, often solely for personal gain rather than performed in the service of some (worthy or unworthy) cause. It is interesting to note that the "good guys" inflicted just as much pain and suffering as did the "bad guys," but the good guys usually triumphed in the end. Such good guys are, by definition, those who achieved a happy outcome. The losers (bad guys) came to an unhappy end. Generally, the good guy killer did not suffer negative consequences for his acts of violence. Of the 54 killers who were major characters in the programs, 46 did not "pay" for their act with their own lives, nor even suffer much punishment. Indeed, it is significant that the major characters who did die were all bad guys. Not one good guy character who killed was a victim of such violence himself!

While across all age groups at least one character in three was guilty of violent conduct, it was the young or midde-aged, unmarried male who was the most typical violent character. These characters committed more than their share of the television violence; in nine out of ten cases, such characters were the killers, and in eight out of ten cases they were the fatal victims. Race and ethnic heritage also played an important part in the portrayal of violent behavior. Nonwhites and foreigners committed more than their share of violent deeds, and were usually the villains. However, unlike their white American counterparts, for nearly every life taken such killers paid with their own. Violence was observed between members of different races, nationalities, or ethnic groups in 28 percent of all violence episodes; in about another third of the episodes the violence occurred between opponents who shared the same ethnic background. However, such relationships could not be determined in the remaining incidents.

The police and other law-enforcement officials were portrayed in the crime shows to be nearly as violent as the criminals. There was, of course, one difference—violence by the police rarely cost them their lives. Police brutality was not usually portrayed; in eight out of ten instances, the level of violence employed by officers of the law was portrayed as no more than was necessary to get the job done. The problem was that the officers had to deal with "bad guys" who initiated violence. However, the law-enforcement officers were depicted as initiating the violence 40 percent of the time. The violent criminals were infrequently turned in for trial, conviction, and sentencing; the elements of due process of law were portrayed to be a consequence of violence in only 20 percent of the cases. Instead "shoot 'em up" solutions were the norm—with the bad guys losing.

The researchers pointed out that it was difficult to observe witnesses to crimes portrayed on television. "Frequent close-ups and medium shots tended to exclude them."[13] Even when witnesses are assumed to be present, showing them and their reactions adds to the cost of production and complicates the scene; it is therefore done only if showing them is necessary to make a specific point in the story. In half of the episodes where violence was shown, no witnesses appeared. When witnesses were shown, they were usually passive. In one-third of the violent episodes witnesses were present but did not react to the violence. The witnesses assisted in or encouraged the violence in 9 percent of the episodes, and in only 8 percent did they attempt to prevent it. In general, violent behavior in the television dramas was rarely overtly objected to by witnesses and rarely punished.

The historical period or setting of the drama was another significant factor in the violence. Seventy-four percent of all contemporary (the 1960s) programs contained violence. However, this frequency paled when compared to those that were set in the past or in the future. Dramas that were set in the past contained violence 98 percent of the time, whereas those that were set in the future *always* contained violence. Overall, the researchers found that the television dramas portrayed America as a violent country filled with many violent strangers. Indeed, America was shown as a nation with a mostly violent past and present but the worst was yet to come; the future seemed likely to be totally violent.

Interpretation of Content Analysis. The Media Task Force examined and interpreted the content analysis data seeking to determine what messages were being broadcast over the airwaves to the viewing public. Once they had identified these various messages, the Task Force went beyond the data and inferred from them the social norms concerning the appropriate use of and proper context for violent behavior portrayed on television. The process they used for these inferences was one of identifying the substantive meaning of a televised event on the basis of incomplete information. As an illustration of the process, suppose that a boy had been turned down by a girl three consecutive times when he had asked her for a date. Might he not draw the inference that she was not interested in dating him? Although the girl had never come right out and said so, he could easily draw such a conclusion and stop asking her out. Thus, the boy "gets the message" and makes an inference based upon incomplete information.

The members of the Media Task Force argued that they used a similar procedure in deciphering the norms of violence implied in the messages contained in the television programming. Their problem was to infer the substantive meanings of these violent messages (i.e., What were the television norms containing violence?) Since under these circumstances it was likely that more than one norm could be inferred from the same message, it was conceivable that one investigator's inference might not agree with another's. It was even possible for them to draw contradictory inferences. The fact that the inferences involved judgment meant that, within reasonable limits, two or more investigators could legitimately differ in their interpretations. To illustrate this, return for a moment to the boy–girl dating situation previously discussed. One inference that the boy who received three consecutive refusals could legitimately make was that the girl was not interested in him. However, based on these same facts, he could also have concluded that she was simply a very popular girl, and that if he kept trying, she might have time to fit him in. In this view, he would eventually get a date with her if he persisted.

Remember, however, that practical factors limit the scope of such inferences. For example, the boy would not have been able to conclude, based upon these facts, that the young lady had been patiently waiting by the telephone for him to call, eagerly expecting a date with him. It is evident that, when the researchers of the Task Force interpreted the messages in the television violence, their inferences were not haphazard, nor were they based upon whim. Their inferences consisted of a process of attributing meaning to events on the basis of factual, although admittedly incomplete data, using logic and trained judgment.

Using this attribution process, then, the Media Task Force set forth a number of the norms concerning violence in television. Among them were:

1. Unmarried young and middle-aged males are more violent than others.
2. Violence can be expected more from nonwhites and foreigners than from whites and Americans.
3. Situations in which strangers are encountered at close range are particularly dangerous; violence is to be expected more from strangers than from family, friends, or acquaintances.
4. Middle-aged men and nonwhites are most likely of all groups to be killed when they become involved in violence.
5. Law-enforcement personnel are just as violent as the most violent citizens.
6. The past and present may have been saturated with violence, but the future will contain even more.
7. While the use of violence may lead to death, the inflicting of physical injury does not cause discomfort or pain.
8. Witnesses to violent behavior seldom intervene.
9. Persons who engage in violent behavior do not need to be concerned about punishment.
10. The use of violence is consistent with being a "good guy" because violence is a legitimate and successful means of attaining a goal. "Good guys" use violence just as much as "bad guys."

Overall, the report concluded that violence was a predominant characteristic of life in television programming. Violence, as portrayed, was useful as a means of conflict resolution and to promote the achievement of personal goals. Violent behavior was a particularly successful means of reaching personal goals, especially when the individual had been cast in a "good guy" role, because that violence was not usually punished. On the other hand, alternative means of conflict resolution—such as cooperation, debate, and compromise—were notable for their absence in television programming. Even when they were present they were shown to be relatively ineffectual.

The Violence Commission National Survey

The Media Task Force did not limit itself to an examination of the world of violence portrayed on television. They also investigated the actual world of violence as it was experienced by residents of the United States. There are two reasons why this examination of the real world was important. First, it was necessary for the Task Force to compare the fictional world of television violence with the real world of violence—the major objective of the new research. Second, it was likely that persons who had experienced direct exposure to violence would be affected by exposure to television violence differently from those who had not experienced it directly. Thus, the Task Force reasoned that: "Experience with violence may be both an independent source of learning and an intervening factor between exposure to and the effects of violence on television."[14]

To examine this "real world" of violence, the Task Force contracted with Louis Harris and Associates, a well-known public opinion research firm. Harris and Associates designed and conducted a national survey using professional interviewers and an area probability sample to estimate the total adult (18 years of age and older) and teenage (14 to 19 years of age) populations of the United States. The area probability sampling procedure required a random selection of census tracts, of clusters within those tracts, of household units within the clusters, and finally of respondents within each household. In total, the samples consisted of 1176 adults and 496 teenage respondents representing households within the United States. The respondents were considered representative of the total adult and teenage populations of the country.

The Louis Harris researchers collected detailed information about respondents' demographic characteristics in addition to the substantive information in three important areas: (1) the respondents' norms concerning violence, (2) the extent and nature of their actual experience with violence, and (3) the media habits and preferences of the respondents. Each of these areas will be examined and the major findings discussed.

Norms about Violence. Norms set standards for behavior and define the limits of that bahavior; they separate the acceptable and the unacceptable in social interaction. Moreover, norms have an explicit controlling function over behavior; conformity to them is rewarded but deviance is punished. Thus, it is generally assumed that most persons seek to act in accordance with established norms.

The survey sought to ascertain adult and teenage norms concerning violence. All respondents in both samples were asked to answer a series of questions that posed hypothetical situations. These items were intended to draw out their norms concerning the use of violence. In all, the respondents were confronted with 16 different situations, which involved eight different assailant–victim relationships and two levels of violence (minor violence and major violence). The eight different role relationships used in the hypothetical situations were:

1. A parent and a child who was at least one year old and healthy.
2. A husband and a wife.
3. A wife and a husband.
4. A public school teacher and a student.
5. A male teenager and a female teenager.
6. A man and an adult male stranger.
7. A policeman and an adult male.
8. A judge and a citizen.

In each situation, the first party was the assailant and the second was the victim. The questions were administered in the following format, where situation A represented an example of minor violence, whereas situation B contained major violence.

A. Are there any situations that you can imagine in which you would approve of a policeman striking an adult male citizen?
   (1) YES   (2) NO   (3) NOT SURE

B. Are there any situations that you can imagine in which you would approve of a policeman shooting an adult male citizen?
   (1) YES   (2) NO   (3) NOT SURE

The findings were similar in both the teenage and adult samples, although the teenagers were more likely to approve of violence. The findings are presented in Table 11.2. As can be seen, only two role relationships won approval from a majority of the American adult population regardless of the severity of the violent act. These were a policeman and an adult male and a judge and a citizen. Thus, the police and judges may engage in minor and major acts of violence with the general approval of a majority of adults. Parents, teachers, teenagers, adult males, husbands, and wives, on the other hand, may engage only in acts of minor violence within these role relationships with varying degrees of approval. Severe acts of violence, however, are disapproved within these role relationships by a majority of the adult population.

What distinguishes policemen and judges in these role relationships from the other characters studied is that they possess an institutionalized authority to engage in violence. For example, the police officer is authorized to use whatever force is necessary to apprehend lawbreakers, including violence. Judges, on the other hand, have the authority and responsibility of meting out punishments which are consistent with the provisions of the law. Such punishments may involve acts of violence: public whipping, the death penalty, and so on.

Interestingly, the role relationship in which the occurrence of violence is least approved is that of husband and wife. The vast majority of adult

TABLE 11.2. THE ADULT RESPONSES TO THE GENERAL QUESTION OF "ARE THERE ANY SITUATIONS THAT YOU CAN IMAGINE IN WHICH YOU WOULD APPROVE OF X DOING B TO Y?" ARE:

	Percent		
	Yes	*Not Sure*	*No*
1. Parent spanking his or her child assuming the child is healthy and over a year old	93	1	6
2. Parent beating his or her child	8	1	91
3. Husband slapping his wife's face	20	2	78
4. Husband shooting his wife	3	0	97
5. Wife slapping her husband's face	22	2	76
6. Wife shooting her husband	4	0	95
7. Public school teacher hitting a student	49	4	47
8. Public school teacher punching or beating a student	5	2	93
9. Policeman striking an adult male citizen	73	5	22
10. Policeman shooting an adult male citizen	71	5	24
11. Teenage boy punching another teenage boy	66	4	30
12. Teenage boy knifing another teenage boy	3	0	97
13. Man punching an adult male stranger	52	5	43
14. Man choking an adult male stranger	24	4	72
15. Judge sentencing a person to one or more years of hard labor	84	6	10
16. Judge sentencing a person to death	53	7	40

Source: Robert Baker and Sandra Ball, eds., *Violence and the Media* (Washington, D.C.: Government Printing Office, 1969) pp. 343–44.

Americans disapproved of even the use of minor violence between spouses, no matter which of them was the instigator.

It should be noted that a small minority of both samples (less than 15 percent), adults as well as teenagers, gave general approval to the use of high-level violence. The adults who were most likely to approve of high-level violence were male residents of metropolitan areas who were between 18 and 35 years of age and who had attained less than a college degree in their education. Among the teenagers who approved of high-level violence, the greatest proportion were black males between 16 and 19 years of age who lived in metropolitan areas.

Briefly stated, the major findings of the national survey were: Adult and teenage Americans approve of violence only when it is carried out by legally constituted authorities. That is, judges and police authorities may use a high level of violence when it is legally permitted. Low-level violence, however, is much more broadly approved of by the majority of both adult and teenage Americans. The only exception to this is the husband–wife relationship; there, even low levels of violence such as slapping the spouse's face is disapproved for either partner.

Actual Experience with Violence. The survey respondents were also asked about their direct experience with violence. They were questioned about personal experiences with any of five violent encounters. Had they, the interviewer asked, experienced them as either the victim, the assailant, or as an observer. The questions asked are presented below:

Victim—Observer Questions

Victim: Have you ever been (repeated 1–5)	(1) slapped or kicked
	(2) punched or beaten
	(3) threatened or actually cut with a
Observer: Have you ever seen	knife
another person (repeated 1–5)	(4) threatened with a gun or shot at
	(5) choked

First, the respondents were asked if they had been a victim, then if they had observed someone else being victimized, and finally, in a different series of questions, if they had been the assailant. Since it was strongly suspected that very few persons would willingly admit that they had committed a severe act of violence against someone else, a slightly different procedure was used to measure experience with violence as an assailant. Some of the questions were changed so that they implied self-defense rather than aggression. The questions about whether or not the respondents had used a gun or knife were placed in the context of self-defense in order to improve the willingness of the respondent to give an honest answer. It should be noted, therefore, that use of a knife or gun for reasons other than self-defense are not reflected in the answers to the questions.

Assailant Experience Questions

Have you ever (repeated 1–4)	(1) slapped or kicked another person
	(2) punched or beaten another person
	(3) been in the situation in which you had to defend yourself with a knife
	(4) been in the situation in which you had to defend yourself with a gun

The data obtained from the responses to the experience questions are presented in Table 11.3. It is clear that for both adults and teenagers the most common experience with violence was as an observer. While low-level violence such as being kicked or slapped was a fairly common occurrence in their lives, more severe forms of violence were rarely observed much less experienced, either as a victim or an assailant. Overall, the vast majority of Americans have not had direct personal experience with severe violence. The Task Force thus concluded

TABLE 11.3. PERCENT OF ADULTS AND TEENS WHO HAVE HAD EXPERIENCE WITH VIOLENCE AS THE VICTIM, ASSAILANT, AND OBSERVER

	Adults			Teens		
Violent Acts	*Victim*	*Assailant*	*Observer*	*Victim*	*Assailant*	*Observer*
Slapped or kicked	0.54	0.30	0.57	0.72	0.49	0.83
Punched or beaten	.30	0.16	.45	.42	0.38	.64
Threatened or cut with a knife	.13	NA	.17	.11	NA	.19
Threatened or shot at with a gun	.12	NA	.16	.06	NA	.14
Choked	.08	NA	.13	.16	NA	.22
Self-defense: Knife	NA	0.05	NA	NA	0.03	NA
Self-defense: Gun	NA	0.09	NA	NA	0.01	NA

Source: Robert Baker and Sandra Ball, eds., *Violence and the Media* (Washington, D.C.: Government Printing Office, 1969) p. 355.

that: "Direct personal experience is not a source of learning about severe violence for the majority of the American adult and teenage populations."[15]

Who, then, were the "violents" in the actual world of violence? That is, who were the people who had experienced severe violence such as choking or threat with a knife or gun—as either victim, assailant, or observer? In the first place, it was found that a person who was a "violent" in one role was likely to be violent in the other two roles. That is, many of the violents in the victim role were also violent as assailants and as observers. Adult violents were mainly males between 18 and 35 years of age, who lived in metropolitan areas and who had obtained less than a college education. Although there were some variations among the teenage violents, the researchers concluded that: "In general, both adult and teenage demographic subgroups with the highest proportion of violents are strikingly similar to the adult and teenage groups with the highest proportion of approvers of violence."[16] This fact, the Media Task Force argued, strongly supported the assumption that norms about violence are directly related to experience with it. They found further evidence of the relationship between norms and experience in the fairly strong statistical association between the two. In short, people who were violent in experience also tended to be approvers of high-level violence and vice versa. Thus, the Task Force argued that it had presented evidence that indicated that norms approving violence was one factor related to the probability of actually experiencing violence

Media Habits and Preferences. The national survey conducted for the Violence Commission contained several questions dealing directly with the issue of the respondents' media habits and preferences. It was not surprising to learn that for Americans television was the medium most often used by both adults and teenagers for entertainment and relaxation. More interesting were the respondents' answers to the items relating to media preferences. One question, for example, inquired:

> How do you feel about the amount of violence portrayed in television programs today, not including news programs—do you think that there is too much, a reasonable amount, or very little violence?

Of those responding to this question, 59 percent said that there was too much violence in television programs, 32 percent indicated that there was a reasonable amount, while only 4 percent thought that there was very little, with another 4 percent undecided. The Media Task Force concluded, on the basis of these data, that "a majority of adult Americans think there is too much violence on television."[17]

Another question asked:

> Apart from the *amount* of violence, do you generally approve or disapprove of the *kind* of violence that is portrayed on TV?

Only 25 percent of those questioned approved of the kind of violence portrayed on television, while 63 percent disapproved, and 12 percent were not sure. On the basis of these data, it was concluded that: "Americans may not be getting what they want in television programming when the issue is the kind of violence portrayed."[18] Yet 25 percent of the adult sample indicated their approval of the kind of violence shown on television. When we examine the characteristics of these respondents, we discover that they are males between 18 and 35 years of age who live in metropolitan areas and have attained less than a college education. Thus, we can see that the demographics of those who approved of television violence were the same as those of the adult "violents" based upon actual experience. In the teenage sample, 53 percent approved of the kind of violence portrayed on television. And again the category with the greatest proportion of approvers was black males between 13 and 15 years old who lived in metropolitan areas. In short, there is almost a complete overlap between the "approvers" of television violence and the actual "violents" in both the adult and teenage samples.

The limitations of such demographic data should be recognized. Even with the substantial overlap between actual "violents" with respect to norms and experiences, and the categories who approve of and prefer violent television content, we cannot infer a cause-and-effect relationship. In other words, we cannot conclude that viewing television violence causes violent norms and behavior; nor can we say that having violent norms and experiences "causes" a preference for violent shows. Because survey data is cross-sectional, it can yield only correlations between characteristics; this allows us to speak of statistical association between the characteristics but not of causality.

Another important limitation of the comparisons of these demographic data is that the unit of analysis is a category, not an individual. It is not possible to make reliable inferences about individuals from collective or central tendency data. If a demographic category has a large proportion of its members classified as "violents" and "approvers" of television violence, it does not mean that all or even most of the individuals who have the same demographic characteristics also have the same norms, experiences, and preferences with respect to violence. The reverse inference would be equally untrustworthy. Unfortunately, those who prepared the report were apparently unaware of this *non sequitur*.

Comparison of the Two Worlds

Thus far in our discussion of the content analysis and the national survey, the television world of violence and the actual world of violence, respectively, have been described in terms of the extent and nature of their violence. When they are compared, however, the differences between the two worlds are quite noticeable. Clearly, the television world of violence does not accurately reflect the real world in many significant aspects. First of all, television exaggerates the probability of being directly involved in violent acts. Additionally, whereas in real life legality is a prerequisite for the approval of violence, in television programs illegal violence is often approved. In real life, most violence occurs between family members, friends, or acquaintances, while in TV-Land the majority of the violence occurs between strangers. In addition, the most frequent type of violence in the television world involves the use of a weapon. But the great majority of adult and teenage Americans have never experienced this type of severe violence. The most common role in the television world of violence is the assailant and the least common is the observer or witness. In real life, however, the situation is reversed; the observer is the most common and the assailant is the least common role. The television world of violence is often set in a time and place other than contemporary America. However, no attempt was made in this study to demonstrate that TV programs accurately or inaccurately reflected the actual world of violence in the American past or the conditions in foreign countries.

It must be kept in mind when comparing the two worlds of violence that a major concern of the Media Task Force was to examine the kinds of implied norms that were depicted by television and the effects of such messages. The Task Force wanted to know if the norms of television modified or changed the actual norms of the viewing audience (especially its younger members) so that violence became commonplace or, worse, an acceptable method of obtaining a goal. What exactly were the audience members learning? The Task Force concluded that the high degree of overlap between preferences for violent media content and real-life violent experiences (coupled with norms in support of such acts) suggested that: "The television world of violence has the capacity to reinforce the 'violents' in the beliefs and actions in the real world."[19] They further hypothesized that the long-term effect of television violence on the "violents" would be in the direction of unrestricted approval of actual violence. They specifically argued that this group might be expected to act violently in conflict situations, when enforcing the law, and when attempting to achieve personal ends. The Task Force further cautioned that long-term exposure to the patterned world of TV violence could affect the norms and behavior of "normal" individuals: there would be an increase not only in the likelihood of their acceptance of violence but also in the probability that these individuals would use violence themselves. In short, the Task Force concluded that watching television violence could both reinforce violent behavior and cause it.

CONCLUSIONS AND IMPLICATIONS

The major conclusion of the Media Task Force was not particularly surprising. They found that television portrayals of violence were "one major contributory factor which must be considered in attempts to explain the many forms of violent behavior that mark American society today."[20] While the research concentration had been on television programming, the Media Task Force did not let the other media off the hook. They too were guilty, but the Task Force believed that television, as the most popular medium, had the most powerful and hence most dangerous effects. However, all of the media had to share in the blame for helping to make American society into a more violent one.

Although the Task Force came to many specific conclusions concerning the effects of the media, these effects can, for convenience, be categorized as either short-term or long-term effects. Simply stated, the overall evidence from the many papers contained in *Violence and the Media* indicated that the major short-term effects were two-fold: (1) Audiences that are exposed to mass media portrayals of violence learn how to perform violent acts; and (2) Audience members are more likely to exhibit that learning if they expect to be rewarded for violent behavior and/or encounter a situation similar to that portrayed. It must be remembered, however, that these conclusions about the short-term effects of media were derived from papers that summarized earlier research; the Media Task Force did not conduct research on the above issues. More importantly, it should be noted that the conclusions they drew concerning short-term effects were already well-established in the scientific literature.

The Task Force's numerous conclusions about long-term media effects, however, contained many more new insights and in many ways anticipated research trends that would become prominent in the late 1970s and early 1980s (see Chapter 13). For example, the researchers stated: "Exposure to mass media portrayals of violence over a long period of time socializes audiences into the norms, attitudes, and values for violence contained in those portrayals."[21] They further added that the probability of such socialization increased as the age of the viewer decreased; the probability also increased as the number of alternate or competitive sources of socialization into violence decreased. The Task Force also noted that persons who had been effectively socialized in this manner by mass media portrayals of violence could be expected to act in accordance with their beliefs. While this view has many implications, a few are quite blatant. First, these persons could be expected to resolve conflict in their lives through the use of violence; hence, the value of nonviolent means of problem solving would be diminished. Such persons would also be likely to use violence as a means to obtain desired goals, and when they engage in violence would probably use a weapon. In addition to engaging in violence, they would probably observe passively when exposed to violence between others. Indeed, it is likely that individuals who have been influenced by the television world of violence would develop the attitude that it is not the responsibility of individual citizens to help each other out of violent or violence-threatening situations. Thus, long-term exposure to mass media portrayals of violence might make members of the audience insensitive to or emotionally neutral to real acts of violence.

Other important long-term effects were also discussed. They included:

1. To the extent that mass media portrayals of violence contain rigid "good-guy"–"bad-guy," right–wrong, and either–or distinctions, young audiences are likely to develop and maintain psychological rigidity.

2. Inaccurate portrayals of class, ethnic, racial, and occupational groups in the mass media can be extremely damaging to communication between groups. When a group is portrayed as violent, members of the group may emulate the portrayal: nonmembers, however, may react to members with hatred, fear, or other emotions, creating additional intergroup conflict and violence. Such portrayals are especially potent if members have no personal contact with one another.

3. Both the extent and intensity of mass media portrayals of violence, especially on television, probably have the effect of creating and/or supporting a view of the world as totally violent. This world view tends to promote widespread toleration of violence, a feeling that it is hopeless to try to control it, and the belief that individuals must be violent in order to survive in a violent world.

These were the major conclusions reached by the Media Task Force. However, they were marred by an important consideration: They were not inferred solely from the research and summary papers contained in the volume. The Task Force did a great deal of extrapolation and often outran the data; that is, there are many conjectures and suppositions in the conclusions. However plausible they may seem, it is difficult to separate them from the research findings. In short, the major conclusions of the study were not directly based on the research conducted, or even on the previous research summarized for the volume. This is the major flaw in the volume as a whole.

Nevertheless, important issues were summarized in the volume, and the research that was conducted did give concrete information concerning the violent content of television. The networks could now no longer delude us with claims that they had been reducing the violence in their programming, as they had said for years. The data clearly contradicted them. Additionally, the content analysis showed that the television world of violence was a patterned one in which violence was portrayed in an unrealistic but potentially dangerous manner.

The Harris survey also added to our knowledge. We learned that a majority of Americans said that they did not approve of either the amount or kind of violence that was portrayed on TV. The American public, it appeared, was not getting the type of programming it wanted. Moreover, it was clear that those persons who watched and approved of violent shows, and those individuals who were violent in actual behavior shared certain characteristics. They were males between 18 and 35 years old, who lived in metropolitan areas and who had an educational level of less than a college degree.

But what did these data really tell us that we did not already know at the time? Not much! As we discussed previously, we can infer no cause-and-effect relationships. We cannot draw reliable conclusions about individuals from grouped data. However, even if we were able to make causal statements about individuals from the survey findings, how much would we really learn? There was nothing new in the demographic descriptions of the "violents"— their characteristics had long been known. Perhaps the most important finding from the survey was that most Americans did not experience violence directly. For the most part, what Americans know about violence they learn from portrayals on TV. Thus, the implications for television's role in providing constructions of reality and socializing the audience about violent behavior are truly significant.

Finally, the comparison of the two worlds of violence showed how different they were—and how unrealistically violence was portrayed on TV. Yet the comparison raises the concern that if television can influence attitudes, values, and behavior, then the two worlds might one day be much more similar.

The editors, Baker and Ball, used a social learning theoretical approach to structure the interpretation of both the research conducted and the research summarized. However, it was not the simplistic stimulus–response assumption that characterized the old magic bullet theory. Indeed, Baker and Ball made this quite clear.

> Common sense and observation refute the claim that exposure alone makes all people think and act violently. We know that millions of adults and children are exposed daily to television entertainment programming but a majority of them do not espouse violent norms or behave violently.[22]

Although the volume discussed both short-term (direct) and long-term (indirect) effects, the editors emphasized the long-term and indirect effects. For example, they stressed the role that television may play in socialization. After all, their findings indicated that teenagers were more approving of violence on television than were adults. This is not surprising given that the teenagers of 1968 had grown up with television, whereas the majority of the adults of that decade had not.

Baker and Ball also discussed the concept of identification and its relationship to social learning. "Identification occurs when an individual emulates another, seeking to be like that person in appearance and behavior."[23] By 1968, the importance of the process of identification for personality and attitude formation was already well-established in scientific literature. Baker and Ball observed that in both the televised and the real worlds of violence, young and middle-aged males dominated the violence. Thus, they concluded that the potential for identification with characters in the television world of violence was greatest for young males. They noted that a common problem in the maturation process of males is the establisment of a male identity. If the young males seized upon "violents" in television portrayals in their search for masculinity, then they would be more likely to imitate the attitudes and behavior of the television world of violence, particularly if young males lack other role models.

Identification may act as an intervening factor between exposure to television violence and the learning of violent attitudes and behavior from this exposure. Thus, young males are more likely than young females to learn violent attitudes and behavior from exposure to the television world of violence. By stressing the long-term and indirect effects rather than the short-term direct effects, the editors were able to contribute to a theoretical approach that remains significant in the 1980s.

In terms of methodology, the research in *Violence and the Media* receives mixed reviews at best. Both the content analysis and the survey sampling were well done. However, when interviewing people in person there are certain factors that become particularly important. One of these is the tendency for respondents to give socially desirable responses to sensitive questions. This could at least partially explain why a majority of respondents said they disapproved of violent shows while at the same time they watched them with pleasure. Asking respondents questions that required them to rely on their memory (e.g., have you ever seen...?) can also be a problem. In addition, particularly in questions like those administered in this survey, there are problems of demand characteristics. That is, the respondent answers the questions in the way the interviewer seems to want it answered.

Moreover, the measurement of the role of assailant was not adequate. The questions concerning severe violence were conducted in terms of self-defense; the use of a knife or a gun for other reasons was never addressed. The researchers assumed that the respondents would not be honest about violent uses of guns and knives, so they did not bother to ask. Not measuring the assailant role is a major problem because we cannot make any assessment of the effects of behavior on norms and attitudes.

Additionally, the data accumulated by the Media Task Force were composed entirely of descriptive statistics. The content analysis and national survey were discussed solely in terms of frequencies and percentages, rankings, demographic groupings, and averages per program or per hour. Trends and tendencies were often noted simply by "eyeballing" the data. In short, the research analysis was descriptive; no inferential statistics were utilized. The discussions overgeneralized from the findings, particularly given the absence of inferential techniques. The analyses simply outran the data.

Yet, *Violence and the Media* has become a classic in the field of mass communication for several reasons. For a number of years (since the 1940 Presidential voting study in Erie County, Ohio) many social scientists had argued that the primary effect of the media was reinforcement. In their discussions reinforcement had taken on the unique meaning of "no effect." Thus, they argued that mass media presentations did not create attitudes, norms, and values among the audience, but rather simply supported or reinforced attitudes, norms, and values already held. This was no effect? Indeed, even if the reinforcement effect *were* the only influence of the mass media, it would have to be viewed as extremely significant, given the widespread exposure that people have to the media in today's society. This was one of the major contributions of *Violence and the Media*: it forced social scientists to reevaluate the importance of the reinforcement effect. In addition, the work forced social scientists to consider that the reinforcement effect and the "causality argument" go hand in hand. In other words, television portrayals can both *create* and *reinforce* attitudes, values, and behavior. Indeed, a portrayal might do several things simultaneously. For some people it may reinforce attitudes, while for others it could help to form and shape attitudes and values, even if those attitudes and values differ from the portrayal. Because ours is such a heterogeneous society, different members of the audience can see different things in the same portrayal, perhaps focusing on different aspects of it and selectively ignoring others.

The public, unlike social scientists, received only a superficial coverage of the research and conclusions. The media chose not to make this book and its contents a subject of public discussion. Nevertheless, *Violence and the Media* had an impact if only because it raised more questions than it answered. Furthermore, those questions were of deep concern to Americans. In fact, the clamor for answers on the issue of television violence and its effects was to grow louder and louder until it could be heard even by politicians.

NOTES AND REFERENCES

1. Executive Order 11412, in *To Establish Justice, To Insure Domestic Tranquility,* Final Report of the National Commission On the Causes and Prevention of Violence (New York: Award Books, 1969), p. vii.

2. Daniel Bell, "The Myth of Crime Waves," in *The End of Ideology* (New York: Collier Books, 1960), p. 151.

3. Robert W. Peterson, editor, *Crime and the American Response* (New York: Facts on File, Inc., 1973), p. 23.

4. Ibid., p. 74.

5. Theodore Sorenson, *Kennedy* (New York: Bantam Books, 1966), p. 528.

6. Robert W. Peterson, op. cit., p. 23.

7. Ibid., p. 43.

8. Ibid., p. 45.

9. Robert Baker and Sandra Ball, editors, *Violence and the Media* (Washington, D.C.: Government Printing Office, 1969), p. 3.

10. Ibid., p. 312.

11. Ibid., p. 314.

12. Ibid., p. 328.

13. Ibid., p. 321.

14. Ibid., p. 341.

15. Ibid., p. 356.

16. Ibid., p. 358.

17. Ibid., p. 332.

18. Ibid., p. 333.

19. Ibid., p. 367.

20. Ibid., p. 375.

21. Ibid., p. 376.

22. Ibid., p. 375.

23. Ibid., p. 368.

Television and Social Behavior:
The Surgeon General's Report

The ink was scarcely dry on the Report of the President's Commission on the Causes and Prevention of Violence when a large-scale research program was funded by the Congress to probe the issue of televised violence more thoroughly. The President's Report had identified the relationship between violence in media content and violence in society as a potentially important and disturbing one, but available data on the role of media content left many questions unanswered. Meanwhile, by the late 1960s, the issue of violence in American society had reached new levels of concern: The urban riots had created confusion and anxiety; street crime had continued to rise sharply; the nation's campuses were in chaos over the Vietnam war and related issues. Most of all, the assassinations of President Kennedy, his brother Robert, and of Martin Luther King, troubled Americans deeply. In the midst of all of these events, television became the nation's most widely attended-to medium. At the same time, the suspicion was well-established in people's minds that the portrayal of violence in mass communication was a cause of violence in everyday life.

Political leaders are always alert to public issues that can have an influence on elections. Violence was just such an issue, and it proved to be a subject that linked research to politics. It was perceived by Senator John O. Pastore (Democrat of Rhode Island) as a problem that might be posing a "public health risk" for members of the American society. If TV violence prompted children to be more aggressive, he reasoned, some sort of political action might be required to modify the practices of the medium.

But what action might be needed? Outright censorship was out of the question, but careful research, showing the facts linking televised portrayals of violence to aggressive behavior, might be enough to change the programming of the industry. After consultation with the research community, it was clear that such facts were not yet clearly available. An impelling case could be made, therefore, that the federal government had a responsibility to provide the funds necessary to resolve the issue once and for all. It was this political situation that prompted the U.S. Congress to take a deep interest in social science research to probe the linkage between violence portrayed in mass communication and aggressive behavior among its consumers. This interest led the Congress to appropriate a million dollars to fund research studies on violence portrayed on television and the behavior of children and adolescents.

After a massive research effort, five volumes of results (plus a summary volume) were published. Popularly (if incorrectly), they are collectively referred to as the "Surgeon General's Report." It is the task of the present chapter to review the highlights of these efforts and to place this massive project into perspective as a milestone in mass communication research.

The so-called Surgeon General's Report on Television and Social Behavior is a monumental collection of more than 40 scientific papers; it includes specially commissioned research in addition to extensive reviews of the relevant literature. Collectively, these independently prepared papers are referred to as the "technical report," and they are divided into five volumes according to their common subject matter and/or their empirical orientations. In addition to these volumes of sponsored research, The Surgeon General's Advisory Committee itself prepared a report (*Television and Growing Up*), in which the Committee states its conclusions about the relationship between viewing televised violence and social behavior. The Committee's argument is that the conclusions it makes were drawn from earlier research and from the papers and reports contained in the five-volume "technical report." It is important to note that this summary volume, *Television and Growing Up*, was released weeks before the technical report and that the conclusions that the Committee draws in that volume were the ones that made headlines.

In evaluating the Committee's work, we should note that its title, The Surgeon General's Advisory Committee on Television and Social Behavior, emphasizes *more* than the issue of violence and the impact of televised violence on the attitudes and behavior of children. The issue of televised violence and its effects, was, however, the central focus of the research program, even though the research conducted for the program examined such diverse topics as television advertising and viewer reaction to it, the amount of time spent watching television, activities displaced by television viewing, the learning of specific information, and the comparative effects of black-and-white versus color television on the information learned from the television program. A wide range of social science methods were used in these studies, including: content analyses, laboratory experiments, field experiments, observation studies, and opinion surveys. Nevertheless, despite the diversity of topics examined and the multiple methods used, it is clear that the product of this research program does not cover the *entire* range of the subject of television and its influence on social behavior, nor was such a claim made by the Committee.

As we noted, the impetus for the Committee's work was provided by a request from Senator John O. Pastore, then Chairman of the Senate Commerce Committee's Subcommittee on Communications. This committee provides legislative oversight to the Federal Communications Commission (FCC). In a letter of March 5, 1969 to Robert Finch, then Secretary of Health, Education, and Welfare, Pastore indicated that he was "exceedingly troubled by the lack of any definitive information which would help resolve the question of whether there is a causal connection between televised violence...violence and antisocial behavior by individuals, especially children."[1] It was as though the recently completed review of the subject by the National Commission on the Causes and Prevention of Violence—both extensive and expensive—had never taken place.

Surgeon General William H. Stewart (on orders from President Nixon) announced on March 12, 1969 that his agency would immediately embark upon a study to "help resolve the question" and that a committee composed of distinguished men and women from appropriate disciplines would be appointed to study the issue. The job of the committee would be to establish scientifically, insofar as possible, what harmful effects, if any, violent television programs have on children. Stewart also announced that a one million dollar budget was being assigned to the project from otherwise undesignated funds in the budget of the National Institute of Mental Health (NIMH), and a report was promised in approximately one year. In addition, NIMH provided staff for the work of the Committee and was responsible for screening proposals, selecting those which would provide the most valuable data, and monitoring the implementation of the studies.

To aid in the selection of members of the Advisory Committee, the Surgeon General sent letters to a variety of academic and professional associations, including The American Psychological Association, The American Sociological Association, and The American Psychiatric Association. He also wrote to the three major national networks: The American Broadcasting Company (ABC), The Columbia Broadcasting System (CBS), and The National Broadcasting Company (NBC). A letter was also sent to the National Association of Broadcasters (NAB). All of these groups, as well as distinguished social scientists and government officials, were asked to recommend "knowledgeable scientists" for membership on the Advisory Committee.

A list of 40 "recognized experts" in the behavioral sciences and mental health disciplines was compiled by the Surgeon General's office from the names received. Then, in a step retrospectively described as "it seemed like a good idea at the time," the Surgeon General sent the list to the presidents of the three networks and the NAB asking them to indicate "which individuals, if any, you believe would *not* be appropriate for an impartial scientific investigation of this nature."[2] CBS declined to offer any advice, but ABC, NBC, and the NAB named seven persons on the list as unsuitable. Eleven members were chosen from the remaining names and another member was chosen whose name had not been on the original list. The reason given for this addition was that representation in one of the scientific disciplines needed to be strengthened.

OVERVIEW OF THE RESEARCH REPORTS

The Committee began its work on June 16, 1969. The recent comprehensive examination of the existing evidence in the area of televised violence made by the National Commission on the Causes and Prevention of Violence, and the reaction it received, reinforced the original decision to sponsor new research. Between August 1969 and April 1970, 40 formal research proposals were submitted and reviewed for possible funding. Those applications selected to receive financial support had to pass a formal review system similar to the one usually used by NIMH to evaluate research proposals. For the Television and Social Behavior Program, groups of four to seven senior scientists in the researchers' field of expertise met, on nine occasions, to review proposals. Each review committee consisted largely of social scientists in the field who were not affiliated with the Television and Social Behavior Program and senior staff members. In addition, one or two members of the Scientific Advisory Committee itself were present at most meetings. The Committee as a whole did *not* select the research projects. In all, 23 independent projects were funded, providing a multidimensional approach to the assessment of television's effects. These 23 projects—many of which involved more than one study and some-times more than one report—form the basis of the technical report.

Volume I: Media Content and Control

Volume I contains the results of six studies, although one of the studies incorporates the separate efforts of many investigators and is the object of discussion in five papers. Overall, a total of 11 reports and papers are contained in the volume, and they are all concerned with the *content* of television and how it comes to be what it is. These reports are *not* concerned with effects. The focus is almost exclusively on content intended as entertainment, rather than on news or educational programs; prime-time evening television and those programs designed specifically for children are dealt with extensively.

Content Analyses of Televised Violence. Some continuity was maintained with earlier research. For example, in Chapter 11 (pp. 277–281) we noted the work of George Gerbner, who had done a content analysis for the National Commission on the Causes and Prevention of Violence; he did a similar one for the Surgeon General's Committee.[3] Gerbner analyzed one week of fall prime-time and Saturday-morning programming in 1969 and compared the results with the analyses done in 1967 and 1968. In all three studies, he used trained coders who enumerated and classified violent incidents by watching videotapes of selected network programs. He defined an instance of violence as "the overt expression of physical force against others or self, or the compelling of action against one's will on pain of being hurt or killed."[4] Note also that he was concerned not only with the quantity of violence but also with its quality or character.

The overall results of the quantity of violence studies displayed, at best, a quality of irony. Killing, compared to 1967 and 1968, declined sharply. But the presentation of aggression, harm, and threat did not. These remained about the same throughout all three years. Thus, the *prevalence* of violence did not fluctuate much from 1967 through 1969. In fact, in each of the three years eight out of ten dramatized entertainment programs contained violence; violent episodes occurred regularly at the rate of eight per hour. Therefore, overall—considering killing and other types of violence together—there was only a slight decrease in violence in prime-time television.

In children's cartoons, however, violence increased. The "children's viewing hours" were the *most* violent of all television hours in 1969, and they were increasing their lead over other types of programs. Violence in cartoons did vary by network; CBS was always lowest. The three-year average was about the same for ABC and NBC, with NBC greatly increasing the level of violence in its cartoons during 1969. It is evident that any overall decline in violence over the three years is attributable to a reduction in violent programming aimed at *adults*. As Gerbner notes:

> It is...clear that children watching Saturday morning cartoons had the least chance of escaping violence or of avoiding the heaviest saturation of violence on all television...Of all 95 cartoon plays analyzed during the three annual study periods, only two in 1967 and one each in 1968 and 1969 did *not* contain violence. The average cartoon hour in 1967 contained more than three times as many violent episodes as the average adult hour...By 1969...the average cartoon hour had nearly six times the violence rate of the average adult television drama hour....[5]

As previously noted, the content analyses dealt not only with the quantity of violence but also with its quality or character—that is, when and where it occurs, who participates, and in what ways different kinds of people are involved. The major findings were: Violence was usually excluded from the familiar; it occurred with much greater frequency when the setting was the past (e.g., westerns) or the future (e.g., space adventure), rather than the present, and when the setting was remote or nonidentifiable. Violence was *least* common in urban settings, as compared to rural, small town, and remote settings. A particularly interesting finding was that, in 1969, violence was typically presented with an absence of suffering.

Violence, and television action in general, tended to be the prerogative of males free of responsibilities. Roughly three-fourths of all leading characters were "male, American, middle and upper class, unmarried, and in the prime of life." Most male roles involved violence. In addition, most televised killings occurred between strangers or slight acquaintances, which is certainly not the case in the real world. Nonwhites, foreigners, and persons of low socioeconomic status, where shown, were portrayed as likely to become involved in violence; but they usually ended up on the "losing side." Women were depicted as lacking social power and influence and much more likely to be the objects of victimization. Between 1967 and 1969, female involvement (as the aggressor) in violence dropped sharply. In fact, this accounts for the slight overall decline in violence in prime-time television. Even though women characters were less violent, men were as violent as ever.

The discussion of the content analyses can be summarized best by noting that the most striking aspect of television violence is its unreality. People, relationships, settings, places and times all depart from real life. Why is violence so portrayed in TV Land? Perhaps placing violence in such uncommon settings and involving people who are strangers is a device that makes violence itself less disturbing to the average viewer and hence more acceptable. In any event, two implications of these unrealistic portrayals can be noted: (1) The reflection thesis, which maintains that television simply mirrors the world as it is, receives little support; and (2) As a guide for attitudes and behavior, television cannot be said to provide much accurate information about real life.

Interviews with Television Professionals. As part of the research, television professionals were interviewed to gain insight into how television content comes to be what it is. Two reports discuss these interviews; Cantor[6] interviewed 24 script writers and producers involved in the production of children's programs, while Baldwin and Lewis reported on the production of drama intended for adults.[7] While the two studies differ in many ways, the picture they convey is largely consistent.

Television professionals see violence as synonymous with action and hence as the best way of holding the attention of both children and adults. They claim to attempt to confine violence to situations where it is appropriate—essential to the plot or character. The television professionals were generally unsympathetic with criticism of television violence. They asserted that violence accurately reflects life (a contention that the content analyses did not support) and that it prepared the young for adulthood. They rebutted critics by citing influences on viewers other than television. They criticized parents for ignoring their responsibilities and argued that the high ratings of certain violent programs indicated parental support. Cathartic benefits of watching television were cited (even though the weight of the evidence did not support this theory).

The professionals *did* admit that television might adversely influence a "disturbed" viewer, but they did not believe that the television industry could be overly concerned with this segment of the population. They suggested that television might be a scapegoat when poverty, racial hostility, distrust of government, and alienation should be the true focus. They argued that on television violent acts were shown as immoral unless they were in self-defense, or on behalf of national security or law enforcement. They argued that the heroes of violent programs used violence only when necessary and in accordance with the law. In sum, television professionals generally believed that violence on the part of viewers was inhibited—either (1) because of cathartic emotional release or (2) because violence was always shown as either justified or punished.

Cantor found an overall indifference on the part of the producers regarding the possible harmful effects of television on children. "While the shows are in production, producers rarely consider the effects they may have on children; most believe those considerations are the networks' responsibility, or maybe the parents', but not theirs."[8] The creators of children's week-night programs expressed a similar indifference.

> Those producing adventure stories deny that they are making shows for children, although these programs are categorized as children's programs by the National Academy of Television Arts. One producer, whose program's ratings and demographic survey data show a large number of children under ten as part of the audience, said, "We are not making a children's story. I don't think anyone in the business knows who their audience is. I think it is presumptuous of anyone to claim they know this. Kids don't know anything. They are not discerning. As long as we are on the air, I don't care."[9]

Networks, of course, do have broadcast standards departments. Each network has a director and about eight staff members who are collectively referred to as "the censors." The general attitude of the "censors" concerning the work of social scientists on the effects of television violence is best summed up by the words of one chief censor: "We laugh at them. I don't see how the work accomplished so far by social scientists is of practical value."[10]

Many network people, in contrast to script writers and producers, verbalized to the researchers interest in reducing violence, but the researchers felt that there was little chance that it could be substantially reduced given the methods of production. What else could be as popular and as effective in holding the attention of both children and adults as violence?

Comparisons with Other Countries. Last in Volume I is an interesting group of papers concerning the social processes and institutional structures through which television content is organized and controlled in the United States, Great Britain, Israel, and Sweden. Michael Gurevitch[11] compares these findings and notes that the proportion of violence in American entertainment programs is greater than that broadcast in any of the other three nations. Yet there is some tendency toward an Americanization of world television; a substantial proportion of the violence on the television of other countries is provided by American programs. However, the relative lack of governmental involvement in broadcasting separates the United States from other countries. In Great Britain, Israel, and Sweden broadcasting is much more tightly controlled by governmental and other public institutions. In addition, in those countries broadcasters gain support either through subsidies or by the licensing of receivers. In the United States, governmental influence is minimal; broadcasters support their enterprise by the sale of advertising and access is free once the viewer obtains a television receiver. Thus, this report gives support to the view that television violence is encouraged and perhaps made inevitable by the competitive economic structure of the American broadcast industry. For the future, however, perhaps public television represents a potential means of altering television content in this country, since public television's content is not dictated by audience size.

Volume II: Television and Social Learning

The second volume of the report consists of six papers: Two are essentially reviews of the literature while the other four report the results of experimental studies. The reports are organized around determining the nature and extent to which social learning occurs as a result of children watching television. More specifically, the reports are concerned with the nature of observational learning, or modeling; that is, the way in which the behavior of children changes as a result of observing the behavior of others. In this case, the children are observing the behavior of actors in television programs.

Modeling and Observational Learning. Virtually all social scientists have acknowledged that attitudes, values, and behavior of any individual may be developed, at least in part, through observational learning. Research studies have shown that simple observation of others can be very effective in changing widely varied aspects of the behavior of children or adults. For example, children's observations of others in films, or on television, have been shown to produce: an impressive level of learning of unfamiliar behavior; an increase in willingness among children to aid others and to share with others; and even a reduction of phobic reaction (e.g., seeing another individual pet a dog in a film may reduce the observer's fear of dogs). These are only a few examples from the impressive body of evidence that supports the conclusion that learning by observation is a critical aspect of the social learning process.

In discussing observational learning, a distinction must be made between *acquisition* of new behavior and *acceptance* of that behavior. In other words, we must distinguish between the ability to reproduce previously unfamiliar behavior (acquisition) and the actual performance of behavior that is the same or similar to that which has been observed (acceptance). A child may *observe and remember* novel behavior without necessarily performing that behavior. If the child can reproduce or describe the behavior he has witnessed (i.e., when asked to do so) the *acquisition* of new behavior has occurred.

The possibility that behavior can be acquired through observation and retained without necessarily being performed *immediately* (or ever) has important implications for our understanding of the effects of television. If a child has acquired some new behavior, he clearly possesses the potential to produce it, particularly if he finds himself in a situation in which such a performance might appear to be useful or desirable (for example, one similar to the situation from which he learned the behavior). Thus, although learning does not necessarily lead to action, it makes more probable the performance of otherwise unlikely responses.

The learning changes the potential range of behaviors a child may display when provoked or when under stress—especially in a new situation. Therefore, the process of observational learning can be seen to involve three stages:

1. The observer must be exposed to the behavior of another individual, either a "live" model (direct exposure to other persons) or a symbolic model (the behavior of others as observed in television and other media);
2. He must acquire and be able to reproduce what he has seen or heard; and,
3. He may or may not accept the model's behavior as a guide to his own actions.

Relating this to the viewing of televised violence, there is no doubt that children are exposed to violence (Stage 1); nor is there any doubt that they can learn by viewing television (Stage 2). What is missing is an adequate explanation describing the conditions under which an observer will accept a model's behavior as a guide to his own actions. Even today, the anwser to this question remains an elusive one.

Experimental Studies of Aggression. The experiments reported in this volume take as their starting point a study carried out by Bandura in 1965; they represent variations and refinements of that classic work. In his project, Bandura had children watch a model perform a series of aggressive acts against a plastic Bobo doll.[12] One group of children observed the model rewarded for this behavior; another group observed the model receive no consequences; and a third group observed the model punished. When the children were subsequently placed in a play situation, those who had viewed the model rewarded or perform without consequences for the behavior showed a high level of direct imitation (i.e., they hit or kicked the Bobo doll in the manner the model had done). Not surprisingly, those who observed the model punished showed relatively few imitative or aggressive responses. Nevertheless, when the children in *all* groups were later asked by the experimenter to reproduce as many of the model's aggressive acts as they could—and were offered attractive rewards for doing so—all groups showed a remarkably *high and uniform* degree of learning.

Note that this evidence does not tend to support the argument advanced by network spokesmen that the depiction of violence has no harmful effects on young viewers so long as violent behavior is ultimately punished. We see that children learn the aggressive behavior and can reproduce it when the situation encourages such behavior.

One point should be clarified. The laboratory experiments concerned with the effects of violence or aggressiveness portrayed in films or on television have focused primarily on two different, although often related, kinds of effects: imitation and instigation. Imitation occurs when what is observed is copied or mimicked. This was shown in Bandura's study of the Bobo doll. There is no longer any doubt that a child may learn a new aggressive or violent form of behavior through observation and imitation. Bandura's work, in addition to the research of many other investigators, has thoroughly documented that fact. As previously discussed, the ability to imitate does not always translate into the performance of actual imitative behavior. Whether or not what is observed will be imitated depends upon a variety of situational and personal factors.

Instigation, on the other hand, occurs when what is observed is followed by a generalized increased aggressiveness. After viewing a boxing match on TV, a child might exhibit increased aggressive behavior—some of which is the result of imitative behavior and some a result of instigation. In other words, the child's aggressive behavior after watching the TV program can be quite different in quality and character from the aggressive behavior displayed in the television program.

Since the fact of imitation was so well-established, no research in the Television and Social Behavior Program was concerned solely with imitation. Instead, the research attempted to provide more precise and extensive evidence about the capacity of televised violence to *instigate* aggressive behavior in children. For the most part, these studies utilized the classic design developed by Bandura in studying imitation.

The study, "Short Term Effects of Televised Aggression on Children's Aggressive Behavior," done by Liebert and Baron,[13] is representative of this approach. The purpose of the study was to determine whether the willingness of children to engage in aggression against other children would be affected by the viewing of violent televised material. One hundred and thirty-six children (68 boys and 68 girls) participated in the study. Sixty-five children were five or six years of age; the remaining 71 subjects were either eight or nine years old. The children were randomly assigned to one of two groups. Both groups of children were shown brief excerpts from publicly broadcast television shows. One group, however, observed the first three-and-one-half minutes of a program from a popular television series, "The Untouchables." The story line contained a chase, two-fisted fighting scenes, two shootings, and a knifing. In contrast, children in the control group viewed exciting, but nonaggressive, sporting events (e.g., hurdle races, high jumping, and so on).

After viewing one of these two programs, children in both groups were placed in a series of situations where they could either *hurt* or *help* another child by pushing one of two buttons. The children were told that if they pushed the green button they would help the other child win a prize; however, if they pushed the red button they would hurt the other child's chances. They were also told that the longer they pushed the button the more they helped or hurt the other child.

The results of this experiment are startling. Witnessing the aggressive episodes increased the willingness of the children to be an aggressor. But the primary effect of the exposure was that those who had observed the violent scenes pushed the red button for a significantly longer period of time than those who had observed the nonaggressive sporting events. It was the magnitude of the hurting response that was increased. It should be noted that *not all* of the young children became more aggressive. Yet the fact remains that most of these "normal" children acted in a much more aggressive manner after a very brief exposure to violence. We do not know how long such effects last, but we cannot overlook this evidence.

Robert Liebert summarized the research reported in this volume and related it to 54 *earlier* experimental studies.[14] His conclusion was that continued exposure to violence is positively related to the acceptance of aggression. Children who view programs or films in which aggression is rewarded are subsequently more violent in their own behavior. According to Liebert, the accumulated evidence shows that

> . . . at least under some circumstances, exposure to televised aggression can lead children to accept what they have seen as a partial guide for their own actions. As a result, the present entertainment offerings of the television medium may be contributing, in some measure, to the *aggressive behavior of many normal children*. Such an effect has now been shown in a wide variety of situations. (Emphasis added)[15]

In general, the studies contained in Volume II were methodologically sound and generally consistent in their findings of a cause-and-effect relationship between viewing televised violence and subsequent aggressive behavior in children. The major criticism directed at these studies has been the fact that they were laboratory experiments. Laboratory experiments are probably the *most* efficient means of obtaining information, but critics charge that such studies represent an *artificial* situation that seriously restricts the possibility of generalizing the experimental findings to everyday life. Statistically significant effects may be obtained from events that occur in the laboratory, but will they, critics ask, have any relation to the behavior of young children in the "real" world *and* over long periods of time? Will aggressive effects present minutes after viewing the program persist one month or one year later? There is no doubt that laboratory studies do give us insight into cause–effect relationships that exist under *specified* conditions, but critics argue that laboratory studies are incapable of providing conclusive evidence about what happens in the "real-life" world. Questions about generalizing from laboratory experiments to the real world remain a subject of controversy.

Volume III: Television and Adolescent Aggressiveness

The question of whether aggressive behavior by adolescents can be attributed, in some degree, to viewing violent television programming is the focus of the research reported in Volume III of the technical report. Eight studies, plus review and commentary, all report analyses of the answers given by *adolescents* to questions asked of them in *surveys*. Note that the methodological focus shifts from small-scale laboratory experiments involving preadolescent children to field studies which examine the attitudes and behavior of adolescents in real-life settings. Thus, these studies address some of the questions of generalizability raised in objection to the experiments. It should also be noted that in some respects it is easier to study adolescents than any other age group. One reason is that, unlike adults, they can be found in groups at schools rather than singly or in pairs at home. Moreover, as subjects they have a distinct advantage over children—they can usually understand and answer questions.

Generally, the studies in this volume all address three problems: (1) the measurement of adolescent television use, (2) the measurement of adolescent aggressiveness, and (3) the correlation or association between viewing violence and aggressive behavior. Even with this common focus, however, the sophistication of the concepts, measures, samples, and modes of analysis vary widely among these studies.

Adolescent Television Use. Three different measures of adolescent viewing behavior were used: (1) total time spent viewing television, (2) program preferences, and (3) frequency of viewing recurrent programs. Total time spent viewing was usually measured by asking the respondent to estimate how much time he or she watched television on an "average" day. Program preferences were usually measured by asking the respondents to list their favorite shows; this measure can also serve as an indicator of whether the individual prefers violent or nonviolent programs. Recurrent viewing was usually measured by providing the respondent with a checklist of recurring programs and asking how often he or she watched each. This indicator also served as a measure of how *often* the individual watched violent programs.

Although each of these measures has something in common, it is obvious that they are *not* measuring exactly the same thing. Therefore, they do not produce consistently similar results. While it might appear that adolescents who view television more frequently would also see more violence than those who view it less often, this is not always the case. An individual who watches a great deal of television may view only as much violence as another individual who watches less often overall but who has a distinct preference for violence.

The most general and consistent finding concerning adolescent use of television was that the amount of time spent watching *decreases* throughout adolescence. Children's viewing is the heaviest during the sixth grade; thereafter, the amount declines steadily. Many factors account for the diminishing of the "TV habit" during this age period. Generally speaking, teenagers increasingly discover other activities that compete with television for their time. Such a tendency is, in fact, particularly evident among those adolescents who have the greatest potential for involvement in other activities—the brighter and more socially skilled and members of more affluent social groups.

While age is indeed an important factor when considering viewing time, it appears *not* to be much of a factor when it comes to preference for violent programs. If there is any tendency, it is for older adolescents to be slightly more likely to name a violent program as their favorite. It is somewhat surprising, given the decline in viewing time among teenagers, that the average amount of time spent viewing by half of all American adolescents on a given day is *three hours or more*. While some do not watch at all, a substantial number watch twice that amount. Overall, a general impression is conveyed that many teenagers spend hours in front of a television set.

Another consistent finding was that of a negative relationship between television use and mental ability. Almost all of the studies reported that intellectually brighter adolescents watched less television and, moreover, were less likely to prefer violent programs. A negative correlation between both I.Q. and/or academic performance and viewing time was obtained consistently. In addition, socioeconomic status also tended to be negatively related to the time spent viewing. Those adolescents whose parents' occupation and education levels placed them in the lower socioeconomic strata spent more time watching television than did those in the higher socioeconomic levels; they also indicated more of a preference for violence.

Adolescents saw the violent shows as being "highly realistic"; they thought they were even more realistic than news or documentary programs. Both boys and girls reported emotional involvement with television violence. But the boys were more likely to identify with violent characters. It must be remembered, however, that the girls lacked aggressive female role models; this alone could explain their failure to identify with violent or aggressive characters.

Adolescent Aggressiveness. Both the measures of aggression and the conceptualizations underlying it were numerous and varied in these studies. This is understandable, even defensible, in view of the fact that there is no simple or uniform consensus definition of aggression. For convenience, the measures of aggression can be placed into four categories:

1. Reports of aggression by others—usually parents, peers, or school officials.

2. Self-reports of aggression and delinquent behavior.
3. Self-reports of aggressive feelings and attitudes.
4. Self-reports of cognitive and affective reactions to aggression.

Some of the studies use a combination of these measures of aggression, whereas others do not.

The two most general findings about adolescent aggressiveness were: (1) Boys, not surprisingly, reported a higher incidence of aggressive behavior than did girls; and (2) Aggressive adolescents were more likely to have come from low socioeconomic-status homes and to have received low grades in school.

Relationships between Viewing Televised Violence and Aggressiveness. The studies in this volume were primarily concerned with the relationship between exposure to televised violence and aggressive tendencies. As previously discussed, some studies used total viewing time as an index of exposure; others employed preference for violent programs; and some used the amount of violence viewed. Most of the relationships obtained were positive, but were of low to modest magnitude. This is particularly true in regard to the strength of the relationship between both total viewing time and preference for violent programs, and aggressive behavior. Stronger relationships, however, were obtained between *amount* of violence viewing and aggressive behavior.

What do these correlations indicate about the relation between viewing televised violence and aggressive behavior? There are three general possibilities:

1. The viewing of violence leads to aggressive tendencies.
2. Aggressive tendencies lead to the choosing of violence viewing.
3. Aggressive tendencies and the viewing of violence are both products of some third condition or set of conditions.

An example of the third alternative is a child who, as a result of certain personality characteristics, may be predisposed toward aggressive behavioral tendencies and toward a preference for violent programs. It should be noted, however, that these three alternatives are not necessarily mutually exclusive. The demonstration that one of the three processes exists would not preclude the occurrence of the others. Each may have an independent effect. In an attempt to find the most *plausible* explanation for the obtained correlations between measures of viewing and aggressive behavior the study "Television Violence and Child Aggression: A Follow-up Study," by Lefkowitz and his associates will be examined in detail. [16]

The Lefkowitz study is somewhat unusual because it was a ten-year longitudinal study. Children in Columbia County, New York, were first tested in their third grade classrooms (in 1959–60) and again ten years later as a part of the Television and Social Behavior Program. There were 436 respondents for whom both third grade and "thirteenth grade" data were available. The subjects were asked to respond to essentially the same questions on both occasions. The researchers had the children rate each other on aggression and then also interviewed their parents in order to establish aggressive tendencies both inside and outside the home. The subjects also made self-reports on their own behavior.

It was found that the popularity of an eight-year-old child in the third grade turned out to be a good predictor of that child's popularity ten years later. The child who is unpopular in the third grade tends to watch television more as he gets older, and continues to be unpopular. More important, the television habits that had been established by the age of eight were found to have influence on the boys' aggressive behavior throughout childhood and into their adolescent years. The more boys viewed violence in the third grade, the more aggressive their behavior was at that time and ten years later. In fact, the relation between third grade TV-watching and later behavior is even stronger than that between third grade TV-viewing and third grade aggressive behavior. Lefkowitz and his associates thus argue that the effects of television violence on behavior is cumulative. Since they also found that there was no relation between later television preferences and earlier aggressive behavior, the authors also argue that this finding supports the claim that frequency of violence viewing is causally related to aggressive behavior ten years later. Although many of these same relationships were also found for girls, they were much weaker and less pronounced.

Another interesting finding was that the more an individual watched violent shows, the more likely he or she was to judge that the situations depicted in television western and crime stories were realistic representations of life. Such a violent and hostile view of the world might lead these subjects to see their own aggressive behavior as normal and a perfectly proper method of solving problems.

Overall, the authors concluded that their findings, over a ten-year period, strengthened the conviction that there was indeed a real relation between viewing violence and behavior. Viewing violence *regularly* appears to lead to aggressive behavior. The significance of the studies in this volume was that they contribute to selecting among the three alternative explanations of the association between violence viewing and aggression. And there is considerably more support for the "viewing induces aggressiveness" position. If the association were due to the initially more aggressive youths preferring violent programs, then there would have been a stronger association between preference and aggressiveness than between exposure and aggressiveness, but this is not the case.

What about the third alternative? Is this relation between exposure to violence and aggressiveness due to some third set of conditions which affects both preference and exposure? When the researchers examined the relationship and took into account a variety of other variables, the relationship between exposure to violence and aggressiveness was not significantly diminished. Neither poor performance in school, nor low socioeconomic status, where norms of aggressiveness are more prevalent, explained any of the relationship. Nor did a variety of other additional variables. It should, however, be kept in mind that there is a multitude of additional factors that might account for the correlation. Noted communication researcher Steven Chaffee, however, concluded:

> There is clearly a preponderance of evidence in these studies to support the conclusion that adolescent aggressiveness and the viewing of violent television programs are statistically associated.[17]

He further clarifies this statement by pointing out that a significant positive correlation was found more often than not and that there was no negative correlational evidence. The correlation held up consistently in varying samples, with different sexes, age levels, and locations, and with a variety of measures of aggressiveness. It remained no matter what variables were controlled.

Yet, overall, these correlations were of modest strength. What can we conclude from the studies we have reviewed in this volume? The best summary is probably as follows: Regular or frequent viewing of violent television programs may cause aggressive behavior. This conclusion should not be surprising, since it would be terribly naive to expect that regular or frequent media experiences would have no influence on the social behavior of developing children. But television violence is only one of many factors that lead to aggressive behavior. It cannot by itself explain aggressive behavior; but its influence cannot and must not be ignored.

Volume IV: Television in Day-to-Day Life

The primary purpose of the 8 projects and 18 papers reported in Volume IV was to provide a current picture of what kind of television people watched in the early 1970s. The projects included field studies, surveys, and laboratory experiments. Discerning these patterns of television use is important, since most people have access to *at least one* television set. The research contained in the volume dealt primarily with households containing children or adolescents; between 98 and 99 percent of these households reported that they had sets, with nearly half of those surveyed watching color sets.

In the early 1970s, television remained primarily a family experience where multiple family members viewed the same set. This was changing, however, because of the increasing number of multiset households. In homes with two sets, one was usually designated "the children's set." While having such a set reduced parent–child conflicts over program selection, it increased sibling conflict. It is not surprising that viewing time for both mothers and children was higher in multiset homes than in single set homes.[18] One study, however, did report that children influencing their parents to watch the violent programs rather than the other way around.[19]

Viewing and Age. Individuals follow an overall pattern of viewing consistent with their age levels. Children begin frequent viewing at about age three, and their level of watching remains quite high until age 12, when it begins to decline. As people marry and begin having their own families, they again begin to spend more time viewing; the level stays rather stable throughout their early- and middle-adult years. After middle-age, when the children have grown and left home, the level rises again.[20]

The studies in this volume reported that most children did watch television every day and that most watched for at least two hours. Many, of course, watched considerably longer. One study found that the viewing time of first grade black boys varied between 5 and 42 hours weekly.[21] Another study, involving nursery school children, documented an average weekly viewing time of 34.55 hours for boys and 32.44 hours for girls.[22] This represented well over one-third of these children's *total waking hours* during the week. In yet another study, Lyle and Hoffman reported that "most elementary school pupils watch television before and after school as well as in the evening."[23] Older children (sixth grade and above) also watch through most of the evening prime time as well as during the earlier "family viewing" period. Children become purposive viewers long before they start school; they have regular viewing times and favorite programs. It is also interesting to note that sex differences in program preferences were evident by the time the children began school. Males showed a preference for violence; indeed, such violent programming, excluding cartoons, increased in importance as the children grew older. The children were found to be very consistent viewers; only two percent did not view on any given day.

LoSciuto reported that most adult Americans watch television daily and that they watched for at least two hours.[24] For adults, however, as much as 20 percent of the population did not watch on a given day. Women tended to watch more than men, probably because more women than men had the opportunity to watch during the day.

The studies in this volume clarified somewhat the relationship between viewing television and socioeconomic status. Before the Television and Social Behavior Program had begun, several studies reported that children of low socioeconomic status tended to spend more time watching television than did children of higher socioeconomic status. One study in the Program supported this conclusion.[25] Lyle and Hoffman, however, in a replication of the classic, *Television in the Lives of Our Children*, found results reminiscent of the 1959 data reported by Schramm, Lyle, and Parker: "At the sixth grade level, bright students tended to be among the heaviest viewers, but at the tenth grade level their viewing was more likely to be somewhat lower than that of their peers."[26] Overall, the viewing differences based upon socioeconomic status were not nearly as great as those found in 1959. It thus appears that there has been some leveling of comparative viewing among children. Several of the researchers (Lyle and Hoffman; Murray) suggest that the brighter children showed more variation in their program preferences. Such diversified program preferences were also related to higher socioeconomic status. Generally, children from higher socioeconomic groups and those who had higher IQ's watched less violence than their age-peers. This may not, however, have been their own choice, since their parents were also more likely to restrict program selection. For most children, however, there was little parental control of television viewing; indeed, despite what many mothers said, most children actually "viewed at will."

The data on adult viewing interestingly parallels that reported for adolescent audiences. Men watch more violence than women. Blacks watch more than Caucasians. The poor and less educated watch more than those who have gone to college. Male high school dropouts were reported to have a particularly high rate of violence viewing. This group is, of course, also higher than average in reports of actual violent behavior.[27]

Family Patterns of Viewing. It should be pointed out that many of the studies in this volume made use of individual or family diaries. One member of the family, usually the mother, recorded for the whole family the amount of time spent viewing and the programs watched. LoSciuto,[28] for example, interviewed a national sample of 252 families and had them keep television diaries. The study is interesting because of some of its peripheral findings indicating that only one-third of the programs watched were viewed all the way through by people who had tuned in. Two out of every five viewers reported that they had watched the program only because it happened to come on the channel they were watching or because someone else in the family wanted to see it. The diary records for the individuals showed a daily average of one hour, 59 minutes, but the respondents said that they watched three hours and 20 minutes on the average day. Other studies report the same discrepancy; the conclusion was reached that Americans consistently tend to overestimate generously the time they spend viewing and feel little social pressure to conceal television viewing.

The obvious problem with diaries as a measure of viewing, however, is that people may neglect, for one reason or another, to record all of the programs viewed. This is especially true when one individual attempts to record the viewing of all family members, often with multiple television sets. It is likely that some omissions will occur. This explanation was often given to clarify the discrepancy between recorded viewing time and verbal estimates of viewing time.

Another interesting study, conducted by Bechtel and associates, examined the validity of such reports of viewing time. They wished to learn whether the viewing habits of individuals were more in line with what they say or with what they report in their diaries. A small sample of 20 families participated in the project for a period of six consecutive days. Each household had a camera installed so that actual behavior in front of the set could be filmed. While this is an intriguing idea, there is little doubt that the presence of the camera affected the subjects' behavior and, in fact, several so reported. But whatever effect the presence of the camera may have had, it recorded only three hours of actual viewing time for every four hours viewing reported by the same individuals in a diary. This gives more credibility to the idea that Americans often overreport their viewing time.

A more interesting finding was that the level of attention to the television screen was constantly varying. The researchers divided the activities they saw while the television set was on into six levels of attention:

1. *Participation* (actively responding to the set or to others regarding content from the set).
2. *Passively watching* (doing nothing else).
3. *Simultaneous activity* (eating, etc.).
4. *Positioned to watch* but reading, talking, or attending to something else.
5. *In the viewing area* but positioned away from the set in a way that would require turning to see it.
6. *Not in the room* and unable to see the set.

Bechtel et al. indicate that as much as half the time the television sets were on, the viewers were doing something which placed them in one of the last three categories. This means that they did not actually "watch," even though they may have later reported that they watched the program. These researchers catalogued an extensive list of activities in which the people who "did watch" were simultaneously engaged. These ranged from eating and talking (the most frequent) to activities such as sleeping, smoking, dancing, preparing meals, dressing and undressing, doing exercises, and crawling.

The data presented by Bechtel et al. are important because they raise some important questions about the nature of television viewing. The most important question is whether viewing time is restricted to "eye contact" time. The authors developed their study from the standpoint of eye contact time, but is that necessarily appropriate? Does a person who performs household chores with the television set on, watching when something catches their interest, qualify as a viewer? The results of the Bechtel study emphasize the problem of establishing the validity of measures of viewing.[29]

Robinson advances this thesis a step further, arguing that viewer time is a continuum of short periods of full attention interspersed with periods of nonattention, or only partial attention. The viewer is alerted to things of interest to him or her by cues from the program itself. If Robinson is right, then the viewer may see only small segments of a program. The viewer may see violence without punishment, victims without criminals, as he or she tunes in and out of the program. What can we then say about the effects of portrayals of violence? Do those who prefer violence see only the violent segments, while those who do not prefer it tune them out?

Considering all of the studies contained in this volume, it appeared that several changes had occurred during the 1960s in the public's attitudes toward, and use of, television. The evidence indicated that more time was spent in the company of television sets than in the 1950s, but that the level of attention fluctuated greatly. Viewers were no longer "glued" to the set; in fact, it appeared that the set was often simply left on with the viewer tuning in and out as the programs changed. This raises the possibility that while television has become even more interwoven with our daily lives, its hold upon our attention has perhaps been reduced. Indeed, one might ask if the public's general affection for television has perhaps fallen despite apparent increases in "viewing time."

Moreover, the public has become more critical of television in one respect. The data gathered showed a high level of antagonism toward commercials. This antagonism was not only in regard to frequency but to their content. The public showed a strong tendency to reject them as deceitful, if not flatly untrue. And this antagonism was stronger among teenagers than among adults.

Overall, the new research indicated that while individuals do spend a great deal of time viewing television, they are primarily seeking relaxation. This in itself does not turn viewers into " escapists, social isolates, or deviants."

Volume V: Television's Effects

The final volume of independent research prepared for the Commission contained a mixed bag of 13 different papers and reports. Unlike the first four volumes, there was no common substantive theme that united the papers except that all of them were based upon ongoing research. The author cautioned that their conclusions were tentative, that the data presented were undergoing further analyses or that follow-up studies were in progress. In all cases, the reports were not intended to be definitive.

Some of the papers did, however, explore the role of televised violence in some new and interesting ways. For example, Ekman and associates[30] videotaped the faces of 65 five- and six-year-old children while they watched television (30 boys and 35 girls). The hypothesis was that the facial expressions displayed by the children while watching televised violence would reflect emotional reactions. The researchers also believed that certain types of facial reactions would be associated with subsequent behavior. They posited that child viewers whose faces expressed happiness or interest while watching violence would be more aggressive than children whose faces expressed sadness, disgust, or fear. Two different measures were used. The first involved a laboratory procedure where the children pushed "help" or "hurt" buttons in the manner previously discussed in the Liebert and Baron study (Volume II); the second was conducted in a more natural play situation.

The researchers found that facial expressions of emotions shown during the viewing of televised violence did indeed predict later aggressive behavior—but for boys only. They concluded, therefore, that it is not the mere presence of televised violence but the boys' emotional responses to it that predict later displays of aggression. However, the question remains: Why did the authors fail to obtain the same success with girls? The authors speculated that the differences may have been due to the fact that the violence shown was male-oriented; in other words, it involved male actors and male roles. There were no female aggressors for the girls to identify with. In addition, we should also consider female socialization in regard to attitudes toward violence. Overall, the girls may have been more frequently censored or punished for approving of aggressive behavior whereas the boys were not. The authors concluded that more studies were necessary to test these possibilities—studies that should include female role models and take into account female socialization.

Another interesting and even more perlexing study was conducted by Foulkes and his associates.[31] They examined whether presleep viewing of a violent program, in contrast to a nonviolent one, affected (reduced or increased) the vividness, pleasantness, aggression, or anxiety components of dream content. Each subject participated in two experimental sessions seven to nine days apart. After arriving at the sleep laboratory, they changed into bedclothes, had electrodes attached to their face and scalp, were exposed to either the violent or the nonviolent film, and slept. The experimental procedure was to awaken each subject after ten minutes of "Rapid Eye Movement" sleep. The subject was interviewed and instructed to go back to sleep after each awakening.

This study was repeated three times, with three separate groups of subjects. Different results were obtained each time. The results of the first experiment indicated that dreams recalled after watching violence were more exciting, more interesting, and more imaginative. There was *increased* general activation. The results from the first replication of this experiment, however, indicated that the exposure to the violent film produced less imaginative and exciting dreams. There was *reduced* general activation. Because of this conflict in results, a second replication was funded by the Commission as a part of the Television and Social Behavior Program in an attempt to resolve the question. The results of this second replication indicated that there was *no difference* whatever in the content of dreams between viewing one of the two films before sleep. The authors indicated that follow-up studies were being planned to further clarify the issue.

The other studies reported in this volume were all projects "in progress" and the papers prepared for the volume were essentially progress reports on these continuing projects. Because of their in-progress status, those papers will not be examined.

Summary Volume: Television and Growing Up

The report prepared by the Surgeon General's Scientific Advisory Committee, entitled *Television and Growing Up*, contains a summary of the technical studies previously reported, recommendations for future research, and the Committee's "definitive" statement about the relationship between the viewing of televised violence and aggressive behavior in children.[32] As previously noted, this volume was the one most often read by scholars and laymen alike; unfortunately, the five volumes of technical research are neither light reading nor, with rare exceptions, particularly enjoyable.

Since the technical reports have already been summarized above, we will turn our attention to the recommendations made by the Surgeon General's Committee. The Committee qualifies its report at the outset by stating their unhappiness with the "narrowness" of the focus of the research program. "Exposure to violence," they argue, "does not exist in a vacuum." They further indicate that the narrowness of concentration "has severely hampered the interpretation of the results."[33] However, in any scientific investigation narrowness of focus is somewhat mandatory. It is this approach which is taught to students in their courses on research methods. No social scientist has yet been able to study all influences on behavior simultaneously. Moreover, the investigators do manage adequate interpretations of their data. That the evidence is not clear, convincing, and irrefutable is not unusual—scientific answers are never absolute or final. A Committee composed of "recognized experts" should have been cognizant of this, but they seemed not to be. Definitive answers can be sought as a goal, but such answers are unlikely to come out of a single series of investigations. In fact, it is widely viewed that definitive answers will perhaps never be found in social investigations. And it should be noted that most scientific studies have a more narrow focus than did the Television and Social Behavior Program.

The Advisory Committee recommended that future research concentrate on the following areas:

1. *Television should be studied in the context of other mass media.* The members of the Committee argued that a positive relationship exists between an individual's use of television and use of other mass media. (This has not been found to be the case.) They thus believed that attempts to isolate the effects of television exposure on social behavior resulted in "possible confounding of attributions."

2. *Television should be studied in the context of the **total** environment, particularly the home environment.* The question posed was: "To what extent does what the young viewer brings to the TV screen determine what he

carries away—which is another way of asking where the television ranks among all other aspects of a child's environment?" The members of the Committee indicated that they were particularly interested in identifying the predispositional characteristics of children who displayed an increase in aggressive behavior in response to televised violence.

3. *Studies should be conducted to distinguish between functional (useful) and dysfunctional (damaging) aggressive behavior.* The Committee pointed out that the "realities of life require a certain set or readiness for aggressive behavior" and that the lines that distinguish between aggression and vigorous competition are often blurred. Even in the early 1970s, most boys were being taught to "stand up for your rights and defend yourself." Thus, the argument is that the viewing of certain aggressive behavior (e.g., vigorous competition) may be beneficial for some viewers, especially perhaps for the shy, timid viewer.

4. *Modeling and imitation of prosocial behavior should be studied.* The Committee argued that if children imitate aggressive acts, they may also imitate prosocial acts; furthermore, this imitation of positive prosocial behavior may balance any negative effects.

5. *We should examine the symbolic functions of violence on television.* Violent content in fiction may sometimes be a vehicle for presenting "messages" to a general audience about important social and cultural issues. Without the use of this violence, it may not be possible to examine these issues.

The Advisory Committee also called for a "more humane definition of violence." While violence was defined primarily in a physical sense in the research program, the Committee argued that it should be expanded to include the "experience of [all its victims]." These victims include those who have been killed or disabled by unsafe drugs that have been approved for public use. (Prescribing birth control pills would thus be defined as an act of violence.) Pollution of the air and water, impure foods, the operation of a factory (if a death or disability occurs) are all violence. The Committee goes so far as to say that the "casting of a vote in Congress, or the signing of an Executive Order" should be defined as violent when such acts have adverse effects "on a few people or a multitude of people." They then suggest that television should be used as a social force to modify society's definition and awareness of violence.

Finally, we come to the Committee's conclusion concerning the relationship between viewing televised violence and aggressive behavior. When the Committee began its work in 1969, it took as the starting point the conclusions derived from a well-known 1961 study (which we discussed in Chapter 10), *Television in the Lives of Our Children:* "For *some* children, under *some* conditions, *some* television is harmful. For *other* children under the same conditions, or for the same children under *other* conditions, it may be beneficial. For *most* children, under *most* conditions, most television is probably neither harmful nor particularly beneficial."[34] To see just how far we have come from these findings, the Committee summarized its findings and conclusions:

> Thus the two sets of findings (laboratory and survey) converge in three respects: a preliminary and tentative indication of a causal relation between viewing violence on television and aggressive behavior; an indication that any such causal operation operates only on some children (who are predisposed to be aggressive); and an indication that it operates only in some environmental contexts. Such tentative and limited conclusions are not very satisfying [yet] they represent substantially more knowledge than we had two years ago.[35]

It cost the American public 1.8 million dollars to gain this "increase" in our collective knowledge. Such is the price of progress.

As a result of this report and the above conclusions and observations, the Committee has been charged with having become an apologist for, and defender of, the broadcast industry. Given the industry's input into the Committee's makeup, the charge is not surprising; the controversy surrounding the Committee and its report will now be examined in detail.

THE FIRESTORM OF CRITICISM AND THE SENATE HEARINGS

In many ways, the real impact of this research came not from the studies themselves but from the controversy that followed the publication of the Committee's report. Even before the Committee's work had been completed, the manner in which the Advisory Committee was selected became a topic of heated controversy.

The May 22, 1970 issue of *Science* magazine contained a report that publicized a previously unknown fact: ABC, NBC, and the National Association of Broadcasters had blackballed seven social scientists distinguished for their past research and expertise on the subject (Albert Bandura, Leo Bogart, Leonard Berkowitz, Leon Eisenberg, Ralph Gerry, Otto Larsen, and Percy Tannenbaum). In response to this revelation, several members of the Advisory Committee threatened to resign but were persuaded to continue serving.

The notoriety prompted an explanation from Robert Finch, Secretary of Health, Education, and Welfare. He argued that the same procedure had been used with the earlier Advisory Committee on Smoking and Health. That is, the tobacco industry had been asked to approve the composition of that Committee in order to forestall any subsequent charge that it had been biased against the industry. In both cases, Finch indicated, the purpose of seeking such advice was to enhance the Committee's credibility and to secure the cooperation of the industry whose product was under scrutiny. What Finch neglected to note at that time was that in the Smoking and Health Advisory Committee, organizations on *both sides* of the controversy had been asked to identify unsuitable parties. Moreover, no individual had been allowed to serve on the committee if he represented any organization or group with an interest in the outcome.

The Advisory Committee appointed to investigate the television question consisted of four psychologists, three sociologists, two psychiatrists, a political scientist, an anthropologist, and an educator. However, all three of the sociologists who served were affiliated with CBS! (Ira H. Cisin and Harold Mendelsohn were active consultants with CBS; Joseph T. Klapper headed the network's Office of Social Research.) Furthermore, two of the psychologists had network affiliations (Thomas E. Coffin was the Research Director at NBC, and Gerhardt Wiebe was a long-time research executive for CBS.) Not only was the broadcast industry given veto power over prospective members but it also placed five of its own people on the Committee.

The reaction from social scientists was immediate and hostile. Leo Bogart's remarks are typical:

> The idea that an industry should not only be represented directly in a scholarly inquiry into its activities, but should also exercise a veto over the membership of the investigating panel, is too stupid and scandalous to escape commentary. It cannot be permitted again in future government-sponsored research on public matters that affect established interests.[36]

In addition to the five persons closely affiliated with the networks, four others were decidedly unfamiliar with the empirical studies of communication effects, although each was well-known and expert in his own field. This left only three persons (a political scientist and two psychologists) who could be said to both possess the necessary technical expertise and be free of affiliations with the television industry. Indeed, the Committee has been described as consisting of "the network five, the naive four, and the scientific three."[37]

Why was the Committee so composed? It might be thought that an ideal investigative team would be a "scientific twelve." The presence of the four members from outside disciplines, however, was the result of a standard policy requiring heterogeneous representation in such panels. But their presence was compromised by the broadcast industry personnel whose participation was considered by many to be a simple function of the power of the industry and the hesitancy of the Nixon Administration to offend it unnecessarily.

While the composition of the Committee provided minimal affront to broadcasters, the shabby treatment of eminent social scientists shocked the scientific community. The blackballing of widely recognized experts *because of* their past work and professional expertise created a deep hostility among social and behavioral scientists. The irony was that it was the broadcasters who paid the price. The broadcast industry made a preemptive strike in a conflict that need never have occurred. In the end, it was the broadcasters who were bloodied.

In addition to the issue of committee composition and selection, the report issued by the Advisory Committee (*Television and Growing Up*) also sparked a controversy. Many of the independent investigators whose works were included among the papers in the technical volumes claimed that their findings had been "irresponsibly distorted" in the Committee's report. Another charge was that "some highly pertinent studies demonstrating that violence viewing causes children to behave aggressively were not even mentioned."[38]

This storm of protest was the impetus for Senate Hearings, chaired by Senator Pastore, March 21–24, 1972, before the Subcommittee on Communications of the Commerce Committee. It became clear from the testimony offered that the final Advisory Committee document reflected a considerable amount of drafting and redrafting, and this redrafting was largely the work of the two network research directors—those with the most at stake in the outcome. Indeed, George Comstock, a member of the NIMH staff, testified that "as much as 90 percent of the report revision was made at the insistence of Klapper."[39]

Besides the more blatant errors and abuses, there are many statements in *Television and Growing Up* that were clearly misunderstood by those untrained in the social sciences. For example, in social science research a call for further study is almost always necessary—to confirm and elaborate findings. However, to reporters untrained in the social sciences this meant that the study failed to prove that violent television presentations had harmful effects. And since *Television and Growing Up* was released prior to the technical reports, the conclusions contained in it were the ones that made news headlines. *The New York Times*, for example, ran a front page story under the headline: "TV Held Unharmful to Youth." Other newspapers and magazines reported the Committee's findings under similar headlines. The cautious and carefully worded conclusions of the Committee were reported in such a way in the news media that the meaning of the Committee's language may have been distorted. The more cynical reader might infer that the carefully drafted wording was intended to mislead the technically unsophisticated.

Because of all the problems associated with the Advisory Committee report, Senator Pastore elected to bypass that report and to examine directly the five volumes of technical research during the hearings. The object—to arrive at an independent conclusion about the relationship between viewing televised violence and aggressive behavior.

Before the end of the hearings, all those who testified before the Senate Committee—even the presidents of the three major national networks—agreed (although it must be admitted, some under heavy pressure from the Committee) that television violence had an adverse effect on children. No one who testified claimed that television violence was the sole cause of aggressive behavior. Indeed, many testifying wished to address other pertinent causes. However, Senator Pastore indicated that the issue at hand was determining the relationship between television violence and aggressive behavior. He pointed out that no one was naive enough to posit a single cause.

The most definitive and incisive testimony given at the Hearings was probably that offered by the Surgeon General himself, Jessie L. Steinfeld:

> While the Committee report is carefully phrased and qualified in language acceptable to social scientists, it is clear to me that the causal relation between televised violence and antisocial behavior is sufficient to warrant appropriate and immediate remedial action. The data on social phenomena such as television and social violence will never be clear enough for all social scientists to agree on the formulation of a succinct statement of causality. But there comes a time when the data are sufficient to justify action. That time has come.[40]

Dr. Steinfeld might just as easily have said: "Warning: the Surgeon General has determined that viewing television violence is dangerous to your child's health."

CONCLUSIONS AND IMPLICATIONS

What are we to conclude from all this? Can we, or should we, separate the research from the controversy surrounding it? The importance of the Television and Social Behavior Program obviously lies in the five volumes of technical reports and not in the Advisory Committee report. The most appropriate way of looking at that report is as the product of a three-way process of interaction— among government, the TV industry, and social science. From this perspective, what was studied and why becomes almost as interesting as what was learned. We can draw three main conclusions from the five volumes of research:

1. Television content is heavily saturated with violence.
2. Children and adults are spending more and more time exposed to violent content.
3. Overall, the evidence supports the hypothesis that the viewing of violent entertainment increases the likelihood of aggressive behavior. This evidence is derived from both laboratory experiments which permit causal inference *and* from surveys that provide evidence of real-life associations in everyday events.

Not all social scientists will agree with the third conclusion. It is easy to criticize most of the studies on an individual basis. For example, in some of the laboratory experiments, the samples studied were quite small. In many of the experiments and all of the surveys, there was an overconcentration on the more articulate and responsible older children and an underrepresentation of younger children (who appear to be especially susceptible to the influence of television). However, the methodological flaws of one study do not usually apply to another. Taken as a whole, the consistent accumulation of evidence allows us, as social scientists, to feel reasonably comfortable with the conclusions reached.

The major problem of the Television and Social Behavior program of research is the way in which the research problem was posed. The Advisory Committee chose to frame the question in terms of direct effects: Does exposure to violence lead children to specific acts of antisocial behavior? As far as the broadcast industry is concerned, this is probably the most acceptable formulation. We must, however, consider the possibility, or probability, that television's most profound influences may be indirect. How does the presentation of life in television programming alter the socialization process, if it does? Does it change the world view of those who are regular viewers? Does it make violence a more common phenomenon in familiar contexts to more people and thus make it more acceptable? Or does the presentation of violence simply make for a more timid, fearful populace? How does the continual flow of violence in the media affect our beliefs, attitudes, and values, and the quality of life in our country? We do not really know what the long-term effects are for individuals or for society.

What, then, should be done about violence on television? Should it be eliminated? No, because violence *is* a part of life, and of art. Besides, the real issue is not the use of violence that honestly reflects the conflicts of the times, "the issue is the deliberate use of cliché violence, violence contrived to formula, violence as a commodity that can be packaged for sale."[41] When violence is packaged in an "acceptable" format, and is presented as real, it distorts reality, and it distorts the perceptions of those who must live in that reality. Violence contrived for the sake of violence—for comic effect, for amusement—without meaning or purpose, does no service to the viewer. It may beguile the audience, but in the end the play may become real—and painful.

In conclusion, *Television and Social Behavior* has an assured place in the history of applied social research. That place is secure because of the large budget, the controversy surrounding the project, and also the broad public and journalistic interest in the wider questions it raises. The reader should be cautioned that this chapter can only hint at the rich detail of the specific findings, theoretical insights, and heterogeneity of research methods and techniques employed. The *Television and Social Behavior* project remains one that is unique in its size, scope, and focus. In many ways, it is a noteworthy exemplar of communication research. Unfortunately, it is also a document that has been discussed much more often than it has been read.

NOTES AND REFERENCES

1. Surgeon General's Scientific Advisory Committee on Television and Social Behavior, *Television and Growing Up: The Impact of Televised Violence*. Report to the Surgeon General, United States Public Health Service (Washington, D.C.: U.S. Government Printing Office, 1971), p. 14.

2. Ibid., p. 15.

3. George Gerbner, "Violence in Television Drama: Trends and Symbolic Functions," in G. A. Comstock, and E. A. Rubinstein, eds., *Television and Social Behavior, Vol. I, Media Content and Control* (Washington, D.C.: U.S. Government Printing Office, 1971).

4. Ibid., p. 31.

5. Ibid., p. 36.

6. Muriel G. Cantor, "The Role of the Producer in Choosing Children's Television Content," in G. A. Comstock and E. A. Rubinstein, eds., *Television and Social Behavior, Vol. I, Media Content and Control* (Washington, D.C.: U.S. Government Printing Office, 1971).

7. Thomas Baldwin and Colby Lewis, "Violence in Television: The Industry Looks at Itself," in G. A. Comstock and E. A. Rubinstein, eds., *Television and Social Behavior, Vol. I, Media Content and Control* (Washington, D.C.: U.S. Government Printing Office, 1971).

8. Muriel G. Cantor, op. cit., p. 19.

9. Ibid., p. 20.

10. Ibid., p. 21.

11. Michael Gurevich, "The Structure and Content of Television Broadcasting in Four Countries: An Overview," in G. A. Comstock and E. A. Rubinstein, op. cit.

12. Albert Bandura, "Influence of Models: Reinforcement Contingencies on the Acquisition of Imitative Responses," *Journal of Personality and Social Psychology*, 1965, 1, 589–95.

13. Robert M. Liebert and Robert A. Baron, "Short-Term Effects of Televised Aggression on Childrens' Aggressive Behavior," in J. P. Murray, E. A. Rubinstein, and G. A. Comstock, eds., *Television and Social Behavior, Vol. II, Television and Social Learning* (Washington, D.C.: U.S. Government Printing Office, 1971).

14. Robert M. Liebert, "Television and Social Learning: Some Relationships Between Viewing Violence and Behaving," in Murray, Rubinstein, and Comstock, op. cit.

15. Ibid., pp. 29–30.

16. Monroe M. Lefkowitz, et al., "Television Violence and Child Aggression: A Follow-up Study," in Comstock and Rubinstein, eds., *Television and Social Behavior, Vol. III, Television and Adolescent Aggressiveness* (Washington, D.C.: U.S. Government Printing Office, 1971).

17. Steven H. Chaffee, "Television and Adolescent Aggressiveness," in Comstock and Rubinstein, op. cit.

18. Jack Lyle, "Television in Daily Life: Patterns of Use," in Rubinstein, Comstock, and Murray, eds., *Television and Social Behavior, Vol. IV, Television in Day-to-Day Life: Patterns of Use* (Washington, D.C.: U.S. Government Printing Office, 1971).

19. Bradley S. Greenberg, Phillip M. Ericson, and Mantha Vlahos, "Childrens' Television Behaviors as Perceived by Mother and Child," in Rubinstein, Comstock, and Murray, op. cit., 1971.
20. Jack Lyle, op. cit.
21. John P. Murray, "Television in Inner-City Homes: Viewing Behavior of Young Boys," in Rubinstein, Comstock, and Murray, op. cit., 1971.
22. Aletha Stein and Lynette Friedrich, "Television Content and Young Childrens' Behavior," in Murray, Rubinstein, and Comstock, op. cit. (Vol. II), 1971.
23. Jack Lyle and Heida Hoffman, "Childrens' Use of Television and Other Media," in Rubinstein, Comstock, and Murray, op. cit. (Vol. IV), 1971.
24. Leonard A. LoSciuto, "A National Inventory of Television Viewing Behavior," in Rubinstein, Comstock, and Murray, op. cit. (Vol. IV), 1971.
25. Jennie J. McIntyre and James J. Teevan, "Television Violence and Deviant Behavior," in Comstock and Rubinstein, op. cit. (Vol. III), 1971.
26. Jack Lyle and Heida Hoffman, op. cit., p. 138.
27. Harold Israel and John P. Robinson, "Demographic Characteristics of Viewers of Television Violence and News Programs," in Rubinstein, Comstock, and Murray, op. cit. (Vol. IV), 1971.
28. Leonard A. LoSciuto, op. cit.
29. Robert B. Bechtel, Clark Achepohl, and Ronald Akers, "Correlates Between Observed Behavior and Questionnaire Responses on Television Viewing," in Rubinstein, Comstock, and Murray, op. cit. (Vol. IV), 1971.
30. Paul Eckman et al., "Facial Expressions of Emotion While Watching Televised Violence as Predictors of Subsequent Aggression," in Comstock, Rubinstein, and Murray, *Television and Social Behavior, Vol. V. Television's Effects: Further Explorations* (Washington, D.C.: U.S. Government Printing Office, 1971).
31. David Foulkes, Edward Belvedere, and Terry Brubaker, "Televised Content and Dream Content," in Comstock, Rubinstein, and Murray, op. cit., 1971.
32. Surgeon General's Scientific Advisory Committee on Television and Social Behavior, op. cit.
33. Ibid., p. 113.
34. Wilbur Schramm, Jack Lyle, and Edwin B. Parker, *Television in the Lives of Our Children* (Stanford, Cal.: Stanford University Press, 1961), p. 13.
35. Surgeon General's Scientific Advisory Committee on Television and Social Behavior, op. cit., p. 11.
36. Leo Bogart, "Warning, the Surgeon General Has Determined That TV Violence is Moderately Dangerous to Your Child's Mental Health," *Public Opinion Quarterly*, 1972, 36,. 491–521.
37. George A. Comstock, *Television in America* (Beverly Hills, Cal.: Sage, 1980), p. 100.
38. Hearings Before the Subcommittee on Communications, of the Committee on Commerce, United States Senate, March 21st through 24th, 1972 (Washington, D.C.: U.S. Government Printing Office, 1972), p. 11.
39. Ibid., p. 41.
40. Ibid., p. 42.
41. Leo Bogart, op cit., p. 519.

13

The Agenda-Setting Function of the Press:
Telling Us What to Think About

Early in the 1960s scholars were rejecting the idea that the media had powerful and immediate effects on their audiences. While some of the earliest research had seemed to point to that conclusion, the large-scale studies of the 1940s and 1950s had not supported such a view. The accumulation of research seemed more consistent with a minimal effects interpretation. At the same time, sensitive observers of the media and their audiences continued to feel that people were influenced in their beliefs and actions because of repeated exposure to the content of mass communications. Such influences might not show up in the kinds of research studies that had been conducted. It was entirely possible, it was felt, that the influences were long-term, subtle, and difficult to pin down by the experiments, survey studies, and other research efforts that had been in vogue. It was time, many communication scholars believed, to look in new directions.

But how could such subtle influences be studied? It was clear that the answer would not be found entirely by following sophisticated theories derived from the social and behavioral sciences. They had not been particularly helpful during the previous thirty years in isolating the effects of the mass media on their audiences. Perhaps it was time to return to the obvious facts about the mass media themselves and how they functioned within the contemporary society. Such a new start might provide clues as to the existence of long-term influences.

One obvious fact about the media in modern society is the constant flow of news. Another obvious fact is that large numbers of people do read their newspapers. Some citizens rely more on television for their news; still others have little interest in daily events. Nevertheless, the mass media still are a significant source of detailed information about what is going on for very large numbers of people.

Another obvious fact is that the news industry seems more interested in some events than in others. It is widely understood that the material presented by the press is selective. That selectivity stems from its limited capacity to provide total surveillance, from factors imposed on those who do the gatekeeping, and from the financial limitations placed on media that must survive as profit-making business enterprises. Such variables go a long way to account for the manner in which the press decides which stories to select, follow up, emphasize, interpret, and present in particular ways.

But the essential point is that there is a constant flow of information from the press to its audience. Day after day, week after week, newspapers provide their readers with information on a list of topics and issues that seem important to those who manage the media. That information, selective or distorted as it may be, provides the most basic source for millions of people about what is taking place in their society. It seemed inconceivable to many media scholars that such a flow of information simply had no effect on those who received it. The idea that the news media powerfully controlled people's attitudes, beliefs, and behavior might not hold water, but the press obviously brings to their attention a selected agenda of topics and issues to respond to and think about.

From that starting point, pieces of the puzzle began to come together. For example, early in the century, Walter Lippmann had noted that since people had only limited opportunities to observe important events in a firsthand manner, they were dependent upon the press to provide them with information on what those events were like. The role of the press, he observed, was to provide us with views of "the world outside" from which we can form "pictures in our heads."[1] Lippmann understood very well that there was often a significant gap between the accounts of the press and what had actually taken place. But aside from the problem of outright distortion, the essential theoretical question that would eventually emerge from such considerations was whether the topics selected by the press to represent the "world outside" limited the kinds of events about which people could form interpretations of what was happening. Furthermore, if the press implied in some way by its presentation of topics that one event was more important than another, did readers come to believe that this was how it was in reality? In other words, were the "pictures in our heads" (whatever their nature and dimensions) ranked in our personal assessments of significance in a manner parallel to the way in which they were covered and differentially emphasized by the press in the daily flow of news?

Those questions address subtle and long-term influences of the news media, and they are not readily reduced to hypotheses that can be tested in a short-term experiment or a one-shot survey. In addition, such questions did not leap fully formed from the analysis of a single scholar or from any specific research study. In fact, they emerged from a complex background of ideas that brought together conclusions from both ancient and modern sources.

The conviction that communication shapes ideas is indeed ancient. Philosophers had long been concerned about the nature and sources of human understanding. In the seventeenth century, John Locke had outlined the relationship between the process of communication and the development of the human mind.[2] As the twentieth century began, the key role of language in human mental activities became a central focus in various branches of anthropology, social psychology, and sociology. Theories in those fields stressed the social sources from which people drew their meanings from the events in the world that surrounded them. The Sapir-Whorf hypothesis from anthropology was grounded on the fact that the languages used by different societies had great differences in structure. Those differences led the people who used them to see, interpret, and understand both the physical and social world in quite different ways.[3] The symbolic interactionism paradigm from social psychology was developed to show the relationship between the internal psychological organization of the individual processes of human communication and the organization of social systems.[4] Sociologists routinely assume that the conceptions of reality people hold as individuals are socially constructed through a process of communication using shared language.[5]

In more recent times, these broad theories and propositions were brought very specifically into the study of the influence of the press—that is, the news media. An important clue as to what kind of influence such media might have on their audiences came from a comment made in a book by Bernard Cohen in 1963. He noted that "The press may not be successful much of the time in telling people what to think, but it is stunningly successful in telling its readers what to think about."[6] This rather simple, and widely quoted, generalization provided an important element in the ideas that would come together into the hypothesis that the press had an important agenda-setting function.

A number of scholars in other disciplines were also thinking along the same lines and they provided additional elements. For example, sociologists Kurt and Gladys Lang observed that while there was considerable doubt that the press had great power to change people's attitudes, the media did provide an immense quantity of information from which people learned about the important issues of the day. Furthermore, the Langs noted, people seemed to learn about such matters as campaign issues in *direct proportion to the emphasis placed on them by their manner of presentation in the media:*

> The mass media force attention to certain issues. They build up public images of public figures. They are constantly presenting objects suggesting what individuals in the mass should think about, know about, have feelings about.[7]

What was needed was someone who could synthesize these various elements into a systematic and researchable hypothesis and test that hypothesis against carefully gathered empirical data.

THE DEVELOPMENT OF THE HYPOTHESIS

In the mid-1960s, a small group of journalism researchers at the University of California at Los Angeles began to notice that whenever a news story that conceivably could have been a major one was played down, its impact on public opinion seemed to be greatly dissipated. The opposite also seemed true. Maxwell McCombs and his colleagues had recently read the Bernard Cohen book, plus other relevant literature, and they were fully aware of both Walter Lippmann's pioneering suggestions of how the press was related to public opinion and the social science background on the social construction of reality generally. The group was increasingly convinced that such influences of the press had to be studied in a long-term perspective.[8]

In 1967, Professor McCombs moved to North Carolina and met Donald Shaw. Together they undertook a program of research on various cognitive effects of the mass media. The research was given financial support by both the National Association of Broadcasters and the University of North Carolina. The concept of the agenda-setting function of the press was not the initial thrust of the research, but within a short time, they decided to study it as a major hypothesis in connection with the 1968 presidential campaign (Hubert Humphrey versus Richard Nixon).

The Exploratory Study

To find out whether there were any grounds for assuming an agenda-setting function of the mass media, a study was designed that would compare media content with voters' beliefs about the presidential campaign. More specifically, the research compared what a sample of voters (in Chapel Hill, North Carolina) *said* were the key issues of the presidential campaign with the *actual content* of the news media to which they were exposed during the campaign. It was a simple design; essentially it was an exploratory effort to see if the agenda-setting hypothesis had any future. It was not a particularly large study. It focused on political news concerning the candidates and issues presented by television, newspapers, and newsmagazines concerning the candidates and issues over a 24-day period in the fall of 1968. This ended early in October, shortly before the election. It also probed the beliefs of 100 respondents concerning the relative importance of the issues of the campaign.

These respondents were selected randomly from lists of registered voters in five of the precincts in the community. These five were used to try to make the sample reflect the economic, racial, and social makeup of the community. A further factor in the selection of the final sample was that it included only voters who had not yet definitely decided how to vote. The grounds for this was the assumption that it was this category that was still open or susceptible to the influence of campaign information. Thus, it was a purposive rather than a random sample, concentrating only on undecided voters. This meant that broad generalizations to the community as a whole, or even to other types of voters, would be unwarranted. Nevertheless, for exploratory purposes, this was an appropriate strategy. If there was no agenda-setting effect among this "most susceptible" category of people, then the whole idea would seem to have little merit.

These respondents were asked to explain what they saw from their own personal perspective as the key issues of the campaign, regardless of what particular candidates happened to be saying at the moment. These were the main data used for comparison with the relative emphasis given the issues by the news media.

The media studied included five newspapers, two network television news broadcasts, and two weekly newsmagazines that reported on the political campaign to the residents of Chapel Hill. Careful definitions were provided to identify what was and what was not a "major" or "minor" report in these media on some aspect of the campaign. For television, a major story had to be one of at least 45 seconds or more in length, or one of the three lead stories in a particular broadcast. A major story for newspapers was defined as any that appeared on the front page or any that appeared under a three-column headline in which at least a third of the story (and a minimum of five paragraphs) was devoted to political news. For newsmagazines, a major story had to be more than one column or any item that appeared in the lead at the beginning of the news section of the magazine. Minor items in these media were stories of a political nature that were smaller in time and space, or less prominent in positioning than the major items.

Refining the Hypothesis

The findings showed that even among the major stories presented by the media, much of the news about a presidential campaign has little to do with the issues. A lot deals with the candidates themselves and assessments of who might win or lose. Nevertheless, an abundance of issue-related news information was provided to the community under study, and it was possible to sort out the relative emphasis given to such topics as foreign policy, law and order, fiscal policy, public welfare, civil rights, and so on. A rank order of emphasis of these topics was worked out for the various candidates and for the political parties. Thus, the manner in which the issues of the campaign had been presented by the news media in both major and minor stories was relatively clear, and a rank order of relative emphasis could be made with some precision.

When the judgments of the sample of voters as to the order of importance of these issues was compared to the relative emphasis given to them by the media, a startlingly high relationship was found. In fact, the correlation between relative media emphasis and voters' beliefs about the importance of the same list of issues was $+.976$! Few correlations of that magnitude are found in social research. McCombs and Shaw concluded from their data that:

> In short, the data suggest a very strong relationship between the emphasis placed on different campaign issues by the media (reflecting to a considerable degree the emphasis by the candidates) and the judgments of the voters as to the salience and importance of various campaign topics.[9]

There was, in other words, a close correspondence between the world outside, as constructed by the news media, and the pictures in the heads of the sample of voters studied. Furthermore, the representation of that world outside (the actual emphasis given to the issues by the candidates) was not particularly distorted. There was clear evidence of an agenda-setting function of the news media. They had not indicated *what* the voters should think about the issues, but they did indicate which issues were to be thought *about* and which were given the greatest *emphasis* by the candidates. The voters themselves perceived those issues in that rank order and adopted it as their own.

In interpreting this extraordinary correlation, one must keep in mind the sampling conditions of the exploratory study. If respondents had been selected on a random basis from the community, the politically inactive would have been included as well as those who had bothered to become registered voters. Futhermore, as we saw in *The People's Choice*, there are abundant grounds to assume that large proportions of voters make up their minds for whom they will vote early in the campaign. An agenda-setting effect would be much less likely among such citizens. The citizen who refrains from a choice until all the issues have been carefully examined (via news reports) is in a minority, but the sample in the exploratory study attempted to focus on just such individuals. Therefore, the significance of the impressive correlation for the larger population remained to be determined. It was clear to everyone concerned that additional research would have to be completed. In any case, there were certainly adequate grounds for hypothesizing that an agenda-setting effect of some kind would be found.

THE CHARLOTTE STUDY

Four years after the 1968 election, Americans were faced with another national campaign to select a president. This time it was the incumbent Richard M. Nixon who was being challenged by the liberal Democrat George McGovern. The 1972 election provided an important opportunity to follow up the exploratory study on agenda-setting. In the fall of 1971, a series of workshops to design new studies were held at the University of North Carolina under the leadership of Donald L. Shaw and Maxwell E. McCombs.

These researchers were convinced that the most appropriate strategy for the accumulation of scientific knowledge in a field was *programmatic* research. That is, one study on a particular topic should lead to another that pushes the frontiers beyond those revealed by the first. In this way, the development of knowledge will be both accumulative and increasingly sophisticated. That was never the pattern in the pioneering efforts in mass communication, as researchers jumped from one topic to another, depending on a variety of factors. In more recent years, with more sources willing to provide funds, programmatic research has been on the increase, and the Charlotte study of agenda-setting provides an excellent example.

Essentially, Shaw and McCombs brought together a research team that designed and completed a panel study that focused on both media presentation of the political issues and voter perceptions of the significance of those issues. Thus, it was of a larger scale than the 1968 Chapel Hill study, but its central focus remained on the agenda-setting functions of the news media during a presidential campaign. This provided continuity with the exploratory study, but at the same time, it provided a number of new perspectives on this kind of influence of mass communication. The nature of the study, its overall objectives, research strategies, modes of analysis, and findings are set forth in a book published in 1977. This work, *The Emergence of American Political Issues: The Agenda-Setting Function of the Press*, prepared by Shaw and McCombs in association with seven other members of their research team, was the first book to attempt to formulate systematically and present extensive data on the agenda-setting hypothesis.[10]

The Research Objectives

Like most of the complex studies reviewed in earlier chapters, the Charlotte study had multiple objectives, although each was related to the underlying process of agenda-setting. In order to understand the various analyses and the results obtained, each of these research goals needs to be understood. The paragraphs below provide a brief overview of the objectives, and each will be discussed in more detail as the findings are summarized.

Defining the Concept. One problem was to refine the definition of the concept and state the relationships between independent and dependent variables more formally. Up to this point, it had been a rather loose generalization indicating that correspondence could be expected between the relative emphasis given to a set of issues by the press and the personal salience assigned to those same issues on the part of voters. That idea was certainly supported by the Chapel Hill data, but the agenda-setting needed to be explicated—that is systematically examined, with every aspect made explicit and clear.

Information Sources for Personal Agendas. An important objective was to try to understand better where people actually obtained information so as to decide on a rank order of salience among the issues of a campaign. Obviously, they obtained much of their information from news and political advertisements presented by the media. But in addition there was the question of other people. That source had emerged in an unexpected manner in *The People's Choice*, when it was concluded that there was a two-step flow of information and influence from the media to opinion leaders and then on by word of mouth to other segments of the population who had little firsthand exposure to the political campaign. Was that also the case for agenda-setting? Did political discussions with friends, family, or neighbors form or modify a voter's conceptions of the salience of the issues? Gaining an understanding of the role of interpersonal communication about the issues was a major objective.

Sequencing over Time as a Major Variable. The influence of time sequence on personal agenda-setting as a dependent variable was still another. In other words, does the order of importance of issues suggested by the news media at one point in time have a continuing influence so that it shapes voters' beliefs about the importance of those issues at a later time? Modern correlational techniques can provide answers to such questions, and unraveling time relationships was one of the objectives of the Charlotte study.

The Personal Characteristics of Voters. What kind of people are most influenced in the agenda-setting process, and why do some more than others turn to the media for information about a presidential campaign? Are those with high levels of uncertainty about the issues, plus a need for orientation, most likely to give close attention to the campaign? If so will they be most influenced by the media in forming their personal rankings of the importance of the various issues? There is also the question of influence on actual voting behavior. It is one thing to form a hierarchy of importance that one attaches to the campaign issues, but it is another to be motivated to go to the polls because some of those issues are seen as critical. Finally, there was a special question of the young voter in the 1972 campaign. The voting age had just been lowered from 21 to 18. How many younger voters actually turned out, and how did they feel about the issues? These questions of individual needs, motivation, and age were all personal characteristics explored in the Charlotte research.

Politics and Agenda-Setting. Finally, when all the data are in, what is the overall picture? How important is agenda-setting in the American political process? Is it another of those negative effects about which we should be concerned, or does it provide benefits to individuals and society? Is it a process that is independent of other social and personal influences of the media, or is it a part of larger and more general relationships that exist between the media and society?

Each of these objectives provides a focus for understanding why the particular data of the study were gathered and examines the implications of the results. But before those tasks can be undertaken, it is necessary to look at where the research was done and among what kinds of subjects.

The Research Site
Charlotte, North Carolina, was selected with specific criteria in mind. For one thing, it is located some distance from major metropolitan communities. It is about halfway between Washington, D.C. and Atlanta, Georgia. At the time,

this meant that it was served by a restricted number of media that could be effectively monitored during the research period. In fact, there were only two newspapers and the usual three television networks. With its 1970 population of 354,000 it was large enough to be diverse but small enough so that samples could be drawn of the entire population of voters.

For another, Charlotte was not a sleepy Southern town. During the previous decade, many changes had occurred: It had grown rapidly, and, indeed, a substantial proportion of its population were transient. Average family income had risen sharply, and many new businesses had made the city their regional headquarters. People moved in and out as young families came in from the countryside and as workers and executives took and left jobs in local branches of national companies and industries. At an earlier time, it was mainly a city of single family dwellings, but, by the early 1970s, a third of its inhabitants lived in apartments.

Finally, unlike many areas of the South, Charlotte was not a Democrat stronghold. In fact, during the previous twenty years the entire county had generally gone Republican. In the election under study, President Nixon won easily over his challenger.

The Panel Design and Sample

The agenda-setting hypothesis assumes that there is some causal relationship between the selective emphasis given to a list of issues by the media and the development of corresponding audience beliefs about their hierarchy of relative importance. The nature of this influence is not understood, but there is clearly a time factor involved. The media must do their part first, and the influence on the audience comes later. It was for this reason that a panel design was selected for the Charlotte project. Panel designs are based on the idea that a sample of respondents will be interviewed at one point in time and then interviewed again later, perhaps repeatedly. Earlier research (*The People's Choice*) had convincingly demonstrated that fears about a Hawthorne effect were without foundation. That is, the fact of being repeatedly observed had little influence on the behavior of those under study.

The original sample was selected from the official voter registration rolls of Mecklenburg County, in which Charlotte is located. The Board of Elections supplied tapes containing more than 150,000 names, and a computer program was used to select those to be included in the study. As is frequently the case, problems were encountered with this sampling frame. Murphy's Law dictates that if something can go wrong, it will! The Law prevails in research as elsewhere. Some people on the list had died, and others had moved away, but these changes were not reflected in the voter registration records. Thus, the transient character of the city prevented the researchers from developing a truly random sample of registered voters.

The plan had been to interview the panel of respondents in June and then

interview the same people again in October, shortly before the election. Still a
third rather brief interview by telephone was scheduled just after the election
was over. But when it came time to actually contact the people whose names
were in the sample for their first interview, many could not be located. Aside
from those who had died or moved, some were simply never home. A few re-
fused to participate. But in spite of these commonly encountered problems, a
total of 380 voters were successfully interviewed in June.

When the interviewers went back again in October, Murphy's Law struck
again. An unusually large number of people had moved away. In fact, only 230
of the original 380 could be found. This was a loss of 39 percent, which was
serious indeed. The researchers discovered furthermore that only a small number of black voters were included in their original sample (there was no way of
knowing this ahead of time as the official list had no racial identifiers). Therefore, before the October interviews, 41 black voters were added to the panel
and interviewed with the June as well as the October questionnaires. About
half of these (24) were included in the postelection interview. Generally, then,
the basic analysis of the Charlotte study was based on 227 registered voters
who were interviewed three times, plus 24 black voters who were added in
October and also contacted in November. For many of the analyses of findings,
the panel of 227 that was interviewed all three times provided the basic data on
the agenda-setting role of the mass media.

The researchers were very much aware of the limitations of their sample
and did not regard it as representative of either the community as a whole or the
population of registered voters that remained in the county. Futhermore, they
were concerned about the effects of the attrition on the characteristics of the
sample between interviews. To see if this attrition had introduced serious
biases, they made a systematic study of the percentage distributions within
those who were interviewed on all three occasions. As it turned out, there were
only trivial differences between the percents who were in various categories of
age, sex, race, income, education, and political party affiliation. In other words,
in spite of Murphy's Law, their final panel design survived and yielded useful
data, even though generalizations to larger populations would have to be
limited.

Findings

The objectives of the Charlotte study have already been set forth in summary.
That overview provides a convenient framework for discussing the results that
emerged from the research findings. The presentation of those findings in *The
Emergence of American Political Issues* was made in ten chapters, each devoted to
particular issues, and each prepared by one or two of the nine members of the
research team. To bring these complex data into a simplified framework, the
sections below attempt to summarize those findings and many of their interpretations within the five research objectives set forth earlier.

Objective 1: Clarifying the Definition. In some ways it would be appropriate to address this objective last as the data from the Charlotte study undoubtedly provides for sharpening and explicating the agenda-setting hypothesis. But since this objective served as a bridge between the earlier formulation of the hypothesis, developed mainly within the context of the Chapel Hill study, and prior, less focused research, it is appropriate to address the issue of clarification first.

It is in the first two chapters of their book that Shaw and McCombs demonstrate their commitment to a programmatic approach and systematic theory development in their study of the influence of mass communication on personal and social life. They set the study of agenda-setting within a framework of accumulating, changing, and evolving theories of mass communication. They make note of the view that continues to dominate the thinking and fears of the public—that the media are very powerful. They then review the major changes in thinking that have characterized media theorists and researchers who had to interpret the findings of their investigation during the late 1940s and the 1950s. As we have noted earlier, they did not confirm the existence of powerful effects. Thus, there was a transition from a belief in all-powerful media to one of minimal consequences. This interpretation of media effects was well entrenched by the beginning of the 1960s.

Shaw and McCombs point out the (widely accepted) conclusion that the earlier research led to a belief in minimal effects because of its strategies of investigation and because of its commitment to a particular conception of the manner in which mass communication presumably achieved its influences on people's behavior. In brief, the commitment of many earlier mass communication theorists was to try to understand the influence of the mass media (particularly in the area of political effects) as generated by the following sequence: First, the media provoked among its audiences an *awareness* of the issues. Second, it provided a body of *information* to the members of that audience. Third, this information provided the basis for *attitude formation or change* on the part of those who acquired it. And fourth, the *attitudes shaped behavior* among those involved in the sequence.

Much of the earlier research, Shaw and McCombs note, had bypassed the first two steps in this sequence and had focused on the attitudinal and behavioral influences that were presumed to take place. When it began to be clear that those kinds of influences were very limited, the baby almost got thrown out with the bath! Instead of advocating that researchers go back to study more intensively the awareness and informational effects of the media, those theorists who subscribed to the law of minimal effects simply declared that the media had virtually no influence on people at all. Needless to say, they were wrong.

Although Shaw and McCombs do not discuss it, it can be pointed out that an important factor that misled earlier communication theorists was the great popularity of the attitude concept. It virtually dominated social psychology since it was introduced early in the century. In particular, there was a firm belief that inner feelings dictated action—that there was a powerful correspondence between attitudes and behavior. In more recent decades, the relationship between attitudes and behavior has been shown to be far less certain. People often behave according to the requirements of a social situation and the expectations of people important to them rather than according to their private convictions.[11] Thus, the commitment of communication theorists to the attitude–behavior paradigm was doomed from the start. Even if the media *had* proved capable of changing attitudes, there was no assurance that people would obligingly alter their behavior.

Shaw and McCombs then place the agenda-setting hypothesis squarely in a cognitive rather than an affective framework. They note that the first two steps in the old awareness-information-attitude-behavior sequence are where research attention is likely to be most fruitful. The media *do* call our attention to events and issues via the flow of news. They *do* provide information about those matters. And people *do* learn about them by attending to the media. The question is not whether attitudes and ultimately behavior are then changed. One need not made such affective assumptions. The more significant question is what people *believe* to be true about those events in the news, with which they can seldom or never have firsthand experience. It is those beliefs about the nature of reality that will guide their actions. As W. I. Thomas pointed out in 1923, people act upon their "definition of the situation." If they believe a situation to be real, they will act as though it is real.[12] In fact, as was pointed out at the beginning of the present chapter, philosophers, sociologists, psychologists, and others have discussed that aspect of human behavior for a long time.

From a general theoretical point of view, the insistence of Shaw and McCombs on a return to the cognitive issues centering on the awareness and information supplying functions of the media has an important consequence. It provides an effective explication and clarification of the broad theoretical paradigm in which the agenda-setting function of the media is located. It becomes one of the processes by which the media in modern society participate in the *social construction of reality* for the populations that they serve. As the authors put it:

> The agenda-setting function of mass communication clearly falls in this new tradition of cognitive outcomes of mass communication. Perhaps more than any other aspect of our environment, the political arena—all those issues and persons about whom we hold opinions and knowledge—is second-hand reality. Especially in national politics, we have little personal or direct contact. Our knowledge comes primarily from the mass media. For the most part, we know only those aspects of national politics considered newsworthy enough for transmission through the mass media.[13]

Thus, the study of the agenda-setting function as conceptualized by Shaw and McCombs returns research on the influence of mass media to the issues suggested by such pioneer public opinion theorists as Charles Horton Cooley, James Bryce, and Walter Lippmann. It focuses our attention on the process by which the media play a significant part in generating a common culture—in this case a consensus of shared beliefs about certain political aspects of our environment that play a significant part in bringing us together at election time.

How, then, is agenda-setting to be defined for the purposes of such research? Certainly, until a body of research is generated to provide a much larger base of findings, it should remain as a *hypothesis*. The authors themselves state the presumed relationship in this manner:

> This book examines that agenda-setting power of the press, the hypothesis that the press itself has some power to establish an agenda of political issues which both the candidates and the voters come to regard as important.[14]

The hypothesis suggests not only an influence on voters but on the candidates as well, although the latter has not been well studied.

In terms of independent versus dependent variables, the press is clearly seen in the causal role. Yet, this should not be taken too literally. The intention is not to portray those who rule the media as making calculated decisions to manipulate the public. The hierarchies of emphasis and importance attached to political topics and issues by the press is seen as an inevitable part of the daily processing and presenting of the news:

> Each day editors and news directors—the gate-keepers in the news media systems—must decide which items to pass and which to reject. Furthermore, the items passed through the gate are not treated equally when presented to the audience. Some are used at length, others severely cut. Some are lead-off items in a newscast. Others follow much later. Newspapers clearly state the value they place on the salience of an item through headline size and placement within the newspaper—anywhere from the lead item on page one to placement at the bottom of a column on page 66.[15]

Thus, the causal chain clearly includes the gatekeepers who make the decisions about giving greater relative emphasis to one story versus another.

But gatekeepers do not act in a vacuum. They process the news according to well-understood criteria that are related in part to their socially derived conceptions of the proper role of the press in society and to the practical necessity of attracting and holding their audiences. Thus, the causal chain becomes very complicated when one attempts to sort out the independent variables that result in the differential emphasis given to the news. In fact, gatekeeping, media agenda-setting, and the construction of individual agendas by members of the public are part of a complex social system. That system includes at least three classes of variables: those that account for selecting a particular event as a news item; those that govern the processing and delivering of the news in a given pattern of selection and emphasis; and those that determine who will be exposed and how they will interpret the media content.

Key factors that shape the agenda provided by the media are the values and beliefs used by reporters as part of the surveillance process. What events should be considered as news? The nature of the medium is another consideration. Newspapers can report in depth while television can devote only a few minutes at most to an important story. Editors provide another level of screening. They have to select from available stories what they can fit into the time or space that they have at their disposal. Sometimes they must cut a story or move it to a back page, even though they may regard it as important. Sometimes there just isn't enough news. This means that less important stories can come to occupy the front page or the first slot on the broadcast. Finally, conceptions of audience interest, profit making, and even the social organization of the news industry have been recognized as factors that shape content of the news and the levels of importance suggested by the media. Thus, the causal chain that sets the media agenda is a complex one indeed.

When the audience receives the messages contained in the news the process of personal agenda-setting results in the assignment or assumption of differential weights of importance. Those weights or degrees of salience are derived in part from the cues provided by the news media. If a story is the lead item in the broadcast, on the front page, or set off by conspicuous headlines, its degree of salience is probably perceived as high. If the cues have the opposite characteristics, the weights and level of salience are more likely to be low. Patterns of attention are subject to variation according to the audience member's needs for orientation, interest in given topics, and other individual characteristics.

One of the features of the agenda-setting hypothesis that makes it attractive as a research topic is that the independent and dependent variables stated in the hypothesis itself can be *measured*. This is not always the case when studying the communication systems that result in a social construction of reality. The cues assigned to a story by the media can be measured by content analyses, and beliefs about salience on the part of the audience can also be measured by appropriate questionnaires. This makes it possible to *test* the agenda-setting hypothesis in a relatively straightforward manner. The degree of correlation between the media-produced agenda and the agenda perceived by the audience provides the basis for deciding whether there has been such an influence.

Generally, then, agenda-setting can best be studied as a hypothesis that relates specific independent and dependent variables. Stated in hypothesis form, it appears to be deceptively simple until it can be seen as a relationship embedded in a complex web of factors that produce both gatekeeping and audience response. Even more broadly, it can also be seen as one part of the social construction of reality, or, more specifically, the social construction of shared meanings that takes place as a result of both interpersonal and mass communication in modern society.

Objective 2: Information Sources for Personal Agendas. The agenda-setting hypothesis began as a relationship between media presentations of the news and personal views of the importance of issues. That is still its central focus. However, there is also a need to consider another form of media content—political advertising by the candidates—as a source from which impressions of the relative importance of issues can be formed. In addition, there is the complicating factor of interpersonal communication. People talk to others about what they have read in their newspapers or seen on television about the campaign and the issues. In other words, news, advertising, and personal discussions are separate sources of ideas about the nature and salience of issues in a campaign. Each can be examined separately.

What were the issues that were presented via the news media in Charlotte? Actually, the specific list of issues and their relative emphasis differed somewhat among the various media. The *Charlotte Observer* presented and emphasized one agenda. Each of the three television networks presented their own version. Yet, each of these media offered at least some information on all of the principal issues that were discussed by the candidates during the campaign. The big issue was Vietnam. The war was constantly in the news during the entire campaign period. As in every election, the economy was important to the voters. A third topic of high news value during the time was the national controversy over school bussing. This issue was important locally as the school system tried to work out an acceptable level of integration. Concern over youth-drugs-morals was also substantial. It was a time of communes, counterculture, youthful rebellion, and, for many young people, a sharp change in sexual mores. These matters were often distressing to the relatively conservative voters of Charlotte. Foreign relations was another important topic, especially with the U.S.S.R. and China. After decades, the Chinese were just beginning to reestablish ties with the west. It was also a time when Watergate was a national preoccupation, along with its implications of government corruption. Such matters were troublesome to voters in Charlotte. Finally, the environmental movement had blossomed a short time earlier, and a major issue was concern over environment-pollution.

These seven, then, were the official agenda that was identified as central to the media coverage of the campaign. There were other topics that were in the news, such as the personalities of the candidates, the events of the campaign itself, other kinds of international events, and an endless flow of general campaign analysis. Leaving these aside, the relative emphasis given to the seven main issues by the news media under study can be seen in Table 13.1.

Table 13.1 shows that there were substantial differences between the levels of emphasis given to the issues in the media agenda as it was offered in June and October. This is to be expected as the candidates worked out and presented their positions. However, the correlations between the media themselves are high (Table 13.2). In other words, the media were presenting a fairly uniform agenda to the voters.

The agenda-setting hypothesis predicts that exposure to the news will bring some degree of correspondence between the levels of importance assigned to the issues during the campaign by voters and the levels of emphasis given to those issues by the media. This is presumably a long-range influence. However, the design of the Charlotte study provided for only a four-month period in which to observe such an effect. Nevertheless, correlations were calculated

TABLE 13.1. THE MEDIA AGENDA: PERCENTS OF CAMPAIGN COVERAGE DEVOTED TO VARIOUS ISSUES BY NETWORK NEWS PROGRAMS AND BY A LOCAL NEWSPAPER DURING JUNE AND OCTOBER

Issue	ABC June	ABC Oct	CBS June	CBS Oct	NBC June	NBC Oct	Charlotte Observer June	Charlotte Observer Oct
Vietnam	27.1	20.7	27.0	19.4	23.4	17.9	16.5	21.3
Youth-drugs	1.0	2.1	0.0	1.6	1.4	1.7	3.3	2.7
Economy	4.0	14.5	4.4	15.9	3.7	12.1	6.9	3.8
Bussing	2.5	4.5	2.2	3.2	1.9	1.2	1.9	1.6
USSR-China	3.0	0.3	2.6	1.9	5.1	3.5	4.1	4.3
Watergate	2.0	9.3	1.8	6.5	4.7	8.4	1.9	9.4
Environment	4.5	0.7	4.0	1.0	2.8	2.6	6.2	4.7

Source: This table is based on information from Table 3-2 from Donald L. Shaw and Maxwell E. McCombs, *The Emergence of American Political Issues: The Agenda-Setting Function of the Press* (St. Paul, Minn.: West Publishing Co., 1974) p. 38.

TABLE 13.2. CORRELATIONS BETWEEN THE AGENDAS AS PRESENTED BY THE SEPARATE MEDIA

	June ABC	June CBS	June NBC	June Ch. Ob.	October ABC	October CBS	October NBC	October Ch. Ob.
ABC	—	.96	.57	.90	—	.89	.64	.64
CBS		—	.61	.94		—	.75	.64
NBC			—	.45			—	.93
Ch. Ob.				—				—

Source: These Spearman Rank-Order correlations are from Table 3-3 in Donald L. Shaw and Maxwell E. McCombs, *The Emergence of Amercian Political Issues: The Agenda-Setting Function of the Press* (St. Paul, Minn.: West Publishing Company, 1974) p. 40.

between the agenda set by the media versus that of the voters in June and again in October. Evidence for such agenda-setting would be an increase in the media–voter correlation over the period. As Table 13.3 shows, by that criterion there was evidence of an agenda-setting effect. For the two television networks, the data indicate that there was an increase in agenda correspondence between June and October. Furthermore, that correspondence was substantially higher for those who viewed television the most. The pattern is different for the newspaper, where correspondence correlations showed a mixed pattern.

The general weight of evidence suggests that the agenda emphasized by the news media became the agenda of importance among the voters. The larger increase in correspondence among those who used television the most supports the conclusion. On the other hand, the data for the newspaper are difficult to interpret. Even though there was an increase in agenda correspondence between medium and voters as a whole, the pattern between heavy and light users was the reverse of that for television.

Candidate advertising is another potential source for agenda information. Little is known about its effect. Paid political advertising on television by the candidates during presidential campaigns has been criticized since it began. No candidate feels that he can dare ignore it, but many are uncomfortable with the idea that it provides an emphasis on personality and image-building rather than an intelligent analysis of the issues. Critics agree and maintain that the candidate with the fattest pocketbook has the best chance of winning through the use of televised ads. Nevertheless, television advertising has become a central part of presidential elections.

While candidates cannot control the manner in which the news media report on them and their discussions of the issues, they can control their advertising campaigns. Therefore, paid television advertisements provide an index of the *candidate's* issue agenda. The degree to which these candidate agendas correspond with voter agendas can be assessed, and that correspondence can show if there is an agenda-setting effect brought about by the advertising.

TABLE 13.3. CORRELATIONS BETWEEN MEDIA AND PERSONAL AGENDAS IN JUNE AND OCTOBER

TV Use	CBS			NBC			Charlotte Observer		
	June	Oct	Change	June	Oct	Change	June	Oct	Change
Great Deal or Some	.33	.68	+.35	.21	.64	+.43	.39	.28	−.11
Little or None	.41	.60	+.19	.05	.20	+.15	.63	.23	−.40
Difference	−.08	.08	+.16	.16	.44	+.28	−.24	.05	+.29

Source: This table is based on Spearman Rank-Order correlations from Table 3-5 in Donald L. Shaw and Maxwell E. McCombs, *The Emergence of American Political Issues: The Agenda-Setting Function of the Press* (St. Paul, Minn.: West Publishing Company, 1974) p. 47.

There is, of course, the problem of sorting out the influence of the ads versus that of the news media if both have similar agendas. Nevertheless, the content of all candidate advertising was analyzed for a three-week period in October during the time when the sample was being interviewed. The frequencies with which certain issues were discussed in both the Nixon and the McGovern ads were calculated so as to obtain candidate agendas for each. These candidate agendas were not identical with those presented by the news media, so the problem of overlap was minimized. The question is to what degree did the issues emphasized in candidate advertising reflect the order of emphasis as perceived by the voters. In other words, did the advertisements influence voters in setting personal agendas?

One important condition is whether or not the voters actually saw the advertisements. Few people deliberately seek out political advertisements on television, so exposure was incidental to viewing for other reasons. As might be expected, those voters who used television a great deal for political news were more likely to have seen the ads than those who used it lightly or not at all.

Overall, the correspondence between voters' agendas and candidates' advertised agendas was low. For the Nixon ads it was +.11 and for McGovern +.37. However, another kind of influence was observed. The advertisements tended to create "affect." That is, positive or negative feelings about the candidates. The numerous Nixon ads led some to such affective responses, but it was the McGovern ads that created the greatest amount of positive or negative feelings. In fact, the results indicated that many people became more negative toward the senator after viewing his ads. This may have been a factor in his defeat.

A third major source of information about a presidential election campaign is other people. From discussions about the candidates and the issues, it is possible to develop a personal agenda based on the interpretations provided by friends, relatives, and other individuals. This may or may not be identical to that supplied by the press.

Included in the interviews with the Charlotte voter sample were items probing how often and to whom they talked about politics. As it turned out, the respondents engaged in a considerable amount of political discussion with family members, friends, and others. Furthermore, as the campaign went on, the proportion who were involved in such interpersonal exchanges increased (from 40 percent in June to more than 60 percent by October).

The researchers found that people discussed politics more with members of their family that with friends or others. This was expecially true of females. However, the category that was most involved in such discussions were younger males of higher income and education. Nevertheless, virtually everyone had some involvement in political conversations. Those who talked the most were also likely to be the highest users of both television and newspapers as sources of political information. There was, therefore, an overlap between the two communication systems—mass media and interpersonal contacts.

The findings on the influence of political discussions were mixed. There was an especially high correlation between the frequent talkers and the agenda provided by the newspaper (.83). On the other hand, correlations with the agenda supplied by television news were low. Therefore, in spite of minor support for the hypothesis that participation in discussions of politics is related to agenda-setting, the evidence was ambiguous.

In summary, the major information source for personal agenda-setting was the news of the campaign as reported by the television networks and to some extent the newspaper. Paid political advertisements on television may help voters develop feelings about the candidates as individuals, but they do not appear to have a strong influence in shaping personal agendas of the issues. Interpersonal discussions of the candidates and the issues may play a part, but the best conclusion is that the press plays the larger role. Shaw and McCombs concluded that ". . . both the press and other people help shape our ideas. Only sometimes the press seems to shout a bit louder. Or perhaps it is only more repetitious."[16]

Objective 3: Time Sequences in the Agenda-Setting Process. Agenda-setting is defined as a process that takes place over time. The assumption is that after voters pay extended attention to the rank order of emphasis given to issues in the press, the agenda of the individual will increasingly resemble that rank order. This implies a causal process. However, as is perennially the case, showing mere correlation between press agenda and voter agenda at a given point in time does not allow a causal inference. It is entirely possible that the interests of the voters play a part in shaping what the press will emphasize. Thus, it is conceivable that the causal influence is in the opposite direction. Which is the chicken and which the egg? Does the press set the voter agenda, or does the voter agenda set that of the press? The fact that they are correlated is important, but it is not conclusive in understanding causal direction.

One way to unravel the chicken-egg question is to see what comes first and what seems to follow at a later time. A rather simple procedure called "cross-lagged correlation" can answer such questions. The idea is rather straightforward, and it can be illustrated by examining the times shown in Figure 13.1. Time 1 is June, when the first interviews were conducted and the newspaper's agenda was first analyzed. Time 2 is October, when the second interviews were completed and the newspaper's agenda was again assessed. As can be seen, the newspaper's agendas are correlated (.43) across the two time periods. The agendas of the voters are even more correlated (.94) between Times 1 and 2. There are also correlations between media and voter agendas at each of the time periods. (.46 and .10, respectively). Thus far, these data do not provide for causal inferences.

The key to understanding the cross-lagged correlation as evidence of a causal relationship is to look at the two diagonals as well as the above correlations in a total configuration. It can be seen that the relationship between the newspaper agenda at Time 1 (June) and the voters' agenda at Time 2 (October) is greater than that of the diagonal running the other way. The comparison is .51 versus .19, with a difference of .32. Statistically speaking, this means that the newspaper agenda offered in June accounts for much more variance in the voters' agenda in October than does the reverse relationship. It is clear that the voters' agenda in June had little in common with the newspaper agenda of October (little variance accounted for). Thus, there is no causal relationship implied between the June voters' agenda and the later agenda of the newspaper. The reverse is true as revealed by the other diagonal. Also, the .51 correlation in that diagonal is larger than either the .46 or the .10 relationship between newspapers and voters on either end of the diagram. The bottom line is that such a configuration of correlations provides evidence to infer a causal relationship between media content in June and voters' ranking of the importance of the issues in October.

While the pattern of correlations shown in Figure 13.1 shows rather clearly the influence of the newspaper on voters' agendas over the four-month period, the same pattern was not found for television. If similar diagrams were constructed for both CBS and NBC network news, the results would not show an agenda-setting influence across time. Thus, the newspaper appeared to play a

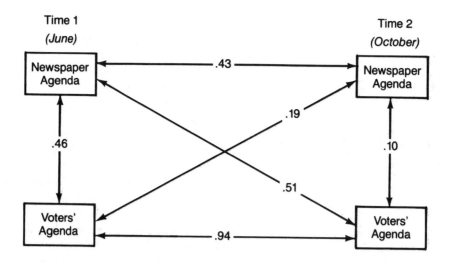

Figure 13.1. Cross-Lagged Correlations Between Newspaper's and Voters' Agendas.
Source: These Spearman Rho coefficients were obtained from Figure 6-1 in Donald L. Shaw and Maxwell E. McCombs, *The Emergence of American Political Issues: The Agenda-Setting Function of the Press* (St. Paul, Minn.: West Publishing, 1974) p. 91.

clear role in shaping voters' agendas during the period studied, but television did not. This type of cross-lagged correlation has become one of the standard ways of looking at agenda-setting at different points in time. In the Charlotte study, it is clear that each of the media did not have a similar effect.

Objective 4: Personal Characteristics and Agenda-Setting. In the search for psychological explanations of agenda-setting, one of the immediate questions is: Why do some voters attend to media content more than others do? For the authors, it appeared that there were three major factors that influenced such different patterns of exposure. First was the voter's level of interest in the content, which is a function of perceived *relevance* to his or her concerns; second is his or her degree of *uncertainty* concerning the issues contained in that content; and finally there is the matter of the *effort* required to locate a reliable source of relevant information. The first two of these factors—perceived relevance and degree of uncertainty—were incorporated into a concept that McCombs and his associates called *need for orientation*. Need for orientation, then, is a personality factor that presumably leads an individual to seek exposure to media content. The simple hypothesis can be formed that the greater such a need, the greater the attention. That, in turn, would lead to an increase in agenda-setting influences. The concept need not incorporate "effort" because mass media are so ubiquitous that this can be regarded as a constant that does not vary much from one individual to the next.

These considerations permit the development of a typology of patterns in the antecedents that lead individuals to have high, medium, or low needs for orientation. Figure 13.2 shows how these antecedents are related. Low relevance, for example, leads logically to a low need for orientation. High relevance and high uncertainty, on the other hand, lead to a high need for orientation. Moderate need for orientation has high-low pattern of antecedents.

Data from the Charlotte study confirm that even when the relevance and uncertainty factors are measured in a variety of ways, differing levels of need for orientation are related to levels of exposure to media content and to the strength of the agenda-setting effect. The typology shown in Figure 13.2, in other words, provides a useful guide in predicting media usage and agenda-setting influences.

Five scales of perceived relevance of issues were used and four scales of uncertainty to measure these factors. Overwhelmingly, those voters with high needs for orientation ranked highest on media usage. These with moderate needs were, in turn, above those with low needs for orientation. The results were virtually uniform across all five scales. The scales also correlated in large part with the agenda-setting effect of the media, although the evidence was not as clear in every instance. The data on the 126 comparisons that were made for both the newspaper and television and for both June and October are too numerous to present in the present summary. However, the overall results

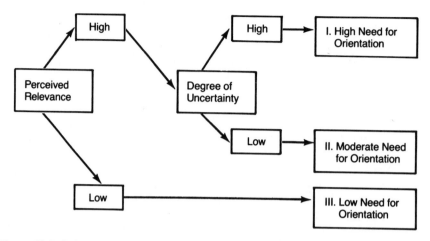

Figure 13.2. Relevance and Uncertainty as Antecedents of Need for Orientation.
Source: This diagram is based on Figure 7-1 from Donald L. Shaw and Maxwell E. McCombs,
The Emergence of American Political Issues: The Agenda-Setting Function of the Press (St.
Paul, Minn.: West Publishing Company, 1974) p. 40.

present a substantial picture of support for the general hypothesis that need for
orientation (combining perceived relevance of media content and degree of
uncertainty) leads to media exposure and then to agenda-setting influences.

Objective 5: Assessing the Political Role of Agenda-Setting. The process of
agenda-setting was initially conceptualized, researched, and formalized within
the context of election campaigns, voting, and mass media reports of political
issues. The Charlotte study was a scientific effort designed to be programmatic
—that is, to build upon previous research on agenda-setting. However, in
many ways its subject matter is uniquely traditional. It looks at the relationship between the Fourth Estate, those in charge of the political process, and
those who are governed. Thus, agenda-setting focuses on the venerable idea of
the "power of the press" as an influence in politics—an old concept indeed. In
fact, the authors suggest that our contemporary mass media, and specifically the
news industries, play a dual role in shaping political activities:

> This means that the mass media are the major artisans of our popular
> political culture, of what the masses perceive to be political reality and the
> political concerns of the day. It also means that the mass media are major
> shapers of our elite political culture. Witness the role of the elite press as a
> source of information among major decision-makers.[17]

In other words, agenda-setting is a part of the communication processes in
society by which individuals develop and share political meanings. Specifically,

it relates media and voters as the latter engage in the social construction of reality in the area of election campaigns, candidate images, and the dimensions of political issues.

At the same time, agenda-setting does not define the media as passive transmitters of information conveying information about political events, candidates, and issues to a waiting public of voters. The media are formulators of meaning in their own right. They are active agents that select, screen, interpret, emphasize, and possibly even distort the flow of information from political events on one side of the system to voters seeking information on the other side. The press injects its own meanings into its reports before it presents them to its audiences. Its consumers, in turn, attend selectively and develop among themselves various shared interpretations ("popular culture") of what the campaign, candidates, and issues are all about. Futhermore, "major decision makers" are described as consumers of this socially constructed reality. The creations of the press become for them important sources of information upon which they base, to some unspecified degree, their political positions and policies. In other words, the press also shapes the "elite political culture."

If this conception of the role of the press is correct, it is a remarkably powerful medium! It not only shapes the public's political beliefs (and indirectly thereby their actions) but the nature of the political process itself by its influences on decision makers. With the press strategically in control of the high ground in the middle, it can exercise its power in both directions through the process of agenda-setting. (Whether the press actually has this power to shape both sides of the political process remains to be seen.)

Meanwhile, several additional conclusions about agenda-setting seem less open to controversy. These need to be summed up. From data presented by authors Shaw, McCombs, and their associates in various sections of their report, a number of generalizations appear to be more or less supported by the findings of the Charlotte study. While they do not list them in the following manner, it may be useful to do so because they seem to provide the beginning point for a more systematic theory of the juxtaposition of independent and dependent variables that are involved in the agenda-setting process:

1. Voters show increasing patterns of use of mass communications as the presidential campaign progresses.
2. Those patterns of increasing exposure to media content show variations among different types of voters characterized by distinctive personal characteristics and social category memberships.
3. Each of the media (newspapers vs. television) plays a different role as an information source for various types of voters.
4. Increasing exposure to the media during a campaign appears to raise interest in politics among voters, and it helps define salient features of the campaign for them.

5. Because of increasing media use, interest, and salience, there is an increase in interpersonal communication about politics during the campaign.

6. Increasing media exposure and involvement in interpersonal communication leads to a rising need for information and orientation regarding politics during a campaign, which in turn stimulates more media exposure and interpersonal communication.

7. The influence of agenda-setting on different categories of voters is, therefore, a product of exposure, type of medium, interest, salience, need for orientation, and interpersonal communication.

The authors do not bring these several generalizations into an overall theoretical formulation. Indeed, given the pioneering nature of their study, it is not at all certain that they should have done so. Their task was to map out the major parameters that seem to play a part in shaping the agenda-setting process and not to test an explanatory theory in a definitive way. Nevertheless, the foregoing appear to represent the heart of the findings of the Charlotte study. Those propositions offered fertile ground for the growth of a research tradition that would follow on the agenda-setting function of the press.

CONCLUSION AND IMPLICATIONS

The study of agenda-setting has now become a well-trodden part of the research territory of the communication scholar. The publication of the Chapel Hill study triggered a substantial interest in the process, and the publication of the Charlotte investigation reinforced that interest substantially. Today, dozens of studies appear every year in the journals devoted to communication specialties. In 1981, a much larger and more sophisticated study was completed by Weaver, Graber, McCombs, and Eyal. It was an analysis of the role of the press in agenda-setting during the 1976 election. In terms of design, it was a much expanded version of the Charlotte study, and it probed many of the same issues in much greater depth.[18]

A thorough review of the literature up to the end of 1985 has been provided by Michael Salwen.[19] His review indicates that in spite of the wealth of studies focusing on the issue, many problems remain in developing an understanding of the process. Additional research is needed to explore the influence of different audience categories and individual characteristics, interpersonal communication, the duration of the effect, differential importance of issues, and above all, the unknown territory of how agenda-setting is related to attitudes and behavior.

In many ways, the emergence of agenda-setting as a central focus of communication research is a product of changes that have taken place in the field. As the present book has shown, the scientific study of the effects of mass communication began outside of journalism or related communication specializations. The Payne Fund Studies were undertaken by psychologists and sociologists in response to a public concern about unwholesome effects of the movies on children. The milestones that followed were also undertaken by social and behavioral scientists who were equipped to conduct quantitative research and reach findings supported by data. The central focus was on children and the potential harm to them that was created by the media. Social scientists have traditionally been disturbed by violence, the power of big corporations, and the exploitation of the underdog. When the opportunity came to subject the media to intensive scrutiny concerning the stimulation of aggressive behavior among the young, and perhaps to lay the blame for violence in society at their door, such social scientists almost trampled over each other in a rush to participate in the formulation of the *Report to the Surgeon General*.

As schools of communication began to turn out research specialists trained in social science methodology, they tended to continue the same lines of investigation that had been opened by the social scientists who had blazed the initial trails in the scientific study of the media. Thus, Schramm explored *Television in the Lives of Our Children*. Gerbner pressed further into the relationship between violence and the media, and other communication specialists continued to study such traditional issues as needs and gratifications, and the diffusion of the news, to mention only a few. Gradually, social scientists dropped out. For example, in sociology today the study of mass communication is regarded as a relatively obscure specialty. Much the same situation exists in psychology. From the 1940s to the 1960s, it was a thriving industry in those disciplines.

As mass communication specialists increasingly turned out their own well-trained research specialists, it was inevitable that they would turn their attention away from the interests of sociologists and psychologists to find a topic more central to the basic interests of their intellectual heritage. The study of agenda-setting is made to order for the communication researcher who looks back to the great traditions of journalism rather than to the founders honored by social and behavioral scientists. Agenda-setting focuses on the classical topics—the Fourth Estate, political decision makers, voters, issues, and the power of the press in shaping our political destiny. These were the issues of James Bryce and Walter Lippmann, not those of the founders of sociology and psychology.

In short, the study of agenda-setting may represent a major turning point in the scientific study of the effects of mass communication. It is clearly an effort to develop hypotheses and to assemble data regarding the classical questions concerning the relationship between the press and society. In that sense, it is a unique product of specialists in journalism, who now use the tools of the scientific method to understand better the workings of their venerable institution.

NOTES AND REFERENCES

1. Walter Lippmann, *Public Opinion* (New York: Macmillan, 1922).
2. John Locke, *An Essay Concerning Human Understanding*, ed. Peter Nidditch (Oxford, Clarendon Press, 1975), p. 402. First published in 1690.
3. Harry Hoijer, "The Sapir-Whorf Hypothesis," *Language in Culture* (Chicago: University of Chicago Press, 1954), p. 94.
4. George Herbert Mead, *Mind, Self, and Society: From the Standpoint of a Social Behaviorist*, ed. Charles W. Morris (Chicago: University of Chicago Press, 1934).
5. Peter L. Berger and Thomas Luckmann, *The Social Construction of Reality* (New York: Doubleday, 1963).
6. Bernard Cohen, *The Press and Foreign Policy* (Princeton, N. J.: Princeton University Press, 1963) p. 13.
7. Kurt Lang and Gladys Engel Lang, "The Mass media and Voting," in Bernard Berelson and Morris Janowitz, eds., *Reader in Public Opinion and Communication*, 2nd ed. (New York: Free Press, 1966) p. 468.
8. Maxwell E. McCombs and Donald L. Shaw, "The Agenda-Setting Function of Mass Media," *Public Opinion Quarterly*, 1972, 176–187.
9. This account of the development of the agenda-setting hypothesis and the early research is based on personal correspondence with Dr. Maxwell McCombs.
10. Donald L. Shaw and Maxwell E. McCombs, *The Emergence of American Political Issues: The Agenda-Setting Function of the Press* (St. Paul, Minn.: West Publishing Company, 1977).
11. These issues from the general standpoint of social psychology have been summarized from Alan E. Liska, *The Consistency Controversy* (New York: John Wiley & Sons, 1975).
12. William I. Thomas, *The Unadjusted Girl* (Boston: Little, Brown, 1923).
13. Shaw and McCombs, op. cit., p. 7.
14. Ibid., p. 86.
15. Ibid., p. 151.
16. Ibid., p. 86.
17. Ibid., p. 151.
18. David H. Weaver, Doris A. Graber, Maxwell E. McCombs, and Chaim H. Eyal, *Media Agenda-Setting in a Presidential Election: Issues, Images and Interest* (New York: Praeger, 1981).
19. Michael B. Salwen, "An Agenda for Agenda-Setting Research: Problems in the Paradigm," Paper presented to the fifth annual Speech Communication Association of Puerto Rico, San Juan, 1985.

14

Television and Behavior, Ten Years of Progress. Part I: Violence and Prosocial and Cognitive/Affective Aspects of Behavior

The year was 1977; the place—Miami, Florida. The occasion was the murder trial of Ronnie Zamora, charged, along with a companion, with the killing of a helpless 80-year-old woman. The essence of the defense was that he had learned from television that this was how people silenced those who threatened them. The elderly victim, his neighbor, had caught Zamora in an act of burglary and had threatened to call the police. But Zamora knew (allegedly from television) that "dead men can't talk." Ellis Rubin, Zamora's flamboyant attorney, introduced a novel defense, "television intoxication," arguing that it was watching violence on TV that led Zamora to act as he did. Zamora was portrayed as a television addict who grew up on a viewing diet consisting mainly of violence and high-action drama. In Rubin's view, television, not Zamora, was the guilty party. The jury, however, disagreed and found Zamora guilty; watching television could not be used as an excuse for murder. Yet many people wondered if television had, in fact, played a role in Zamora's violent behavior. Indeed, were there other young Zamoras sitting in front of their sets consuming violence—human time bombs waiting to be set off? It was not a comforting idea. There were other TV-violence cases that had captured the attention of the public. A group of teenagers in Florida had set homeless old men on fire after watching such a portrayal in a "Sunday Night Movie." A young woman in Boston had been the victim of a similar fate; she was dragged by a gang of violent youths to a vacant lot, beaten, and burned with gasoline. Her death occurred two days after the television movie portraying such behavior aired.

Moreover, the level of violent crime remained high during the decade of the seventies, and we appeared to be making little progress in solving the problem. While no one was blaming television solely for this social problem, the issue of televised violence and its link with antisocial behavior remained a salient concern with much of the public and with many media researchers.

By the 1980s, concern with television's effects was no longer focused mainly on the issue of violence; perhaps watching television was affecting our lives and those of our children in many other ways. For example, as more women (including those with young children) moved into the work force,

353

television appeared to become a convenient babysitter for many. Given that children spent so much time in front of the set, was television becoming a major agent of their socialization? If so, how would televised portrayals of women, minorities, alcohol, and other drugs affect our children's perceptions? Just what lessons were being taught via the omnipresent 21-inch screen? Additionally, seasoned teachers complained that the children of the "television generation" expected a level of humor and entertainment and rapid-paced style of teaching that was quite different from earlier generations. Many parents worried—how was television affecting their children's cognitive development? It was within this atmosphere of concern that *Television and Behavior: Ten Years of Scientific Progress and Implications for the Eighties* came into being.

HISTORY OF THE PROJECT

It is widely believed among both academics and the public that *Television and Behavior* is simply an update of the information presented in the 1972 Surgeon General's report discussed in Chapter 12. Indeed, the 1982 report is often viewed as the "unfinished business" of the earlier report. That, however, is not the case. The 1972 report focused primarily (but not exclusively) on the issue of televised violence and its effects on children. However, in its summary report, called *Television and Growing Up*, the Surgeon General's Advisory Committee recommended that other areas of television influence be investigated. Of special importance to the Committee were that (1) childrens' modeling of prosocial behavior be studied; (2) television influence be studied in the home environment (not in the laboratory); (3) the relationship of television viewing to the cognitive and emotional development of children be examined; and (4) that we consider how television programming could be used to promote good health. These were just a few of the Committee's many recommendations for future research. The scientific community responded to the Committee's call; a massive research effort was undertaken both in this country and abroad, which yielded an enormous amount of information. Indeed, in the decade following the publication of the first Surgeon General's report, approximately *90 percent of all research publications on television's influences on behavior appeared*! It was this body of evidence that would be reviewed. This massive accumulation of reports consists of more than 3000 titles, three-fourths of which appeared after 1975.

There was so much information available, and so little in the way of synthesis and evaluation, that Julius B. Richard, then Surgeon General, suggested that such a synthesis and evaluation of the scientific literature be undertaken by the National Institute of Mental Health (NIMH). That agency had provided leadership and had sponsored research in the area for more than a decade. Indeed, it had directed the massive *Television and Social Behavior* project published in 1972. The new project began in early 1979. It was headed by Dr. David Pearl, Chief, Behavioral Sciences Research Branch, Division of Extramural Research Programs, National Institute of Mental Health. Seven consultants were selected to advise and work the NIMH staff on this project. Some of the consultants were media specialists, others were behavioral scientists, child development researchers, or mental health experts. The Advisory Group played a key part in the entire review process. The nature of the report was influenced by several early decisions. First, because of the large body of existing literature, no new studies would be undertaken for the project. Instead, the project commissioned comprehensive and integrative reviews of the existing literature to present the state of the art in coherent and unified form. Second, it was decided to focus on a much broader spectrum of television and behavior than what was offered by the 1972 report. Although the effects of televised violence on aggressive behavior among children would continue to be of interest, it would receive much less emphasis in the new project. The new report was to be given the lengthy title *Television and Behavior: Ten Years of Scientific Progress and Implications for the Eighties*. Decisions on areas to be covered and on the selection of scientists responsible for those areas were based on the recommendations of the Advisory Group.

ORGANIZATION OF THE REPORT

Two volumes were prepared, both edited by David Pearl, Lorraine Bouthilet, and Joyce Lazar, all of NIMH. Volume I is a summary of the major conclusions report intended for public consumption, while Volume II is a lengthy and detailed technical work intended for the research community. It consists of 24 separate reports prepared by independent researchers and 6 introductory papers prepared by the consultants, making a total of 30 reports and papers. The independent researchers who prepared the comprehensive and critical syntheses of the scientific literature were among the most knowledgeable researchers in communications research. Each prepared summaries in their own areas of specialization. The NIMH staff and consultants then provided comments and suggestions to the authors for revisions. However, the Advisory Group did not impose its opinions and values on the authors; it simply assumed an editorial function in regard to the clarity and soundness of each paper. Thus, the reports are independent products of the authors, representing their own surveys of the scientific literature as well as their evaluation, and in some cases, their own work. Even though no new research was commissioned especially for this project, research findings published for the first time are presented in some of the papers. The emphasis, however, is on review and evaluation of the existing relevant scientific literature.

It should be noted that much of the research reported was conducted with children and adolescent subjects; however, the 1982 report, unlike the 1972 report, is not limited to the influences of the medium on youth. The two reports do share an emphasis on entertainment programming. The rationale behind this focus is that such programs are those watched by most of the audience most of the time. Thus, television news and news reporting are generally not covered, nor is public affairs programming emphasized.

In general, the 1982 report covers seven broad areas of media research. These areas are: (1) television and health; (2) violence and aggression; (3) prosocial behavior; (4) cognitive and affective aspects of viewing; (5) the family and interpersonal relations; (6) social beliefs and social behavior; and (7) television's effects on American society. Obviously, all of these broad areas contain many important subareas. Each will be examined in some detail.

As has been indicated, this summary and evaluation of research was massive, to say the least. We have noted that it covers 90 percent of all research that has ever been published on the influence of television on social behavior. It was not possible to review all the findings of this milestone project in one chapter. Therefore, for purposes of the present book, we decided to devote two separate chapters to the work. Furthermore, the organization of materials in the original report was developed for needs rather different from those of the present book, and it was necessary to regroup the material into a somewhat different sequence. For those reasons, the present chapter is devoted to that material most closely related to the earlier Surgeon General's report, while Chapter 15 presents a review of those additional topics that were identified as important in the second project. In the present chapter, we review research findings and generalizations dealing with violence and aggression, prosocial behavior, plus various cognitive and affective aspects of television. Chapter 15, which follows, is devoted to television and health, television and the family, social beliefs and social behavior, plus television's effect on American institutions.

VIOLENCE AND AGGRESSION

In general, the section on aggression and violence in Volume II continues the long-term debate concerning the relationship between televised violence and aggressive behavior. What is new is that an attempt is made to settle the issue. In addition to the introductory article, four other papers are devoted to the issue. The history of the violence controversy is reviewed in one paper, while the remaining three focus on the following: (1) trends in violent content; (2) measurement of violence; (3) effects of TV violence; and (4) what processes produce the relationship between televised violence and aggression? The report on the fourth issue assumes that there is a positive relationship between televised violence and aggression, a conclusion that all the reports, with one major exception, support.

History of the Violence Controversy

Since the early days of television in the 1950s, the greatest single concern of the public about the medium has revolved around the issue of violence and its effect on behavior, especially with respect to children. As discussed in Chapters 11 and 12, two separate federal efforts have been devoted to the investigation of the problem of television violence. These efforts took place in the late 1960s and early 1970s: one was the National Commission on the Causes and Prevention of Violence and the other was the Surgeon General's Scientific Advisory Committee on Television and Social Behavior. Both groups reported a link between TV violence and aggressive behavior. Yet the question of TV violence and its effect remained controversial. Perhaps some of the controversy resulted from the cautious conclusion of the Surgeon General's Committee, which appeared to lead to different interpretations of the research results. Indeed, most newspaper writers and critics reported that television had no effect on aggressive behavior, whereas many but not all social scientists considered that a link between TV and violence had been established.

> Most television researchers look at the totality of evidence and conclude, as did the Surgeon General's Advisory Committee, that the *convergence* of most of the findings about televised violence and later aggressive behavior by the viewer supports the positive conclusion of a causal relationship. A few researchers, looking at each piece of research individually and finding flaws in design and/or methodology, conclude that the case has not been made for a causal relationship. [1]

In addition, as discussed in Chapter 12, other controversies, such as the makeup of the Committee, arose to cloud the scientific issues.

So, in fact, the question of the effects of TV violence remained unresolved in many people's minds. Moreover, it is likely that the public lost some confidence in the ability of social scientists to resolve the issue. Yet, concern over the relationship between violence and TV viewing did not die, and the year 1975 brought several new developments. For one thing, Congress took up the question of violence on television along with its investigation of obscenity and sexual provocation and pressured the Federal Communications Commission (FCC) to "do something." As a result, the FCC commissioners negotiated with the networks for the establishment of "family viewing hours" in the early evening. Writers and producers, however, challenged the arrangement on the grounds that it violated First Amendment rights and infringed on their right of trade. The courts ruled for the artists, but the networks continued the family hour on an informal basis.

At about the same time, citizen groups began raising protests against some programming practices. Broadcasters should reduce the amount of violence, said the American Medical Association, because it threatened the social health of the country. The National Parent-Teachers Association began monitoring television content and sponsored public forums concerning its effects throughout the country. In addition, an activist group called the National Citizens Committee for Broadcasting began linking advertisers with violent content. This resulted in some advertisers acting to reduce their association with violent programming. Additionally, a 1980 national survey indicated that violence on television continued to concern the American public; 70 percent of the respondents indicated that there was too much violence and that it was a "serious" or "very serious" problem.[2] As a result of this public concern and protests by citizen groups, all three major networks became involved in research on the social influence of the medium. Their approach, however, was in many ways reminiscent of the tobacco industry's efforts to solve their image problems through research. It was aimed at gathering evidence supporting their claims.

Effects of Televised Violence

Most researchers seem to agree that there is a causal relationship between televised violence and later aggressive behavior. That conclusion was significantly strengthened by research in the decade following the publication of the original Surgeon General's report. Indeed, in the following years, several important *field* studies found that televised violence results in aggressive behavior. The emphasis was on field studies, since the violence-aggression connection was well established in the laboratory and according to researcher L. Rowell Huesmann was "beyond challenge at this point".[3] Much more controversial were the data collected outside the laboratory. The argument being: If there is no effect in the "real world" (as opposed to a laboratory setting), then there is no major impact upon society.

Studies Linking Violence-Viewing and Aggression. J.L. Singer and D.G. Singer carried out two independent investigations that involved three- and four-year-old children over the course of a one-year period.[4] They carefully measured a number of variables at four different points in time. The Singers concluded that the children's television viewing at home was definitely related to the various types of behavior they showed during free-play periods at daycare centers. They found consistent associations between heavy viewing of violent television programs and unwarranted aggressive behavior in the children's free-play. Indeed, a variety of different multivariate analyses of their data all lead to the same conclusion—"television viewing, particularly violence viewing, is a cause of heightened aggressiveness in children of that age."[5]

Another study of special significance is a five-year longitudinal study by E.D. McCarthy and associates.[6] In this research, data from 732 children were obtained that clearly supported the hypothesis that viewing television violence is related to aggressive behavior. In fact, all their data on children's aggressive conduct (e.g., fighting with peers, conflict with parents, delinquency) were positively correlated with viewing violence on TV. They also found that the total amount of television viewed was positively related to aggressive behavior. This finding was particularly interesting because older studies (see Chapter 12) had found no relationship between total amount of viewing and aggression. Moreover, several other recent studies have reported the same findings.[7]

Another long-term study by researchers Eron and Heusmann collected extensive data on children in several countries.[8] At the time of the report, results were available for grade-school children in the United States, Finland, and Poland. As Table 14.1 indicates, in each of these countries significant positive relationships were found between television violence and aggression for *both* boys and girls. In earlier studies (see Chapter 12) the relationship was found only for boys. (Perhaps the appearance of more aggressive female role models for girls was a critical factor.) Additionally, the simple frequency of television also correlated highly with aggression.

One other study should be mentioned if for no other reason than that it was funded by the Columbia Broadcasting System.[9] William Belson collected data on 1650 teenage boys in London. Although his data were not longitudinal, he concluded on the basis of analysis of matched subgroups, that "the evidence . . . is very supportive of the hypothesis that high exposure to television violence increases the degree to which boys engage in serious violence."[10]

In summary, it should be noted that these are only a few of the studies that establish a link between televised violence and aggressive behavior. Moreover,

TABLE 14.1. CORRELATIONS BETWEEN TELEVISION VIOLENCE VIEWING AND PEER-NOMINATED AGGRESSION

	All Subjects	Males	Females
U.S.A. ($N = 758$):			
1st grade	.212****	.160*	.210***
2nd grade	.234****	.204**	.245****
3rd grade	.232****	.191**	.205**
4th grade	.224****	.184*	.260****
5th grade	.261****	.199*	.294****
Finland ($N = 220$):			
1st grade	.141	.026	.139
2nd grade	.163	.266*	.022
3rd grade	.257***	.038	.052
4th grade	.228*	.381***	—.158
Poland ($N = 237$):			
1st grade	.227**	.296**	.070
3rd grade	.293****	.259**	.236*

$p > $ *.05. $p > $ **.025. $p > $ ***.01. $p > $ ****.005.

Source: David Pearl, Lorraine Bouthilet, and Joyce Lazar, eds., *Television and Behavior: Ten Years of Scientific Progress and Implications for the Eighties,* Vol II (Washington, D.C.: Government Printing Office, 1982) p. 128.

at least three researchers have recently compiled summaries of existing research that relates violence viewing to aggression. While such compilations have their flaws, they convincingly show the "overwhelming nature of the evidence for a positive relation between violence viewing and aggression."[11]

Conflicting Evidence. Yet, not all people nor even all social scientists agree that there is a causal relationship between televised violence and aggressive behavior. Indeed, the concept of causality in the social sciences has also been the object of much analysis. Because it is a complex concept, there is no single, unassailable theory or approach; inferential errors may occur in either direction. In one case, a likely causal relationship may be rejected because the researcher employs too rigorous a standard of judgment. Likewise, a questionable relationship may be accepted because of a weak standard. In any event, much of the dispute about the meaning of research on violence and aggression stems from such differences in judgment.

One major study that has added fuel to the causality debate as well as the one over violence is by J. Ronald Milavsky and associates.[12] It appears as one of the papers in this volume. The results of this major study were first published in the *Television and Behavior* report, although a more detailed book appeared later. The Milavsky study was sponsored and carried by the National Broadcasting Company (NBC). In fact, all of its authors were employed by NBC's Department of Social Research. The Study was designed as a panel survey, covering a three-year period (1970–1973), and some 3200 young people were interviewed as part of the project. Data were collected on both elementary school boys and girls as well as teenage high school boys. The study focused on "purposive aggression," which was defined as "physical or verbal acts intended or known in advance to cause injury to others, rather than on rough play or accidents that might result in injury as an unintended or unforeseen consequence."[13] This definition is obviously more restrictive than those used in other research.

The researchers measured aggression in elementary school children six times during a three-year period; the high school boys were measured five times. These measures were "peer nominations" for the elementary students and "self-reports" for the teens. Both groups of students reported on which television programs they watched. However, for purposes of analysis, the investigators chose only those programs that they could classify as violent. The researchers obtained small positive correlations between measurements taken at the same time, but none between those taken at different times. The finding of small correlations in same time measurements is consistent with the results from other cross-sectional studies.

The investigators wanted to learn whether the effects of television were short-term or whether they had cumulative effects and produced consistent behavior patterns in real world settings. The study, however, provided "no evidence that television violence was causally implicated in the development of aggressive behavior patterns in children and adolescents over the time periods studied."[14] Thus, while the authors did not disagree that viewing violence on TV is associated with short-term aggressive behavior, they found no relationship between patterns of aggressive behavior and televised violence. They concluded that the effects are not cumulative or long-term. Yet, at the same time, they correctly limit their findings to the time and circumstances of that particular study.

It is not difficult to predict that this study, with its wealth of data, would provoke much discussion. It stands in opposition to a large body of cumulative evidence that indicates a relationship between televised violence and aggressive behavior. Besides, even though the study was carefully planned and methodologically sophisticated, critics were quick to criticize the statistical model used to test the hypotheses. As Eli Rubenstein argued: "Milavsky and his colleagues chose to establish causality in accord with a statistical model whose complexity and relative newness will permit honest differences of opinion about its appropriateness for this extensive set of data."[15]

All the other papers, however, argue that there is a *positive* relationship between viewing televised violence and aggressive behavior. Indeed, L. Rowell Huesmann concludes that:

> While the strength of the relation changes as a function of situational determinants, population characteristics, and measurement techniques, the evidence seems overwhelming that television violence viewing and aggression are positively correlated in children.[16]

What Produces the Relationship Between TV Violence and Aggression?

Many researchers do not now question the validity of the relationship between viewing violence and aggressive behavior. Instead, they argue that researchers must move beyond it to the real issue of what processes produce that relationship. Four different possibilities have been suggested: observational learning, attitude changes, physiological arousal, and justification processes.

Observational Learning. According to the observational learning model, children learn to behave aggressively from watching violent actors on television the same way that they learn cognitive and social skills from watching parents, siblings, peers, and others. Bandura's original experiment (discussed in Chapter 12) suggested the validity of the thesis and, although observational learning had been successfully demonstrated in the laboratory many times, questions remain about its role in field settings. Indeed, it was not until 1977 that the results of a longitudinal study were first published in the area. Its findings provided substantial evidence for observational learning as the most plausible explanation for the link between televised violence and aggressive behavior. Since then, several other field studies have concurred with those findings. These field studies have clarified the way that observational learning may be linked to other factors. Some of the findings, for example, indicate that observational learning is most likely related to age; specifically, it is a significant factor for young children, but it loses some importance in adolescence. Research indicated that children as young as two years were facile at imitating televised behaviors and, in fact, some imitation was observed in even younger children.

Another factor frequently believed to be implicated in observational learning is the extent of the viewer's identification with the actor or actress being modeled. However, it cannot be assumed that girls will identify with female actors or that black children identify with black actors. Indeed, some research has indicated that girls as well as boys are more likely to identify with male actors; likewise, at least some black children tend to identify with white actors. Generally speaking, we can say that a child is most likely to imitate a model perceived to possess realistic and valued characteristics.

Along these lines, some researchers have recently attempted to tie observational learning more closely to cognitive-processing psychology. Researchers Tulving and Thompson's concept of encoding *specificity* in human memory seems particularly relevant. They argued that the likelihood of an item being recalled depends upon the specific encoding context (acquisition context) being reproduced, including even apparently irrelevant aspects. The major idea is that forms of aggressive behavior can be elicited by the presence of specific cues in the environment—cues that were also present in the televised violence. Indeed, in one study, a number of cases were analyzed in which juveniles seem to have imitated specific criminal acts portrayed on television; e.g., the Boston incident in which a gang burned a woman to death.[17] In each instance, it was found that highly specific visual cues present in the television program (e.g., a woman carrying a bright red gasoline can) were also present in the environment in which imitated behavior occurred.

Overall, the research on observational learning and cognitive processes suggests that children who watch large numbers of aggressive behaviors on television programs may store, and at a later time retrieve and perform, those behaviors when appropriate cues (from the portrayals) are present. Even aspects of the scene that seem irrelevant (e.g., color) may be the triggering cues. The recall of an aggressive behavior that provides a solution to a problem a child faces may lead to modeling of that behavior in the child.

Attitude Change. Another way in which television violence is thought to exert its influence on children (as well as adults) is by influencing their attitudes. Research indicates the more televised violence a child watches, the more favorable is the child's attitude toward aggressive behavior. Overall, attitudes of heavy television viewers toward aggression tend to be more positive than those of lighter viewers because heavy viewers perceive that aggressive behavior is the norm. In fact, it has been found that the more aggressive a subject is, the more aggressive he or she thinks others are.

A major study, using a longitudinal design, found that children's attitudes toward aggression could be changed if adults discussed the program with them.[18] Heavy-viewing children were selected and randomly divided into experimental and control groups. The children in the experimental group were exposed over the next two years to two treatments designed to mitigate the effects of television violence. The first treatment was begun at the start of the second year; three small group sessions were held in which the investigators tried to teach the subjects how unrealistic television violence was. The children viewed brief excerpts from violent shows and participated in a highly structured discussion of the actors' behaviors. The control group viewed nonviolent educational excerpts, followed by discussion of their content.

In addition, the researchers used a more formal attitude change procedure at the beginning of the third year. They had each experimental subject write a paragraph on "Why TV violence is unrealistic and why viewing too much of it is bad." In two sessions, the children in the experimental group wrote the paragraph, received suggestions and rewrote it, were taped reading the paragraph, and watched a television tape of themselves and their classmates reading the paragraphs. The subjects were told that the tapes were going to be shown to school children in Chicago. The control group made a tape about "What you did last summer."

Six months after the final experimental session, the last data were collected on all the children. The mean peer-nominated aggression score for the experimental group became significantly lower than the score for the control group, as indicated by Table 14.2. In addition, the viewing of violence was a much more important predictor of aggressive behavior for the control group than for the experimental group. In short, the experimental group was much less aggressive than the control group. Since the children were randomly assigned to each group, the researchers concluded that the changes in the children's attitudes were the result of their intervention.

Not every single study during the 10-year period found a positive relationship between viewing violence and positive attitudes toward aggression, but it was concluded that *overall* the evidence suggested that television violence can change one's attitudes toward aggression and that one's attitudes in turn influence one's behavior. At the same time, we should point out that the cognitive paradigm on which this type of interpretation rests has not been particularly fruitful in the study of the effects of the media (See Chapter 17).

Arousal Processes. Some researchers hypothesize that arousal processes are the intervening factor between viewing violence and attitude change. However,

TABLE 14.2. EFFECT OF THE INTERVENTION ON MEAN LEVEL OF AGGRESSION OVER
THE COURSE OF 1 YEAR

		Mean Peer-Nominated Aggression (Peeragg)		
		Before (1978)		*After (1979)*
Experimental Group ($N = 59$)		154.0		175.3
Placebo Group ($N = 58$)		158.0		242.8
Analysis of Covariance	**Source**	**df**	**F**	**Signif.**
Covariates				
	Sex	1	1.23	—
	Grade	1	0.00	—
	Peeragg 1978	1	61.12	.001
Effects				
	Group	1	6.40	.013
Error		112		
Total		116		

Source: David Pearl, Lorraine Bouthilet, and Joyce Lazar, eds., *Television and Behavior: Ten Years of Scientific Progress and Implications for the Eighties,* Vol. II (Washington, D.C.: Government Printing Office, 1982) p. 133.

there is a great deal of confusion about the nature of arousal. Some researchers argue that television is making children hyperactive by "overloading" them with stimulation, while others claim that television is anesthetizing children by "overloading" them with stimulation. However, there has been a great deal of interest in what has been considered a major consequence of arousal—desensitization. For example, boys who regularly watched a heavy diet of television violence showed less physiological arousal when they looked at new violent programs than did control subjects.[19] While such findings are difficult to replicate in field studies, it should not be a great surprise that emotional and physiological responsiveness to scenes of violence habituates in a manner similar to other responses. Arousal will be discussed in more detail in a later section.

Justification Processes. According to this hypothesis, people who are aggressive like to watch violent television because they can use it to justify their own behavior as being normal. The process is similar to attitude change but it operates in the opposite direction. In this view, watching television violence does not stimulate the child's aggressiveness; it results from it. Because aggressive behavior should make a child feel guilty, the guilt can be relieved if aggression is normal. Thus, a child who behaves aggressively watches violent television shows to justify his or her own aggressiveness. However, so little research has been done testing this hypothesis that at the present time it cannot be evaluated.

Catharsis Theory. In direct opposition to the previous approaches, catharsis theory posits that aggression will be *reduced* after watching violence on television. Through catharsis the need or desire to be aggressive is supposed to be dissipated by watching violent television. However, since almost all the evidence points to an increase in aggressive behavior, rather than a decrease, the theory is contradicted by the data.

In general, then, researchers have moved beyond the question of whether or not there is a positive relationship between viewing TV violence and aggressive behavior. Currently, many are now investigating a number of theories that may explain what produces the relationship. Five potential processes are currently under study: observational learning, attitude change, emotional and physiological arousal, catharsis, and justification processes. The weight of the evidence strongly suggests that observational learning and attitude change induced by television violence are contributing to the positive relationship. Meanwhile, the concept of arousal remains an attractive possibility. Significant relations between arousal, television violence, and aggression have been found. Future research will seek to clarify exactly what role arousal processes play in aggressive behavior. The justification hypothesis remains essentially untested. Finally, the available data convincingly contradict the catharsis model. There is no evidence that vicarious participation in aggression obtained by watching it on TV reduces aggressive behavior. On the contrary, the evidence suggests that it actually increases the likelihood of aggressive acts.

Methodological Issues in the Study of Televised Violence

Another complex and controversial aspect of research on televised violence deals with methodological issues. Just how do we define, measure, and analyze television violence itself? As authors Nancy Signiorelli and associates point out: "Over the past twenty years, violence has probably been defined almost as many times as it has been studied."[20] However, a key element in the evaluation of the relationship between violence and aggression is an objective and reliable measure of violence on television.

Measurement of Violence. There have been two basic ways in which researchers have assessed violence in television programs. These are through the use of: (1) content analyses using trained coders and specific rules and definition and (2) rating or consensual measures in which people rate the amount of violence in programs. The raters may be television researchers, television critics, or "ordinary people." Even children have been used as raters. Sometimes definitions of violence are given to the raters, but many investigators believe that definitions are not necessary. The longest and most extensive content analysis of television programs is the Cultural Indicators Project developed by George Gerbner and his colleagues. The project has two parts. The first is the "message system analysis," which consists of an annual content analysis of one week of prime time and weekend daytime dramatic programs. Gerbner calls the second "cultivation analysis." It is concerned with determining conceptions of social reality that television programming may foster in viewers.

It would almost seem a truism that all assessments of violence must begin by defining it. While there are differences among the various definitions, all include physical force, killing, or injuring. Some definitions include psychological violence; others do not. Some also include violence against property, accidents, and that portrayed in the comics. A few even include acts of nature, such as floods and earthquakes. (The rationale for including "acts of nature" is that writers and producers have deliberately put in violent "natural" events.) Thus, the amount of violence reported to be in a program will depend greatly on the definition being used. However, it should be noted that neither the Cultural Indicators Project nor CBS (the two major analysts of televised violence) includes psychological violence, damage to property, or acts of nature in their definitions.

Another definitional problem is that of the "unitization" of violence—that is, when does it begin and when does it end? In other words, in order to count the number of violent actions, it is necessary to know when a violent action starts and stops. Although any decision in this area is somewhat arbitrary, it is the researcher's task to operationalize the decision in the most appropriate way. In the tradition of content analysis research, the Cultural Indicators Project states that a "violent action is a scene of some violence confined to the same participants. Any change in the cast of characters starts another episode."[21] CBS defines a violent action in an apparently similar manner. In this case, it is: "One sustained, dramatically continuous event involving violence, with essentially the same group of participants and with no major interruption in continuity."[22]

The primary difference in the two definitions is the word "essentially" in the CBS instructions; it makes the definition more ambiguous. Moreover, since the criteria for determining the "essential" set of agents are not specified, the CBS study seems to permit an unnecessarily subjective manipulation of the unit of analysis. In fact, the instructions to coders are rather vague on this issue, stating that:

> A violent incident is not absolutely synonymous with an "act." One incident might include brief breaks in the action, as in a protracted chase scene, interrupted by pauses for regrouping and reloading, or acts of violence by more than one person, as, for example, in a fight scene involving several people.[23]

Because of these definitional differences, the findings of these two major studies are different. However, they differ in a predictable way. That is, CBS finds much less violence than does the Cultural Indicators Project.

The Violence Index Controversy. Another area of controversy concerns the Violence Index developed by the Cultural Indicators Project, which has been reported annually since 1967. It should be noted that indices are widely used for a variety of purposes. For example, most Americans are aware of such examples as the Dow Jones Index of stock values, the Consumer Price Index, and the Pollution Index. In short, the usefulness of an index lies in its ability to reduce a broad array of data to a single number that can be used in making cross-sectional and trend comparisons.

An index has been defined as "a type of composite measure that summarizes several specific observations and represents some more general dimension."[24] The Cultural Indicators Project's Violence Index is composed of three sets of direct observational data: the prevalence, rate, and role of violence. Prevalence is the percentage of programs in a particular sample containing any violence. Rate, on the other hand, is the frequency of violent actions in units of programming and in units of time so that we can look at rate per hour or rate per program. Finally, role is defined as the portrayal of characters as violent offenders or victims of violence or both. From this measure we could calculate the percentage of violent characters out of all characters in a show or sample of shows, or the percent of victims out of all characters in a program or sample as well as various other items of information.

There has been a lengthy controversy about this index; even its users agree that it is arbitrary. However, that is true of all indices. Moreover, CBS criticizes the Violence Index as being faulty on exactly the grounds that make it an index; i.e., it includes a set of measures rather than only a single indicator. Their argument is that the number of violent actions may change unexplainably because the different measures may move in different directions. But this criticism does not wash; much the same could be said of any set of comprehensive indicators such as the GNP, the Dow-Jones, and many labor statistics. Criticisms notwithstanding, the Violence Index is useful to illustrate trends and to facilitate comparisons.

Trends in Television Violence

What, then, are the major trends in the portrayal of violence on television that can be identified from the data of the Cultural Indicators Project? Is such violence increasing or decreasing? Perhaps the most notable characteristic of televised violence is its overall stability and regularity, despite fluctuations by network, genre, and time period. Indeed, the percentage of programs containing violence has been quite consistent since the index was first used in 1967. Table 14.3 shows that during the years 1967–1979, there were no significant differences in the proportion of programs that include violence, whether we look at the entire sample, at prime time, or at weekend daytime.

Basically, the number of violent acts per program tells a similar story, but there are important exceptions by time period. Overall, for all TV shows, the yearly means show no significant differences. But for prime-time programs, we see a significant trend—there is a pattern of increases in the number of violent

TABLE 14.3. PERCENT OF PROGRAMS CONTAINING VIOLENCE AND NUMBER OF
VIOLENT ACTS PER HOUR (1967–1979)

Year	Percent of Programs Containing Violence			Number of Violent Acts per Program		
	All Programs	Prime Time	Weekend-Daytime	All Programs	Prime Time	Weekend-Daytime
1967	81.3	75.0	93.8	4.98	5.11	4.72
1968	81.6	75.4	93.3	4.53	3.89	5.73
1969	83.5	70.3	98.3	5.21	3.63	6.98
1970	77.5	62.3	96.0	4.49	3.31	5.92
1971	80.6	75.8	87.8	4.69	3.85	5.95
1972	79.0	71.7	90.0	5.39	4.90	6.13
1973	72.7	59.7	94.9	5.29	4.47	6.68
1974	83.3	77.6	92.1	5.44	5.66	5.11
1975*	78.1	66.7	94.9	5.38	5.51	5.18
1975	78.4	69.7	91.1	5.64	5.47	5.89
1976*	76.5	67.7	89.4	4.86	5.22	4.34
1976	89.1	80.3	100.0	6.18	5.61	6.90
1977**	76.9	66.2	90.6	5.20	5.46	4.87
1978	84.7	74.6	97.9	5.79	4.52	7.46
1979	80.9	70.3	91.9	4.98	5.37	4.58
Total	80.3	70.8	93.6	5.21	4.81	5.77
Significance of differences between means	.38	.47	.47	.61	.32	.001
Significance of linearity	.74	.92	.83	.09	.02	.29
Significance of deviations from linearity	.32	.40	.40	.77	.69	.000

* Spring sample; all others are fall sample
**Does not include second week of prime time programming used in sampling experiment
Total *N* = 1603 programs (935 prime time, 668 weekend-daytime)
Source: David Pearl, Lorraine Bouthilet and Joyce Lazar, eds., *Television and Behavior: Ten Years of Scientific Progress and Implications for the Eighties*, Vol. II (Washington, D.C.: Government Printing Office, 1982) p. 168.

acts per program. There were relatively few violent acts between 1968 and 1971, but the mean number of violent acts per program has not been less than 4.4 since 1971. Thus, the changes that have occurred in last decade have been in the direction of more violent acts on prime-time programs. On the other hand, children's shows (weekend-daytime) show a significant nonlinear trend. There is a cyclical regularity in the number of violent acts. First it is up; then it is down; then it's up again. Moreover, the fluctuations seem to be getting more extreme. The 1978 figure was the highest, whereas the 1979 figure is the second lowest. In general, however, the amount of violence in television remains remarkably consistent. The television industry, obviously, did not live up to their earlier promises to reduce the amount of violent content in programming. In fact, at this point in time it is probably unrealistic to take seriously the industry's promises to reduce the levels of violence portrayed in their content.

PROSOCIAL BEHAVIOR

During the decade of the 1970s, considerable research examined whether or not television content could produce prosocial behavior—the obverse of the television-aggression linkage. After all, if viewing violence could produce aggression, then it followed logically that viewing altruistic, friendly, or cooperative situations should result in prosocial behavior. Prosocial was defined as that which is "socially desirable and which in some way benefits another person or society at large."[25] This definition obviously involves a value judgment based on the wider social context.

Observational learning theory, which we have seen is often linked with the violence issue, has been applied to prosocial behavior. According to the theory, television can have diverse effects—depending on the content of what is watched. Indeed, if one of the main ways in which people learn is by observing others, then it follows that people should learn a variety of behaviors by viewing others on television. Television does provide its viewers with access to a very wide range of observational learning experiences.

Researcher J. Philipe Rushton has categorized television content that is prosocial into four types: (1) altruistic, which includes such behaviors as generosity, helping, and cooperation; (2) friendly behavior; (3) self-control behavior, which includes resisting temptations and delaying gratification; and (4) portrayed behavior that helps adults and children cope with fears. Rushton reviewed 42 studies. Some were laboratory experiments, while others were carried out in field settings. Nonetheless, results from both types of studies came to similar conclusions.

Altruism
The studies that address altruism agree that children who watch this type of behavior on television become more altruistic themselves. For example, in a series of experiments, several hundred boys and girls from six to nine years old were shown five-minute videotapes in which a child played a bowling game and won gift certificates.[26] On one of the tapes, the character donated the certificate to charity; on the other set the character did not. Subsequently, the children were watched through a one-way mirror to see how much of their winnings they donated to a similar charity. The results showed that children were strongly influenced by what they had seen on television, and modeling of altruistic

behavior was clearly demonstrated. Children who had watched generosity on the videotape gave more of their certificates to the charity than those who had watched selfishness portrayed.

Several other studies, using similar procedures, have replicated these findings. One study found that children from five to seven years old were influenced by television models to share both candy and money.[27] Moreover, these findings are not limited to American children. Another study showed that eight- to ten-year-old British children were influenced to donate tokens to a charity by watching television models do so.[28] Critics, however, point out that these studies all took place in a laboratory setting and that the laboratory is not like the typical television-watching situation. However, field studies have been carried out (eight such studies were reviewed by Rushton). While the results were not as clear-cut, the totality of results from these studies supports the conclusion that altruistic behavior can be learned by watching televised models who display such patterns.

Friendly Behavior

All of the seven studies of friendly behavior described in this report used nursery school children as subjects. Both laboratory studies (N=2) and naturalistic ones (N=5) were included. For example, a 1976 study carried out in Canada investigated whether prosocial television content could increase young children's friendliness toward ethnic minorities.[29] After viewing special Sesame Street inserts containing nonwhite children, a sample of children who were three, four, and five years old showed a strong preference for playing with minority children as opposed to white ones. Children who had not seen the special program inserts did not show such preferences. The children, all English Canadian, also watched inserts with a French Canadian boy and indicated an equally strong preference for him after seeing the special program inserts. Again, the control group showed no such preference.

The goal of one very dramatic field study was to see if television programs could be used to enhance social interaction among nursery school children who tended to isolate themselves from their peers.[30] Thirteen extremely solitary children were selected for this study. One group of these isolated children viewed a specially prepared film shown over a television console. The film portrayed several scenes in which children interacted in a nursery school setting and were rewarded for it. For comparison purposes, a control group of children watched a film about dolphins. The results were, to say the least, dramatic. Children who viewed the televised scenes increased the number of their interactions with others from an average of two per day to an average of twelve per day. The control group, on the other hand, showed no increase in their interaction with other children. A follow-up at the end of the school year indicated that the changes were durable over time—the subjects were still interacting with other children.

Self-Control

Most of the studies on the effects of showing self-control behaviors on television are laboratory experiments. However, some field studies have been done. One example is a 1972 study in which girls who were eight and nine years old were told the rules of an electronic bowling game. They were also told that they could win money by scoring high.[31] Before playing the game, the children watched a television program in which they saw a young girl model playing the same game. Some of the girls, however, saw a film in which the model broke the rules in order to win money. The other girls viewed a film that was identical except that the model abided by the rules. The results were as expected; the girls who saw cheating on the film cheated twice as often as the other girls.

Some studies looked at a particular form of self-control, in the form of delayed gratification. For example, in a 1974 New Zealand study, 72 children who were eight years old were used as subjects to determine if viewing television could affect patterns of delayed gratification.[32] The normal behavior of the children was established by asking them if they would prefer a small reward, such as money, immediately, or a larger one by waiting for seven days. Later, some of the children watched television programs showing an adult female model engaging in delayed gratification behavior and explaining why she had acted in such a manner. The control group of children did not view such programs. The results showed that the children who had watched the examples of delayed gratification were subsequently more likely to choose to delay their gratification for a larger reward. Moreover, when the children were retested four weeks later, their behavior still showed the effects of the exposure to the television films.

Effects of Showing People Coping with Their Fears

Fourteen studies that show the capability of televised presentations to modify people's fears were included in the report. Some of the studies used adult subjects, while others worked with children.

One pioneering study dealt with young children who ranged from three to five years old.[33] These children were all afraid of dogs. To determine which children were afraid of the cocker spaniel dog used in the study, the researchers measured their willingness to approach and play with it on several occasions. Then, over an eight-day period, some of the children were shown eight three-minute film programs showing other children playing with dogs. A control group of similarly fearful children saw movies of Disneyland. The children were then given the chance to approach a live dog. Previously fearful children who viewed the film with the dog were more likely to approach and play with the dogs than were the children in the control group. In addition, the reduction in fear generalized to dogs quite different from those seen in the film, and the reduction remained when they were retested four weeks later. Similar results were obtained by other researchers using young children and a large German shepherd dog as the film stimulus.[34] Although both groups of children showed high levels of fear in the pretest, eight of the nine boys in a film group were subsequently willing to approach, pet, and feed the live German shepherd dog. In contrast, only three of the nine boys in the control group did so.

Bandura and his associates studied the influence of film programs on fear of snakes in adolescents and adults.[35] Only persons whose dread of snakes was so severe that it interfered with activities such as camping and gardening were tested. The subjects watched a 35-minute film in which children, adolescents, and adults interacted with a king snake. The results were clear: those who watched the film were significantly less fearful. Indeed, the behavioral measurements of fear were stringent and involved actually holding a snake and allowing it in their laps unrestrained. These findings were replicated in 1973.

Another interesting study involved 60 children age four to six who were preparing to undergo elective surgery for hernias, tonsillectomies, or urinary-genital tract difficulties.[36] The goal of the study was to reduce their fears about the surgery. The children were divided into two groups and were shown either a film of a child being hospitalized and receiving surgery or an unrelated control film. The treatment film depicted various events that hospitalized children encounter. Although both groups received extensive preparation by the hospital staff, there was a significant reduction of preoperative (night before) and postoperative (3 to 4 weeks postsurgery examination) fear arousal in the experimental group. The parents also reported more problem behavior in the children who had not seen the medical film.

It should be noted that although fourteen different studies were reviewed regarding the use of television or film presentations to help individuals cope with fear, many other studies dealing with the same subject were published during the 1970s. All reached the same conclusion: such presentations have a vast therapeutic potential.

The general conclusions regarding television and prosocial behavior seemed reasonably clear. Forty-two studies, both laboratory and field, supported the same generalization: television and film programs can modify viewers' social behavior in a prosocial direction. Friendliness, cooperation, helping, generosity, observance of rules, delayed gratification, and a lack of unreasonable fears can all be increased by the use of televised materials. J. Philipe Rushton argues that these studies "suggest that television is an effective agent of socialization, that television entertainment is modifying the viewers' perception of the world and how to live in it."[37]

There seems little doubt that people learn from watching television, and, more importantly, what they learn depends on what they watch. If viewers see prosocial behavior displayed on TV programs, then this is what will be learned as appropriate, normal behavior. If, however, aggression and antisocial behaviors are shown, then they may be judged as normative by viewers. If this seems like an extreme position then one should consider that such a view is quite consistent with the logic behind the billions of dollars spent annually by advertisers. They believe, correctly, that repeated exposure to their brief messages will change the behavior of the public toward their products.

This massive body of research clearly implies that television can no longer be viewed as mere entertainment. As a major source of observational learning experiences, it determines what people judge to be appropriate behavior in a variety of situations. Indeed, Rushton concluded "television has become one of the most important agencies of socialization that our society possesses." And, as the studies in this section indicate—television can have beneficial effects for our society; it is a potential force for good. In short, television has the power to affect the behavior of viewers in a positive, prosocial direction.

COGNITIVE AND AFFECTIVE ASPECTS OF TELEVISION

One of the key advances in research on television in the seventies was the recognition that the medium must be understood more broadly. In particular, its relation to the cognitive and affective development of children needed to be examined. Children begin to pay attention to the medium by the time they are from six to nine months old. From that point on, television is an increasingly frequent intruder into the life of a child. Today's children grow up in an environment where television talks, entertains, and promotes products for their consumption. They must organize these experiences along with those of the physical and social environment.

Just how does TV affect the cognitive growth of children who often spend more time watching television than they spend in school or in conversation with adults or siblings? Also, to what extent do the structural properties of television as a medium influence the way new information from other environments is processed? It may be that the very nature of thinking itself is being modified by the heavy visual stimulation that characterizes regular viewing.

The broad field of television and its relation to cognitive and emotional functioning includes many topics: cognitive processing, effects of the forms and codes of television technology, physiological arousal in television viewing, and emotional development and functioning. In the following sections, a brief summary of the research in each of these areas will be examined.

Cognitive Processing

Research in the area of cognitive processes blossomed during the decade of the 1970s. Approximately 75 major books and articles were published on the topic during that period. The research reviewed for the present project examined how individuals perceived, remembered, and comprehended what was seen and heard on television; almost all of the research subjects were children.

Paying Attention to Television. A child lounges in front of a television set staring at it intently. What is attracting the child to the set? What is on the screen that has so captured the youngster's attention? In an effort to find an answer to these questions, researchers have unobtrusively observed children in a playroom with the television on, usually through a one-way mirror. In addition to the TV set, the room has toys and games that might distract the children. Researchers have been quite ingenious in the measurement techniques they have developed to measure and count accurately the times a child is watching, while at the same time keeping a record of what is on the screen when the child is looking. The results of these studies have been informative chartings of the attention paid by children to TV as a function of attributes of the presentation, age, and individual differences.

One principle used to explain attention to television is called "attentional inertia." It has been defined as "the longer people look at the television screen the greater the probability that they will continue to look."[38] Inertia also characterizes *not* looking. "The longer children have directed their attention elsewhere, the less likely they are to begin looking at television."[39] Attentional inertia has been found in children of all ages as well as among college age adults.

Such inertial tendencies of viewers do not, however, override differences in viewing styles or the content and presentational characteristics of programs. Even among preschool children, attention varies according to the content of the presentation. In fact, the age of the child is directly related to the length of time they look at the set. Six-month-old infants gaze only occasionally at television programs, whereas at age one children actually watch about 12 percent of the time that a set is turned on. There is a dramatic jump in viewing between the ages of two and three years, rising from 25 to 45 percent of the time. Moreover, parents have confirmed these findings, indicating that their children begin to watch a lot of television at around two and a half years. By age four, children are watching about 55 percent of the time, even when they are in a playroom with many distracting toys. These figures are group averages; not all children watch the same amount. We do not know the reasons for the differences, although one study found that they were not related to intelligence or personality as measured by standard tests.

Children were also attracted to television by specific features of programs. For example, their attention was obtained and maintained by women characters, women and children's voices, auditory changes, peculiar voices, activity or movement, camera cuts, sound effects, laughing, and applause. Negative attributes—those that terminated looks at television—included voices of men, extended zooms and pans, animals, and still pictures. Auditory cues were found to have strong effects in attracting attention. Apparently, children quickly learn which sights and sounds go together, so that what may appear to be a peripheral background sound actually may be an attention-getter. For example, "chase" music implies a chase scene, which is exciting and fun to watch. Thus, children do not attend to just any content on television, rather they are psychologically active and selective, and they shift their attention according to the sense and meaning of what they see and hear.

Comprehension. When children are paying attention to the TV set, do they understand what is going on? As might be expected, there is substantial variation in comprehension, with age being the single most important factor. Young children do not appear to understand much of television's offerings. Of course, this improves with age and with general experience and knowledge of the television medium. However, young children frequently remember discrete scenes or events (actions less than a scene). What they do not understand are relations between the scenes. But older children and adults typically "chunk" programs into larger units that encompass several scenes. Flexibility in chunking appears to be a characteristic of mature perception. It is a cognitive ability that young children do not possess. This factor raises some serious questions for the television industry. For example, younger television viewers tend to focus only on acts of aggression without being able to be aware of possible cause-effect sequences. Thus, young children miss the implications of the aggression within the story line, recalling only the acts themselves. Several researchers in this area emphasized thet programming for children should pay special attention to the cognitive limitations of children in grasping cause-effect relationships.

One important implication of these findings pertains to the ways children come to like or dislike characters and, by inference, whether they imitate their behavior. For example, if children understand the relation between a character's aggressive behavior and their antisocial motives and consequences, they do not like aggressive characters. But, when they do not understand the relations between aggressive behavior and antisocial motives, they may like the television character and even model the character's behavior. Thus, children's programs should make motives and consequences clear.

Forms and Codes of Television

Historically and traditionally much of the research about television has examined the content (and its effects) rather than the form of the medium. Yet the content of the medium is not unique to the medium. Aggression, stereo-types, and prosocial behavior can be presented easily by other media or in other ways. Television, however, is a visual medium in which techniques that have no counterparts in the real world are used to produce a stream of constantly changing images. Special effects, such as camera cuts and slow motion, are used in unique ways—with sound effects, accompanying music, unusual cries and noises, canned laughter, and faceless narrators. Of course, television is also a verbal medium, but the verbal and linguistic conventions of television are not unique; they are the language conventions of the real world. However, the ways in which language is used to convey content (rather than the content it conveys) is an important *form* of television as a medium.

During the decade of the 1970s, there was new interest in studying television's form and codes (also referred to as conventions.) One of the major reasons for this interest is the belief that television effects may at least partly be the result of form as well as content. It may be that fast action, loud noises, and unusual camera effects are just as responsible for behavioral effects as is violent content. Obversely, the slow pace of some programs may be more important than content in producing prosocial conduct.

Two laboratory studies provide support for the idea that the formal features of television can instigate aggressive behavior in children, even in the absence of violent content.[40] The first study showed three different kinds of programs: one high in both violence and action, one low in violence and high in action, and one low in both. It was not possible to find a program high in violence and low in action. The second study used advertisements with different levels of salient formal features—action, pace, visual special effects—in the commercial breaks of a nonaggressive program. There was no aggression in the program or in any of the commercials. In each study, pairs of preschool children were observed in a play situation containing a variety of toys before and after viewing the experimental programs.

In spite of the diverse content and formats of the programs and commercials, both studies came to the same conclusion: children tended to be more aggressive after high-action programs than after low-action or no television program at all. Interestingly, violent content did not add to the level of aggression produced by high levels of action alone. These findings support the hypothesis that the high-action format can lead to increased aggression without the modeling effects of violent content in the same way that it aroused more attention with or without violence. One alternative interpretation of the data is that children learn to associate high action with violent control through experience with the medium. Hence, they respond to the action scenes as if they did contain violence, even though there are no explicit content cues.

It is debatable whether form and content can be clearly distinguished, even though they may be defined independently. In practice, form of presentation and content of message systematically co-occur. Thus, the two effects are confounded in real world situations, and all studies of content that attribute effects to one may also include the effects of the other. The only possibility of understanding the two and their interaction lies in theory and research that focuses on form independent of content, and vice versa.

Arousal

Research on the arousal effects of television increased during the decade of the seventies, mainly as a consequence of new theoretical concepts and better techniques of measurement. Yet, while accelerating, research in this area is still relatively limited. Arousal has been measured in several ways, depending upon the theoretical stance of the investigator. However, in three well-known theories (i.e., behavior, activation, and emotion), arousal has been defined as "a unitary force that energizes or intensifies behavior that receives direction by independent means."[41] Thus, while arousal may be conceived of as an energizer, it is *not* a guide. Usually, it simply motivates the person to act, most often in accordance with established patterns of behavior.

There is disagreement among investigators concerning the source of arousal. Some believe that arousal originates in the reticular activating system of the brain ("cortical arousal"), while others argue that the autonomic nervous system ("autonomic arousal") is the major source of arousal and emotions. Cortical arousal is involved in attention, perception, alertness, and vigilance. Autonomic arousal, on the other hand, is related to affect and the emotions. As a rule there is a high degree of correlation in the activity in the reticular and autonomic systems. However, they are measured in different ways. Cortical arousal is usually measured in alpha wave blocking on the electroencephalogram. Autonomic arousal is measured by blood pressure, heart rate, vasoconstriction (usually measured in skin temperature decrease), and skin conductance.

Television as the Unwinder. It is well documented that everyday life is highly stressful for many people. As workers return home from their busy days, millions of them turn to television as their major leisure activity. But is it because television offers relief from stress?

In terms of arousal considerations, the prediction that television relieves stress is straightforward. A person who is "uptight" maintains an inappropriately high level of arousal. This is clear from neuropsychological research. Moreover, the condition most conducive to maintaining arousal at a high level is a psychological one; it is the continued preoccupation with the events responsible for the stress—the thinking of and ruminating over the events of the day. Disruption of this "rehearsal process" should have the beneficial effect of reducing arousal and stress.

Research indicates that the "intervention potential" of television can reduce arousal. However, this effect is dependent on the content of the program. That is, if the program contains portrayals similar to the viewer's daily events, and thus rehearses them, it will not be calming. This was demonstrated by a study in which annoyed and tense adults were exposed either to violent programs or neutral, nonviolent programs.[42] As might be expected, those adults exposed to violent programs showed no reduction in the level of arousal, whereas those exposed to neutral content showed lowered arousal levels as well as reduced aggressiveness. In addition, a 1976 study found that exposure to media violence tends to perpetuate an existing propensity for aggression.[43]

We might ask, Why do people turn to television for relaxation, especially when it has so many exciting and violent programs? Recent research shows that acutely aroused people seek out shows that do not perpetuate arousal. They may choose intuitively, or on the basis of past experience, but in general, exposure to an absorbing program has a beneficial soothing effect on an irritated person. In this way, viewing helps to control antisocial behavior.

Television for Excitement. There is no doubt that exposure to television can be highly arousing and may foster intense emotional reactions. Many types of content can elevate level of arousal—suspenseful drama, sporting events, even comedy (if it creates true hilarity). Also, the portrayal of aggressive behavior can be very arousing. However, the one type of content that consistently produces the highest level of arousal in both men and women is explicit erotica.

Outside the area of entertainment programming, little is known about the arousal effects of television presentations. It may be assumed that news reports on wars, plane crashes, natural disasters, and other "bad news" foster emotional reactions that are associated with substantial increases in arousal. This assumption, however, has not yet been directly tested; but there is some research that pertains to the issue. Two studies showed that when harm-inflicting actions were believed to have actually happened, there was far more arousal for much longer periods of time than if they were believed to be fiction.[44] This suggested that news reports might be highly arousing.

Who is most likely to be aroused by watching television? Basically, people who are bored are likely to have the strongest reaction. Researcher Dolf Zillman argues that:

> . . . persons who experience low levels of arousal—because of monotonous environmental conditions, repetitive nonstrenuous tasks, or similarly unstimulating circumstances—are likely to respond more intensely than others to affect-inducing stimuli.[45]

Zillman added that persons who are initially rather unaroused can be expected to obtain more pleasure from watching television than those who are comparatively aroused. Indeed, the "unaroused" are drawn to television for "the excitement of it."

Transfer of Excitation and Its Consequences. The transfer of excitation theory proposes that already aroused persons, when stimulated to another emotional response, will become more excited than they would have without the residual arousal. Moreover, the emotions tapped need not be the same. Lingering arousal from fear may intensify anger, or sexual arousal may intensify sadness, and so forth. Of course, the person is not aware of this arousal. The theory has been supported in a number of studies.

Such arousal transfer effects can occur after exposure to television.

Aggressive behavior has been related to viewing violent scenes on TV. The effects could conceivably result from arousal or excitatory features of the scenes, rather than the violence.[46] Several studies have investigated this issue. In the first, male adults were provoked, then exposed to a neutral, an aggressive, or an erotic film. The subjects then had an opportunity to get even with their tormentor. A pretest determined that the neutral film was neither arousing nor aggressive; that the aggressive film was somewhat arousing; and that the erotic film was highly arousing but entirely nonaggressive. Thus, if aggressive cues are the critical mediators of effects on aggressive behavior, aggressiveness should be higher after exposure to the aggressive stimulus than to either of the others. However, if residual excitation from exposure to communication critically influences postexposure behavior, the intensity of aggressive reactions should be a simple function of the excitatory potential of the communications. Thus, the erotic film should produce more aggressiveness than the aggressive film, which in turn should produce more than the neutral one. The findings, displayed in Figure 14.1, confirmed the expectations based on the transfer model.

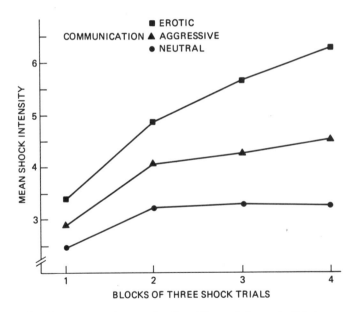

Figure 14.1. Retaliatory aggression as a function of the excitatory potential of communications. Exposure to communication was interpolated between provocation and retaliation. Excitation, measured in peripheral manifestations, was at a higher level after exposure to the erotic communication than after exposure to the aggressive communication and, in turn, at a higher level after exposure to the aggressive communication than after exposure to the neutral communication. (From Zillmann 1979; copyright 1979 by Lawrence Erlbaum Assoc.)
Source: Reprinted in D. Pearl, L. Bouthilet and J. Lazar, eds., *Television and Behavior: Ten Years of Scientific Progress and Implications for the Eighties, Vol. II* (Washington, D.C.: Government Printing Office, 1982) p. 60.

It is noteworthy that those findings have been replicated and refined.[47] Other recent studies have extended the earlier work on males to females and to mixed-sex situations.[48]

This transfer of the excitation paradigm is significant for the "winning formula" of suspenseful drama. If drama is to be an enjoyable experience— pleasant and emotional—it must rely on a previously induced distress that leaves residual excitations. The more negative the initial reaction, the more residual arousal there will be to intensify later experience. Enjoyment, then, may be greatly enhanced by residual arousal from preceding stimulation. The recognition of this principle has three interesting consequences for television:

1. Moving television drama relies on and benefits from stimuli that induce strong arousal reactions.
2. Sex and violence are proven arousal inducers; without them, dramas are likely to become unexciting and flat. For children and adults, violence arousal reactions appear to increase with the reality of its portrayal.
3. Because these arousal inducers foster exciting drama that attracts the large audiences upon which television commercially depends, any curtailment of the use of violent materials will likely result in an increased use of sexual materials, and vice-versa.

We should also keep in mind that while a heightened state of arousal *may* lead to aggressive actions on the part of the viewer, it does not always do so. The increased level of excitement may be channeled into various types of behavior, depending on the circumstances.

The Habituation Issue. During the seventies, the depiction of both aggressive and sexual behavior became increasingly explicit and "graphic." Apparently, stronger and stronger materials were called upon to provide excitement to the viewers. This was a result, some argued, of the audience's arousal reactions becoming *habituated*. Habituation has been defined in the following manner: "Initially strong excitatory reactions grow weak or vanish entirely with repeated exposure to stimuli of a certain kind."[49]

The possibility of habituation to sex and violence may have significant social consequences. Will we forever be searching for stronger and stronger arousers? If so, this does not bode well for media content in the future. But there is another immediate problem that the habituation issue forces us to confront. Research evidence suggests that exposure to violent content on television does lead to increased tolerance for violence. For example, two studies have shown convincingly that children (both boys and girls) were more tolerant of hostile and aggressive behavior among their peers after exposure to a violent film.[50] When exposed to a nonaggressive or no film, they were less tolerant of peer aggressiveness. However, these studies did not measure arousal, so habituation can only be assumed.

A 1973 study, however, did measure arousal directly.[51] Boys (age 5 to 14 years old) with differing amounts of exposure to violence-laden television drama were used as subjects. Specifically, the boys fell into two groups—those with little exposure to televised violence and those with extensive exposure. All boys viewed a violent movie and were measured for arousal. Heavy television viewers were found to be less responsive autonomically than light viewers, thus supporting the hypothesis that extensive exposure to violence desensitizes. Such findings point toward a causal connection between consumption of violent programming and decreased reactivity, but they do not establish it. The correlational nature of the data does not permit causal inferences, and the findings are open to alternative causal explanations. For example, the findings are equally consistent with the hypothesis that autonomically subdued respondents seek violent programs more often than others. It appears that this uncertainty in interpretation can be resolved only through longitudinal studies.

Habituation to sexual stimuli is also possible, but it is less lasting. Experiments in which adult male subjects were heavily exposed to erotica showed that they became less responsive both autonomically and sexually than the control subjects. After a few weeks of heavy exposure to erotic materials, subjects preferred nonerotic materials such as *Reader's Digest*. However, "spontaneous recovery" did take place; after eight weeks, subjects were again aroused by erotic materials. In fact, arousal levels reached preexperiment levels.

The evidence on excitatory habituation can be summarized as follows: (1) There are indications that massive exposure to arousing materials can substantially reduce excitatory reactions. (2) There may be spontaneous recovery from reduced responsiveness after the massive exposure stops.

Emotional Functioning and Television

Not much research has been done in this area, but it is an area that is beginning to attract the attention of researchers. Much of the research done can be described briefly under the following topics: recognition of emotions, emotional responses, emotional reactions to characters, and personal states and television use.

Recognition of Emotions. The ability to recognize emotions felt by others aids viewers in understanding television content. Only a few emotions are recognized by children—happiness, anger, sadness, and fear. They are unable to distinguish more complex emotions like contempt, shame, or guilt. Some television programs (e.g., "Mister Rogers' Neighborhood," "Inside/Out") have attempted to teach children to recognize their emotions and the emotions of others. Informal evaluations indicated that these shows were successful, but no scientific data were available for general perusal.

Emotional Responses to Television. A number of studies indicated that television programming does arouse emotions in children. Those most often aroused were interest-excitement, joy, surprise, distress, and fear. The response varied by content and age. For example, younger children were more responsive to action and danger themes and less responsive to love and romance themes. Older children, while certainly not immune to danger themes, were more responsive to love and romance themes. Moreover, emotions aroused during viewing were often evident immediately after viewing had ceased, and sometimes even for hours. For example, fear after watching a horror movie could persist for hours or even days. This finding has echoes of the same conclusion reached in the Payne Fund studies half a century earlier.

Emotional Reactions to Television Characters. Both children and adults often come to love or hate television characters. Several studies have shown that high school and college students develop strong emotional attachments to television characters, and these effects persist for some time.[52] Other studies have found, not surprisingly, that children prefer some characters over others.[53] Usually, the greater liking is felt for characters who are most similar to the viewer in terms of age, sex, ethnicity, and interests. However, liking is tempered by the character's importance to the show as well as other variables. Of course, liking is important to the "identification with characters" concept. For example, one study of college students showed that identification with a character produced greater emotional reactions in the viewer at crisis points of the film.[54] Thus, it appears that those viewers who identify with characters are more likely to experience greater arousal during viewing.

Personal States and Television Use. Researcher Aimee Dorr suggested that the study of the emotional states elicited by television might benefit from the "uses and gratification approach." This theoretical orientation assumes that viewers choose television programs that satisfy their needs and that those needs are accompanied by emotional states. In fact, most of the research that has employed the uses and gratification approach has sought to learn why audiences use a particular medium or why they seek out a particular type of content within a medium. For example, television is thought to be used for relaxation, escape, social interaction, arousal, passing time, and even learning.

In addition, the approach assumes that members of the media audiences are not passive but are active in seeking content selectively according to their needs. For example, researchers using this approach have suggested that lonely youth might watch more television for "company." However, this issue needs to be clarified. Researcher Dorr noted that whereas it was reasonable to expect a lonely youth to seek out more television, it was also possible that such heavy viewing might further preclude the young person's acquisition of appropriate social skills. This observation was supported by data. A 1980 study of third, fourth and fifth grade school children compared heavy viewers with light viewers as well as examined type of program content viewed.[55] It was found that those who watched a good deal of fantasy-aggressive program content also were reported by the teachers to be more unhappy and troubled in behavior at school. More sophisticated research is needed that takes into account complex interactions, where viewing preferences may reinforce types of emotional responses and social experiences.

In summary, research on the influence of television on emotions and emotional development is still in an early stage. Yet, it is clear that television viewing can produce emotional responses. However, we do not know the long-term effects of vicarious emotional experiences through television. Much research is needed in this important area. It has been suggested that the combined visual and auditory messages presented by television allow children to become involved in events long before any similar real-life experience. Moreover, through television they engage in a diversity of experiences that go beyond ordinary realities. In other words, they may become emotionally "adulterated." The effects of such vicarious experiences may be cumulative; they may also be quite significant for the developing child. In any event, they are certainly different from those experienced by children growing up in pretelevision eras.

CONCLUSIONS AND IMPLICATIONS

The most widely *publicized* finding of the 1982 report concerned televised violence. Various popular media (e.g., *Time, Newsweek*) uniformly highlighted the single conclusion that violence on television leads to aggressive behavior by children. From such reports plus various news broadcasts of May, 1982, one might have assumed that televised violence was the only concern addressed, insofar as all the other relevant issues and areas covered by the report were virtually ignored.[56]

As might be anticipated, the major television networks issued statements calling the 1982 report "inaccurate," but they did not bother to identify the inaccuracies. The American Broadcasting Company (ABC) did publish a 32-page critique of the report entitled "A Perspective on Television and Violence," but nothing in the critique refuted the major findings of the report.[57] Typically, only the question of televised violence was addressed. In addition, by calling the evidence "correlational," the networks' defense sounded remarkably similar to that of the tobacco industry after being confronted with evidence linking their product to lung cancer.

It must be granted that the evidence concerning televised violence and aggressive behavior is complex; yet the convergence of that evidence from so many studies is overwhelming. Indeed, most social and behavioral scientists now accept the conclusion of the 1982 Surgeon General's report that links televised violence to later aggressive behavior.[58] Since research has now demonstrated this association in both field and laboratory studies, most researchers have shifted the focus of their work beyond this issue to investigate what processes produce the relationship. In this area, much work remains to be done. It will probably continue to be a major focus of research during the next decade.

Another major finding regarding the link between televised violence and aggressive behavior is that the sole culprit may not be portrayed violence per se. Some research suggests that aggression can be stimulated by high levels of action, even without high violence content. Thus, television's form and codes may be partly responsible for aggressive behavior. This finding should stimulate researchers to investigate this intriguing problem for years to come.

Additionally, the 1982 report emphasized the concept of *arousal* and its relationship to aggressive behavior. Findings suggest that some television viewing can heighten a state of general arousal. This increased level of excitement may then be channeled into aggression. Therefore we are faced with the possibility that exciting television programming, regardless of content, may for a number of reasons induce aggressive behavior. Obviously, the well-documented link between televised violence and aggressive behavior is far from simple. New questions are constantly being raised regarding this perennial issue.

As we have indicated, the topic of prosocial behavior also received considerable research attention. A number of studies investigated the obverse of linkage between televised violence and aggression. Overall, it was concluded that programming providing numerous prosocial portrayals can induce similar behavior in the viewer. Both laboratory and field studies consistently found that behavior such as friendliness, cooperation, delay of gratification, and generosity could be enhanced by exposure to appropriate television content. Such findings support the general explanation that observational learning takes place when people view television. There now seems little doubt that individuals learn from viewing television and that what they learn depends upon the content that they watch. In short, television can no longer be dismissed as mere entertainment. It is a major source of observational learning for millions of people. In that role it may be one of the most important agencies of socialization in our society.

NOTES AND REFERENCES

1. Eli A. Rubenstein, "Introductory Comments," in D. Pearl, L. Bouthilet and J. Lazar, *Television and Behavior: Ten Years of Scientific Progress and Implications for the Eighties* (Vol II), (Washington, D.C.: U.S. Government Printing Office, 1982), p. 104.

2. J. Immerwahr, J. Johnson, and J. Doble, *The Speaker and the Listener: A Public Perspective on Freedom of Expression*. (New York: Public Agenda Foundation, 1980).

3. L. Rowell Huesmann, "Television Violence and Aggressive Behavior," in D. Pearl, L. Bouthilet and J. Lazar, op. cit. (Vol II), 1982, p. 127.

4. J.L. Singer and D.G. Singer, *Television, Imagination and Aggression: A Study of Preschoolers' Play*. (Hillsdale, N.J.: Erlbaum, 1980).

5. Ibid., p. 127.

6. E.D. McCarthy, et al., "Violence and Behavior Disorders." *Journal of Communication*, 1975, 25(4), 71–85.

7. For a review of these studies, see L. Rowell Huesmann, op. cit., p. 128.

8. L.D. Eron and L.R. Huesmann, "Adolescent Aggression and Television." *Annals of the New York Academy of Sciences*, 1980, 347, pp. 319–331.

9. W. Belson, *Television Violence and the Adolescent Boy* (London: Saxon House, 1978). Cited in Pearl, Bouthilet, and Lazar, op. cit. (Vol. I), p. 15.

10. Ibid., p. 15.

11. L. Rowell Huesmann, op. cit., p. 128.

12. J. Ronald Milavsky, Ronald Kessler, Horst Stipp, and William S. Rubens, "Television and Aggression: Results of a Panel Study," in D. Pearl, L. Bouthilet, and J. Lazar, op. cit. (Vol. II), 1982, pp. 138–157.

13. Ibid., p. 139.

14. Ibid., p. 154.

15. Eli A. Rubenstein, op. cit., p. 105.

16. L. Rowell Heusmann, op. cit., p. 105.

17. C.W. Turner and M.R. Fern, "Effects of White Noise and Memory Cues on Verbal Aggression." Paper presented at the meetings of the International Society for Research on Aggression, Washington, D.C., 1978.

18. L.R. Huesmann, L.D. Eron, R. Klein, P. Brice, and P. Fischer, "Mitigating the Imitation of Aggressive Behaviors," Technical Report. Department of Psychology, University of Illinois at Chicago Circle, 1981.

19. V.B. Cline, R.G. Croft, and S. Courrier, "Desensitization of Children to Television Violence." *Journal of Personality and Social Psychology*, 1973, 27, 360–365.

20. Nancy Signiorelli, Larry Gross, and Michael Morgan, "Violence in Television Programs: Ten Years Later," in D. Pearl, L. Bouthilet, and J. Lazar, op. cit. (Vol II), 1982, p. 158.

21. Ibid., p. 164.

22. Ibid.

23. Ibid.

24. Ibid., p. 165.

25. J. Philipe Rushton, "Television and Prosocial Behavior," in D. Pearl, L. Bouthilet, and J. Lazar, op. cit. (Vol. II), 1982, p. 249.

26. J.H. Bryan, "Children's Cooperation and Helping Behavior," in E.M. Hetherington, ed., *Review of Child Development Research* (Vol. 5), (Chicago: University of Chicago Press, 1975).

27. R. Elliot and R. Vasta, "The Modeling of Sharing: Effects Associated with Vicarious Reinforcement, Symbolization, Age, and Generalization." *Journal of Experimental Child Psychology*, 1970, 10, 8–15.

28. J.P. Rushton and D. Owen, "Immediate and Delayed Effects of TV Modelling and Preaching on Children's Generosity." *British Journal of Social and Clinical Psychology*, 1975, 14, 309–310.

29. G.J. Gorn, M.E. Goldberg, and R.N. Kanungo, "The Role of Educational Television in Changing the Intergroup Attitudes of Children." *Child Development*, 1976, 47, 277–280.

30. R.D. O'Connor, "Modification of Social Withdrawal through Symbolic Modeling." *Journal of Applied Behavior Analysis*, 1969, 2, 15–22.

31. G.M. Stein and J.H. Bryan, "The Effects of a Televised Model upon Rule Adoption Behavior of Children." *Child Development*, 1972, 43, 268–273.

32. G.C.R. Yates, "Influence of Televised Modeling and Verbalization on Children's Delay of Gratification." *Journal of Experimental Child Psychology*, 1974, 18, 333–339.

33. A. Bandura and F.L. Menlove, "Factors Determining Vicarious Extinction of Avoidance Behavior through Symbolic Modeling." *Journal of Personality and Social Psychology*, 1968, 8, 99–108.

34. J.A. Hill, R.M. Liebert, and D.E. Mott, "Vicarious Extinction of Aviodance Behavior Through Films: An Initial Test." *Psychological Reports*, 1968, 22, 192.

35. A. Bandura, E.B. Blanchard, and B. Ritter, "The Relative Efficacy of Desensitization and Modeling Approaches for Inducing Behavioral, Affective, and Attitudinal Changes." *Journal of Personality and Social Psychology*, 1969, 13, 173–199.

36. B.G. Melamed and L.J. Siegel, "Reduction of Anxiety in Children Facing Hospitalization and Surgery by Use of Filmed Modeling." *Journal of Consulting and Clinical Psychology*, 1975, 43, 511–521.

37. J. Philipe Rushton, op. cit., p. 255.

38. W. Andrew Collins, "Cognitive Processing in Television Viewing," in D. Pearl, L. Bouthilet, and J. Lazar, op. cit. (Vol. II), 1982, p. 10.

39. Ibid.

40. For a description of these studies, see Mabel Rice, Aletha C. Huston, and John C. Wright, "The Forms of Television: Effects on Children's Attention, Comprehension, and Social Behavior," in D. Pearl, L. Bouthilet, and J. Lazar, op. cit. (Vol. II), 1982, pp. 24–38.

41. Dolf Zillman, "Television Viewing and Arousal," in D. Pearl, L. Bouthilet, and J. Lazar, op. cit. (Vol. II), 1982, p. 53.

42. D. Zillman and R.C. Johnson, "Motivated Aggressiveness Perpetuated by Exposure to Aggressive Films and Reduced by Exposure to Non-Aggressive Films." *Journal of Research in Personality*, 1973, 7, 261–276.

43. E. Donnerstein, M. Donnerstein, and G. Barrett, "Where is the Facilitation of Media Violence: The Effects of Nonexposure and Placement of Arousal." *Journal of Research in Personality*, 1976.

44. For a description of these studies, see Dolf Zillman, op. cit., pp. 57–58.

45. Ibid., p. 58.

46. Ibid.

47. P.H. Tannenbaum and D. Zillman, "Emotional Arousal in the Facilitation of Aggression through Communication," in L. Berkowitz, ed., *Advances in Experimental Social Psychology* (Vol. 8), (New York: Academic Press, 1975).

48. For a description of these studies, see D. Zillman, op. cit., pp. 61–63.
49. Ibid., p. 61.
50. Ibid.
51. V.B. Cline, R.G. Croft, and S. Courrier, "Desensitization of Children to Television Violence," *Journal of Personality and Social Psychology*, 1973, 27, 360–365.
52. For a description of these studies, see Aimee Dorr, "Television and Affective Development and Functioning," in D. Pearl, L. Bouthilet, and J. Lazar, op. cit. (Vol. II), 1982, pp. 72–73.
53. Ibid., p. 72.
54. P.H. Tanenbaum and E.P. Gaer, "Mood Change as a Function of Stress of Protagonist and Degree of Identification in a Film-Viewing Situation," *Journal of Personality and Social Psychology*, 1965, 2, 612–616.
55. Aimee Dorr, op. cit.
56. Eli A. Rubenstein, "Television and Behavior: Research Conclusions of the 1982 NIMH Report and Their Policy Implications," *American Psychologist*, July, 1983, 820–825.
57. Ibid.
58. Ibid.

15

Television and Behavior, Ten Years of Progress. Part II: Health, Family, Social Beliefs, and American Institutions

During the late 1970s, research concerning the effects of television on viewers expanded to include issues that went far beyond those discussed in the previous chapter. In large part, the earlier preoccupation with issues of violence versus prosocial behavior, or even with cognitive versus emotional influences, represented attempts to determine to what extent television was one of the "bad guys" among the media, creating harm to those who attended to its content. Beyond those concerns were other, less explored questions, such as the possible influence of the medium on health, family life, gender roles, the status of ethnic and racial groups, and beliefs about the aged. Even broader questions were in the background. What was the role of television in teaching about such matters as leisure, religion, and citizenship?

In other words, as research interests have broadened, it is increasingly recognized that television has a potentially significant role in shaping people's interpretations in many areas of social life. The research community recognizes that insufficient attention has been paid to its broader role as part of the general communication processes of society by which we collectively shape *meanings*. Television, as do each of our media, plays a significant part in the social derivation and achievement of consensus concerning interpretations of reality for almost every aspect of our physical and social world.

For these reasons, the report, *Television and Behavior: Ten Years of Scientific Progress and Implications for the Eighties* assembled research findings on a long list of topics.[1] While Chapter 14 focused on studies dealing with violent, prosocial, cognitive and affective aspects of behavior, the present chapter extends the list to include health, family issues, social beliefs, and social institutions. All these have received less research attention than the topics discussed in Chapter 14. Nevertheless, during the period covered by the report, a large number of studies were completed.

More specifically, health is a topic of general concern to Americans. A number of recent studies have probed the lessons presented in television content concerning such matters as diet and its consequences. In an age when the use of alcohol is declining in our society, how does the medium present the consumption and use of beer, wine, and spirits? How does it portray the use of automobiles, including safe versus reckless driving and the use or nonuse of seat belts? How are health workers, such as nurses and doctors, depicted?

Another area of widespread concern is the American family. What are its norms? How should family roles be defined? Furthermore, how does attention to the content of television influence the way family members relate to each other? Has watching TV programs cut seriously into interaction among members of families? Have parents lost control over, or should they even bother to supervise, what their children view?

Television presents depictions of all kinds of people in cartoons, soap operas, situation comedies, advertisement, serious drama, old movies, documentaries, and even in the news. All such content provides lessons in what various social categories are like and how others evaluate them. What is television currently teaching about sex relationships, about gender roles for males and females, about various racial and ethnic groups, and about older people in our society? Furthermore, how is it training members of the oncoming generation for their roles as consumers? Children have to learn *some* set of social beliefs about each of these topics and activities. In many cases, television can be their primary, or even their *only*, source of information.

Finally, researchers are beginning to believe that television's influences extend beyond the behavior and beliefs of individual members of its audience. Long-range and subtle influences are possible with respect to our laws, our political system, and even our practice of religion. Currently, such questions are on the frontier of research. But as older questions, such as whether or not TV violence can stimulate aggressive behavior, yield to an accumulation of research evidence, these broader issues are being pursued with vigor.

Threading through the research studies now accumulating around all foregoing issues are two basic concerns: one is with the role of television as a large-scale and effective *agent of socialization* within our society. The other concerns the *validity of the lessons* being taught. Is television a subtle but effective teacher for millions of viewers regarding the topics presented in the present and the preceding chapters? Furthermore, is its content presenting correct and socially desirable or distorted and undemocratic views of American life? As we will see, research now accumulating suggests that there are grounds for concern.

TELEVISION AND HEALTH

One of the Recommendations of the original Surgeon General's Committee on Television and Social Behavior was that we should "consider and stimulate television's health-promoting possibilities."[2] In 1972, virtually nothing was known about the portrayal of health-related issues in television programming. Few answers were available as to what kind of health portrayals were available to viewers and whether or not such messages were likely to encourage healthy or unhealthy life-styles. Media researchers were quick to follow up on this suggestion, and their zeal produced a plethora of published articles in the subsequent years.

Three lengthy summary articles in the section of the report review the status of health-related research. The first one is concerned with the content of television programs; it focuses on portrayals relevant to health and health-related behavior.[3] Another paper examines television campaigns that were designed to promote better health.[4] The reasons for the successes as well as the failures of several recent TV campaigns are also reviewed. The third and final paper analyzes the use of television by persons in institutions (e.g., mental institutions, nursing homes)—as well as its effects on such persons.[5] In the following sections, we will discuss each report.

Health Portrayals

George Gerbner, Michael Morgan, and Nancy Signiorelli wrote the paper entitled "Programming Health Portrayals: What Viewers See, Say and Do." This report reviewed the multitude of studies on health portrayals on television; both direct and indirect health messages were included in their analysis. Among the direct messages analyzed were the portrayals of medical conditions as well as physician and patient behavior in televised dramas. Indirect messages included an analysis of life-style behaviors, such as smoking, alcohol use, risky driving, or use of seat belts. Gerbner and his associates pointed out that "lifestyle illnesses" account for about half of the deaths in the United States each year. Indeed, advances in medical sciences have led to a shift in the type of illness most likely to be fatal. Many acute, often infectious diseases have been conquered, whereas many chronic ones, in which life-style plays a major role, continue to take their toll. Nutrition and dietary patterns, smoking and alcohol use are included in the risk factors for life-style diseases. Thus, their portrayal may have some relevance to viewers' health-related practices, particularly if a consistent message is often conveyed.

What Viewers See. The average viewer watches television about 30 hours each week.[6] During that time, he or she is exposed to health-related concepts and behavior many times in both programs and commercials. The nature of those portrayals, however, is usually determined by dramatic or sales functions, rather than scientific or therapeutic criteria. In one study, health-related topics were found to occur in 7.2 percent of the total broadcast time.[7] Most of these appearances were in entertainment programs or commercials. There were few informational programs dealing with health issues. In addition, 70 percent of the health information provided was considered to be inaccurate, misleading, or both, while only 30 percent was rated useful. Viewers were 10 times more likely to see a message urging the use of pills than one concerning drug abuse.

Some of the brief public service messages, including those on heart disease, smoking, and crisis centers, were considered to be useful and informative. But information about most major health problems, such as cancer, stroke, accidents, hepatitis, maternal death, malnutrition, and venereal disease was virtually nonexistent. Thus, according to this survey, television was performing nowhere near its potential in offering health information.

Both prime time (8 to 11 P.M.) and children's weekend-daytime (8 A.M. to 2:30 P.M.) network dramatic programs were dominated by themes involving action, power, and danger. Both also portrayed many acts of violence, which, as Gerbner pointed out, is definitely related to health. Few accidental fatalities occurred in the world of prime-time television despite all the risky driving, fires, and explosions. In real life, automobile accidents are a leading cause of death for young adults in the United States. However, while automobiles and trucks were common on television, seat belt use was seldom seen. Indeed, one study found only a single instance of characters using seat belts, and even that depiction was followed by a wild driving stunt in which the driver did not use a belt.[8]

Prime-time characters were rarely shown to have any type of physical impairment; in fact, almost none even wore glasses. Only 2 percent of major characters were physically handicapped. They tended to be older, less positively presented, more likely to be victimized, and were almost never shown on children's programs. Characters suffering from mental disorders, however, did appear on prime-time programs with some frequency—about 17 percent of prime-time programs involved a depiction or theme of mental illness. Moreover, about 3 percent of major characters were identified as mentally ill, and, in the late evening programs, this percentage doubled. The mentally ill were also disproportionately depicted both as "violents" and as the victims of violence. Of the dramatic characters in prime-time programs, 40 percent of "normals" were violent compared to 73 percent for the mentally ill. Similarly, 44 percent of the "normal" characters were victims of violence, whereas the figure for mentally ill characters was 81 percent. No other group of fictional characters suffered, nor was shown to deserve, that fate so often. Those most likely to be portrayed as mentally unstable in television programs were sales and clerical workers, manual laborers, criminals, and scientists. Those least subject to mental illness were policemen, owners and proprietors, farmers, and ministers. Overall, the portrayal of the mentally ill was very unrealistic; television was certainly not reflecting "reality" as far as this topic was concerned.

Nutrition and Obesity. Eating and drinking appeared frequently on television programs. In general, eating and drinking occurred about 10 times per hour. Moreover, 75 percent of all dramatic characters ate and drank or talked about doing so. In the portrayal of nutrition patterns in prime-time programs, eating was anything but balanced or relaxed. Of all eating-drinking episodes, characters "grabbing a snack" (39 percent) occurred nearly as often as breakfast, lunch, and dinner combined (42 percent). For children's weekend-daytime programming, the incidence of snacking rose to 45 percent, while regular meals declined to 24 percent of all eating-drinking episodes. In addition, the snack was most often a high-calorie, high-fat food; fruits were consumed only 4 or 5 percent of the time.

The beverage most frequently consumed on television was alcohol. In fact, the kinds of drinks consumed were inversely proportional to those in real-life settings. On TV, alcohol was consumed twice as often as coffee or tea, 14 times as often as soft drinks, and 15 times as frequently as water. Indeed, alcohol is hard to escape in TV-land. One study found it shown or mentioned in 80 percent of prime-time programs (not counting commercials).[9] Moreover, a 1980 study reported that alcohol use was present in 12 of the 15 most popular programs.[10] It was estimated that the average child viewer would see approximately 3000 drinking episodes a year! Furthermore, the drinkers were not the villains or the bit players; they were the good, steady, likeable characters.

While obesity is a problem which plagues around 45 percent of the American population, fat people are rarely seen on television. In a study done in 1979, less than 6 percent of male characters and 2 percent of female characters portrayed on television were found to be obese. Not one of those was a leading character.[11] The results of another survey found that 11 percent of the characters were overweight, but none of the obese were children, teens, or young adults.[12] When fat people were portrayed, they were usually members of a minority group. Sixteen percent of the black and 80 percent of the Asian-American characters were obese. On the other hand, the causes of obesity are seldom made clear. Many characters portrayed on television consume large amounts of snacks, sweets, and alcohol, but few have weight problems. They eat and drink but stay slim. Just what the effects of such depictions are remains unclear, but it is unrealistic, to say the least.

Smoking has become an uncommon occurrence in contemporary television portrayals, although it is still frequently seen in the reruns of old movies. A recent analysis of the major characters today found that few smoked—only 11 percent of the men and 2 percent of the women.[13] The highest levels of smoking occurred in dramatic presentations, but even there it was only 13 percent of the male and 4 percent of the female characters. In general, situation comedies had little smoking, whereas crime and adventure shows portrayed somewhat more. There were, however, no instances of television characters expressing anti-smoking sentiments or refusing to smoke.

Health Portrayals on the Daytime Serial. Health portrayals are so frequent on daytime serials that they are worthy of special mention. Coping with illness and its effects is one of the major themes of the soap opera. Nearly half of all characters become involved in health-related problems. These include psychiatric disorders, heart attacks, pregnancies, automobile accidents, attempted homicides, attempted suicides, and infectious diseases, in that order. The major killers, however, were homicides, car accidents, and heart attacks. In spite of the fact that men were sick and got hurt more often than women, illnesses were more often fatal for women. Cardiovascular diseases claimed four times as many women characters as men. In addition, half of all pregnancies resulted in miscarriages, while 16 percent resulted in the death of the expectant mother. Mental illness also struck women more frequently and usually resulted from guilt, trauma, or the inability to cope with crises.

However, the world of the soap opera was a just one. While illness, like the rain, might fall on the good and the bad characters alike, it was the good people who were likely to survive. The bad deserved their fate. In another twist of facts, the extent of a person's suffering seems to be related to their survival, except that unlike the real world, suffering seemed to enhance one's chances of recovery.

Not only were medical facts distorted in the daytime serials, but characters with professional occupations were greatly overpresented. In fact, one study reported that more than two thirds of all professionals portrayed were medical practitioners.[14] Another reported that about 80 percent of the men in the serials were doctors.[15] Finally, health was also found to be the most frequent topic of conversation among characters. This led Gerbner and associates to argue that: "It may be that daytime serials comprise the most prolific single source of medical advice in America."[16]

Doctors on Prime Time Television. Professionals also played a disproportionately large role in the world of prime-time television, where doctors and nurses dominate. In fact, television doctors and nurses were five times more numerous than they are in real life. Only police and criminals were more numerous than health professionals in the world depicted in television programming. Most doctors and nurses were white, young, or middle-aged—and always attractive. As might be expected, 9 out of 10 doctors were male, whereas virtually all nurses were female.

Television doctors are good guys. Very few were portrayed as evil (fewer than 4 percent). That was half the rate for other professionals. In addition, they were smarter, fairer, and more rational than other characters, including nurses. In addition, television doctors were symbols of power and dominance. However, they were portrayed as using their power carefully; they were ethical, kind, and willing to take risks to help their patients. Unlike busy physicians in the real world, television doctors thrived on private relationships with their patients, while 61 percent of their work was done on house calls or in other field settings. But even with all these admirable qualities, doctors were seldom shown to have a personal life. That is, they were rarely shown at home with the family.

Television's Effects on Health

Not much is known about the actual influence of television on health. One study, however, indicated that television is thought by its audience to be an important source of health information.[17] Approximately 600 teenagers in two cities were interviewed about their source of information about family planning. Twenty-four percent of the teens said that most of what they knew had been learned from television. No other source of information had such a high percentage. Another analysis of a similar group found that 45 percent of the youngsters could remember at least one specific family planning message from television.[18]

Evidence from several studies suggested that improper health attitudes may be a result of reliance on television for health information. In a study sponsored by General Mills, respondents were asked to name two or three main sources of health information.[19] Nearly a third of the respondents named television programs; only doctors and dentists, at 45 percent, were named more often. Those who named programs were distinctly different from those who did not. They tended to be more complacent about their health, to hold "old" health values, to be nonexercisers, and to be poorly informed about health issues.

These levels of information and misinformation cannot be attributed to television alone; the situation is much more complex. The less-educated and low-income groups of our society use television more heavily than other groups; but they are also the groups most deprived of reliable information about many subjects. In addition, they are unresponsive to other sources of information. The General Mills report indicated that these groups sorely need valid information about health. Thus the important issue may not be whether television, in part, "causes" poor health but whether it uses its vast influence to perpetuate or to break it.

The General Mills study also concluded that a major determining factor in the attitudes of Americans about health is "denial and unwillingness to believe that catastrophic illness could attack one's own immediate family." The authors indicated that it is possible that spending a lot of time "living" in the world of television, where (except for soap operas) illness is rare, may help cultivate such denial. Finally, they argued that the extremely high level of public confidence in doctors and the medical profession in general might underlie the "philosophy of denial" and the "live for today" attitudes they found to be so widespread.

The development of this view of doctors as omnipotent saviors may begin early in life. Indeed, two studies reported that young children who are heavy viewers of television are more likely than lighter viewers to hold images of doctors and medical professionals that resemble television portrayals.[20] Even among adults, heavy viewers are more likely to express confidence in doctors, particularly heavy viewers of doctor shows. Thus, television may contribute to a syndrome in which confidence in the medical profession justifies "live for today" attitudes and a lack of interest in preventive medicine. If a problem develops, a doctor can cure it. However, it could be argued that those in poor health simply watch more television. Indeed, they do; but the data also suggest that television may help to perpetuate unhealthy beliefs, values, and life-styles.

Moreover, the mere act of watching television itself may have health implications. Most viewing occurs in a relaxed atmosphere and offers a perfect opportunity for resting, eating, smoking, and drinking. For example, one study of teenagers found that more than 80 percent "usually eat" while watching television.[21] In addition to eating, persons who watch are also likely to smoke, even though there is a relatively low level of smoking on programs and no cigarette commercials. Thus, watching television may have certain characteristics that may affect, or even counter, the lessons relayed by its content.

In summary, there are indications that heavy exposure to television's portrayal of health matters may contribute to the public's health-related knowledge and behavior. Even the act of viewing itself may have health implications. Although the findings are preliminary, they confirm without question the idea that television has tremendous potential for influencing health and that its role deserves serious, sustained research.

Health Campaigns on Television

Douglas S. Solomon reviewed health campaigns on television and analyzed the reasons for their success or failure. "In a campaign, there is a deliberate effort to convey a particular message about health and to persuade the audience to heed that message."[22] This is, of course, very different from entertainment programs where any learning about health is only incidental. There have, however, been some health campaigns on daytime soap operas.

There is still debate about the ability of campaigns to change attitudes and behavior. Some communication researchers believe that most campaigns are ineffective; others believe that a carefully planned campaign can achieve the desired results. A number of campaigns have been conducted over the past few years encompassing community mental health, drug abuse, smoking, use of seat belts, dental health, cancer, venereal disease, and alcoholism. For the most part, the results have been encouraging.

The Stanford Study of Heart Disease in Three Communities. An interesting example of a televised health campaign is the Stanford Heart Disease Three Community Study.[23] The program was conducted, beginning in 1970, by an interdisciplinary team of researchers. They explored the possibility of reducing cardiovascular risk in a community through education programs in the mass media. Two communities were exposed to intensive mass media campaigns in English and Spanish. The Spanish programs were not merely translations of the English but were specifically tailored to the Spanish-speaking community and its culture. One community also received face-to-face instruction for a small group of persons considered to be at high risk. A third community served as a control. People from each of the communities were examined for cardiovascular problems before the program began and twice thereafter at one-year intervals. They were also asked what they knew about cardiovascular disease and what they were doing about it. In addition, the researchers took physiological measures such as blood pressure, weight, and plasma cholesterol. After one year, the estimated risk of heart attack and stroke had been reduced only in the community receiving both the personal instruction and the televised programs. But by the end of the second year, the community receiving just the televised program had come down to the same level. In the control community, however, risk had increased. The researchers concluded that mass media campaigns could clearly be effective, but that more research was needed on how to refine the techniques and target the message. For example, ways to reduce smoking and to increase participation in physical exercise needed to be devised. Thus, the study used television to teach specific behavioral skills, and the evidence is clear that the program worked.

The Feeling Good Series. The "Feeling Good" series, an experimental TV series on health produced for adults by the Children's Television Workshop (CTW), was a more typical example of a televised health campaign. Many considered it to be a failure, but the programs produced a number of behavior changes.[24] The series, broadcast in 1974 and 1975, consisted of 11 one-hour programs and 13 half-hour programs. The overall objective of the program was "to motivate viewers to take steps which could enhance their own health and that of their families." In all, they measured 33 behavioral goals that were emphasized in the program. Of these, there was strong evidence of behavioral change in 10 goals (meaning statistical significance when compared to a control group), partial evidence in 14 goals, and no evidence in 9 goals. The goals associated with strong evidence of change included eating more fresh fruit or fruit juice, performing breast self-examination, having an eyesight examination, encouraging someone else to have a PAP test, and sending for health information offered on television.

A number of important lessons were learned from the "Feeling Good" series. One was that it is difficult but not impossible to have an impact on both health knowledge and behavior with a television series that stresses prevention. The researchers felt, however, that the format needed improvement. One-hour programs were simply too long. In addition, many of the message-designed strategies selected, such as songs, humor, and strong emotional appeals, were not effective in conveying health information to adults. Instead, it was concluded that documentary segments and straightforward information presentations would be more useful in effecting change. In any event, the "Feeling Good" series should certainly not be characterized as a failure.

Generally, then, the evidence regarding televised health campaigns remains mixed. One problem in evaluating such campaigns is that most of them employ a combination of media to achieve their objectives. For example, some antismoking campaigns have used print, television, and radio to reach the public. Thus, it is difficult to untangle the influence of a single medium. However, televised health campaigns will probably be used extensively in the future. If they are effective, they could be a significant factor lowering the costs of health care. Vast numbers of people can be reached through television and at a comparatively low cost per person. Additionally, cable television will make it possible to reach more people and more targeted audiences.

Television and Persons in Institutions

There have been relatively few studies involving the use of television by persons in institutions, and little is known of the effects of the medium upon people in such special environments. Researchers Rubenstein and Sprafkin argued that patients in general hospitals, mental hospitals, and homes for the aged "all are engaged in other than 'normal' viewing under other than normal circumstances," and so the effects of TV viewing on these special audiences may be "unique."

Several studies reviewed by Rubenstein and Sprafkin focused on mental patients in psychiatric settings. It was reported that directors of psychiatric centers generally believe that watching television has a positive effect on patients and that such viewing may have potential as a modest therapeutic procedure in mental hospitals. The TV viewing, however, seemed to be more beneficial for chronic and geriatric patients than for acutely ill or adolescent patients. Not surprisingly, several studies found that television viewing was a dominant leisure-time activity and that television sets were turned on an average of over 12 hours per day.[25] Not all mental patients, however, react to TV in the same way; in one study, 34 percent became more relaxed, whereas 38 percent appeared bored. Moreover, others became agitated or upset and some even talked back to the television. Another interesting study found that some schizophrenic patients incorporated television program material into their psychotic delusions.[26]

Overall, it was concluded that television is a significant factor in the daily lives of institutionalized patients, but more evidence is needed regarding the issue of whether it can be useful in treatment programs. The unanswered question remains: How might television be modified to increase its positive (therapeutic) effects, not only for mental patients but also for those in other institutional settings?

THE FAMILY AND INTERPERSONAL RELATIONS

Among the recommendations of the 1972 Surgeon General's Committee was that future research on television be conducted "in the context of. . .the home environment." That recommendation was taken to heart by some researchers during the 1970s, although compared with other areas discussed in this chapter relatively little was accomplished. Nevertheless, research conducted on the family can be divided into two broad categories: (1) detailed content analyses of the portrayal of families on TV and (2) Television's effects on family and social interactions.

Television's Families
Since its inception, one of the dominant themes of television programming has been the portrayal of family life. From 1946 through 1978, 218 fictional families appeared in various series devoted to the portrayal of family life. Such series are defined as "prime-time, network shows in which the main characters in each episode are members of a family and in which the major proportion of interaction is among family members, usually in a home setting."[27] Obviously, the scope of this definition includes a variety of show formats. Most have been half-hour situation comedies, but the rubric "family series" also includes family dramas, family drama-comedies, serials, adventure series, and even some cartoons (e.g., "The Flintstones," "The Jetsons"). Many of the television families have become part of our collective history and culture. Millions of Americans fondly recall the Rileys ("The Life of Riley"); the Nelsons ("The Adventures of Ozzie and Harriet"); the Andersons ("Father Knows Best"); the Cleavers ("Leave it to Beaver"); the Ricardos and Mertzes ("I Love Lucy"); the Kramdens and Nortons ("The Honeymooners"); the Bunkers ("All in the Family"); "The Waltons"; "The Jeffersons", and the Bradfords ("Eight is Enough"). Moreover, in recent years, "family series" have experienced a resurgence in popularity led by "The Cosby Show" and "Family Ties," which according to measurements taken by the Nielsen Rating System were one and two in program popularity in 1986.

Why study these fantasy families? Researchers argue that by shaping our cultural norms—and thereby our individual ideas, attitudes and values about what kind of family life is desirable—they impact upon "real-life" families. After all, these TV families can demonstrate to us how husband and wife are supposed to behave as well as how parents and children are expected to relate to each other. Thus, we can judge our own family against the normative models offered by television.

So, then, how are TV families portrayed? Researchers Lynda Glennon and Richard Butsch present new research on that issue as well as summarize earlier work.[28] They conducted a content analysis of all 218 family series, with a special focus on the social class of the portrayed family. Occupation of the head of the household was used as the indicator of social class. Their data found an overrepresentation of middle-class families and a corresponding underrepresentation of the working-class family. Many of television's families were quite successful and glamorous. They lacked the mundane problems that most real families must face. Indeed, the middle-class families appeared to be quite successful economically. Many had servants, usually a maid. On the other hand, two dominant recurring themes emerged in portrayals of working-class life. One theme was the father and husband as "inept, dumb or bumbling" (e.g., "The Honeymooners," "All in the Family"), a characterization that seldom appeared in middle-class family portrayals. The second theme was upward mobility. It was not always present and usually appeared only where the working-class family was given some dignity. Membership in the working-class was presented as a one-generation phenomenon; it was portrayed as something to escape and its desirable features ignored. The investigators believed that both of these themes served to weaken the legitimacy of the working-class family life-style.

Middle-class families, on the other hand, were portrayed in two different fashions. In one type of portrayal both parents were "superpeople" who were able to deal effectively and rationally with any problem. However, in some shows the husband was intelligent, mature, and strong, but the wife was a giddy fool (e.g., "I Love Lucy").

The researchers speculated on possible effects of such family portrayals. They suggested that working-class children might be left with the impression that their fathers were inadequate, inferior, and the laughingstock to the rest of the world. Also, the upward mobility theme implied that it was easy to attain success and to move almost without effort into the midde class. Furthermore, the idealized portrayals of middle-class families might lead viewers to question the adequacy of their own families. Indeed, it has been hypothesized that viewers learn family roles and ways to solve family problems by watching TV families. Some researchers also argue that television may be changing attitudes about how parents and siblings should behave. However, little research has been done to test these assumptions.

Television's Effect on Family Life and Social Interaction

Research on the effects of television on family and interpersonal behavior is generally sparse. The research that has been done focuses on social behavior at the individual level, undoubtedly because of the convenience of obtaining data from individuals rather than groups. At best, relational and family system characteristics are examined in the findings only by implication. The relatively small number of studies in the decade of the 1970s can be organized into three areas of concern for television and family relations: (1) the impact of parents on the use of television; (2) the effects of television use on family functioning and interaction; and (3) the mediation effects of parental intervention in enhancing or diminishing the impact of television viewing.

Before turning to each of these three areas, it should be noted that the studies in the foregoing areas tend to suffer from certain methodological problems. For example, samples were often small and atypical; many of the studies lacked theoretical focus; and some even lacked control groups. It is hoped that in the future more researchers will turn their attention to this important (although difficult to research) area.

The Impact of Parents on the Use of Television. Virtually all studies agreed that parents are concerned with the violent and sexual content of television. Far fewer are concerned with the amount of time their children spent viewing television. One reason given for this relative lack of concern is that parents might underestimate their child's viewing time and might not be aware of which programs the child was watching (or how violent the content of the program was). Indeed, several studies found that children gave estimates of their own viewing time that were twice as great as those given by their mothers.[29] Of course, the researchers were assuming that it is the mothers who distorted reality and the children who gave valid responses. This remained an untested assumption.

There was also evidence that mothers might not recognize the extent of their child's emotional response to program content. Children tended to perceive more violence in the same set of TV programs than their mothers did. In fact, mothers typically underreported how frightened their children were after watching scary programs. In addition, parents, did not exert much control over their children's television viewing. In fact, some noted media researchers concluded that "television watching by youngsters is largely devoid of parental influence."[30] For example, in one study 39 percent of sixth graders reported that their families had *some* rules about television, while only 18 percent of tenth graders said that they were restricted by *any* rules about amount of viewing.[31] Even less common was guidance on specific programs that children were or were not allowed to watch. In fact, it was found that both mothers and children (ages 9 to 14) reported very little parental guidance, with 85 percent of both groups saying "none."

The Effects of Television Use on Family Interaction. Families spend many of their waking hours watching television. Thus, it follows that television has influenced family behavior if for no other reason than that it affects the proximity of family members to one another. Television is believed to have effects on family life because of the large areas of family functioning that are not governed by societal norms but, rather, by rules that evolve in the course of their interaction. Thus, it is possible that when more general societal norms are absent, members of a family may accept behavior portrayed on TV as legitimate, or even use it as a model for their own interaction.

A relatively large proportion of television viewing is done with other members of the family. Nielsen data from 1975 indicated that 70 percent of prime-time viewing was cowatching by an adult and child. The proportion is only 20 percent for Saturday morning. However, the number of television sets in the home did affect this pattern; in households with multiple sets, children tended to watch together while parents viewed together.

TV also seems to have changed the ways in which family interaction occurs. There is less conversation and less interaction when the set is on. The data also suggest that TV experiences are more private. While the family views together, they are isolated from other members when watching. This separation is magnified for both children and adults who live in homes with multiple sets.

There is also a potential for family conflict when more than one person wants to watch television. Generally, it has been assumed that the norms of society prevail when these decisions are made: parents win over children, older children win over younger, etc. Yet, researchers have found that in a surprisingly large number of cases parents defer to their children, who decide what the family will view. Other studies have indicated that commercials directed toward children have led to parent-child conflict because the children acted with great displeasure when they did not receive a cereal, toy, etc. that was advertised during their favorite program. Moreover, it has been found that family members may turn to television to cope with tense family situations. A sample of 64 persons was asked questions like: "Is anyone you live with too critical or faultfinding?" and "Are you often moody?" The results indicated that there was a positive relation between TV time and family tension.[32] The researchers interpreted this to be supportive of the hypothesis that television is used to cope with tense family situations.

Television viewing has also been linked with the inability to communicate effectively with family members (and others). It has been hypothesized that this inability to communicate arises from the passivity learned in responding to a televised world. One participant in a study described his experience with television in this way:

> Perhaps the single greatest factor in my life was television. I was taught manners by my mother and not much by my father, but I was taught almost everything by television...The largest factor that TV played in my life is that no feedback is required. I have always been good at listening and learning but poor at speaking to others.[33]

Overall, the above findings represent only a beginning in this very critical area of study. Unfortunately the studies in this area have neither the methodological sophistication of many recent media studies nor theoretical depth. It was suggested that sociological theory developed on marriage and the family might add depth to future studies.

The Mediation Effects of Parental Intervention. As we saw in the previous chapter (in the section on viewing TV violence), intervention in the form of discussions about how unrealistic television is can diminish the impact of such programs. But what about intervention by parents? Can actions by parents enhance or diminish television's effects on their children? Some evidence indicates that they can. For example, a 1974 study, using disadvantaged preschoolers, found that those children who viewed Sesame Street with their mothers and discussed it with them were more likely than others (who did not discuss the programs with their mothers) to increase their learning of cognitive skills.[34] In a similar study, parents of 276 grade school children were asked to watch TV with their child and explain the content of a Saturday morning newscast. This parental intervention did stimulate the child's attention to the newscast and also enhanced recall.[35]

Whereas this area of research shows great promise, much remains to be done before we can draw sound conclusions. Moreover, it is a difficult area to research. For example, it is difficult to recruit a representative sample of mothers and to get them to cooperate in carrying out the manipulation strategies under natural conditions. Most experiments have used relatively simple interventions, such as discussion. Moreover, there is a strong need to conceptualize more clearly the ways parents (and other agents of socialization) could enhance or mitigate television's effects. There have been relatively few attempts to do so. Nevertheless, there are six ways that parents can use to help their children attain critical viewing skills:[36]

1. *Limited viewing.* Parents can limit the amount of time children spend viewing television.
2. *Content control.* Parents can encourage or discourage viewing of particular programs.
3. *Purposeful viewing.* Parents can arrange planned viewing of programs with prosocial messages.
4. *Direct mediation.* Parents can provide explanatory comments and interpretations.
5. *Indirect mediation.* Parents can model critical viewing skills by discussing programs with others in the presence of the child.
6. *Springboard techniques.* Parents can show children how television information can be applied to, and have implications for, many events in everyday life.

While the relative lack of parental attention or interaction is unfortunate, it is encouraging that television programming now often includes public service announcements urging parents to watch with their children and to talk about what they see on television.

SOCIAL BELIEFS AND SOCIAL BEHAVIOR

The papers in this section are concerned with television and socialization. Specifically, does television contribute to the socialization process and to the learning of various social roles? Most of the studies are based on content analyses, and, as a result, we now have a detailed "demography" of television's fictional characters. With this collective portrait accomplished, researchers have turned their attention to the examination of the effects of televised portrayals on various social roles. These include patterns of expectations associated with gender, age, race, occupation, and consumer behavior. Do these televised portrayals lead viewers to stereotype role occupants in a manner consistent with the televised messages? And, does the world view of heavy viewers differ from that of light viewers? These issues are examined in this section.

Sex and Gender

No role area has been as extensively analyzed by communication researchers as that of sex and gender roles. Indeed, in terms of the number of publications appearing, it is clear that there was massive interest in the topic during the 1970s. Most of the studies conducted in this area were content analyses, although some experimental and field studies looked at the effects of television content.

Content Analyses. Perhaps the single most important point developed from the content analyses was that men greatly outnumber women on television. There are about three times as many males shown. The ratio of males to females in leading roles was even higher in the early 1970s, but the number of women increased at the end of the decade. Moreover, the number of men and women characters varied with the type of program. There were approximately equal numbers of men and women in situation comedies, family dramas, and soap operas; but men outnumbered women 5 to 1 in action adventure shows, and 4 to 1 in Saturday morning cartoons.

Various content analyses also examined age, race, and occupation as related to sex roles. On the average, women characters were younger than men. Most of the females were in their twenties or early thirties, whereas the males were usually about ten years older. Black men appeared more frequently than black women. Hispanic men greatly outnumbered Hispanic women, although the number of Hispanics was a very small part of the total.

The men portrayed on television were employed in a wide variety of jobs. One study of Saturday morning fare, for example, found men in 42 different jobs. Women, on the other hand, occupied only 9 different jobs.[37] Another study found twice as many women characters as men characters in low-prestige jobs.[38] The late 1970s brought the appearance of a few new programs in which females had difficult and demanding jobs. The women, however, were usually single, sophisticated, often divorced, and their work glamorous. Some analysts observe that such new roles are really not very different from past roles because the women usually depended on men, were portrayed as more emotional than men, and there was more concern for their safety.

What personal traits differentiated men from women on television? In general, males were portrayed to be more rational, smarter, independent, more powerful, more tolerant, and more stable. Females, on the other hand, appeared warmer, more sociable, more attractive, more peaceful, and less competent. Moreover, women were often treated as sex objects and were more likely than men to use their bodies seductively. Yet, by the late seventies, this was changing in that men were being portrayed more frequently as sex objects—especially in the action-adventure programs, where they were often called upon to prove their physical prowess.

During the 1970s, there was an increase of sexually suggestive behavior and innuendo. There were few, if any, visual portrayals of explicit erotic behavior on commercial television programming. However, there were numerous cues for the viewer about the events that presumably would happen or had happened off screen. For example, sexual intercourse was frequently implied. It is significant that most references to intercourse on television, whether verbally insinuated or contextually implied, occurred between unmarried partners. Indeed, this occurred five times as often as references to sexual activity between married couples. References to intercourse with prostitutes came in second. Together, these accounted for almost 70 percent of all allusions to intercourse on prime-time television programs.[39] Sex was also commonly linked with violence. For example, most verbal references to sex in action-adventure (police) programs resulted from discussion of rape or other sex crimes. And even when they were not prostitutes or victims of sex crimes, women characters used their eroticism to entrap men.

Marriage and family were not nearly as important to television's men as they were to its women. One study found the viewer could not tell if 46 percent of men were married, compared to 11 percent of the women; and could not identify if 53 percent of the men were parents, compared to 19 percent of the women. Also, less than 20 percent of male interactions have been found to focus on marital or family relationships.[40] There was no question about it—careers came first. However, among those TV characters whose marital status was clear, men appeared more successful than women, even at their marriages. Men were simply more successful at everything than women—whatever the area of endeavor. Researchers generally agreed that whereas both male and female roles were stereotyped, there was more stereotyping in the female role. However, some of the differences may be attributed to the smaller number of female characters. If there were more females on television, the writers and producers could give them more varied characteristics.

Content Effects. In terms of TV effects on sex-role socialization, research has focused primarily on stereotyping. In other words, does the viewer select roles for men and women that are like the stereotypes portrayed on television? The data seem to indicate that viewers do indeed stereotype. A 1974 study asked children three to six years old to indicate whether a woman or man would be in a certain occupation and found that children who were heavy viewers tended to stereotype men and women much more than children who were light viewers.[41] The same pattern has emerged from several studies. That is, again and again the heavy viewers gave the stereotyped answer.

On the other hand, television can have the opposite effect. That is, children can learn counterstereotyped roles from some programs. In one study, children were shown women in nontypical occupational roles (e.g., police officer, school principal). Those children who understood the content of the program thought the nontypical occupations were appropriate for a woman.[42]

Generally, then, television's effects appear to be that heavy viewing usually perpetuates sex-role stereotyping. However, by altering the ways in which women are presented in programs, such rigid sex-role stereotyping can be decreased.

Sex Education. No study has directly examined the impact of television on a child's sexual learning. However, the research that has been done points to a number of characteristics of the medium and its messages that make it likely that children's sexual socialization is affected. These are: (1) the adult nature of most programming children watch; (2) children's limited access to information and/or ideas inconsistent with the portrayals; (3) the "realism" of the portrayals; and (4) the overwhelming consistency of the messages about sexuality.

Children watch a lot of television, but they are not the intended audience for most of what they choose to watch. Because the programs are directed principally at older audiences, they often deal with aspects of life that usually, in other contexts, are considered to be off-limits to children. A clear example of this curious situation is television's portrayal of most aspects of sexuality. Obviously, children are not as sophisticated as adult viewers. They have limited experience as a basis for placing the portrayals in perspective, and they are less aware of the differences between fantasy and reality. For the young viewer, the sexual portrayal is often far different from anything else in a limited life experience. Thus, because they are still in the process of developing cognitive and social skills, boys or girls may not adequately assess and evaluate what they see. Moreover, they usually lack other sources of information on sexual behavior to compare with the television messages.

Additionally, the sexual and values attitudes usually presented in TV programming seem remarkably "real." Most of the programs children watch are fictional. Yet much time, money, and skill are spent by the programs' creators in locating the action in realistic settings and portraying the actors in situations that seem true to life. Thus, TV programs present seemingly realistic information about human relationships, including their sexual aspects.

Furthermore, the overwhelming consistency of the sexual attitudes and values portrayed adds to television's effectiveness as a sex educator. The impact of programming is seldom the result of a specific scene or even a program. It is the cumulative result of many messages received over time. During the 1970s, researchers reported that most of the images of sexual life were similar, thus making it more likely that television was affecting children's sexual socialization. Indeed, many parents believe television to be a major source of sex education for their children. In a 1978 study, about half of the 1400 parents interviewed indicated that their children learned more about sex from television than from any other source except themselves.[43] In fact, they related that television was more important than peer communication in affecting their children's learning about sexuality. This viewpoint was especially evident among parents who themselves were heavy viewers (27 to 35 hours a week). Heavy-viewing parents said they believed television to be an accurate source of information about sexuality for their children. Light viewers, on the other hand, did not tend to view television sexual information as accurate.

In heavy viewing families, parents did not talk about sexuality with their children. The same parents also believed that it should not be discussed outside the family. This lack of communication about the subject within the families of heavy viewers, along with the consistent messages of television programming, implies that TV entertainment may be an important sex educator indeed. Researcher Elizabeth Roberts summarizes:

> Our concern with television's sexual curricula is of more than speculative interest. At the simplest level, one implication of the research is clear: television is a sex educator of our children and a potentially powerful one. Contemporary television entertainment is saturated with sexual lessons, lessons which are likely to have an impact on young viewers' sexual development and behavior.[44]

Race and Ethnicity

For the hundreds of thousands of Americans who live in sections of the country where few minority citizens reside, television's portrayal of racial and ethnic minorities in news and fiction is the primary source of information about them. Much attention has been given to the portrayal of blacks, but little attention has been paid to Hispanics or any other group, except frequency counts. In addition, the studies done, consistent with other areas of research, have generally been content analyses rather than studies of the effects of content.

Content Analyses. The proportion of black characters on TV was about 10 percent during the 1970s, a near equivalent to their actual proportion in the population. This is in contrast to the 1950s, when there were only a few black characters shown, all of whom were classic comic stereotypes like Amos and Andy. Hispanics were far fewer, reported as 2.9 percent (1970–1976) and 1.5 percent (1975–1977). Orientals comprised 2.5 percent between 1970 and 1976. Native Americans comprised less than half of one percent during the same period.[45]

Both black and Hispanic TV characters were found mainly in situation comedies. Approximately 41 percent of all black characters appeared in just six shows. The same kind of concentration was also found with Hispanic characters, with 50 percent in only four shows. During the 1950s and 1960s, blacks were overrepresented as criminals. This was no longer true, however, in the 1970s. But blacks were less likely than whites to have jobs and, when employed, more likely to have lower status jobs.

An analysis of the occupation of Hispanic characters on television revealed a heavy emphasis on unskilled or semiskilled labor. Furthermore, of the 53 Hispanics found in three sample weeks, 22 were comic portrayals and 22 were either lawbreakers or law enforcers. Thus, there were three significant images of Hispanics: the clown, the criminal, and the cop.

Overall, substantial information has been gathered concerning the way in which blacks are portrayed on television. But information about Hispanics is just emerging, as are the characters themselves.

Content Effects. The concerns in this area are twofold: (1) do the portrayals of minorities affect white children's attitudes and reactions toward them; and (2) do the portrayals affect the self-image of minority children? Research has indicated that white children who have little or no interaction with blacks report that television has given them information about their physical appearance, speech, and dress. Studies of "Sesame Street" give evidence that white children who were regular viewers had more positive attitudes toward other races than children who had not been exposed to the programs. Additionally, a 1976 study with white nursery school youngsters manipulated segments of a program containing nonwhite characters. Only one-third of the control group (who viewed solely white actors) subsequently selected minority playmates from photos. However, more than two-thirds of those exposed to multiracial segments made similar choices.[46] Thus, it can be concluded that television is a factor in socialization regarding race and ethnicity for many white children, especially those who have limited contact with minorities.

Researchers have also studied the self-image of minority group children who watch programs such as "Sesame Street" and "Villa Alegre". In general, all of these public television shows have had a favorable effect on cultural pride, self-confidence, and interpersonal cooperativeness of minority children. It has also been found that movies depicting successful black athletes, entertainers, and others enhanced the self-concept of black children. Contrary to popular belief, black children exposed to a white-dominated medium did not develop destructive self-images. There was no research published during the 1970s that examined the impact of the commercial portrayal of Hispanics on the socialization of either Hispanic or Anglo children. It is likely, however, that there will be a strong emphasis on this question in the 1980s.

Aging and the Elderly

The topic of television and aging is of particular interest for two major (but rather ironic) reasons. First, people over 65 watch more television than any other age group (even more than children). There is virtually unanimous agreement that television is of utmost importance in the lives of many elderly people. It is their most frequently named activity. Second, older people are infrequently seen on television, but, when they are shown, they are often portrayed in a negative fashion. It was not until the decade of the 1970s that researchers concerned themselves with the characteristics of the elderly shown on television.

Content Analyses. A 1979 study by Gerbner and associates analyzed the image of aging on prime-time programs for the years 1969–1978. [47] Of the over 9000 characters that were portrayed, only 3.7 percent of major and minor characters were 65 or older. The ones that were shown were portrayed as comparatively unattractive and unhappy. Other studies reported even fewer elderly characters, usually only a little over 2 percent. Also, through stereotypic characterizations, television tended to perpetuate myths of old age. Many studies indicated that television presented a picture of the television elderly as being verbally hostile, cranky, ugly sexless, senile, confused, helpless, stubborn, eccentric, and foolish. These attributes, however, emerged primarily from prime-time programming. In sharp contrast, the daytime soap operas presented the older person as important, attractive, and independent.

Older men greatly outnumber older women in prime-time television, even though in "real" life there are more older women than men. One researcher reported that a viewer could expect to see an old man about every 22 minutes on prime-time television, while one would see an elderly woman only every four or five hours. In addition, females were shown to age earlier and faster than males. In general, older women were portrayed in a more negative fashion than older men and were almost never portrayed as "successful." The exception again was the soap opera. Here, women's roles were stronger, and older women had very positive, serious roles. A mention should be made of game shows, since they are a favorite of the older viewing audience. A 1975 study found that not only were older people rarely contestants but also that they seldom were even in view when the camera panned the studio audience. They had usually been seated in the rear.[48]

Occasionally, elderly people were found to be shown performing moderate-to-high physical activity (e.g., energetic dancing, riding a motorcycle, or alluding to a vigorous sex life). However, researchers believe that these "reversed stereotypes" may do more harm than good for the image of the elderly because viewers generally interpret these actions as comical or inappropriate.

Content Effects. The major concerns in this area are: what are the effects of television on the elderly population and also how do the portrayals of the aged population affect attitudes and reactions toward them? In a 1980 study, researchers examined the self-perceptions of elderly individuals and related this to the amount of television viewed.[49] They found that positive perceptions of television portrayals of the elderly enhanced the self-concepts of older people. Likewise, negative portrayals lowered self-esteem. Also, frequent viewers, when compared to less frequent viewers, were more likely to view the elderly in general as hindrances to society; heavy viewers also had lower self-concepts than lighter viewers.

Several studies by Gerbner and his associates found that young people who were heavy viewers tended to stereotype the elderly much more than did young people who were light viewers. Specifically, among heavy viewers, the young were more likely to believe that older people were "not open-minded, not bright, alert or good at getting things done." Heavy viewing also led to other inaccurate beliefs about old people, such as the idea that the number of elderly persons was decreasing or that old people did not live as long as they used to and, in general, were less healthy than was the case 20 or 30 years ago.

It has been argued that the greatest fault in television with respect to aging is that it does not accurately reflect real life in either the numbers of old people portrayed or in the way they are shown. The National Council on Aging has argued that television is the channel through which elimination of stereotypes about aging must occur. On a more hopeful note, a 1980 study found that the number of older characters on television had increased and that the television industry appeared more willing to confront issues on aging as subject matter.[50]

Training Consumers

Consumer socialization has been defined as "the developmental process by which young people acquire the knowledge, attitudes, and skills relevant to their functioning in the marketplace."[51] In the study of television's effects on consumer roles, most of the research has dealt with advertisements and has used children as subjects. Only a small amount of research has been done on entertainment programs or employed adults as subjects.

Responses to advertising differ substantially across various social categories. Consumers can be categorized according to race, sex, socioeconomic status, and social context. The most crucial variable, however, is age, since information-processing abilities and product needs vary through the life cycle. Researchers in the area of consumer socialization have generally used three broad age categories: childhood (up to age 12), adolescence (12 to 17), and adulthood (18 and older).

Children's Responses to Advertising. Many researchers have been concerned with the consequences of children's annual exposure to about 20,000 television commercials, especially those Saturday morning ads that are targeted to young audiences. Generally, young children (under 12) like to watch Saturday morning commercials, whereas adolescents are undecided. The younger children enjoy the humor and entertaining qualities of TV commercials.

Age is also an important factor in children's belief in advertising claims. Young children usually believe the claims, but older ones are more skeptical. Trust by children is related to the product. They are more distrustful of claims made about toys they know about than they are about medical or nutritional products. Heavy-viewing children are also more likely to believe advertisements than are light viewers.

Some researchers have tried to determine the role of television advertising in the development of children's awareness of, and preference for, toys and food products. In some cases, they simply asked children or their parents where they learn about desired products. According to a 1977 study, mothers of young children ranked television first as a learning source for products in general, followed by friends and catalogs.[52] A similar study supported this conclusion; mothers and children both cited television as the most important source for cereal and toy information.[53]

Children often desire to have advertised products. Several studies have found a high positive correlation between viewing commercials and liking frequently advertised foods. One study reported that children who saw an advertisement for a toy tended to prefer playing with the toy than with a friend. In fact, they would rather play with a not-so-nice friend if he or she owned the toy than with a nice friend who did not possess the toy.[54]

A significant finding with young children is that they often take advertisements literally. In a laboratory study, children aged four to seven were shown an ad for Cocoa Pebbles cereal where cartoon characters Fred Flintstone and Barney Rubble claimed that the cereal was "chocolatey enough to make you smile." Among the reasons for wanting to eat the cereal, two-thirds cited the chocolate taste, three-fifths wanted it because it would make them smile, and more than half desired the cereal because Fred and Barney liked it.[55]

In another study, an advertisement that showed a circus strongman lifting a playhouse and eating the cereal was presented to youngsters. When asked, nearly two-thirds of the four- to seven-year-old children thought that the cereal would make them stronger. One-third even said that the cereal would make them strong enough to lift really heavy objects.[56] Again, children who were frequent viewers of the Saturday morning cereal advertising at home were much more likely to believe the strength claims than those who were not heavily exposed.

Several studies have indicated that children do not evaluate food advertising critically. In fact, young children tended to accept as true claims made in four ads identified by the Federal Trade Commission (FTC) as possibly deceptive. Again, a significant difference was found between heavy and light viewers. Heavy television viewers were less certain about the validity of nutrition claims in food commercials and had lower nutrition knowledge.[57]

Adolescents' Responses to Advertising. Most of the studies investigating the response of adolescents to advertising consist of survey research rather than experimental studies. Typically, the studies have involved self-administered questionnaires, with large samples of middle school and high school students. A major methodological weakness in most of these studies is that advertising exposure is not measured directly. As a rule, the investigators simply measure total hours of viewing television. This is at best an indirect and crude indicator of exposure to TV ads. The major conclusion is that adolescents' awareness of brands and brand slogans was only "mildly or moderately related" to television viewing. Yet, in one study where actual viewing of alcohol advertisements was measured, there was a strong positive correlation between viewing the commercial and being aware of the slogans, symbols, and content presented in those commercials.[58]

Studies have also focused on how adolescents see the typical consumers of various brands and products. To some extent, heavy viewers tended to believe that more people needed or used highly advertised products such as over-the-counter medicines, mouthwash, deodorants, and alcohol. There were also weak positive associations between exposure to television commercials and the belief that these health products were effective.

In general, it was concluded that "television advertising has a distinct but hardly overwhelming impact on...adolescent consumers."[59] This could, however, result in part from weakness in the research; i.e., using total hours viewing as an indicator of exposure to ads. Several studies that measured actual exposure to ads found that adolescents who were highly exposed tended to prefer advertised brands. One example of this tendency is the positive relationship between watching beer and wine commercials and citing these brands as favorites. Furthermore, aside from brand preferences, TV ads led to more accepting attitudes regarding the practice of using certain restricted products such as alcohol.

Adults' Responses to Advertising. Advertising is believed to have a strong influence on the knowledge of brand names and advertising claims among adults. For example, one study found that half of the public was aware of Crest toothpaste's endorsement from the American Dental Association within two weeks after it was announced in their advertising.[60] Another study found that more than half of the public knew the heavily promoted slogans of Budweiser beer, United Airlines, and General Electric.[61] It has been found that viewing alcohol ads correlates strongly with knowing the brand names, slogans, symbols, and themes of beers, wines, and liquors. Several surveys have demonstrated weak to strong positive associations between advertising exposure and purchases of the advertised items. Also, brands that are advertised frequently tend to achieve higher sales. This should not be surprising since the producers of television materials invest more dollars and human resources in the production of commercials than in the production of programs. It has been argued that commercials are "the medium's best shot" and, indeed, its most effective vehicle for influencing beliefs, attitudes, and behavior. This is especially true for young children who do not understand the selling purpose of commercials. It is rather ironic that it is the entertainment "filler" between commercials that has attracted the most research. Whatever effects television entertainment has on Americans' belief systems, stereotypes, and behavior, they are for the most part "unintended side effects." After all, the intended effect is on consumer behavior.

EFFECTS OF TELEVISION ON AMERICAN INSTITUTIONS

As the previous sections reveal, the majority of studies by social and behavioral scientists have concentrated on the effects of the medium on individuals. A broader, and equally important question, concerns the influences of television on social institutions. In his chapter, "Television and American Social Institutions," George Comstock summarized research on TV's influences on such aspects of social life as religion, law and norms, leisure, public security, and citizenship.[62] The present section draws heavily from his work.

Religion

Comstock noted that little research has been done on the effects of television on religious behavior. A 1972 study found that television has reduced the amount of time devoted to conventional religious practices.[63] It has been argued that television itself promotes secularization and thus lessens the importance of organized religion. Yet, the audience for Sunday morning religious broadcasts is a sizeable one, averaging some 13 million persons. Some faithful who cannot attend a local service obviously tune to TV religion; others may have found televised preaching more to their liking than what they found in a church. For one thing, religion on television has more in common with entertainment than with the typical church service. In addition, the rise of cable television has seen evangelical leaders use TV to increase their followings and their empires. This topic will obviously be of interest to researchers in the future.

Laws and Norms

Comstock advanced three main arguments to explain television's effects on laws and norm: (1) Television is a disruptive force due to its heavy emphasis on aggression and antisocial behavior; (2) television is a powerful reinforcer of the status quo; and (3) television contributes to a homogenization of norms. Each of these arguments will be reviewed.

Television as a Disruptive Force. Due to its frequent portrayal of violence, viewers are likely to accept aggression as normal behavior. Support for this argument does exist, since violence on television is correlated with aggressive behavior. As discussed in Chapter 14, this connection is now well documented in both laboratory and field studies. In addition, there have been instances in which singular portrayals appear to have led to antisocial acts like those depicted. A notable example was the increase in airline bomb threats that followed a broadcast of *Doomsday Flight*. Such findings are said to show that television may contribute to a disruption of the social order.

Television as a Reinforcer of the Status Quo. Television portrayals assign roles of power and authority, success and failure, and dependence and vulnerability in a manner that matches real-life social hierarchies. Thus, it is argued that such televised portrayals perpetuate power, on the other hand, and subservience, on the other. However, the proposition that television reinforces the status quo is actually a speculative one that is virtually untestable. Indeed, the proposition is so wholistic that it is somewhat like asking about the effects of Christianity, Confucianism, and the automobile.

Television as a Contributor to Homogenization of Society. There can be no doubt that television has become a shared experience for people from all walks of life. It is true that there are differences in viewing time and attitudes toward TV among social categories, yet viewing is sufficiently similar among all segments of the population for television to be considered a common national experience. This shared experience is said to lead to the assimilation of middle-class values throughout the population. Thus, it is argued that television reduces differences among social strata. In this sense, it is said to contribute to a "homogenization" of society.

While speculation is abundantly available on this issue, definitive data are conspicuous by their absence. Furthermore, it should be pointed out that these arguments are not mutually exclusive. Perhaps they are all correct but simply point out different types of effects that televised portrayals may have on our society.

Leisure

Television has profoundly changed the way Americans spend their leisure time. In fact, viewing ranks third behind sleep and work as a consumer of time. Moreover, the impact of the medium on leisure time is not the same in all segments of society. Those of lower socioeconomic status—blacks, women, and the elderly—view more. Thus, television occupies an even greater proportion of their time than it does for the more affluent. Yet, there is no doubt that most groups and strata engage in extensive viewing.

A UNESCO study of the way time is spent in modern society has made a major contribution to an understanding of the impact of television on leisure time.[64] Diaries of 24-hour time allocations were obtained from large samples of employed adults in fifteen industrialized cities in The United States, Western Europe, and Latin America. Set owners were compared to those without television and it was found that time spent viewing television reduced time that would otherwise have been spent at social gatherings away from home, in conversation with other family members and others, with other media, on households tasks, and on other leisure time activities.

Television has also affected the economic viability of other media and activities, stifling some and leading to the reshaping of others in the attempt to meet television's competition.[65] For example, TV has drastically reduced the audience for movies. Moreover, there is evidence that it has probably contributed to an increase in violence and explicit treatment of sexual themes in films. Because of the competition between movies and television, filmmakers employed the predictable means of telling stories in ways less acceptable in a medium that functions in a living room. Television also appears to have brought about the demise of such mass-audience magazines as the *Saturday Evening Post, Collier's*, and *Look*, probably by providing a new and superior means by which advertisers could reach consumers. However, magazines that were devoted to specialized audiences prospered because they served well-focused interests incompatible with the more general and inclusive character of television audiences. But it is possible that the specialized cable channels will have similar effects on the more specialized magazines. Time will tell.

Television is believed to have been an important factor in the decline of film and such media as comic books. It certainly changed the nature of radio. Some claim that even the newspaper has been affected by the growth of television. Until the 1970s, per capita daily newspaper circulation kept pace with population growth. Then, in the 1970s, it began to lag. How much television contributed to this trend is not known. However, some media researchers believe that the trend reflects the growing proportions of persons who grew up with television and who watch it for news as well as entertainment.

These effects of television, however, are not solely the result of television-consuming time that might otherwise be spent pursuing other media. They are due, at least in part, to the ability of television to perform the same functions or services of alternative media more economically and perhaps more conveniently.

Leisure options outside of the media have also been changed by television. For example, it has been argued that television demolished minor league baseball. Between 1950 and 1970, attendance plunged from 42 to 10 million. Why? Because the people could now sit in their living rooms and watch the major leagues play as well as watch sports figures of national significance. Yet, while television may harm a sport by keeping people away from the stadium, it also may support it through fees paid by the broadcaster to carry it. Thus, television can create new fans for rising sports like tennis and soccer. It has even been argued that television made football our most popular sport and created a new national holiday—Super Bowl Day.

Public Security

Does television affect our public security? This might seem like a far-fetched question, yet, it has frequently been noted that terrorist acts and outbreaks of violence tend to occur in a series or cluster. For example, the hijacking of planes to Cuba and other destinations has often increased sharply after prominent television coverage of a similar incident. The same was true with the urban riots of the late 1960's and early 1970's. More recently, tampering with an over-the-counter medication (Tylenol) apparently stimulated copycat incidents with Contac and Excedrin. The copying appears to have spread to foods like Jif peanut butter and Lipton's Cup-a-Soup. In its coverage, television may actually provide useful clues as to how one commits such an act. So, an individual may not only receive an idea of what to do from TV but also how to do it. On the other hand, public safety may be enhanced when such events occur because people who might ordinarily buy such products tend to be deterred by televised coverage of the events.

In some instances, television coverage itself may be the goal. For decades, political and other types of demonstrators have sought television coverage to be sure "the whole world is watching!" Thus, coverage shapes as well as reports the events. Attempts to gain television coverage on behalf of a cause or goal may result in actions that affect public security directly. Such examples raise many questions about the ethics of television broadcast policies; they surely deserve to be the subject of debate during the next several years.

Even the way in which world events are covered can have an effect. For example, television coverage of the Vietnam War is believed to have played a major role in generating public opposition to the war. One broadcast in particular may have been pivotal. On February 2, 1968, NBC televised, in gruesome color, the assassination on a Saigon street of an unarmed prisoner of war by a South Vietnam general. Such media events led General Westmoreland, when he returned to the U.S. after the American withdrawal from Vietnam, to declare that television had made war untenable to the public because of the graphic display of its ugliness. In line with this, George

Comstock has argued: "It has often been said that television drama sanitizes violence by avoiding gruesome consequences; it could also be argued that television news *desanitizes* war." (italics added.)[66]

Citizenship

Television, it is agreed, has reshaped American politics. There are few who would disagree that the medium has affected the behavior of politicians and the conduct of political campaigns. Examples include devising campaign strategies to maximize favorable exposure on television, the importance of communications and advertising experts in the mapping of campaigns, and the devotion of major portions of campaign budgets to television. In addition, because of the enormous journalistic forces that it deploys, television has largely removed the suspense from any vote. As a result, the parties have turned to the devices of show business to hold the attention of viewers.

In a similar fashion, TV coverage has changed the function of political conventions. Television coverage of the primaries has narrowed the options open to convention delegates. By the time of the convention, the field has been narrowed to only one or two contenders. The medium's focus on winners and losers has virtually disqualified some candidates. Before the advent of television, many candidates remained viable nominees until the convention voting had ended. The competitive network coverage of the primaries has converted what were once state or regional contests into national events. This ability to reach the public has changed the nature of the nominating process. As a result of the coverage, the number of primaries has doubled, further reinforcing TV's ability to influence the selection.

In spite of these effects on the selection process for candidates, televised election coverage does not seem to have a large role in either directly changing the allegiance of voters from one candidate to another or in influencing voter choice indirectly. Instead, television's role is to crystallize and reinforce voters' decisions and inclinations. But as George Comstock has argued: "[television's] extensive political coverage alerts the nation to the forthcoming political choice. In this respect, it certainly peforms a major and importance task."[67]

Despite television's extensive coverage of national politics, two political scientists reported that they found no relationship between the exposure of voters to network news and their knowledge of issues and candidates in a presidential election.[68] However, television tends to cover visually interesting content pertaining to the candidates such as welcoming parades, handshaking, and ethnic events. Thus, there is a limited amount of time available for the coverage of issues.

Overall, researchers have argued that television coverage of politics has two major consequences for our society. First, the image of the candidates has become crucial to voter decision. Second, the event-and-image bias of television news has made political advertising more important and effective in conveying information about the position that candidates hold on the issues. Brief political statements purchased by the candidate and aired at specified times reach more viewers because they are aired in regular commercial spots and are not avoided by them. If voters are ignorant of a candidate's position, and if the issue is central to their vote decision, such political commercials have the potential for great influence. But whereas voters consistently name television as their principal source of news in a presidential campaign, newspapers are the preferred medium of the well educated, of professionals, and of white-collar workers—the segments of the population most likely to vote.[69] Newspaper coverage is also more effective than television news in making voters aware of specific issues.

On the whole, the evidence marshalled by Comstock points toward a relatively restrictive view of the influence of TV in the electoral process. However, historical trends indicate that the mass media will have greater influence in the future. Faith in party system has been declining, and the number of voters not aligned with a party has been increasing. There is also evidence that there is a growing reliance on issues and ideology to make voting choices. Examples of this are the increasing proportion of the voting population who consider themselves to be independents as well as those who split their votes among candidates of opposing parties in different races (split-ticket voting). In addition, within each party, the proportion of members who hold noncentrist positions has been increasing. We may infer from these changes a politics of the future in which information plays a greatly enhanced role. Conversely, reinforcement and crystallization, in the sense of cultivating prior loyalties, presumably will have a reduced role. It also implies a politics that is volatile, with the uncertain voter becoming the norm rather than the exception. In such circumstances, the influence of the mass media is likely to grow. If the influence of television in the political arena does increase, and its coverage continues to deal with personalities and politics as drama rather than as competing on issues, such trends could present major problems for our society and its political future.

CONCLUSIONS AND IMPLICATIONS

The 1982 version of *Television and Behavior* is in essence a summary of 90 percent of the published research on the medium's influence on our lives at the time of publication. For the most part, the report covers research published during the 1970s, although a few of the titles appeared in 1980. The fact that one decade could produce such a massive amount of literature accents the interest in the role of television in American society.

If a single statement could epitomize what was found in this research summary, it is the following:

Almost all the evidence testifies to television's role as a formidable educator whose effects are both pervasive and cumulative. Television can no longer be considered as a casual part of daily life, as an electronic toy. Research findings have long since destroyed the illusion that television is merely innocuous entertainment. While the learning it provides is mainly incidental rather than direct and formal, it is a significant part of the total acculturation process.[70]

Coinciding with the research findings is the large place that television has in American daily life. It must be kept in mind that about half of the present U.S. population has never experienced life without it. In short, television is now a deeply embedded social institution in American society. And, as such, it has changed or influenced most other institutions—from the family to the functioning of the government.

One of the most significant developments signalled by the NIMH report is that media research moved beyond the violence theme and started to investigate the possible interaction between the viewer and what is seen on the television screen. This was quite a departure from the first Surgeon General's report.

The 1982 report also signaled another major development in media effects research. It reflected clearly the shift to a new theoretical point of departure for research—the meaning paradigm emphasizing the role of mass communication in the social construction of reality within our society. It became clear to many researchers that among the potentially damaging influences of television is the way it may shape the viewer's perceptions of the real world. As we have seen in this chapter, concern ranges from the portrayal of women and minority groups in stereotypic fashion to the portrayal of family life (and how that might affect our expectations and evaluations of our own family) to health portrayals and how these affect our views and behavior regarding what is a healthy life-style. Why are all these types of portrayals important? As Rubenstein argues:

> To the extent that television shows minority groups in demeaning roles, women in excessively passive and subordinate positions, older people as senile and burdensome, or an overrepresentation of doctors, lawyers, police officers, or other professionals, the young viewer—especially the heavy viewer—is seeing a distorted image of the real world.[71]

Of course, the real concern is that these portrayals have real-life effects. For example, the mentally ill are often portrayed as dangerous and violent, even though the vast majority are not. However, this type of portrayal is believed to be related to the stigma that the mentally ill must shoulder. Thus, in the long run, it is assumed that what has been shown on the television screen makes life more difficult for those classified as mentally ill or who have suffered from such conditions in the past.[72]

The present review of *Television and Behavior* leads to a major flaw evident in many of the research reports. The report presents many descriptive content analyses, but it is short on studies that document the effects of that content. Proof of impact is obviously much more tedious, qualified, and time-consuming than describing what has been shown. Perhaps this is the reason why such documentation has not been pursued with vigor. At the same time, such documentation is not impossible. The focused theories derived from the meaning paradigm predict, generally speaking, the type of effects a given content should have. It is now time to resist simply assuming effects from content and turn to demonstrating that they actually exist.

In addition, even the content analyses themselves are not without flaws. Obviously, it is important to know the content (and thus the messages and meanings) of television programming. For that reason, content analyses should be rigorously conducted. Yet, so many of them are based largely on simple counts of frequency or quantity of a phenomenon portrayed. Moreover, it is often assumed that if people in a given social category, group, or role are omitted or neglected in portrayals by the medium, this condition will lead to a devaluation of such people in real life. This proposition is difficult to evaluate. For example, if Hispanics are not seen on television, some people may believe that it is because they are not worth seeing. But, if few bankers are seen, it is doubtful they will be devalued for that reason.

Another real problem with content analyses as they are presently done is that they are based on samples of television characters. Researchers then draw influences about the behavior of members of the audience from those samples. Such a procedure does not take into account patterns of viewing typical among those who watch television. But audiences do not watch representative samples of characters; instead, they are highly selective in what they view. This means that generalizations based on average stimuli have little meaning because audience members do not watch in such patterns. In other words, content effects for individuals can be predicted only, if at all, from knowledge of what they actually view—not from what is available on the TV screen.

Overall, *Television and Behavior: Ten Years of Scientific Progress and Implications for the Eighties* is a noteworthy document for several major reasons:

1. It shifts the focus away from the relatively narrow confines of violence on television to a larger concern. Thus, a broader area of television-influenced behavior is examined.
2. There is also a shift from examining short-term direct effects to searching for long-term indirect effects, which are, of course, more elusive and of considerable more importance to our society.
3. The above change in focus was brought about by a shift in paradigms from the cognitive approach to the meaning paradigm that focuses on the role of communication in the social construction of reality. (This is discussed in more detail in Chapter 16.)

4. The report promoted the view of television as an important educator, albeit an informal rather than a formal one.

Obviously, there are connections among these four reasons. For many years, the high visibility and continued emphasis on televised violence has obscured other important issues. In particular, it is important to look at the totality of television viewing as a continuing form of informal education. The 1982 report has given us a clearer view.

Still, some people will argue that the issue of television influence is "much ado about nothing." Their argument is that television is nothing more than a mirror reflecting what we are as a society and as human beings. However, research in this report has found that, at least in several major areas, this argument does not hold true. Many distortions of reality occur on television. In addition, even if television were only reflecting our society, that would tend to have the effect of reinforcing the status quo—not an insignificant effect in itself. Finally, if television is but a mirror of life, it may, nevertheless, like Alice's looking-glass, possess some intriguing and life-changing qualities. Only time and research will tell.

NOTES AND REFERENCES

1. David Pearl, Lorraine Bouthilet, and Joyce Lazar, eds., *Television and Behavior: Ten Years of Scientific Progress and Implications for the Eighties* (Vol I). (Washington, D.C.: U.S. Government Printing Office, 1982), p. 2.

2. Ibid., p. 87.

3. George Gerbner, Michael Morgan, and Nancy Signorielli, "Programming Health Portrayals: What Viewers See, Say and Do," in David Pearl, Lorraine Bouthilet, and Joyce Lazar, eds., Television and Behavior (Vol. II) (Washington, D.C.: U.S. Government Printing Office, 1982), pp. 291–307.

4. Douglas S. Solomon, "Health Campaigns on Television," in D. Pearl, L. Bouthilet, and Joyce Lazar, op. cit. (Vol. II), 1982, pp. 308–321.

5. Eli A. Rubenstein and Joyce N. Sprafkin, "Television and Persons in Institutions," in D. Pearl, L. Bouthilet, and J. Lazar, op. cit. (Vol. II), 1982, pp. 322–330.

6. George Gerbner, Michael Morgan, and Nancy Signiorelli, op. cit., p. 292.

7. F.A. Smith, G. Trivax, D. A. Zuehlke, P. Lowinger, and T. L. Nghiem, "Health Information During a Week of Television." *New England Journal of Medicine*, 1972, 518–520. Cited in Gerbner, Morgan, and Nancy Signiorelli, op. cit., pp. 291–307.

8. George Gerbner, Michael Morgan, and Nancy Signiorelli, op. cit., p. 297.

9. J. Dillon, "TV Drinking: How Networks Pour Liquor into Your Living Room." *Christian Science Monitor*, June 30, 1975. Cited in George Gerbner, Michael Morgan, and Nancy Signiorelli, op. cit., p. 297.

10. E. Futch, M. J. Geller, and S. A. Lisman, "Analysis of Alcohol Use on Prime-

Time Television." Unpublished paper, State University of New York at Binghamton, 1980. Cited in Gerbner, Morgan, and Signiorelli, op. cit., p. 297.

11. George Gerbner, Michael Morgan, and Nancy Signiorelli, op. cit., p. 296.

12. L. Kaufman, "Prime-time Nutrition," *Journal of Communication*, 1980, 30 (3), 37–46.

13. George Gerbner, Michael Morgan, and Nancy Signiorelli, op. cit., p. 297.

14. M. Downing, *The World of Daytime Television Serial Drama.* Unpublished doctoral dissertation, University of Pennsylvania, 1975.

15. M.G. Perloff, "Television Soap Bubbles," *New Republic*, 172, May 10, 1975, 27–30.

16. George Gerbner, Michael Morgan, and Nancy Signiorelli, op. cit., (Vol. II) p. 295.

17. P.V. Miller, A.J. Morrison, and F.G. Kline, "Approaches to Characterizing Information Environments." Paper presented at the meetings of the International Communication Association, New Orleans, 1974.

18. F.G. Kline, P.V. Miller, and A.J. Morrison, "Adolescents and Family Planning Information: An Exploration of Audience Needs and Media Effects." In J. Blumer and E. Katz, eds., *The Ways of Mass Communications.* (Beverly Hills: Sage, 1974).

19. General Mills, Inc., *The General Mills American Family Reports, 1978–79: Family Health in an Era of Stress.* (Minneapolis: General Mills, 1979).

20. See H. L. Arenstein, *The Effect of Television on Children's Stereotyping of Occupational Roles.* Unpublished Master's thesis, Annenberg School of Communications, University of Pennsylvania, 1974. Also see J. McLaughlin, "The Doctor Shows," *Journal of Communication*, 1975, 25(3), 182–184.

21. George Gerbner, Michael Morgan, and Nancy Signiorelli, op. cit., p. 301.

22. Douglas S. Solomon, op. cit., p. 13.

23. J.W. Farquar, et al., "Community Education for Cardiovascular Health." *The Lancet*, 1977, June 4, 1192–1195.

24. K.W. Mielke and J.W. Swinehart, *Evaluation of the Feeling Good Television Series.* (New York: Children's Television Workshop, 1976).

25. See D.W. Jeffers, R.E. Ostman, and C. Atkinson, "Mass Media Availability and Use in a Mental Institution." *Journalism Quarterly*, 1979, 56, 126–133. Also see, R.E. Ostman, D.W. Jeffers, and C. Atkinson, "Madness and the Mass Media." Paper presented at the convention of the Popular Culture Association, Cincinatti, April, 1978.

26. H. Wadeson and W.T. Carpenter, "Television in the Hospital: Programming Patients' Delusions." *American Journal of Orthopsychiatry*, 1976, 46, 434–438.

27. Lynda M. Glennon and Richard Butsch, "The Family As Portrayed on Television, 1946–1978," in D. Pearl, L. Bouthilet, and J. Lazar, op. cit. (Vol. II), 1982, p. 265.

28. Ibid.

29. Jack M. McLeod, Mary Anne Fitzpatrick, Carroll J. Glynn, and Susan F. Fallis, "Television and Social Relations: Family Influences and Consequences for Interpersonal Behavior," in D. Pearl, L. Bouthilet, and J. Lazar, *op. cit.* (Vol. II), 1982, pp. 272–286.

30. Ibid.

31. P.J. Mohr, "Parental Guidance of Children's Viewing of Evening Television Programs." *Journal of Broadcasting*, 1979, 23, 213–228.

32. P.C. Rosenblatt and M.R. Cunningham, "Television Watching and Family Tension." *Journal of Marriage and the Family*, 1976, 38, 105−111.

33. J.M. McLeod, et al., op cit., p. 280.

34. G.S. Lesser, *Children and Television: Lessons from Sesame Street*, (New York: Random House, 1974).

35. J.M. Mcleod, et. al., op. cit., p. 283.

36. D. Pearl, L. Bouthilet, and J. Lazar, op. cit. (Vol. I), 1982, p. 36.

37. L. Busby, "Defining the Sex Role Standard in Commercial Network Television Programs Directed Toward Children." *Journalism Quarterly*, 1974, 51, 690−696.

38. J. McNeil, "Feminism, Femininity, and the Television Series: A Content Analysis." *Journal of Broadcasting*, 1975, 19, 259−269.

39. For a discussion of this study and other similar ones, see Elizabeth J. Roberts, "Television and Sexual Learning in Childhood," in D. Pearl, L. Bouthilet, and J. Lazar, op. cit. (Vol. II), 1982, pp. 209−223.

40. Ibid.

41. A. Beuf, "Doctor, Lawyer, Household Drudge." *Journal of Communication*, 1974, 24(2), 142 −145.

42. M. Miller and B. Reeves, "Dramatic TV Content and Children's Sex-Role Stereotypes." *Journal of Broadcasting*, 1976, 20, 35−50.

43. E.J. Roberts, D. Kline, and J. Gagnon, *Family Life and Sexual Learning.* (Cambridge, Mass.: Population Educated, Inc., 1978).

44. Elizabeth J. Roberts, op. cit., 1982, p. 222.

45. Bradley S. Greenberg, "Television and Role Socialization: An Overview," in D. Pearl, L. Bouthilet, and J. Lazar, op. cit. (Vol. II), 1982, pp. 179−190.

46. G. Gorn, M. Goldberg and R. Kanugo, "The Role of Educational Television in Changing the Intergroup Attitudes of Children." *Child Development*, 1976, 47, 277−280.

47. For a discussion of this study, see Bradley S. Greenberg, op. cit., pp. 186−187.

48. Ibid.

49. F. Korzenny and K. Neuendorf. "Television Viewing and Self-Concept of the Elderly." *Journal of Communication*, 1980, 30 (1) 71−80.

50. R.H. Davis, *Television and the Aging Audience.* (Los Angeles: Andrus Gerontology Center, University of Southern California, 1980).

51. Charles K. Atkin, "Television Advertising and Socialization to Consumer Roles," in D. Pearl, L. Bouthilet, and J. Lazar, op. cit. (Vol. II), 1982, p. 191.

52. T. Barry and A. Sheikh, "Race as a Dimension in Children's TV Advertising: The Need for More Research." *Journal of Advertising*, 1977, 6, 5−18.

53. C.K. Atkin, op. cit., p. 193.

54. M. Goldberg and G. Gorn, "Some Unintended Consequences of TV Advertising to Children." *Journal of Consumer Research*, 1978, 5, 22−29.

55. C.K. Atkin, op. cit., p. 197.

56. Ibid.

57. S. Sharanga, *The Effect of Television Advertising on Children's Nutrition Attitudes, Nutrition Knowledge and Eating Habits.* Unpublished doctoral dissertation, Cornell University, Ithaca, New York, 1974. Cited in Pearl, Bouthilet, and Lazar, Vol. II, op. cit., p. 197.

58. C.K. Atkin, op. cit., p. 198.

59. Ibid., p. 198.

60. L. Bogart, *Strategy in Advertising*. (New York: Harcourt, Brace and World, 1967).
61. C. Laren and H. Wales, "Slogan Awareness in the Chicago Market." *Journal of Advertising Research*, 1970, 10 (6), 38–43.
62. See George Comstock, "Television and Social Institutions," in D. Pearl, L. Bouthilet, and J. Lazar, op. cit. (Vol. II), 1982, pp. 334-348.
63. Ibid., p. 337.
64. A. Szalari, ed., *The Use of Time: Daily Activities of Urban and Suburban Populations in Twelve Countries,* (The Hague: Mouton, 1972).
65. George Comstock, op. cit., p. 341.
66. Ibid., p. 341.
67. Ibid., p. 341.
68. T. E. Patterson and R. D. McClure, *The Unseeing Eye*. (New York: Putnam, 1976).
69. H. Mendelsohn and G. J. O'Keefe, *The People Choose a President*. (New York: Praeger, 1976).
70. D. Pearl, L. Bouthilet, and J. Lazar, op. cit., (Vol. I), p. 87.
71. Eli A. Rubenstein, "Television and Behavior: Research Conclusions of the 1982 NIMH Report and Their Policy Implications." *American Psychologist*, July, 1983, p. 882.
72. Melvin L. De Fleur and Everette E. Dennis, *Understanding Mass Communication* (Boston: Houghton Mifflin Company, 1985) pp. 393-400.

16

The Lessons of the Milestones

It is obvious that the question to be asked at this point is, *what have we learned from these thirteen major research efforts?* It is also obvious that the answer to that question will not be easy to formulate. From one point of view, the cup is at least partly full; an impressive number of empirical generalizations, concepts, theoretical paradigms, hypotheses, research strategies, and methodological techniques were produced by these projects and programs. From another point of view, the cup is still partly empty; many aspects of mass communication remain to be discovered. Compounding the difficulty is the fact that it is not always easy to separate the achievements of the thirteen efforts reviewed in the present book from those of numerous other investigations. In many cases, the latter were stimulated by the milestone studies. In turn, smaller-scale efforts sometimes played a part in shaping the directions of the major studies we have reviewed. But in spite of these considerations, there are a number of identifiable contributions that either had their origins in the milestone projects or were greatly advanced by them.

A useful approach to bringing together such a summary of significant contributions is to identify broad categories of findings that can provide a framework for interpreting the influence of these thirteen projects on the study of mass communication in American society. For example, numerous *empirical generalizations* have been formulated on the basis of observational evidence obtained in each of these important studies. These are mainly descriptions of regularities, patterns, or relationships among variables that the original investigators observed in the behavior of audiences or other components that make up our system of mass communication. How can these generalizations be assessed? They appear to have been valid and reliable in their time, but do they still describe the process and influences of mass communications in contemporary society, or has the situation changed so much that many such generalizations are obsolete? If so, are such generalizations without value?

A second issue is the current status of the *focused theories* of mass communication that describe and explain some specific aspect of the process or its effects on people. These, in particular, stimulate the research process to move forward on what is often referred to as a "cutting edge." Focused theories identify problems with known boundaries and set forth reasonably clear propositions that can be tested against well-defined data. It is in this category that some of the milestone studies have made very clear contributions.

Nevertheless, the question of their applicability to contemporary society remains relevant.

Finally, the milestone studies were conducted with certain *broad theoretical paradigms* as guides to what needed to be investigated and explained. These paradigms defined some theoretical approaches as appropriate and ruled out others. Generally, such paradigms were formulated in the social sciences, such as psychology and sociology, for the purpose of explaining the basics of human nature or the social order. Since investigators from those fields pioneered the study of mass communication, the paradigms they brought to the task have played a key role in such research ever since. Thus, their relationship to the study of mass communication needs to be traced. In particular, we need to look closely at what happened when it became evident that a particular paradigm was inconsistent with the accumulating facts in the study of media influences, and what occurred when investigators shifted from one paradigm to another.

Finally, a very different set of issues related to the milestone studies are those pertaining to *methodology*. In what ways have these thirteen studies shown us better ways to conduct research on the effects of mass communication? The question of applicability to contemporary society is less significant here. A more appropriate question is: how has communication science been enriched by the development of the measurement strategies, controls, research designs, or modes of statistical analysis used in the milestone studies? In some cases, those contributions were true innovations, in the sense that they had never been used before in any kind of social research. Their use in mass communication research was a contribution not only to the study of the media but to social science as a whole. In other cases, techniques that had proved valuable for other types of research were borrowed, brought into the field, and adapted to the study of mass communication. Both sources of methodological innovations are important, as they add significantly to the tool kit of the communication researcher.

LOOKING BACK: A REVIEW OF MAJOR FINDINGS

What can be said in overview about this legacy of research? Clearly, each of the milestone studies left its own unique contribution to the developing area of mass communication, but, clearly, some were more important than others. Taken together they provide an enormous amount of information about the effects of the media under study as they existed at the time and on the specific populations who made up their audiences. A few broke new theoretical ground, opening pathways that are still being explored today. Still others had their greatest impact on the general public—often confirming their fears of the new media among us—but in the long run providing a basis for continued financial support for research. Several introduced valuable methodological techniques. All were important in altering the perspectives of communication scholars concerning the role of the mass media in modern society and their impact on us as individuals.

Before attempting to assess the collective impact of this series of major studies, it will be helpful to review very briefly, one at a time, the salient conclusions that emerged from each. Therefore, the sections that follow provide a thumbnail sketch of their major goals, findings, and conclusions.

The Payne Fund Studies

Of the thirteen separate studies of this massive program, we chose two to illustrate the range of research strategies and interests that were used in the series as a whole. One was the set of psychological field experiments conducted by Peterson and Thurstone to study the impact of exposure to one or more films on childrens' attitudes toward social issues. The other was the more qualitative approach of Blumer, who used a biographical technique to probe the influence of the movies on childrens' daily behavior, such as in their play, imitation of the actors, daydreaming, fantasy, and emotional life.

Peterson and Thurstone concluded that exposure to a single movie did little to shape childrens' attitudes toward racial and ethnic categories. However, two or three films on the same topic produced significant modifications. Furthermore, such influences tended to persist for long periods. These conclusions initially impressed behavioral scientists because they were based on an experimental approach that was favored by those who wanted to study human conduct within the traditions of the physical sciences. Also impressive was the use of inferential statistics, a relatively recent innovation. Perhaps more than anything, the new attitude measuring procedures that Thurstone himself had pioneered seemed especially sophisticated.

The Blumer studies are undoubtedly more intriguing now than they were at the time. They were essentially qualitative rather than quantitative. They did not use elaborate experimental designs or inferential statistics, and this made them seem less scientific to a research community that was enthusiastically converting to the strategies of the physical sciences. Today, however, when the limitations of experiments and surveys are more apparent, and when qualitative research has found an accepted role in scientific studies of human behavior, Blumer's studies reveal a depth of sensitive insights and information on children's imitation of role models, adolescent emotional development, and the problems of young people interpreting the adult world. Children copied the speech patterns, hairstyles, and mannerisms of the stars; acted out the plots they saw on the screen; had a rich fanatasy life related to the movies; and underwent profound emotional experiences while viewing. Many of these influences today would be discussed in terms of *modeling* (using the actors as models for personal behavior) and *meaning* (using the norms, inter-pretations, and social meanings provided by the movies as valid construc-tions of reality). Blumer's contributions to such issues were not recognized at the time because the meaning paradigm was itself not yet fully developed.

Understandably, in the decade that followed, the Payne Fund studies fell into disrepute. As new and even more impressive methodologies were developed in the social and behavioral sciences, the Payne Fund research was found wanting by comparison with the new standards. Critics pointed to their lack of control groups, problems in sampling, shortcomings in measurement, and other difficulties that placed technical limitations on their conclusions. The public, however, neither understood nor cared about such issues. To laypeople, these experiments seemed impressive and showed that—just as had been feared—the movies were a bad influence on children. Such interpretation was supported by the results of some of the other studies, which showed that the movies had unwanted influences on school attendance, academic performance, retention of factual material (such as ideas about tobacco, liquor, and sex), childrens' sleep, moral concepts, fantasy life, and juvenile crime. It was a damning list. The end result was to reinforce the legacy of fear concerning the mass media that was the result of their role in World War I as instruments of manipulative propaganda.

Thus, in retrospect, the Payne Fund studies can either be denounced for their methodological shortcomings, applauded because they forced future researchers to use more refined methods, criticized because of their theoretical naiveté, or celebrated for their anticipation of concepts, theories, and paradigms that would be further developed in later decades. However, they cannot be ignored; their importance to the foundation of the field is indisputable.

The Invasion from Mars

A decade after research started on the Payne Fund studies, a new medium had successfully challenged newspapers and movies for the attention of Americans. Radio was a wonderful new source of information, entertainment, and news. It was glamorous and trusted. It was thought to have great influence on its listeners. In October, 1938, that aura of trust was rudely challenged by the now-famous broadcast depicting an invasion of hostile Martians, and the idea that radio could strongly influence its audience was demonstrated forcibly: Of the six million who tuned in, a million were severely frightened or panicked.

The study conducted by Hadley Cantril for the Office of Radio Research at Princeton illustrates an important feature of several of the early media studies. It was not actually conducted in an effort to understand the influence of mass communication in a direct sense. It was designed as a study of panic behavior. The fact that the panic occurred as a result of mass communication was not seen as all that important. It simply represented an opportunity to learn more about a particular form of collective behavior of considerable interest to psychologists. Many of the early contributors to mass media research conducted their investigations to probe issues of concern to their parent disciplines, rather than as direct attempts to develop the study of mass communication as a research field in its own right. Thus, there was an accumulation of quite unrelated studies of such topics as public opinion formation and change, violence, political influences, panic behavior, and persuasion. All were done in a context of mass communication, but there was no systematic attempt to build later studies on the theoretical foundations of those completed earlier because of their great differences in disciplinary origin. In the Cantril study, the emphasis was on comparing the individual differences and social category characteristics of two types of listeners—those who discovered that the broadcast was a play and simply sat back to enjoy it, versus those who were terrified by their belief that the Martians had arrived to destroy us all. Data were gathered that had a bearing on the social aspects of listening, and they showed that social relationships had some bearing on response to the broadcast. However, the main effort was on the personal and social characteristics that led to a selective mode of response.

Methodologically, the study can be either denounced or praised. By the standards of well-designed and meticulously conducted research, it was sloppy in many respects. The number of subjects was small; they were not selected by a standard sampling design; and they were not interviewed immediately after the broadcast. Additional data were obtained in later surveys and content analyses, but it was the initial sample of 135 people who were the main focus of the analysis. However, the study had to be rushed into the field as soon as possible. There were no models to follow, and there certainly had been no opportunity for planning in advance. The fact that the study was done at all is remarkable. While these problems do not erase its methodological shortcomings, they make them quite understandable.

The variables of greatest interest to the researcher were such psychological factors as "critical ability" and "suggestibility"—classics from the field of collective behavior. Neither was measured directly. Amount of formal education was used as an index of critical ability. Suggestibility was felt to be related to such phenomena as religiosity, emotional insecurity, phobic personality, lack of self-confidence, and fatalism—all drawn from the psychological lexicon.

The general conclusion was that listeners possessing critical ability were able to sort out the broadcast as a play. Those who were low in that factor were more suggestible and reacted in fear. In part, a subject's response was shaped by the social setting in which listening occurred, and there were a number of background situations that appeared as important facilitators of panic. However, the lasting contribution of the study is not in what it tells us about panic but in the attention it gives to individual differences and to membership in social and demographic categories. It concluded that these were the key variables that led to different modes of attention, perception, and response to the broadcast. Thus, although he did not realize it at the time, Cantril made an important contribution to the emerging paradigm of selective influence based on individual differences in personal characteristics and membership in social categories.

The People's Choice

Few studies in the history of social science have had a greater impact on a field than did the study of mass media influences on voters in Erie County, Ohio, during the presidential election of 1940. First, it provided a long list of empirical generalizations that described the detailed attention of voters to mass communications during a political campaign of several months' duration. Second, it advanced a number of new concepts, measuring procedures, research strategies, and theoretical explanations of media influences on the voting decision. Finally, it prompted a fresh look at social relationships as an important part of the mass communication process—a set of factors conspicuously absent from earlier paradigms.

From a methodological standpoint, the panel design was both innovative and sophisticated. It provided an important set of controls that enabled researchers to assess the results of repeatedly interviewing the same sample. This brought an important aspect of experimental logic into survey design. Panel techniques came into wide use in fields that involve polls and surveys.

The People's Choice was also important for its focus on multivariate analysis. The techniques used for apportioning the influence of such factors as socioeconomic status, religion, occupation, urban-rural residence, and age seem crude by current standards. Today we can accomplish with SPSS and a few strokes of a keyboard what it took months and even years to do in the 1940s. Nevertheless, the logical foundations and worth of such analyses were demonstrated in an unusually clear manner in the Erie County investigation. The study also clarified the role of social category memberships in political predisposition and the influence of the mediated campaign in achieving activation, reinforcement, and (limited) conversion. But perhaps most important of all was the unanticipated discovery of the role of social relationships in the mass communication process. The "two-step flow" hypothesis stimulated research not only in mass communication but in the diffusion of information and innovation in a number of related fields.

Overall, it is difficult to find a parallel in the history of social science research of a study so cleverly designed, so meticulously conducted, and so rich in substantive yields as *The People's Choice*. It was truly a milestone in its time, and whatever the eventual fate of its empirical generalizations, specific theories, and contributions to the development of paradigms, it will remain as a model of outstanding social science research.

Experiments on Mass Communication
in World War II: The Film Studies

Few researchers have access to as many subjects as they want, when and where they want them, and with the power to order them to cooperate. Just such unusual conditions prevailed for the behavioral scientists of the U.S. Army who studied the use of films for indoctrination and training during World War II. The main thrust of the research was to see if the films could change the beliefs and orientation of new recruits. The most important of the films consisted of the *Why We Fight* series, prepared for the purpose of informing the men about the war—why it was being fought, the nature of the enemy, and what it would take to win. Their purpose was not only to provide factual knowledge but to raise the morale and commitment of the recruits to the war effort. Other training films were also studied.

The basic experimental design used was the "before and after, with control group." In assessing the impact of the films on their audiences, factual knowledge, opinions about specific topics, general attitudes, and overall motivation were measured with carefully designed instruments.

As it turned out, the films were not very effective—at least in the sense of achieving dramatic changes among those who viewed them. It was clear that the recruits did learn many important facts about the war, the enemy, and so forth. And because those facts were learned, many of the men formed more favorable opinions about a number of specific issues. Influences of this kind were most likely to occur among recruits with a higher intellectual ability, who presumably could learn facts more easily. Thus, the comparison of audience members with distinctive patterns of individual differences guided much of the analysis. But there was little evidence of more dramatic results. The films were ineffective in improving certain attitudes, motivation, or morale.

At the time, the research team, the filmmakers, and the Army were disappointed and rather surprised that the *Why We Fight* series had such limited effects. While a number of interpretations and speculations were advanced as to why the results were not more significant, the findings did not fit well with the prevailing belief that carefully designed communications, with just the right content and structure, could achieve change in general attitudes and other dispositions—and presumably corresponding changes in overt behavior. But in spite of the lack of support of such cognitive assumptions in the film experiments, the finding of limited effects was in the long run one of the important outcomes of the American Soldier studies. In time, the continuing failure of additional research to support a powerful effects cognitive model forced a search for new interpretations of the nature and influence of mass communication.

The World War II studies provided a foundation in theory and method for an important research direction that was to be continued by some of the members of the Army's research team led by Carl Hovland. This was the idea of an experimental approach to testing various message structures to see if one was more effective than another. For example, the Army researchers had conducted experiments on radio presentations to soldiers, posing the contrasting conditions of hearing "both sides" versus only "one side" of a persuasive argument. The findings suggested that such structural conditions interacted with initial predispositions in complex ways to modify opinions and possibly attitudes. It seemed like a very promising line of research to continue—to see if there were optimum message structures, appeals, or other conditions that could be used as effective tools of persuasion.

The Yale Experiments on Communication and Persuasion

With the war over there was much to do. For students of communication there was basic research to be conducted to learn how to change people's beliefs, attitudes, and behavior—an essential task in building a better world. If a systematic theory of persuasion could be developed, the promotion of prosocial behavior might be effectively accomplished. The experimental approach seemed to Hovland and his associates the best strategy for conducting basic research and developing a systematic theory of persuasion. It was this kind of thinking that led to a lengthy search of what we have termed the "magic keys" around which messages might be designed so as to alter beliefs, opinions, and attitudes so as to achieve the desired changes in behavior.

A long list of factors was explored in more than 50 experiments on opinion and attitude change over a period of five years. The main categories of analysis were derived from Harold Lasswell's well known characterization of the proper study of communication as the analysis of who says what, to whom, over what channel, with what effect. Thus, the Yale Program of Research on Attitude Change and Communication focused on variables related to (1) the communicator, (2) the content of the communication, (3) the audience, and (4) actual responses made by members of the audience.

The methodology was the controlled experiment. These were essentially stimulus-response situations in which little contact was allowed between members of an audience. Before-and-after assessments of each individual's beliefs or predispositions were completed; experimental conditions (or control conditions) of varying message content or structure were imposed; and the data were examined to see if the message had achieved change.

Many empirical generalizations emerged. Some surprising findings came out of experiments using fear appeals (messages with low fear arousal were more effective in achieving change than those that provoked high fear). Other generalizations emerged concerning source credibility, one side versus both sides of an argument, and other aspects of message organization and content. The personality characteristics of the audience member were also discovered to be related to type and direction of changes in opinions and attitudes achieved by persuasive communication.

This was a theoretically sophisticated program in the sense that every effort was made to relate the findings from the experiments to prevailing theories of learning, conceptualizations of attitude and opinion, and even basic theories of personality. In addition, it was hoped that these extensive efforts would lead to a much more comprehensive understanding of the process of persuasion. Today, the Yale studies still seem impressive as carefully designed, tightly controlled, and meticulously conducted experiments that yielded interesting findings. Undoubtedly, they will continue to serve as models for researchers who elect the laboratory-type experiment as a strategy for studying issues of communication and persuasion within a cognitive framework.

Did they locate the "magic keys" to persuasion that can serve as sure guides to the promotion of prosocial behavior? In retrospect, it doesn't seem so. The program did yield many new and provocative findings, but the nagging question still to be answered is exactly how such laboratory studies of artificially controlled conditions relate to the less controlled conditions of persuasion in daily life. Thus far, there is no consensus among researchers on that issue. Certainly, the findings from the studies do not fit together into a comprehensive theory of persuasion that lends itself to modifying people's behavior through achieving changes in their attitudes.

In retrospect, the Yale studies probably set too lofty a goal. While they were imaginative and thorough, the underlying idea that it is possible to discover ways to manipulate people through the systematic use of clever words and message structures according to a formalized theory of persuasion was simply too much to ask. It is tempting to draw parallels between such research goals and the ancient search for the philosopher's stone that could turn baser metals into gold. However, the comparison is unfair. Whereas the Yale studies did not provide final answers, they did yield important clues and hypotheses to be pursued. Therefore, the significance of these experiments is that they developed an important foundation on which further research into the psychological and social dynamics of persuasion can be pursued.

The Two-Step Flow of Communication

Programmatic research, in which one study leads to another that pursues hypotheses or theoretical issues uncovered in the first, is common in the physical sciences. Such linkages between studies are rare in the study of mass communication. The work of Katz and Lazarsfeld reported in *Personal Influence* was a notable exception to that rule. Here the research effort was focused on the phenomenon of social relationships among members of the audience that had been unexpectedly encountered while conducting the Erie County study (*The People's Choice*).

The somewhat serendipitous discovery that the mass communication process seemed to involve a "two-step flow" of information and influence represented a rather radical change of thinking. Before 1950, those trying to develop theories of mass communication had given little thought to the idea that the kinds of social relationships described by the term "primary group" had anything to do with mass communication. Most previous research had been based on the assumption that members of an audience responded to the media as individuals. By the 1940s, the naive assumptions of the magic bullet theory, based on assumptions of uniformity among members of the mass society and their uniform modes of response, were no longer seen as realistic among communication theorists. In their place was an emphasis on individual psychological and demographic factors that shaped the responses of members of the audience in selective ways. This kind of thinking guided major research on mass communication from Cantril's study of the Martian broadcast to the Yale Program of Research on Attitude Change and Communication.

In 1955, however, the publication of *Personal Influence* presented communication theorists with considerable evidence that close and intimate social relationships had to be presumed among the members of the audience. People not only passed on information that they had acquired from direct exposure to the media, they also influenced the opinions and decisions of those to whom the information was passed. An important new area of mass communication research, therefore, was to map out the interpersonal channels followed in two-step flow from media to mass and to identify what kind of people influenced others in the process.

As it turned out, the flow of influence was mainly horizontal. It was not a case of high status persons passing on information and influence to those below them in the hierarchy. People were more likely to be influenced by persons at their own level. At the same time, the factor of perceived "expertise" was significant. In the study of who influenced housewives in their purchasing choices at the supermarket, it was those women actively raising large families to whom other women turned for advice. For fashions, hairstyles, and cosmetics, it was to younger women in the labor force. In each case, the opinion leaders were seen as more knowledgeable than those to whom they gave advice. The link to the media was that the more knowledgeable opinion leaders were presumably more attentive to advertisements, articles, stories or other media content pertaining to the choices than those whom they influenced.

Many of the empirical generalizations that emerged from the research are no longer relevant to contemporary society. For example, the proportion of women who remain as traditional housewives has been drastically reduced since the time of the study. The demographics of movie attendance have also shifted significantly. Other specific findings are now similarly obsolete. However, the major contribution of the *Personal Influence* research remains as important today as it was at the time. The evidence seemed to support the two-step flow hypothesis—that "ideas often flow *from* radio and print *to* opinion leaders and *from* them to less active sections of the population." This meant that it was important to study social relationships among audience members as a vital part of the mass communication process. This relatively simple idea had been over-looked largely because it was not consistent with conceptions of the mass society and the emphasis on the psychological characteristics of the individual member of the audience that had dominated mass communication research since it began.

Project Revere

During the years in which the data from *Personal Influence* were being analyzed, another major study of social relationships among members of an audience was being planned and conducted. From 1952 to 1954, a team of sociologists with substantial funding from the U.S. Air Force studied the airborne leaflet as a kind of communication medium of last resort. It was thought to be the only way to get messages to large numbers of people when other, more normal, channels of communication were not available. The assumption made by the research team was that such a medium would have its main use in times of war, such as in Korea where cities and industries had been disrupted by dropping leaflets warning of forthcoming bombing attacks. Or, they had frequently been used to deliver propaganda messages to various kinds of populations.

It was not known to the team at the time, but evidence that came to light many years later strongly suggests that it was not really the Air Force that was behind the study and that goals other than use in situations such as Korea were at stake. The new information makes it seem very likely that Project Revere was actually funded by the CIA as part of a larger series of social and psychological studies.[1]

Although anything associated with the CIA sounds sinister to many people today, the reasons for funding research of this type by such an agency during the time were both prosocial and in the national interest. The probable covert reasons for the study did not become clear until the Freedom of Information Act made public certain previously secret CIA files.

We now know that at the beginning of the 1950s, the American military and intelligence communities were deeply concerned by the fact that the Russians had developed a substantial lead in the design and production of intercontinental ballistic missiles capable of delivering nuclear bombs to certain cities in the continental United States. It was the first time that such a threat existed for the country, and the U.S. did not have the means either to prevent such strikes or to retaliate effectively. In other words, certain areas of the nation were vulnerable.

The American public was not aware of either the details of this "missile gap" or its military implications. It was not the kind of thing to inspire either stability or confidence. But, given those conditions, there was an urgent need to develop and understand ways of communicating with large populations scattered into the hinterland from cities that would become targets if the unthinkable happened. It was not the kind of research that could be conducted openly by the military without important questions being raised. Doing it through a university research group, however, right out in the open, and under the auspices of the Air Force that had a natural interest in airborne leaflets for propaganda purposes, gave it a less ominous look.

Final answers as to who funded the project and exactly why are still impossible to obtain, but if the information gleaned from old CIA files many years later is correct, then Project Revere had a greater significance than was realized at the time. In any case, it did provide at least some important information on the effectiveness and limitations of airborne leaflets as a communication medium vital to the management of disrupted populations. People under such circumstances have to be given instructions as to where to obtain food, medical help, shelter, and so on. The problem is how well does it work?

One important consideration was "how many" leaflets per person were needed to get a simple message across. Relatively elaborate studies were undertaken to try to develop guidelines. As it turned out, it was possible to incorporate the concept of "repetition" into the study of this simple medium. This made possible the use of classic theories from psychophysics and the development of mathematical models that would predict the amount of learning of the message that would take place under specific conditions of repetition. One of the clearest findings from this part of the research was the "curve of diminishing returns" related to message repetition. Geometric increases in the availability of the message did not result in corresponding gains in message learning. In fact, after a point, doubling or redoubling the repetitions had virtually no effect whatever in getting more people to learn the message.

From a methodological standpoint, the level of precision of these studies has seldom been equaled in communication research. The amount of funding for the studies was undoubtedly a factor, because each step and operation could be carried out with limited concern for the costs of sampling designs, pretesting, control procedures, interviewer training, measurement, and statistical analysis. In addition, with notable exceptions, the use of mathematical representations of the theories being tested has not characterized more recent research on mass communication issues. The development and testing of such theories was at an advanced level by comparison. Thus, the Revere studies remain a model of theory development, systematic research strategies, and carefully used research procedures. Like several of the studies reported in the present survey of milestones, they did not focus on a traditional medium, but they offered important insights into problems that are shared by all media.

One of those problems is what happens to the message after it is initially presented to its audience. The Revere studies showed that once received, the information presented by the leaflets was passed on through a process of "social diffusion." This was in some cases accomplished by handing leaflets from one person to another and in other cases by relating the content by word of mouth. It was in many ways similar to the idea of a two-step flow of communication, but there were important differences. Children were considerably overrepresented among the original recipients of the air-dropped leaflets. Once received, however, they gave them to adults, who often passed them on still further, or at least told others of their content. Thus, the typical channels of social diffusion of the leaflet message was from children who received one directly, to their parents, and then to other adults within the family. Passing it on to neighbors and acquaintances was also important, but few contacted strangers.

Another problem shared by other media concerns what happens to message content during the process of social diffusion (which is a significant part of the two-step flow). One of the Revere studies was directly concerned with that issue. It showed that the quality of information passed from person to person is limited. A simple six-word message was released in a community and passed from person to person under conditions designed to stimulate high motivation both to pass it on and to learn it accurately. The results showed that the message deteriorated, following patterns identical to those noted in classical laboratory studies of "rumor" messages that are told and retold in serial transmission.

The pattern of message deterioration under such conditions has been called the *embedding* pattern, and it consists of "leveling" (growing shorter and more concise), "sharpening" (focusing on a limited number of salient terms), and "assimilation" (distorting to cultural expectations and stereotypes).[2] Such findings are especially important for those concerned with research on "diffusion of the news," which has a long tradition in the social sciences and in communication studies. They also have obvious importance if clear and complete communication is needed to manage a disrupted population with the aid of airborne leaflets.

Generally, then, three major studies were completed by sociologists just before, during, and immediately after the Second World War. These were *The People's Choice, Personal Influence*, and *Project Revere*. All three focused on social relationships as a significant part of the mass communication process. In addition, each did other things that also were important. However, as a result of their substantial attention to the part played by social interaction and social ties between members of the audience, it was no longer possible to study the process and effects of mass communication strictly within a perspective of individual psychological variables.

The Seduction of the Innocent

In many ways it may be difficult to understand the contribution made by Frederick Wertham's study of crime comic books to the developing field of mass communication research. It is probably fair to say that the scholarly community was never impressed, except in a negative way, with either his methodology or his conclusions. This less than favorable reaction was based on a number of factors: Wertham's assumptions about the process of mass communication were primitive—reading the content of crime comics changes childrens' attitudes and beliefs (to pathological forms), and these in turn channel behavior (in unwanted and antisocial ways). The methodology was a combination of selective content analysis, clinical case studies of disturbed children, psychological testing, anecdotal discussions, and opinionated interpretations laced liberally with personal values. There was implicit throughout the discussion an emphasis on comic book publishers as villains and their products as dangerous to the moral health of youth. In short, *Seduction of the Innocent* was not and cannot now be regarded as a model of dispassionate or objective analysis.

In spite of its rejection by the scientific community, Wertham's analysis of the comic book industry and its products was important. It was part of a determined campaign to discredit a medium of mass communication. Wertham's forum was not the technical journals of the academic world but the popular media of middle class America. His articles in widely read magazines, plus the book itself as a selection of the Book of the Month Club and the *Reader's Digest* Book Club, brought his message to millions of people who neither understood nor cared about the need for probability sampling, the limitations of the clinical method, or other technical issues. Wertham told his story of the horrors of the crime comics in a spellbinding way, and millions of people were persuaded that he was right.

The public had long distrusted the media in all their forms. Wertham's condemnation of the comic book industry was consistent with those established orientations. His attack was so strong, and so convincing, that the comic book industry was virtually destroyed. Even today, it is a shadow of what it was before Wertham's assault. He was not alone in condemning the industry, but he provided what seemed to many citizens to be important scientific evidence.

In short, the true significance of Wertham's *Seduction of the Innocent* was that it made the public completely receptive to further research on the dangers of mass communication, particularly at government expense. Many academicians received grants from federal agencies and even private foundations during the 1960s and 1970s, when studies of violence and agression represented the cutting edge of media research. Such concerns rested squarely on convictions shared by the public that the media were up to no good and that something had to be done. Wertham's book is a milestone in that it played a key part in establishing a political climate that made such expenditures seem both necessary and logical.

Television in the Lives of Our Children

During the 1950s, America became a nation of television fans. Early in the decade home TV sets were rare; by the end of the period, there was a receiver in 88 percent of American households. The question was, what were the programs received by 150 million television sets doing to the nation? In particular, the recurring question that concerned American families was how this lively new medium was influencing children.

Wilbur Schramm and his associates tried to answer that question by focusing on the uses children made of TV, the functions it performed for them, and the satisfactions they received from viewing. Armed with theories of selectivity, they envisioned the new medium as a kind of cafeteria from which children chose content consistent with their interests. It was a conception of an active audience using a medium to meet its needs and to obtain gratifications rather than a passive one being acted upon.

It was truly a massive study; data from more than 8000 people in 10 communities in the United States and Canada were examined. A significant strategy used in the study was that of *comparison*. Communities without television still existed in Canada. One of these was compared with a similar community that did receive a signal. Other studies were done in American metropolitan areas and small towns. Various categories of children were compared with each other in all such settings.

The researchers concluded that children watched television for three primary reasons: to be entertained, to acquire new information, and to participate in social activities associated with viewing. The most significant were the entertainment and information functions. Like adults, children wanted to escape from boredom. Watching attractive people in exciting adventures was an enjoyable pastime. The acquisition of information was often not a deliberate goal. One of the important concepts that emerged from the study was that of "incidental learning." As in Blumer's early study of the movies, Schramm and his associates showed that children unwittingly learn many details about adult behavior and the world while being entertained. Today, this has become a very important idea.

While psychological factors were studied (e.g., intelligence and frustration) as variables accounting for selective viewing and influences, the major thrust from a theoretical point of view was on social categories and social relationships. Social class, age, and sex were seen to influence the selection of content. Similarly, the nature of the social relationships young viewers enjoyed with their parents and peers also shaped viewing patterns and influences.

Findings from a detailed content analysis showed that the adult world shown on the screen was heavy in violence, light in intellectual content, and deeply concerned with crime as entertainment. Yet, in an analysis of the effects produced by the medium, there were no dramatic and disturbing findings such as those described by Wertham regarding comics. There were only minor physical effects (eyestrain), some emotional effects (fright), and numerous cognitive effects (learning new material and about the adult world). Overall, the study revealed a complex but not particularly threatening relationship between children and television. Certainly, the conclusions were far from a universal condemnation of the new medium as harmful; essentially the conclusions were that some children under some conditions watching some television were affected negatively. For others, the same content could be beneficial. But for most children under most conditions television seemed neither harmful nor beneficial.

Not everyone was happy with the results of this rather bland view of television in the lives of children. To critics of the medium, it seemed that it failed to prove what they already knew—that television was bad and harmful to the young. To those expecting more dramatic results of *some* kind, the work seemed to do little more than provide further support for a minimal effects interpretation. It just seemed inescapable that an activity that (as the authors noted) occupied more time in the first 16 years of life than anything except sleep simply must have strong influences. Thus, while many empirical generalizations emerged from the findings, this first major probe of the new medium did little to set aside the more political questions that were beginning to be associated with the effects of television.

Violence and the Media: The Task Force Report

Public discontent with the media, especially television, peaked during the 1960s. In part it was a response to the events of the times. The war in Vietnam not only set America against its military foes, it set its people against one another. Violence in the society escalated: crime rates rose; students rioted; inner cities exploded in turmoil; there were frequent demonstrations; flags, draft cards, and brassieres were burned in protest; drug use expanded as a problem; skyjacking began; political leaders were assassinated. It was a frightening time.

Much of this activity was shown dramatically on television's evening news night after night. It was an ancient custom to kill the messenger who brought bad news. Apparently, a somewhat parallel association between the bearer of the news and the upsetting events grew during the 1960s. Americans loved television, but as the medium brought them daily portrayals of these mounting miseries, the legacy of fear returned in force, and suspicion grew that television was one of the *causes* of the nation's increasing violence, delinquency, and crime.

Politicians responded to the rise in violence with new crime control legislation. At the end of the decade, President Johnson appointed a special Commission on the Causes and Prevention of Violence. This Commission established a Media Task Force to assess the role of mass communication in stimulating violence in the society. Their major concern was television.

The Task Force report contains a major section devoted to the topic of violence and the media. Included was new research that was sponsored by the Task Force. One major study was a content analysis of violence portrayed in prime-time TV programs. Another was an elaborate survey of the actual experiences of the American public with violence.

The world of prime-time television was shown to be filled with violent action. Approximately 80 percent of the network programs studied during typical weeks during two consecutive years contained violent incidents. A rich set of conclusions and generalizations described the details of violence as they appeared in televised portrayals. The overall conclusion was that violence was a predominant characteristic of television programming, and it was used in the programs, especially by the "good guys," as an effective and approved means of conflict resolution. To the public, this was a disturbing report.

The survey of actual violence in American society also yielded elaborate details and numerous generalizations concerning both the norms governing violent acts and the actual experiences of people with violence. Essentially, Americans approved of violence only when it was carried out by legally constituted authorities. The only exceptions were low-level violence, such as parents spanking a child, or, in some situations, people striking each other in disputes (except between husband and wife). Even in such cases, however, approval was by no means universal.

In short, there was a significant difference between the norms and level of violence as shown on TV and the same phenomena in actual daily life. This difference led the Task Force to conclude that television had to be considered as a possible contributing factor in explaining why there were so many forms of violent behavior in American society. The Report also emphasized the need for further study of the long-term effects of mass communication, especially television. They indicated the possibility that exposure to television content played an important role in *socialization*. As children see violence portrayed day after day, week after week, and on over a span of years, it seemed very likely that this would influence their attitudes and conceptions of norms toward violent and aggressive behavior.

Such a position was entirely consistent with Blumer's pioneering interpretations of media influences, Schramm and Parker's concept of "incidental learning," and De Fleur's "cultural norms theory."[3] From such diverse sources, plus milestones yet to be discussed, has emerged the contemporary meaning paradigm. That is, the media are seen as providing constructions of what society is like, the nature of its norms, and what behaviors are appropriate in various circumstances. Presumably, from media portrayals of social life children internalize those conceptions as their own. Note, however, that in the actual Task Force report, the older cognitive paradigm assuming that media content shapes attitudes (which then shape behavior) was seen as the actual mechanism of influence.

While the Task Force Report presented an objective summary of its conclusions regarding the content of network television, and regarding the nationwide survey of violent experiences, its interpretations of what these generalizations implied (such as the socialization influences) often went considerably beyond the data. In other words, the conclusions of the authors were in some instances based more on their personal opinions than on objective findings. But in spite of this feature of the Report, it forced social scientists to take a fresh look at mass communication, especially television, as related to the long-term socialization process. It raised forcibly the possibility that the media were causal factors in the long-term creation of beliefs, attitudes, and internalized norms as people developed conceptions of reality through exposure to communications. In particular, while it raised more questions than it answered, it clearly brought the issue of violence on television and its influence on children to center stage. Because of rising concern from both the scientific community and the public, that issue was to receive special research attention.

Television and Social Behavior: The Report to the Surgeon General

Public concern with violence in American society rose to new heights during the last years of the 1960s. That concern had a realistic basis. Almost daily the news showed campus riots, assassinations and their aftermath, drugs, crime, and ghetto upheavals. The old legacy of fear that the media were a causal agent in these troubles, now reinforced by magazine articles, books, and other reports by media critics (such as Dr. Wertham) provided an interpretive framework. It seemed to many people that mass communication, and especially television, was a cause of much of the violence in society. It was disturbing to think that if television was indeed the source from which children learned to be aggressive and solve their problems by violent means, then everyone was at risk whenever a child sat down in front of a TV set. People believed that something should be done to reduce that risk.

As always, when action is needed on a social problem, the public turns to the federal government for solutions. Increasing demands were made on Congress to do something. Such widespread concern seldom goes unnoticed by political figures who want to be reelected. By 1969, Senator Pastore had convinced his colleagues to fund large-scale research on the relationship between the violence portrayed on television and the behavior of children and adolescents. The million dollars appropriated for the studies was something of a record.

The management of the project was placed in the hands of the U.S. Surgeon General and was coordinated and administered under his direction by the National Institute of Mental Health (NIMH). The report prepared by that agency to the Surgeon General as to what they found—often called the Surgeon General's Report—was in five volumes. It contained 40 scientific papers, ranging from original studies commissioned by NIMH to summaries of existing literature. In addition, the Advisory Committee to the Surgeon General prepared a separate report (*Television and Growing Up*), based on the five volumes, setting forth the group's conclusions about the relationship between viewing violence portrayed on television and social behavior.

The entire project created numerous controversies. There were not only the usual debates among research specialists about methods and theoretical implications, but conflicting interpretations by the press and the public of what the conclusions really meant. Additionally, there was political infighting over such issues as membership on the Advisory Committee and the implications of condemning a major medium.

After the dust had settled, and the results of the many studies had been widely examined, it did appear that the research had advanced our knowledge about the effects of violence shown on television. The Advisory Committee summed up by saying that there was a tentative indication of a relationship between viewing violence on television and aggressive behavior among certain categories of children. They were careful to point out that this was a preliminary conclusion subject to further verification by additional research and that it certainly did not apply to all children. In fact, they noted that it characterized mainly those who were already predisposed to be aggressive and who were in particular environmental circumstances.

The careful and guarded, but scientifically responsible, conclusion pleased almost no one. It did, however, point to the importance of conducting further research, not only on the issues of the effects of exposure to portrayals of violence on television, but on the influence of other kinds of content. As we will see, this may have been one of the most important outcomes of the project, as the pace of research on television's influences on society and individuals increased enormously in the decade following the NIMH project. In fact, ten years later, it was necessary to release a new report to bring the public and the research community up to date. The highlights of that effort will be reviewed after looking briefly at another important milestone.

The Agenda-Setting Function of the Press

In spite of the limited effects shown in much of the research on violence, and in many earlier studies of the influence of mass communication, there remained a conviction that (1) the media could create significant effects, but (2) somehow some of their more important influences had not been uncovered by past projects. By the early 1970s, at least some communication theorists began to feel that another, and possibly simpler, approach might have better results in revealing media influences. One such group, led by Maxwell E. McCombs and Donald L. Shaw, was particularly interested in the influence of the press, that is, traditional newspapers and television news programs. They decided to investigate the level of importance audiences attach to issues as a result of the way they are presented in the news.

It was a significant focus for research for two reasons. First, it was a modern counterpart of one of the oldest assumptions made by many nineteenth-century scholars who studied the relationship between the press, public opinion, and politics. Since mass newspapers began, many political analysts have attributed to the press the power to influence the thinking and actions of the electorate regarding candidates and issues. McCombs and Shaw believed that only research could settle the question as to whether or not such influence actually exists. Second, issues that are seen as important or unimportant are probably evaluated and acted upon in different ways by voters who attend to the news. This seemed to be a logical point from which to begin their research. While judging issues to be more or less important does not imply approval or disapproval, such evaluations may form a framework for judging the merits of particular political leaders or their proposed programs. Ultimately, such opinions and conclusions may be the basis for political action, such as voting for one candidate or another.

There are several obvious facts about the news media in American society that influenced researchers' formulation of their basic research questions. One obvious fact is that there is a continuing flow of news that reaches very large audiences. It is also obvious that the news is selectively prepared and presented by the press in such a way that a *daily agenda* of issues, topics, and items is placed before the public for their consideration. A third obvious fact is that the press does not treat all news items equally. Some are presented as leading stories; others are given minor recognition. To assume that this daily flow of selectively packaged and widely attended news content has no influence on people did not seem to make sense. A number of scholars interested in this area of mass communication were convinced that there had to be *some* kinds of effects created by this large-scale communication activity. If those effects were not of the direct kind that had been looked for in earlier media research (attitude change, behavioral change), there might well be long-term and indirect influences that could be uncovered. Therefore, while it might be true that the news media do not directly shape our thinking and actions toward the issues and topics they present, their daily agenda places before us a selective list of things to think about that are differentially emphasized. By focusing our collective attention on that list, the media agenda might well become the personal agenda of concern of members of the audience.

In other words, the research question centered on the relationship between media versus audience agenda. If the press continued to give particular topics prominent treatment in their agenda over a long period of time, would the audience come to believe that such topics indeed were important? This was the essential underlying hypothesis that is associated with the agenda-setting function of the press. The idea paralleled an older proposition from the 1940s suggested by Lazarsfeld and Merton called the "status-conferral" function of the press—namely, if a person is given attention by the press, then surely he or she must be important. Conversely, if a person is important, then surely he or she will be given attention by the press. In either case, status is derived from the level of attention given to the person by the press.

Beyond the idea that press and audience agendas are related, there is the question of so what? As we have already implied, there may be a relationship between the convictions of what issues and topics are important as seen by voters and the fate of political programs and candidates attempting to address those issues. While this very long-term and indirect set of influences offers fertile ground for research, definitive studies remain to be done.

McCombs and Shaw took their research question into the field in two major stages. First a preliminary study conducted in North Carolina during the 1968 presidential election showed a very high correlation between the relative emphasis given to issues by newspapers and network TV news and judgments of a sample of voters about the importance of those issues. There seemed to be grounds, in other words, for concluding that (among those studied) there was a close correspondence between the world outside, as constructed by the media, and the pictures in the heads of the sample of voters studied.

The ideas derived from the smaller study were followed up by a much larger investigation of the way in which voters in Charlotte, North Carolina perceived the issues and candidates as reported in newspapers and network television news during the presidential election of 1972. Their results, published in 1977 in *The Emergence of American Political Issues: The Agenda-Setting Function of the Press*, were complex. Essentially they clarified the research question and provided data on the sources people actually used to decide on the salience of issues, how the personal charcteristics of voters are factors in attending to news about the campaign, how time sequences in the press agenda influence the audience agenda, and how agenda setting by the press may influence the larger political process.

The 1972 study of agenda-setting was clearly a milestone in mass communication research. Like many of the studies that break new ground, the work can be critized in several respects. Certainly, it had methodological flaws. The researchers encountered numerous problems in designing their samples and in developing rigorous measurement techniques. However, the study made use of innovative statistical techniques, such as cross-lagged correlations, to study influences on voter's beliefs from one time period to another. But above all, both the first study and the second stimulated considerable interest in the way in which the press tells us daily what to think about. It seems clear that the press does set peoples' agendas of political concern. A considerable amount of research is now being directed toward how these media play a part in constructing the meaning of our political environment through the differential hierarchies of importance that they assign to the topics covered in the news.

Television and Social Behavior: Ten Years of Scientific Progress

Public concern with violence in American society remained high during the late 1970s. Crime was still a very serious problem, with few signs of improvement. Public suspicion remained that television was a causal factor in violence and aggression. Indeed, as the decade moved to a close, there were several spectacular examples of teenagers imitating violent behavior portrayed on television; that did little to reduce such fears. For example, in a widely publicized murder trial, "television intoxication" was used as the basis for the legal defense of a youthful offender. The claim was that the client had seen so many murders on TV that he could no longer distingush between right and wrong regarding such activity. It was a defense that exaggerated the evolving meaning paradigm. Fortunately, the strategy was unsuccessful, but the possibility that it could occur did little to calm the public. Generally, then, the legacy of fear was alive and well and clearly concerned with TV as the society looked ahead to the 1980s.

At the same time, concern about the influence of television no longer focused on violence alone. Children were spending increasing amounts of time in front of their screens, but no one knew just what lessons were being offered or what was being learned. The concerns of both experts and parents ranged from alcohol and drugs to television's impact on cognitive development.

We noted earlier that following the release of the 1971 *Report to the Surgeon General*, the volume of research probing the influence of television on behavior increased greatly. Many of the studies undertaken followed the recommendations of the Surgeon General's Advisory Committee as set forth in the original report. Generally speaking, those recommendations called for research to move beyond the violence theme to include a broader spectrum of television's possible influences. The scientific community took up the task with considerable enthusiasm to a point where *90 percent of all research ever published on television's effects on social behavior appeared during the 1970s!* Because of the richness of this new research base, no further studies needed to be commissioned by NIMH as they planned their next major report.

To pull these more recent findings together into a new report on television and social behavior, 24 of the most knowledgeable researchers in the field were selected by the federal agency and asked to prepare comprehensive and integrative reviews of the existing literature. These were published in 1982 in: *Television and Social Behavior: Ten Years of Scientific Progress and Implications for the Eighties*.

The report is in two volumes edited by David Pearl, Lorraine Bouthilet, and Joyce Lazar. However, 24 of the reports making up the volumes were prepared by the two-dozen individual researchers who had been selected. Six summary reports were provided by the consultants. Whereas no new research was commissioned for the project, several of the reports do contain findings that had not previously been published.

This new version of *Television and Social Behavior* covers seven broad areas of media research. These are: (1) violence; (2) health; (3) prosocial behavior; (4) cognitive and affective aspects of viewing; (5) the family and interpersonal relations; (6) social beliefs and social behavior; and (7) television's effects on American institutions. Obviously, the project had far broader objectives than the 1971 effort. In some ways, it is as comprehensive as the original goals of the Payne Fund series with which media research began. Certainly, it was far more than simply "unfinished business" of the earlier report.

When the findings and conclusions were released, the media predictably focused mainly on the issue of televised violence and aggressive behavior. The remaining six topics received little publicity. Even though the media did not find to their liking the conclusion that portrayed violence tended to lead to aggressive behavior, the case for television as a causal factor had become far stronger. Most of the participating researchers accepted the generalization, and the NIMH team interpreted the evidence in that manner.

Complicating this issue was the finding that the content of violent programming on television may not be solely responsible for the medium's part in stimulating aggressive behavior. New research found that aggression could be stimulated by high levels of action in a program, even without a substantial amount of portrayed violence. In other words, television's *form* as well as its violent *content* may be partly responsible for the link between violence and aggression. Thus, new questions were raised regarding this perennial issue.

On a positive note, it was found that television content can produce prosocial behavior. What viewers learn from television depends upon what they watch. If they see prosocial behavior as a response to a particular situation, then they will learn that this is appropriate and normal. However, if aggression and antisocial behavior are shown as responses, then those forms will be learned as appropriate. Hence, television appears to have as much potential for "good" as for "bad."

Television's role as an informal educator was scrutinized with respect to a number of issues: minorities, women, drugs, alcohol, risky driving, and family life. Thus, the report contains numerous content analyses of the "lessons" taught on such topics. However, it includes only a limited number of studies that attempt to deal with the actual *effects* of such content on audiences. In many cases, the classic error of content analysis is committed, as effects are simply assumed from the nature of what was portrayed. However, the report does indicate a need to concentrate on such effects in future research.

The 1982 report also focused on an important theoretical development in media research—the shift from a domination of the cognitive paradigm to the emergence of the portrayal of cultural norms and shared interpretations of reality. The new perspective, which has been given various names (we have referred to it as the meaning paradigm), emphasizes long-term and indirect influences of media content rather than short-term direct effects. This basic theoretical shift will have a significant impact on the nature of most media research in the future. In particular, it will focus attention on the role of the medium as a long-term agent of socialization in society. Such research should increasingly reveal how television defines and transmits cultural norms as well as values and shared meanings for a variety of social situations.

THE IMPLICATIONS OF THE FINDINGS

The thirteen studies we have reviewed have yielded a substantial body of information about media effects. If we could also include the results of literally thousands of smaller efforts that were addressed to similar issues during the same period, the size of that body of knowledge would be impressive indeed. However, that information is by no means unified or systematic. It was assembled by scholars from various disciplines, working on many different aspects of mass communication for a variety of purposes. This diversity makes it especially difficult to synthesize and interpret. In summary, therefore, our current body of knowledge about the effects of mass communication is both large and impressive, but also both complex and perplexing.

One way of attempting to understand the implications that this body of knowledge has for the scientific study of mass communication today is to look at three conceptually distinct but interlocking issues. These are: (1) the status of the hundreds of empirical generalizations that have emerged from this half century of research; (2) the question of the contemporary utility of the more limited number of focused theories that were formulated and tested in the milestone studies; and (3) the relationship between both of the first two issues and the underlying paradigms concerning the nature of human beings and the social order that have guided major theory developments in mass communication.

Empirical Generalizations

We noted in the first paragraphs of Chapter 1 that those who try to develop valid and reliable generalizations to describe the effects of mass communication are confronted with a set of obstacles. Those obstacles are generated because of the ever-changing nature of what is under study. The media industries undergo virtually continuous change. The most obvious form of that change is in technology. Many media devices that were state of the art only a few years ago now seem quaint and outdated.

Less visible but equally significant are social and cultural changes in the society as a whole. These continually reshape the nature and requirements of audiences as they collectively redefine their goals and priorities. Fads and fashions, along with new social movements and subcultures, constantly emerge in a dynamic and creative society. These change people, and, because of those changes, they make new demands on the media for various kinds of content that is consistent with their modified tastes, beliefs, and modes of gratification.

Still other changes are reflected in demographic indices. Our population is not the same from year to year in terms of age, education, rural versus urban residence, religious affiliation, and political orientation. Currently, Americans are getting older, better educated, healthier, more urban, less orthodox, and more conservative. Such trends both create and reflect alterations in shared conceptions of what the media should offer and how their content should be evaluated.

Finally, both formal and informal norms that regulate our media undergo change. Legal controls that restrict or foster media business organizations, or what can or cannot be printed, broadcast, or exhibited, obviously come and go. Informal norms that define liberal versus conservative morality bring public outcries against the media during some periods but not others.

This dynamic nature of society and the media systems within it influences the status of empirical generalizations derived from media research. Namely, what appears to be a valid generalization at one time may be obsolete a short time later. These inescapable facts of *societal change, media system modification*, and *obsolescence of generalizations* from mass communication research poses a very considerable restriction on the study of this subject matter. Put metaphorically, it is difficult to locate eternal verities using the strategies of science while searching through the shifting sands of change.

The problem of social and technological change and the short shelf life of empirical generalizations can be seen clearly in even the most casual review of the history of every major medium. Each had its Golden Age before it declined in the face of new media. The newspaper peaked about the time of World War I; the film during the 1930s and 40s; large circulation magazines during the 1950s; radio just before television took over during the 1960s; and network TV was at its height during the 1970s, before inroads began from cable, VCR's, and so on. Even college textbooks may be in for rough days ahead as various kinds of computer-assisted instructional systems continue to be developed.

But even assuming that all this is true—that generalizations become obsolete as society changes and the media change—the important question is *so what?* Is this really an obstacle to the development of a body of scientific knowledge concerning the effects of mass communication? If so, just what are those obstacles, and even more important, can they be overcome?

To answer these questions, we need to begin with a brief review of two issues concerning the nature of science as a procedure for developing trustworthy knowledge. First, what is the distinction between science as *methodology* and as accumulated *knowledge*? Second, what very basic assumptions are required before science can even be considered as an appropriate means for developing knowledge? By looking at these two issues, the field of mass communication research can be placed in perspective along with others that attempt to use science as a mode of inquiry in the study of a changing empirical world.

To address the first issue, a distinction is often made between the procedures of observation and control used by scientists and the actual *findings* of their investigations. This is the familiar dual definition of science as (1) strategies, methods, and techniques for making systematic observations and (2) trustworthy conclusions reached on the basis of those observations. It has long been accepted, then, that science is both methodology and accumulated knowledge.

There is little doubt that the methods of science can be used effectively by communication researchers in their media studies. Indeed, it is done every day. And, as the present book notes, there has been a considerable development of procedures and techniques. However, methods are *means*, not ends. If the subject matter that is under study cannot meet the assumptions posed by the second major characteristic of science (as a body of valid and reliable knowledge), then those who study that subject matter face serious restrictions no matter what methods they use.

Just what are the fundamental postulates of science that pose restrictions on the accumulation of valid and reliable knowledge about mass communication and its effects? Actually, there are three that need to be considered. These are the postulates of *order, cause and effect*, and *tentative truth*. Each needs to be reviewed briefly in terms of its implications for mass communication research.

Perhaps the most fundamental assumption of science is that of order. In such fields as biology, physics, and chemistry, scientific research has traditionally proceeded from the assumption that the phenomena under study are governed by orderly laws that remain constant. For example, few botanists doubt that the photosynthesis that took place in the plants eaten by dinosaurs millions of years ago is the same process that makes vegetation green today. Similarly, chemists fully believe that the salt used by ancient people to preserve or flavor their food was made up of exactly the same elements of sodium and chloride as those that we sprinkle on our french fries at lunch. In other words, such phenomena in the physical world are thought to be constant and predictable in their relationships. Without such an assumption of order, such sciences could not be developed. Imagine the chaos that would result if the atomic table shifted its values from time to time in relatively unpredictable ways. Or, imagine what a problem it would be to develop a reliable science of physics if the laws pertaining to the attraction of bodies were undergoing rapid and somewhat erratic modification. Unfortunately, because just such a situation exists in the society-media relationship, it is very difficult to produce empirical generalizations that will hold over an extended period. The valid life of such generalizations is usually only a few years at best, sometimes only a few months.

The inability to meet the assumption of order is a serious problem, because if a field cannot depend upon constancy of relationships among the phenomena that it studies, it will have difficulty in meeting the second postulate of science—that of the existence of *cause and effect sequences*. Scientists do not assume that events just "happen" in random ways. Chemical reactions, trajectories, orbits, diseases, and other phenomena under study are presumed to be produced because potentially identifiable antecedent factors bring about specific consequences in a universe of orderly relationships. It is further assumed that those causal sequences can be understood and conceptualized in the form of hypotheses and, later, as propositions in valid theories (as empirical research findings support one such formulation or another). But in a shifting and dynamic milieu, a straightforward postulate of cause and effect based on constancies of order is less certain, to say the least. Thus, the scientific study of the influences and effects of changing media in a changing society is especially difficult.

The third postulate of science at first seems more hopeful. The assumption that scientific truths are always regarded as tentative implies that researchers in all fields have always been willing to let "the facts" have the final say. The rule is that when any conclusion (interpretation, hypothesis, generalization, theory) is inconsistent with observable facts, then it is primarily the conclusion that is suspect rather than the assembled evidence (given adequate observational controls).

The postulate of tentative truth is unique to science and one that separates it sharply from revelation or tradition as alternative sources of valid knowledge. History is replete with examples of traditional interpretations or revealed conclusions that survived against an overwhelming assembly of contrary factual evidence. But science is very different. It is understood that the truths that are uncovered today have to be replaced with other truths tomorrow if the latter are found to be more consistent with the facts.

Before jumping on the postulate of tentative truth as the way out of the dilemma for mass communication research, we should be aware that one of its features presents a problem. Namely, this postulate rests firmly on the previous two! The willingness of scientists to reject formulations that seem inconsistent with observations stems from their conviction that there *is* order in what they are studying and that a particular formulation may need revision in order to describe more correctly cause and effect relationships that exist among those phenomena. They definitely do *not* assume that there will be a different underlying order next week or next year. That would require a postulate of *inconstancy* rather than one of constant relationships. Such a postulate would negate and be inconsistent with the previous two.

But where does all of this discussion leave mass communication research? Does it mean that it must be studied outside of the scientific model? Is the fact that its empirical generalizations are often of the variety "true today but maybe not tomorrow" a total obstacle to the development of a science with respect to this subject matter? Hopefully, the answer is probably not!

There are other sciences that deal with a changing universe of phenomena. Meteorology and geology are examples. Storm systems, highs, lows, rain, drought, and other events studied by the weather sciences present a constantly changing picture. Indeed, the pace of change can be swift. On a very different time scale, the geologist also faces constant change. Over eons, mountains thrust up only to be eroded away; layers are deposited over other layers to form complex stratified deposits; even the continents themselves, which seem so stable, are said to be moving around on the surface of the earth. But in spite of these circumstances, both sciences develop explanations and predictions for the phenomena they study. What are they doing, and what lessons do they provide for the study of mass communication?

The critical feature that enables them to develop theories in spite of a disorderly universe is that they look beyond their empirical data to search for regularities, or *patterns*, among their generalizations that suggest causal influences. By this means, they can develop focused theories of limited categories of phenomena—theories based on principles that transcend the vagaries of shifts in the daily relationships among whatever elements they have under study. In other words, the fact that generalizations obtained from media research have a short shelf life may not pose an insurmountable obstacle if focused theories can be generated at the next level of abstraction.

Focused Theories

The relationship between empirical generalizations and a specific theory induced from a pattern among them can be illustrated by the classic story of King Louis' clock. During the seventeenth century Louis XIV of France was deeply interested in astronomy. It is a science where accurate measurement of time is crucial. A master clock was built in Paris to the most exacting standards available at the time. Then he had a second clock made whose pendulum was a precise duplicate. It beat in perfect time with the master clock. In 1671, in order to make certain astronomical observations, Louis sent Monsieur Jean Richter to the island of Cayenne, in French Guiana (which is close to the equator).

From the first, nothing went right, and it seemed that Richter's observations were dreadfully in error. Then, to everyone's astonishment, it was discovered that his duplicate clock was losing approximately two and a half minutes per day! Eventually, it became clear that clocks with a given pendulum length beat slower at the equator than they do in Paris and at intermediate rates in between (empirical generalizations).[4]

The only thing that could account for such a pattern of discrepancies was the explanation (theory) that the equator was farther away from the center of the earth than Paris, and the closer one got to the poles the lesser the distance to that center. This meant that the force of gravity was not as strong at the equator. It was a novel idea. If true it would mean that the world is not actually a globe but is somewhat squashed down at the poles and fatter at the equator. This theory of the world's shape turned out later to be totally consistent with Newton's famous laws of gravitation (paradigm), and the mystery was solved.

The point is that a *pattern* of empirical generalizations provided a basis for inducing an explanation that was not present among any of the individual generalizations themselves. This same process of induction from patterns led communication researchers to formulate a number of specific theories that can both explain and predict what will happen in the American society under certain conditions of exposure to mass communications.

An example of a focused theory in mass communication that emerged from patterns discovered among time-bound generalizations was the theory of selectivity based on social relationships (discussed in some detail in Chapter 1). As the review of the milestone studies reveals, little attention was paid to social relationships among audience members during the earlier decades of research on the effects of mass communication. Much of that work had sought explanations of selective response to the media within an individualistic framework of psychological variables. During the period, demographic variables were also seen as influencing audience members in selecting, interpreting, and acting upon media content. However, before 1950, no major investigation had been completed on the role of social ties and group memberships as influences on how people would select or respond to mass communications.

In a very preliminary way, communication researchers during the 1930s began to notice that social activities among members of an audience sometimes modified the way they responded to the media content. The first among the milestone studies to explore such an idea was Cantril's; he observed that the social conditions of listening to the Martian program (tuning in at the suggestion of frightened friends vs. listening alone) tended to result in a different kind of interpretation of the meaning of the event, leading to differences in the actions taken. At that point, the idea was little more than an interesting but theoretically insignificant empirical generalization.

In 1940, the Erie County study uncovered an unanticipated set of influences on political interpretations, decisions, and actions brought about by social relationships among members of the audience. A more significant role for social relationships was suggested. This was systematically studied in both the Decatur studies of personal influence and in the Project Revere series. Since that time, the "social relationships theory" (that people attend to, interpret, and respond to the content of mass communications selectively in ways influenced by their group memberships and social ties) has provided a set of principles guiding the expectations and research designs of investigators studying the process and effects of mass communication. The development of this theory was no different than that concerning the shape of the earth.

The social relationships theory is only one example of how an accumulation of empirical generalizations provides the basis for the induction of a focused theory. Other examples are the theories of message structure and appeals that were the result of Hovland's Yale Program, the content distortion and repetition theories of Project Revere, the incidental learning theory of Schramm and his associates, the theory that exposure to violent media content stimulates aggression in some kinds of audience members (from the NIMH projects), and finally, the theory of the agenda-setting function of the press.

These focused theories are an invaluable legacy from the milestones in mass communication research. In retrospect, some now seem more attractive, valid, or otherwise significant than others. Nevertheless, they have provided the guiding principles around which much of the remaining body of research has accumulated. But an important point is that *none of them have been made obsolete by changes in media or society*! In other words, even though many of the empirical generalizations on which those formulations rest now seem hopelessly dated or even completely obsolete, they provided the basis for the development of the focused theories. Once that step was taken, from the concrete level of observation to the abstract level of theory, the difficulties and limitations discussed earlier (about the changing nature of society, media, and effects) do not make the theories obsolete. Their principles can still be used to explain those aspects of communication behavior that the theories address. It may be quite true that the media have changed, and society is different now than at the time the selective influence theories were formulated, but people still select and react to media content based on their individual differences, their social category memberships, and their social relationships with others. Generally, then, even though a particular theory was formulated some decades ago from observations on behavior that might not recur, it may still be perfectly valid and reliable today, or even tomorrow. Needless to say, continuous retesting against contemporary data is the ultimate test.

Underlying Theoretical Paradigms

As one moves from focused theories to the level of broad theoretical paradigms, the problem of the obsolescence of empirical generalizations becomes much less relevant. This is because the paradigms are at a level of abstraction that is considerably higher than that of the focused theories. Indeed, the paradigms are the parent conceptual sources from which the focused theories are presumably drawn.

Paradigms are sets of postulates. They are taken as "given" and are not presumed to be open to acceptance or rejection. The mass society paradigm was set forth in Chapter 1. It was a list of assumptions about the nature of broad changes within the society that were producing a new type of social order. It was assumed that mass society is characterized by particular kinds of ties, social controls, and conflicts that occur among its members, and that these serve as fundamental influences on their communication behavior. These postulates pose principles so general that they are presumed to apply to many kinds of specific theories about many kinds of media, presenting many kinds of content, to many kinds of people. They are not time-bound to particular conditions.

While paradigms are essential, they are in one sense cruel taskmasters from which researchers find it difficult to escape. This is because they cannot be tested in any direct sense. Their assumptions are accepted as given before research planning even starts. Thus, it is one's underlying paradigm that places limits on the specific theories that can be induced from patterns of empirical generalizations.

The Shift to the Cognitive Paradigm. A change of basic paradigms can have a wrenching influence on a field. For example, early in the present century, sociologists abandoned the mass society paradigm. They replaced it with several alternative sets of postulates about the nature of the social order. These ranged from structural functionalism, to conflict perspectives and symbolic interactionism. Suddenly, the study of mass communication had to change. The old magic bullet theory based on mass society concepts became totally obsolete (although it took some people a long time to realize it). The same thing was true when psychologists developed paradigms stressing learning in a social environment as a source of human nature. These replaced assumptions that human behavioral tendencies were acquired at birth. As the study of learning processes became a central focus, the "nature vs. nurture" debate began to lose its force. The psychological study of the human individual became a search for the social origins of personality factors that were presumed to shape overt behavior. At first, the psychoanalytic paradigm looked like it might become dominant, but it never caught on in media research. Instead, communication scholars based their theories on the cognitive paradigm that stresses how sensory input shapes perception, belief, attitudes, values, remembering, thinking, and, ultimately, action.

All this had a profound impact on the study of mass communication. Specific theories of media effects were sought within the postulates of the cognitive paradigm, and the search was under way for the components of personality that determined how people would be influenced by the media. We noted earlier that for decades it was accepted as beyond question that the mass media could achieve behavioral change only if its message content formed or altered individual opinions and attitudes (which, in turn, were the keys to the psychodynamics of overt behavior). That idea, anchored in the cognitive paradigm, was pursued relentlessly from the field experiments of Peterson and Thurstone in the 1920s to the studies of violence and the media in the 1970s. Indeed, many are still held captive by such assumptions.

The Emergence of the Meaning Paradigm. Yet, as the 1970s began, the cognitive paradigm had to be reassessed. For the most part, it had yielded only the minimal effects view of the media that we have discussed at some length. It was a position that satisfied almost no one. To at least some scholars, and to most lay people, it seemed that in spite of the results of research, the media were capable of a considerable amount of influence over various aspects of peoples' lives. For one thing, advertising campaigns obviously had a significant impact on consumer decisions. Hard-headed business executives would not spend millions on such advertising if they did not enhance profits. For another, political campaigning had become heavily dependent on mass communication, and candidates who presented themselves effectively via television and other media had better prospects of winning. Again, in the tough political arena, such strategies were not built on pipe dreams but on results. Other evidence of media influence could be seen in ever-changing language usages, fads, fashions, media-created heroes, popular music, and spectator sports. It seemed like everyone in the world believed that the media had important effects on people, but communication researchers were curiously unable to demonstrate them in their studies.

Such considerations, among many others, led to another wrenching shift in basic paradigms. Communication researchers began to look less for short-term and immediate changes in people based on opinion and attitude manipulation and more for subtle, but nevertheless significant, influences brought about by long-term exposure to media content.

Essentially, the new paradigm stressed a different set of postulates. These assumptions were derived from classic sources in anthropology, social psychology, and sociology. They postulated that the location of the individual in systems of communication was a critical condition for many kinds of effects. Some of these assumptions were derived from anthropological research done on primitive peoples in the 1920s. A number of anthropologists had concluded that a given people's language and its culturally defined meanings strongly shaped their interpretations of the world and their subsequent behavior.[5] Other postulates extended back even further, to the turn-of-the-century concept of the primary group as a significant communication milieu that helped shape the interpretations of individuals concerning the world around them.[6] Still others, coming from the early 1930s, maintained that the process of symbolic interaction in a society in which meanings are shared through the use of significant symbols is the source from which individuals derive their conceptions of self and their interpretations of their social order.[7]

Thus, the new paradigm had deep and extensive roots in classical social science, and had for decades been discussed in those sciences as the process of the social construction of reality. A simpler term is "meaning paradigm" which notes that our conceptions of norms, interpretations, and action requirements are meanings derived from participation in various kinds of communication processes. Clearly, these can include mass communication. Thus, the meaning paradigm has its origins in many disciplines, including communication itself. Walter Lippmann implied the basic idea of the paradigm in his classic statement about the role of the press in the 1920s, when he noted that newspapers (the main medium of the time) selectively portrayed "the world outside" and by doing so created "pictures in our heads."[8]

Essentially, then, the meaning paradigm assumes that participation in *both* interpersonal and mediated communication processes brings us information that shapes our understanding of our environment, broadly conceived. Those meanings include such matters as norms, social controls, and the life-styles of many kinds of people. In other words, they define for us, correctly or incorrectly, the way the social order works. They also contribute to our understanding of much of the physical world—especially those aspects of that world with which we have little or no contact. But perhaps more important, meanings derived from exposure to communications provide us with definitions of how we can cope with and how we should behave in the complex and often perplexing social environment in which we live.

Insofar as the mass media are a significant part of the communication systems in which we participate, they offer us guidelines for understanding what other people are like, what they want, what we ourselves ought to want, and what will happen to us if we conform or deviate. These are the "pictures in our heads" of what social reality is all about. Other meanings derived from media sources provide interpretations of virtually every aspect of the world around us. These internalized conceptions are major influences in shaping our behavior.

A shift from the cognitive to the meaning paradigm has both costs and benefits. One of the costs is that as research increasingly focuses on cultural norms and meanings that are *external* to the individual, investigators will pay less attention to individual differences that are *internal* among members of audiences. That is, attention is now focused on the "lessons" about social life provided by the media and how they "teach" those lessons through a process of socialization. As the pendulum of scientific inquiry swings increasingly in that direction, it is likely that less attention will be focused on cognitive factors as intervening variables. That is, less attention will be paid to the manner in which mass communications play a part in the acquisition or modification of underlying attitudes, needs, values, knowledge, skills, etc. even if they clearly *do* play a significant role in shaping individual decisions and actions.

A case can be made that a substantial decline in interest in the cognitive paradigm would not be beneficial in the long run. While it has indeed been difficult to explain the influences of the mass media on the basis of cognitive factors alone, they obviously remain as critical variables shaping many kinds of individual decisions and behavior. For that reason, cognitive factors will play a part in the learning patterns and internalizations of individuals in their exposure to the content of the media. The lesson emerging from this brief consideration of the two paradigms is that in the long run, *an adequate theory of the role of the media in the processes of socialization in society must include both the cognitive and meaning paradigms.*

As the process of socialization moves increasingly to center-stage in the attempt to unsort the long-range influences of mass communication, it is important to understand the nature of that process. Like many other master concepts in the social sciences, it has different meanings for different people.

To the anthropologist, socialization is *enculturation*—that process of active or passive teaching and learning by which one generation in a society passes on to the next their entire design for living. This literally includes their whole culture—material artifacts, language, social institutions, skills of production and distribution, legends, myths, art, and so on. The whole society participates in greater or lesser degree in this process of cultural transmission. There are many variations from one society to the next. In some, particular persons such as the paternal uncle or the grandmother have specific teaching responsibilities; this is may be not the case in others.

To the sociologist, the term has a more restricted meaning. It refers to a process in which individuals are prepared to enter and play acceptable parts in various kinds of *groups*. They learn norms, roles, systems of ranking, and procedures of social control. Supporting such social skills are beliefs about self, about others, definitions of deviance, and about the society in general. However, sociologists look to specific agents of socialization and the ways in which they transmit particular lessons to particular categories of recipients. The agents may include parents, peers, the schools, and, of course, the media. The lessons may focus on such matters as criminal orientations, sex roles, and racial and ethnic stereotypes. Different types of recipients may be inner-city youth, males, or the white middle class.

Psychologists tend to be more concerned with the manner in which people learn to control and modify personality factors, especially *urges* to behave in ways that are socially unacceptable. An example is provided by the theories of Freud. The task of civilization, he said, was to "cage the beast within." Individuals have to learn to accept society's standards of right and wrong if their inborn libidinal sex drives are to be held in check. While many psychologists would reject the theories of Freud, they are interested in such matters as how viewing pornography might disrupt society's efforts to channel individual sexual conduct into approved patterns. They are concerned about how violence shown on TV might disrupt a society's socialization efforts intended to keep children's aggressive drives in check.

Whereas these views of socialization differ considerably in both focus and scope, they have essential similarities. They conceptualize socialization as a teaching/learning process, in which one or more agents plays a role in transmitting some aspect of culture or approved pattern of behavior to individuals who are then changed in some way. Viewed from this perspective, the importance of both the major paradigms discussed before—media portrayals of meanings and the role of cognitive variables in behavior—can be understood. Those who control the media do serve as agents of socialization, whether they intend to or not. The programs they design and present are portrayals of social life that inevitably contain lessons on how to behave. Those who attend to that content can scarcely be expected to come away totally uninfluenced by the experience. It should scarcely be surprising, then, to find that when particular lessons are presented often, those who attend to them will undergo some process of change.

Thus, the meaning paradigm can yield a number of focused theories that are based on the particular kinds or categories of content provided by media portrayals. One example that can be derived from the paradigm is the *cultural norms theory* that was set forth by De Fleur in 1970. Essentially it states that:

...the mass media, through selective presentations and emphasis of certain themes, create impressions among their audiences that common cultural norms concerning the emphasized topics are structured or defined in some specific way. Since individual behavior is usually guided by cultural norms (or the actor's impression of what the norms are) with respect to a given topic or situation, the media would then serve *indirectly* to influence conduct.[9]

While the theory is more complex than the foregoing statement it can be seen that the emergence of socialization as a concept important in understanding media effects is not particularly new. In fact, at least certain aspects of this idea were discussed by Merton and Lazarsfeld as far back as the 1940s.[10] Furthermore, there seems little doubt in face of the impressive accumulation of research today that such a theory is essentially correct. The second Surgeon General's Report (Chapter 14 and 15) summarizes data from numerous content analyses showing that television presents views of norms on a range of topics from diet to family life. There appears to be increasing evidence that such presentations do influence people's definitions of social situations and consequently their actions.

Similar theories can be derived concerning such topics as the meanings and desirability of certain occupations, nuclear war, terrorism, space exploration, and numerous other aspects of contemporary life portrayed by the media. The major task is to link extended exposure to a body of consistent content with tendencies to behave according to particular patterns.

LOOKING AHEAD

What all this implies is that after decades of research, and the accumulation of a mass of empirical generalizations and focused theories, a radical change of paradigms became necessary to develop new theories explaining the long-term, subtle, but significant influences of mass communication. The major point is that those influences on our behavior do not depend directly on a number of cumbersome constructions of inner psychological processes that researchers have for the better part of a century assumed are the major shapers of our responses to the mass media. At the same time, that older paradigm remains important in understanding many forms of behavior, whether related to media or not.

There is no certainty that the meaning paradigm will remain dominant. In the changing milieux of the media, functioning in a changing society with an evolving culture, it may eventually look as outmoded as the mass society paradigm with which it all started. Yet, it represents the point to which more than half a century of research on mass communication has brought us.

The meaning paradigm, like all such sets of postulates, is sufficiently general in its assumptions that it overcomes the limitations of the ever-changing universe faced by those who search for the effects of mass communication. The task ahead is to use the paradigm, explaining and predicting specific aspects of the relationship between the mass media, particular forms of content, and the behavior of audiences. This will require the development of new focused theories.

In brief, then, the lessons of the milestones are reasonably clear. First, a change in basic paradigms has led the search for focused theories of media effects in new directions. However, that change in paradigms is by no means complete, and many investigators will (and should) continue to study more traditional problems. Second, any search for answers as to how the mass media influence people must come to grips with certain facts that characterize the use of science as a means of assembling knowledge regarding the effects of mass communication. These can be summed up in four major propositions:

1. We cannot assume constancy in the way people respond to and are influenced by mass communication because we live in a rapidly changing society with a dynamic culture.
2. Inconstancy is present because new technology develops at an increasing pace, which means that the media change quickly due to the adoption of communication innovations.
3. Inconstancy is also present because audiences constantly change due to the evolution of culture and society—new social movements, changing subcultures, the spread of new values, the influence of demographic trends, and the continuing influences of industrialization and urbanization.
4. The first three propositions imply that inconstancy will always be present in the kinds of effects and influences produced by the media, as different kinds of people respond to changing media content presented through new technologies.

Thus, while it will be possible with use of any new paradigm to develop focused theories that attempt to explain in a very general way how people are influenced by mass communication, it will probably never be possible to indicate exactly *what* ideas, beliefs, or behaviors will be influenced, among *whom*, or by what *modes* of media presentation.

NOTES AND REFERENCES

1. Melvin L. De Fleur and Otto N. Larsen, *The Flow of Information* (New York: Harper and Brothers, 1958). See the new introduction in the reprint by Transaction Press, 1987.
2. Gordon W. Allport and Leo Postman, *The Psychology of Rumor* (New York: Holt, 1947).

3. Melvin L. De Fleur, "The Cultural Norms Theory," in *Theories of Mass Communication* (New York: David McKay, 1970), pp. 129–139.

4. Arthur N. Strahler and Alan H. Strahler, *Modern Physical Geography*, 2nd ed. (New York: John Wiley and Sons, 1983), pp. 5–6.

5. Edward Sapir, "Language and Environment." *American Anthropologist* 14, 1912, pp. 226–242. See also: Benjamin Lee Whorf, *Language, Thought and Reality*, John Carroll, ed. (Cambridge, Mass.: MIT Press, 1956). In particular, see pp. 134–159.

6. Charles Horton Cooley, *Social Organization* (New York: Charles Scribner's Sons, 1929). This book was originally published in 1907.

7. George Herbert Mead, *Mind, Self, and Society* (Chicago: University of Chicago Press, 1934).

8. Walter Lippmann, *Public Opinion* (New York: Macmillan, 1921).

9. Melvin L. De Fleur, "The Cultural Norms Theory," in *Theories of Mass Communication* 2nd ed. (New York: David McKay, 1970) pp. 129–139.

10. Paul F. Lazarsfeld and Robert K. Merton, "Mass Communication, Popular Taste, and Organized Social Action," in Lymon Bryson, ed., *The Communication of Ideas* (New York: Harper and Brothers, 1948) pp. 95–118.

Name Index

463

Subject Index

Melvin L. De Fleur has recently accepted the John Ben Snow Endowed Chair in the S. I. Newhouse School of Public Communications at Syracuse University. His books include several in sociology, the field in which he received his doctoral training. Among them are *Sociology: Human Society* and *Social Problems in American Society*, now in their fourth and second editions respectively. His works in communication include *Understanding Mass Communication*, third edition (with Everette Dennis) and *Theories of Mass Communication* (with Sandra Ball Rokeach), another Longman Inc. publication. The latter has been translated into Spanish, Portuguese, Chinese, and Malayan and is now going into a fifth edition. His earlier work, the *Flow of Information*, has just been reprinted by Transaction Press as part of their series, "Classics in Communication."

His interests include private flying (holding a commercial license and instrument rating) and fishing. He believes that some of his best ideas are developed while on his boat, the *Emile Durkheim*, where telephone lines cannot reach, or while wading a peaceful river casting flies to hungry trout.

Shearon Lowery is an Associate Professor of Sociology at Florida International University in Miami. Besides the interest in media effects, her research has included studies of crime and other forms of deviant behavior. Her book, *Crime and the Elderly* (written with others), was published in 1985. She is currently conducting a study of children who kill, paying special attention to the possibility of media influences.

Outside of her professional life, she is devoted to thoroughbred horses and is an aficionado of horse shows, riding competitions, and the track. Her household includes many animals, including a German Shepherd dog named Inga, who was actually born in Germany and understands commands in two languages. An activity particularly close to her heart is the preservation of the rare spotted leopard cat, the Egyptian Mau. To further the development of this breed she operates Sansih Cattery through which she breeds and shows this strikingly beautiful cat.